The Movies

The Movies

Extracts from The Movie
The illustrated Who's Who of The Cinema

Bloomsbury Books

An imprint of Godfrey Cave Associates Limited, London

First published in this casebound edition by
Bloomsbury Books
an imprint of Godfrey Cave Associates Limited
42 Bloomsbury Street, London WC1B 3QJ

© Orbis Publishing Limited London 1982
Godfrey Cave Associates Limited 1984

This edition produced and published by arrangement
with Orbis Publishing Limited 1984

ISBN 0 906223 46 6

Bound in Great Britain by
R. J. Acford

Chapter 14

Business is booming

In Britain the cinema expanded, though a slump in British film production allowed Hollywood to extend its empire to England. Meanwhile in the USA finance flooded back into production

By the late Thirties the superficial boom in British production was nearly ended. The old Quota Act was coming up for renewal in 1938, and in anticipation of this American producers set about making top-class films in England.

The crucial necessity of selling films in the USA had already defeated both Michael Balcon and Basil Dean. The only producer who still had a chance of breaking into the American market was the larger-than-life Alexander Korda. In 1937 Korda made a bid for equal co-ownership of United Artists with Sam Goldwyn. Had the deal come off it would have given him a vital foothold in America, but at the eleventh hour it fell through.

Korda's production empire included real assets such as a large studio, contract players and some of the most outstanding talent in the business. The enterprise made glossy and enjoyable films and was heavily backed by the Prudential Assurance Company along conventional shareholding lines.

At the same time as Korda was pursuing this orthodox production practice, a small and virtually unknown group had been channelling vast sums of money into film production through an elaborate system of bank loans secured by guarantees from marine underwriters. In this way many production units without capital, studios or personnel of their own – 'tramp' producers as they have been called – were extravagantly financed on a film-by-film basis without any supervision from their backers in London's business world. Financiers were speculating on film production.

Korda had set the fashion for lavish production but he always kept his books in order. The day of reckoning was bound to come, however, for a number of the 'tramp' producers whose spending was on a scale comparable to that of Korda. Unfortunately the financial scandal that resulted from movie speculation came to light. The bad publicity and the resulting reluctance on the part of businessmen to invest in production harmed Korda as much as the rogue producers. Shorn of control of his studios, and confined to making more economical pictures, Korda now had little chance of regular American distribution.

After a decade of the quota regulations, the potential had gone out of British production companies. On the other hand the cinema business was booming. Throughout the Thirties audiences grew and grew. Funds poured into the exhibition side of the business which remained profitable even during the Depression. Gaumont-British and Associated British Cinemas both became highly profitable circuits and were organized as large vertical combines, with their own production, renting and exhibition branches.

Gaumont-British Picture Corporation, run by the Ostrer family, was made up of three companies: the Gaumont and Gainsborough studios in London, a nation-wide film distribution network and the Gaumont-British cinema circuit. By 1929 the company controlled 287 cinemas throughout Britain. Their chief competitor was ABC, headed by the tough, aggressive John Maxwell, who later tried to wrest control of Gaumont-British from the Ostrer family. At the beginning of the Thirties ABC owned 88 cinemas, the prolific British International Pictures studio at Elstree and the distribution firm Wardour Films. During the winter of 1933–34, the company was reorganized as the Associated British Picture Corporation and by 1938 it had increased its number of cinemas to 325.

Another major film exhibitor was the energetic and likeable Oscar Deutsch, whose chain of Odeon cinemas was built up over the decade, his first cinema having been built at Perry Bar, Birmingham in 1930. A new approach to urban planning in the Thirties created large suburbs which contained ideal sites for the new Odeons. These cinemas were broadly uniform in their functional art-deco appearance and created a modern brand image for the circuit.

In 1937 Odeon merged with County Cinemas to form a circuit of 250 cinemas and had first call on all United Artists and Korda films. At this point Odeon became the third circuit in size and worth £6 million as a company. Towards the end of 1939, the Odeon board was enlarged to include two members of the new General Cinema Finance Corporation; one of them was the future mogul J. Arthur Rank.

A Methodist millionaire with flour-milling and other business interests, Rank had entered films in the early Thirties to improve the production of religious films. In 1936 his company moved into feature production and studio ownership. His arrival on the board of Odeon and was his first step into exhibition – a business he all but monopolized.

While film exhibition was flourishing, production was depressed. A government committee under the then Lord Moyne studied the problem and tried to accommodate the opposing interests of the big combines (Gaumont-British and ABC) and the independent producers like Basil Dean. The problem continued to be the quality of British films and the difficulty of selling them in America. The new Quota Act was finally passed in 1938. The committee who had framed the legislation had attempted to ensure higher quality in British films by insisting

Above: MGM stamped its familiar lion logo on its British films. Below: Conrad Veidt and Annabella played nobles in Richelieu's France in the black and white romance Under the Red Robe. *Bottom: Henry Fonda, Annabella and the crew of* Wings of the Morning

that a film should meet certain minimum costs in order to be eligible for distribution as a quota film.

As might have been hoped, the introduction of the minimum-cost clause killed off the cheap 'quota quickie'. It also put a premium on expensive films and led to the production of some high-quality pictures. But film production as a whole did not revive. In the first year of the new quota regulations, no feature films emerged from eight of the British studios. The labour union claimed that unemployment among technicians stood at 80 per cent. Fewer 'quota quickies' meant, moreover, that film production continued to decline numerically.

Worse still for those who had hoped for a truly national picture-making industry, statistics revealed that all but 25 per cent of films made in 1938 were American productions of one kind or another. The dilemma central to the British film industry remained unsolved: quality films were expensive and to cover their costs they had to be exported to the USA. Once again the effort to achieve this had put the industry in the hands of the American major companies.

In order to forestall the British government's moves against them, the American majors had begun serious production in Britain on a large scale. Twentieth Century-Fox made a horse-racing drama, *Wings of the Morning* (1937), that had the distinction of being the first British film in Technicolor. The film starred Henry Fonda and the popular French star Annabella and was produced by Robert T. Kane, who had been Paramount's chief in Paris at the start of the Thirties. Kane retained Annabella for his next English production, *Under the Red Robe* (1937). This historical romance was another prestige picture, with Conrad Veidt starring opposite Annabella. The film brought together the great talents of cameramen Georges

Above: filming A Yank at Oxford with (left to right) American director Jack Conway, British producer Michael Balcon and star Robert Taylor. Right: John Maxwell, a Scottish solicitor turned film mogul. Below: Conrad Veidt and Valerie Hobson who had been a hit in The Spy in Black were teamed here in a similar wartime spy film, Contraband. Top right: Jimmy Hanley played a young mechanic bribed to lose a boxing match. Far right: Robert Donat in Vidor's The Citadel

BIGGEST *Personality* of BRITISH FILMS

The Spectacular Success of John Maxwell

The final article in our series dealing with British Film Personalities tells of the phenomenal achievements of the Chairman of British International Pictures, who certainly seems to be the leader for whom the British Film Industry has waited so long

by the EDITOR of "FILM WEEKLY"

Périnal and James Wong Howe, under the direction of the Swedish director Victor Sjöstrom.

Columbia embarked on production at Korda's Denham studio, making several good thrillers, among them *Q–Planes* and *The Spy in Black* (both 1939), which promoted the beautiful Valerie Hobson into a star, after she had been neglected for several years by British producers.

MGM made perhaps the biggest impact of all. The plans they announced when Michael Balcon joined them as head of production early in 1937 included *A Yank at Oxford* and one film he was to make in Hollywood. But Balcon and MGM were to part company within 18 months of agreeing a long-term producer's contract.

A Yank at Oxford was a massive undertaking that involved a mixed American/British cast. A vast and varied collection of writers that included John Monk Saunders, Sidney Gilliat, Hugh Walpole, Ben Travers, Herman J. Mankiewicz and F. Scott Fitzgerald had a shot at the script. Jack Conway was the director and the film sold well on both sides of the Atlantic.

Balcon's old friend Victor Saville took a different approach to MGM. As an independent producer he had prudently acquired the film rights to A. J. Cronin's recent best-selling novel *The Citadel*, a book that MGM wished Balcon to produce. Saville was not inhibited by the MGM regime and he soon found himself producing both *The Citadel* (1938) and *Goodbye, Mr Chips* (1939). Once again the directors, King Vidor and Sam Wood, were American but the main star of both was the British actor Robert Donat. These two films were highly successful and earned Saville his passport to Hollywood where he was to remain when MGM pulled out of Britain at the outbreak of war.

During the late Thirties other top British film-makers like Hitchcock, Wilcox and Korda found their way to Hollywood. Balcon, however, turned his back on the American market and was to spend the rest of his career in the British cinema. He stepped into Basil Dean's shoes at Ealing Studios where Dean had come under increasing criticism from the board. Balcon assembled many of his former Gaumont team and continued the Ealing tradition of providing vehicles for music-hall comics, but in certain other films he introduced a more realistic treatment of ordinary people and themes. *There Ain't No Justice* (1939), an unassuming film starring Jimmy Hanley as a young boxer, was scarcely noticed as a forerunner of what later became known as the Ealing style.

By the end of the decade, British film technicians and directors, who had proved themselves in the tough training school of 'quota quickies' and documentary film production, were ready to undertake the difficult task of filming the war. On its own the 1938 Quota Act is unlikely to have fostered a prosperous national industry. Early in 1939, an important daily newspaper carried the headline 'Films Act Has Failed'. The following day its correspondence columns had a letter from Basil Dean saying bitterly, 'I told you so'. Whether the making of quality American films would have expanded in the Forties is hard to say; with the outbreak of war the American majors withdrew from Britain and the character of the native industry was to change beyond recognition.   RACHAEL LOW

Spending spree

The eyes of the industrial world are on Metro-Goldwyn-Mayer, shining example of a company that refuses to be licked! An inspiration to the nation! In the worst year of history Leo of M-G-M has backed optimism with results. The hell with depression!

SHOWMEN!
TAG ON
TO
SUCCESS!
Leo leads the way—

Top: Hollywood presented a brave face to the economic crisis of the Thirties, and companies like MGM entered a great period of prosperity once the Depression was over. Above: Thurman Arnold, the Washington politician who sought to break the monopolies of the Hollywood majors. Below: extras stand in line waiting to be hired; unionization of film actors had improved the lot of the extras

President Roosevelt's New Deal, announced to the nation in 1934, proved to be a mixed blessing for Hollywood. The new measures to alleviate economic hardship and curtail unemployment began to take effect. People were spending money again and more of it went on the movies. By 1935 all the major studios were back in profit and MGM, with its galaxy of stars, was the undisputed leader.

Part of the philosophy of the New Deal was that collective action in business was preferable to cut-throat competition. But cut-throat competition was exactly what Hollywood thrived upon. The struggle for power, prestige and profit had always been the name of the picture-making game but the circumstances were such that Hollywood had to fall in line with government legislation.

Another major change brought about by the second phase of the New Deal was the passing of the National Labor Relations Act of 1935, which guaranteed unions the right to bargain collectively and establish maximum wages and minimum hours. The first beneficiaries of this new legislation in Hollywood were the studio craftsmen. Earlier in the decade, extras had been lucky to find work, let alone earn a paltry $1.25 per day. Now, under the terms of the National Industrial Recovery Act, their job security and rates of pay improved enormously.

For the Hollywood moguls the reforms of the New Deal were the thin end of the wedge. Union shops sprang up throughout the industry. In May 1937 the Screen Actors' Guild was recognized as the bargaining agent for all actors, and stars could at last begin to negotiate their way out of long-term contracts. Similarly, the following year, the Screen Writers' Guild was given the right to represent scriptwriters. Shortly afterwards the Screen Directors' Guild also won recognition. By the outbreak of World War II, practically all studio employees below the rank of executive producer had become unionized.

The revival of the economy meant that money was more freely available. When David O. Selznick began his much vaunted production of *Gone With the Wind* in December 1938, Hollywood had never been so buoyant. The directors Frank Capra, John Ford, Leo McCarey, William Wyler, Ernst Lubitsch and Howard Hawks were at their peak, and shooting pictures as distinguished as any that had ever been made in the movie capital. A check on the best picture nominees in the 1939 Oscar race reveals that *Dark Victory, Ninotchka, Stagecoach, The Wizard of Oz, Wuthering Heights, Mr Smith Goes to Washington* and *Gone With the Wind* were all among the contenders.

Every studio boasted its big stars and financial hits. Every studio stepped up production. The more wealthy among them indulged in the luxury of filming in the great outdoors thanks to the new Technicolor process. The more economically-minded jumped on the bandwagon of the double-feature bill, producing less expensive films for a new kind of cinema programme in which two 80-minute movies were presented instead of the traditional main feature and shorts combination.

Over at the Walt Disney studios, artists toiled hour after hour, month after month to have *Snow White and the Seven Dwarfs* (1937) ready for release. This was to be an even more revolutionary notion in cinema programming since it was the first time filmgoers had been offered a full-length cartoon as a main feature.

At MGM, Mayer and Thalberg paid tribute to showmanship with *The Great Ziegfeld* (1936) and re-staged the spectacle of the 1906 earthquake in *San Francisco* (1936); at Paramount, Cecil B. DeMille filmed the building of the *Union Pacific* railroad in 1939; 20th Century-Fox flooded a studio mock-up of the Indian sub-continent in *The Rains Came* (1939), and Chicago was burned to the ground in Henry King's *In Old Chicago* (1938); RKO erected massive sets for the Charles Laughton version of *The Hunchback of Notre Dame* (1939); and Sam Goldwyn had his special effects men create the mightiest wind in Hollywood for John Ford's high-adventure *The Hurricane* (1937).

Even though Hollywood was spending money on such a grand scale and enjoying box-office success, the movie business in the late Thirties was in a constant state of flux. The foreign market, so long a reliable source of income, was under threat. Distribution of films in Spain had been drastically hit by the Civil War which had begun in 1936. Hitler's annexation of the Sudetenland in 1938 provided problems for US distribution in Central Europe and, despite deals made with the Nippon Finance Ministry, release of American films in Japan was far from ideal in Hollywood's view.

Finally, the Roosevelt administration was to give Hollywood further cause for anxiety in the pursuit of antitrust legislation. Measures were being proposed in key industries that would break up existing monopolies. And the movie business, which had acquired its monopolistic control of distribution and exhibition by some extremely dubious strong-arm tactics, began to be seriously worried about having to surrender its cinema chains, or divorce them from production and distribution combines.

It was not surprising, therefore, that Hollywood felt threatened when Thurman Arnold, the head of the Department of Justice Antitrust Division, charged the big five studios with 28 separate offences against the antitrust laws and sought 'theatre divorcement' and the 'abolition of all monopolistic practices in the motion picture industry'. But the majors resisted such moves until the late Forties.

The Thurman Arnold suit of 1938 did not change things immediately. The studios, with their backs to the wall, used every means at their disposal to hold on to the block-booking system, even claiming that the 3000 cinemas they controlled were but a small percentage of the total cinemas, and omitting to mention that these were almost all first run cinemas and were therefore the most lucrative.

It was to be a decade later, after innumerable court wrangles and investigations by the FBI, that Hollywood's struggle against the antitrust laws ended. In 1948 the Supreme Court ruled that 'theatre divorcement' was to become law and the structure of the industry was to undergo major changes.   ROY PICKARD

Hollywood invades Britain

The foreign invasion of British films in the Thirties was on a large scale. Indeed, so many Europeans were employed by Alexander Korda at Denham studios that the trio of Union Jacks hoisted outside the building was said to stand for the only three British workers in the place. But it was the Americans who aroused the strongest feelings in Britain. They were feared as potential economic invaders who might take over the more profitable parts of the home film industry; they were envied for the greater popularity of their films, even with British audiences; and they were admired for their greater technical expertise.

Here come the Yanks

During the decade British companies continued the well-established practice of luring American stars across the Atlantic. The first feature made at Pinewood, *Talk of the Devil* (1936), starred Americans Ricardo Cortez and Sally Eilers – though otherwise it was an entirely British production. Helen Chandler, Sylvia Sidney and Fay Wray, Bela Lugosi, Raymond Massey and Edward Everett Horton were other stars who worked in Britain.

The really big stars almost never made the crossing: they had more important commitments in Hollywood. But stars who had passed their peak or who had never shone that brightly in the Hollywood firmament were happy to work in Britain. Ruth Chatterton's last two films, *The Rat* (1937) and *A Royal Divorce* (1938), were both British, as was Cary Grant's *The Amazing Quest of Ernest Bliss* (1936), made when he was still a rising star. Exceptionally, Edward G. Robinson was in great demand back home when Warners loaned him out at such short notice for *Thunder in the City* (1937) that it seems to have been one of that studio's many tactless exercises of authority over its contract players.

Hollywood directors who worked in Britain were often in decline. Among them was William Beaudine, a top director of silents (including Mary Pickford's *Sparrows* of 1926). Beaudine settled down to making bright British

comedies – like *Windbag the Sailor* (1936) with Will Hay – before returning to Hollywood and the Bowery Boys. Another director past his best, William K. Howard, whose films had included *Transatlantic* (1931) and *The Power and the Glory* (1933), was entrusted in Britain with *Fire Over England* (1937). It was a lavish historical costume picture climaxing in the defeat of the Spanish Armada, and to photograph it Howard recruited his favourite American cameraman, James Wong Howe. William Cameron Menzies was a major American art director when Alexander Korda tempted him over with an offer to direct the spectacular *Things to Come* (1936) – based on an H.G. Wells novel about an apocalyptic world war and requiring strong pictorial stylization.

At the time of the 1927 Films Act, several American companies went into 'quota-quickie' production for themselves, appointing American executives to oversee output. The films made by Paramount British, under Walter Morosco, included *Service for Ladies* (1932), the first to be directed in Britain by Korda. Fox British, under Albert Parker (formerly a leading director), made a stream of economical 'quota quickies' at Wembley and discovered James Mason – giving him his first role in the crime story *Late Extra* (1935).

Warners at Teddington

But it was Warner Brothers that made the biggest move into British production, vastly improving the existing studios at Teddington in 1931 and promising that major pictures of international appeal would be made with top stars. George Arliss was one scheduled to make films in Britain but the company lost his services soon afterwards when he joined Darryl F. Zanuck at 20th Century, and Teddington was only used for low-budget films that were rarely released in the USA. Irving Asher headed production and made some important acting finds that he sent on to Hollywood; they included Errol Flynn, Ian Hunter and Patric Knowles who were put into major Warner films like *The Adventures of Robin Hood* (1938).

Ever economical, Warners remade some of their Hollywood successes in Britain – *The Man*

Above: Robert Donat in Goodbye, Mr Chips, *a triumph for Anglo-American collaboration. Left: Annabella and Henry Fonda in the race-track romance,* Wings of the Morning

265

From *Blankley's* (1930), a mild comedy, was repeated as *Guest of Honour* (1934) with Henry Kendall taking the part that John Barrymore had played in the original. American directors like Beaudine, William McGann and John Rawlins were given plenty of work at Teddington, and players like Laura La Plante, Glenda Farrell, and James Finlayson were active there. But Warners also used many British directors and stars, and one exceptional murder thriller, *They Drive by Night* (1939), with Emlyn Williams, had little or no American participation, while Max Miller's films gave the company its biggest successes.

With *Wings of the Morning* (1937), 20th Century-Fox's British outpost, offered an early example of a frequent ploy to widen a film's appeal in Britain and the Empire by making the American star (here Henry Fonda) play a Canadian. Fox also tried to make an international star of Gracie Fields by starring her in a South African 'Western', *We're Going to Be Rich* (1938), before returning her to the indigenous subjects that made her so popular with British audiences.

The MGM lesson

MGM, who also announced major production plans in Britain, retained its traditional methods of big-budget film-making. The script of *A Yank at Oxford* (1938) eventually called upon some thirty writers, working both in Britain and Hollywood. The film had an American director (Jack Conway), cameraman (Hal Rosson) and supervising editor (Margaret Booth), while Robert Taylor played the lead supported by Maureen O'Sullivan and Lionel Barrymore. British participation was secondary (though Vivien Leigh was striking in a small role) and American production procedures provided a useful lesson for British technicians in such areas as dubbing.

MGM's subsequent pictures did give more scope to British talent and especially to Robert Donat who was persuaded to sign for six films in England. But he was still directed by and co-starred with Americans: King Vidor on *The Citadel* (1938) with Rosalind Russell, and Sam Wood on *Goodbye, Mr Chips* (1939) with Greer Garson. The pictures could as easily have been filmed at Culver City as Denham: the Welsh

Robert Donat

Charles Laughton called him 'the most graceful actor of our time'. Graham Greene said he was 'the best film actor we possess'. Sadly Donat's career was brutally cut short

Right: Donat and Eugene Pallette haunted by the 'Glourie Ghost' in The Ghost Goes West. *Far right:* The Citadel *gave Donat the part of a young doctor who must amputate a trapped miner's arm to save his life; he encounters greater difficulty, later, in maintaining his professional ideals in high society*

Robert Donat had everything an actor could hope for – except health. Beneficent spirits, attending his cradle, endowed him with good looks, a fine voice, exceptional elegance of demeanour. A malevolent spirit gave him chronic asthma.

Born in 1905 of mixed parentage – a Yorkshire mother and a Polish father who had settled in Manchester – Donat came to the screen in a period when it was the poor sister of the stage in Britain. It was natural that he should long for the theatre, and indeed he was to become one of its notable players. He made his stage debut in Birmingham in 1921 and by 1930 had reached the West End. But he was made for the cinema. Alexander Korda recognized Donat's gifts and in 1933 cast him, after a few banal roles, as Thomas Culpeper in *The Private Life of Henry VIII*. Donat was overshadowed by the bravura of Charles Laughton as the King; but looking back one sees how much his grace and easy charm added to the film. A year later he was in Hollywood playing

mining village of *The Citadel* was a studio creation, not location work; and Irving Thalberg had originally bought *Chips* as a vehicle for Charles Laughton, who would have made it in Hollywood as he did *The Barretts of Wimpole Street* (1934).

War calls a halt

The two films were world-wide successes, gaining Donat Oscar nominations for Best Actor: he won for *Chips*, beating MGM's reigning star, Clark Gable, who was nominated for *Gone With the Wind*. MGM's British programme was proving a winner; for its fourth picture, *Busman's Honeymoon* (1940), Robert Montgomery came over to play Dorothy L. Sayers' sleuth, Lord Peter Wimsey. He was accompanied by the director Richard Thorpe and co-star Maureen O'Sullivan, but the declaration of war caused a temporary suspension of production and Thorpe and O'Sullivan hurried back home. Montgomery stayed on to work under the talented British director Arthur Woods who had made *They Drive by Night*. But *Busman's Honeymoon* was Woods' last picture: an RAF pilot, he died in action soon afterwards.

Montgomery had also planned to make *The Earl of Chicago* (1939) with Richard Thorpe in Britain, but it was transferred back to Hollywood along with other MGM British projects in the pipeline. MGM's only other British picture of the war period was *Adventures of Tartu* (1943), directed by Hollywood's Harold S. Bucquet, and starring Robert Donat – as a British spy in Czechoslovakia – after he had been taken to court to enforce his contract.

Warners meanwhile continued filming in Britain, responding to the outbreak of hostilities with such propaganda efforts as *The Prime Minister* (1941) – starring John Gielgud as Disraeli – and *Flying Fortress* (1942), with Richard Greene as a Yank in the RAF. Then on July 5, 1944, a flying bomb wrecked the Teddington studios: after 152 films Warners' British output came to a halt. Other Hollywood companies like RKO were active in the war years and it was probably Columbia that did most to keep up British spirits by putting George Formby into such comedies as *Much Too Shy* (1942), *Get Cracking* and *Bell Bottom George* (both 1943).   ALLEN EYLES

Above: Laurence Olivier defeating the Spanish Armada in Fire Over England. *Left: Victor McLaglen as a boxer and Gracie Fields as his wife, a singer, in* We're Going to Be Rich. *Opposite page: James Mason in his first film,* Late Extra *and (right) Bristol-born Cary Grant, who returned to Britain in 1936 to film* The Amazing Quest of Ernest Bliss *(left)*

the lead role in *The Count of Monte Cristo* and rags and beard could not disguise his qualities. In 1929 Donat had married Ella Annesley but they were to divorce in 1946.

Back in Britain Donat was Richard Hannay in Alfred Hitchcock's *The Thirty-Nine Steps* (1935), then starred in René Clair's comedy *The Ghost Goes West* (1935) as both the young owner of a Scottish castle and his ghost-ancestor, who is doomed to haunt the castle when it is transported to the USA. Clair was brought over to England by Korda, as was Jacques Feyder, director of *Knight Without Armour* (1937) – in which Donat played the Englishman faced with the job of getting a widowed countess (Marlene Dietrich) to Moscow after the revolution.

Always Donat was the romantic hero, resourceful, brave, the ideal star of the Thirties and Forties. Perhaps if health had not handicapped him he might have gone back in triumph to Hollywood and become a truly great star. As it was, his illness, increasing diffidence and self-doubt, and contractual problems combined to cost him the lead roles in such prestigious films as *Captain Blood* (1935), *Anthony Adverse* (1936), and *The Adventures of Robin Hood* (1938). Instead he stayed to work in Britain and there had a brief period of glittering fame in the late Thirties.

He had not been happy in Hollywood in any case, but he had made an impression and when MGM extended their empire to include production in Britain they made him one of their leading players. King Vidor directed him in *The Citadel* (1938) and drew from him a performance of considerable range as the young doctor who moves from Wales to fashionable London. In 1939 came the film with which the name of Robert Donat has been linked ever since: Sam Wood's *Goodbye, Mr Chips*. Insisting on the role, he audaciously broke away from the smooth, confident face; the easy, elegant movements of the ideal film star. He played a master at an English public school, at first helplessly ragged by his pupils, then taught self-assurance by his beautiful wife (Greer Garson), desolate as a widower and finally a whiskery old sentimentalist. It was a character of fantasy, but still solid enough for Donat to deliver a superb performance and win the Best Actor Oscar. Decades afterwards, Donat's *Chips* is still remembered.

He never did as well again. Turned down for military service, he gave a decent but uninspired performance in the flag-waving *The Young Mr Pitt* (1942); and returned to action in *Adventures of Tartu* (1943), a piece of flummery in which he played a wartime British sabotage agent. It was not worthy of his powers. But increasingly Donat was engaged in the fight against illness. He was unremarkable as the husband who resumes marriage with Deborah Kerr after war-enforced separation in *Perfect Strangers* (1945) – both his and Korda's last film for MGM – but more commanding as the defence counsel in *The Winslow Boy* (1948). In 1949 he produced, adapted (from Walter Greenwood's play), directed and starred in a tame but pleasant Northern comedy *The Cure for Love* for Korda. Donat played a soldier pursued by a coarse, overbearing fiancée (Dora Bryan) and a sweeter girl (Renée Asherson) who wins him in the end; in 1953 Donat married Miss Asherson in real life but they parted in 1956.

He was touching as the film pioneer Friese-Greene in the Festival of Britain picture, *The Magic Box* (1951) but, by now very ill, had to refuse roles in *No Highway* (1951) and *Hobson's Choice* (1954). Oxygen cylinders were kept in the wings for him when he acted in T.S. Eliot's play *Murder in the Cathedral* in 1953 and there was mordant irony in his casting as the dying country parson in *Lease of Life* (1954). In 1958 he summoned up the last of his strength to play the mandarin in *The Inn of the Sixth Happiness*. A month later he was dead.

Donat could have been one of the universal stars of cinema. Illness, however, corroded the latter years of his comparatively brief life. It could not destroy his brilliant gifts but it shortened his career and, one might say, blunted it.   DILYS POWELL

Filmography
1933 Men of Tomorrow; That Night in London (USA: Overnight); Cash (USA: For Love or Money); The Private Life of Henry VIII. **'34** The Count of Monte Cristo (USA). **'35** The Thirty-Nine Steps; The Ghost Goes West. **'37** Knight Without Armour. **'38** The Citadel. **'39** Goodbye, Mr Chips. **'42** The Young Mr Pitt. **'43** Adventures of Tartu (USA retitling for TV: Tartu). **'45** Perfect Strangers (USA: Vacation From Marriage). **'47** Captain Boycott (guest). **'48** The Winslow Boy. **'49** The Cure for Love (+dir; +co-sc; +prod). **'51** The Magic Box. **'54** Lease of Life. **'56** The Stained Glass at Fairford (short) (voice only). **'58** The Inn of the Sixth Happiness (USA).

All About Bette

'What a fool I was to come to Hollywood where they only understand platinum blondes and where legs are more important than talent'

On December 3, 1930, Bette Davis arrived in Hollywood. Originally from Lowell, Massachusetts (she was born in 1903), she had studied drama at the John Murray Anderson school, acting in summer repertory. She had won a modest but growing reputation as a promising young actress in two Broadway plays – *Broken Dishes* and *Solid South* – and had come to the attention of Universal studios, who put her under contract.

It was hardly an auspicious time for someone like Davis to break into films; she was pretty enough, in an odd way, but hardly fitted any of the moulds by which either the studios or the public judged beauty. The fact that she was, or wanted to be, a serious actress was irrelevant, if not actually a handicap to success. When she got off the train, no-one from the studio was there to meet her. In fact, a representative *had* been at the station but later reported that he had seen 'no-one who looked like an actress.' When head of the studio Carl Laemmle saw the first film in which she was cast, *Bad Sister* (1931), he said, 'Can you picture some poor guy going through hell and high water in a picture and ending up with *her* at the fade-out?'

Five undistinguished films later, Universal dropped her contract. Just as she and her

Above: even in publicity portraits Bette Davis avoided the glamorous extravagances of most other Hollywood actresses. Right: The Man Who Played God provided her with a prestigious role as the fiancée of a concert pianist (George Arliss)

mother were packing to return to New York and the theatre, George Arliss, then a leading star at Warner Brothers telephoned. A friend of his, Murray Kinnell, had worked with Davis in her fifth film *The Menace* (1932) and had thought she might be right for Arliss' upcoming *The Man Who Played God* (1932). In his autobiography, Arliss recalled:
'I did not expect anything but a nice little performance. But . . . the nice little part became a deep and vivid creation . . . I got from her a flash that illuminated mere words and inspired

them with passion and emotion. That is the kind of light that cannot be hidden under a bushel.'

Warners, however, either didn't see that light, or didn't care; she was put under contract, but given a series of roles in mediocre pictures which today have few, if any, redeeming qualities except Davis' presence.

She was, of course, noticed by critics and the public, and her reputation as a solid actress continued to grow. She was a convincing vixen in *Cabin in the Cotton* (1932), and man-

aged to make even the most ludicrous Southern dialogue – 'Ah'd luv ta kiss yo, but ah jes washed mah hayuh' – sound believable. She fought with director Archie Mayo over the way she should play her mad scene in *Bordertown* (1935); she won, as she often did in battles with directors, and was proved right, as she often was in such cases, when the film was well received. Critics pointed to the subtlety of her portrayal of 'a fiery-souled, half-witted, love-crazed woman' (*Film Weekly*) in their reviews.

Davis has claimed that 'There wasn't one of my best pictures I didn't have to fight to get.' *Of Human Bondage* (1934), from the novel by Somerset Maugham, was one of the first. Director John Cromwell wanted her for the role of Mildred, a scheming waitress who ensnares a sensitive medical student, but Warners was reluctant to loan her to RKO for the film. Bette hounded Jack Warner every day for six months, and he finally gave in simply to be left in peace. She recalled in her autobiography *The Lonely Life*:

'My employers believed I would hang myself playing such an unpleasant heroine . . . I think they identified me with the character and felt we deserved each other.'

It is, seen now, perhaps not one of Davis' best performances; her Mildred is so constantly overwrought and nasty that one begins to wonder what even the obsessed student Philip Carey (Leslie Howard) could see in her. Put in historical perspective, however, the performance is both effective and courageous; at a time when 'movie star' meant glamour and sympathy, Davis had dared to look terrible and to be unsympathetic. All were surprised when

she was not even nominated for an Academy Award. When she won an Oscar for *Dangerous* (1935), she claimed it was given her because she had been overlooked the previous year.

In spite of the acclaim she received for *Of Human Bondage*, Warners threw her into five melodramas of variable quality before giving her the script of *Dangerous*. Davis says that she thought it 'maudlin and mawkish, with a pretense at quality', and that she had to work hard to make something of her role as an alcoholic actress bent on self-destruction. She is undoubtedly right about the screenplay, but she gives a performance of such intensity that one overlooks everything that is going on around her on screen.

Those critics who had begun to complain that she was fast developing a set of mannerisms and was playing too broadly for the screen were suprised at her tender and restrained Gaby in *The Petrified Forest* (1936). Yet, in spite of her obvious power at the box-office and her critical standing as a serious actress, Warners insisted that she make an empty comedy, *The Golden Arrow* (1936), and a flat and confused version of Dashiell Hammett's *The Maltese Falcon* called *Satan Met a Lady* (1936). Davis was understandably angry. To preserve her self-respect and her popularity, she wanted to make fewer films each year and to act only in those with scripts she thought intelligent. Warners reply was to cast her in something called *God's Country and the Woman* (made in 1936 with Beverley Roberts as the female lead), with the promise that if she made it she could have the part of Scarlett O'Hara in *Gone With the Wind* (1939). She refused and the studio put her on suspen-

Left: a role Davis fought to get – Mildred in Of Human Bondage, *co-starring Leslie Howard. Centre: Davis (with Miriam Hopkins) in* The Old Maid *– a study of repressed love. Top left:* Dark Victory *was one of her strongest melodramas: Humphrey Bogart played a minor part. Top: as the rich flirt Madge, she bewitched her father's employee Marvin (Richard Barthelmess) in* Cabin in the Cotton

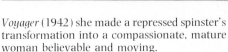

sion for three months. She held out, refusing two other scripts offered her, with the comment 'If I continue to appear in mediocre pictures, I'll have no career worth fighting for'.

With the Davis–Warners feud at an impasse, Ludovico Toeplitz, who produced films in England, offered her a two-picture contract at £20,000 for each film, with script approval. She signed, but upon her arrival in London found herself under injunction from Warners. They claimed that she was contracted to work exclusively for that studio and was not allowed to make films for others. The entire film industry watched the ensuing court battle (which all actors applauded) as the outcome would determine how the studio system would work in the future. Davis lost her suit and was forced to return to Warners or to give up films until her long-term contract expired – but she

---

'I have never known the great actor who . . . didn't plan eventually to direct or produce. If he has no such dream, he is usually bitter, ungratified and eventually alcoholic'

---

did not lose out in the long run. Warners paid her legal fees and began to take her more seriously; the standard of her material temporarily rose.

Her first film upon her return to Hollywood was *Marked Woman* (1937), an above-average social-problem (prostitution) film which gave her a chance to show a wider range of emotion than usual. *Jezebel* (1938) began a long series of films specially tailored for Davis. They were for the most part what was then called 'women's pictures', melodramatic soap operas turning on romantic conflict and sacrifice. It would be a mistake, however, to dismiss them in the

light of the wider freedom of expression allowed in today's films. In the Thirties and Forties such films were taken seriously and accorded more than a little respect. The best of them attempted to illuminate areas of emotion, sexuality and human situation which could not be portrayed on the screen at that time in any other way. Those that Davis made were certainly among the best – she continuously fought for a certain level of intelligence in plot and dialogue, and insisted on as much realism as possible in her portrayals of disturbed or troubled women.

In *Jezebel* she was convincing as a wilful Southern belle who is made to suffer for her own strange peversity. In *Dark Victory* (1939) she alone lifted a maudlin tale of a woman slowly dying into an illuminating study of human understanding and sacrifice. In *Now*

Voyager (1942) she made a repressed spinster's transformation into a compassionate, mature woman believable and moving.

In 1946 she decided to set up her own production company with the films thus made to be released through Warners. A single film came from her company – *A Stolen Life* (1946) in which she played twins, one good, one evil, both in love with the same man. She found she was uncomfortable in the role of producer: 'I never really *produced*,' she said, 'I simply meddled as usual. If that was producing, I had been a mogul for years.'

From 1946 onward, Davis seemed to have a problem finding suitable material, and her popularity began to slip. *Winter Meeting* (1948) is a talky film about a poetess meeting a naval

Left: Bette with William Dix in The Nanny, *one of her best later roles. Above left: Her performance as stage star Margo Channing (here with Celeste Holm and Hugh Marlowe) helped* All About Eve *achieve a record of 14 Academy Award nominations (it won six). Above: Davis in full regalia as* The Virgin Queen *– her second portryal of Elizabeth the First*

forays back into 'women's films' such as *Where Love Has Gone* (1964), she was offered and accepted a series of ghoulish roles in progressively worse movies.

Davis' most notable recent achievement was an Emmy award for the TV series *Strangers: the Story of a Mother and Daughter*. She also tours the lecture circuit with her older films, and remains the determined figure she always was:

'I'll never make the mistake of saying I'm retired. You do that and you're finished. You just have to make sure you play older and older parts. Hell, I could do a million of those character roles. But I'm stubborn about playing the lead. I'd like to go out with my name above the title.'

She is still known as 'the finest actress of the American cinema'. There are those who have disputed that she acted at all, maintaining that all the characters she played were drowned by her own strong personality. It is a moot point, depending upon one's standards and definition of screen acting, although one could reply that she has played the widest range of roles in the widest range of mood of any actress ever to work in American films. Whatever the final judgment of her abilities as an actress, however, it cannot be denied that, whatever she does on the screen, it is impossible to take one's fascinated eyes off her.   DAVID OVERBEY

Quotations from The Lonely Life, *by Bette Davis (New York, G.P. Putnam's Sons, 1962)*

officer who wants to be a priest. *Beyond the Forest* (1949) was forced upon her by Warners in spite of her warning that 'I'm too old and too strong for that part'. The film was savaged by the critics and the public stayed away. Nonetheless, it is one of the most enjoyable bad movies ever made. ('There never was a woman like Rosa Moline, a twelve-o'clock girl in a nine-o'clock town.') Davis pulls out all the stops and turns in one of the finest Bette Davis caricatures ever seen. She asked for her release from the studio and got it, although Jack Warner was considering her for Blanche in *A Streetcar Named Desire* (later made in 1951).

She was completing a rather ordinary melodrama about divorce, *Payment on Demand* (1951) at RKO, when she was offered the part of ageing actress Margo Channing in *All About Eve* (1950). Davis later recalled:

'I can think of no project that from the outset was as rewarding from the first day to the last . . . It was a great script, had a great director, and a cast of professionals all with parts they liked . . . After the picture was released I told Joe [Mankiewicz, the director] he had resurrected me from the dead.'

Davis was never better in a role that allowed

'There was more good acting at Hollywood parties than ever appeared on the screen'

---

her to play an actress larger than life, and at the same time to reveal the self-pity and vulnerability beneath. But this upswing in her career was not maintained; throughout the decade she was cast in poor roles.

Still, as had happened with *All About Eve*, a film came along which once more revitalized her career: Robert Aldrich's *What Ever Happened to Baby Jane?* (1962). She obviously more than enjoyed playing 'Grand Guignol', and the film was overwhelmingly popular everwhere in the world. Perhaps the one unfortunate aspect of its success was that, in spite of minor

Left: Bette became one of the murderer's victims in the whodunnit Death on the Nile. *Above: as the crazy, former child star in* What Ever Happened to Baby Jane? *she slowly destroyed her crippled sister*

Filmography

1931 Bad Sister; Seed; Waterloo Bridge; Way Back Home (GB: Old Greatheart). '32 The Menace; Hell's House (reissued as: Juvenile Court); The Man Who Played God (GB: The Silent Voice); So Big; The Rich Are Always With Us; The Dark Horse; Cabin in the Cotton; Three on a Match. '33 20,000 Years in Sing Sing; Parachute Jumper; Ex-Lady; The Working Man; Bureau of Missing Persons. '34 The Big Shakedown; Fashions of 1934 (GB: Fashion Follies of 1934; USA retitling for TV: Fashions); Jimmy the Gent; Fog Over Frisco; Of Human Bondage; Housewife. '35 Bordertown; The Girl From 10th Avenue (GB: Men on Her Mind); Front Page Woman; Special Agent; Dangerous. '36 The Petrified Forest; The Golden Arrow; Satan Met a Lady. '37 Marked Woman; Kid Galahad (USA retitling for TV: The Battling Bellhop); That Certain Woman; It's Love I'm After. '38 Jezebel; The Sisters. '39 Dark Victory; Juarez; The Old Maid; The Private Lives of Elizabeth and Essex. '40 All This and Heaven Too; The Letter. '41 the Great Lie; Shining Victory (uncredited guest); The Bride Came COD; The Little Foxes; The Man Who Came to Dinner. '42 In This Our Life; Now, Voyager. '43 Watch on the Rhine; Thank Your Lucky Stars; Old Acquaintance. '44 Mr Skeffington; Hollywood Canteen. '45 The Corn is Green. '46 A Stolen Life; Deception. '48 Winter Meeting; June Bride. '49 Beyond the Forest. '50 All About Eve. '51 Payment on Demand; Another Man's Poison (GB). '52 Phone Call From a Stranger; The Star. '55 The Virgin Queen. '56 The Catered Affair (GB: Wedding Breakfast); Storm Center. '59 John Paul Jones; The Scapegoat (GB). '61 Pocketful of Miracles. '62 What Ever Happened to Baby Jane? '63 La Noia (IT). '64 Dead Ringer (GB: Dead Image); Where Love Has Gone; Hush . . . Hush, Sweet Charlotte. '65 The Nanny (GB). '67 The Anniversary (GB). '69 Connecting Rooms (GB). '71 Bunny O'Hare. '72 Lo Scopone Scientifico (IT) (USA: The Scientific Cardplayer). '76 Burnt Offerings. '78 Return From Witch Mountain; Death on the Nile (GB).

Bette
DAVIS
JEZEBEL

with
HENRY FONDA   GEORGE BRENT
MARGARET LINDSAY DONALD CRISP FAY BAINTER
RICHARD CROMWELL HENRY O'NEILL SPRING BYINGTON JOHN LITEL
A WILLIAM WYLER PRODUCTION
A WARNER BROS. PICTURE

Directed by William Wyler, 1938
Prod co: Warner Brothers. **exec prod:** Hal B. Wallis. **ass prod:** Henry Blanke. **sc:** Clements Ripley, Abem Finkel, John Huston, Robert Bruckner, based on the play *Jezebel* by Owen Davis Sr. **photo:** Ernest Haller. **ed:** Warren Low. **art dir:** Robert Haas. **cost:** Orry-Kelly. **mus:** Max Steiner. **lyr:** Harry Warren, Al Dubin. **r/t:** 106 minutes.
Cast: Bette Davis (*Julie Marston*), Henry Fonda (*Pres Dillard*), George Brent (*Buck Cantrell*), Donald Crisp (*Dr Livingstone*), Fay Bainter (*Auntie Belle*), Margaret Lindsay (*Amy*), Henry O'Neill (*General Bogardus*), John Litel (*Jean La Cour*), Gordon Oliver (*Dick Allen*), Spring Byington (*Mrs Kendrick*), Margaret Early (*Stephanie Kendrick*), Richard Cromwell (*Ted Dillard*), Theresa Harris (*Zette*), Janet Shaw (*Molly Allen*), Irving Pichel (*Huger*), Eddie Anderson (*Gros Bat*), Symie Beard (*Ti Bat*), Lou Payton (*Uncle Cato*), George Renevant (*De Lautrec*).

Bette Davis regarded the lead role in *Jezebel* as poor compensation for not being cast as Scarlett O'Hara in *Gone With the Wind*.

While the publicity campaign to cast *Gone With the Wind* was in full swing, Warner Brothers happened to purchase, as part of an intricate deal, the rights to a play by Owen Davis Sr called *Jezebel*. It had not been very successful on the stage, and they had previously turned it down. But the similarities between it and *Gone With the Wind* were too obvious to be discounted. Both had a fiery, perverse, self-destructive heroine, a correct Southern gentleman with whim the heroine is hopelessly in love, a sweet and gentle other woman that the Southern gentleman marries in preference to the extravagant heroine, a suitable ration of physical disaster (plague in *Jezebel*, the burning of Atlanta in *Gone With the Wind*), lots of talk about the faded glory of the South and the ruthless North's probable victory in the Civil War, and a colourful assortment of gamblers and adventurers.

When *Jezebel* was announced for production late in 1937 Selznick was predictably aggrieved, and began firing off letters and cables to Harry Warner alleging unfair trade practices. Warners took little notice – although it is possible that they made some cuts in scenes that were particularly similar to those in *Gone With the Wind*.

Warners meant *Jezebel* to be as good as, if not better than, *Gone With the Wind*; and they certainly meant it to be first. To ensure quality they cast around Bette Davis (who had always been the centre of the concept) Henry Fonda as Pres Dillard, the gentleman she loves in vain, and, less excitingly, George Brent as her faithful beau Buck Cantrell who steps in to console her. Most importantly, William Wyler was assigned to direct the picture. Bette Davis felt she had been slighted by him at an earlier stage in her career, and intended to veto him as director. But he was suitably apologetic, and she decided that they could, after all, contrive to get along.

She later thought this the wisest decision she ever made, though at the time they continued to have their clashes. Wyler was already famed as an actors' director, but nobody who worked with him ever seemed to know how he achieved such fine results. He had no patience with incompetent actors, and was by no means easy for even the talented to work with, because he steadfastly refused to give readings of lines or describe exactly what he wanted. He seemed to goad and torment actors as much by his silence as by his tantrums, forcing them to search deeper and deeper into their roles and into themselves. This, naturally, could be a very uncomfortable process, and many actors described working with him as a kind of slow torture. Yet nearly all of them, including Bette Davis, admitted that they were never better than under his direction. This was the first of three films she made with him: the others were *The Letter* (1940) and *The Little Foxes* (1941).

Because of the (unadmitted) competition with *Gone With the Wind* there was some urgency about shooting the film, which, in any case, was not intended to be one of Warners' more expensive pieces. If it had been, surely, considering the central importance of the red dress the heroine wears to the ball, it would have been shot in colour. But Wyler, always a perfectionist, went way over schedule and budget, and there were plans to take him off the picture half-way through. Bette Davis intervened and flatly refused to work with anyone else; the film was completed as intended, even though Wyler sometimes shot a scene as many as 45 times to get a line or gesture absolutely right.

Even with the delays, the film opened some nine months before *Gone With the Wind* had started shooting. It was one of Warners' biggest box-office films of 1938 and Bette Davis' greatest personal success (and unarguably her best role) since *Of Human Bondage* (1934), winning her a second Oscar.

Though the film anticipated *Gone With the Wind* it nevertheless stands effectively on its own merits. Even today it lives up to the opinion of the contemporary *National Board of Review* writer who observed that its special quality was that it worked, not as 'the usual romantic Southern tale', but as 'a penetrating study of character in a setting whose conventional surface handsomeness does not nullify its essential truth and solidity'.

JOHN RUSSELL TAYLOR

Below: Wyler (in dark suit) directs Fonda and Davis in the ball scene

Julie Marston is the spoilt and wilful fiancée of a staid young banker, Pres Dillard. Because he will not indulge all her whims, she decides to embarrass him at the 1850 Olympus Ball, where their engagement is to be announced. All the unmarried girls traditionally wear white; she determines to wear red (1).

She creates a scandal, but makes herself look foolish — especially since Pres forces her to go through with the whole process of being shunned and slighted (2). She wheedles another admirer, Buck Cantrell, into taking her home. Pres breaks off their engagement and leaves New Orleans. A year later he returns and Julie is convinced he will now marry her. She arranges

a big coming-home party for him on her family's estate. However, he arrives with a sweet young Yankee bride (3).

At the party (4) Julie tells Buck that Pres has insulted her, and incites him to challenge Pres to a duel. This he does, but Pres is summoned back to New Orleans, where a plague of yellow fever has broken out, before it can be fought. His younger brother Ted takes his place (5) and kills Buck.

Hearing that Pres has been stricken with the plague, Julie travels to the city from the relative safety of the country to nurse him (6). When he is sent to a quarantine island, where most people go to die, Julie begs his wife Amy to be allowed to go with him. She promises that if he survives, she will bring him safely back to his wife.

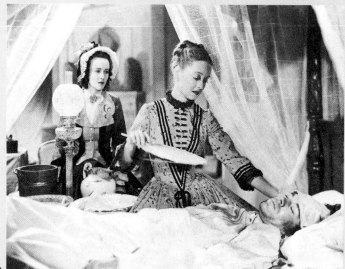

273

The Power Behind the Stars

Driven by a desire to vindicate the family name, Myron Selznick changed the Hollywood film industry by freeing top stars from the tyranny of the studios. His brother, David O. Selznick commented: 'My brother is the only man in history to make a fortune from revenge.'

Myron Selznick remains an enigmatic figure in the history of Hollywood, his name overshadowed by that of his publicity-minded younger brother David. While David O. Selznick continually strove to produce films of quality – and get his name in the papers – Myron preferred to operate away from the glare of the spotlights.

Myron was an agent. In the Twenties agents had occupied a subordinate position in show business. They were often failed actors or carnival grafters who wore loud clothes, smoked smelly cigars and were as trustworthy as race-track touts. When they were allowed inside studios, they entered by the back door.

Myron Selznick owed his success to an instinct for filling a power vacuum. During the Twenties, and into the Thirties, the six or eight men who controlled the major studios acquired enormous strength. All the top stars and directors were under long-term contracts and hence subject to the whims of these Titans. If a famous actor tried to seek more pay and better terms, he could find himself suspended by his own studio and blacklisted by the others.

Myron Selznick thought this system should be changed. Movie stars were too important –

Above left: Myron Selznick made the actor's agent a powerful force in Hollywood. Left: director William Wellman (smoking a pipe), a Selznick client, poses with some of the camera crew of Wings.
Some of the stars on Myron's books were (below, left to right) William Powell, Ida Lupino, Henry Fonda, Merle Oberon, Raymond Massey, ZaSu Pitts, Charles Laughton, and Lupe Velez and (opposite page top, left to right) Katharine Hepburn, Laurence Olivier, Fay Wray and Fredric March

and their careers much too brief – for them to be working at salaries far below their worth. Myron took up their cause. He did so not out of love for actors (he could tolerate them, but just barely); his underlying motive was revenge. He wanted to punish the moguls for ruining his father.

From easy street to skid row
His father, Lewis, had left the 'Zeleznick' family home in Kiev, Russia, at the age of 12 and laboured in a London factory to earn his passage to America. Before he was 24, he had founded a bank and three jewellery stores in Pittsburgh, Pennsylvania, where Myron was born on October 5, 1898.

Always ambitious for bigger things, Lewis moved his family to New York in 1910 and opened a huge jewellery store. When this failed, he invested in Universal Pictures but quarrelled with Carl Laemmle and joined World Film Corporation. Once more he was unable to get along with his partners and he departed to form Lewis J. Selznick Enterprises, taking with him World Film's brightest star, Clara Kimball Young. The Selznick fortunes soared, and the family took up residence in a 17-room apartment on Park Avenue.

Lewis brought his sons into the business early. Each day after school, Myron and David went to his office and listened to him conduct business in flamboyant style. When Myron was 21 his father appointed him vice-president in charge of production. The young man gave a press interview in which he said expansively: 'We're one big happy family, and there is no red tape in our family. Anyone can see me at any time.'

The crown prince was due for a fall. His father had made important enemies on his way to the

top, especially Adolph Zukor, the iron-willed boss of Famous-Players-Lasky (later Paramount). Zukor managed to undermine the Selznick operation. When Lewis pleaded for loans to keep his enterprise afloat, his fellow magnates turned their backs on him.

Lewis J. Selznick was ruined. He filed for bankruptcy in 1923, his wife sold her jewellery, their furniture was auctioned, and Myron and David were unemployed.

Myron tried to find work in Hollywood. All the studios turned him down. His father's old enemy, Carl Laemmle, told him: 'Get out of the picture business; you don't know anything about it, and you'll never get anywhere in it.' Myron found a position with independent producer Joseph Schenk, but his combativeness lost him the job. Locked out of the movie business, Myron decided to become an agent.

Milking the moguls

He began his own agency in 1928. His first important client was Lewis Milestone, the Russian-born director in whose house Myron had lived when he was broke. Milestone had filed for bankruptcy to avoid paying $200,000 to Warner Brothers for breach of contract. It was a clever ploy, except that no other studio would hire him.

Milestone was about to seek work in Europe when Myron found a producer who refused to go along with the studio boycott. He was a shy young Texan who was willing to top Milestone's salary at Warners. Milestone later discovered that he had signed with the film magnate Howard Hughes.

Another Myron Selznick client was the director William Wellman. He was making main features for Paramount at a paltry $250 a week. Assigned to direct *Wings* (1929) in

Texas, Wellman mentioned to Myron that the studio had overlooked the fact that his contract had expired.

'Go on location,' Myron instructed the director. 'Take all the time you need. Make the picture you want. You've got 'em where it hurts.'

Wings opened to great acclaim, and only then did Wellman inform Paramount that he had been off salary for months. Selznick stepped in and negotiated a contract that earned his client a four-figure weekly salary.

Myron's delight was doubled because Paramount was owned by Adolph Zukor, the man who had ruined his father. Myron raged:

'I'll break them all! I'll send those thieves and four-flushers to the poorhouse. Before I'm done, the artists in this town will have all the money.'

The artists soon discovered that they had a powerful ally. First with partner Frank Joyce, then on his own after 1935, Myron built the biggest talent agency in Hollywood. During the mid-Thirties, his clients included: Katharine Hepburn, Carole Lombard, Myrna Loy, Merle Oberon, Maureen O'Sullivan, ZaSu Pitts, Ginger Rogers, Lupe Velez, Fay Wray, Fred Astaire, Clive Brook, Gary Cooper, Henry Fonda, Charles Laughton, Boris Karloff, Fredric March, Laurence Olivier and William Powell.

His clients realized that Myron would do battle for them against any producer, including David O. Selznick. Myron was a major stockholder of his brother's independent production company, but that did not stop him from exacting stiff terms. Myron instructed the agents on his staff: 'When you talk to David, he's a producer, not my brother.'

Not only could Myron negotiate tough con-

tracts; he also had a showman's touch for recognizing fresh talent and guiding careers towards success. His most famous achievement was the casting of Vivien Leigh in the plum role of Scarlett O'Hara in *Gone With the Wind* (1939). This was a blow to another of Myron's clients, Carole Lombard, who had been eager to play opposite her sweetheart, Clark Gable. Myron quelled her ire by negotiating a contract with RKO that brought her $150,000 a picture plus a percentage of the profits. It was one of the first profit-sharing deals for a star, demonstrating Myron's creative talent for deal-making. He was also adept at 'packaging' – combining an important book or play with two stars, a director and a writer, all of them Selznick clients, from which he exacted his ten per cent commission. The package technique was later employed by Selznick's successors, giant agencies like MCA and William Morris, and is now standard in the Hollywood movie industry.

Myron's immense success brought him no contentment. He became notorious as an alcoholic and brawler; his bouts with John Barrymore and others became part of Hollywood legend. He adored his wife, the actress Marjorie Daw, but was often unfaithful to her. She sued him for divorce, asking for custody of their daughter and a share of his wealth, which she estimated at $10 million.

His power as the premier agent of Hollywood began to wane because of his growing inattention to business. His famous clients began drifting off to newer, more aggressive agencies. The drinking began to tell, and in early 1944 he suffered internal haemorrhages. On March 23 he died in Santa Monica Hospital of portal thrombosis. He was 45 years old.

BOB THOMAS

Harry Cohn

'I don't have ulcers - I give them'

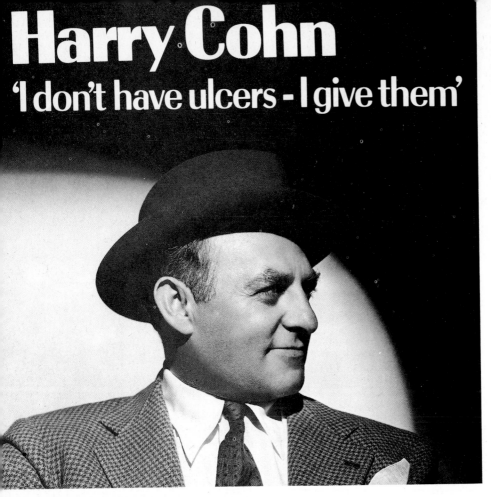

Harry Cohn, one of Hollywood's most successful moguls, hauled Columbia studios from Poverty Row into the big time. He was a man whose ruthlessness kept his employees in a state of constant fear, who regarded the business of movie-making as 'better than being a pimp'

The great days of the studio system were richly populated by colourful figures. Yet Harry Cohn barged to the front of them – more energetic and ruthless, and more enigmatic as a character than any of his extraordinary contemporaries. He was a man who inspired every emotion except indifference.

Harry Cohn was born in 1891, shortly before the movies. He lived through their greatest years, dying in 1958 during their decline. He came from a family of orthodox Jews, son of a German immigrant who worked as a tailor on the East Side of New York. By the time Cohn was 30, he had founded CBC (later Columbia Pictures), of which he was to be head of production and President. He was the only person to hold both positions in a major Hollywood film company.

But CBC (named after co-founders Cohn, Joe Brandt, and Harry's brother Jack Cohn) did not begin life as a major company – and here lies the true fascination of Cohn's career: he represents what was once – and for many people still is – the American Dream. He hauled himself and his studio from poverty. Columbia never rivalled MGM or Paramount for glamour during the golden Thirties and Cohn remained in constant awe of Mayer, but when the economic tide turned against the big studios, Columbia – one of the small studios in the area known as 'Poverty Row' – remained secure.

In January 1924, four years after it was founded, CBC became Columbia and within a further two years had offered shares on the open market. Slowly the company gained respectability, though Cohn insisted that it should remain in the heart of the 'Row'. It would expand, but only in the vicinity of its original Hollywood headquarters – an area Cohn knew only too well. He first acquired a small, two-stage studio in Gower Street. Over the next decade Columbia nibbled away at the surrounding blocks, buying up lot after lot; building sound stages, additional offices and workshops, and making the company self-contained. Although still small by the standards of the five majors, Columbia emerged as the most important of the minor studios.

Honest Harry

During the formative Twenties, Cohn retained iron control over the West Coast development while his brother controlled the New York side of the business. The distance of several thousand miles kept them from each other's throats – but the telephone lines were 'blue' with their exchanges.

What seems most remarkable about Harry Cohn's rise to power and wealth is that it appears to have been achieved without dishonesty. He paid his taxes scrupulously and accounted – with devastating accuracy – for all studio expenditure. He bargained and wheedled to get the best deal for the studio. Many actors and actresses found themselves loaned out to another studio, but the colossal cash gains from this went into Columbia's coffers, not the stars' bank accounts. The reasons for this respectability and penny-pinching stem from Cohn's childhood; his parents believed in unremitting hard work and honesty, and in those far off days there was no room for wastage. In addition, their son was gifted with the one quality that all self-made millionaires share – tireless energy. Cohn's working day was, literally, that. And once the studio day ended, the entertaining he did at home was concerned purely with business. His entire life was spent controlling all aspects of studio policy and production. He took lunch in the studio, visited the sets and viewed every movie. He would fine someone for leaving on an unnecessary light and negotiated major contracts personally.

In such matters, Cohn – whose dictatorship was absolute – was ruthless. His treatment of those unable – or, like Jean Arthur, unwilling – to contest his bullying was utterly heartless. Careers could be smashed, and artists given ten minutes to get out of the studio. No women's liberationist would complain of Cohn's attitude, since he treated his actresses and other women with the same contempt as he treated the men. He preferred to deal with men as he could not bear tears, and an actor such as Glenn Ford, who retaliated physically to Cohn's abuse, was subsequently treated better both professionally and socially.

Cohn modelled his office on that of the fascist dictator Benito Mussolini whom he had visited in Rome. It was not so much that Cohn admired Il Duce's politics, but he liked his style. Cohn's office was long and dominated by a massive desk – the lighting favoured him, shining intimidatingly at his visitors who had probably already been kept waiting in an outer office for hours. Once inside they would be told of their next assignment, of a loan-out to another studio, whether they could get married,

Rod Steiger (left) as the tyrannical movie producer in The Big Knife, *and (below, on the left) Broderick Crawford as the millionaire junk-dealer in* Born Yesterday – *both portrayals were inspired by Harry Cohn*

or even see the person they loved. Kim Novak found her romance with Sammy Davis Jr terminated when Davis, a coloured entertainer and therefore considered 'bad' for her image, was told to choose between working in lucrative nightclubs or continuing the affair. He preferred to carry on singing.

Working with Capra

In building Columbia, Cohn naturally had valuable help – and strokes of good fortune. The most significant of these was his early association with writer-director Frank Capra who first worked for Columbia on silent movies. Most importantly, he helped usher the studio into the sound era and it was at this time, according to Capra's autobiography *The Name Above the Title*, that his boss stopped calling him 'Dago'. Cohn learned respect for the man, if not for his Sicilian ancestry, and the two shared an artistic collaboration throughout the late Twenties and the Thirties. Other great directors worked with Cohn: Hawks on *The Criminal Code* (1931) and the masterpieces *Twentieth Century* (1934) and *Only Angels Have Wings* (1939); Ford on *The Whole Town's Talking* (1935); even Welles on *The Lady from Shanghai* (1946). But only Capra worked consistently and fruitfully for Columbia.

After the runaway success of *It Happened One Night* (1934), most of the ensuing Columbia–Cohn–Capra pictures of the Thirties were also successful, and the studio acquired a respectability from which its location on Poverty Row could not detract. Many of the fifty-plus Oscars that found their way behind Cohn's massive desk resulted from these halcyon days.

Despite such success, Cohn lost Capra (who left and formed his own company in the Forties) as he had lost the wonderful Barbara Stanwyck and the equally talented Jean Arthur who was terrified by his manner. She refused to have direct contact with him, was frequently suspended and finally ceased working for the studio: hardly surprising for a sensitive actress who could find herself in a conversation with a man liable to walk off to the private bathroom adjoining his office and urinate with the door open so that the chat could continue. The action typifies a man who had a daily manicure, dressed in the most expensive clothes and was obsessed with personal cleanliness, yet behaved like a hoodlum.

Lovely Rita

Cohn, however, was to find a replacement for Barbara Stanwyck and Jean Arthur. If not his greatest actress, beautiful Rita Hayworth became his greatest star. She came to prominence in *Only Angels Have Wings* (1939), co-starring with Arthur who was then in comparative decline. At the time Hayworth was receiving only $250 a week – a salary that was to rise ten-fold in the following years as she entered the realms of the great Hollywood love goddesses. Working for Columbia, and on loan-out, in dramas, comedies and musicals, Hayworth earned Cohn a fortune, but his interference with her love life – typically, he supervised her contract, her work and her lifestyle – alienated her. He also alienated his male leads, Glenn Ford and William Holden. He groomed them, paid them handsomely and seemed genuinely fond of the trio – his 'children' – yet resented their independence. By the late Forties and the Fifties, he had lost control of these and other artists.

Hayworth's swansong for Cohn and Columbia was *Pal Joey* (1957). The wheel had come full circle and she was to be replaced as the studio's top star by the latest Cohn discovery, Kim Novak, who supported her in the film just as Rita herself had supported Jean Arthur 18 years previously. Frank Sinatra, Hayworth's other co-star on *Pal Joey*, remarked that, for him, Hayworth *was* Columbia – 'She gave them class'.

Cohn did nothing in a small way. He gambled furiously, often as much as $10,000 a day. This obsession was halted by the money men in the East when the total losses for one single season reached $400,000. His lifestyle was modified only by his certain 'knowledge' that he would die in his sixties, but during the last decade of his life Cohn refused to relinquish control of the studio, since the only alternative he could envisage was an even earlier death. He resented the independence of producers and directors such as Stanley Kramer and Fred Zinnemann as much as he did that of his stars, yet he could not resist the tide of a changing Hollywood.

Cruel but kind

Boorish and bullying, Cohn was also capable of great kindness. Even his most intimate colleagues and workers could be struck dumb by his outbursts of cruelty, only to find on another occasion that a mammoth hospital bill for an ageing mother had been settled by Cohn personally. Cohn would accept no thanks for such an action and would warn the recipient never to tell anyone of his generosity. Also, as the studio gradually slimmed down its personnel, Cohn made sure that the old Columbia staff had jobs to go to.

He was the model for Broderick Crawford's politician in *All the King's Men* (1949) and his crude junk-dealer in *Born Yesterday* (1950) – both Columbia pictures – and Rod Steiger's studio boss in *The Big Knife* (1955). Cohn remains an enigma. He has never been described as a happy man, and his cruelty became legendary. But at his gaudy funeral, the tributes flowed with a mixture of affection, hypocrisy and disbelief that the man had finally succumbed. It is said that most people attended it to make sure he was dead. In the history of the cinema, however, Harry Cohn and Columbia deserve a prominent place.

BRIAN BAXTER

Some of the actresses Cohn's Columbia loved and lost: Jean Arthur (top left), overjoyed when her contract expired; Kim Novak (top) whose love-life was ruled by the studio; Barbara Stanwyck (above) who sued for more money; Rita Hayworth (below with Harry) who angered Cohn by eloping with Aly Khan

Poverty Row

In a board meeting at Monogram Pictures an executive once remarked that the company was 'standing on the brink of an abscess'. Between this Goldwynism and Jean-Luc Godard's gesture of dedicating his first feature to Monogram, lies the truth about Poverty Row

It is a striking aspect of Hollywood's economic history that the companies which dominated the industry by the early Thirties are those that still hold power today. And although there has always been competition, none of the new-comers has proved able to join the ranks of Warners, Paramount, Universal, United Artists, MGM and 20th Century-Fox.

It was not always so. In the early Thirties there was a plethora of small companies known collectively as 'Poverty Row'. With a bit of luck any of them might have climbed the ladder to 'major' status. They had, after all, the shining example of Columbia who graduated to 'major' status in the Thirties.

Many Poverty Row outfits were survivors from the silent era. They experienced the crippling difficulties of the Depression and did not constitute the kind of enterprises bankers were prepared to rescue: they either amalga-mated or died.

Poverty Row represented an actual place: roughly a block's length on Gower Street, parallel to Sunset Boulevard. One of the tougher resident studios on the block was

Tiffany whose history dated back to 1922; it released 26 pictures in 1930 – only three less than Columbia. Tiffany's films for that year included *Journey's End*, a co-production with a British company shot with Hollywood's super-ior sound equipment and an imported cast, and *Medicine Man*, an abortive attempt to make a comedy star out of Jack Benny.

Hollywood and bust

Fortunes changed so fast, however, that by the summer of 1932 Tiffany had to throw in the towel. Its final two releases were taken over by another minor, the somewhat inaptly named World Wide Pictures. Indeed it was characteristic of these small fry to give them-selves impressive names and trade marks. There were other big-sounding outfits: Mayfair, Maj-estic, Liberty and Supreme; all of them made cheap pictures on rented studio space.

Distribution of Poverty Row product was a complex business. In the first place these films were competing against the B pictures made by the major studios. But the pattern of the B-film industry was the same as that of main features: film-making was done in Hollywood, while the point of distribution and the office for the sales staff was in New York. From here films would be booked out to the cinema circuits or re-leased through independent regional distribu-tors (known as 'exchanges'). In some situ-ations Poverty Row films were slotted into programmes at independent cinemas; else-where movie houses owned by the Hollywood majors frequently played B pictures other than their own. But it was the independent cinema owners in small towns who really welcomed

Above: the corner of Hollywood's Sunset Boulevard and Gower Street in the early Twenties when the appearance of many small studios earned it the nickname 'Poverty Row'

the Poverty Row product as cheap and reliable programme material.

Well-known stars were a rarity on Poverty Row, only working there when they could not find work higher up the ladder. To create stars would have taken better merchandizing and more prestigious pictures than these com-panies were capable of, but occasionally they were able to capitalize on the reissue of certain films after their leading actors had become major stars.

Allied Pictures Corporation (not the same as the later firm Allied Artists) had a typical stroke of luck with *A Shriek in the Night* (1933) that had starred Ginger Rogers before she became a big name at RKO. PRC (Producers Releasing Corporation) had given Alan Ladd sixth billing in *Paper Bullets* (1941), but when the company relaunched the picture two years later, as *Gangs Inc*, Ladd appeared from the credits to be the top star; the fact was that he had become a new sensation at Paramount in the meantime.

At first sight Grand National seemed to be on to a good thing when James Cagney, rebelling against the big studio system, signed up with the company in its first year of existence. Even with Cagney's name on the payroll, however, finance was still hard to come by and Grand National's two films with the star, *Great Guy* (1936) and *Something to Sing About* (1937), lacked the gloss of major studio films. After

Animating the Ape

Filming *King Kong* involved many ingenious trick effects. Ray Harryhausen, world-famous special-effects man, describes the film's technical innovations

In 1933 RKO presented *King Kong* as 'the Eighth Wonder of the World'. Of course audiences knew that he was not actually alive. Yet Kong, like his prehistoric companions, looked so amazingly lifelike that the public, for almost half a century, has credited him with a reality and personality of his own.

The illusion was basically achieved by the extensive use of the process of stop-motion animation. Successive still poses are photographed on motion picture, frame by frame. The process is similar to that of the animated cartoon, but unlike the cartoon the subject to be given movement is made in a full three-dimensional form; and this dimension gives an appearance of greater reality.

Over the years I have come to prefer the word 'Dynamation' for this process capable of giving the illusion of a living form to something which could in all probability not be found in nature, or photographed in the ordinary way. I have adopted this term because Charles Schneer, my associate for many years, and myself found so often that the word 'animation' was interpreted to mean the use of cartoon animation.

On screen King Kong appears 50 feet (15.24m) tall. In reality he stood a mere 18in (45cm) – a scale model. He was the creation of Willis J. O'Brien, a wizard at technical effects since 1914, who had devised the prehistoric creatures for *The Lost World* in 1925. The great ape's interior skeleton was constructed of steel, with complicated friction ball-and-socket joints. His flesh was of rubber; and his exterior was covered in clipped rabbit fur (which gave the animators some problems because it tended to show their finger-marks). The figure would hold in any position in which he was placed: to keep him upright, as his weight moved from foot to foot, required a baseboard with holes into which he could be firmly fixed and yet remain mobile.

For some close-up scenes – for instance where Fay Wray is held in the creature's hand, or actors are seen struggling as he grips them in his teeth – full-size animated sections of the beast were required. For the scene where the ape chews people, a huge model was constructed, and operated by motors and compressed air. It required 40 bear hides to cover it,

Top: Fay Wray as King Kong's victim. Above: the diminutive Kong – an 18-inch model worked and moved by hand – photographed against a painted backdrop of the jungle. Below: the sequence filmed above is back-projected onto a screen in front of which the actress Fay Wray is positioned (on a dummy tree branch), and the entire sequence is filmed by the camera (bottom left)

Above: Kong shaking people off a tree trunk. The ape model is worked by hand against a painted backdrop and the sequence is filmed through a painted glass plate edged with real foliage. The whole sequence is printed together with the matte shots (top left) of actors walking up a ramp

and four men to make it move convincingly. The eyebrows raised or lowered at will; the great 'twelve-inch' eyeballs rolled and blinked, and the jaws seemed to change expression as they clamped down on the unfortunate natives. Similarly, internally operated sections of arms and legs were built in full-size, all to maintain the impression of Kong's gargantuan appearance.

To combine these disparate elements, so different in scale, required some very elaborate mathematical work, and the use of the whole repertory of special photography as it was then known – though the work on *Kong* in itself developed the range of special effects. A usual method was to obscure a part of the camera lens with a painted glass while filming one element of the scene – perhaps the animated miniature. The 'blackout' would mean that a certain portion of each frame remained unexposed. The film could therefore be run back to the start; a different mask was placed over the lens to correspond to the material already shot; and the film was then exposed for a second time, to photograph the setting.

This technique is the basis of the 'matte' shot; and already in 1933 very much more sophisticated developments of the system were available, using colour filters. The principle was that an image photographed under orange-yellow light would pass through orange-dyed positive film and print as normal on the negative film. On the second exposure, blue light reflected from the scene's background would be blocked out by the image on the (orange-dyed) positive film and register as a negative image on the negative film. Through this technique, for example, figures could be made to interact with backgrounds in a way that could not have been filmed normally.

King Kong was one of the earliest – at RKO the first – films to use much back projection. This technique, employed extensively in the later Thirties and Forties, involved projecting a filmed background onto a large translucent screen, while the actors performed and were filmed in front of it. *King Kong* made use of a new form of cellulose back-projection screen which won its inventor, Sidney Saunders, an Academy Award. Previously sand-blasted glass screens had been employed, and apart from giving rather poor technical results, exposed actors and crew to grave peril from breakage.

Almost an inversion of this process was the projection of live-action shots of actors onto a tiny screen within a miniature model of the setting. This was used for the sequence in which we see Fay Wray dangled from the Empire State Building by Kong. Subsequently known as 'miniature projection' the technique was used again by Willis J. O'Brien in another gorilla movie, *Mighty Joe Young* (1949).

The spectacular jungle scenes were achieved by the use of paintings on three or four separated planes of fine plate glass. Miniature sets – trees made of paper and lacquer, thin copper, the twisted roots of old vines – were then sandwiched in between them. The technique was probably to an extent influenced by the work of early Victorian illustrators, in which the impression of depth is achieved by a dark foreground, a medium-toned middle ground and a pale, diffused background. The method produced an illusion of great depth in the fabulous, mystic jungles.

Thus it was that a team of twentieth-century necromancers employed all the magic of the painter, the model-maker, the camera, the laboratory, and the tricks of the animator – as well as intense patience – to achieve a work of magnificent scenic value and fantastic imagination that has stood the test of time. They had achieved a milestone in the creation of the grand illusion.   RAY HARRYHAUSEN

Above and right: in this scene of the ape on the rampage in New York, the illusion of perspective is achieved by matching a painted backdrop of the Hudson River shoreline to a glass painting of skyscrapers and in turn to the model of Kong. The model aircraft were moved on wires, and a doll replaced Miss Wray

The Art of Animation

Reynaud's skipping girl bounce slightly each time her feet hit the ground.

Thus, when moving pictures proper arrived, there was a pre-existing tradition of animation. It took slight ingenuity and the example of Georges Méliès' magic films to suggest the idea of photographing series drawings onto film, frame by frame, to give movement to the cartoonist's creations.

Above: Winsor McCay's Gertie the Dinosaur. *Left: Dave Fleischer's feature* Gulliver's Travels. *Below left: the Phenakistiscope, a toy demonstrating a primitive form of animated cartoon in the 1830s. Below: Disney's* Snow White and the Seven Dwarfs

Animation is older than cinema itself. There were moving drawings long before the days of *The Great Train Robbery*. But film made many new techniques available to artists and cartoonists, and by the mid-Thirties animated films in many different styles were being produced all over the world

Animation is the oldest art of moving pictures. In the eighteenth century crude mechanical movement was produced in the images projected by the magic lanterns of travelling showmen. Sixty years before the Kinetoscope and the Cinématographe, scientists demonstrated the basic optical principles from which the cinema was to be developed by means of toys which used short sequences of cartoon drawings to produce the illusion of movement. In these toys – the Phenakistiscope and Stroboscope of 1832 and the Zoëtrope, first described in 1834 – the essential principle of the animated cartoon is already fully stated.

In the 1880s the Frenchman Emile Reynaud (1844–1918) succeeded in projecting onto a screen the moving drawings produced by his invention the Praxinoscope; and by 1892 he was able to present his Pantomimes Lu-

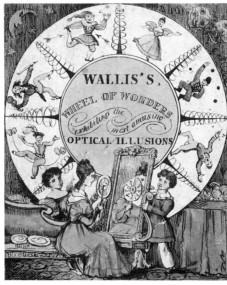

mineuses – little plays performed by animated cartoon characters, the direct forerunner of modern film animation.

Apart from his technical ingenuity, Emile Reynaud, as an artist, was the first great animator, accurately reproducing in his little drawings the sense of real-life movement. A present-day animator, Richard Williams, still marvels at the lifelike way that the braids of

(1907), experimented with giving life to normally inanimate objects. In 1910 Emile Cohl made *Le Tout Petit Faust* (*The Little Faust*) in which little dolls or puppets were animated instead of drawings. The great master of puppet animation, however, was the Russian Ladislav Starevitch (1892–1965) who made a series of delightful films of anthropomorphic insects and animals that recalled the work of the nineteenth-century French illustrator Grandville. In the Soviet Union Starevitch's most notable follower was Alexander Ptushko (b.1900) whose feature *The New Gulliver* (1935) achieved international reputation. In this, as in his later *The Little Gold Key* (1939), Ptushko combined live actors with his animated dolls.

Ptushko's example inspired a whole school of puppet animation in the Soviet Union and, much later, in Czechoslovakia. Elsewhere the practice was sporadic. In France Jean Painlevé and René Bertrand used plasticine dolls for *Barbe Bleue* (1938). In Britain Len Lye and Humphrey Jennings collaborated on *Birth of a Robot* (1936). In Holland production was more consistent thanks to the work of the Hungarian Georg Pal (b.1908) and Joop Geesink (b.1913), their work often being sponsored

Early this century the English-born pioneer of American cinema, J. Stuart Blackton (1875–1941), originally a newspaper cartoonist, made *Humorous Phases of Funny Faces* (1906) and *The Magic Fountain Pen* (1909). More significant, however, was the work of Emile Cohl (1857–1938), a well-known newspaper cartoonist in Paris and already 50 years old when he made his first cartoon film, *Fantasmagorie*, in 1908. In the course of the next ten years, first in France and then in the USA, Cohl made hundreds of short films. Working in the most basic of graphic styles, he had a gift for giving vigorous characterization to little creatures who were often no more than circles, lines and dots traced on the film.

From strip to screen

These pioneer days of the cinema coincided with the great period of the comic strip, and newspaper cartoonists in every country – in England, for example, Harry Furniss and Tom Webster – undertook the laborious work of bringing their characters to life on the screen. The most successful was the American artist Winsor McCay (1871–1934) whose masterpiece was *Gertie the Dinosaur* (*c*.1909), originally filmed for use in a vaudeville act in which McCay talked to, petted and fed the large, flirtatious and bashful prehistoric beast.

Other characters, even before Mickey Mouse and his entourage, rivalled the status of live film stars. Prototypes were: Baby Snookums, originated between 1912 and 1914 by Emile Cohl and George McManus; Colonel Heeza Liar, John Randolph Bray's skit on Theodore Roosevelt; Bud Fisher's long-lasting Mutt and Jeff; George Herriman's Krazy Kat; and Max

Fleischer's Koko the Clown and Betty Boop. The greatest cartoon star of silent films, however, was Felix the Cat, created by the Australian-born Pat Sullivan (1887–1933).

Mickey Mouse, animated for Disney by Ub Iwerks, came in 1928; and his popularity and the success of the first Silly Symphonies enabled Disney to effect a revolution in animation. Throughout the Thirties Disney dominated the field, and his technical and industrial innovations and achievements culminated in the first cartoon feature film, *Snow White and the Seven Dwarfs* (1937), followed by the innovatory *Fantasia* (1940).

No-one could rival Disney; but the audiences now demanded cartoons in every cinema programme, and each major company established its own animation production. Fired by Disney's success with *Snow White*, the Fleischer studio later embarked on feature production with the admirable *Gulliver's Travels* (1939); but after the commercial failure of *Mr Bug Goes to Town* (1941) the Fleischers concentrated on the production of shorts.

Puppet masters

There were other styles of animation. Influenced by the trick films of Méliès, a number of early film-makers, including Segundo de Chomon in *El Hotel Electrico* (1905, The Electric Hotel) and J. Stuart Blackton in *Haunted Hotel*

Top: Disney's Fantasia *combined cartoon and classical music to remarkable effect. Above right: Alexander Ptushko's* The New Gulliver. *Right: the animal puppets of Ladislav Starevitch. Below: cartoon images drawn by Emile Reynaud for his Praxinoscope*

by big industrial firms. After 1940 Pal worked in the USA, lending his ingenuity to science fiction films like *Destination Moon* (1950).

Lotte Reiniger (b.1899), whose creative career now spans more than sixty years, went back to one of the most venerable forms of light show, the oriental shadow theatre. Even before she began her first experiments in 1918, other film-makers had used crude cut-out silhouettes for film animation; but Reiniger, an artist of genius, transformed the style. Using scissors as

freely as other artists might use pen or brush, she created a world of exquisite, filigree beings who were animated, step by step, on a 'trick table' largely developed by herself and her collaborators – husband Carl Koch (1892–1963), Walter Ruttmann and Bertold Bartosch. In 1926 Reiniger made the first *true* feature-length animated film, *Die Arbenteuer des Prinzen Achmed* (*The Adventures of Prince Achmed*), a work whose quality has not diminished more than half a century later. With the coming of sound she experimented with music and her *Harlekin* (1931, *Harlequin*), *Carmen* (1933) and *Papageno* (1935) are perfect choreographic creations. Since World War II she has worked in Britain and, occasionally, Canada.

Making waves
Reiniger's main creative collaborator on *Prince Achmed* was Bartosch (1893–1968) who excelled in producing effects of atmosphere, snow scenes, sea waves and the like. Before working with Reiniger, Bartosch had made a number of advertising films. Afterwards he went on to make his masterpiece *L'Idée* (1932, *The Idea*), a tragic, symbolist allegory of man's struggle for the Ideal, based on illustrations by Franz Masereel and with music by Arthur Honegger. Bartosch combined cut-out silhouettes on the lines of the Reiniger technique with subtle effects achieved by control of photographic exposure and diffusion of the light source.

It was watching Bartosch at work on *L'Idée* that stimulated the Russian emigré illustrator Alexandre Alexeieff (b.1901) to try his hand at animation. Working with his future wife, Claire Parker, he made his most remarkable contribution with the 'pinboard' – a soft board studded with thousands of headless pins which are raised or deflected so that the reflection of light on their surfaces produces an image

Above: some of the animated cut-out silhouettes created by Lotte Reiniger. Above right: Len Lye and Humphrey Jennings' Birth of a Robot. Right: one of Georg Pal's characters from his Puppetoon series

that may be subtly changed. The technique enabled Alexeieff and Parker to give the images of their *Une Nuit sur le Mont Chauve* (1933, *Night on a Bare Mountain*) the range and subtlety of a dry-point etching. Later they were to use their pinboard for *En Passant* (1943), made for the National Film Board of Canada, *Le Nez* (1963, *The Nose*) and *Pictures at an Exhibition* (1972).

The early work of Bartosch and Alexeieff was among the most sophisticated animation of the inter-war period, comparable with the abstract films made in Germany in the early Twenties. The earliest abstract animated film appears to have been *Opus I* shown by the painter Walter Ruttmann (1887–1941) in 1921. It is now not quite clear what system of animation Ruttmann used for this 'absolute' film and its successors, *Opus II*, *Opus III* and *Opus IV*, which occupied him between 1921 and 1925. Ruttmann also provided the 'Hawk Dream' sequence of Lang's *Die Nibelungen* (1924), and later worked with Lotte Reiniger.

Meanwhile, two other painters, who had been associated with the Dada group in Zurich, were also seeking a form of dynamic graphic art through animated film. Viking Eggeling (1880–1925), a friend of Modigliani and Arp, completed only one film, *Diagonal Symphonie*,

which had its first public show in Berlin at the moment he was dying of blood poisoning. For his contemporaries the film revealed new spatial relationships in abstract art.

Hans Richter (1888–1976) was deeply involved with Eggeling and his experiments. Both, in Richter's words, 'saw in the completely liberated (abstract) form not only a new medium to be exploited, but the challenge towards a "universal language"'. Richter's *Rhythmus 21*, completed in 1921 (the year that Eggeling had made the first version of *Diagonal Symphonie*) was followed by *Rhythmus 23*, *Rhythmus 25* and *Rhythmus 26*. Later Richter incorporated his experiments into advertising films, and for the rest of his life – especially after his emigration to America in 1940 – was an inspirational figure for the young avant-garde film-makers of successive generations. Oscar Fischinger (1900–67), an engineer and draughtsman, was inspired by the work of Eggeling and Richter to embark on his series of eight *Studies* (1927–32), numbered 5 to 12.

Lye's painted film
The film work of Len Lye (b.1901), a New Zealander, was altogether more intuitive. He had been variously inspired by Oceanic Island art, Australian travelogues and Soviet art, and spent a year on a South Sea island before making his way to England in the mid-Twenties. The Film Society helped him with the costs of a ten-minute cartoon, *Tusalava* (1929); then he managed to interest John Grierson in his revolutionary (and attractively inexpensive) notion of painting directly onto film. The results were *Colour Box*, *Kaleidoscope* (both 1935) and *Trade Tattoo* (1937).

Lye moved to the USA in 1944. Though he later seemed discouraged by lack of interest in his work, he resumed film-making in the late Fifties. His influence has, perhaps, been strongest through the work of his successor, Norman McClaren, who followed him to John Grierson's GPO Film Unit in 1937, and whose work in abstract film has been seminal to the development of animation since the beginning of the Forties.

DAVID ROBINSON

THE BEGINNING OF
DISNEY'S WONDERFUL WORLD

Walt Disney was born in Chicago on December 5, 1901. He attended classes at Kansas City Art Institute, and served in the Ambulance Corps in World War I. After the war he worked for a commercial art studio, where he first met Ub Iwerks who was later to be his most important collaborator. In 1920 he began to make animated advertising films for the Kansas City Film Advertising Company, and began to produce his own 'Laugh-O-Grams'. His 'Laugh-O-Gram' company went into liquidation, however, and in 1923 he went to Hollywood with his brother Roy (1894–1971) and established his own studio. From 1923 to 1927 he made the *Alice in Cartoonland* series, combining live and animated action, for the distributor M.J. Winkler. After 1925 he was joined by Ub Iwerks, who worked with him on developing the *Oswald the Lucky Rabbit* (1927–28) and *Mickey Mouse* series (1928–53).

In 1928 Disney formed Walt Disney Productions, and broke into sound with *Steamboat Willie* (1928). This and *Skeleton Dance* (1929), which inaugurated his Silly Symphonies, gave him an ascendancy over every other American

animation firm which was never seriously to be challenged. In 1932 he first used colour in *Flowers and Trees*; and in 1937, with *The Old Mill*, revealed the full potential of the three-dimensional effects he could give his animation pictures with his Multiplane process – involving the accurate focusing of animated images arranged in a sequence of planes.

Throughout the Thirties Disney was producing an average of 18 cartoon shorts a year,

Previous page: the cover of Mickey Mouse Weekly, *13 November, 1937, featuring a gallery of Disney characters. This page: Walt Disney (left) and four of his most innovative early films.* Steamboat Willie *(below left) and* Skeleton Dance *(bottom left) combined superb animation with exciting experiments in sound;* Flowers and Trees *(below) was the first film in three-strip Technicolor, and* Snow White and the Seven Dwarfs *(above) the first feature-length cartoon*

and developing his world-famous repertory company of Mickey and Minnie Mouse, Donald Duck, Pluto, Goofy and their supporting players. In 1937 he released his first feature-length cartoon *Snow White and the Seven Dwarfs*. It was followed by *Pinocchio* and *Fantasia* (both 1940), *Dumbo* (1941) and *Bambi* (1942).

The innovations of *Fantasia* (1940) in interpreting classical music through realistic or abstract animated images are better appreciated today than they were on their first appearance when Disney was charged with overweening pretensions.

THE DISNEY LEGACY

Richard Williams, Oscar-winning animator of *A Christmas Carol* (1972), reveals Disney's unequalled contribution to the development of animated film

Every working animator is deeply indebted to Walter Elias Disney. Even those who most dislike the content and graphic style of the films made by his studio still owe him an enormous amount. Disney did not invent the medium, but in a matter of some twelve years – between 1928 and 1940 – he transformed it into a highly sophisticated, perfected tool.

The technical innovations for which he was responsible are astounding. It is hard for us today to appreciate the impact of sound – which Disney first used with cartoons in 1928 – but when people saw *Steamboat Willie* (1928) and *Skeleton Dance* (1929), saw these little drawings dancing and singing and talking, the shock was tremendous. A lot of new artists were attracted into the field just by that alone. Then again, the introduction of colour, in

The immediate pre-war period was unhappy for Disney. In 1941 dissatisfaction among the staff over pay differentials and film credits resulted in a bitter strike by members of the Cartoonists Guild. Art Babbitt was sacked, but after long legal wrangling reinstated. He returned to the studio for a token year; Disney had lost a friend and a key collaborator.

The Reluctant Dragon (1941) inaugurated an unfortunate period of combining live action with cartoons. Its immediate successors were *Saludos Amigos* (1942) and *Three Caballeros* (1944) – both aimed at capturing a new Latin American market to make up for lost European

audiences – and *Song of the South* (1946). Between 1942 and 1946 the Disney studios did much work for the government, including the remarkable propaganda piece, *Victory Through Air Power* (1943).

Following World War II, Disney's output became more and more diverse. Apart from feature-length cartoons of continued technical excellence, he inaugurated the True Life Adventure Series of nature documentaries and embarked on the production of live-action films – distinguished by his acute ability to cater to popular tastes.   DAVID ROBINSON

The post-World War II work of the Disney studios will be dealt with in detail in a later chapter.

All illustrations copyright Walt Disney Productions.

Left: Pinocchio desperately tries to escape the whale's enfolding jaws. Above left: Mickey, the sorcerer's apprentice, uses magic to avoid doing the housework in the first section of Fantasia. *Above: Bambi with his mother just before she is killed by hunters and he is left alone to fend for himself in the forest*

Flowers and Trees (1932) was a revelation.

The next step forward was *The Three Little Pigs* (1933). Animators agree that this was the first time there had been *acting* instead of just movement in animated films. Felix and Krazy Kat and the rest had been characters, of course; but here were three little pigs, each one acting differently, expressing a different and distinguishable personality. In the succeeding four years between that film and *Snow White and the Seven Dwarfs*, the Walt Disney studios worked out the entire vocabulary of animation. There have been no real advances in animation since that time – only artistic and stylistic developments.

When Art Babbit, one of the greatest Disney pioneers, conducted a seminar at our studios (Richard Williams Animation), he told us:

'We have to *advance backwards* to 1940 to achieve the level of craftsmanship attained by Disney at that time; and *then* we will advance forwards to the Seventies and Eighties.'

The elements of good animation are *timing* and *spacing*. The timing is a matter of rhythm, like music – the ability to anticipate things or to drag back, like passing notes in music. At Disneys they discovered the formulas for giving weight, giving lightness, for making actions stronger. When you get out of a chair, for instance, you go *down* before you go up. When you go forward, you first press back. A lot of this is commonsense; but the Disney studio formulated it, learned how people act and react and how many drawings to use.

Spacing – the matter of where you place those drawings – is crucial to the final effect. Ken Harris, another of the great animators, who is now 81, still corrects my animation, showing that by just moving the thrust of a head slightly, it becomes *correct*. 'It's just not *quite* in the right place, Dick', he will say, 'I hope you don't mind'. And he's always right. There's nothing magical or mysterious about it; they just learned it there at Disneys. Mastering spacing and timing is a matter of achieving plasticity in the movement – weight, spring, life. It is something quite distinct from graphic qualities. There are people who can create marvellous graphic qualities, but cannot animate, cannot give a sense of weight or of movement to things.

When Disney was starting out in Hollywood in the Twenties, the real business of animation and the best people were all in New York. Disney imported several of them to Hollywood – including his old collaborator Ub Iwerks who was the most brilliant inventor. Disney was lucky, ironically, that it was the Depression period. All the veterans say that they might never have gone to Disneys but that they were starving. They accepted his offer of jobs, and then stayed on because they were fascinated. Disney had the brains to reward his best men well, and they just found they spent their whole lives there.

Disney next sought out the best young artists from all over the States. Thousands went through the studio; and they ended up

with maybe twenty who had flair for animation. By the time of *The Jungle Book* (1967) – the animation in that brought the rest of us to our knees – there were nine old men left, all from the class of '33 or '34, people who had come in with the Depression and learned from the old New York guys. They were much more sophisticated artists. Nobody else came through the ranks because nobody else was needed.

Disney, back in the Thirties, had chosen the right people and formed a good school. He provided a hot-house atmosphere; artists could do things over and over again until they got them perfect – which is how you learn.

A lot of what they discovered has been forgotten by the animation world; but it is still there at Disneys, and with the Disney veterans. When Art Babbitt came here to London, we closed our studio down and all went back to school. The notes we made during that time are an absolute textbook of Disney animation discoveries. If I want to animate someone skating, I can work it all out for myself; or I can just turn to the Babbitt notes, and there it all is, perfectly formulated.

Disney laid down the principles and the standards which prevail today. Some singular artists, like Norman McLaren, have been able to go their own way. Some others have tried to ignore Disney; but for a real animator it would be madness to disregard his legacy.

RICHARD WILLIAMS

From an interview with David Robinson, December 1979

Stars in Line

From ink-wells and paintboxes, they poured into Hollywood in the Thirties to charm their way into every moviegoer's heart . . .

The pen and ink world of the animated cartoon film curiously paralleled the flesh and blood world of the feature film during the Thirties. Like their human counterparts, many great cartoon stars of the silent era failed to find a voice in the age of the talkie, and fell fatally by the wayside. In their place new stars rose to join the few survivors.

When *Steamboat Willie* came whistling round the river bend on November 21, 1928, the first star of the sound cartoon was born. He was Mickey Mouse – devised by Walt Disney and brilliantly animated to music and sound effects by Ub Iwerks. But the Aesop's Fables gang was not far behind. This merry if motley menagerie from the Van Beuren studio scoffed their synchronized way through *Dinner Time* on December 17, while just nine days later Oswald the Lucky Rabbit came roaring in on *Sick Cylinders* with music and effects by courtesy of the Universal Jazz Band.

Oswald, whose cartoon career had begun in 1927 with *Trolley Troubles*, had proved less than lucky for the Disney–Iwerks team that had created him. But for Walter Lantz, Friz Freleng, Hugh Harman and Rudolf Ising, the ex-Disney animators who had stayed on with Universal after their director had departed to make a fresh start with Mickey Mouse, Oswald was a success. As a rabbit he was little more than Felix the Cat with extended ears – a black blob in white gloves which had three little lines on the backs and buttons, standard issue for

all cartoon characters since the days of Bud Fisher's Mutt and Jeff.

Felix the Cat himself, the great cartoon hero of the Twenties, failed to make the switch to sound, and a comeback in colour in *The Goose That Laid the Golden Egg* (1936) was to no avail. Oswald not only survived the switch to sound, but swung on through the Thirties to notch up over two hundred cartoons. After early efforts like *Chili Con Carmen* (1930), he starred in a string of stories in which he was title-billed: *Oswald in the Navy* (1930) and *Oswald in Wonderland* (1931), for example. Somewhere in mid-career Oswald's skin was turned from black to white in an attempt to capture the new cuteness of the Disney bunnies seen in the Silly Symphonies. *The Wily Weasel* and *The Playful Pup* (both 1937) are typical of this period and symptomatic of Ozzie's ultimate slide into obscurity.

Krazy Kat was another survivor from the silent era. Originated in the Sunday 'funnies' by eccentric cartoonist George Herriman, Krazy had first come to life on the cinema screen in 1916, one of many newspaper-strip characters animated by W.R. Hearst's International studio under the creative supervision of young Gregory La Cava. Revived in 1925 at Columbia, Krazy became the studio's only cartoon character of the period. The top animation team of Ben Harrison and Manny Gould found no problem in synchronizing Krazy to sound and brought out their oddly titled *Ratskin* in August 1929.

Although comic-art purists found little of their beloved Herriman original in the animated version, enough *kraziness* remained in the Kat's capers to make many of the visual gags still seem outstanding today. The titles are characterized by terrible puns, such as *Svengarlic* (1931), *Hic Cups the Champ* (1932) and *Broadway Malady* (1933). But the mid-Thirties brought to Krazy that same softening of style that had affected Oswald (as well as a girlfriend called Kitty Kat) and 14 years of fast fun petered out in the sentimentality of *The Little Lost Sheep* (1939).

The Fleischer studio, run by brothers Max (producer) and Dave (director), was the top animation studio of the early Thirties. With years of experience in synchronizing pictures to

Above: Oswald the Lucky Rabbit. Above right: Koko the Clown. Below: Felix the Cat. Right: Mutt and Jeff with Theda Bara. Far right: Betty Boop and Bimbo. Opposite page, top left: Paramount star Popeye, and (top centre) with Olive Oyl and Bluto. Top right: Porky Pig. Above right: Bugs Bunny and Daffy Duck. Bottom right: Looney Tunes' famous sign-off

music (their first Song Car-Tune was shown in 1924) they embarked on a monthly schedule of Screen Songs with *The Sidewalks of New York* in 1929. These cartoons starred their regular characters Koko the Clown and Bimbo. The latter, a dog, was promoted to solo stardom in Talkartoons, beginning with *Noah's Lark* (1929). *Dizzy Dishes* (1930) introduced Bimbo's girlfriend, a chubby but decidedly sexy female dog – 'bitch' seems hardly a suitable word for Betty Boop, who was soon to change into a 'human' character and become queen of the cartoon screen. Just plain Betty at first, her black-button nose became a pert point, her long droopy ears became ear-rings, her skirt grew short enough to show not only one saucy garter but even saucier knickers, and her voice grew so much like Helen Kane's that the radio star sued – and lost. What Helen Kane failed to do, however, the Hays Office did; sexy Betty was toned down to suit the family audience. But before she went the way of all flesh, Betty left posterity a string of inventive, funny and often outrageous cartoons.

Betty Boop has one other claim to fame: she introduced the movie-going world to Popeye the Sailor Man. A pilot picture featuring E.C. Segar's hero from the comic-strip Thimble Theatre was released as part of the Betty Boop series; Betty herself stealing a scene from the scraggy Olive Oyl as she swings a grassy hip in the hula-hula. Max Fleischer's gamble on his favourite comic-strip hero as an animated character paid off so swiftly that two months later the first purely Popeye cartoon, *I Yam What I Yam* (1933), was in the cinemas. One a

month followed throughout the Thirties, and the formula never changed. For the classic 'boy meets girl, loses girl, wins girl' situation substitute the names of Popeye and Olive Oyl, throw in brutal Bluto as the villain and add a can of spinach as a catalyst. The films made a star of Billy Costello, the vaudevillian who provided Popeye's screen voice; a hit song of Sammy Lerner's salty signature tune; and an international success of Segar's comic strip Newspapers and comics fell over themselves striving to sign up the rights, and the spin-offs in the juvenile market were second only to those of the much-merchandised Mickey Mouse. Popeye's finest films were three double-length Technicolor adventures beginning with *Popeye the Sailor Meets Sindbad the Sailor* (1936), followed by similar slapstick meetings with Ali Baba and Aladdin.

The Thirties were the heyday of the Hollywood studio system and each studio had its own animation set-up and star. Popeye was Paramount's, and over at Warner Brothers there was Bosko the Talk-ink Kid, who was created by Freleng, Harman and Ising – the Oswald team – and made his debut in *Sinkin' in the Bathtub* (1930), first of the Looney Tunes. As a sample of the human race, Bosko was a bit like Mickey Mouse but without his ears, or Felix the Cat in a derby hat, but the early Looney Tunes were decidedly adult, as titles like *The Booze Hangs High* (1930) reveal. After 40 adventures Harman and Ising moved on to MGM and took Bosko with them to star in their Happy Harmonies series. Suitably softened, as suited the studio of the stars, Bosko began his MGM career in the Hays-approved *Bosko's Parlor Pranks* (1934). Another star of the Technicolored Happy Harmonies was an ultra-cute mouse who featured in *Little Cheeser* (1936) and overcame sentiment with science-fiction in a superb sequel, *Little Buck Cheeser* (1937), a burlesque of the strip 'Buck Rogers'.

Meanwhile, back at Warners, a second series – the Merrie Melodies – had been started with *Lady Play Your Mandoline* (1931). Like Looney Tunes, it was firmly based on the music library owned by the studio. Having lost Bosko, producer Leon Schlesinger replaced him with Buddy, a white boy who was not much more than a reversed negative of black Bosko. Deliberately created as a star, Buddy failed like so many of his real-life equivalents.

In his place grew up the real cartoon stars, characters conceived as little more than one-offs but who caught the fancy of the public. One of these was the stuttering Porky Pig who tried to recite 'The Midnight Ride of Paul Revere' in a cartoon called *I Haven't Got a Hat* (1935). Porky soon ousted the unfunny Buddy to star in his very own *Porky the Rainmaker* (1936) and became the stuttering utterer of

Warner's famous cartoon trade mark, 'Th-th-that's all, folks!' Out of one of Porky's vehicles, *Porky's Duck Hunt* (1937), flew the first truly crazy cartoon character of the talkie era: originally known as 'that crazy darnfool duck', Daffy Duck quacked his way into all-time stardom. In one of *his* pictures, *Daffy Duck and Egghead* (1937), another star was born. Egghead evolved into Elmer Dudd who evolved into Elmer Fudd. And *Porky's Hare Hunt* (1938) saw the debut of the wisecracking character who would eventually top the Warner Brothers' cartoon tree: Bugs Bunny. Radio man Mel Blanc provided all the voices.

By the end of the decade, cartoon films had begun to evolve their own stars – stars who had grown from the special art of animation rather than out of the comic strips. Around the corner lay the Forties with the flowering of the Looney Tunes crew captained by Bugs and Daffy, and the soon-to-be-born Tom and Jerry and Woody Woodpecker. Of all the cartoon stars who had come from outside animation only Popeye remained – and remains (still making films for television) – because, simply, he yam what he yam!   DENIS GIFFORD

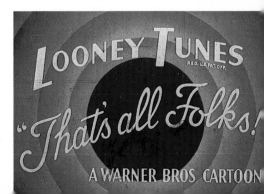

Key films of 1937

Baltic Deputy. USSR. **prod co:** Lenfilm. **dir:** Alexander Zarkhi, Josif Heifits. **sc:** Alexander Zarkhi, Josif Heifits, Leonid Rakhmanov, D.Del. **photo:** M. Kaplan. **art dir:** Nikolai Suvorov, V. Kalyagin. **mus:** N. Timofeyev. **with:** Nikolai Cherkasov, M. Domansheva, Boris Livanov, Oleg Zhakov, A. Melnikov.
Few Soviet films of this period attained the humanity of this film which, through its leisurely narrative pace, depicts the involvement of an individual in the revolutionary cause. Cherkasov's portrayal of 75-year-old Professor Polezhayev brought him to fame as a major actor.

Les Bas-Fonds (*The Lower Depths*). France. **prod co:** Films Albatross. **prod:** Vladimir Zederbaum. **dir:** Jean Renoir. **sc:** Jean Renoir, Charles Spaak, Jacques Companeez, Y. Zamyatin, from the play by Maxim Gorky. **photo:** Fedote Bourgassoff, Jacques Mercanton, Jean Bachelet. **ed:** Marguerite Houllé-Renoir. **art dir:** Eugène Lourié; Hugues Laurent. **mus:** Jean Wiener, Roger Desormière. **with:** Jean Gabin, Louis Jouvet, Vladimir Sokoloff, Robert Le Vigan, Suzy Prim, Junie Astor, Jany Holt.
Less sombre than Gorky's original play and even occasionally Chaplinesque, this portrayal of a disgraced aristocrat's descent into the 'lower depths' was described by the critic André Bazin as 'an improbable game of hide-and-seek between vaudeville and tragedy, realism and parody.'

Un Carnet de Bal (*Christine*). France. **prod co:** Productions Sigma. **prod:** Jean Lévy-Strauss. **dir:** Julien Duvivier. **sc:** Julien Duvivier, Jean Sarment, Pierre Wolff, Yves Mirande, Bernard Zimmer, Henri Jeanson. **photo:** Michel Kelber, Philippe Agostini, Pierre Levent. **ed:** André Versein. **art dir:** Serge Pimenoff, Jean Douarinon, Paul Colin. **mus:** Maurice Jaubert. **with:** Harry Baur, Pierre Blanchar, Fernandel, Louis Jouvet, Raimu, Marie Bell, Françoise Rosay, Robert Lynen, Milly Mathis.
A film of ambivalent nostalgia in which a woman seeks out the fate of all the men whose names appear on a dance card retained from her youth. Generally considered (with Pépé-le-Moko) as the peak of Duvivier's achievement.

Dead End; directed by William Wyler – see special feature in Chapter 13.

Drôle de Drame (*Bizarre, Bizarre*). France. **prod co:** Corniglion-Molinier. **prod:** Charles David. **dir:** Marcel Carné. **sc:** Jacques Prévert, from the novel *His First Offence* by J. Storer Clouston. **photo:** Eugen Schüfftan, Louis Page, Henri Alekan. **ed:** Marthe Poncin. **art dir:** Alexandre Trauner. **mus:** Maurice Jaubert. **ass dir:** Pierre Prévert. **with:** Michel Simon, Louis Jouvet, Jean-Pierre Aumont, Françoise Rosay, Jean-Louis Barrault, Pierre Alcover.
A comic fantasy set in Edwardian London with Jouvet as a suspicious Anglican bishop and Simon as a botanist who secretly writes thrillers

Edge of the World. Britain. **prod co:** Rock Studios. **prod:** Joe Rock. **dir/sc:** Michael Powell. **photo:** Ernest Palmer, Skeets Kelly, Monty Berman. **ed:** Derek Twist. **mus dir:** Cyril Ray. **with:** John Laurie, Belle Chrystall, Eric Berry, Finlay Currie, Kitty Kirwan, Niall MacGinnis.

Michael Powell emphatically graduated from a string of 'quota quickies' with this poetic, semi-documentary lament on the elemental harshness of life on the Shetland isle of Foula.

Fire Over England. Britain. **prod co:** Pendennis/London Films. **prod:** Erich Pommer. **dir:** William K. Howard. **sc:** Clemence Dane, Sergei Nolbandov, from the novel by A.E.W. Mason. **photo:** James Wong Howe. **ed:** Jack Dennis. **art dir:** Lazare Meerson, Frank Wells. **mus:** Richard Addinsell. **mus dir:** Muir Mathieson. **with** Laurence Olivier, Flora Robson, Leslie Banks, Raymond Massey, Vivien Leigh, Tamara Desni, Morton Selton, James Mason.

A stirring historical drama with Elizabethan England awakening late to evidence of European expansionism. A love-lorn Olivier saves Flora Robson's Good Queen Bess from Spanish treachery.

La Grande Illusion (*The Great Illusion*). France. **prod co:** Réalisations d'Art Cinématographique. **prod:** Frank Rollmer, Albert Pinkovitch. **dir:** Jean Renoir. **sc:** Jean Renoir, Charles Spaak. **photo:** Christian Matras. **ed:** Marguerite Houllé-Renoir. **art dir:** Eugène Lourié. **mus:** Joseph Kosma. **with:** Jean Gabin, Pierre Fresnay, Erich von Stroheim, Dalio, Julien Carette, Gaston Modot, Jean Dasté.
An anti-war masterpiece about the imprisonment of a group of French officers in a German fortress. Erich von Stroheim's subtle portrayal of the camp commandant enriches the film's profound philosophical study of a moment in mankind's history, the end of an era, the collapse of the old structures and the uncertainty of the new ones.

Lost Horizon. USA. **prod co:** Columbia. **prod/dir:** Frank Capra. **sc:** Robert Riskin from the novel by James Hilton. **photo:** Joseph Walker. **aerial photo:** Elmer Dyer, Ganahl Carson. **ed:** Gene Havlick, Gene Milford. **art dir:** Stephen Goosson. **sp eff:** E.Roy Davidson, Ganahl Carson. **mus:** Dmitri Tiomkin. **mus dir:** Max Steiner. **with:** Ronald Colman, Jane Wyatt, John Howard, Margo, H.B. Warner. Sam Jaffe, Edward Everett Horton, Thomas Mitchell.
The famous tale of a hidden valley where people live to incredible ages. Capra's usual sharp sense of charactization, modified by an over-conscious sentimentality, made it a truly escapist romance and a box-office success.

La Marseillaise. France. **prod co:** Société de Production et d'Exploitation du Film La Marseillaise. **prod:** André Zwoboda. **dir:** Jean Renoir. **sc:** Jean Renoir, Carl Koch, N. Martel-Dreyfuss. **photo:** Alain Douarinou, Jean Bourgoin, Jean-Marie Maillois, Jean-Paul Alphen, Jean Louis. **ed:** Marguerite Houllé-Renoir. **art dir:** Georges Wakhévitch, Léon Barsacq, Jean Perrier. **mus arr/lyr:** Joseph Kosma. **with:** Pierre Renoir, Léon Larive, William Aguet, Lise Delamere, Nadia Sibirskaia, Andrex.
This film of the French Revolution is a portrayal of ordinary people

caught up and participating in the Revolution, and it captures the spirit of the times in the clash between different sets of values.

Oh, Mr Porter! Britain. **prod co:** Gainsborough. **prod:** Edward Black. **dir:** Marcel Varnel. **sc:** Marriott Edgard, Val Guest, J.O.C. Orton from the story by Frank Launder. **photo:** Arthur Crabtree. **ed:** R.E. Dearing, Alfred Roome. **art dir:** Vetchinsky, Maurice Carter. **sd:** W. Salter. **with:** Will Hay, Moore Marriott, Graham Moffatt.
A classic of comic invention working on the traditional English romanticizing of branch lines and ancient engines. The most famous of Will Hay's Gainsborough Studio comedies, it contains a typical personification of a figure of authority with an air of seediness which was Hay's trade mark.

Nothing Sacred: directed by William Wellman – see special feature in Chapter 12.

Quality Street. USA. **prod co:** RKO. **prod:** Pandro S. Berman. **dir:** George Stevens. **sc:** Allan Scott, Mortimer Offner, from the novel by Sir James M. Barrie. **photo:** Robert de Grasse. **ed:** Henry Berman. **with:** Katharine Hepburn, Franchot Tone, Eric Blore, Fay Bainter, Cora Witherspoon, Joan Fontaine.
A Hepburn showpiece; a period film in which she poses as her own non-existent niece to win back forgetful Tone's love. The use of play-acting within the film is characteristic of her long association with the former stage-director George Cukor.

Snow White and the Seven Dwarfs. USA. **prod co:** Walt Disney. **prod:** Walt Disney. **sup dir:** David Hand. **sc:** Ted Sears, Otto Englander, Earl Hurd, Dorothy Ann Blank, Richard Creedon, Dick Richard, Merrill de Maris, Webb Smith, from the Grimm Brothers fairytale. **seq dir:** Percy Pearce, Larry Morey, William Cottrell, Wilfred Jackson, Ben Sharpsteen. **sup anim:** Hamilton Luske, Vladimir Tytla, Fred Moore, Herman Ferguson. **char des:** Albert Hurter, Jose Grant. **art dir:** Charles Philippi, Hugh Hennessey, Terrell Stapp, McLaren Stewart, Harold Miles, Tom Codrick, Gustaf Tengren, Kenneth Anderson, Kendall O'Connor, Hazel Sewell. **anim:** Arthur Babbitt, Grim Natwick, Wolfgang Reitherman, Ward Kimball, Stan Quackenbush. **mus:** Frank Churchill, Leigh Harline, Paul Smith.
Perhaps the most famous of Disney's films: it was his studio's first full-length feature cartoon. Its simple narrative, animal sketches, tuneful music, gentle humour and genuinely frightening passages combine to ensure its continuing popularity.

The Spanish Earth. USA. **prod co:** Contemporary Historians Inc. (New York). **dir/sc:** Joris Ivens. **photo:** Joris Ivens, John Fernhout. **ed:** Helen van Dongen. **mus:** Virgil Thompson, Marc Blitzstein. **sd:** Irving Reis (comm). **with:** Ernest Hemingway (comm).
Sponsored by liberal American intellectuals in support of the Spanish Republican cause, this early example of Western 'agit-prop' documentary takes its emotive strength equally from Hemingway's impassioned narration and Ivens's remarkable footage.

Stage Door. USA. **prod co:** RKO. **prod:** Pandro S. Berman. **dir:** Gregory La Cava. **sc:** Morrie Ryskind, Anthony Veiller, from a play by Edna Ferber, George S. Kaufman. **photo:** Robert de Grasse. **ed:** William Hamilton. **art dir:** Van Nest Polglase, Caroll Clark. **mus:** Roy Webb. **with:** Katharine Hepburn, Ginger Rogers, Adolphe Menjou, Gail Patrick, Constance Collier, Lucille Ball.
The snappiness and wit of Ferber and Kaufman's play about the hectic vicissitudes of life in a theatrical boarding house are admirably served by La Cava's knowing direction.

A Star Is Born. USA. **prod co:** UA. **prod:** David O. Selznick. **dir:** William Wellman. **sc:** Dorothy Parker, Alan Campbell, Robert Carson from a story by Carson, Wellman. **photo:** W. Howard Greene. **ed:** Hal Kern, Anson Stevenson. **art dir:** Lyle Wheeler, Edward Boyle. **mus:** Max Steiner. **sd:** Oscar Lagerstrom. **with:** Janet Gaynor, Fredric March, Adolphe Menjou, May Robson, Andy Devine, Lionel Stander.
The original, non-musical version of the thrice-filmed showbiz yarn had March and Gaynor playing the Hollywood couple passing each other on the ladder of stardom.

Stella Dallas. USA. **prod co:** Goldwyn/UA. **prod:** Sam Goldwyn. **dir:** King Vidor. **sc:** Victor Heerman, Sara Y. Mason, Harry Wagstaff Gribble, from a novel by Olive Higgins Prouty. **photo:** Rudolph Maté. **ed:** Sherman Todd. **art dir:** Richard Day. **mus:** Alfred Newman. **with:** Barbara Stanwyck, John Boles, Anne Shirley, Barbara O'Neil, Alan Hale, Edmund Elton.
A poignant and forceful remake of

Henry King's 1925 film of the same name about a woman of humble origins who sacrifices everything for the sake of her daughter's social ambitions. Vidor's direction and Stanwyck's acting are faultless.

You Only Live Once. USA. **prod co:** Wanger/UA. **prod:** Walter Wanger. **dir:** Fritz Lang. **sc:** Gene Towne, Graham Baker, from a story by Towne. **photo:** Leon Shamroy. **ed:** Daniel Mandell. **art dir:** Alexander Toluboff. **mus:** Alfred Newman. **ass dir:** Robert Lee. **with:** Sylvia Sidney, Henry Fonda, Barton MacLane, Jean Dixon, William Gargan, Warren Hymer.
An early version of the Bonny and Clyde legend that added a plea for justice to romantic fatalism as Fonda and Sidney go on the run with the law, and destiny, on their heels.

Chapter 16
Images of France

Outside of Hollywood, the Thirties belonged to the French cinema, and the atmosphere of romantic fatalism created by France's famous directors seemed appropriate to the prevailing mood of the time

The structure of the film industry in France changed markedly with the arrival of sound in 1930. The extra costs of talkie production eliminated many of the smaller film companies, though others continued to proliferate throughout the decade, albeit undercapitalized and short-lived; in 1936 alone, for example, 175 new film companies were founded.

Financial considerations also led to the creation of two massive and vertically-integrated companies (embracing production, distribution and exhibition) formed out of the pioneering companies of Charles Pathé and Léon Gaumont. Both the resulting companies, however, withdrew from film production in the mid-Thirties, partly as a result of the illegal financial manipulations of Bernard Natan who had taken over the Pathé company in 1929.

From an output of some fifty feature films in 1929, French film production doubled by 1931 and more than tripled by 1933. But the native film industry never supplied any more than 25 per cent of the movies distributed annually in France. Moreover these were years of chaos and disorder in the industry: technical crews struggled with the limitations of unwieldy new sound-recording equipment; cinema owners required considerable capital to convert their buildings to sound; and producers contrived to add sound to projects conceived originally as silent films. For a while the cumbersome business of multi-language shooting occupied the studios until dubbing and subtitling enabled French films to be distributed abroad with ease. In retrospect it seems almost a miracle that the cinema survived at all.

Certainly in the confusion of the early years of the decade, much of the specifically French quality of the national film production was lost. France had a slow start in talkies since patent rights to the most successful sound systems were owned by American and German companies. The early Thirties had also seen the establishment of large-scale multi-language production in Paris, both on the part of the American Paramount company and the German Tobis company, operating from suburban studios at Joinville and Epinay respectively.

The upheavals of sound were followed, from the middle of the decade onwards, by further crises which reflected the contradictions of contemporary French society as much as the inherent problems of the film industry itself.

In this climate a sense of national identity was difficult to achieve and sustain even after the era of multi-language production had come to an end. Germany, in particular, was a major foreign influence. On the one hand co-productions with Ufa at the Neubabelsberg studios in Berlin continued to provide work for French directors, writers and actors throughout the decade. On the other hand, the advent of Hitler to power in 1933 caused a mass emigration to Paris of German producers, directors and technicians. Figures as important as Erich Pommer, Fritz Lang, Billy Wilder, Robert Siodmak, G.W. Pabst and Eugen Schüfftan worked, some of them for several years, in the French film industry. It has been estimated that up to a third of French cinema in the Thirties was strongly shaped and influenced by emigrés like, for example, Max Ophuls who spent eight years in France during the decade.

In the new situation of sound-film production, many of the characteristic features of earlier French cinema were lost, in particular the visual experiment associated with the various avant-garde movements of the Twenties.

The interaction of film with Surrealism in France had reached a climax by 1930 with the premiere of Luis Buñuel's *L'Age d'Or* (*The Golden Age*), a masterly indictment of society which provoked riots when first shown in Paris. In the same year the Vicomte de Noailles financed Jean Cocteau's *Le Sang d'un Poète* (1930. *The Blood of a Poet*), but with the increased costs of sound-film production this kind of private patronage of independent film-making came to an end. *Le Sang d'un Poète* was Cocteau's first venture into film and though attacked and derided by the Surrealists on its first appearance, the film now stands as a major achievement and a statement of the personal vision which would be fully orchestrated in *Orphée* (1950, *Orpheus*) some twenty years later.

Sound meant that other key figures of French silent cinema, such as Abel Gance, Marcel l'Herbier and Jean Epstein were reduced to merely commercial film-making. Gance, for example, alternated remakes of some of his earlier successes – he made a sound version of his famous *Napoléon* in 1935 – with routine assignments which offered only rare opportunities to show his full talents. L'Herbier made a couple of lively thrillers, adapted from the novels of

Above left: if any one face typified the look of French cinema in the Thirties it was that of Jean Gabin; in this film he played a gangster hiding from the law. Top: Jean-Louis Barrault as Napoléon, and Jacqueline Belubac as Josephine, in Les Perles de la Couronne. *Above: Fernandel in his first serious role in Pagnol's* Regain

Above: Abel Gance's J'Accuse *was a 1937 sound version of his 1919 anti-war classic. Right: Jean Grémillon's* Gueule d'Amour *was a Hollywood-style romance with Gabin at the mercy of a femme fatale. Below: poster for Marius. Bottom: in La Kermesse Héroïque a Flanders town is occupied by Spanish troops who are first seduced and then routed by the townswomen. Bottom right: the delightfully nostalgic* Un Carnet de Bal *related a woman's search for the beaux of her youth*

Gaston Leroux, – *Le Mystère de la Chambre Jaune* (1930, The Mystery of the Yellow Room) and *Le Parfum de la Dame en Noir* (1931, The Perfume of the Lady in Black). Otherwise l'Herbier's output was restricted to dull historical spectacles, while Epstein's work of the Thirties was equally compromised by unsuitable scripts and financial restraints.

One thread of continuity is provided by the career of René Clair, the master of silent cinema whose writings of the late Twenties opposed the notion of sound (and particularly talking) films but who was one of the first in France to exploit the new form with wit and inventiveness.

The five Clair comedies released in the early Thirties create a distinctive universe where the entanglements of his characters are presented with good-humoured sympathy, and where good eventually triumphs over evil. His first sound film, the internationally successful *Sous les Toits de Paris* (1930, *Under the Roofs of Paris*) with its treatment of characters living on the fringes of society, is an early precursor of what was later to be called 'poetic realism'. Generally, however, Clair's comedies are much lighter and involve a great use of the interplay of dream and reality.

Clair is at his weakest when attempting abstract statements about society, as at the end of *A Nous la Liberté* (1931), or politics, which form the background of *Le Dernier Milliardaire* (1934, *The Last Millionaire*). But despite the reticence and restraint which characterizes all his work, Clair's films of the early Thirties remain genuinely moving and affectionate works.

He left for England in 1935 and was absent from

France for 12 years except for a brief period during 1939 when he began, but failed to complete, *Air Pur* (Pure Air).

Another great loss to the French film industry was that of Jean Vigo, who died in 1934 at the age of 29. Vigo was one of France's most talented and promising young film-makers, whose entire output amounted to two documentaries and two longer fictional works.

After a penetrating study of Nice, *A Propos de Nice* (1930), which blends documentary and surrealist elements, and a short film about a champion swimmer, *Taris* (1931), Vigo made the two films on which his reputation principally rests. Both were dogged by misfortune. The 47-minute *Zéro de Conduite* (1933, *Nought for Behaviour*) was banned by the French censor until 1945, and the feature-length *L'Atalante* (1934) was re-edited and redubbed by its producers while Vigo himself lay dying.

Through both films runs a unique vein of poetry. The world of childhood has seldom been so accurately captured as in *Zéro de Conduite* and the combination in *L'Atalante* of realistically detailed barge life with larger-than-life elements (such as the figure of the mate, brilliantly played by Michel Simon) is a splendid fusion of fantasy and reality.

The outstanding film-maker throughout the decade, however, is Jean Renoir – the son of the painter Auguste Renoir. Like Clair, he had worked extensively during the silent period but the Thirties, when he made some fifteen films, were the richest years of his career. His work is enormously varied and combines elements drawn from his father's Impressionist style and from the naturalism of the nineteenth-century novel or theatre.

Renoir's work during the early years of the decade is marked by his collaborations with the actor Michel Simon. The first film they made together was a farce called *On Purge Bébé* (1931, Purging Baby). Next they did two splendidly amoral tales designed to exploit the actor's remarkable talents: Simon excels as Legrand in *La Chienne* (1931, The Bitch), a timid cashier turned painter who murders his faithless mistress and allows her lover to be executed for the crime. He is equally impressive as Boudu, the tramp in *Boudu Sauvé des Eaux* (1932, *Boudu Saved From Drowning*) who rewards his rescuer by seducing both his wife and his mistress. The anarchism celebrated in the figure of the tramp links the Renoir film with Vigo's *L'Atalante* and to some extent with the mood at the end of Clair's *A Nous la Liberté*. It is a measure of Renoir's versatility that he could subsequently follow adaptations of Simenon – *La Nuit du Carrefour* (1932, Night at the Crossroads) and Flaubert's *Madame Bovary* (1934) – with *Toni* (1934) a sober study of migrant workers shot on location and in a style which anticipates some aspects of post-war Italian neo-realism.

In the great theoretical debate about sound, and particularly talking pictures, two highly successful French dramatists declared themselves opposed to

the traditional view of the primacy of the image. Sacha Guitry and Marcel Pagnol both initially turned to the cinema simply as a means of recording their own work written for the theatre. Both of them had plays adapted for the cinema by other directors in 1931 and then began to direct their own work for the screen a few years later. The results were paradoxical. Their best films, far from being stage-bound, show a freedom shared only by Renoir among their contemporaries.

Guitry was a prolific dramatist who wrote some hundred and thirty plays; most of his Thirties films are simple adaptations, but in his original work written for the screen he shows a freedom of construction, a light and playful style of performance and an inventive approach to the relationship of image and sound which would later be acknowledged as an influence by post-war directors like Alain Resnais. Among Guitry's notable films are: *Le Roman d'un Tricheur* (1936 Story of a Cheat), *Les Perles de la Couronne* (1937, Pearls of the Crown), *Remontons les Champs-Elysées* (1938, Let's Go Up the Champs-Elysées) and *Ils Etaient Neuf Célibataires* (1939, They Were Nine Bachelors).

The work of Pagnol, too, has its surprises. His first contact with the cinema was through his own adaptations of his famous Marseilles trilogy – *Marius* (1931), *Fanny* (1932), and *César* (1936, directed by Pagnol himself). He later made his own film adaptation of his play *Topaze* in 1936, which has subsequently been much filmed.

The success of these works in the tradition of filmed theatre allowed Pagnol to build his own studio and exercise total control over production, even to the extent of completely remaking films that displeased him, either through defects of sound, as in *Merlusse* (1935) or in *Cigalon* (1935).

Pagnol's major films of the Thirties, however, were all adapted not from his own plays, but from novels and stories by the popular author Jean Giono. *Angèle* (1934) and *Regain* (1937, *Harvest*) with Fernandel, and *La Femme du Boulanger* (1938, *The Baker's Wife*) with the great Raimu, were filmed away from the studios on location in Provence so as to make the most of the landscape. The construction and the direction of these films is characterized by a freedom that now strikes us as extremely modern and undated.

Less successful in the Thirties, despite his enormous talent, was the director Jean Grémillon who experienced difficulties in establishing himself in feature film production.

His first sound film, *La Petite Lise* (1930, Little Lise), was a box-office failure and from then on he was condemned to make films that were guaranteed commercial projects or, subsequently, to seek work abroad in Spain and Germany.

Working at the Ufa studios in Berlin, Grémillon made two films from scripts by Charles Spaak. Both *Gueule d'Amour* (1937) starring Jean Gabin and *L'Etrange Monsieur Victor* (1937, The Strange Mr Victor) with Raimu had considerable merits. It was,

Sans lendemain

however, typical of Grémillon's ill-fortune that when, in 1939, he had the opportunity to direct the ideal couple of the period – Jean Gabin and Michèle Morgan – in Jacques Prévert's scenario *Remorques*, the plan to make the film was disrupted by the outbreak of World War II.

While Grémillon was forced to seek work abroad, the French studios were filled with refugees from Germany. Max Ophuls achieved some impressive melodramas that portrayed the misfortunes of beautiful women: *Divine* (1935), *La Tendre Ennemie* (1935, Tender Enemy), *Yoshiwara* (1937), and *Sans Lendemain* (1939, No Tomorrow).

What distinguished the French cinema of the Thirties artistically was its sheer literacy. The lead was given by Jacques Feyder, the Belgian-born director who returned from Hollywood to make three films that re-established his European reputation (first acquired during the silent era). The films were *Le Grand Jeu* (1933, The Great Game), *Pension Mimosas* (1934) and *La Kermesse Héroïque* (1935, Carnival in Flanders) and the team of technicians Feyder assembled to make them included the designer Lazare Meerson, the photographer Harry Stradling and a young assistant, Marcel Carné.

All three films starred Feyder's wife, Françoise Rosay, and were scripted by Charles Spaak, another Belgian who had earlier worked with Feyder on *Les Nouveaux Messieurs* (1928, The New Gentlemen). The writer's contribution, not only to the surface brilliance of the dialogue but also to the structural organization of the plot, was vital. It was to be the first of several writer-director collaborations that characterized the French cinema of the period.

Left: in Sans Lendemain *Edwige Feuillère played a typically tragic Max Ophuls heroine who makes desperate sacrifices to retain her lover and her small son. Above: the director Julien Duvivier. Below:* Le Parfum de la Dame en Noir: *the heroine is 'haunted' by her first husband, whom she believes dead. Below: Raimu at the centre of a typical peasant group in* La Femme du Boulanger. *Bottom left: Gabin's death in* Pépé-le-Moko, *an early film noir set in North Africa*

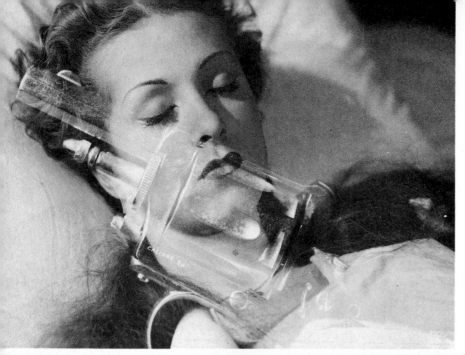

Above: surrealistic images found their way into mainstream cinema – here a dream sequence with Danièle Darrieux in Anatole Litvak's Mayerling *(1936). But the overtly surrealist films appeared earlier in the decade. Right:* Le Sang d'un Poète *was Jean Cocteau's first film; using trick shots and bizarre images like the 'animated' statue of the poet's muse, he explored the act of artistic creation. Below right and bottom: the dream-like imagery of Buñuel's* L'Age d'Or; *the first shot illustrates his anti-clerical sentiments and the second his erotic fetishism*

Spaak himself went on to work with another veteran of silent cinema, Julien Duvivier. They made two films starring Jean Gabin: both *La Bandera* (1935) and *La Belle Equipe* (1936, The Fine Team) captured the confused aspirations of the period when the left-wing Popular Front government came to power in France.

Duvivier's other major script collaborator was the more superficial but nonetheless brilliantly witty writer Henri Jeanson. Together they worked on the gangster film *Pépé-le-Moko* (1936), a striking example of the romantic pessimism of the time, starring Jean Gabin and the nostalgic *Un Carnet de Bal* (1937, *Christine*) in which a woman seeks out all the men whose names appear on an old dance card to discover what fate has befallen them.

To return to the work of Jean Renoir in the latter half of the Thirties is to confirm him as the greatest director of the decade. He was, in every sense, the complete author of his films and was far less dependent than either Feyder or Duvivier on the quality of scripts written by others.

Many of his greatest films like *Une Partie de Campagne* (1936, A Day in the Country), *La Bête Humaine* (1938, Judas was a Woman) and *La Règle du Jeu* (1939, The Rules of the Game) were made from his own scripts. *Le Crime de Monsieur Lange* (1935, The Crime of Monsieur Lange), however, announces a new orientation for his work since it was made in collaboration with the poet and scriptwriter Jacques Prévert.

The two of them captured the essential socialist optimism of the Popular Front period and subsequently Renoir found himself caught up in political activity to the extent of making *La Vie Est à Nous* (1936, *People of France*), an explicit propaganda piece for the Communist Party.

The following year he made *La Grande Illusion* (1937, *The Great Illusion*), a passionate anti-war statement and a triumph of human observation, controlled rhetoric and total professionalism. At the end of the decade Renoir completed his masterpiece *La Règle du Jeu*, a perceptive dissection of a divided society which amounts to his personal statement on the eve of world war.

If the genius of Renoir is of a kind that defies classification and generalization, the talent of Marcel Carné, by contrast, is defined by a single period and style. Carné was the protégé of Feyder and had proved himself a brilliant organizer of artistic collaborators like the designer Alexandre Trauner and the composer Maurice Jaubert. Before he was 30, Carné had completed five star-studded features, four of them from scripts by Jacques Prévert.

After his debut with *Jenny* (1936), he made the striking comedy *Drôle de Drame* (1937, *Bizarre, Bizarre*), a comparatively rare example of Prévert's purely comic gifts. Carné and Prévert's two masterpieces *Quai des Brumes* (1938, *Quay of Shadows*) and *Le Jour se Lève* (1939, *Daybreak*) are both fatalistic pieces in which Jean Gabin loses all chance of happiness with the woman he loves after a confrontation with two personifications of evil, respectively portrayed by Michel Simon and Jules Berry. The combination of Prévert's anarchic poetry and Carné's technical prowess creates an unforgettable mixture that is echoed in the Carné-Jeanson collaboration *Hôtel du Nord* (1938).

The achievements of Clair and Vigo in the early Thirties and, later in the decade of Feyder, Duvivier, Renoir and Carné, together with their writers Spaak, Jeanson and Prévert, combine to make this a seminal period in the development of French cinema. Its influence extends not only to post-war France but also to Italian neo-realism.

ROY ARMES

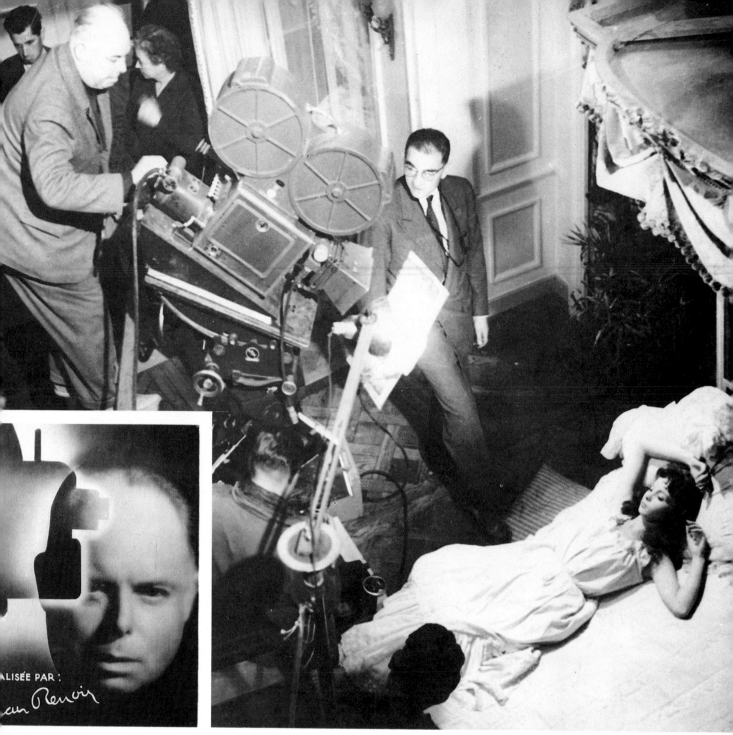

The artistry of Jean Renoir

Jean Renoir died on February 12, 1979 at his Beverly Hills estate. He was 84. Hardly anyone today would question that he was the greatest French film director. His work and his vision of the world, no less than his personality, have delighted several generations of moviegoers

Above: even in his seventies, Renoir was eager to involve himself in every aspect of direction. Here he checks a high-angle shot of Françoise Arnoul for a scene from what was to be his last film Le Petit Théâtre de Jean Renoir. *She plays Isabelle, a pretty, young wife, who cuckolds her rich old husband in the third episode of the film*

Renoir's career, more than that of any other director, summarizes the whole evolution of the cinema, from the first hesitant steps of silent films to the French *nouvelle vague* (of the late Fifties), encompassing advances in sound recording, colour and even television techniques. At each stage of his life he was open to suggestions from those around him, while retaining a fine sense of his own artistic integrity. The critic and theorist André Bazin has written that Renoir always knew 'how to adapt to the evolution of the cinema and the taste of his contemporaries' – not out of some vain opportunism but because 'the need to renew himself was part of his genius'. The 38 films which he directed between 1924 and 1969 have profoundly influenced the art of the screen and most have stood the test of time.

That said, Renoir's work curiously defies investigation and confounds the kind of critic who is fond of attaching labels to works of art. It seems to advance without any guiding line or internal logic; it cannot be pigeon-holed. Renoir would change his style without warning and cheerfully contradict himself from one film to another – if not within the same film.

Between 1931 and 1939 (his most prolific period) he tackled every type of film with

UN FILM DE JEAN RENOIR
UNE PARTIE DE CAMPAGNE
D'APRÈS GUY DE MAUPASSANT
SYLVIA BATAILLE
GEORGES D'ARNOUX · JEANNE MARKEN · JACQUES BOREL · PAUL TEMPS · GABRIELLE FONTAN

Top left and top right: Catherine Hessling, Renoir's first wife, dances in Nana *and dies in the snow in* La Petite Marchande d'Allumettes *their last film together. Above left and left: Rodolphe (Jacques Borel) flirts with Mme Dufour (Jeanne Marken) in* Une Partie de Campagne *(1936). Above: Jean Gabin as engine driver Jacques Lantier in the grim railway setting of* La Bête Humaine

equanimity: naturalistic melodrama in *La Chienne* (1931, The Bitch), thriller with *La Nuit du Carrefour* (1932, Night at the Crossroads), broad farce in *Boudu Sauvé des Eaux* (1932, Boudu Saved From Drowning), respectful adaptations of great writers such as Flaubert, Maupassant, Gorky and Zola, examinations of French society like *La Vie Est à Nous* (1936, People of France) and *La Marseillaise* (1937), moving human dramas like *La Grande Illusion* (1937, The Great Illusion), culminating in that modern sequel to the enchantments of Beaumarchais and Marivaux that is *La Règle du Jeu* (1939, The Rules of the Game). Though superficially a 'mad imbroglio', it is a perfectly constructed film which (with Orson Welles' *Citizen Kane*, 1941) is the source of everything of importance in modern cinema. With a couple of exceptions, all these films were, in their day, received with total incomprehension by both public and critics.

It seems almost impossible, therefore, to encompass Renoir's multiple, abundant, unclassifiable and contradictory *oeuvre* – its broad contrasts are an expression of its richness. If one sees Renoir as a sensualist, it immediately becomes apparent that he does not disdain general ideas, abstraction or intellectual rigour. He could be sarcastic, goodnatured, licentious, nonchalant, endearing – according to subject, mood and circumstances. In a film like *Le Testament du Docteur Cordelier* (1959) he seemed obsessed by human failings and sought to place spiritual pursuits beyond the whims of the flesh. Immediately afterwards he made *Le Déjeuner sur l'Herbe* (1959, Picnic on the Grass), which was a hymn to nature and to the joy of living. The 'mixture of irony and

tenderness, humour and sensuality' which Renoir discerned in his father, the painter Auguste, applied equally well to himself. Renoir was, as it were, a cross between a peasant, whose temperament and work had their roots in the soil, and an artist, whose vocation was universal. His comedies were caustic, his dramas light-hearted. His life, too, was in the image of his films – one of constant wandering, of inspired disorder.

'I must insist on the fact that I set foot in the world of the cinema only in order to make my wife a star, intending once this was done to return to the pottery studio. I did not foresee that once I had been caught in the machinery I should never be able to escape'

It was long believed that the adjective 'realist' sufficed to account for the diversity of his gifts. Historians and critics wished (and still wish) to make Renoir the leader of a so-called French 'realist' school, including personalities as unlike him as Carné, Duvivier, Grémillon and Pagnol. No doubt his path at some time crossed theirs. He made, for instance, at least

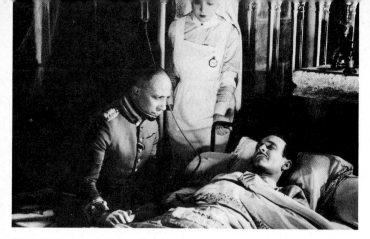

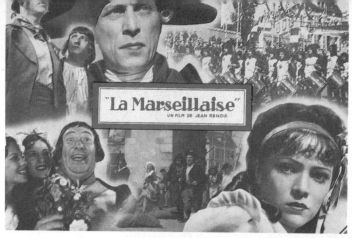

one film strongly influenced by the theories and sensibilities of Pagnol – *Toni* (1934). But this does not prove that Renoir was a realist. If one means by realism the direct, objective reproduction of reality, without any reworking, the kind of reproduction whose logical conclusion was the invention of first photography and later cinema (whose initial claim was to describe 'life as it is'), it is clear that Renoir was not a realist in that sense. He never ceased to affirm the primacy of the narrator over the narration, the painter over the painting, man over nature. Contrary to those mediocre directors naively concerned with 'getting close' to the reality (psychological, social, political) of their time, it would appear that Renoir contrived to get as far away from it as possible. He saw such a reality as a constraint. He did not so much wish to destroy it as to restructure it in a more agreeable and harmonious fashion. Renoir's early films twisted reality, were all flights into imaginary worlds and fairy-tales.

Early in his career, Renoir demonstrated that the vocation of cinematography lay in fantasy, even science fiction (*Charleston*, 1927), bending plots and characters to fit the conventions of fantasy. So the heroine of *La Fille de l'Eau* (1924, *The Whirlpool of Fate*), recklessly

Top left: Rauffenstein, the prison commandant (Erich von Stroheim), visits the bedside of Boeldieu (Pierre Fresnay) in La Grande Illusion. *Top right:* La Marseillaise – *a re-creation of the French Revolution. Above right: Renoir's first American film –* Swamp Water. *Right: the Tucker family contemplate their devastated home in* The Southerner. *Above: boats on the Ganges – a scene from* The River

takes refuge in escapist day-dreaming to console herself for the indignities of everyday life, just as the main character in *La Petite Marchande d'Allumettes* (1928, The Little Match Girl), will do one cold Christmas night. In the same way *Nana* (1926) is firmly ensconced in a self-made woman's mythomania, while *Mar-*

'In my view cinema is nothing but a new form of printing – another form of the total transformation of the world through knowledge'

---

quitta (1927), a humble street-singer, imagines she is a grand-duchess. As for the madcap soldiers of *Tire au Flanc* (1928, Skiver), their substitute for the dull routine of the barracks is

rowdyism, irreverence, wrangling, lechery and finally a wild Bacchanalia.

Almost all of Renoir's characters seek comfort in dreams: Maurice, the wretched clerk of *La Chienne*, fleeing the drab greyness of his middle-class life and seeking solace in art and a doomed love affair; the federates of *La Marseillaise* heroically pursuing a revolutionary ideal which never ceases to elude them; Monsieur Lange, who, in *Le Crime de Monsieur Lange* (1935, *The Crime of Monsieur Lange*) creates a romantic universe made to his own measure; *Madame Bovary* (1934) and her romantic fancies, and *Toni* with his unrequited love for the beautiful, fickle Josefa. What are the prisoners of *La Grande Illusion* looking for if not to escape, to regain their freedom even if they know that by doing so they will only be plunged back into a chaotic world at war.

In each case, for better or for worse, imagination attempts to triumph over reality. For some characters, indeed, the price to be paid for this relentless quest will be their own lives. In the later films, fantasy, humour, gaiety – the 'superior form of civilization', as one of the characters in *Eléna et les Hommes* (1956, *Paris Does Strange Things*) calls it – will carry the day. Camilla in *Le Carrosse d'Or* (1952, *The Golden Coach*) and Nini in *French Cancan* (1955), will find their vocation in art: they have both understood that they are not made 'for what is called life', that their place is 'among the acrobats, the clowns, the mountebanks', that their happiness lies not in the petty concerns of reality but in the *grande illusion* of the stage. Renoir shared with his father the conviction

'To a film director who will take the trouble to use his eyes, everything that constitutes our lives has a magical aspect. A metro station can be as mysterious as a haunted castle'

that the task of a true artist is not to copy nature, however faithfully, but to re-create it. He has commented:

'What will remain of any artist is not his imitation of nature, since nature is changeable and transient; what is eternal is his approach to nature, what he can achieve by the reconstruction, and not the imitation of nature.'

In *The River* (1951) Renoir asked his director of photography, his nephew Claude Renoir, to paint the turf, as he found it 'not Indian enough'. In *La Bête Humaine* (1938, *Judas Was a Woman*) Renoir compared the locomotive to 'a flying carpet in the Arabian Nights', and wanted to retain only the poetic side of Zola's original novel to the detriment of its naturalistic message. Neither of these actions or statements can possibly be described as being realist in motivation. Renoir has declared more than once: 'It's by not being realistic that one has the greatest chance of capturing reality', and has said, even more dogmatically, 'All great art is abstract'. This so-called realism, which a whole critical tradition hoped to attach to his work at any price, is for Renoir, only the façade of fantasy, a mask which must be ripped off to uncover the work's true dimension. Life is a dream, a 'rich comedy with a hundred different acts'; and the film-maker (like every artist) must try to feel the upsurge of the imaginary at the heart of the real, the quest for the irrational that makes the world go round. This is the key to Renoir's aesthetics and philosophy. At the opposite pole to realism, his art is an art of magic and fantasy.

Renoir's last film *Le Petit Théâtre de Jean Renoir* (1969, The Little Theatre of Jean Renoir) gives a crucial insight into the director's genius. It is just the film one would expect from a creator whose *oeuvre* is complete and who chooses nonchalantly to recapitulate its principal themes, as one might leaf through an

Above: the finale of French Cancan. *Opposite page, top left: a gust of wind scatters the picnickers in* Le Déjeuner sur l'Herbe. *Top right: a scene from* The Golden Coach. *Right: Jean-Louis Barrault in* The Testament of Dr Cordelier. *Far right: Jean-Pierre Cassell and Jean Carmet in* The Vanishing Corporal

album of memories. The film's premise is put in a nutshell by wise old Duvallier who introduces each section of the film. 'Life', he exclaims, 'is only bearable because of constant

'I was afraid, and still am, of photographing Nature as it is. I think one has to look very hard, and by means of camera-angles and lighting enlarge the significance of a setting, a countryside or a human face'

little revolutions . . . revolutions in the kitchen . . . in bedrooms . . . on village squares . . . storms in teacups.' This is, according to Renoir, the way of the world: in his films the bonds of society are slightly stretched, irregularities are committed by certain characters who are cleverer than others, risks are calmly taken by free spirits. Some find undreamed of happiness by the end, some die pointlessly; it hardly matters since, as Duvallier says, all that will remain when all is said and done are the lyrics of a bitter-sweet song, which generations to

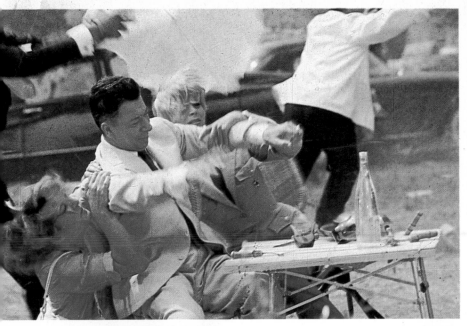

come will sing in chorus:

> When everything is ended
> When your hopes have died
> Why lament the days gone past
> Why regret the vanished dreams . . .

The discreet exit that Renoir contrived with *Le Petit Théâtre de Jean Renoir* is in keeping with his character. The film critic Jean Collet wrote:

'When the red curtain falls on the stage of the Little Theatre, as it fell at the end of *The Golden Coach*, we have the feeling that Renoir is leaving us with a fragile secret, a secret that was lost and found again a thousand times.'

Renoir said something similar about his father's work, at the end of the painter's life. As he looked with emotion at his father's 'extremely simplified palette' composed of 'a few tiny droppings of colour' it seemed as if the artist had been approaching 'the secret of universal harmony as if it were the most natural thing in the world'.

CLAUDE BEYLIE

Quotations from My Life and My Films, by Jean Renoir, translated by Norman Denny. (Collins. 1974).

Filmography

1924 Une Vie Sans Joie (re-edited and shown in France as Catherine in 1927) (sc. only); La Fille de l'Eau (GB: The Whirlpool of Fate) (+prod; +des). '26 Nana (+prod). '27 Charleston/Sur un Air de Charleston/Charleston-Parade (unfinished) (+prod); Marquitta (+prod); La P'tite Lili (actor only). '28 La Petite Marchande d'Allumettes (co-dir; +co-prod; +sc); Tire au Flanc (+co-sc). '29 Le Tournoi/Le Tournoi dans la Cité (+sc); Le Petit Chaperon Rouge (actor only); Le Bled. '31 On Purge Bébé (+sc); La Chienne (+sc). '32 La Nuit du Carrefour (+sc); Boudu Sauvé des Eaux (USA: Boudu Saved From Drowning (+sc). '33 Chotard et Cie (+sc). '34 Madame Bovary (+sc); Toni (+co-sc). '35 Le Crime de Monsieur Lange (USA: The Crime of Monsieur Lange) (+co-sc). '36 La Vie Est à Nous (USA: People of France); Une Partie de Campagne (+sc;+act) (not released until 1949). '37 Les Bas-Fonds (USA: The Lower Depths) (+co-sc); La Grande Illusion (USA: Grand Illusion; GB: The Great Illusion) (+co-sc); Terre d'Espagne (+comm;+sc;+narr) (French version of USA doc. Spanish Earth); La Marseillaise (USA: Marseillaise) (+co-sc). '38 La Bête Humaine (USA: The Human Beast; GB: Judas Was a Woman) (+sc;+act). '39 La Règle du Jeu (USA: The Rules of the Game) (+co-sc; +act). '40 La Tosca (+co-sc) (some scenes only) (IT). '41 Swamp Water (GB: The Man Who Came Back) (USA). '43 This Land Is Mine (USA) (+co-sc). '44 Salute to France (short) (co-dir; +co-sc) (USA). '45 The Southerner (+sc) (USA). '46 The Diary of a Chambermaid (+co-sc) (USA); The Woman on the Beach (+co-sc) (USA). '51 The River (+co-sc) (IN). '52 Le Carrosse d'Or/La Carozza d'Oro (GB: The Golden Coach) (+co-sc) (IT-FR). '55 French Cancan (USA: Only the French Can) (+sc). '56 Eléna et les Hommes (USA: Paris Does Strange Things; GB: The Night Does Strange Things (+sc;+lyr); L'Album de Famille de Jean Renoir (short). '59 Le Testament du Docteur Cordelier (USA: The Testament of Doctor Cordelier; GB: Experiment in Evil) (+sc;+narr); Le Déjeuner sur l'Herbe (USA: Picnic on the Grass; GB: Lunch on the Grass) (+sc;+co-prod). '62 Le Caporal Epinglé (USA: The Elusive Corporal; GB: The Vanishing Corporal) (+co-sc). '68 Le Direction d'Acteurs par Jean Renoir (as himself) (short). '69 Le Petit Théâtre de Jean Renoir (+prod; +sc;+narr) (FR-IT-GER); The Christian Liquorice Store (actor only) (USA).

JEAN RENOIR

"Le plus important film français jamais réalisé"
La Critique Internationale

LA RÈGLE DU JEU

Le chef-d'oeuvre de **JEAN RENOIR**

A weekend party assembles at the château of the Marquis de la Chesnaye (1). Among the guests are André, an aviator, who is in love with Christine (the Marquis' wife), Geneviève, the Marquis' mistress and Octave, an old friend of the family.

When his gamekeeper captures a notorious poacher (2), the Marquis, on a whim, decides to employ the poacher as a servant.

The weekend diversions include a morning hunt and an evening fancy-dress masquerade (3). During the former the Marquise is shocked to learn of her husband's infidelity. She tells André that she is willing to go away with him, but when the Marquis surprises them together, a fight breaks out between the two men (4). At the same time, the gamekeeper becomes aware of the poacher's attentions to his flighty wife (5), Lisette, and chases him through

the château with a gun (6).

Christine decides that, after all, she would prefer to go away with Octave who has always loved her. However, Lisette points out to Octave that he is far too old to satisfy Christine. He feels the truth of this and sends André out into the garden to meet her.

Christine, wearing a coat borrowed from Lisette, is spotted by the gamekeeper, who has now become reconciled with the poacher. The gamekeeper mistakes her for his wife and shoots André, believing that he is making love to Lisette. The Marquis explains to his guests that the gamekeeper has shot André having mistaken him for a poacher. The guests feign belief but privately decide that it was the Marquis who did the shooting to rid himself of a dangerous rival. They file back into the château (7).

7

6

Directed by Jean Renoir, 1939
Prod co: La Nouvelle Edition Française. **prod:** Claude Renoir. **sc:** Jean Renoir, Carl Koch. **photo:** Jean Bachelet, Jean-Paul Alphen, Alain Renoir. **ed:** Marguerite Renoir, Marthe Huguet. **art dir:** Eugène Lourié, Max Douy. **cost:** Coco Chanel. **mus:** Roger Desormières, Joseph Kosma, from Mozart, Monsigny, Saint-Saëns. **sd:** Joseph de Bretagne. **ass dir:** Carl Koch, André Zwoboda, Henri Cartier-Bresson. **r/t:** 113 minutes. Paris premiere, 7 July 1939. Released in the USA as *The Rules of the Game*.
Cast: Marcel Dalio (*Robert, Marquis de la Chesnaye*), Nora Gregor (*Christine de la Chesnaye*), Jean Renoir (*Octave*), Roland Toutain (*André Jurieux*), Mila Parély (*Geneviève*), Paulette Dubost (*Lisette*), Julien Carette (*Marceau, the poacher*), Gaston Modot (*Schumacher, the gamekeeper*), Pierre Magnier (*the General*), Eddy Debray (*Corneille, the major-domo*), Pierre Nay (*Saint-Aubin*), Odette Talazac (*Mme de la Plante*), Richard Francoeur (*La Bruyère*), Claire Gérard (*Mme de la Bruyère*), Anne Mayen (*Jackie, Christine's niece*), Léon Larive (*cook*), Lise Elina (*radio reporter*), Nicolas Amato (*South American*), Tony Corteggiani (*Berthelin*), Camille François (*radio announcer*), André Zwoboda (*engineer at Caudron*), Henri Cartier-Bresson (*English servant*), Jenny Hélia (*kitchen servant*).

In a currently distributed print of *La Règle du Jeu*, a mysterious caption has been inserted at the beginning claiming that the film 'is intended as entertainment not as social criticism'. It seems that, even today, the nature of this potent work is still misunderstood. In *My Life and My Films*, Renoir recalled:

'During the shooting of the film I was torn between my desire to make a comedy of it and the wish to tell a tragic story. The result of this ambivalence was the film as it is.'

Of all the characters that assemble at the Marquis' château, only two act without duplicity and guile. One is the aviator André, a romantic idealist infatuated with Christine, the Marquis' beautiful wife. He has just made a spectacular crossing of the Atlantic, and was upset that Christine did not welcome him in Paris. The other, Octave (played by Renoir himself), is a friend of the Marquis and his wife, with a special fondness for the latter. However, in procuring for André an invitation to the house party he is not entirely without blame for the eventual tragedy. Indeed it may be said that none of the characters acts with any really malicious intent – but are simply weak or incapable of controlling their wayward caprices. Even the gamekeeper, whose jealousy results in André's accidental death, cannot help himself. Yet the characters' excusable – even at times

endearing – fallibilities stem finally from selfish irresponsibility. In the dissolute social world the film depicts, the 'rules of the game' solely concern the hollow observance of 'appearances'; any idea of living according to a stable form of morality has been lost.

When the film was first shown in Paris, in July 1939, it caused a riot and attempts were made to burn down the cinema. The distributors called for cuts in certain offending scenes, but even when these were made, the public found others to jeer at. The film ran for a mere three weeks. In October of that year the French government banned it, claiming it was morally unacceptable. The ban was lifted some months later but re-enforced when the Germans occupied Paris, and it remained in existence until the end of World War II. Though it was championed by a few discerning French critics, most found the film's mixture of drama, comedy and farce unpalatable and chaotic, while others viewed it as a calculated attack on the *haute bourgeoisie*. Moreover, owing to the presence in the cast of the Jewish actor, Dalio, and Nora Gregor, an Austrian refugee, the film was attacked by both the anti-Semitic and the nationalist press.

At the end of the war it was feared that a complete version of the film was lost for ever. Then, by a series of chance discoveries and the dedicated work of two young French

enthusiasts under Renoir's supervision, it was re-assembled. With hindsight, it is easy to see why Renoir's film met with such violent antipathy: France was about to find herself plunged into war, into a conflict which she was not to prove herself capable of sustaining for long – perhaps due to the very debilitating social inconsistencies that Renoir had depicted in his film.

Renoir's original choice for the role of the Marquise had been Simone Simon, but the film's limited budget precluded her participation. Then, by chance, at a theatre Renoir met Nora Gregor, the Austrian stage actress. Despite his colleagues' vigorous opposition (her French was far from perfect) he insisted on engaging her for the role. Renoir's obstinacy seems justified: the actress' statuesque bearing is extremely effective in the scene where her aviator lover arrives at the château; whereupon she rises to the occasion to deliver a homily to her other guests on the beauties of platonic friendship. Also effective is the moment when, elegantly scanning the scene of the hunt through binoculars, she chances to see her husband embracing his mistress.

The hunt is splendidly executed. Shot in greyish light and using natural sounds, it turns into a savage, senseless massacre of wild life. This is followed by a ball where, with unconscious irony, many of the

guests opt to wear skeleton costumes and cavort in a dance of death. The intrigues of the guests and the underlings intermingle. Few of the residents seem unduly surprised when the jealous gamekeeper causes havoc by chasing his rival through the house with a gun; they treat the incident almost as an entertaining diversion and remain obsessed with their own petty intrigues. Occasionally the film's underlying theme is illuminated by a casual remark: 'Sincere people are such bores', or 'We live in a time when everything is a lie'.

In the final scene – when the gamekeeper sees the aviator in the grounds of the château with the woman he takes to be his wife, and shoots him – the guests are quick to rationalize the event according to their own ethics. They feel that the murder was surely committed by the Marquis who was justified in preventing the aviator eloping with Christine.

After *La Règle du Jeu*, Renoir went to Italy to begin work on *La Tosca* (1940). Renoir was forced to abandon the film after a few days, owing to the worsening political climate, and left for the USA.

With *La Règle du Jeu* he had made his most personal statement about a society he knew well. Although received acrimoniously, the film's accuracy and validity have been established over the passing years.
DEREK PROUSE

A Propos de Vigo

Jean Vigo (1905–34) directed only four films but is recognized as one of the major artists of the cinema. His first job was as a cameraman at the film studios in Nice, and it was there that he made his first film *A Propos de Nice* – a free-wheeling semi-surrealist documentary of the town and its inhabitants. Commissioned to make a series of films about sports, Vigo completed only *Taris* – a short about a champion swimmer – before proceeding to make his most famous film, *Zéro de Conduite*. Vigo's only other feature-length film, *L'Atalante* shows how his work had moved from early avant-garde experimentation towards the 'poetic realism' of mid-Thirties French cinema. From her personal memories and family papers, Vigo's daughter provides here a portrait of the man and his times

In thinking about Jean Vigo, the term 'grandfather' does not spring instantly to mind. Yet he had a family and would have been a grandfather today, had he lived. To remember this helps to put into perspective the idolatry, the mythology with which certain post-war film critics have invested his memory. Vigo was not just a brilliant young film-maker whose career was tragically cut short (he died of tuberculosis on October 5, 1934); he was also a family man whose feet were firmly grounded in the realities and events of his day.

Jean Vigo was born in Paris on April 25, 1905, the son of militant anarchist parents Eugène Bonaventura Vigo and Emily Cléro. Vigo's father, better known by his pseudonym

Miguel Almereyda, was co-editor of the magazine *Le Libertaire* (The Libertarian) before going on to found a weekly called *La Guerre Sociale* (The Social War) and then a daily paper – *Le Bonnet Rouge* (The Red Bonnet). The political meetings to which Jean's parents took him as a boy left their mark on him – as did his father's spells in prison for his political beliefs.

The last of these terms of imprisonment proved fatal – in circumstances which suggest murder rather than the official verdict of 'suicide'. But in spite of the continued investigations by his son's various biographers, and Jean Vigo's own dossier of 'facts', compiled with care and anguish, by which he hoped to vindicate his father's name, the truth of the matter has never been clearly established.

After his father's death Jean Vigo began his life as a boarding-school pupil at Millau. Far away from his family, he had, however, the warm affection of Gabriel Aubès and his sister Antoinette – photographers who lived in nearby Montpellier. Their friendship must be reckoned a formative one, for they introduced him to the language of images.

The Aubès did their best to protect him from the scandal and rumours arising out of his father's death, and it was they who enrolled Vigo in the grammar school at Millau under the name of Jean Salles. Neither his own diary nor the accounts given by his fellow-pupils at Millau or Chartres (where he later moved to be nearer his mother) support the theory that he was a sad and lonely child. The love he had known and the relationships he had formed during the earliest years of his life had shaped a character which, although to some extent 'worked over' by other influences, was to emerge more or less intact in all the projects that he was involved in – and, of course, in the films he made.

After his school-days at Chartres, Vigo enrolled at the Sorbonne, but no sooner had he begun his studies than his illness forced him to go to a sanatorium at Font-Romeu (in the Pyrenees) to recuperate. It was here that he became friendly with the writer Claude Aveline, who was to become his executor, the founder of the celebrated Jean Vigo Prize (for film-making) and my own tutor. It was here, too, that he met Lydou Lozinska; they were married in Nice in January 1929.

As a child Vigo had grown up in the heady

Top left: Dita Parlo as Juliette and Jean Dasté as Jean, the newly-weds aboard the barge in L'Atalante *(1934). Inset: Jean Vigo. Left: Michel Simon as Père Jules, skipper of the barge, with Dita Parlo. Below: a typically arresting image from* A Propos de Nice *(1929)*

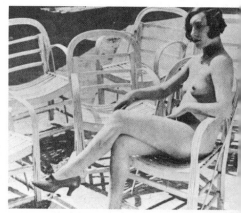

met and made firm friendships with people who shared his passions in life and cinema – Luis Buñuel, the Prévert brothers, Jean Painlevé, Charles Goldblatt, Boris Kaufman, Henri Storck, Pierre Merle, Maurice Jaubert, Albert Riéra, Jean Dasté and Gilles Margaritis. All these friendships were mutually enriching for the film work of the individuals concerned, and their influence is what makes Vigo's own films even more impressive.

There is no doubt that Vigo's work has aged well. Viewed today, *L'Atalante* appears quite modern. Vigo's cinema constantly surprises the viewer with its beauty, its rigorousness and its unique facility for creating living characters. Indeed it is the environment, rather than any particular psychological background, that gives Vigo's characters their depth. In the films his sense of place is as vivid as his characterizations. Without it the people in his films would have no origins, no social situations from which to develop.

The barge in *L'Atalante*, long and lithe, gliding through the water is a repository of the lives and dreams of its passengers. The berths, the quaysides, the banks of the canal Saint-Martin. Shots of trains, railways and pylons constitute an image of Paris that is hard, aggressive, even repellent. It is a city where theft is commonplace, where people are lynched or stand in line unemployed, looking for an escape.

There are at the same time some peaceful places in this film – Père Jules' cabin, for example. A sense of happiness, however transitory, permeates the film and brings together the inhabitants of the barge, even though tensions can be detected just below the surface.

Throughout the film, however, the pleasure Vigo took in making it is transmitted via the crew and the actors to the viewer. *L'Atalante* can provoke audiences to tears or laughter, and it seems to me that this is the most beautiful present an artist can give the world.

I have only spoken of *L'Atalante*, but everything I have said about it can also be applied to the two documentaries *A Propos de Nice* and *Taris, Champion de Natation* (Taris, Champion Swimmer) and finds its climax in *Zéro de Conduite*. The richness of Vigo's work comes, then, directly from his character; as a group of films they continue to live long after their creator's untimely death.   LUCE VIGO

Translated from the French by Martyn Auty

atmosphere of his parents' social world, constantly exposed to the ideas generated by them and their friends. His own adult married life was, in a way, a re-creation of this lifestyle. And although the couple had their share of problems (Jean's poor health and a shortage of money – though alleviated by contributions from Lydou's father – figured largely among them), hardship never forced them into leading a cloistered life.

As for film-making, Vigo's correspondence testifies as to how much he needed to be a part of that profession. He drew on the support of Francis Jourdain, and of film-makers like Germaine Dulac and Claude Autant-Lara. Thanks to the latter he became fourth assistant cameraman in L.H. Burrel's crew at the Franco-Film studios in Nice.

At the same time he discovered the films of Dziga Vertov, Sergei Eisenstein, Henri Storck and Joris Ivens. Like Ivens in Holland, Vigo founded a cine club (his was in Nice). The club was called *Les Amis du Cinéma* and was soon affiliated to the International League of Independent Cinema.

A letter received by Vigo from the mayor's office in Nice testifies to the battle he waged with officialdom in his 'defence and illustration of the cinema'. The letter reads:

'Sir, I have received your letter of October 8, 1930, requesting authorization to use a cinema hall for the monthly presentation of films that have been forbidden by the censor's office. I have consulted with the Chief of Police on this matter, who informs me that he cannot give a favourable response to your request . . .'

The cine club saw its task as one of making the public aware of developments in cinema: films that were considered avant-garde; as well

as films that were already classics in the repertory of movie history. Retrospectives of various kinds were planned. Films would be shown, often behind locked doors, in their original versions without the cuts required by the censor, and in accordance with the wishes of the film-makers.

The programmes of Vigo's cine club reveal the interests of the group of 'cinéphiles'. They showed Germaine Dulac's *Etude Cinématographique sur une Arabesque* (1928), unreleased films by René Clair, like *Paris Qui Dort* (1923, The Crazy Ray) and two shorts from 1928 *La Tour* (The Tower) and *Les Deux Timides* (The Bashful Pair). Several films by Henri Storck were also featured: *Train de Plaisir* (1929, Pleasure Train), *Images d'Ostende* (1929, Pictures of Ostend), *Une Idylle à la Plage* (1930, Seaside Idyll), and Buñuel's *L'Age d'Or* (1930, The Golden Age) was screened in its original version.

Vigo did not only watch films, however, he

Top: the beginnings of anarchy in the classroom in Zéro de Conduite (1933), a film that later influenced Lindsay Anderson's If . . . (1968). *Above left: a teacher, and his principal (played by Delphin) in Zéro de Conduite. Below: even in the documentary* Taris (1931) *Vigo's style was more poetic than realist*

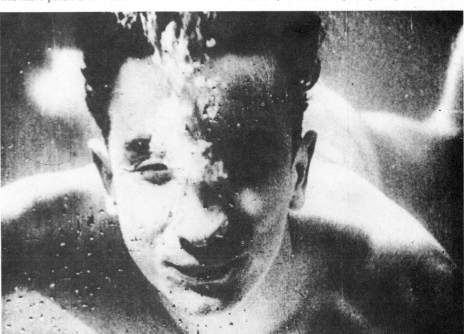

Directed by Marcel Carné, 1938
Prod co: Ciné-Alliance/Gregoire Rabinovich. **prod:** Simon Schiffrin. **sc:** Jacques Prévert, from the novel by Pierre Mac Orlan. **photo:** Eugen Schüfftan, Louis Page, Marc Fossard, Pierre Alekan. **ed:** René le Hénaff. **art dir:** Alexander Trauner. **mus:** Maurice Jaubert. **r/t:** 90 mins. Paris premiere 18 May 1938. Released in the USA as *Quay of Shadows*.
Cast: Jean Gabin (*Jean*), Michèle Morgan (*Nelly*), Michel Simon (*Zabel*), Pierre Brasseur (*Lucien*), Aimos (*the tramp*), Robert le Vigan (*Michael Krauss*), René Genin (*ship's doctor*).

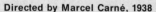

The films which Carné directed from Prévert's screenplays prove such closely integrated collaborations (involving both Trauner's designs and the music of either Jaubert or Joseph Kosma) that any discussion of authorship (ie who holds the creative responsibility for the film) becomes difficult.

Prévert, perhaps still best known as a poet, had come to film from a close association with the Surrealists and the subversive 'Octobre' theatre group. Carné, on the other hand, had begun his working life in insurance and saw himself primarily as a technician. In addition to his three years as a film critic, Carné had been assistant to Feyder (on *Le Grand Jeu* and *La Kermesse Héroïque*) and Clair (on *Sous les Toits de Paris*).

The combined work of Carné and Prévert is commonly characterized by the phrase 'poetic realism' but on close scrutiny it proves to be more poetic than realist. For instance, *Quai des Brumes* transforms its specific setting (Le Havre) into a shadowy limbo-land – a moment between past sufferings and unrealizable aspirations.

The film's principal concession to realism rests in its choice of proletarian settings and lowly characters (all social outcasts, all oppressed) whose purpose is to illustrate a romantic fatalism more commonly associated with high tragedy and the fall of the mighty.

Significantly, Prévert changes the setting of Mac Orlan's novel from Montmartre to a busy seafaring port. The silhouette of a large freighter at anchor is clearly discernible behind the opening credits, and Carné's final montage sequence is of the same ship, the *Louisiane* (which might have taken Jean to freedom and a new life), belching out the signal for its departure.

Most of the film's settings – the hotel where Nelly and Jean consummate their passion, and Panama's isolated shack on the peninsula tip – are poised yearningly on the water's edge, and the characters who pass through them spend much of their time gazing out of their windows at the vast beyond. Refugees from their past lives and from conventional society, they are united by the common dream of an impossible elsewhere to which the seaport's out-going craft offer an illusory passage.

In this respect, the harbour's real ships hold the same purely symbolic value as the facsimiles, like the ship in a bottle which reminds the bar-keeper of his past in the land of permanent sunshine, or the cardboard steamer aboard which Jean and Nelly pose for a photograph – the closest either will ever get to departure.

For if all the characters dream of escape, none of them has any place to go. Or perhaps it is only the suicidal painter who knows the one possible destination. When Nelly talks of returning to Zabel she tersely sums up their common situation: 'If I go back, it will be terrible; just as it will be if I don't.' Yet if all the film's human flotsam are trapped within miserable lives overshadowed by the threat of sudden, violent death, they are still polarized between the good and the evil. Despite the mist and fog of the settings, the iconography of the film makes it impossible for the spectator to get lost: the gangsters wear black hats and over-long topcoats and assume Capone postures around their black limousine. Moreover the ugliness of Zabel, the film's least convincing figure, is denounced by several of the other characters as being a reflection of his soul. In contrast both Nelly and Jean are lit in such a fashion as to convey their latent energy and passion. If Jean appears menacing as he first steps out of the fog to thumb a ride to Le Havre, if Nelly in black beret and shiny raincoat can at first glance be mistaken for a whore, script and camera soon establish their affinities of soul (pure) and situation (fugitive). The effect is to endow Gabin's taciturn veteran and Michèle Morgan's involuntary *femme fatale* (both prototype portrayals) with a strange innocence.

The painter may be right to declare that 'life is bad' and Jean may be right in saying that there can be no understanding between men and women. Nelly, however, does have a point when she adds that 'there can be love'. The film becomes the expression of a kind of transcendental pessimism, in which love has the power to redeem and to transform despair into irrational hope. Jean's dying kiss asserts the power of love to conquer even death, while the small stray dog which has followed him throughout the film and which provides its final image embodies the survival of hope over experience.

JAN DAWSON

takes him to Panama's, a bar-cum-shack at the end of the harbour. Here Jean meets Michael Krauss, a suicidal painter who bequeathes him his money, clothes and identity papers before swimming to oblivion. Jean befriends Nelly (2), a 17-year-old orphan fleeing from her guardian who turns out to be none other than Zabel. Nelly is pursued by a gun-toting Lucien to the Panama bar. Jean beats up Lucien for molesting Nelly (formerly a girlfriend of the gangsters) during an early-morning stroll. That night at a fairground (3) Jean publicly humiliates Lucien.

Through a friendly ship's doctor, Jean arranges passage on a ship leaving the next day for Venezuela. Only after they have spent the night together in a waterfront hotel (4) does Jean announce to Nelly that he intends to leave. But when Jean's uniform is discovered near Maurice's mutilated body, Nelly seeks to protect Jean. She confronts Zabel (5) who admits murdering Maurice out of jealous love for Nelly. Zabel attacks Nelly but Jean, who has followed her to Zabel's shop, tackles Zabel (6) and kills him in a fight. As Jean leaves, Lucien guns him down in the street (7). With his dying breath Jean declares his love for Nelly.

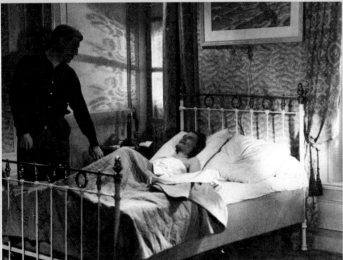

Jean, an army deserter, arrives hungry and penniless in the port of Le Havre. In a nightclub, the gangster Lucien Legardier and his henchmen attempt to learn from their 'fence', Zabel, the whereabouts of their missing associate Maurice Brevier. Outside the same club Jean falls in with a drunken tramp (1), who

The Marius Trilogy

According to the actor Fernandel, Marcel Pagnol's approach to film-making was somewhat specialized: 'It generally involved a train trip to Marseilles to sit in a café over a bottle of *pastis* discussing the weather and this and that, then, if there was any time left, to do some filming.'

Marcel Pagnol's *Marius* trilogy – comprising *Marius* (1931), *Fanny* (1932), and *César* (1936) – is perhaps the French cinema's most charming celebration of the Provençal way of life. The characters living around the old port of Marseilles, where the trilogy is set, are richly observed and superbly played. The cast came to the films after a long and greatly acclaimed success with the stage version of *Marius*. They embody all of the characteristics that the inhabitants of that raffish and rakish town like to think of as essentially their own: much given to extravagant and fanciful garnishing of the truth; prone to passionate explosions of anger and equally warm reconciliations; deft and cunning in the avoidance of work in favour of a few rounds of *pastis* and a game of *belote*.

At the heart of the story is César – played by the incomparable Raimu – running his little bar in the port, swigging his *pastis* and cheating at cards. He is devoted to his only son Marius, who breaks his heart when he sleeps with Fanny and then, unaware that she is pregnant, leaves her for the sea. Although Pierre Fresnay, who played Marius, was the only member of the cast without a truly authentic Marseilles accent, he conveyed most movingly the plight of a man torn between two loves: Fanny and the sea. Another impeccable performance was given by Charpin who played Panisse, the old sail-maker who has always loved Fanny. Then there is Fanny herself, loyal and vulnerable and concerned only for Marius' happiness. She was played by Pagnol's wife, Orane Demazis.

Pagnol had already refused other offers to adapt his plays for the screen, but when Paramount's French outpost gave him the necessary reassurances, he agreed – only to have his fears revived with the news that a Hungarian, Alexander Korda, had been assigned to direct *Marius*. Pagnol, with no previous film experience, kept a vigilant eye on Korda during production, however, and they actually became good friends. It is in fact extraordinary that a film whose charm and fascination depends so strongly on its meticulous depiction of the Provençal lifestyle should have been made by a Central European – not a Frenchman.

Reports differ widely as to how the artistic responsibility for the film was divided. Pagnol's original conception of the cinema was as filmed theatre; he considered that, with the advent of sound, the cinema was admirably equipped to serve the theatre and widen its horizons. It seems logical, therefore, to ascribe the more effective moments in *Marius* to Korda, who was dedicated to the cinema.

Marius is undoubtedly the best of the three films; the potent atmosphere it establishes makes the shortcomings of *Fanny*, directed by Marc Allégret, and *César*, directed by Pagnol himself, of little importance – one has already become deeply beguiled and involved in the fortunes of the main protagonists. In *Marius* panning shots round Marius' bedroom, which resembles a ship's cabin, convey the strength of his obsession with the sea and the vividness of his inner life compared with the ordinariness of his daily existence. And the blinking light from the lighthouse that shines into Fanny's room, during an intimate scene between the lovers, hints at the omnipresence of her rival, the sea; frequently there is an evocative isolation of an object or an eloquent intrusive sound imaginatively inserted to make a telling emotional impact. *Fanny* and *César* stay closer to the theatrical structure of the writing, despite the occasional, rather obvious, attempts to open out the action.

César is really a tying-up of events: Fanny's reconciliation with Marius after the death of Panisse; and César's reconciliation with Marius – eked out by a somewhat contrived complication that Marius might be a smuggler. But it is the trilogy's high points that remain in the memory: César's lesson in how to mix a drink; the famous card game with César making frantic references to his heart to indicate to his partner the suit he wishes to be led; and his heart-rending reading of Marius' letter when he attempts to find between the lines some measure of comfort for Fanny.

DEREK PROUSE

MARIUS, directed by Alexander Korda (and Marcel Pagnol), 1931
Prod co: Films Marcel Pagnol. prod: Robert T. Kane. sc: Marcel Pagnol, from his own play. photo: Ted Pahle. ed: Roger Spiri-Mercanton. art dir: Alfred Junge, Zoltan Korda. mus: Francis Gromon. r/t: 130 minutes.

FANNY, directed by Marc Allégret, 1932
Prod co: Films Marcel Pagnol/Etablissements Braunberger-Richebé. prod: Roger Richebé. sc: Marcel Pagnol, from his own play. photo: Nicolas Toporkoff, Roger Hubert, Georges Benoit, André Dauton, Coutelan, Roger Forster. ed: Jean Mamy. art dir: Gabriel Scognamillo. mus: Vincent Scotto, Georges Sellers. ass dirs: Pierre Prévert, Yves Allégret, Eli Lotar. r/t: 140 minutes.

CESAR, directed by Marcel Pagnol, 1936
Prod co: Films Marcel Pagnol. prod: Charles Pons. sc: Marcel Pagnol. photo: Willy, Gricha, Roger Ledru. ed: Suzanne de Troye. Jeannette Ginestet. art dir: Marius Brouquier. mus: Vincent Scotto. r/t: 168 minutes.

Cast: Raimu (*César*), Pierre Fresnay (*Marius*), Charpin (*Panisse*), Orane Demazis (*Fanny*), Alida Rouffe (*Honorine, Fanny's mother*), Paul Dullac (*Escartefigue* in Marius and César), Mouries (*Escartefigue* in Fanny), Robert Vather (*Brun* in Marius and César), Pierre Asso (*Brun* in Fanny), Alexandre Mihalesco (*Piquoiseau*), Edouard Delmont (*Le Goelec*), Milly Mathis (*Claudine*), André Fouché (*Césariot*), Bassac (*Dromart*).

2

César presides over his little bar in the port of Marseilles, arguing, boasting and playing cards with his cronies. His son, Marius, is in love with Fanny but still yearns to sail off to distant, romantic lands (1). César's friend Panisse also loves Fanny and he and Marius nearly come to blows over her (2). Fanny and Marius spend a night together and César, in the know, suggests to Fanny's mother that the children get married (3). But an old salt tells Marius (4) that there is a place waiting for him aboard a ship, and Fanny persuades Marius to give in to his heart's desire and go.

Fanny faints as Marius sails off and César carries her home (5). Pregnant by Marius, she turns in desperation to Panisse, who is delighted to accept the child as his own – though César nearly hits him when he hears of it (6). Fanny marries Panisse but when the child, Césariot, is a year old, Marius returns and realizes that it must be his. César, however, persuades him to leave again.

Twenty years pass. Panisse dies (7) and Fanny tells Césariot that Panisse was not his father. Césariot is shattered, but tracks down his real father who now runs a garage in Toulon.

When he returns, he tells César that Marius is a smuggler. César is outraged and bitterly upbraids his son when he comes to Marseilles. When it emerges that a colleague of Marius' had told this story to Césariot as a joke, Marius is exonerated, and, at long last, reunited with Fanny (8).

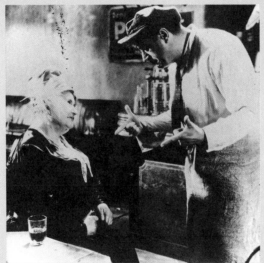
3

5

6

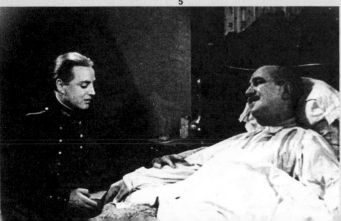

Familiar faces of the French screen

The French cinema is full of romantic heroes, lovelorn waifs, busybody dowagers, engaging rogues and shoulder-shrugging shopkeepers. Here are a few of the well-known actors and actresses who have brought these and other roles to life and done the most to popularize the Gallic image in the movies

Raimu

Raimu – or Jules Muraire César Raimu, to give him his unfamiliar full name – was born in Toulon in 1883, and it was in that Provençal town that he first appeared as a music-hall and revue performer. He later went to Paris where his first great theatrical success was in Marcel Pagnol's *Marius* in 1929 – a triumph that he repeated two years later on the screen. Thereafter, throughout the Thirties, he was responsible for some of the most impressive and subtle performances in the French cinema. His bulky build, his wary but compassionate looks, his ability to convey both aggression and vulnerability made him a perfect interpreter of Pagnol's depictions of life in the South of France. In Julien Duvivier's star-studded *Un Carnet de Bal* (1937, *Christine*) he was hilariously effective – amidst the general sombreness – as a small-town mayor who marries his own cook and conducts the ceremony himself.

Apart from the *Marius* trilogy, perhaps Raimu's most superbly rounded performance was in Pagnol's *La Femme du Boulanger* (1938, *The Baker's Wife*). He played the baker who is shattered when his young wife leaves him for another man. Another big success for Raimu was Pagnol's *La Fille du Puisatier* (1940, *The Welldigger's Daughter*), but after that, until his death in 1946, he found little material that was equal to his genius – with the possible exception of his last film, Pierre Billon's *L'Homme au Chapeau Rond* (1946, The Man in the Round Hat). Even to indifferent material, however, the actor never failed to bring his own special integrity and warm perception of character.

Françoise Rosay

The imposing presence of Françoise Rosay lent a special lustre to many of the key French films of the Thirties. Born in 1891, she first came to the screen in 1913 and went on to play in 94 films. Her superb sense of comedy was particularly evident in Bernard-Deschamps' *Le Rosier de Madame Husson* (1931, Madame Husson's Rose-Tree). But she had an even greater success in her husband Jacques Feyder's masterpiece, *La Kermesse Héroïque* (1935, *Carnival in Flanders*), in which, as the First Lady of seventeenth-century Flanders, she enlists the women of the town to outwit the invading Spaniards.

Rosay's gift for sardonic black comedy found perfect expression in Claude Autant-Lara's *L'Auberge Rouge* (1951, *The Red Inn*): here she played the landlady of a sinister provincial inn where she and her husband (Carette) murder their guests for financial gain. She was not restricted to the French screen, however. As a young girl she had studied in both England and Germany and was consequently equipped to bring her great talent to the films she made in both these countries, including *The Halfway House* (1944) for Balcon, and *Fahrendes Volk* (1938, Travelling People).

Michel Simon

Michel Simon was a unique character actor, brilliant in his portrayals of seedy, secretive, shabby Frenchmen. Born in Geneva in 1895, he moved to Paris when he was 16 and eked out a living by giving boxing lessons and selling contraband cigarette-lighters in the streets. He made his theatrical debut as an acrobat and clown and entered films in the early Twenties. His first notable screen appearance was in 1925, in Marcel l'Herbier's *Feu Mathias Pascal* (*The Late Mathias Pascal*). With the advent of sound it became evident that Simon's vocal delivery was as strikingly individual as his extraordinary physical bearing, and his range and virtuosity quickly became apparent in such films as Jean Renoir's *La Chienne* (1931, The Bitch), and in the same director's truly anarchic *Boudu Sauvé des Eaux* (1932, *Boudu Saved From Drowning*). In 1934 he scored perhaps his greatest triumph in Jean Vigo's hauntingly poetic *L'Atalante* as the bargee surrounded by a family of cats.

Thereafter he lent his distinctive, even bizarre, presence to many more famous films of the Thirties, including Marcel Carné's *Drôle de Drame* (1937, *Bizarre, Bizarre*) and *Quai des Brumes* (1938, *Quay of Shadows*), and Christian-Jaque's *Les Disparus de Saint-Agil* (1938, The Lost People of Saint-Agil). Simon remained in demand after the war and his career continued into the early Seventies. He died in 1975.

Top, far left: Raimu in La Femme du Boulanger. *Above left: Françoise Rosay in* La Kermesse Héroïque. *Above:* Circonstances Atténuantes *(1939) starred Michel Simon and Arletty. Top: Simon in* Boudu Sauvé des Eaux. *Above right: the suave side of Jules Berry. Top right: Berry as the devil in* Les Visiteurs du Soir. *Above, far right: Michèle Morgan in* La Symphonie Pastorale. *Right: Louis Jouvet's second version of* Knock.

Michèle Morgan

It was the director Marc Allégret who first realized the unique potential of Michèle Morgan. She was born in Neuilly and went to drama school in Paris. Then in 1937, when she was 17, Allégret gave her a part in *Gribouille* (The Simpleton). But it was in a subsequent Allégret film, *Orage* (1937, Storm), that the actress first found a role on which she could impose her personality, though Charles Boyer, the star, was most favoured by the camera. It was left to Marcel Carné to put to full dramatic effect the cinematic power of Michèle Morgan's cool pellucid gaze and purity of expression – in *Quai des Brumes* (1938). She was excellent in the role of the shy ward of court who falls in love; the enigmatic aspect of the actress's face was somehow heightened by dressing her in a simple beret and a shiny raincoat. Her next two films were indifferent but she then consolidated her success in Jean Grémillon's *Remorques* (1940) and Feyder's *La Loi du Nord* (1942, Law of the North).

After a series of mainly undistinguished films made in America during the war, Michèle Morgan returned to France to make Jean Delannoy's *La Symphonie Pastorale* (1946, The Pastoral Symphony), based on the novel by André Gide. The film was a success both in France and abroad, though it was evident that Delannoy was intent on presenting his star as a kind of cold, statuesque Garbo and Morgan's famous look seemed in danger of losing its fascination. But it was revitalized in René Clair's *Les Grandes Manoeuvres* (1955, The Grand Maneuver) and André Cayatte's *Le Miroir a Deux Faces* (1958, The Mirror Has Two Faces).

Jules Berry

Born in Paris in 1889, Jules Berry entered the cinema after a long apprenticeship on the stage in Brussels. With his dapper appearance, elegantly studied gestures and insinuating voice, he was one of the actors most in demand during the Thirties. In 1936 alone he appeared in 11 movies and in 1938 was in 14, while continuing to act in the theatre. It is hardly surprising that he regularly forgot his lines – but he improvised so brilliantly that the only people to be aware of the lapses were his disconcerted fellow actors.

Of the 90 films he made during his 22-year career his performances in the Thirties are best remembered: his crooked industrialist in Renoir's *Le Crime de Monsieur Lange* (1935, The Crime of Monsieur Lange); the immaculate ladies' man in Abel Gance's *Le Voleur de Femmes* (1937, The Wife Stealer); the stage dog-trainer in Carné's *Le Jour se Lève* (1939, Daybreak). But his triumph was his vigorous, loud-laughing devil in Carné's *Les Visiteurs du Soir* (1942, The Devil's Own Envoy), exulting over the plight of his victims.

He died, an ageing, extravagant Don Juan, in April 1951. Although crippled with arthritis he had still managed to appear in five films during the previous year.

Louis Jouvet

Louis Jouvet made his first film appearance – as Shylock – in 1913 at the age of 26, but the real cinema debut of this eminent stage actor and producer came 19 years later when he scored a moderate success in Louis Gasnier's version of Pagnol's *Topaze* (1932), and a considerable triumph in *Knock, ou le Triomphe de la Médecine* (1933, Dr Knock) which he also co-directed. Thereafter his lean, wolf-like features and clipped, sardonic diction were to be seen in several of the decade's greatest achievements – perhaps most notably in *La Kermesse Héroïque* (1935), in which he played the devious, lecherous chaplain. After the failure of the unreleased *Haut en Bas* (1936, From Top to Bottom) Jouvet renounced the cinema, but Jean Renoir persuaded him to return to play the ruined baron in *Les Bas-Fonds* (1937, The Lower Depths). Of the 19 films he made between 1936 and 1940 – often as a means of financing his own stage productions – the most notable were G.W. Pabst's *Mademoiselle Docteur* (1937, Street of Shadows); *Drôle de Drame* (1937); and *Un Carnet de Bal* (1937), in which he was memorable as the shifty nightclub-owner.

His last big success was in Henri-Georges Clouzot's marvellously atmospheric *Quai des Orfèvres* (1947, Jenny Lamour). Then in 1951, just before his death, he remade *Knock* (this time directed by Guy Lefranc), the film that first made his name on the screen.

Arletty

The actress who best reflected the poetic, urban, twilight world of Marcel Carné and his writer Jacques Prévert was undoubtedly Arletty. The faintly husky voice, the guarded gaze at once provocative and mocking, an aura of jaded elegance and sophistication – all admirably suited the fatalistic mood of lovers in the grip of an inexorable destiny that characterized many of Carné's films.

Arletty was born Arlette-Léonie Bathiat in Courbevoie on the Seine in 1898. She worked as a factory hand and as a typist before going on the stage in 1920. She was eventually discovered in the music-hall and made her screen debut in Jean Choux's *Un Chien Qui Rapporte* (1931, A Retriever Dog). Her enigmatic presence then graced such films as Carné's *Le Jour se Lève* (1939).

Her range was wide enough to include an hilarious performance in *Fric-Frac* (1939); and in 1954 she was superbly effective as the lesbian in Jacqueline Audry's *Huis Clos* (*Vicious Circle*). But perhaps the most haunting image of Arletty is during the final scenes of Carné's *Les Enfants du Paradis* (1945, *Children of Paradise*) as she watches the mime of Jean-Louis Barrault from her theatre box. In later years, Arletty was tragically stricken with blindness.

Fernandel

The lugubrious features of Fernandel found their best expression in his roles of the Thirties. Born in Marseilles in 1903, he came to the screen from vaudeville and revue theatres and in 1931 had his first success in *Le Rosier de Madame Husson*. As the only virgin to be found in the village where the local *grande dame* (Françoise Rosay) is holding a fête to boost flagging morality, Fernandel wins the prize money and squanders it on a lewd spree: a witty and ironic comment on French hypocrisy. His air of gauche innocence was equally well exploited in Autant-Lara's *Fric-Frac* (1939, Burglary) in which he played a pedantic jeweller's assistant who comes up against a gang of Parisian crooks. He falls under the spell of one of its members (Arletty) to whom he had the effrontery to utter a mild reproach couched in that rarely used tense, the past subjunctive. Arletty shoots him a glance of mingled astonishment and suspicion and, in her impeccable Parisian argot drawl, enquires of her companions, 'Is this character French?'

Fernandel's greatest international success in this period was in *La Fille du Puisatier* (1940) in which he was delightful as Raimu's apprentice. The comedian's work later coarsened but he triumphed with Henri Verneuil's *Le Mouton a Cinq Pattes* (1954, *The Sheep Has Five Legs*) and, in the Fifties and Sixties, as the priest in the popular Don Camillo series. He died in 1971.

DEREK PROUSE

Jean Gabin

Perhaps one element of Jean Gabin's enduring popularity was the fact that, to the French, he embodied the average man who became a star. The main reason for his powerful impact on the public was, however, more complex. Although such directors as Carné and Renoir learned how to present the actor's rugged good looks to their best advantage, it was Gabin's own ability to use his face and gestures with a rare and telling economy in front of the camera which gave the appearance of real life. Like Spencer Tracy, his close American counterpart, Gabin perfected this technique.

He was born into a family of theatrical artists in Paris in 1904, but began work in a foundry. He then entered the music-hall and acted in musicals and operettas before starting a career in movies in 1930. His performance in Renoir's *Les Bas-Fonds* (1937) brought him some fame, but it was in Julien Duvivier's *Pépé-le-Moko* (1936) that he won international acclaim. Many successes followed: as one of the prisoners-of-war in Renoir's *La Grande Illusion* (1937, *The Great Illusion*), the deserter in *Quai des Brumes* (1938), the locomotive-driver in *La Bête Humaine* (*Judas Was a Woman*), a foundry worker in the magnificent *Le Jour se Lève* (1939). This last film epitomized Gabin's unique role in the French cinema: the ordinary man who finds himself matched against forces of society which he fails to comprehend. After killing the mountebank (Jules Berry) who has thwarted his love, he locks himself in a bleak room awaiting his doom, and the scene with the last cigarette butt ranks as one of the most poignant depictions of a man at the end of his tether that the cinema has produced. Gabin remained a star into the Seventies and eventually made 65 films. He died in 1976.

Top: Tricoche et Cacolet *(1938) – a story about two confidence tricksters – gave Fernandel ample opportunity for outlandish characterization. Above left: Arletty, an actress ideally suited to the poetic realism of Marcel Carné's films, as Garance in* Les Enfants du Paradis, *with Pierre Brasseur. Left: Jean Gabin, best known for his portrayals of world-weary, working-class heroes for Carné, Renoir and Duvivier. Renoir said of him 'Gabin could express the most violent emotion with a mere quiver of his impassive face'*

Chapter 17

Blood and thunder

Action on the high seas, glittering spectacle in Ancient Rome and grand-scale disaster movies
rekindled the public's passion for epics and swashbucklers

With the advent of sound several of the staple genres of the silent screen went into eclipse, notably Westerns, swashbucklers and historical epics. But when, in 1934, Hollywood rewrote and strictly enforced the Hays Code, which had been drawn up in 1927, the film companies, returned to such 'safe subjects'. These were films which were generally set in distant eras, far-off countries, and societies whose moral codes stressed romance, patriotism, gallantry and clean-cut action rather than sex, violence and sensationalism.

They were also films which brought out the best in Hollywood's unrivalled team of craftsmen and technicians: the costume designers, art directors, stunt arrangers, fencing masters, composers and special-effects men. It was these artists who were responsible for the feel and shape of the action films and for providing a constant stream of spectacle and excitement to take the minds of the audiences off Depression and unemployment, international uncertainty and rumours of war.

The most purely escapist films were the swashbucklers – entrancing, exhilarating excursions into pure style. Warner Brothers set the revival in motion with their remake of *Captain Blood* (1935), but the history of the swashbuckler owes much to the talent of Douglas Fairbanks Sr. The archetypal characters of dashing hero, double-dyed villain and damsel in distress, the elaborate sets, the acrobatic set pieces and the stylized plots were established by Douglas Fairbanks in an unforgettable series of films that began with *The Mark of Zorro* (1920) and ended with *The Iron Mask* (1929) almost a decade later. The new cycle of swashbucklers adhered to this pattern, but added sound and colour to provide the finishing touches.

Errol Flynn, cast by Warner Brothers at short notice in *Captain Blood*, proved the ideal successor to Douglas Fairbanks Sr. The combination of lithe, animal grace, clear-eyed youthfulness, pure English-speaking voice and athletic prowess was irresistible. Warners assembled a memorable supporting cast headed by Olivia de Havilland, as a radiantly lovely heroine, and Basil Rathbone,

sneering, arrogant, virile and flamboyant, as a definitive villain. Fred Cavens provided the thrilling sword-play, Anton Grot designed the stylized, semi-Expressionist sets, Erich Wolfgang Korngold wrote the symphonic score, the whole wealth of skills being blended together by maestro Michael Curtiz into the classic pirate adventure. Galleons, with sails billowing, engaged in thunderous sea battles, swords clashed on the sea-shore, and a tyrannical governor was overthrown, all in sun-drenched Caribbean settings.

With occasional changes of personnel, the same talented team went on to create two more swashbucklers which set the standard that all rivals and successors would have to aim for. *The Adventures of Robin Hood* (1938), shot in lustrous Technicolor, still ravishes the senses and stirs up the blood. The action highlights of the film are the outlaws' attack on a gold shipment in Sherwood Forest and the climactic sword fight between Flynn and Rathbone ranging all round Nottingham Castle.

The Sea Hawk (1940) starred Flynn as a privateer, modelled on Sir Francis Drake. It was a film of sumptuous visual style, spell-binding skill, breath-taking action and full-hearted commitment. Two stirring sea-battles between actual-size ships were staged in the new Warners studio tank and a furious final duel between Flynn and the villain Henry Daniell was fought, with the protagonists dwarfed by huge flickering shadows on the walls.

The Warners style was closely copied by 20th Century-Fox when they produced two swashbucklers with their leading male star, Tyrone Power. Rouben Mamoulian's elegant *The Mark of Zorro* (1940) utilized Fred Cavens' sword-play and a score that echoed Korngold's style. Several Warners

Above: Tyrone Power as Zorro (a 'hybrid' of Robin Hood and the Scarlet Pimpernel) battling with the villainous Basil Rathbone. Comparisons with the 1920 version were inevitable, but if Power lacked Fairbanks Sr's prowess, Mamoulian's agile, thrusting camerawork more than compensated. Below: another Fairbanks classic was remade in the Thirties; this version of The Three Musketeers *featured Walter Abel, Paul Lukas and Moroni Olsen as the duelling heroes of Dumas' story*

The Three MUSKETEERS

Top: The historical disaster movies of the Thirties were every bit as dramatic as the swashbucklers; for In Old Chicago *Henry King staged the great Chicago fire and the ensuing flood most spectacularly. Above: Errol Flynn as Robin Hood in the Technicolor* Adventures of Robin Hood – *a quintessential swashbuckler that has stood the test of time owing to the zest and humour of Flynn's performance. Below right: George Stevens' rousing and riotous adventure set on the North-West Frontier contained plenty of action and comedy, but Hecht and MacArthur's script bore little relation to Kipling*

grace, speed and humour, those of the historical epic were size, scale and seriousness. The latter was also frequently used to point up a moral, religious or even political message. The great showman Cecil B. DeMille was the acknowledged master of the historical epic.

Although he prided himself on imparting moral uplift, DeMille's promotion of Christian values was virtually lost beneath the glittering spectacle and the slyly titillating scenes of eroticism and sadism. *The Sign of the Cross* (1932), *Cleopatra* (1934) and *The Crusades* (1935) remain his finest achievements. They celebrate on the one hand an almost pagan sensuality, with shimmering photography and languorous camera movements weaving scenes of luxurious seduction. In *Cleopatra*, amid clouds of incense, showers of rose petals, fluttering doves and strutting peacocks, scantily-clad slaves attended Claudette Colbert as she wallowed naked in a bath of asses milk. On the other hand the films appeal to a primitive blood-lust, featuring cruel games in the Roman arenas and the torture or slaughter of captive Christians. Bloody battles are frequent set pieces – monstrous siege-engines roll inexorably forward over human bodies, torrents of flame pour from city walls onto the soldiers beneath and battalions of knights wade through corpses with swords whirling around their heads.

supporting players embellished a dream-like sequence of horseback chases, sword-fights and sardonic encounters. Henry King's *The Black Swan* (1942) was Fox's answer to *Captain Blood*, complete with flame-haired Maureen O'Hara and villainy from George Sanders. It was a brawling, sprawling, rumbustious, rollicking yarn that lived up to its preface:

'This is a story of the Spanish Main – where villainy wore a sash and the only political creed was love, gold and adventure.'

Other swashbuckling stars emerged too. Louis Hayward starred in two spirited adaptations from novels by Alexandre Dumas: *The Man in the Iron Mask* (1939, dir. James Whale) and *The Son of Monte Cristo* (1940, dir. Rowland V. Lee). Both brought to their exciting proceedings an atmospheric touch of Gothic mystery, with secret passages, cobwebbed catacombs and torture chambers. Rowland V. Lee also directed a lively, streamlined version of *The Three Musketeers* (1935) for RKO. Here the accent was very much on action and once again Fred Cavens staged some impressive fencing sequences.

Douglas Fairbanks Jr took up his father's mantle to star in one of the finest films of the decade, John Cromwell's *The Prisoner of Zenda* (1937), the purest and noblest fable of love and honour ever committed to celluloid. Ronald Colman, Madeleine Carroll, Raymond Massey and Fairbanks Jr could not have been bettered as the protagonists in this timeless Ruritanian romance, and the film climaxed with one of the best and wittiest of screen duels, choreographed by Ralph Faulkner (who, along with Cavens, had a virtual monopoly of fight arranging in the Thirties). Fairbanks Jr followed this in 1941 with a lively double role in Gregory Ratoff's *The Corsican Brothers*.

Where the keynotes of the swashbuckler were

History hit the screen with a clash of steel and a flash of gunpowder – and British India became the new lawless frontier

There were, of course, second-rate historical epics. RKO's *The Last Days of Pompeii* (1935), despite an impressive final holocaust, devoted most of its length to the tedious and sanctimonious story of the moral regeneration of a brutal gladiator, told with none of the spice or flair of DeMille. Only Josef von Sternberg's unfinished *I Claudius* (1937), with its marvellous performance by Charles Laughton, suggests a possible rival to DeMille's pre-eminence.

In the late Thirties, however, DeMille turned his eye on American history and dramatized the expansion of the United States in *The Plainsman* (1936), *The Buccaneer* (1938) and *Union Pacific* (1939) which, although replete with battles, charges and train wrecks, lacked both the erotic and sadistic edge of his earlier films. In the same vein, the decade ended with David O. Selznick's *Gone With the Wind* (1939), the single most famous film of the era and the one which celebrated the rebirth of the nation after the trauma of civil war.

Hollywood boasted two other profitable lines in epics. The box-office success of Henry Hathaway's *The Lives of a Bengal Lancer* (1935), in which Gary Cooper put down a native uprising on the North-West Frontier of India, began a vogue for imperial epics to which almost every studio contributed.

Warner Brothers countered with *The Charge of the Light Brigade* (1936). The film offered a tiger hunt, a wild horse drive and had Errol Flynn leading the climactic charge which was unforgettably staged by Michael Curtiz. Fox presented *Wee Willie Winkie* (1937) in which Shirley Temple brought peace to the Indian North-West Frontier under the expert direction of John Ford. At the same time Universal produced *The Sun Never Sets* (1939) and RKO made *Gunga Din* (1939), adapted from Rudyard Kipling's famous poem.

Even Republic Pictures, home of Gene Autry and Captain Marvel, contributed *Storm Over Bengal* (1938). These Indian adventures, whose location

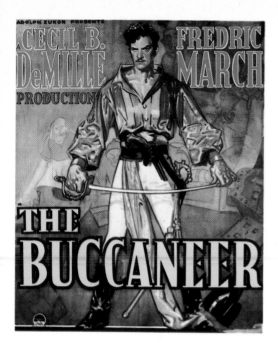

work was usually done at Lone Pine, California, contained generous action sequences and constituted another exotic form of escapism. But their insistence on a racial hierarchy headed by the white man, their implicit (and sometimes explicit) justification of the British Imperial presence in India and Africa tended to reinforce the political *status quo*.

Disaster epics were equally successful action pictures. They might be classified as films that sought to live up to Sam Goldwyn's celebrated injunction to a scriptwriter, 'I want you to begin with an earthquake and work up to a climax'. Invariably they brought together a group of characters with individual and collective problems and caused these problems to be resolved in one way or another by a spectacular final holocaust.

Such films also had a heavily moralistic message. Mankind had fallen into evil ways and so God was punishing them, but out of the ruins of the old a new civilization would arise built on the basic principles of decency, humanity, hard work and good government. The Hollywood special effects departments had a field day, creating ever more grandoise disasters. They succeeded in destroying New York by tidal wave (*Deluge*, 1933), San Francisco by earthquake (*San Francisco*, 1936), Chicago by fire (*In Old Chicago*, 1938), the South Sea island of Manikura by hurricane (*The Hurricane*, 1938), a Chinese province by locust plague (*The Good Earth*, 1937) and the Indian city of Ranchipur by damburst (*The Rains Came*, 1939).

The epic form also appealed to other countries, particularly those with totalitarian regimes, which used the cinema to rewrite and restage dramatic episodes from their countries' pasts, imbuing them with nationalistic and militaristic messages.

The Italian silent cinema had been famous for its historical epics and had re-created virtually every story from the classical past: from Spartacus to Nero, from the Fall of Troy to Julius Caesar, from Oedipus Rex to Attila the Hun. The cinema of the Fascist era could not manage an output of epics comparable to that of the great age of Italian cinema, but Carmine Gallone's *Scipione l'Africano* (1937, *Scipio the African*) was a lavish re-creation of the Roman general's victorious campaigns in North Africa, intended to justify Mussolini's African campaigns. Other directors turned to the epic in order to escape contemporary reality and avoid entanglement with the controversial present. Many films, such as the 1937 version of *Gli Ultimi Giorni di Pompeii* (*The Last Days of Pompeii*), were remakes of silent successes. The historian Richard Griffith has written that 'they reflected nothing but the frozen values of a paralyzed society. Even the Fascists were bored by them'.

Both Stalin's Russia and Hitler's Germany promoted historical epics to glorify the submission of a people to their national destiny and to hold up for admiration the all-powerful, all-knowing, all-seeing leader. In Russia the two-part film *Peter the Great* (1937/38) and in Germany the Fridericus series of films about the Prussian king Frederick the Great preached just that message. Eisenstein's Soviet epic *Alexander Nevsky* (1938) was a passionately nationalistic and anti-German drama about the thirteenth-century Russian prince who defeated an invasion by the Teutonic knights.

In Germany the foremost historical epic was *Condottieri* (1937, *Knights of the Black Eagle*) filmed by a German company on location in Italy and directed by Luis Trenker. As a piece of pure film-making the movie is outstanding for its majestic use of Italian settings and buildings, crystal-clear photography, a soaring symphonic score and graphically-staged battles and sieges.

Although the totalitarian countries carried on the production of epic films into the war, the USA's entry into World War II signalled the demise in Hollywood of these kinds of historical action films. Swashbuckling movies set on the Spanish Main, imperial epics located on India's North-West Frontier and historical epics set in Ancient Rome, all seemed suddenly irrelevant, and the disaster movies had literally been overtaken by reality. War films and Westerns enjoyed an instant revival – the former for obvious reasons, the latter because they laid stress on America's national consciousness, ideals and traditions. The historical epic, the swashbuckler, the imperial drama and the disaster film were out for the duration of the war.

JEFFREY RICHARDS

Top left: Although one of the top Hollywood stars of the Thirties, Fredric March was not an obvious choice for the title role in Paramount's The Buccaneer *as he had turned down several swashbuckler roles earlier. Above: swashbucklers came full circle when Douglas Fairbanks Jr starred in the dual role of* The Corsican Brothers. *Bottom left:* La Corona di Ferro, *the apogee of the Italian costume epic, was made by Alessandro Blasetti who had directed little else but historical films throughout the Thirties. Below: not to be outdone by Hollywood, the Soviet cinema mounted epic battles like this one in* Peter the Great

The Admirable Briton

He was the brave custodian of the British Empire, a dashing, stiff-upper-lipped gentleman-soldier committed to defending the faith and protecting the natives. And when his story was put onto the screen in the Thirties, he was more dashing, stiff-upper-lipped and gentlemanly than ever before . . .

It seems, on the face of it, rather odd that the USA, which had seceded from the British Empire in 1776, should in the twentieth century have given the definitive visual form to the myths and archetypes of British imperialism. But in the Thirties, in a succession of exciting, lavishly produced epic adventures, Hollywood did just that. All of the films successfully glamorized the British Empire and its representatives and preached a consistent ethic of service, duty, dedication and selfless heroism. The characters conformed strictly to type, embodying the required attributes. The British officers and administrators were handsome, modest, brave, hardworking and self-sacrificing: the natives divided into the loyal and devoted servants, willing to lay down their lives for the white sahibs; and the suave, educated princes, bent on stirring up revolt and bringing slaughter and devastation to the peaceful inhabitants of India (where most of the films were set).

The cycle began with Henry Hathaway's *The Lives of a Bengal Lancer* (1935), in which Gary Cooper, Franchot Tone and Richard Cromwell, Americans all, play Lancer officers on the North-West Frontier of India. It derives almost nothing from its ostensible source – Major Yeats-Brown's best-selling book of travel notes and reflections – but tells instead a story of action, intrigue and adventure, culled from the literary tradition of Rudyard Kipling, A.E.W. Mason, and Talbot Mundy. Strong in its justification of British rule in India and the exaltation of the life of military service, the narrative traces the process by which two outsiders, Cooper and Cromwell, are initiated into the British imperial mission and the traditions of discipline and self-effacement that it demanded. The inevitable C. Aubrey Smith, doyen of the British colony in Hollywood, is on hand to explain to them this ideal – the

Above: in defiance of history, Captain Geoffrey Vickers (Errol Flynn) leads his Bengal Lancers in The Charge of the Light Brigade. *Above right:* The Lives of a Bengal Lancer, *first of Hollywood's Empire films of the Thirties. Right: Ronald Colman as the self-sacrificing Robert Clive in* Clive of India

provision of peace, order and good government for millions of natives; Cooper and Cromwell demonstrate their acceptance of it by helping to defeat rebel Afghans and earning decorations, though in Cooper's case it is a posthumous VC. The glamour of the uniforms, the grandeur of the locations and the excitement of riding, hunting and fighting sequences combined to make the film a box-office success for Paramount.

Into the valley of death

Other studios were impressed by Paramount's triumph with *The Lives of a Bengal Lancer* and hastened to follow suit with imperial films. Warner Brothers, for example, jettisoned the script of their Crimean War epic, *The Charge of the Light Brigade* (1936), and fabricated a story in which the Bengal Lancers are transferred to the Crimea in time for the climactic charge. Although critics cavilled at the liberties taken with history, audiences were swept along by the sheer gusto of the film, which is an intoxicating blend of romance, action and drama, teaming a stunningly handsome Errol Flynn and a meltingly lovely Olivia de Havilland. The director, Michael Curtiz, brought the action to a triumphant climax in his staging of the charge, a sequence which has perhaps never been equalled. Horses thunder across the plain, sabres flash in the sunlight, cannons roar to right and left and the Union Jack waves proudly over the carnage; it was all sufficient, as one critic observed, 'to persuade the most ardent pacifist of war's undoubted glamour'. Another critic, entitling his article 'Hooray, you're dead', was genuinely alarmed that Hollywood was now selling heroism with the same success that it had sold sex, crime, horror and history:

'Heaven forbid they sell us heroism for it is a terribly dangerous thing and if it is offered, we

shall buy it like strong drink. The Germans and the Italians seem to be quite drunk but we must try to keep sober.'

He would have been in no way reassured to learn that *The Lives of a Bengal Lancer* was a favourite film of both Hitler and the Spanish dictator Primo de Rivera.

Fox's Indian summer

Darryl F. Zanuck's 20th Century Pictures, later 20th Century-Fox, was perhaps the most anglophile Hollywood studio in the Thirties, and kept up a constant stream of imperial adventures. Richard Boleslavsky's *Clive of India* (1935) cast Ronald Colman as one of the heroes of British India, sacrificing everything for his duty: 'India is a sacred trust. I must keep faith.' Henry King's *Lloyds of London* (1936)

celebrated the exploits of the merchant marine, the emergence of maritime insurance and the heroism of Nelson. King also directed *Stanley and Livingstone* (1939), re-creating the epic search of explorer Henry Morton Stanley (Spencer Tracy) for the lost missionary hero David Livingstone (Cedric Hardwicke). John Ford's *Four Men and a Prayer* (1938) showed how the four sons of a disgraced British Indian army officer (C. Aubrey Smith) set out to clear their father's name. Perhaps the best of Fox's British Empire output is Ford's *Wee Willie Winkie* (1937). Kipling's short story – the hero of which suffers a sex change from Percival to Priscilla for the film to accommodate Shirley Temple – was crossed with the plot of *Little Lord Fauntleroy* (child and widowed mother from the USA humanize starchy old British grandfather). But the film enabled Shirley to be instructed in the nature of the British imperial

mission by her grandfather (C. Aubrey Smith). It is ironic that John Ford, who as a professional Irishman hated the British Empire, should have contributed to the imperial cycle; he was also, however, a military romantic, and responded with great sympathy to the parades and patrols, regimental balls and full-dress funerals, flag-raisings and inspections that punctuate the film and give visual expression to the message of discipline and duty.

RKO's contribution, *Gunga Din* (1939), was virtually an imperial swashbuckler. It teamed Kipling's *Soldiers Three*, a smiling, sword-fighting, unflaggingly energetic trio played by Cary Grant, Douglas Fairbanks Jr and Victor McLaglen, with Sam Jaffe as the humble water-carrier Gunga Din, in a series of exhilarating adventures, culminating in their successful averting of the massacre of a British regiment by Hindu fanatics.

The best of British

Curiously enough, Hollywood produced more imperial epics than Britain did. But Britain's contribution was a notable imperial trilogy – *Sanders of the River* (1935), *The Drum* (1938), and *The Four Feathers* (1939) – produced by Alexander Korda, an enthusiastic and patriotic proponent of Britain's imperial role. All three films were directed by Zoltan Korda and designed by Vincent Korda. All three involved extensive location shooting – in Nigeria, India and the Sudan respectively – and *The Drum* and *The Four Feathers* were photographed in glowing Technicolor. Amid a satisfying ritual of chases, fights, escapes, battles and rescues and stirring displays of pageantry (parades, processions and formal banquets), well-acted dramas are played out with the principal characters once again demonstrating the qualities of the 'admirable Briton'.

In *Sanders of the River* District Commissioner Sanders (Leslie Banks) puts down, virtually single-handed, a native uprising in Nigeria and rescues his faithful singing ally (Paul Robeson). In *The Drum*, an Indian Prince (Sabu) joins forces with the stalwart Carruthers and his wife (Roger Livesey and Valerie Hobson) to thwart the evil machinations of his uncle (Raymond Massey). In *The Four Feathers*, a disgraced British officer (John Clements), assisted by the pro-British Karaga Pasha (Amid Taftazani), redeems his honour with deeds of gallantry during the 1898 Sudan campaign.

Judged together, these three films unques-

tionably championed the continuation of the British Empire – but offered no sound political, economic or constitutional reasons for its existence. The Empire was justified in the apparent moral superiority of the British, demonstrated by their adherence to a code of gentlemanly conduct and the maintenance of a disinterested system of law, order and justice. In each of the films the exercise of power by the British is supported by the consent of the governed, as represented by the Paul Robeson, Sabu and Amid Taftazani characters; and defined by the opposition of self-seeking, power-hungry native despots who, if left alone, would prey unmercifully on their own people (King Mofalaba in *Sanders of the River*, Ghul Khan in *The Drum*, the Khalifa in *The Four Feathers*). Since all three Korda films were made with the active cooperation of the colonial authorities and the British Army, the scripts must have been officially approved. Yet in them there is nothing of the major imperial innovations of the interwar years, the development of the commonwealth, the constitutional changes in India or of the institution of colonial development policies in Africa. The Korda films and their Hollywood counterparts depict British rule as timeless and eternal: whether they are set in 1856 like *The Charge of the Light Brigade*, or 1938 like *The Drum*, uniforms, attitudes and aspirations are identical. For the cinema of the Thirties, the British Empire was frozen forever somewhere around the 1890s, with Victoria the Queen-Empress on the throne, the Russians menacing the North-West Frontier, and the Bengal Lancers on

Left: Spencer Tracy and Cedric Hardwicke as Stanley and Livingstone. *Above left:* Lloyds of London, *a tribute to Britain's naval supremacy. Above:* Gunga Din, *in which the White Man's Burden becomes his ally. Top: no imperial film was complete without C. Aubrey Smith, here with 'sons' David Niven, George Sanders, Richard Greene and William Henry in* Four Men and a Prayer

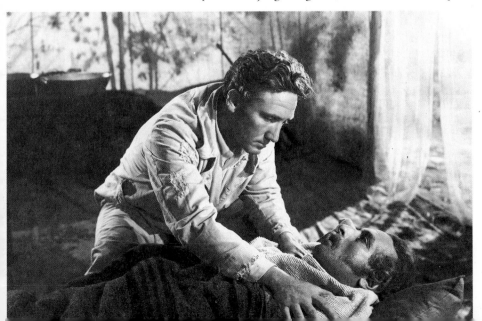

guard protecting the population of India from foreign aggression and domestic exploitation.

The setting sun

The outbreak of World War II brought an end to the imperial epics. The last two contributions from Hollywood were Rowland V. Lee's *The Sun Never Sets* (1939) and Henry Hathaway's more appropriately titled *Sundown* (1941), in which heroic British District Commissioners in Africa fight against fascist villains who are stirring up the tribes. Both films contrasted benevolent British paternalism with totalitarian tyranny. But soon it became clear that the war was promoting a new ethos which rendered imperial epics out of date. World War II was a war for democracy, a crusade for racial equality, self-determination and freedom. Its enemies were the cruel and racist tyrannies of the German, Japanese and Italian empires. It would be wrong to equate the British Empire with the Axis powers – but they did share a fundamental belief in racial hierarchy with the whites at the top. This became an embarrassing feature of Hollywood films at a time when, for instance, India's role as a bulwark against Japanese aggression was crucial. Consequently the Office of War Information (OWI) in America scotched MGM's plans for a film version of Kipling's *Kim* and banned the reissue of *Gunga Din* which, on its initial release, had been banned in India, Japan

Above: trouble in Sudan in Korda's The Four Feathers. *Below: in* The Real Glory *David Niven, not so much the 'admirable Briton' as the 'admirable American', defends the American-held Philippines against rebels*

and Malaya for offending against 'racial and religious sensibilities'.

Interestingly, the OWI also banned the reissue of Samuel Goldwyn's production, *The Real Glory* (1939). Another Hathaway picture, this stirring tale of three American officers – Gary Cooper, David Niven and Broderick Crawford – who help the American military garrison in the Philippines to suppress a native revolt, was the American imperialist equivalent of *The Lives of a Bengal Lancer*. Its box-office success had indicated why American audiences accepted British imperial epics with such readiness – for it was simply the most obvious manifestation of a strain of militarist and racist imperialism in American history and society. Elsewhere this tendency was celebrated in epic Westerns with wagon trains of white settlers dispossessing the American Indians of their ancestral lands and US cavalry regiments waging war against the tribes. At a time when the Western itself was unfashionable, imperial epics had filled the gap. They were in a very real sense British Westerns. No less an authority than R.J. Minney, co-author of the play and film *Clive of India*, described *The Lives of a Bengal Lancer* as 'a Wild West picture in an Indian setting'; and at least three imperial epics – *The Lives of a Bengal Lancer*, *Four Men and a Prayer* and *Gunga Din* – were later remade as cavalry Westerns – *Geronimo* (1962), *Fury at Furnace Creek* (1948) and *Sergeants Three* (1962). The war was destined to change the course of colonialism and, with the sun setting on the British Empire in the mid-Forties, the old-style imperial epic became a thing of the past.

JEFFREY RICHARDS

Memories of

Ronald Colman

Ronald Colman was a screen heart-throb from the mid-Twenties to the late Forties. More than any other actor he personified the heroic English gentleman-adventurer, bringing his urbane, romantic manner and distinguished looks and voice to the roles he played in films like *Bulldog Drummond* **(1929),** *Clive of India* **(1935) and** *The Prisoner of Zenda* **(1937). Here Juliet Benita Colman, his daughter from his marriage to the lovely English film actress Benita Hume, recalls Ronald Colman in some of his real-life roles – soldier, star and father**

Our family lived in Beverly Hills and Santa Barbara, California, until my father's death in 1958. It was an unusually private existence by Hollywood standards, full of books, teas, piano, croquet, animals, treasure hunts. He was 53 when I was born, and I was 13 when he died, unaware of him as a star – having at that point seen only two of his films – or indeed of anything that had been part of those 53 years. But I knew Ronald Colman intimately as a father, for he was rarely away and I was the only child; and I knew him vicariously as a husband (my mother, whom he married in 1938, died in 1967). Later I researched those other years for his biography.

He was born in Richmond, Surrey, in 1891, and first went on the stage as an amateur

beard. They played the entire sequence apparently looking at each other. 'Cut!' shouted Joseph L. Mankiewicz, who was directing. 'Now, you son of a bitch,' said Edna, 'will you *look* at me?' 'Why Edna, what on earth are you doing in that beard?' came Ronnie's reply. Needless to say, his camera habits did not change.

Although, during our years together, I never realized he was a star, I vividly remember first being brushed by the magic that affected fans over three decades. One afternoon when I was 11 years old, we sat after tea by his library fire and he introduced me to Edgar Allan Poe. 'It was many and many a year ago, In a kingdom by the sea . . .' he read. No longer in a room in California, I was transported to somewhere in the famous Edmund Dulac illustration of a lady with pearls in her hair, the sea at her feet, and the turreted kingdom behind her. 'Read it again!' I begged, and he sat with that weighty book of poetry on his lap and read 'Annabel Lee' seven or eight times, making such magic of it that 25 years later I still have the taste of that afternoon – the warmth of the fire on my cheek and the gleam of his smile in my mind's eye.

JULIET BENITA COLMAN

Above: a hand-coloured fan-annual shot of Colman and Lily Damita in the silent The Rescue *(1929). Above left: as Sidney Carton in* A Tale of Two Cities *(1935). Top: as* Bulldog Drummond *(1929) – his first talkie. Below: as* The Prisoner of Zenda *(1937) with Douglas Fairbanks Jr. Right: with his wife Benita Hume and daughter Juliet in the late Forties*

while working for the British Steamship Company. In 1914, aged 23, he became one of Kitchener's Contemptibles. At Messines he was hit by shrapnel, and when he regained consciousness he found that his colleagues had withdrawn to a nearby hill. His knee shattered, and with ammunition still flying, he started dragging himself through the mud towards safety. He suddenly thought of the imminent possibility of being hit again and found dead with his back to the enemy. That would never do. He turned around and painfully reversed off the field of battle, determinedly facing the Kaiser's troops.

Six years later – now a professional actor in English theatre and films – he married an actress who had made a name for herself in a stage-musical, *The Joy-Ride Lady* – a title which proved all too prophetic of her lifestyle. When, two lean years later, he was discovered in New York by the director Henry King, and went to shoot King's *The White Sister* (1923) opposite Lillian Gish in Italy, the marriage had soured considerably. On location he enjoyed everything from the garlic in the spaghetti to the lilt of the Italian language, and thrived amid the gregarious, professional American film team. His wife was a fish out of water, jealous of his success and incapable of coping with it. One evening – the last night of the marriage – she ran hysterically from their hotel room shouting, 'My God, I've killed him!' King and Gish rushed in to find him on the floor. When he came to he claimed he'd fallen and hit his head.

Filming *The Late George Apley* (1947) with his close friend Edna Best, he irritated her during their scenes together with his habit of avoiding her eyes. It was unconscious on his part, something he had evolved over the years as part of his relationship with the camera, so subtle that only his partner in a scene would notice. Edna chided him about it constantly. 'But my dear Edna', he would answer, 'of course I look you in the eye!' At their daughter's wedding in the film they walk down the aisle exchanging some words. With the crew clued in, Edna walked in immediately before shooting began wearing a long black

Filmography

1917 The Live Wire (unreleased short) (GB). **'19** The Toilers (GB); A Daughter of Eve (GB); Sheba (GB); Snow in the Desert (GB). **'20** A Son of David (GB); Anna the Adventuress (GB); The Black Spider (GB). *All remaining films USA:* **'21** Handcuffs or Kisses. **'23** The White Sister; The Eternal City. **'24** $20 a Week; Tarnish; Her Night of Romance; Romola; A Thief in Paradise. **'25** The Sporting Venus; His Supreme Moment; Her Sister From Paris; The Dark Angel; Stella Dallas; Lady Windermere's Fan. **'26** Kiki; Beau Geste; The Winning of Barbara Worth. **'27** The Night of Love; The Magic Flame. **'28** Two Lovers. **'29** The Rescue; Bulldog Drummond; Condemned/ Condemned to Devil's Island. **'30** Raffles; The Devil to Pay. **'31** The Unholy Garden; Arrowsmith. **'32** Cynara. **'33** The Masquerader. **'34** Bulldog Drummond Strikes Back. **'35** Clive of India; The Man Who Broke the Bank at Monte Carlo; A Tale of Two Cities. **'36** Under Two Flags. **'37** Lost Horizon; The Prisoner of Zenda. **'38** If I Were King. **'39** The Light That Failed. **'40** Lucky Partners. **'41** My Life With Caroline. **'42** The Talk of the Town; Random Harvest. **'44** Kismet (retitling for TV: Oriental Dream). **'47** The Late George Apley. **'48** A Double Life. **'50** Champagne for Caesar. **'53** Shakespeare's Theater: The Globe Playhouse (short) (narr. only). **'56** Around the World in 80 Days (guest). **'57** The Story of Mankind.

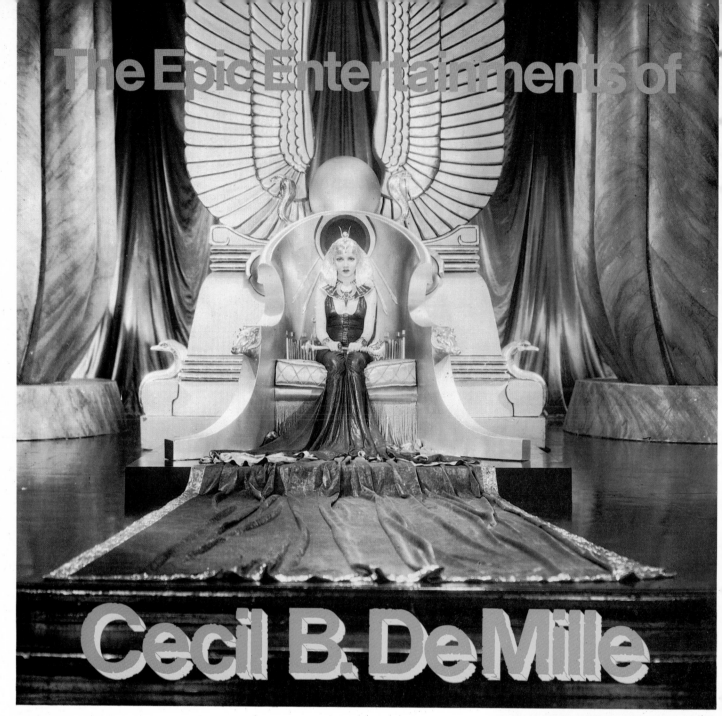

Cecil B. DeMille

During the Thirties DeMille rescued his floundering career with grand re-creations of the power and debauchery of Ancient Rome and with Westerns that celebrated the American pioneering spirit

When sound first came to the movies, the career of Cecil B. DeMille, Hollywood's greatest showman, had reached an unprecedented crisis. From his first film, *The Squaw Man* (1913), he had unerringly mirrored changing fashions in public taste. During World War I he made contemporary war stories like *The Little American* (1917), which depicted the sinking of the *Lusitania*. Thereafter, in the changing moral climate of the early Twenties, he specialized in spicy marital dramas such as *The Affairs of Anatol* (1921), visions of opulence centring on the bathroom and bedroom. He

then undertook his most ambitious project to date, *The Ten Commandments* (1923), a block-busting epic costing $1.5 million.

Although he was a household name, De-Mille's professional position was far from secure. Arguments over the cost of *The Ten Commandments* initiated a widening rift be-tween DeMille and his business associates at Famous Players-Lasky – especially Adolph Zukor. DeMille left under a cloud to form his own company in 1925. However, despite the success of an epic life of Christ, *The King of Kings* (1927), many of his company's films failed at the box-office and his backers and partners lost confidence in him. As DeMille explained him-self in his autobiography:

'The trouble in 1928 was that I did not have

Above: DeMille's Cleopatra; the star, Claudette Colbert, was one of his favourite leading ladies in the Thirties. Right: Cecil Blount DeMille in favourite directorial garb – riding boots, jodhpurs and open-necked shirt

DeMille contracted to make three pictures with MGM. *Dynamite* (1929) was made in both silent and sound versions (he still was not convinced): *Madame Satan* (1930), a musical, was a box-office flop, and in something of a panic he attempted to repeat earlier successes with his third version of *The Squaw Man* (1931), but this, too, failed disastrously. At this time DeMille attempted to form an organization known as the Directors' Guild with Lewis Milestone, King Vidor and Frank Borzage. The Guild's aim was to place creative control of picture-making with the directors rather than the financiers. DeMille claimed:

' . . . the conditions under which motion pictures are now generally produced are not conducive to the best creative work, and must, if long continued, result in a deadly uniformity of ideas and methods, thus seriously retarding the highest commercial and artistic development of the craft.'

This move by DeMille highlights one of his fundamental contradictions: by forming the Guild he was attempting to gain for himself an artistic freedom from financial constraint which was impossible in such a highly capita-

enough 'picture money' to be completely independent and make only the kind of pictures I wanted to make.'

In 1928 he embarked upon *The Godless Girl*, a moral tale set in a girl's reform school. The shooting of this film is a typical example of DeMille's methods. His production team spent months researching reform schools and a realistic set was constructed on the lot. True to DeMille's passion for authenticity this set was to be burnt down at the end of the film with the actors (literally) escaping the flames – a procedure which was planned to the second. Despite the fine timing, when one wing of the set fell down on cue (pulled by special wires) two girls were trapped. They luckily managed to escape by climbing up a gable and down the other side.

DeMille was convinced that the success of *The Jazz Singer* (1927) was only temporary and that *The Godless Girl*, which he had shot silent, would be a hit, but his backers insisted that sound should be added. The quarrels that ensued finally prompted him to sign with MGM. On his departure a soundtrack was added to the film.

Top: Charles Laughton as the Emperor Nero, with Claudette Colbert and Fredric March, in The Sign of the Cross, *one of DeMille's finest epics. Above:* The Plainsman *marked DeMille's successful return to the Western. Below: the last spike is hammered in to complete the Western Union railroad in* Union Pacific

lized industry, yet as a fervent Republican, DeMille had absolutely no wish to change the industry's structure.

Louis B. Mayer, head of MGM, was, not surprisingly, unhappy about this move; his unhappiness was compounded by DeMille's box-office failures. After an extended trip to Russia and Europe, lack of money forced DeMille to mortgage his property and swallow his pride; he approached his first company (which had, in the meantime, become the Paramount Pictures Corporation) and Lasky and Bud Schulberg (the head of production on the West Coast) persuaded Zukor to let DeMille back into the fold. He was assigned to direct a Roman epic entitled *The Sign of the Cross* (1932) on a budget of only $650,000; he received a meagre salary of $450 per week. (In 1916 DeMille had been drawing a salary of $1000 per week plus a share of the profits.) DeMille was forced to adopt a more rigorous production operation: Nero's palace, far from being an authentic, life-size reproduction, was largely constructed in miniature with special flights of stairs and ramps of sufficient size for the cast to walk on. DeMille was not allowed to marshal thousands of extras as he had in the old days; instead, the cameraman used a prism lens which gave the effect of doubling the number of people in a crowd. However the Roman circus was genuinely full-size: it seated

7500 and had a vast arena. DeMille brought the picture in on budget (apparently stopping shooting in the middle of a take so as not to exceed it) and it was a box-office smash.

Clearly a great deal of this success was due to the film's sexual content, which included the attempts of Poppea (Claudette Colbert) to seduce Marcus Superbus (Fredric March) and his futile efforts to seduce a Christian girl called Mercia (Elissa Landi) in the course of which he forces her to attend an orgy with him. DeMille writes that William Hays, the industry's moral guardian, was very upset about a dance in the orgy scene and telephoned to ask him what he was going to do about it. 'Not a damn thing,' DeMille replied, and didn't. DeMille's insistence that 'I will always resist, as far as I am able, the claim of any individual or group to the right of censorship' is ironic in view of his support of Hays' appointment, which he defended on the grounds that some pictures were '. . . bad art as well as bad morals and bad taste'.

The film's success reinstated DeMille within the industry. After two pot-boiling films (*This Day and Age* in 1933 and *Four Frightened People* in 1934) he launched himself into another epic, *Cleopatra* (1934). This time DeMille's passion for authenticity was rampant – even Cleopatra's hairpins were museum copies – in addition to his pleasure in sexual symbolism and innuendo, which he justified on commercial grounds. A slave girl danced almost naked with and on a golden bull, and the film was a box-office if not a critical success. From then on, with the exception of *The Greatest Show on Earth* (1951), all DeMille's films were historical.

His position at Paramount was now assured, not only because of these successes but also because Ernst Lubitsch had become production director at the studio (both Lasky and Schulberg had long since departed) and he was a great admirer of DeMille's silent films. Lubitsch's presence was a godsend; although DeMille's next picture, *The Crusades* (1935), failed miserably, he was able to abandon the ancient world for a while to make *The Plainsman* (1936), based on the lives of Wild Bill Hickok and Calamity Jane – but *not* with any historical accuracy in terms of events. DeMille built sets covering six acres of the Paramount lot and was once again able to use as many extras as he wanted for the battle scenes. Reviewing the film, *Variety* weekly wrote: 'It's cowboys and Indians on a broad, sweeping scale: not a *Covered Wagon* but realistic enough.' Realistic or not, it was a financial

success, as was his later *Union Pacific* (1939) which dealt with the construction of the Western Union railroad. His researchers went through the company's records going back 70 years. In Utah he built a complete reproduction of the town of Cheyenne and imported by bus over a thousand Navajo and Cheyenne Indians. During shooting, DeMille was taken ill and after an emergency operation he directed from a stretcher, but large sections of the film had to be shot by Arthur Rossen and James Hogan. The film's enormous success led Paramount to grant him a four-year contract and virtual independence. His next two films, *North West Mounted Police* (1940) and *Reap the Wild Wind* (1942) were both hits, the latter breaking Paramount's record for grosses at the box-office previously held by DeMille's silent version of *The Ten Commandments*.

DeMille then became carried away with the idea of filming the story of a missionary and naval commander, Dr Corydon E. Wassell, who had run a Japanese blockade in order to rescue nine wounded sailors despite orders to abandon them. The subject especially appealed to DeMille, who practised what would today be described as something of a 'macho' lifestyle. Prior to his film career he had loved attending Pennsylvania Military College, where the regimen included daily Bible readings and cold baths; until his last years he went every day for a nude swim in his pool. The film he made, *The Story of Dr Wassell* (1944), was a success, but the critics, as DeMille admits, did not like it. In

Top left: Loxi Claiborne (Paulette Goddard) sights a ship running on the rocks in Reap the Wild Wind, *a seafaring drama set in Georgia in the 19th century. Right: Charlton Heston as Moses in DeMille's second version of* The Ten Commandments, *his last biblical epic. Below: Samson (Victor Mature) brings the house down on his Philistine captors at the climax of* Samson and Delilah

ploying some 12,000 extras and 15,000 animals for the Exodus scene alone. DeMille was, of course, well versed in the organization and control of huge productions. He habitually directed from a platform, with a megaphone, and in sequences with thousands of extras used to communicate his instructions to his assistant directors in amongst the action by radio telephone. The film's final cost was $13 million and by the end of 1959 it had grossed over $83 million and been seen by more than 98 million people.

DeMille's career is significant for his production of Biblical epics and other films on a grand scale. He acknowledged the influence of the silent Italian epics on his work, and his contribution to the genre was both formative and substantial. However the artistic value of his films, of which he himself was quite convinced, probably lies in his silent work, not simply because, despite his Christian beliefs, he undoubtedly began to serve Mammon in his later work, but also because his despotic professional personality blinded him to the possibilities of fine art on small budgets. The *New Yorker*'s review of *Samson and Delilah* read:

'It may be said of Cecil B. DeMille that since 1913, when he teamed up with Jesse Lasky to create *The Squaw Man*, he has never taken a step backward. He has never taken a step forward either, but somehow he has managed to survive in a chancy industry where practically everybody is incessantly going up, down, or sideways . . . '

This, sadly, probably sums up his career.

SHEILA WHITAKER

Below: DeMille's career was financially successful, but not until The Greatest Show on Earth *did a film of his win a Best Picture Oscar. Here, the circus manager (Charlton Heston), injured in a train crash, is tended by a murderer (James Stewart) who, to escape dectection, wears the makeup of a clown*

the *Nation* James Agee wrote:

'. . . Cecil DeMille's [film] is to be regretted beyond qualification. It whips the story, in every foot, into a nacreous foam of lies whose speciousness is only the more painful because Mr DeMille is so obviously free from any desire to alter the truth except for what he considers to be its own advantage.'

This is an interesting point with regard to DeMille's complex character. His devout Christian beliefs and adherence to the Episcopalian Church, his increasingly right-wing political opinions and his somewhat unusual sex life – he was a foot fetishist and openly maintained relationships with two mistresses (Jeanie Mac-Pherson and Julia Faye) for many years – combined with his strict moral sense, inevitably produced violent contradictions in himself, his actions and his films.

DeMille's devotion to the American way of life led him to become passionately involved in the anti-communist movement that took hold in the USA after World War II. He was one of the first to name the respected left-wing writer John Howard Lawson as a leader of communist infiltration.

DeMille's career ended in grand style: *Samson and Delilah* (1949), *The Greatest Show on Earth* and *The Ten Commandments* (1956). The script of this film took three years to write and it was shot in Egypt after two years' preparation. It was a monumental production, em-

Alexander Nevsky

Eisenstein's picture of heroism

1

' . . . a completely contemporary picture, so close are the feelings that inspired the Russian people in the thirteenth century in repulsing the enemy to the feelings that inspire the Soviet Russian people now, and doubtless to all the feelings that inspire all those towards whom the grasping claw of German aggression is spreading . . . Let them not cringe before fascism, let them not kneel before it without protest, let them stop the unending policy of concession and appeasement towards this insatiable mon-

Directed by Sergei Eisenstein, 1938
Prod co: Mosfilm. **sc:** Sergei Eisenstein, Pyotr Pavlenko. **photo:** Eduard Tissé. **art dir:** Isaak Shpinel, Nikolai Solovyov, Konstantin Eliseyev, from drawings by Eisenstein. **mus:** Sergei Prokofiev. **ass dir:** Dmitri Vasiliev, Boris Ivanov, Nikolai Maslov. **r/t:** 112 minutes. Moscow premiere, 23 November 1938.
Cast: Nikolai Cherkasov (*Alexander Nevsky*), Nikolai Okhlopkov (*Vasili Buslai*), Alexander Abrikosov (*Gavrilo Olexich*), Dmitri Orlov (*Ignat*), Vasili Novikov (*Pavsha, governor of Pskov*), Vera Ivasheva (*Olga*), Nikolai Arsky (*Domash*), Varvara Massalitinova (*Amelfa*), Anna Danilova (*Vasilisa*), Vladimir Ershov (*Grand Master of the Teutonic Order*), Sergei Blinnikov (*Tverdilo*), Lev Fenin (*bishop*), I. Lagutin (*Ananias*), Naum Rogozhin (*black monk*).

Alexander Nevsky was the first film to be completed by Eisenstein since *The Old and the New* (1929) as well as being his first sound film. It offered an opportunity for the realization of the ideas on sound expressed in the 1928 *Declaration* by Eisenstein, Pudovkin and Aleksandrov. In this the authors warn that a mere:

'. . . *adhesion* of sound to pieces of montage reinforces their inertia.

'*Only a contrapuntal use* of sound in relation to the piece of visual montage offers new possibilities for the development and perfection of montage. *The first experiments with sound must be directed towards a sharp contrast between it and the visual images.* And only such a "storm" will produce the sensation needed to create a new *orchestral counterpoint* of visual and sound images.'

This concept of 'orchestral counterpoint', is exemplified in the Battle on the Ice sequence by the interaction between Eisenstein's powerful imagery and Prokofiev's dramatic musical score.

Alexander Nevsky was also the film that marked Eisenstein's return to official respectability. After *October* (1927) and *The Old and the New* Eisenstein had gone abroad, but his film projects there remained unfinished. Returning to the USSR, he fell foul of Boris Shumyatsky, administrative 'tsar' of the Soviet film industry. When he was eventually permitted to begin filming *Bezhin Meadow* the project was halted by Shumyatsky in March 1937, after two million roubles had already been spent on its production. This was an expensive mistake, not only for Soviet film art, but also for Shumyatsky: he was purged as a 'captive of the saboteurs' in January 1938.

This gave Eisenstein his opportunity. He began filming *Alexander Nevsky* on June 5 and completed it on November 7. The film had its premiere a fortnight later. In the process of its rapid editing Eisenstein fell asleep one evening. While the director slept, an incomplete print was removed to the Kremlin and shown to Stalin, who was eager to see it. He liked what he saw, and this made it difficult for Eisenstein to add the missing sequences. Thus his most success-

ful film remained for him the most unsatisfactory – at least from an artistic point of view. At the time, Eisenstein noted:

'*Nevsky* is brazenly effective despite *itself*. *Everyone* can see its staginess *above all*, its length, the rhythmic breaks and failures. *Everyone* can see them, not just the specialists . . . And it is effective *nonetheless*. Why? . . . There's only a single thought and everything revolves around a *single* thought. There's not a word, a remark, an episode or a scene where the dialogue and the plot are not concerned with the enemy and the need to defeat him.'

The story of the Russian people's successful struggle against the Teutonic Knights was an allegorical warning to the Nazis. Alexander's final address to the liberated citizens of Pskov renders this explicit:

'Go and tell all in foreign parts that Rus lives. Let people come to us as guests without fear. But he who comes with the sword shall perish by the sword. On this Rus stands and will stand forever!'

Alexander Nevsky was, in Eisenstein's words:

4

332

ster. Let the sceptics remember that there is no force of gloom and darkness that could stand against the combined efforts of all that is best, healthiest, most progressive and forward-looking in mankind.'

The article in which Eisenstein penned these words was called 'Patriotism Is My Theme': it remained unpublished in the USSR because, in August 1939, the Nazi–Soviet Pact was signed. The film no longer served a useful political purpose and was removed from circulation. But by then both

the director and Nikolai Cherkasov, who played Alexander, had been awarded the Order of Lenin, the highest order that the Soviet Union can bestow.

Following the German invasion of the USSR on June 22, 1941, *Alexander Nevsky* was re-released. It is a tribute to both Eisenstein and his politically most successful film that the Soviet government soon instituted a new battle honour for bravery at the front – the Order of Alexander Nevsky.

RICHARD TAYLOR

Thirteenth-century Russia is laid waste by the Mongol hordes from the East, while the Teutonic Knights (1) invade from the West, capturing the ancient city of Pskov and committing atrocities against the population (2). The men of Novgorod call on Alexander Nevsky to lead the Russian forces. The people take arms (3).

On the eve of battle, Ignat entertains the men with the tale of the hare and the vixen: as the hare cannot outpace her, he runs between two closely planted tree

trunks. Following him, the vixen is trapped and the hare deflowers her. This tale inspires Alexander's battle strategy. The Russian armies lie in wait (4), luring the Teutonic Knights (5) onto the frozen surface of Lake Peipus (6); the weight of their armour cracks the ice and they drown in the freezing water. This is the famous Battle on the Ice.

At the head of his victorious forces, Alexander enters Pskov to be fêted by the population (7). Russia is free.

Sword-play and satire

Period epics with samurai warriors were as popular in the Thirties as they had been in the Japanese silent cinema, but film-makers began to satirize their own traditions and to develop genres based on the new taste for realism

The Japanese cinema of the Thirties is still a relatively closed book to western filmgoers. At first viewing it is surprising to find such a varied and rich output during a time of extreme political and social stress – the imposition of rigid governmental doctrines and the conflict in China which led to the war in the Pacific.

As in other politically repressive regimes, some artists conformed whilst others simply tried to continue making their own kind' of personal films and succeeded to a remarkable degree. Another factor to be taken into consideration is the late coming of sound to the Japanese cinema. Although Heinosuke Gosho made the first sound film in 1931, a rather raucous local comedy called *Madamu To Nyobo* (*The Neighbour's Wife and Mine*), he and others, including Ozu and Mikio Naruse, continued to produce silent films well into the mid-Thirties. The late arrival of sound films was partly due to the resistance of the *benshi* (highly skilled commentators who used to narrate and explain silent films for audiences) who naturally saw talking films as their ultimate enemy, and the fact that it took several years for provincial cinemas to be supplied with sound equipment.

As a consequence, there is a striking continuation of silent-film experimentation from the Twenties into the Thirties, with an emphasis on action, free-wheeling camerawork and exotic subject matter. Tsuruhiko Tanaka's *Beni Komori* (1931, *The Red Bat*) is a typical example of the *chambara* (sword-play) school, which began in the Twenties. In this particular film the hero battles with dozens of opponents. Each fight is shot with a camera mobility quite unknown in the West at this time. The camerawork contains rapid panning movements, dissolves and even a split-screen effect.

Streets ahead of Hollywood
Tomu Uchida's *Keisatsukan* (1933, *Police*) anticipates the American, location-shot detective thriller by over a decade in its daring street-shooting, including some extraordinarily lengthy tracking and panning movements, whereas Minoru Murata's *Muteki* (1934, *Foghorns*), set in Yokohama in the 1870s, combines action with a seamy realism culled unashamedly from American and European sources, notably the films of the German director F.W. Murnau.

Of greater importance, however, was the drama of everyday life, though a surviving, battered print of *Made to Order Cloth*, directed by Daisuke Ito, reveals the vividness of samurai dramas in the Thirties. This film has a full quota of virtuoso fights and contains a tense night scene in which police with lanterns besiege an inn where the hero is hiding.

The celebrated film director Teinosuke Kinugasa is well-known and highly regarded for his silent films – but though there is less experimentation in a film like *Hebihimesama* (1940, *The Snake Princess*) than in his masterpieces *Jujiro* (1928, *Crossways*) and *Kurutta Ippeiji* (1926 *A Page of Madness*) – the director does maintain a continuous flow of lively imagery with many well-staged chases, moments of exotic fantasy and climaxes rendered in several vertiginous crane-shots. Kinugasa's famous 1932 version of the much-filmed *Chushingura* (*The Loyal 47 Ronin*) is reputed to be a most impressive action film but is rarely seen.

Sending up the samurai
Mansaku Itami stands apart from his colleagues in that he is the prime satirist of the period drama and is known to have admired Clair's satirical style. Of his two surviving films from this period, *Akanishi Kakita* (1936) and *A Capricious Young Man* (1935), it is the latter which reveals his gifts most fully, being a wry, almost deadpan account of two travellers who become involved with rival kingdoms and settle the matter by instituting a search for a mythical golden egg. Itami has a wonderful sense of the ridiculous. His parody of the historical adventure film extends to the formal conventions of the genre, as in the scene where, after entering through a trapdoor (situated unexpectedly under a princess' bed) the two interlopers proceed to flatter and apologise to her in the most conventional, unctuous fashion imaginable.

The war films of the period dealing with the Chinese conflict contain a good deal of action, though normally the enemy is unseen, represented as a vague, abstract mass 'out there'. Outstanding examples are *Nishizumi Senshachoden* (1940, *Tank Commander Nishizumi*) and Tomotaka Tasaka's military films *Gonin No Sekkohei* (*Five Scouts*) and *Tsuchi To Heitai* (*Earth and Soldiers*, both 1939). Though the films subscribe to the Japanese military code, they are curiously muted, even downbeat in their effects: groups of troops advance across desolate terrains in long shot and then close in for flurries of battle action, caught in long, winging tracking movements which prefigure the shooting style of Akira Kurosawa in later decades.

On the evidence of these films of the Thirties, with both period and contemporary subjects, it becomes clear that the Japanese pioneered a form of neo-realism years before the Italian experimentation of the post-war period. Ozu's family dramas may be better-known in the West but there is much to discover in the pre-war work of Gosho, Naruse and Yasujiro Shimazu. The latter's *Tonari No Yae-Chan* (1934, *Our Neighbour, Miss Yae*), for example, records the banalities of daily life with a humour that slowly darkens in the course of the film. Gosho, in a film like *Aibu* (1933, *Caresses*) uses hundreds of short shots to build up a pattern of living which gives it the density of a novel; he also reveals a dry, rather American sense of the absurd in the embarrassing family encounters of *Hanayome No Negoto* (1933, *The Bride Talks in Her Sleep*) and its sequel *Hanamuko No Negoto* (1934, *The Groom Talks in His Sleep*).

Naruse's silent films are full of delicate framing devices used to point up character, and none of this technique is lost in his first major sound film *Tsuma Yo Bara No Yo Ni* (1935, *Wife, Be Like a Rose*). This delightful film is remarkable for its formal organization of movement within shots and for its climax, achieved in a flurry of images that ends with the daughter's line, 'Mother, you've lost' as the father leaves to return to his mistress.

Despite a rather rosy view of its shanty-town milieu, Kajiro Yamamoto's *Tsuzurikata Kyoshitsu* (1938, *Composition Class*) is astonishing for the fact of having been shot on real, grubby locations, without the stifling influence of the studio common in other countries at the time.

Unknown master
The most recent discovery from this period, however, is the work of Hiroshi Shimizu, whose career covers 150 films from the Twenties to the Fifties. Almost completely unknown in the West, Shimizu developed a marvellously precise visual style (characterized by long-distance shooting and a stealthily tracking camera) and he perfected a kind of anecdotal, improvised method which is often very funny and totally personal.

In *Hanagata Senshu* (1937, *A Star Athlete*) a lengthy comic sequence is constructed around a group of marching students on the road by tracking either before or behind them as various other characters come and go. He clearly loved roads and children and *Arigatosan* (1936) is simply the account of a bus journey through rural Japan, shot entirely either in the actual bus or out of doors, with a few comic and pathetic incidents and a lyrical

Top left: Shimizu's The Four Seasons of Childhood, *a portrait of pre-war youth. Top right:* Akanishi Kakita *one of several satires on Japanese history by Itami. Above:* Police, *made towards the end of the silent period, portrays two childhood friends who end up on opposite sides of the law. Above right: boy meets girl-next-door in Shimizu's* Our Neighbour Miss Yae. *Right:* The Story of Tank Commander Nishizumi. *Far right: in Naruse's* Wife, Be Like a Rose *the daughter attempts to reconcile her estranged parents*

feeling of moving through a landscape in a particular time and place.

Finally Shimizu's *Kodomo No Shiki* (1939, *The Four Seasons of Childhood*) is a masterly study of children's reactions to their own rural world and to the doubtful financial squabbles of surrounding adults. In its rapt feeling for the earth, populated by distant figures in the landscape, Shimizu's work has some affinities with the early films of the Indian director Satyajit Ray. By the end of the Thirties, it now seems clear that Shimizu had perfected a visual language wedded to a poetic sensibility that has made his comparative oblivion a tragedy for lovers of cinema everywhere.

JOHN GILLETT

Action! The films of Michael Curtiz

'Curtiz liked blood so much, he insisted the tips be taken off the swords.' Errol Flynn's viewpoint of Michael Curtiz's temperament was possibly coloured by the mutual antipathy that finally split up their successful partnership; but it is supported by Olivia de Havilland's assertion that 'Curtiz was, until his later years, always an angry man'. Certainly his own attempts at self-promotion were clumsy and arrogant: a manic-depressive by nature, he seldom allowed himself the luxury of any social contact, but his addiction to work combined with an efficient, economic and rapid productivity, made him a perfect craftsman for Warner Brothers. Between 1930 and 1939, Curtiz directed 46 features.

Born Kertész Mihály in Hungary in 1888, he entered the Hungarian film industry in its infancy and directed some of the country's first feature films, *Az Utolsó Bohém* (The Last Bohemian) and *Ma és Holnap* (Today and Tomorrow) in 1912. His career was interrupted in 1919 when he became a political exile and fled to Austria. Jack Warner saw his *Die Slavenkönigen* (1924, *Moon Over Israel*) and invited the director to America. He rapidly acclimatized himself and began to churn out films in all genres, with particular success in horror movies whose suspense was created through ghoulish humour and Expressionistic lighting.

First blood

In 1935 Michael Curtiz (as he was known as in the USA) was assigned a large budget and expensive sets, and Robert Donat was approached to star in *Captain Blood*. Curtiz had filmed many romantic love stories and costume dramas in Hungary, and was the ideal choice to bring to the screen the grandeur and dramatic sweep of Sabatini's novel of a gentleman pirate. Pirate films had not been in vogue since the heyday of Douglas Fairbanks Sr, the athletic swashbuckling hero of silent films, but Warners realized their excellent potential for giving Thirties audiences plenty of action and excitement.

When Donat withdrew owing to illness and contractual misunderstandings, Curtiz remembered a young actor who had worked with him on a B feature, *The Case of the Curious Bride* (1935), and Errol Flynn was summoned back from his honeymoon to test for a role which catapulted him to overnight stardom. Flynn's screen presence as the dashing, inspiring, devil-may-care hero outweighed his limited experience as an actor, compensated for in any case by the excellence of Basil Rathbone and Olivia de Havilland. The narrative – Peter Blood, a doctor, is forced into piracy when he opposes James II – was concise and well-paced. Curtiz also engineered a remarkable technical collaboration that brought ingenious process photography and miniature work, precise editing, and an outstanding first score by Erich Korngold to the film. *Captain Blood* established a highly successful formula that the studio returned to constantly during the next decade, but it was also to prove a typecasting trap for Flynn who was unable to break away from his swashbuckling image for the rest of his career.

The oversized personality of the hero was one of the staple ingredients of the swashbuckler, which had no pretentions to great art but an instinctive appeal to child, critic and intellectual alike. Its genesis lay in the novels of Dumas and Sabatini, and its realization flourished in the hands of Belgian fencing masters and European expatriate directors and musicians. The success of the genre in talkies depended largely upon the contributions from Hollywood's 'English' colony – including Flynn (a Tasmanian with an English accent), Rathbone and Ronald Colman – who carried

off their roles with grace and bravado, presenting the tongue-in-cheek material with balanced earnestness. Curtiz summed up the basic appeal of this type of film: 'I don't see black and white words in a script when I read it, I see action.'

He applied the formula to other swashbucklers, Westerns and comedies with Flynn but their working relationship became increasingly strained and tense. Their next collaboration, *The Charge of the Light Brigade* (1936), involves some awkward romantic entanglements, while titles used as establishing shots slow the pace; but the final charge is a supreme technical achievement.

Colour photography was in more frequent use by 1938 when Flynn starred as Robin Hood. It was the logical and ultimate embellishment of the swashbuckler; and the sharper, primary colours of the three-colour stock that was used gave *The Adventures of Robin Hood* a wonderfully rich texture. The film had been begun by William Keighley and second-unit director B. Reaves Eason (best known for filming the famous chariot race in the 1925

Ben Hur). But after completing most of the Sherwood Forest scenes in six to seven weeks, Keighley was taken off the film by producer Henry Blanke, who felt that his approach was too light-hearted. Curtiz was called in and shot some additional exterior footage as well as all the interiors.

The result was a classic: lavishly bedecked, brilliantly photographed, with a jolly, rousing score by Korngold; and its highlight is the superbly orchestrated final duel between Flynn's Robin and Guy of Gisborne (Basil Rathbone). The playing – Flynn, Rathbone and Olivia de Havilland were excellently supported by Claude Rains, Alan Hale, Eugene Pallette, Ian Hunter and Patric Knowles – was a combination of enthusiasm and total conviction. Flynn's daredevil charm and assurance were enough to carry a variable performance, but the final triumph belonged to Curtiz's professional skill. His castle set afforded Flynn an opportunity to lay claim to the mantle of Fairbanks with a spectacular swing across the dining-hall astride a chandelier to set the room ablaze with action.

Below: Curtiz staged the climax of The Charge of the Light Brigade *in the San Fernando Valley, California: one man and many horses were killed during filming. Above left: Errol Flynn, Curtiz and David Niven discuss the script. Above: Flynn as Sir Geoffrey Thorpe in* The Sea Hawk, *eleventh of 13 films he made with Curtiz*

Good Queen Bette

Curtiz's *The Private Lives of Elizabeth and Essex* (1939) was a much less satisfying experience for Flynn; action took second place to words and he was acted off the screen by Bette Davis as the ageing Elizabeth I. The ambiguous screen relationship between the Queen and her courtier, bedevilled by court intrigue, was certainly more 'Hollywood history' than textbook fact, but Davis' performance was sensitively shaped – the tempestuous outward nature of the monarch tellingly counterpoints her tender, feminine inner-self, while the makeup is determinedly unattractive. Off-screen, Flynn was well aware of his disadvantaged role, and he felt correctly that the

action scenes – such as the opening triumphant return from Cadiz, Essex's ill-fated campaign in Ireland, and the storming of the palace – were not enough to compensate. He is also reputed to have behaved badly towards Davis during filming. He did manage to have the title changed before release to include the name of his character, but to little avail as the praise went to Bette Davis' performance and to Curtiz's effective presentation of the scheming courtiers.

The final Flynn–Curtiz swashbuckler, *The Sea Hawk* (1940), again had its basis in a Sabatini novel – about English captains loyal to Elizabeth I (Flora Robson) who wage an undeclared war with Spain. Korngold supplied the music and the climax was another specta-

Above: Dolores Costello in Curtiz's part-talkie spectacular, Noah's Ark *(1928). Above right: Curtiz's* Kid Galahad *(1937), a typically tough Warners boxing melodrama*

cular duel – between Flynn and Henry Daniell – but contemporary propaganda also crept in with some veiled allusions to the need for opposing military aggression.

The Casablanca story

By the time America entered World War II, Flynn had begun a new partnership with Raoul Walsh. Curtiz was able to establish himself as Warner's resident 'prestige' director, promoting patriotism and the war effort in the musicals *Yankee Doodle Dandy* (1942) and *This Is the Army* (1943), and in high-powered dramas like *Casablanca* (1942) and *Mission to Moscow* (1943). *Casablanca* has proved an ageless film, beautifully constructed, superbly played and carrying an emotional impact of continuing relevance.

Multi-faceted characterization of all protagonists, major and minor, binds a gripping plot through which the action is perfectly distributed; precise editing ensured the con-

stant tempo and the elimination of any irrelevance. Curtiz's master-stroke was in giving full rein to Bogart's jaded, worldly-wise cynical appeal as the bitter lover with little faith in the general good, who chooses to sacrifice his love for Ilsa (Ingrid Bergman) in favour of her and her husband's lasting happiness. Bogart does so with the immortal words:

'I'm no good at being noble, but it doesn't take much to see that the problems of three little people don't amount to a hill of beans in this crazy world.'

Another form of choice – the overriding ambition of a mother that destroys her marriage, alienates her vicious daughter, and involves her in murder, blackmail and corruption – provided Joan Crawford with an Oscar-winning showcase in *Mildred Pierce* (1945). The more sordid aspects of *Mildred Pierce*'s dealings with Monty Berrigan (Zachary Scott) were handled with particular taste.

The last of Curtiz

The latter half of the Forties provided Curtiz with a change of pace, initiated by *Life With Father* (1947), a beautifully observed cameo of family life in New York during the 1880s, scripted by Donald Ogden Stewart. But although Curtiz remained active for another 15

Filmography

Films made in Hungary as Kertész Mihály: **1912** Az Utolsó Bohém; Ma és Holnap. **'13** Hazasodik az Uram; Rablélek; Atlantis (act; + ass. dir) (DEN). **'14** A Hercegnö Pongyolában; Az Éjszaka Rabjai (+ act); Aranyáso; A Kölcsönkért Csecsemok; A Tolonc; Bánk Bán. **'15** Akit Ketten Szeretnek (+ act). **'16** Doktor ur; A Fekete Szivarvany; A Magyar föld ereje; Az Ezust Keckse (+ co-sc); Farkas; Karthausi; A Medikus; Makkhetes. **'17** A föld Embere; A Karuzslo; A Béke Utja; A Senki Fia; A Szentjóbi Erdö Titka; A Vörös Sámson; Arendás Zsidó; Az Utolsó Hajnal; Az Ezredes; Halálcsengö; Zoárd Mester; Egy Krajcár Története; Tartárjárás (+ sc); Tavasz a Télben. **'18** Szamárbör; Alraune (co-dir); A Csunya Fiu; A Napraforgós Hölgy; A Skorpió; A Wellingtoni Rejtély; Az Ördög; Judás; Kilencvenkilenc; Lu, A Kokott; Lulu; Varázskeringö; Vig Özvegy (+ sc). **'19** Jön Az Öcsem; Liliom (unfinished). *Films made in Austria as Michael Kertesz:* **'19** Die Dame mit dem Schwarzen Handschuh. **'20** Boccaccio (+ prod); Die Dame mit den Sonnenblumen (+ sc); Die Gottesgeisel; Der Stern von Damaskus. **'21** Cherchez la Femme; Dorothys Bekenntnis/Frau Dorothys Bekenntnis; Mrs Tutti Frutti (A-IT); Wege des Schreckens/Labyrinth des Grauens. **'22** Sodum und Gomorrah/Die Legende von Sünde und Strafe (Pt 1: Die Sünde) (+ co-sc); Sodum und Gomorrah/Die Legende von Sünde und Strafe (Pt 2: Die Strafe) (+ co-sc); Samson und Delila, der Roman Einer Opernsängerin (prod. ass. as Kertész Mihály only) (GB: Samson

and Delilah). **'23** Der Junge Medardus (co-dir); Der Lawine (USA: Avalanche); Nemenlos/Der Scharlatan/Der Falsche Arzt. **'24** Harun al Raschid; Die Slavenkönigin (USA: Moon Over Israel). **'25** Das Spielzeug von Paris (A-FR) (USA: Red Heels). **'26** Der Goldene Schmetterling (A-DEN) (USA: The Road to Happiness); Fiaker Nr 13 (A-GER). *All remaining films in USA as Michael Curtiz:* **'26** The Third Degree. **'27** A Million Bid; Good Time Charley; The Desired Woman. **'28** Tenderloin; Noah's Ark. **'29** The Glad Rag Doll; The Madonna of Avenue A; The Gamblers; Hearts in Exile. **'30** Under a Texas Moon; Mammy; The Matrimonial Bed (GB: A Matrimonial Problem); Bright Lights; A Soldier's Plaything (GB: A Soldier's Pay); River's End. **'31** Damon des Meeres (GER. language version of Moby Dick, USA 1930); God's Gift to Women (GB: Too Many Women); The Mad Genius. **'32** The Woman From Monte Carlo; Alias the Doctor (with scenes by another director); The Strange Love of Molly Louvain; Doctor X; The Cabin in the Cotton (co-dir). **'33** 20,000 Years in Sing Sing; The Mystery of the Wax Museum; The Keyhole; Private Detective 62; Goodbye Again; Female (co-dir); The Kennel Murder Case. **'34** Mandalay; The Key; Jimmy the Gent; British Agent. **'35** The Case of the Curious Bride; Black Fury; Front Page Woman; Little Big Shot; Captain Blood. **'36** The Walking Dead; The Charge of the Light Brigade; Stolen Holiday. **'37** Kid Galahad (retitling for TV: The Battling Bellhop); Mountain Justice; The

Perfect Specimen. **'38** Gold Is Where You Find It; The Adventures of Robin Hood (co-dir); Four Daughters; Four's a Crowd; Angels With Dirty Faces. **'39** Dodge City; Sons of Liberty (short); Daughters Courageous; The Private Lives of Elizabeth and Essex (retitling for TV: Elizabeth the Queen); Four Wives. **'40** Virginia City; The Sea Hawk; Santa Fe Trail. **'41** The Sea Wolf; Dive Bomber. **'42** Captains of the Clouds; Yankee Doodle Dandy; Casablanca. **'43** Mission to Moscow; This Is the Army. **'44** Passage to Marseille; Janie. **'45** Roughly Speaking; Mildred Pierce. **'46** Night and Day. **'47** Life With Father; The Unsuspected. **'48** Romance on the High Seas (GB: It's Magic). **'49** My Dream Is Yours (+ exec. prod); Flamingo Road (+ exec. prod); It's a Great Feeling (guest appearance as himself only); The Lady Takes a Sailor. **'50** Young Man With a Horn (GB: Young Man of Music); Bright Leaf; The Breaking Point. **'51** Jim Thorpe – All American (GB: Man of Bronze); Force of Arms. **'52** I'll See You In My Dreams; The Story of Will Rogers. **'53** The Jazz Singer; Trouble Along the Way. **'54** The Boy From Oklahoma; The Egyptian; White Christmas. **'55** We're No Angels. **'56** The Scarlet Hour (+ prod); The Vagabond King; The Best Things in Life Are Free. **'57** The Helen Morgan Story (GB: Both Ends of the Candle). **'58** The Proud Rebel; King Creole. **'59** The Hangman; The Man in the Net. **'60** The Adventures of Huckleberry Finn; Olympia (IT-USA) (USA: A Breath of Scandal). **'61** Francis of Assisi. **'62** The Comancheros.

years, his career had reached a summit and the assignments slipped from prestige pictures to minor musicals, remakes and some absolute 'turkeys'. The break up of the studio system, culminating in Curtiz's departure from Warners in 1954, directly affected this decline, aided by a poor business sense. He continued to work steadily with stars like Cooper, Holden, Bacall, Ladd, Loren and Wayne, but little of his output – with the notable exceptions of *The Best Things in Life Are Free* (1956), *The Proud Rebel* (1958) and *The Comancheros* (1962) – was worthy of his name or time. He died in Hollywood in 1962.

Although Michael Curtiz has never really achieved the critical stature of John Ford, Alfred Hitchcock and Ingmar Bergman, there is no disputing the craftsmanship and skill with which he packaged his films. Many of them epitomize the best film-making to emerge from Warners in the Thirties and Forties.

KINGSLEY CANHAM

Left: Sheree North in The Best Things in Life Are Free, *one of Curtiz's many musicals. Above left: Claude Rains, Paul Henreid, Humphrey Bogart and Ingrid Bergman in* Casablanca, *filmed by Curtiz without a script so that the outcome was not decided until the final day's shooting. Above: the classic duel between Robin (Errol Flynn) and Guy of Gisborne (Basil Rathbone) in* The Adventures of Robin Hood

The Further Adventures of *Errol Flynn*

Flynn, born in Tasmania in 1909, tried his luck as a gold-prospector, hunter, diamond-smuggler and policeman before making his first film in Australia. In Hollywood, after a debut as a corpse, he became the greatest action star of the Thirties and gained an equally famous reputation for carousing. Unable to shake off either tag, his life and career fell gradually apart

During his apprenticeship at Warners, the studio tested Flynn in other genres – Curtiz's comedy *The Perfect Specimen* (1937), Anatole Litvak's period drama *The Sisters* (1938) – but soon settled on the premise, attributed to Jack Warner, that Flynn had either got to be fighting or fornicating. In spite of his English accent, he became an accomplished Western hero, making *Gold Is Where You Find It* (1938), *Dodge City* (1939), *Virginia City* and *Santa Fe Trail* (both 1940) for Curtiz before they parted company.

Warners then assigned veteran film-maker Raoul Walsh as Flynn's 'house director', beginning with *They Died With Their Boots On* (1941), in which Flynn played General Custer. But not all of the seven vehicles that Flynn and Walsh completed together were A-budget projects or quality films. *Northern Pursuit* (1943), for example, in which Mountie Flynn tracks down a Nazi pilot stranded in Canada, was short on plausibility and demoted characterization to the lowest level, while the dialogue was loaded with simplistic wartime propaganda. Flynn had been rejected for military service on health grounds and, like John Wayne, was confined to fighting his battles on the studio back-lots. Warners' scriptwriter and director Vincent Sherman felt that the criticism levelled at him during this period and the

Above: Flynn as Custer, winning the American Civil War before falling with the Seventh Cavalry at the Little Big Horn in Raoul Walsh's They Died With Their Boots On

general hostility of critical notices upset him:

'Everybody used to think that he didn't give a damn about being an actor, or he kidded the whole thing. I think just the contrary was true. I think he was highly sensitive about it, and I think he was deeply hurt when they said things like this. The next day – that's when

Flynn's implausible war heroics in Objective, Burma! *(above) and other films seriously damaged his career. By the time of* The Roots of Heaven *(top) self-torment and drink had eroded his abilities and looks. He is best remembered as the charming, dashing hero (right) of films like* San Antonio *(1945)*

he'd start drinking. He'd come in at nine but he wouldn't come out of his dressing room until eleven. He had some phoney doctor who was always coming in and giving him shots . . .'

Late in 1942 Flynn was charged with statutory rape by two teenage girls and although he was acquitted in January 1943, the episode made him the object of dirty jokes ('In like Flynn' became a catchphrase for sexual conquest) and lewd stories for the rest of his life. Drink and drugs became a permanent feature of that life and a series of unsuccessful marriages added to his instability and financial problems.

His last major film at Warners was *Objective, Burma!* (1945). Flynn's unlikely heroics in this and other war pictures had saddled him with the label of 'the man who won the war single-handed', and he fell out with both Walsh and the studio, who now offered him little more than formula roles. He became a yacht-dweller – wandering the world between assignments – and was seldom out of the headlines for long; on his travels he met another studio rebel, Sterling Hayden, who was fleeing from the McCarthy witch-hunt. But Hayden had both a natural love of the sea and a stronger instinct for survival. By the mid-Fifties Flynn was reduced to sleep-walking through dross like *Istanbul* (1956), seemingly irretrievably bent on self-destruction. Henry King restored some dignity to the man and baled out his shattered career by giving him fourth billing as Mike Campbell in his adaptation of Hemingway's *The Sun Also Rises* (1957). Flynn responded gamely, portraying a drink-sodden loser, jaded, faded, but with a degree of charm and

self-awareness, ultimately worthy of some sympathy and respect. Ironically, Flynn next portrayed John Barrymore – an erstwhile carousing companion and friend – in the prophetically titled *Too Much, Too Soon* (1958), but the film was poorly scripted, and weakly directed.

A third stint as a drunk, in John Huston's *The Roots of Heaven* (1958), produced another persuasive performance, but it, too, was a box-office failure. Flynn hit rock bottom, making a deal with a 'quickie' producer and writing a vehicle for himself and his girlfriend of the time, 17-year-old Beverley Aadland. Entitled *Cuban Rebel Girls* (1959), it was a disaster, and a sad end to the career of the dashing hero who had been the screen's greatest Robin Hood, General Custer and Peter Blood. The film's director, Barry Mahon, later wrote:

'Errol Flynn was probably the greatest symbol of masculinity and virility developed in the modern age. Errol didn't feel he was successful as an actor. He always wanted to win an Academy Award but the roles he was cast in never gave him a chance. He had this great resentment of his own industry for not accepting him for what he really wanted to be, yet he was the personification of film glamour.'

Flynn died of a heart attack on October 14, 1959 during a visit to Vancouver, trying to sell his beloved yacht to raise some money.

'Not drink, not drugs, not sex. It is curiosity. This has got me into all my troubles, successes and failures. I cannot resist looking into a garbage can, or a good book, a new or an old bottle or bar, or emptying a full paper bag.'
KINGSLEY CANHAM

Filmography
1932 Dr H. Erben's New Guinea Expedition (guide in doc) (AUS). '33 In the Wake of the Bounty (AUS). '35 Murder at Monte Carlo (GB). *All remaining films USA unless specified:* '35 The Case of the Curious Bride; Don't Bet on Blondes; I Found Stella Parrish; Captain Blood. '36 Pirate Party on Catalina Isle (short); The Charge of the Light Brigade. '37 Green Light; The Prince and the Pauper; Another Dawn; The Perfect Specimen. '38 Gold Is Where You Find It; The Adventures of Robin Hood; Four's a Crowd; The Sisters; The Dawn Patrol. '39 Dodge City; The Private Lives of Elizabeth and Essex (retitling for TV: Elizabeth the Queen). '40 Virginia City; The Sea Hawk; Santa Fe Trail. '41 Footsteps in the Dark; Dive Bomber; They Died With Their Boots On. '42 Desperate Journey; Gentleman Jim. '43 Edge of Darkness; Thank Your Lucky Stars; Northern Pursuit. '44 Uncertain Glory. '45 Objective, Burma!; Peek at Hollywood (short) (as himself); San Antonio. '46 Never Say Goodbye. '47 Cry Wolf; Escape Me Never; Always Together (guest); The Adventures of Don Juan/New Adventures of Don Juan. '48 Silver River. '49 It's a Great Feeling; That Forsyte Woman (GB: The Forsyte Saga); Montana. '50 Rocky Mountain; Kim; Adventures of Captain Fabian (+ sc). '52 Maru Maru; Cruise of the Zaca (short) (+ dir; + narr); Deep Sea Fishing (short) (+ dir); Against All Flags. '53 The Master of Ballantrae (GB); William Tell (+ co-prod) (unfinished). '54 Il Maestro di Don Giovanni (Crossed Swords) (IT); Lilacs in the Spring (GB); King's Rhapsody (GB). '55 Let's Make Up (guest); The Dark Avenger (GB) (USA: The Warriors). '56 Istanbul. '57 The Big Boodle (GB: Night in Havana); The Sun Also Rises. '58 Too Much, Too Soon; The Roots of Heaven; Hello God. '59 Cuban Rebel Girls.

Chapter 18
Scarlett fever

The actual filming of Margaret Mitchell's *Gone With the Wind* was relatively uneventful, but the casting and the advance planning were as historic and as well-publicized as the final film

In May 1936 David O. Selznick's East Coast story editor, Katherine Brown, sent her boss a pre-publication copy and a synopsis of *Gone With the Wind* with an enthusiastic recommendation that he purchase the rights. Selznick, however, was more than reluctant, and understandably so. A month before its publication no-one could have foreseen that Margaret Mitchell's novel would fast become a publishing phenomenon and a national craze.

There had not been a successful film about the Civil War since D.W. Griffith's *The Birth of a Nation* (1915). Furthermore best-selling novels did not always make hit films. Even in summary form, the plot seemed over complicated. The hundreds of characters, the many huge settings and the sprawling action indicated that it would have to be a costly production were it to be filmed at all.

Although several studios were interested initially, the insistence of Mitchell's agents that the bids stay extremely high discouraged even the wealthy MGM studio. However, when Jack Hay Whitney, Chairman of the Board of Selznick International, wired Selznick that no matter what the decision in Hollywood, he himself intended to purchase the rights for the company, Selznick relented and paid the then-unequalled price of $50,000 for the book – a sum which was to be one of the lesser expenses in the production of the film.

Once he had acquired the rights, Selznick characteristically threw himself into the project and pursued it with obsessional energy for the next three years. Even after the premiere in Atlanta, Georgia on December 15, 1939, Selznick continued to fire off his famous memos to everyone involved in the sale and distribution of the film.

The playwright and film scenarist Sidney Howard was the first writer Selznick engaged to work on the script of *Gone With the Wind*. George Cukor was hired to direct and Selznick sent both men to Atlanta to discuss the film with Margaret Mitchell, for Selznick was adamant that his *Gone With the Wind* should be faithful in spirit and in letter to hers.

Even before a first script was finished, William Cameron Menzies was engaged to design the production, beginning with those sets they knew they would need no matter what the final form of the scenario. When a completed script was ready, Menzies was to sketch the entire film shot by shot, including camera set-ups, lighting and colour motifs. Lee Garmes was hired as director of photography. The film was, at this point, budgeted around $1.5 million, which remained the highest figure spoken of at Selznick International until the autumn of 1938 when MGM became involved (as a result of Selznick's desire to borrow Clark Gable for the male lead) and the budget rose to $2.25 million.

For over a year after he purchased the rights, Selznick went ahead assembling a script and getting a production design completed, but was stalled in almost every other aspect of the project. In May 1938, because of his company's financial difficulties, he was tempted to accept Louis B. Mayer's offer

to buy the project outright (with a substantial profit for Selznick International) and to hire Selznick himself to produce the film at MGM. His mistrust of his father-in-law (Mayer) and his fear of losing his independence led him to refuse the offer, although in his collected memos Selznick shows himself to be fully aware of the advantages of such a deal. MGM, after all, had greater production facilities and a more prestigious roster of stars for the cast. Above all, they had Clark Gable, who was the public's overwhelming choice for the role of Rhett Butler.

Surprisingly, Clark Gable was not Selznick's first choice. He wanted Gary Cooper, then under contract to Samuel Goldwyn, partially because it would have allowed him to release *Gone With the Wind* through United Artists. Goldwyn did not so much refuse Selznick's request for the loan of Cooper as ignore it. Selznick then considered other actors, including Warners' Errol Flynn. Warner Brothers, after initial indifference, agreed to loan Flynn if Selznick would cast Bette Davis as Scarlett. In her autobiography, Davis claimed that she was attracted to the part of Scarlett but that the thought of Flynn as Rhett Butler appalled her. Controversy still surrounds the differences of opinion between Selznick and Warners, but Davis found compensation in a similar role in *Jezebel* (1938), elements of which film were so close to the story of *Gone With the Wind* that Selznick bombarded Warner Brothers with bitter memos accusing them of profiting from his production and insisting that certain sequences be cut from their film.

In the 'Search for Scarlett' 1400 actresses were interviewed and 90 were screen tested, but eventually Selznick's brother Myron found the ideal but unknown lady

Finally, however, giving in to public pressure, he made a deal with MGM for Gable's services, the terms of which were to continue to rankle with him for the rest of his career. In exchange for Gable and $1.25 million, MGM was to have the distribution rights and 50 per cent of the profits (which, 25 years after initial release, totalled $41 million).

Although the great hunt for a Scarlett has become a major part of the *Gone With the Wind* story, none of the casting was automatic or easy. Leslie Howard now seems the obvious choice for Ashley Wilkes and was one of the first actors considered, but Howard was reluctant to play 'yet another weak and ineffectual character' and had to be promised a producer's function on Selznick's upcoming production *Intermezzo*, before he would sign. Other actors considered were Ray Milland, Melvyn Douglas (who almost got the part after a splendid test) and even Humphrey Bogart.

A great many actresses were also considered and tested for Melanie Hamilton, and at one point Joan

Above: an artist's impression of the ideal Scarlett, published under the heading 'Is this Scarlett?' and showing an uncanny resemblance to the then-unknown Vivien Leigh. Below: fan magazines thrived on Selznick's 'Search for Scarlett', printing pictures of the top contenders – though this strikingly modern portrait of Paulette Goddard hardly evoked the image of a Southern Belle

*Top: William Cameron Menzies'
sketches for the scenes of
Sherman's attack on Atlanta and
the city's subsequent evacuation.
Above: Margaret Mitchell, the
author of* Gone With the Wind.
*From the start she wanted as little
as possible to do with the
production, although she answered
all Selznick's inquiries courteously.
She stoutly refused, however, to
undertake Selznick's proposal for a
sequel to be called 'Daughter of
Scarlett O'Hara'*

Fontaine peevishly refused with the remark, 'If you want someone to play Melanie, I suggest you call my sister'. Cukor did and found Olivia de Havilland exactly what he wanted, but she was under contract to Warner Brothers who, after the Davis debacle and the *Jezebel* trouble, wanted nothing more to do with *Gone With the Wind*. De Havilland persisted, however, and Warners gave in when Selznick offered to loan them James Stewart, whose services he had for a single film. Even the smaller roles of Dr Mead, Ellen O'Hara, Belle Watling and Careen O'Hara were first intended for Lionel Barrymore, Lillian Gish, Tallulah Bankhead (who had, amazingly, been an early contender for the role of Scarlett) and Judy Garland.

Still it was the casting of Scarlett that provided the biggest problem and which garnered the most publicity. For the $50,000 Selznick admitted spending on the search for the perfect Scarlett, he had the entire nation talking about *Gone With the Wind*. But the talent hunt cannot be entirely and easily dismissed as merely the greatest publicity stunt ever pulled off in Hollywood. From reading his countless memos on the subject, it is clear that Selznick was sincere in wanting to find an actress who would please as many readers of the novel as possible.

While Gable was Rhett in the public imagination, no current female star held an equal place as Scarlett, although it was clear often enough whom they did not see in the role. When Norma Shearer was unofficially announced for the part at one point, letters and telegrams of outrage deluged Selznick. Shearer's fans refused to allow her to play anyone who was not a 'lady', while fans of Scarlett O'Hara scoffed at the idea of their heroine as a 'grande dame'. Furthermore Selznick thought that if he could find an unknown, the part and the film would make a new and valuable star for the studio.

Thousands of unknown girls from all over the USA, but primarily, for obvious reasons, from the South, were interviewed and many were tested. Each day hundreds of letters arrived at Selznick International with photographs, many of the girls in Southern Belle gowns and not a few without any gowns at all. Every major star in Hollywood was considered and a number of them submitted to the indignity of a screen test. Every studio's list of young female contract players was combed.

Katharine Hepburn wanted the part badly but refused to test and was rejected, as were all who did test, including Susan Hayward, Lana Turner and Lucille Ball. Seriously considered were Joan Bennett, Miriam Hopkins, Joan Crawford, Margaret Sullavan, Jean Arthur, Ann Sheridan and Carole Lombard. Selznick had just about decided to give the role to Paulette Goddard (if she could produce proof she had actually married Charles Chaplin, and thus avoid any scandal), when Selznick's agent brother Myron introduced him to Vivien Leigh.

Selznick was later to claim that he had never seen her before, although he mentions her by name after seeing *A Yank at Oxford* (1938) while looking for an actress to cast in *Young at Heart* (1938). Nonetheless he liked what he saw, tested her immediately, and when it was clear that she was as good as she looked, could handle a Southern accent, and that her eyes would match the colour of Scarlett's in the novel, she was signed to a seven-year contract.

While the search for the perfect cast went on, so did that for a perfect script. In 1937, Selznick had given Sidney Howard a copy of the novel with his own notations and kept in close communication with the writer and with Cukor who was advising him. Selznick admired the script, but it would have taken over five hours of screen time to film. Howard, however, considered that he had done what he had contracted to do and refused to stay in Hollywood to write another version.

Rejecting the idea that *Gone With the Wind* become two films, Selznick began himself to compress the script. He then hired playwright Oliver Garrett to revise Howard's work. Dissatisfied with that, Selznick soon found himself with three scripts. Summarizing the situation in his memos, he noted: '. . . the Sidney Howard script, the so-called Howard-Garrett script, and the script that we are shooting . . . We have everything that we need in the book and in the Howard and Howard–Garrett scripts. The job that remains to be done is to telescope the three in to the shortest possible form.'

Along the way, Scott Fitzgerald, Charles MacArthur, Edwin Justus Mayer, Ben Hecht, John Van

Druten and others were hired to rewrite single scenes, supply lines of dialogue, or to search through the original novel for alternative dialogue. But Selznick recognized Howard's contribution by giving him sole screen credit for the screenplay.

The directorial credits are just as muddled. George Cukor was involved deeply in pre-production and directed three weeks of the actual shooting at which time he was discharged. Several reasons for his replacement have been suggested, and probably all played their part. Gable objected that Cukor, even then known as a 'woman's director', paid far more attention to Leigh and de Havilland than to himself. Selznick maintained that Cukor had a firm grasp on the intimate aspects of the story but none on the more epic sequences. The producer also complained in memos that Cukor was changing lines of dialogue from the 'finished script' – this from a man whose daily revisions often arrived *during* the shooting of a scene.

Cukor left *Gone With the Wind* to do *The Women* (1939), although he continued to advise and direct both Leigh and de Havilland on the interpretation of their roles in secret throughout the making of *Gone With the Wind*.

Cukor was replaced by Victor Fleming, who was Gable's choice from a list of directors submitted to him by Selznick. Fleming's stated intention of making *Gone With the Wind* 'a flamboyant melodrama' seemed to fit Selznick's own ambitions for

Which director shot which scenes has long been a guessing game among devoted fans of *Gone With the Wind*

the film. The shooting went fairly smoothly for some weeks. They had started filming on January 26, 1939, though the key scene of Atlanta burning had been shot on December 10, 1938, the night of the instant casting of Vivien Leigh. By July 1 all the film was in the can and Selznick began to immerse himself in the task of promoting and planning the movie's distribution. During the shooting the strains of working at a high pitch on a complicated and costly production began to tell. At one point, for example, Leigh (who never cared for Fleming) balked at doing a scene. Fleming rolled the script in his hand into a tube shape, threw it at Leigh and told her graphically what she could do with it. He then stalked off.

Production stopped for two days until Fleming could be placated and enticed back to work. Selznick began to worry about Fleming's health and ability to continue, and asked Sam Wood to prepare himself to take over. Fleming did eventually collapse. Wood directed during the two weeks that Fleming was absent and continued to shoot upon his return. And so the cast often found themselves being directed by Fleming in the mornings and by Wood in the afternoons. Selznick estimated later that about 33 minutes of Wood's work remained in the final film. At the same time, no matter who was directing the major sequences, there were never less than three second units shooting 'atmosphere' and action sequences elsewhere on the sets or on the various locations.

In a letter to Frank Capra, then president of the Screen Directors' Guild, Selznick explained that he had given full credit for directing the film to Victor Fleming (both Cukor and Wood had refused to take screen credit) in spite of the fact that, as he put it, 'I alone had the reins of the picture in my hands'. He went on to suggest that if the full truth were known,

either William Cameron Menzies or he –Selznick– deserved directorial credit far more than any director who had worked on the film.

The hundreds of memos, letters and notes that Selznick sent to everyone involved in *Gone With the Wind* suggest that he was right. He insisted that Walter Plunkett redesign Gable's costumes and produce no less than 27 copies of Scarlett's calico dress in order that the same costume could be seen in various stages of deterioration during the film. He further instructed his cameramen (and though Ernest Haller received sole credit after the early departure of Lee Garmes, there were many who worked on the picture) to follow his specifications of lighting and filters. Even though the Technicolor company provided advisors, Selznick required that they follow his and Menzies' notions of what was possible in colour. He even ordered the makeup and costume departments to rebuild Vivien Leigh's bosom. In short, there was no detail, however small, which he did not have a hand in shaping, making *Gone With the Wind* the prime example of a producer's film, perhaps even a case for arguing Selznick as *auteur* – a term usually reserved to describe the artistic creation and control of a director.

DAVID OVERBEY

Above: a production shot from the set of Tara, the O'Hara's mansion. The camera crane is positioned to follow Vivien Leigh and Olivia de Havilland down the staircase in a single sweeping movement – a shot that conveys the feeling of elegance appropriate to the theme. Below: cheering crowds line the streets as the stars arrive for the Gone With the Wind *premiere in Atlanta, Georgia. Clark Gable is accompanied by his third wife Carole Lombard*

That Scarlett Woman!

Vivien Leigh's legendary rise to stardom can be traced back to the evening of December 10, 1938, when Atlanta – simulated by a group of old sets – was going up in flames a second time. The long-delayed filming of *Gone With the Wind* (1939) was finally under way, even though the Scarlett O'Hara role remained to be cast – an extraordinary risk for producer David O. Selznick to run. Between setting up the takes, Myron Selznick, one of Hollywood's foremost agents, approached his brother, beckoning from the shadows of the old Pathé back-lot a slender young woman with beautiful eyes. 'Dave,' uttered Myron, for press agents, film fans and raconteurs to quote slavishly for decades to come, 'I want you to meet Scarlett O'Hara.'

That, at least, is the story of how Vivien Leigh came to be cast in the role coveted or claimed at one time or another by every rising, established or waning female star in Hollywood. Perhaps the only exceptions were Barbara Stanwyck (who was aware that her screen persona made her unsuitable for the part) and Hedy Lamarr (whose Viennese accent cancelled her out).

The carefully orchestrated three-year search ended in a *coup de théâtre* with the revelation that an English actress, with only a few films to her credit, was to play the Southern heroine of the novel that, since 1936, had outsold the Bible in the USA. The fact that Vivien Leigh was not American failed to outrage the many

Scarlett O'Hara fan clubs in the Deep South; the unforgivable miscasting would have been to let a Yankee play the role!

After diction lessons, Vivien Leigh successfully added the right touch of molasses to her clipped English delivery. She was also coached (at first officially, later privately) by George Cukor, Selznick's original choice to direct *Gone With the Wind*. She battled constantly with Victor Fleming (the director who replaced Cukor after three weeks), failed to make friends with co-star Clark Gable, threw tantrums on the set and off, and won an Oscar.

The truth about Scarlett?
Her achievement still stands, even if there remains some doubt as to how she came to play the role. Another version of the story is that Victor Saville, the British director who had directed Leigh in *Storm in a Teacup* (1937) rang her London flat one day and said:

'Vivien, I've just read a great story for the movies about the bitchiest of all bitches, and you're just the person to play the part.'

Resolved to try for the part of Scarlett, Leigh

Convent-educated, married at the age of 19 to Ernest Leigh Holman, a man of retiring habits. Vivian Hartley (alias Vivien Leigh) claimed to have little in common with the role of Scarlett O'Hara (top right). But her bewitching blend of innocence, beauty and guile fitted the character like a glove

followed Laurence Olivier – then her paramour, later her husband – to California, where he was to play Heathcliff in Samuel Goldwyn's production of *Wuthering Heights* (1939).

It seems that she was probably seen by – and made a strong impression on – David O. Selznick and Cukor, and was kept under wraps while the continuing search for Scarlett garnered a million dollars' worth of publicity. She was then made to appear, like a rabbit out of Myron Selznick's hat, to snatch the part.

The English rose of Hollywood
At 26 she became a priceless commodity in the industry. David O. Selznick, the sole proprietor of her contract, doled out her talents parsimoniously: first to MGM for *Waterloo Bridge*

1940), then to Alexander Korda, who had originally discovered Leigh in Britain, for *That Hamilton Woman!* (1941). There followed an absence from the screen dictated by war and sickness. She reappeared as Bernard Shaw's Egyptian kitten of a queen in *Caesar and Cleopatra* (1945), looking ravaged and mature enough to play Shakespeare's Cleopatra.

She was Tennessee Williams' own choice for the part of Blanche DuBois in his play *A Streetcar Named Desire*. The play was filmed in 1951, and this time Leigh's Southern drawl was so convincing that it seemed to issue from a dark, bruised recess of her being. A sense of inevitable decline is captured in the curtain line: 'After all, I've always depended on the kindness of strangers' – a melancholy echo of that other famous exit line: 'After all, tomorrow is another day', which summed up the headstrong, vixenish, egotistical Scarlett.

Living close to the edge

Various screen tests for Scarlett have survived and been screened: Leigh's has disappeared into some clandestine collection, but we have Cukor's word that no-one, not even Leigh herself during the actual shooting of the film, could match her miraculously intuitive approach on that first brush with the part.

Bottom: Alexander Korda capitalized on Leigh and Olivier's much-publicized affair by casting them as Lady Hamilton and Lord Nelson in That Hamilton Woman! *Above right: severe bouts of depression marred her performance as Anna Karenina which failed to match Garbo's earlier portrayal. Centre right: Leigh as the Egyptian queen in* Caesar and Cleopatra. *Bottom right: Blanche in* A Streetcar Named Desire, *clinging to her fading beauty and her dreams of romance in a brutal world, was her last great screen appearance. The film's sexual frankness caused a storm of controversy*

Around her Scarlett one perceives, even now, not just the whims and caprices of a spoiled beauty, but real hovering demons; the same which would overwhelm her later in her private life. As early as *Fire Over England* (1937), she seemed a needlessly neurotic lady-in-waiting, but while she was young such traits could be taken as eccentricities. Watching Vivien Leigh glow in inferior pictures like *The Roman Spring of Mrs Stone* (1961) or *Ship of Fools* (1965), there is the strong impression of a trained performer drawing perilously close to lived experience; in *The Deep Blue Sea* (1955), she is almost too genuine for comfort playing a woman caught between suicide attempts.

Vivien Leigh's own life had been one of extremes. Born in 1913 in India, separated in childhood from her mother, she struggled with bouts of hysteria and depression before contracting tuberculosis in 1945. She fought the disease throughout her life until finally succumbing to it in 1967. But these bare facts do not explain her peculiar 'poetic' nervousness.

Tennessee Williams celebrated a certain breed of women as 'ladies who died when love was lost'. This definition, though it misses Scarlett, encompasses Blanche, Anna Karenina, Mrs Stone and Mrs Mary Treadwell of *Ship of Fools*, and may stand as a fitting, if melancholy, epitaph for Vivian Leigh herself.

CARLOS CLARENS

Filmography

1935 Things Are Looking Up; The Village Squire; Gentleman's Agreement; Look Up and Laugh. '**37** Fire Over England; Dark Journey (cut version issued as The Anxious Years); Storm in a Teacup; (USA: 21 Days Together). '**38** A Yank at Oxford. '**39** St Martin's Lane (USA: Sidewalks of London); Gone With the Wind (USA). '**40** Waterloo Bridge (USA). '**41** That Hamilton Woman! (GB: Lady Hamilton) (USA). '**45** Caesar and Cleopatra. '**48** Anna Karenina. '**51** A Streetcar Named Desire (USA). '**55** The Deep Blue Sea. '**61** The Roman Spring of Mrs Stone (USA). '**65** Ship of Fools (USA).

Memos of a Movie-making Mogul

Driving ambition and a passionate interest in every aspect of film-making were the chief characteristics of David O. Selznick. On the road to becoming one of Hollywood's most powerful independent producers, he furthered the careers of George Cukor, William Powell and Myrna Loy, and virtually discovered Fred Astaire and Katharine Hepburn. But *Gone With the Wind* was the achievement of a lifetime

In 1931, when David O. Selznick was 29 years old, he sent one of his famous memos to his employers at Paramount complaining that he had not been granted sufficient control:

'A motion picture is like a painting. Instead of oil paints, it uses talents and personalities to tell its story. But each artist must paint his own picture and sign it.'

Selznick never doubted whose signature should appear on each of the films he was associated with. Indeed, when younger he had spent some time in creating a signature digni- fied enough for the films he intended to produce. His parents had neglected to give him a middle name, so he went through the alphabet until the letter 'O' (which he later claimed stood for Oliver) struck him as giving the proper tone to plain David Selznick.

His insistence throughout his career that *his* should be the decisive voice, that *his* vision and taste should dominate the films he produced no matter who the original author or director, came from his belief that he understood both films and audiences better than anyone else. He had, after all, grown up in the industry.

He began by working for his father's own Selznick Pictures, where he did everything, at one time or another, from designing advertis- ing posters to editing and directing. This gave him a supreme self-confidence and convinced him that in the American production system everyone hired became part of a team to be managed by and to carry out the producer's will. It also made him uneasy with employers and partners, especially after his father had been manipulated by business competitors into a state of bankruptcy.

David O. Selznick subsequently became the archetypal 'creative producer'. He was in- volved in every aspect and every detail of each film he produced, from the basic structure of the narrative to the colour of the nail varnish worn by the leading lady. In spite of current attitudes in film criticism which stress the importance of the director's vision and style, the films of Selznick indicate how much Amer- ican cinema could be a producer's cinema. For his major films, he often replaced director after director, writer after writer, and set designer after set designer, until he found those people who could give him exactly what he wanted. He soon became notorious for his long memos (often running as long as the scripts for the films themselves) which described in great detail what *should be done* or what was wrong with what *had been done*. The films which he produced thus resemble one another; the style, the production values, the performances, all have in common the 'Selznick touch'.

> *'It is my opinion, generally speaking, and from long observation, that there are only two kinds of merchandise that can be made profitably in this business – either the very cheap pictures or the expensive pictures'*

His ambition – to have his own studio and to be a power in Hollywood – was realized with the creation of Selznick International in 1936, just 12 years after he had made his first independent low-budget feature, *Roulette* (1924). During those dozen years, he had put his unflagging energies, his sure knowledge of every part of film production, and his imagi- nation to work towards that ambition. After his father's company had failed, he followed his brother Myron to Hollywood, where he at first took what jobs he could find (assistant editor at MGM, for instance) as a pretext for demonstrating his greater abilities to his em- ployers. While at MGM he managed to produce two Tim McCoy Westerns for not much more than the price of one. He was soon hired by Paramount, first as assistant to the studio head B.P. Schulberg, and then as a producer in his own right. He brought his pictures in on schedule, and often turned 'programmers' into profit-making main features. He also made a number of professional and personal contacts at Paramount, including directors John Crom- well and Merian C. Cooper, whom he would take with him when the time came to move on. That time came in 1931 when he fully under- stood that no matter how highly regarded he might be at Paramount, all important deci- sions would continue to be made by others.

David Sarnoff's Radio Corporation of America had just acquired RKO studios, and

Above: newlyweds David and Irene Selznick with the bride's parents, Mr and Mrs Louis B. Mayer. Top: Ingrid Bergman lays a friendly hand on Selznick's shoulder as he jokes with Shirley Temple and his future second wife, Jennifer Jones

Sarnoff hired Selznick as head of production, with a promise that he would be able to do as he liked. In addition to a young and talented production team, Selznick surrounded himself with writers and directors he had observed at

> *'RKO had an amazing faith in me at a time when my previous employers did every- thing to run me down, and when very few other companies in the business had an appreciable respect for my ability'*

work at Paramount. He made dialogue direc- tor George Cukor into a fully-fledged film director. While Selznick retained, as ever, the right to make final decisions, he listened to the opinions of those around him. Thus, although he at first found Katharine Hepburn unattrac- tive and unpromising, he listened to Cukor and helped to make her into a major star. Selznick also hired Fred Astaire despite advice that the

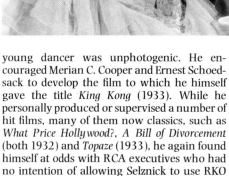

Left: Selznick confers with Jennifer Jones on the set of A Farewell to Arms. Above: Ingrid Bergman, seen by Selznick in the Swedish version of Intermezzo, starred in his remake and gained international fame. Below left: Powell and Loy were teamed by him for the first time in Manhattan Melodrama

young dancer was unphotogenic. He encouraged Merian C. Cooper and Ernest Schoedsack to develop the film to which he himself gave the title *King Kong* (1933). While he personally produced or supervised a number of hit films, many of them now classics, such as *What Price Hollywood?*, *A Bill of Divorcement* (both 1932) and *Topaze* (1933), he again found himself at odds with RCA executives who had no intention of allowing Selznick to use RKO merely as an instrument for releasing his own productions. Selznick again resigned.

Although he had earlier married Irene Mayer, daughter of MGM chief Louis B. Mayer, Selznick had refused to play the Hollywood game of nepotism. Now, however, Mayer found himself in need of someone to take charge of MGM production as his previous production head, Irving Thalberg (with whom Mayer never got along anyway) was seriously ill. With a huge salary and access to MGM's full roster of stars and technicians, Selznick accepted the offer and began to turn out expensive, star-filled melodramas based on plays and novels – *Dinner at Eight* (1933). *David Copperfield* and *Anna Karenina* (both 1935). He brought Cukor to MGM (where the director had a long and successful career), 'discovered' Mickey Rooney (for *Manhattan Melodrama* in 1934) and was the first to co-star William

Powell and Myrna Loy (in the same film). But even with his own production unit at MGM, Selznick was still not his own boss; his decisions might always be overridden by Mayer or by Loew's head office in New York. Once more he resigned.

Making a deal by which his own productions would be released through United Artists, he assured himself that films he produced would reach cinemas, most of which were

---

'I hear rumours that Miss Hepburn is under twenty-one, which we should take immediate action to confirm, to find out whether it is necessary to get the approval of the courts. I understand she is prone to exaggerate her age and likes to be thought much older than she is'

---

then controlled by the major studios. Not surprisingly his taste in the projects he chose to undertake, and the style in which he made them, differed little from that shown at MGM. He continued to transfer classic and popular novels and plays to the screen, producing them in glossy and expensive style, and casting them with a combination of established stars and his own discoveries. Although his production pro-

gramme at Selznick International falls under the gigantic shadow of his *Gone With the Wind* (1939), that programme included *A Star Is Born*, *Nothing Sacred* (both 1937), *Intermezzo: a Love Story* (1939) and Alfred Hitchcock's first American film, *Rebecca* (1940).

After the release of *Gone With the Wind*, Selznick spent the rest of his career trying to find a project with which he could top it. In 1944, he met Jennifer Jones, a young actress

---

'I am getting to the end of my patience with criticism based on the assumption that actors know more about scripts than I do'

---

working in his *Since You Went Away* (1944). She was to remain a constant obsession. Even on those films in which she acted and he did not produce, Selznick sent off to their directors a never-ending stream of memos about how Jones should look, act and be treated.

In 1946, Selznick decided he had found a novel which could be turned into a film with the epic scope of *Gone With the Wind* – Niven Busch's novel *Duel in the Sun*. The film was released in 1946 with much hyperbolic fanfare. It was laughed at by most critics, some of whom dubbed it 'Lust in the Dust', but it was also hugely successful at the box-office and revitalized the careers of Jennifer Jones and Gregory Peck, its two stars. Seen now, this Western holds up very well indeed as an operatic and melodramatic entertainment; its production matches its content, with the over-saturated colours of every sunset somehow fitting exactly the over-saturated emotions of the characters.

Although there were a number of projects which were never realized (including *War and Peace*), Selznick continued to search for bigger and 'more important' subjects, especially those which had a part for Jones, now Mrs Selznick. While waiting for the right property to turn up, he personally produced two smaller films after *Duel in the Sun* – Hitchcock's *The Paradine Case* (1947) and Dieterle's *Portrait of Jennie* (1948). The latter reveals Selznick's creative state of mind at the time. Although the story is modest,

Above: Gregory Peck and Jennifer Jones in Duel in the Sun. *Above right: A Farewell to Arms, set in Italy during World War I, was Selznick's last production. Below: Selznick hired Alfred Hitchcock to direct* Rebecca *in Hollywood; it won an Oscar for Best Film in 1940. Bottom: Jones and Montgomery Clift in* Indiscretion of an American Wife, *the director De Sica's first English-language film*

concerning a man falling in love with the portrait of a girl from an earlier time, the film has an epic climax – a full-scale hurricane. Even in his smaller films, then, the ghost of *Gone With the Wind* continued to haunt him.

Selznick also became involved in several co-productions throughout the late Forties and Fifties. Although he did not 'interfere' much with *The Third Man* (1949), he had whole sequences of Michael Powell's *Gone to Earth* (1950) re-shot in Hollywood by Rouben Mamoulian for release in the USA. He also expressed interest in working with one of the Italian neo-realist directors. He once approached Roberto Rossellini, perhaps in an effort to protect his star Ingrid Bergman, perhaps in a misguided attempt to recapture the prestige which had eluded him for at least a decade. Certainly nothing could be more opposite to the aims of neo-realism than Selznick's own glossy productions; nonetheless he proceeded to co-produce (with Columbia) *Stazione Termini* (1953, *Indiscretion of an American Wife*), directed in Italy by Vittorio De Sica and starring Jennifer Jones. The result was a critical and financial disaster.

Selznick's final film was a co-production with 20th Century-Fox, an expensive epic adaptation of Hemingway's *A Farewell to Arms* (1957), directed by Charles Vidor (who had earlier done the first sequences of *Duel in the Sun*) and starring Jennifer Jones and Rock Hudson. One can again assume that the ghost

of *Gone With the Wind* appeared to the producer, for the new film diminished its personal story to make way for battles and marches through snow-covered mountains. Its lack of success with critics and public caused Selznick to retire from film production.

Still, it is not by those last few films that one should judge Selznick's career. He worked in every genre except horror and science fiction, and in each created at least one recognized classic. He knew how to entertain mass audiences, and yet do it with a certain sensitivity and taste.   DAVID OVERBEY

Quotations from Memo From David O. Selznick, *edited by Rudy Behlmer. Copyright © 1972 Selznick Properties, Ltd (New York, Viking, 1972)*

Filmography

1923 Will He Conquer Dempsey? (short); Rudolph Valentino and His 88 American Beauties (short). **'24** Roulette. **'27** Spoilers of the West. **'28** Wyoming (GB: The Rock of Friendship); Forgotten Faces (sup. only). **'29** Chinatown Nights (assoc. prod. only); The Man I Love (assoc. prod. only); The Four Feathers (assoc. prod. only); The Dance of Life (assoc. prod. only); Fast Company. **'30** Street of Chance; Sarah and Son; Honey; The Texan; For the Defense; Manslaughter. **'32** Lost Squadron/The Lost Squadron; Symphony of Six Million (GB: Melody of Life); State's Attorney (GB: Cardigan's Last Case); Westward Passage; Roar of the Dragon; What Price Hollywood?; The Age of Consent; Bird of Paradise; A Bill of Divorcement; The Monkey's Paw; The Conquerors; Rockabye; The Animal Kingdom (GB: The Woman in His House); The Half-Naked Truth. **'33** Topaze; The Great Jasper; Our Betters; Christopher Strong; Sweepings; Dinner at Eight; Night Flight; Meet the Baron; Dancing Lady; King Kong (exec. prod.). **'34** Viva Villa!; Manhattan Melodrama. **'35** David Copperfield; Vanessa, Her Love Story; Reckless; Anna Karenina; A Tale of Two Cities. **'36** Little Lord Fauntleroy; The Garden of Allah. **'37** A Star Is Born; The Prisoner of Zenda; Nothing Sacred. **'38** The Adventures of Tom Sawyer; The Young in Heart. **'39** Made for Each Other; Intermezzo: a Love Story (GB: Escape to Happiness); Gone With the Wind (+uncredited sc; +uncredited dir). **'40** Rebecca. **'44** Since You Went Away (+ sc); I'll Be Seeing You. **'45** Spellbound. **'46** Duel in the Sun (+ uncredited dir). **'47** The Paradine Case (+ sc). **'48** Portrait of Jennie (GB: Jennie). **'49** The Third Man (co-prod. only) (GB). **'50** Gone to Earth (USA: The Wild Heart) (co-prod. only) (GB). **'53** Stazione Termini (USA: Indiscretion of an American Wife; GB: Indiscretion) (co-prod. only) (IT-USA). **'57** A Farewell to Arms (co-prod. only).

DAVID O. SELZNICK'S PRODUCTION OF MARGARET MITCHELL'S

"GONE WITH THE WIND"

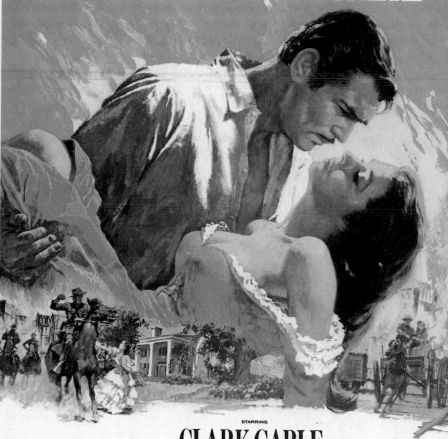

STARRING

CLARK GABLE
VIVIEN LEIGH
LESLIE HOWARD OLIVIA de HAVILLAND

A SELZNICK INTERNATIONAL PICTURE · DIRECTED BY VICTOR FLEMING · SCREEN PLAY BY SIDNEY HOWARD · METRO-GOLDWYN-MAYER INC. · Music by MAX STEINER

© PORTAL PUBLICATIONS, SAUSALITO, CALIF. 94965

1939

A monument to the studio system, *Gone With the Wind* was planned from over 3000 full-colour sketches by William Cameron Menzies, involved a cast of 2400 extras and was completed in just under a year – a schedule that would astonish today's multi-million-dollar productions. The film itself lived up to Selznick's ambitions and everyone else's expectations. The shots that follow give an impression of this most lavish, colourful and romantic movie

Directed by Victor Fleming, 1939
Prod co: Selznick International. **prod:** David O. Selznick. **sc:** Sidney Howard, from the novel by Margaret Mitchell. **photo:** Ernest Haller. **des:** William Cameron Menzies. **ed:** Hal C. Kern, James E. Newcom. **art dir:** Lyle Wheeler. **cost:** Walter Plunkett. **mus:** Max Steiner. **Technicolor assoc:** Ray Rennahan, Wilfred M. Cline, Natalie Kalmus. **sp eff:** Jack Cosgrove. **r/t:** 222 minutes. Atlanta (USA) premiere, 15 December 1939.
Cast: Clark Gable (*Rhett Butler*), Vivien Leigh (*Scarlett O'Hara*), Leslie Howard (*Ashley Wilkes*), Olivia de Havilland (*Melanie Wilkes*), Laura Hope Crews (*Aunt 'Pittypat' Hamilton*), Ona Munson (*Belle Watling*), Harry Davenport (*Doctor Meade*), Hattie McDaniel (*Mammy*). Thomas Mitchell (*Gerald O'Hara*), Barbara O'Neill (*Ellen O'Hara*), Victor Jory (*Jonas Wilkerson*), Evelyn Keyes (*Suellen O'Hara*), Ann Rutherford (*Carreen O'Hara*), Alicia Rhett (*India Wilkes*), Rand Brooks (*Charles Hamilton*), Carroll Nye (*Frank Kennedy*), Jane Darwell (*Mrs Merriwether*), Albert Morin (*Rene Picard*), Mary Anderson (*Maybelle Merriwether*), Leona Roberts (*Mrs Meade*), Butterfly McQueen (*Prissy*), Everett Brown (*Big Sam*), Zack Williams (*Elijah*), Oscar Polk (*Pork*).

A DAVID O. SELZNICK
PRODUCTION OF
MARGARET MITCHELL'S
GONE WITH THE WIND
A SELZNICK INTERNATIONAL PICTURE
RELEASED BY
METRO-GOLDWYN-MAYER

1

2

3

Georgia 1861. The American Civil War is about to begin, but beautiful, wilful Scarlett O'Hara who lives at Tara refuses to listen to talk of war (2). While her nurse, Mammy, helps Scarlett dress for the party at Twelve Oaks, she chides her for her unladylike behaviour (3). At the party Ashley Wilkes' engagement to Melanie Hamilton is announced (4) and the handsome dashing stranger, Rhett Butler, tells the assembled gentry that the South cannot win the war (5). Scarlett slips away from the party to declare her love for Ashley (6) but he rejects her.

War is declared and Ashley and Melanie decide to marry at once. In a fit of pique Scarlett marries the callow Charles Hamilton and thus becomes Melanie's sister-in-law (7).

Charles soon dies of measles. Scarlett then goes off to visit Aunt 'Pittypat' Hamilton and Melanie in Atlanta where, at a charity ball for the war effort (8), Rhett begins to court her. She is attracted to him and flirts (9) but still believes she loves Ashley who has returned on leave; Scarlett promises to watch over Melanie when he goes back to war. Shortly afterwards Ashley is reported missing.

When General Sherman's troops attack Atlanta the city is evacuated as it burns, and Rhett arrives in time to save Scarlett, Melanie and her new-born child from the fire and the looters (10, 11), but leaves them on the road to Tara (12) and returns to fight alongside the losing army.

At Tara, they find that Scarlett's mother has died of typhoid nursing 'poor white trash' and Gerald, her father, has gone mad with grief. The plantation at Tara is nearly destroyed but Scarlett and Melanie survive (13). Ashley returns to Melanie. Scarlett continues to nurse a passion for him though he tells her there is no hope for them. But

7

8

10

11

14

15

16

5

6

9

she is never beaten and the fear that she may lose Tara to the carpetbagger Jonas Wilkerson (**14**) only makes her more intent on survival.

Scarlett, wearing a dress improvised from her mother's curtains (**15**), goes to Atlanta to borrow money from Rhett. She later marries local lumber merchant Frank Kennedy for money and remains in Atlanta where Melanie helps her convince Ashley to stay and run the lumber business together. Scarlett's conduct is once again the talk of the town. When Scarlett is almost raped, only to be saved by the faithful family retainer Big Sam, Frank and Ashley decide to clear out the local riff-raff. Rhett steps in and prevents Ashley from being arrested but Frank is killed in the fracas. Later, giving in to much persuasion, Scarlett agrees to marry Rhett (**16**).

Rhett, who had spent some time in prison on suspicion of murder, builds a grand new house on the fortunes he amassed during the war. Once installed, however, Rhett and Scarlett are cold-shouldered by the Southern gentry, but when Scarlett gives birth to a daughter, Rhett starts to ingratiate himself with the local aristocracy. But this occasions many stormy rows between man and wife.

Scarlett could be happy with Rhett (**17**) were it not for her persistent attachment to Ashley. When Bonnie Blue, Scarlett and Rhett's infant daughter, is killed in an accident, their marital problems come to a head. Shortly afterwards Melanie also dies and Scarlett realizes that Ashley has only ever loved Melanie and that she truly loves Rhett. But it is too late; she begs him to let them try again but Rhett leaves (**18**). Undaunted, however, Scarlett resolves to make a new start for 'tomorrow is another day' (**19**).

13

18

19

The Clark Gable Story

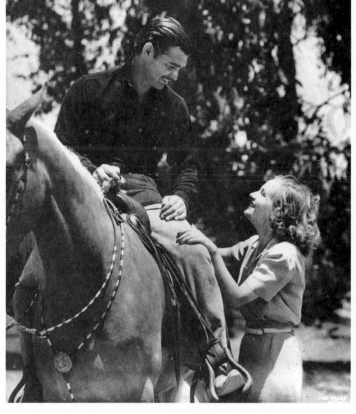

There was no nonsense with Gable. He was rough, tough and ready for anything. And when it came to women . . . well, frankly, he didn't give a damn. But who would have guessed that the King of Hollywood owed his early breaks as an actor to the care and encouragement of the women who wooed him?

When the age of talking pictures dawned in Hollywood, the two greatest romantic male stars of the silent era – Wallace Reid and Rudolph Valentino – were already a memory. Douglas Fairbanks Sr was ageing fast; so was Richard Barthelmess; and that other cavalier, John Gilbert, was in decline. The kings of the silents were all dead or dying. It was time to push the young princes forward and cry out 'Long live the King!'

The most promising heir apparent, ignored at first because he had protruding ears, became the public's choice for King. Twelve Clark Gable pictures were released during 1931, and there was little doubt that MGM, the studio that made most of them, was grooming him for stardom. In the second of those films, *Dance, Fools, Dance*, Gable played a brutal gangster giving Joan Crawford a bad time, and in his seventh role that year, in *A Free Soul*, he beat up Norma Shearer. In the silent days he would have been an out-and-out villain, but the film heroines of the Thirties were showing masochistic tastes, and thought of rugs as something not just to be walked on but dragged over.

William Clark Gable was born in Cadiz, Ohio, on February 1, 1901, the only child of

farmer and oil-driller William H. Gable and his wife Adeline. His mother died when he was just seven months old, and his grandparents looked after him for two years until his father married again. William Jr's stepmother, Jennie Dunlap, was the best thing that could ever have happened to him; always a rough diamond, he learned from her the strength of tenderness. He worshipped her.

When young Gable finished his sophomore year at high school, he wanted to go to Akron with an older friend and work in a tyre factory, and his stepmother persuaded her husband to let the boy go. All through his life, women (usually older ones) put him on the right track and helped him forward. It was in Akron that he saw his first stage play, and he was entranced. He went backstage afterwards and got an unpaid job after factory hours as a call boy at the theatre, and was even sometimes given a few small parts with lines.

Gable was hooked. Not even when his stepmother died and his father compelled him to work with him in the Oklahoma oil fields could he forget the magic of the theatre. When he was 21 his grandfather gave him $300 and Gable took off for Kansas City, where he joined

a company known as the Jewell Players.

The image everyone associates with Gable is such a virile one, and he played so many cowboys, reporters, oil-men, truckdrivers, auto-racers, boxers and soldiers in his time that he never had any trouble convincing his audiences and fans that he was anything but a hard-working male with square ideas. Certainly no-one would have guessed that at an early age he had drunk of theatre wine and really had little interest outside the stage. He was eager to learn more of the show world, and again it was the women he met who helped him. Among them was Franz Dorfler, an aspiring young actress who took him home to her parents when his stock company failed in Oregon, and saw to it that he was looked after. He marked time in Portland where he was variously employed, first by a newspaper and then a telephone company, until he got a job with an acting group. It was headed by actress and stage director Josephine Dillon, 14 years his senior, who was aware of what he had to offer as an actor and helped him refine his talents. She took him with her to Hollywood, where, on December 13, 1924, they were married.

Gable learned more about the craft of acting from her than he did from anybody else. She taught him physical grace so that he did not move like an oil-rigger; his deportment, both on and off stage, was exemplary. She bought him clothes, took him to a dentist so that he could smile unashamedly, showing off the deep dimples at the sides of his mouth, and persuaded him to drop the name 'William', and call himself Clark Gable. She also got him his first roles in films – mostly as an extra, though he did receive his first screen credit when he played Alice Joyce's brother in *White Man* (1924), and also had a bit part in *The Plastic Age* (1925), with Clara Bow.

Gable was aware that he needed more finesse as an actor and returned to the stage. He played juvenile for Lionel Barrymore in a production of *The Copperhead*. Then, separated from his wife, he let the ladies of the theatre take turns sponsoring him. Jane Cowl took him on as a spear-carrier in her production of *Romeo and Juliet*; Pauline Frederick cast him as the public prosecutor in her revival of *Madame X*, and as a nightclub owner in *Lucky Sam McCarver*. Gable often accompanied Miss Frederick socially; she bought him a new suit and paid for the further expensive dental work he needed. Apart from acting he had other duties to perform, as he grumpily explained, 'Miss Frederick is forever complaining she has a sore back. She likes me to rub it for her.'

After other minor roles he made his debut on the Broadway stage on September 7, 1928, in *Machinal*, playing the star's lover and attracting very good notices. On tour with another play in Texas, he met Mrs Ria Langham, a Houston socialite and several times a divorcee. She was very wealthy, and she liked what she saw when she looked at Clark Gable and followed him back to New York. Like others before her, she took him on as a 'special project'. Josephine Dillon had given him the essentials, but Mrs Langham, 17 years older than Gable and blessed with social contacts, gave him the polishing touches. She took him to the best tailor, the best bootery, the best barber, the best everything. He developed manners, confidence and ease. After they saw Spencer Tracy in the play *The Last Mile*, Mrs Langham decided that the role of Killer Mears was custom-made for Gable. Reputedly, she arranged for him to take the part in the West Coast production of *The Last Mile*, and he was a sensation. As a result, Darryl F. Zanuck tested him for *Little Caesar* but complained about the shape of his ears, and did not sign him to a contract. Minna Wallis, however, did. She was not only a top agent but also the sister of the producer Hal Wallis. She got him the role of a nasty young villain in a Pathé Western, *The*

Painted Desert (1931), with William Boyd and Helen Twelvetrees. She then persuaded William Wellman to hire him for the part of a villainous chauffeur in Warner Brothers' *Night Nurse* (1931), in which he gave Barbara Stanwyck such a brutal beating that audiences were left gasping.

The release of *Night Nurse* was delayed for over a year, and by the time it came out Minna Wallis had got Gable a two-year contract, with options, at MGM. His first picture there was in a small role as Anita Page's husband, a hard-working laundryman in *The Easiest Way* (1931). His success in the part led him directly into *The Secret Six* (1931), in which he and John Mack Brown played reporters investigating underworld crime. The studio was pushing Brown because he had been a top athlete before entering films and had big movie star potential. Frances Marion, however, the scriptwriter of *The Secret Six* and the highest-paid person in her profession at that time, immediately saw Gable's galactic potential. Her husband, George Hill, was the film's director, and they quietly decided to give the stronger lines and better scenes to Gable rather than to Brown. The ruse worked. Gable's rough, tough, but sympathetic role was made to fit. Studio interest was diverted from Brown to Gable and the order went out to give him the big star build-up.

He fitted in well at MGM; his best friends there were the public relations man Howard

Far left: Gable as Rhett Butler in Gone With the Wind. *Left: with his third wife Carole Lombard. Above left: the rising star of 1931 in* A Free Soul *with Norma Shearer and Leslie Howard and* Possessed *(above) with Joan Crawford and Skeets Gallagher. Below: Fletcher Christian to Charles Laughton's Bligh in* Mutiny on the Bounty

Strickling and the director Victor Fleming, in whose company he frequently hunted and fished, golfed and sailed. The studio paid for the perfect set of dentures it was finally necessary for him to have; and also paid for surgery to pin back his ears.

Meanwhile Josephine Dillon had agreed to a divorce. She spoke of him with reluctant but calculated reticence:

'Clark told me frankly that he wished to marry Ria Langham because she could do more for him financially. He is hard to live with because his career and ambition always come first.'

Ria Langham became the second Mrs Clark Gable in New York on March 30, 1930, and they were married a second time in California on June 19, 1931, because of a legal hitch. Ria Langham queened it in Beverly Hills film society, which was fitting enough because by the end of 1931 her husband was the acknowledged King of Hollywood. He was a star who would be in the box-office top ten from 1932 to 1943, again from 1947 to 1949 after he

had returned from the war, and for one more year in 1955.

Most of the time MGM reserved Gable, drawing on his powerful masculine image, to co-star with their galaxy of female stars, and he developed powerful screen partnerships with three of their greatest stars. Joan Crawford and he were together in eight features, Myrna Loy was with him seven times, and Jean Harlow was with him six times.

Gable's off-screen relationships with Miss Loy and Miss Harlow were always platonic, friendly but strictly professional. Miss Crawford later confessed, however, that on several occasions when they were both free from personal obligations they nearly ran away and married, but on each occasion came to their senses in time – their careers mattered more.

Gable also starred with Lana Turner in four films, with Norma Shearer in three, with Rosalind Russell in three, Constance Bennett twice, and Helen Hayes twice. He made one appearance each with Greta Garbo and Jeanette MacDonald. He was, in fact, at some time or another teamed with every MGM female star except Marie Dressler.

Gable was at his best, however, in a man's world, leading the *Mutiny on the Bounty* (1935), sorting out the problems of the Air Force in *Command Decision* (1948), scouting Indian country in *Across the Wide Missouri* (1951). Also, say the name of Clark Gable and to most people it means Rhett Butler in *Gone With the Wind* (1939), or Peter Warne, the newspaper reporter he played in *It Happened One Night* (1934); yet he hadn't wanted to play them or *Bounty's* Fletcher Christian. These were the three pictures for which he was honoured with Oscar nominations (winning for *It Happened One Night*) – virtually the only three he fought against playing.

During the filming of *Gone With the Wind*, Gable was more excited when Ria divorced him for a settlement of $286,000. He was a free man before shooting was finished and drove with Carole Lombard to Kingman, Arizona, where they were quietly married on March, 29, 1939. They had known each other for nearly three years; it was no secret that they had been living together for most of that time, and were both still ecstatically happy. They bought a ranch in Encino and settled down; it seemed as if they would always be the perfect couple. World War II came, however, and Lombard threw herself into war work. She went out on the first War Bond tour after Pearl Harbor in 1942. Returning home, the plane crashed into a mountainside and everybody on it was killed.

Gable was half-crazy with grief. Lombard had teased him about getting involved in the war and now it was all he wanted to do. He took time off from the nearly completed *Somewhere I'll Find You* (1942) to get a firm hold of himself. Then he finished the picture, and eventually joined up in August 1942. He was assigned to Officers Candidate School in Miami, Florida, and went overseas with the Eighth Air Force in 1943. Seven months later he received the Distinguished Flying Cross and Air Medal for 'exceptionally meritorious achievement while participating in five separate bomber combat missions' over Germany. Gable was promoted to the rank of major and, discharged shortly afterwards, returned to work for MGM.

The studio did not know what to do with him: Gable had changed – so had the image of the movie hero. *Adventure* (1945), his comeback film co-starring him with Greer Garson, was a tedious, manufactured comedy. *The Hucksters* (1947), with Deborah Kerr and Ava Gardner, had its moments but was largely a bore. Next to *Parnell* (1937), *Homecoming* (1948) – his third post-war film – is probably his most tiresome and embarrassing picture. The next two were better: Gable seemed to be at ease in uniform with an all-male cast in *Command Decision* (1948); and in *Any Number Can Play* (1949), here as a casino owner. Most

Above left: Gable and Jean Harlow in Wife vs Secretary *(1936). Above: on the set of* Lone Star *(1952) with Ava Gardner. Above right: in* Across the Wide Missouri *(1951). Below, far left: with Spencer Tracy and Myrna Loy in* Test Pilot *(1938). Below left: with Barbara Stanwyck in* To Please a Lady *(1950). Below right: with (back row) Eli Wallach, Arthur Miller, John Huston, (front) Montgomery Clift, Marilyn Monroe, while making* The Misfits – *the last film for both Gable and Monroe*

of his later films were disappointing, however. Even *Mogambo* (1953), Ford's remake of *Red Dust* (1932), with Ava Gardner and Grace Kelly, which did very well at the box-office, was tame in comparison to the earlier version and had little 'bezazz' except Miss Gardner.

Gable was bitterly discontented during this period. He was also lonely, and committed a terrible and expensive error when, on December 21, 1949, he married a fourth time. The bride was Lady Sylvia Ashley, the widow of Douglas Fairbanks Sr. It is said that three weeks after the wedding Gable knew that he'd made a mistake. They were not divorced, however, until 1951 – an event which cost Gable a neat bundle. That same year Dore Schary replaced Louis B. Mayer as head of production at MGM. The stars began falling out of the MGM heavens and Gable's contract, expiring in 1954, was not renewed.

He became the most expensive freelance actor in the business, working for a percentage of the gross. His pictures, though largely ineffective, were better than any he had made at MGM after returning from the war, and they made money. Gable also fell in love, and married for the fifth time. His new wife was beautiful Kay Spreckels; there was much about her that was not unlike Carole Lombard and for the first time since Lombard's death Gable was really happy.

His last film, *The Misfits* (1961), written by Arthur Miller and directed by John Huston, was one of the best pictures he ever made. He played an ageing cowboy who is seeking one

Filmography
1923 Fighting Blood (series). **'24** White Man; Forbidden Paradise. **'25** Déclassée/The Social Exile; The Pacemakers (series); The Merry Widow; The Plastic Age; North Star. **'31** The Painted Desert; Dance, Fools, Dance; The Easiest Way; The Finger Points; Laughing Sinners; The Secret Six; A Free Soul; Night Nurse; Sporting Blood; Susan Lenox: Her Fall and Rise (GB: The Rise of Helga); Possessed; Hell Divers. **'32** Polly of the Circus; Strange Interlude (GB: Strange Interval); Red Dust; No Man of Her Own. **'33** The White Sister; Hold Your Man; Night Flight; Dancing Lady. **'34** Men in White; It Happened One Night; Manhattan Melodrama; Chained; Forsaking All Others. **'35** After Office Hours; Call of the Wild; China Seas; Mutiny on the Bounty. **'36** Wife vs Secretary/Wife versus Secretary; Screen Snapshots No. 10 (short); San Francisco; Cain and Mabel; Love on the Run. **'37** Parnell; Saratoga. **'38** Test Pilot; Too Hot to Handle. **'39** Idiot's Delight; Gone With the Wind. **'40** Strange Cargo; Boom Town; Comrade X. **'41** They Met in Bombay; Honky Tonk. **'42** Somewhere I'll Find You. **'43** Combat America (military training short); Wings Up (propaganda short, incorporating footage from Combat America); Aerial Gunner (military training short). **'45** Adventure. **'47** The Hucksters. **'48** Homecoming; Command Decision. **'49** Any Number Can Play. **'50** Key to the City; To Please a Lady. **'51** Across the Wide Missouri; Callaway Went That-a-Way (guest) (GB: The Star Said No). **'52** Lone Star. **'53** Never Let Me Go (GB); Mogambo. **'54** Betrayed. **'55** Soldier of Fortune; The Tall Men. **'56** The King and Four Queens. **'57** Band of Angels. **'58** Teacher's Pet; Run Silent, Run Deep. **'59** But Not for Me. **'60** It Started in Naples. **'61** The Misfits.

last perfect moment on earth and finds it in a beautiful divorcee (Marilyn Monroe).

Gable had a good time making *The Misfits* but it was not an easy picture to work on. Filming it on location in Reno, the cast and crew had to put up with weather conditions of sheer hell – it was usually over 105°F. The action was far too strenuous for a man of Gable's years but he refused a double; Monroe, meanwhile, was exasperatingly difficult, never on time and unprofessional. But Gable was content. His wife was pregnant, and he went around announcing, 'It's going to be a boy'.

It was a boy – named John Clark Gable – but his father never lived to see him. Two days after completing his part in *The Misfits*, Clark Gable suffered a massive heart attack and died on November 16, 1960, aged 59.

Between 1957 and 1961 many of the screen heart-throbs of the Thirties and Forties died, including Ronald Colman, Gary Cooper, Tyrone Power, Errol Flynn and Humphrey Bogart. But it was Gable's death that really signified the end of that generation of all-male, all-action movie heroes – for Gable alone had been the King of Hollywood.

DeWITT BODEEN

Writ large in the movies' screen credits are the established 'authors' of Hollywood cinema – the directors, writers and producers around whom film history has been written and rewritten. The small print of those same credits, however, carries the names of those whose largely unheralded contribution to the 'look' of a film is often just as important and personally expressive – the art directors

Until the remarkable success of *Gone With the Wind* (1939), when the crucial individual contribution of William Cameron Menzies was acknowledged, the art director was the last person in the Hollywood studio hierarchy to be given fitting recognition for his efforts.

Menzies' major role in the production of *Gone With the Wind* far exceeded the art director's usual responsibility. His working relationship with David O. Selznick had already won him a unique titular up-grading to

production designer. His willingness to undertake detailed story-boarding (the pre-production sketching of sequences shot-by-shot) and second-unit direction showed how much he wished to be creatively involved at all stages of production. The strength of this desire was often to project him into the director's or producer's chair before the end of his multi-faceted career.

The role of most leading Hollywood art directors of the period was vastly different.

Figures such as Anton Grot, Cedric Gibbons, Van Nest Polglase and Hans Dreier were contracted exclusively to one studio, and through their work created a consistent 'look' that defined the identity of, say, an RKO or MGM picture.

The very term 'art director' covers a multitude of functions. Having read the script and perhaps liaised with the director assigned to the film, the art director had to be able to develop – through sketches to sets – an appropriate visual continuity, and so help to

Above: The approach to Peter Blood's house as sketched by Anton Grot for the opening sequence of Curtiz's Captain Blood. *Below left and right: Grot's strong influence on the eventual composition of a shot may be seen by comparing his drawing of Elizabeth I's throne room for* The Private Lives of Elizabeth and Essex *(1939) with a still from the film*

impart a consistent mood and style to the finished film. He had to be conversant with painting, sculpture, stage design, interior decoration, construction crafts and architecture. Apart from the essentials of imagination and flair, he had to possess an acute appreciation of the specific demands of cinema. He had to understand the requirements of actors, lighting, and the moving camera – and have an eye for matching sets to locations and fully integrating special effects into the finished product.

During the Thirties (and through to the breakdown of the studio system during the Fifties) designers in Hollywood were departmentalized under a supervising art director. Their individual functions on any given picture were often limited to such specializations as sketch artistry, scenic design, or the preparation of blueprint plans. Thus, in assessing the work of a designer it is often impossible to identify individual achievements – however a few men are justly renowned for their undoubted talent and influence.

Let there be light

A contract signed in 1914 between Jesse L. Lasky and New York theatrical impresario David Belasco bought the services of the designer Wilfred Buckland for Lasky's partner

– the director Cecil B. DeMille. Buckland became the first 'credited' art director to work in Hollywood. He not only possessed new ideas on architectural design, but also on lighting; instead of relying on natural sunlight, the common practice at the time, Buckland used Klieg arc lights to achieve the striking effects to be found in, for example, DeMille's *The Cheat* (1915) and *Joan the Woman* (1916). Even then the art director's role was played down, and the style Buckland created became famous as 'Lasky lighting'. Ironically, Buckland had probably the shortest career of the pioneer art directors. He retired in 1927, on bad terms with DeMille, having designed sets for the canine stars of *Almost Human* (1927). He later worked virtually anonymously as a sketch artist for various studios.

While Buckland and others like Cosmopolitan's Joseph Urban were recruited from the theatre, some go-ahead Hollywood producers cast envious eyes towards Europe for art directors. Thus, in 1912, Ben Carré arrived from France (after numerous collaborations with the film director Louis Feuillade) to strike up a fruitful partnership with the director Maurice Tourneur, who has ever since been hailed as one of the foremost visual stylists of the silent cinema for films such as *The Blue Bird* (1918) and *Treasure Island* (1920). The Polish illustrator Anton Grot was working in films in New York and New Jersey from 1913, and Hans Dreier was imported by Paramount in 1923 from German cinema.

Castles in the air

The silent era was a heyday of sorts for film design. Many of its extravagances may never be rivalled even with today's mega-million budgets, and were triumphs of the architecture illusion that epitomized Hollywood opulence in the Twenties. Some splendid examples are: the Norman castle in Allan Dwan's *Robin Hood* (1922), on which Buckland, Grot and Menzies, among others, worked; Richard Day's recreation of Monte Carlo for Erich von Stroheim's *Foolish Wives* (1922); Ben Carré's subterranean labyrinths in Rupert Julian's *The*

Left: Wilfred Buckland's design and dramatic lighting effects – borrowed from the New York stage – enhanced DeMille's The Cheat, *starring Fannie Ward. Above: an example of MGM's 'house style' – the art-deco foyer of* Grand Hotel, *designed under Cedric Gibbons' supervision. Below: Charles D. Hall and Herman Rosse collaborated on the design of the laboratory in Whale's* Frankenstein, *bringing Bauhaus modernism to deepest Transylvania*

Phantom of the Opera (1925), for which Charles D. Hall provided the above-ground sets; the jokily phallic minarets that decorate the city in Raoul Walsh's *The Thief of Bagdad* (1924) dreamed up by Grot and Menzies.

As the studios grew and became more budget-conscious, art direction conformed to the all-round rationalization. Multi-purpose sets were left standing on the back-lots for constant re-use. Departmental delegation became the norm, but even so it was the supervising art director – not the art director – who often claimed more than his fair share of what little credit was going.

MGM's maestro of elegance

Cedric Gibbons – after architectural training and several years with the producer Sam Goldwyn – was installed as supervisor at MGM from its formation. He had a clause inserted in his contract guaranteeing that his name would appear on the credits of every MGM film produced in the USA – and so it did, on over 1500 films, until his retirement in the mid-Fifties. His associate art directors and designers, however, often received no screen credit at all for their work, even if Gibbons' sole contribution to a film was his signature of approval on sketches or blueprints. Gibbons' only directorial credit, on *Tarzan and His Mate* (1934), should have gone to Jack Conway who substantially re-shot the film before its release. Such practices – not necessarily abuses of authority, more a form of bureaucratic shorthand – also occurred at other studios. Both Richard Day and Van Nest Polglase suffered

shadow over substance even if his Expressionist leanings had not been so clear. Here was an art director willing to paint shadows on his sets if need be. His Teutonic moodiness suffused sets in all genres, chiming perfectly with the manic streak of Warners' jack-of-all-trades director Michael Curtiz in films like *The Mad Genius* (1931), *Captain Blood* (1935) and *Mildred Pierce* (1945).

Charles D. Hall had come from the English stage and Fred Karno touring shows to be Chaplin's regular art director. However, he soon settled at Universal to create the studio's Gothic house style in a succession of horror films directed by Paul Leni, James Whale and Tod Browning. The laboratory in *Frankenstein* (1931) and Boris Karloff's modernistic domain in *The Black Cat* (1934) were imitated later in countless pale adaptations. Hall's superb set for *The Old Dark House* (1932) remained standing for subsequent regular re-use on a rental basis. His trade mark of tongue-in-cheek gloom also served him in the late Thirties as art director for Hal Roach and the Laurel and Hardy comedies, and necessarily to the end of his chequered career in the late Fifties, by which time he had freelanced his way through a slough of sci-fi and Cold War movies, and even an Abbot and Costello feature.

Hans Dreier's arrival at Paramount led to two wonderful partnerships, with Josef von Sternberg and Ernst Lubitsch, that won for most of the studio's Thirties productions a reputation for glowing opulence. His prodigiously inventive 'European' settings created a

Ben Carré once worked at the Paris Opera, but his sketches for the underground sequences of Julian's The Phantom of the Opera *were pure products of his artistic imagination.*
Right: a studio production shot reveals the scale of Hans Dreier's sets of Victorian London for Mamoulian's Dr Jekyll and Mr Hyde. *Below: a Welsh mining village faithfully reconstructed in the Hollywood hills – Richard Day's Oscar-winning exterior set for Ford's* How Green Was My Valley

virtual dream continent, as Lubitsch testified:
'There is Paramount Paris, and Metro Paris, and of course the real Paris. But Paramount's is the most Parisian of all.'

Dreier's tenure lasted until 1951, by which time many of the associate talents fostered under his supervision had left and made their own reputations.

The painter and the executive

Differing responses to increasing specialization were shown by Ben Carré and Van Nest Polglase. Carré was at Fox for the first half of the decade, where he created, without credit, the spectacular fiery fantasy sequence for *Dante's Inferno* (1935). Yet he tired of the remoteness of the executive chair, and in 1937 retired from art direction to return to his craft roots, becoming a prolific scenic artist.

Van Nest Polglase, however, thrived on his supervisory responsibility at RKO. Though the

from Gibbons' unwillingness to share credit until they were in a position to exercise their own rights to professional recognition at 20th Century-Fox and RKO respectively.

But the threat of anonymity rarely curbed the imaginations of Hollywood's art directors. Most of them worked diligently to satisfy the recognizable aesthetic predilections of their supervisors and (thus) their studios. It soon became evident that Gibbons favoured white sets, evenly lit; that he scorned shadows and distorted perspectives, and his associates generally complied with his tastes. His gradual adoption and adaptation of art-deco styles and motifs did not only affect his collaborators – his sets became widely influential in domestic interior design.

Over at Warner Brothers, Anton Grot favoured the other extreme. His relatively low budget would have decreed an ascendancy of

studio was renowned for its regular wholesale personnel changes, Polglase retained his position there until the end of the decade. He was able to call on associate talents of the calibre of designers Carroll Clark and Perry Ferguson in creating the gleaming deco palaces which served as nightclubs, casinos and ballrooms in the wonderful series of Astaire/Rogers musicals, or the varied settings of films like *The Informer* (1935), *Mary of Scotland* (1936), *Gunga Din* and *The Hunchback of Notre Dame* (both 1939). He kept a safe distance from the riskier projects like *King Kong* (1933), so was out of the way when the studio axe fell on Perry Ferguson and Hilyard Brown following the supposed extravagances of *Citizen Kane* (1940). Eventually a drink problem lost him his post to Albert D'Agostino, though he continued to work as a freelance until 1957.

The all-round genius

Richard Day's career was also lengthy and prolific, stretching from shared credits on Erich von Stroheim's silent masterpieces to collaborations with the art director Jack Martin Smith in 1970, and ending with Joseph Sargent's made-for-TV movie *Tribes*. He had left what Vincente Minnelli called 'Gibbons' medieval fiefdom' at MGM in 1930 to work for Goldwyn and United Artists and gained distinction for his amazing versatility – ranging from the stagey naturalism of the single sets for Vidor's *Street Scene* (1931) and Wyler's *Dead End* (1937) to the surreal flights of fancy of *The Goldwyn Follies* (1938). By the end of the decade he had succeeded William Darling as supervisor at 20th Century-Fox. As the studio merry-go-round accelerated, Day was succeeded in turn by Lyle Wheeler, whose own reputation had soared after his association with Menzies on *Gone With the Wind*.

The magic of Menzies

William Cameron Menzies owed his introduction to the movies to Anton Grot, whose assistant he became on the 1918 Pathé film *The Naulahka*. Recognition of this truly visionary artist grew throughout the silent period, when he worked with stars of the calibre of Fairbanks, Pickford, Norma Talmadge and Valentino. He received the very first Academy Award for art direction in 1928 for his work on Roland West's *The Dove*. His sense of involvement with the *kinetic* aspects of design in addition to its traditional decorative function

brought him into the Thirties with an itch to direct. He got his first chance in 1931 on *Always Goodbye* but ended up having to share his credit with another director – a fate that frequently befell him owing to his indifferent direction of actors. His varied contributions to films such as *Alice in Wonderland* (1933), which he co-scripted (and designed without credit), *Cavalcade* (1933), on which he was second-unit director and designer, and his total control over the elegantly futuristic *Things to Come* (1936), commended him to David O. Selznick, who teamed him with Lyle Wheeler on several projects, culminating in *Gone With the Wind*.

Throughout the Forties, Menzies was studio-hopping with director Sam Wood – whose rather pedantic style was much enlivened by his designer's contribution – and also acting as

Above: Day's experience of bringing Europe to Hollywood dated back to his collaboration with Stroheim on Foolish Wives, *for which he created a meticulous imitation of the Casino at Monte Carlo. Right and below: William Cameron Menzies' superb watercolour designs for Walsh's* The Thief of Bagdad

a producer. Selznick called on Menzies to plot some sequences for *Duel in the Sun* (1946). Whatever Menzies' screen credit on a particular movie, he invariably involved himself deeply in every aspect of its 'look'. His low-budget Fifties films as director reveal an endearing playfulness with the image and with special effects; the experimentalist streak he had exhibited throughout his career in various short films and series eventually led him into a flirtation with TV. But if he went out with a relative whimper, his name is nonetheless revered by later generations of film-makers.

Menzies was not the only art director, nor even the first, to graduate to the director's chair. Alfred Hitchcock quickly made this transition in England, and never forgot the value of pre-production story-boarding and design. In Hollywood the roster includes such notables as Mitchell Leisen, Paul Leni, Eugène Lourié, Daniel Haller, Nathan Juran and Harry Horner. Having reached a position from which the potential for film 'authorship' is widely acknowledged, each of these would surely, however, stress the point that their former colleagues within, or at the head of, Hollywood studio art departments often deserved similar status. The 'look' they created for a film or a studio is the intangible element that, time and again, makes a Hollywood movie naggingly memorable.

PAUL TAYLOR

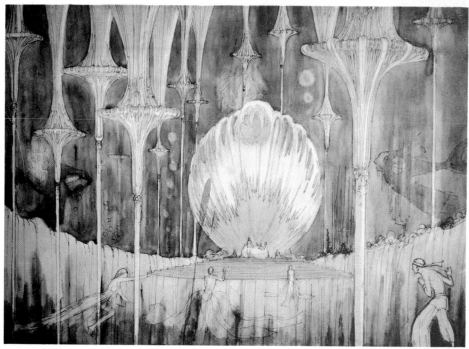

Key films of 1938

The Adventures of Robin Hood. USA. **prod co:** Warner Bros. **dir:** Michael Curtiz, William Keighley. **sc:** Norman Reilly Raine, Seton I. Miller. **photo:** Sol Polito, Tony Gaudio, W. Howard Greene. **ed:** Ralph Dawson. **art dir:** Carl Jules Weyl. **mus:** Erich Wolfgang Korngold. **with:** Errol Flynn, Olivia de Havilland, Basil Rathbone, Claude Rains, Patric Knowles, Alan Hale, Eugene Pallette.
The majestic spectacle of this rousing action film was immeasurably enhanced by the new three-colour Technicolor process. The Academy Awards went to the art director, editor and composer, though it is Flynn who is best remembered, for his verve and athleticism.

Alexander Nevsky; directed by Sergei Eisenstein – see special feature in Chapter 17.

Angels With Dirty Faces. USA. **prod co:** Warner Bros-First National. **assoc prod:** Sam Bischoff. **dir:** Michael Curtiz. **sc:** John Wexley, Warren Duff, from a story by Rowland Brown. **photo:** Sol Polito. **ed:** Owen Marks. **art dir:** Robert Haas. **mus:** Max Steiner. **sd:** Everett A. Brown. **with:** James Cagney, Pat O'Brien, Humphrey Bogart, Ann Sheridan, George Bancroft, the Dead End Kids.
The Dead End Kids are caught squarely between the morality of a neighbourhood saint (Pat O'Brien as the priest) and a sinner (Cagney as the local gangster) in a typical Warners 'social comment' movie.

La Bête Humaine (*Judas Was a Woman*). France. **prod co:** Paris Film. **prod:** Robert Hakim. **dir/sc:** Jean Renoir, from the novel by Emile Zola. **photo:** Curt Courant. **ass photo:** Claude Renoir, Jacques Natteau. **ed:** Marguerite Houllé-Renoir, Suzanne de Troye. **art dir:** Eugène Lourié. **mus:** Joseph Kosma. **sd:** Robert Teisseire. **with:** Jean Gabin, Simone Simon, Fernand Ledoux, Julien Carette, Jenny Helia, Colette Regis, Jean Renoir.
At once a naturalistic drama and a work of great lyricism, Renoir's film updates Zola's themes to Thirties France, while remaining true to the spirit of the original, and emphasizes the novel's critical social vision.

Blockade. USA. **prod co:** United Artists. **prod:** Walter Wanger. **dir:** William Dieterle. **sc:** John Howard Lawson. **photo:** Rudolph Maté. **ed:** Dorothy Spencer. **art dir:** Alexander Toluboff, James Basevi. **mus:** Werner Janssen. **mus dir:** Boris Morros. **with:** Madeleine Carroll, Henry Fonda, Leo Carrillo, John Halliday, Vladimir Sokoloff, Reginald Denny.
The only commercial Hollywood feature film to deal with the global implications of the Spanish Civil War, and to take a clear stand on the side of the Republicans. It was somewhat marred by an ill-fitting espionage sub-plot but remains apt testimony to John Howard Lawson's left-wing commitment.

Block-Heads. USA. **prod co:** Hal Roach Productions. **dir:** John G. Blystone. **sc:** Charles Rogers, Felix Adler, James Parrott, Harry Langdon, Arnold Belgard. **photo:** Art Lloyd. **ed:** Bert Jordan. **sp eff:** Roy Seawright. **mus dir:** Marvin Hatley. **with:** Stan Laurel, Oliver Hardy, Patricia Ellis, Minna Gombell, Billy Gilbert, James Finlayson.
Stan returns from World War I to find Ollie married and settled down, but chaos soon follows. Their relationship is more fully developed and self-conscious than in the earlier works and their brand of comedy is as uniquely personal as ever.

Bluebeard's Eighth Wife. USA. **prod co:** Paramount. **prod/dir:** Ernst Lubitsch. **sc:** Charles Brackett, Billy Wilder, from the play by Alfred Savoir. **photo:** Leo Tover **ed:** William Shea. **art dir:** Hans Dreier. **with:** Claudette Colbert, Gary Cooper, Edward Everett Horton, David Niven, Elizabeth Patterson, Herman Bing, Warren Hymer.

Claudette Colbert becomes the eighth wife of a millionaire and delights everyone with her wit and aristocratic airs. The film marks the beginning of the long and fruitful Brackett/Wilder partnership.

Bringing Up Baby. USA. **prod co:** RKO. **prod/dir:** Howard Hawks. **assoc prod:** Cliff Reid. **sc:** Dudley Nichols, Hager Wilde, from a story by Oscar Wilde. **photo:** Russell Metty. **ed:** George Hively. **art dir:** Van Nest Polglase, Perry Ferguson. **mus:** Roy Webb. **with:** Katharine Hepburn, Cary Grant, Charlie Ruggles, Barry Fitzgerald, May Robson, Fritz Feld.
Hawks' particular refinement of the screwball-comedy genre was the comedy of humiliation – with academic Grant the victim of a madcap plot involving lost dinosaur bones and a pet leopard called Baby. The film has crackling dialogue, gags galore and Hepburn gleefully surveying the wreckage.

The Childhood of Maxim Gorky. USSR. **prod co:** Soyuzdetfilm. **dir:** Mark Donskoi. **sc:** Mark Donskoi, Ilya Gruzdev, from memoirs by Maxim Gorky. **photo:** Pyotr Yermolov. **mus:** Lev Schwarz. **with:** Alexis Liarski, Varvara Massalitinova, Mikhail Troianovski, Dimitri Sagal, Elena Alexeieva.
The first section of Donskoi's three-part adaptation of Gorky's autobiography deals with his courageous and inspiring struggle as a child against poverty, injustice and oppression. Donskoi captures the heroic spirit and broad sweep of Gorky's canvas.

The Citadel. USA. **prod co:** MGM. **prod:** Victor Saville. **prod sup:** Harold Boxall. **dir:** King Vidor. **sc:** Ian Dalrymple, Frank Wead, Elizabeth Hill, Emlyn Williams, from the novel by A.J. Cronin. **photo:** Harry Stradling. **ed:** Charles Frend. **art dir:** Lazare Meerson, Alfred Junge. **mus:** Louis Levy. **ass dir:** Pen Tennyson. **with:** Robert Donat, Rosalind Russell, Ralph Richardson, Rex Harrison, Emlyn Williams, Penelope Dudley-Ward, Cecil Parker.
A major MGM-British production that followed up the success of A Yank at Oxford. *Cronin's best-selling novel about a crusading doctor was faithfully brought to the screen by Vidor.*

La Femme du Boulanger (*The Baker's Wife*). France. **prod co:** Films Marcel Pagnol. **prod:** Charles Pons. **dir/sc:** Marcel Pagnol, from the novel *Jean le Bleu* by Jean Giono. **photo:** Roger Ledru, Georges Benoît. **ed:** Suzanne de Troye, Marguerite Houllé-Renoir, Suzanne Cabon. **mus:** Vincent Scotto. **with:** Ginette Leclerc, Raimu, Fernand Charpin, Maximilienne, Alida Rouffe, Odette Roger, Charles Moulin.
A Rabelaisian vision of Provençal village life. The illicit love affair between a shepherd and the local baker's wife provides Pagnol and his cast with ample opportunity for wry observation, biting satire and telling characterization.

Hôtel du Nord. France. **prod co:** SEDIF. **prod:** Jean Lévy-Strauss. **dir:** Marcel Carné. **sc:** Henri Jeanson, Jean Aurenche, from a novel by Eugène Dabit. **photo:** Armand Thirard, Louis Née. **ed:** René Le Hénaff, Marthe Gottié. **art dir:** Alexandre Trauner. **mus:** Maurice Jaubert. **with:** Jean-Pierre Aumont, Louis Jouvet, Arletty, Annabella, Paulette Dubost, François Périer.
A typical portrait of doomed young love from the fatalistic sensibility of Carné. The film is built around the lives of a group of characters inhabiting a Parisian hotel and is greatly embellished by Trauner's evocative sets.

Jezebel; directed by William Wyler – see special feature in Chapter 14.

The Lady Vanishes. Britain. **prod co:** Gainsborough. **prod:** Edward Black. **dir:** Alfred Hitchcock. **sc:** Sidney Gilliat, Frank Launder, from the novel *The Wheel Spins* by Ethel Lina White. **add dial:** Alma Reville. **photo:** Jack Cox. **ed:** Alfred Roome, R.E. Dearing. **art dir:** Alec Vetchinsky, Maurice Carter, Albert Jullion. **mus:** Louis Levy. **sd:** Sidney Wiles. **with:** Margaret Lockwood, Michael Redgrave, Paul Lukas, Dame May Whitty, Googie Withers, Cecil Parker.
An essentially English Hitchcock thriller concerning the disappearance of an old lady and the search for an espionage secret hidden in a folk song. Charming for its eccentric performances and its blend of model-work and drama in the interior of the trans-European express train.

Olympia (*Berlin Olympiad*). Germany. **prod co:** Tobis. **prod/dir/ed:** Leni Riefenstahl. **ass:** Walter Ruttmann. **photo:** Hans Ertl, Walter Frentz, Guzzi Scheib, Willy Zielke. **mus:** Herbert Windt.
The Olympic Games have frequently acted as a focus of global political tensions and the film records of them have often either reflected or contributed to the atmosphere of contest and conflict. This presentation of sport on film is one of the most overtly propagandist and, insofar as it celebrates Nazi ideals of strength and vitality, is a genuinely fascist film.

Pygmalion. Britain. **prod co:** Gabriel Pascal Productions. **prod:** Gabriel Pascal. **dir:** Anthony Asquith, Leslie Howard. **sc:** Cecil Lewis, Anthony Asquith, W.P. Lipscomb, Ian Dalrymple, Anatole de Grunwald, from the play by George Bernard Shaw. **photo:** Harry Stradling. **ed:** David Lean. **art dir:** Laurence Irving, John Bryan. **mus:** Arthur Honegger. **ass: dir:** Teddy Baird. **with:** Leslie Howard, Wendy Hiller, Wilfred Lawson, Marie Lohr, Scott Sunderland, Jean Cadell, David Tree, Everley Gregg.
The career of Hungarian emigré Gabriel Pascal consisted entirely of four adaptations from Shaw. This, the first, was a rare but effective collaboration between Asquith and the actor Leslie Howard, though its merits remain largely those of performance and theatrical reproduction.

Quai des Brumes; directed by Marcel Carné – see special feature in Chapter 16.

South Riding. Britain. **prod co:** Victor Saville Productions for London Film Productions. **prod:** Alexander Korda, Victor Saville. **dir:** Victor Saville. **sc:** Ian Dalrymple, Donald Bull, from the novel by Winifred Holtby. **photo:** Harry Stradling. **ed:** Jack Dennis, Hugh Stewart. **art dir:** Lazare Meerson. **sp eff:** Lawrence Butler, Edward Cohen. **mus:** Richard Addinsell. **sd:** A.W. Watkins, Charles Tasto. **with:** Ralph Richardson, Edna Best, Edmund Gwenn, Ann Todd, John Clements, Marie Lohr, Milton Rosmer, Glynis Johns, Gus McNaughton.
A highly faithful adaptation of the famous novel of rural power politics, this film, with its beautifully photographed landscapes, is very much in the 'English' tradition established by the pioneer director Cecil Hepworth. The film is less successful in dealing with the numerous social issues which it tries to raise.

Three Comrades. USA. **prod co:** MGM. **prod:** Joseph L. Mankiewicz. **dir:** Frank Borzage. **sc:** F. Scott Fitzgerald, Edward E. Paramore, from the novel by Erich Maria Remarque. **photo:** Joseph Ruttenberg. **sp eff:** Slavko Vorkapich. **ed:** Frank Sullivan. **art dir:** Cedric Gibbons, Paul Groesse. **mus:** Franz Waxman, Chet Forrest, Bob Wright. **sd:** Douglas Shearer. **with:** Robert Taylor, Margaret Sullavan, Franchot Tone, Robert Young, Guy Kibbee, Lionel Atwill.
The pacifism of the original Remarque novel is admirably suited to Borzage's spiritual theme of life-in-death. The story concerns three survivors of World War I 'lost' in the crazy milieu of the Twenties.

You Can't Take it With You. USA. **prod: co:** Columbia. **prod/dir:** Frank Capra. **sc:** Robert Riskin, from a play by George S. Kaufman, Moss Hart. **photo:** Joseph Walker. **ed:** Gene Havlick. **art dir:** Stephen Goosson, Lionel Banks. **mus:** Dmitri Tiomkin. **with:** Jean Arthur, Lionel Barrymore, James Stewart, Edward Arnold, Mischa Auer, Ann Miller, Spring Byington, Donald Meek.
A fast-moving screwball comedy with a serious underlying theme typical of its director. Capra contrasts two families – the carefree Vanderhofs and the rich careworn Kirbys – to emphasize how it is better to love one's friends than to chase after wealth, status and power.

Chapter 19

Lonesome trail

After a big-guns opening to the sound era, Westerns fell from popularity in the Thirties until 1939's bumper crop of cowboy pictures proved that old genres never die

In the Western actions usually spoke louder than 'words', but when the sound revolution occurred the craze was for films with plenty of dialogue – comedies and musicals. So in the early days of talkies the immediate outlook for the Western was bleak. To make matters worse the sound engineers claimed that recording outdoors would be difficult, if not impossible.

In the ensuing uncertainty, the big Western stars of the silent cinema – Tom Mix, Ken Maynard, Tim McCoy – were dropped by their studios. Only Universal persevered, pumping out more of its Hoot Gibson Westerns and later snapping up Maynard and McCoy. But it was the director Raoul Walsh and the crew of *In Old Arizona* (1929) who quashed any reservations about applying sound to outdoor subjects.

The film was a modest Cisco Kid drama based on a story by O. Henry with a typical twist in which the Kid neatly revenges himself on a double-crossing señorita and outwits the law at the same time. The incidental sounds were laid on somewhat heavily, but audiences were thrilled at the clear recording of lips being smacked after a character had swallowed a drink, of eggs and bacon frying, and of horses' hoofs fading away as riders departed. There was also a zestful performance by Warner Baxter as the laughing bandit who serenaded his faithless señorita with the song 'My Tonia'. Baxter won the Academy Award in 1929 for Best Actor and *In Old Arizona* was the smash hit that restored

Westerns to favour.

The same year saw Victor Fleming's painstaking screen version of the thrice-filmed story *The Virginian* (1929) in which Gary Cooper made a suitably laconic hero forced to hang the friend who has turned cattle-rustler.

The Western was so strong a box-office prospect that by 1930 it was seen as a suitable candidate for wide-screen experimentation. MGM made *Billy the Kid* (1930) which was shot in the 70mm Realife process; Fox released its epic *The Big Trail* (1930) which ran 158 minutes in its Fox Grandeur version and 125 minutes in the standard 35mm version (both were shot simultaneously). Warners contributed *The Lash* (1930), a romantic adventure set in the California of the 1850s with Richard Barthelmess as a Spanish nobleman who turns bandit in order to overthrow a crooked American land commissioner. This movie was released in yet another wide-screen process: 65mm Vitascope.

Despite the resurgence of interest in Westerns, these three films flopped at the box-office owing to resistance on the part of exhibitors to the cost of installing wide-screen systems in their cinemas. Experimentation with 65mm and 70mm film gauges had raised the production cost enormously, and because of their failure the Western was once again brought into disrepute as far as the big producers were concerned.

Billy the Kid (dir. King Vidor) was a straightforward, slow, austere account of the young outlaw's

Top: William S. Hart, the foremost star of silent Westerns, hands over to the talkie star, John Mack Brown. The gun used for this historic occasion is reputed to have belonged to the real-life outlaw Billy the Kid. Left: Indian chiefs survey the range in Raoul Walsh's The Big Trail

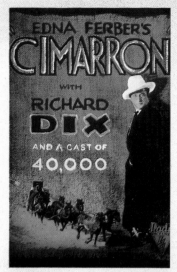

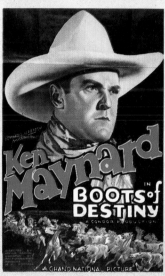

Top: Cimarron *portrayed the life of an Oklahoma family between 1890 and 1915. Above: Ken Maynard, an early cowboy star, continued well into the Thirties in B pictures like this 1938 Western. Below: wagons roll westwards in* The Big Trail

life, using the Grand Canyon for its locations. Although the film altered the facts by allowing a reformed Billy to go off with his girl at the end, the high death count up to that point set a harsh tone that did not appeal to audiences. John Mack Brown played Billy but it was not a role that suited him and he was to gain more charisma later in the decade as a star of series Westerns.

The Big Trail (dir. Raoul Walsh) was made to celebrate the centenary of a pioneering wagon-train journey that had set out from Independence, Missouri. The movie was shot under conditions almost as gruelling as those endured by the original travellers. It contained spectacular scenes of a buffalo hunt, a massive Indian attack on a circle of wagons, the fording of a swollen river and the lowering of cattle and wagons down a sheer cliff-face, in settings ranging from rainstorms and blizzards to desert heat. Unfortunately the human-interest was feeble and the casting of the unknown John Wayne as the wagon-train scout was a gamble that did not pay off at the box-office, although Wayne acquitted himself well. The final image fittingly celebrates the might of nature – the film's most impressive theme – as Wayne strides out of frame to be reunited with the heroine (Marguerite Churchill) and the camera tilts upwards to take in the towering trees of the forest setting.

The only Western ever to win the Academy Award for the year's Best Picture was *Cimarron* (1931). But this was more than a Western: based on one of Edna Ferber's vast, sprawling, generation-spanning sagas, it was an epic about the development of Oklahoma. It began with a spectacular reconstruction of the Cherokee Strip land-rush and continued through to the oil boom of the twentieth century. The success of *Cimarron* spawned such imitations as *The Conquerors* (1932) with the same star, Richard Dix, and *Secrets* (1933), with Mary Pickford and Leslie Howard. The latter film was the only main feature Western among the sixty or so released in 1933.

Before the genre went into the wilderness of the B

movie there was one notable, medium-scale Western, *Law and Order* (dir. Edward Cahn, 1932) which drew heavily on the story of Wyatt Earp bringing law to Tombstone and of the gunfight at the OK Corral. Walter Huston brought his usual authority to the central role and the script was written in part by his son John Huston. Cahn's direction provided some powerful sequences as, for example, the coverage of a lynch mob's arrival on horseback, townsfolk thronging the balconies around the jail-house, then edging forward slightly (the camera edging with them) to press in on Huston who is waiting on the steps outside. Cahn composed a striking finale to the film, shooting the march towards the final showdown with his camera set low, tracking backwards in front of Huston and his men as they stride purposefully forward.

After this production, however, it was left to the B picture units and the Poverty Row studios to keep the Western alive, though usually in the series format. In 1935, however, minor Westerns doubled in number in response to public demand, and two important developments in the genre occurred. First there was the arrival of Gene Autry, a former radio singer, who made his debut as a singing cowboy in the serial *The Phantom Empire* and the feature *Tumbling Tumbleweeds* (both 1935). Songs and comedy became major ingredients in Autry's work and his bland easy-going personality set the tone for the relaxed quality of his films which non-metropolitan audiences found especially to their liking. His stories were set in a fantasy land where contemporary and period details merged – aircraft, for example, could co-exist comfortably with old-fashioned stagecoaches.

The second key development was the Hopalong Cassidy series starring William Boyd as the blond knight of the range. Boyd was an accomplished performer who could handle action as ably as he could deliver lines; responding to a query about his guns in *Bar 20 Rides Again* (1935), he says, 'I just wear them to keep my legs warm'. The Hopalong Cassidy series was a success and encouraged Para-

mount, who had distributed it, to venture into big Westerns again.

So in 1936 King Vidor made *The Texas Rangers* with Fred MacMurray as the former stagecoach robber who joins the lawmen and brings an old partner (played by Lloyd Nolan) to justice. More significant, however, was Cecil B. DeMille's *The Plainsman* (1936) a lavish pot-pourri that starred Gary Cooper as Wild Bill Hickok, Jean Arthur as Calamity Jane, James Ellison as Buffalo Bill, John Miljan as Custer and Frank McGlynn Sr as Abraham Lincoln. Its robust action scenes, filmed by the second-unit director Arthur Rosson, blended awkwardly with studio close-ups of the stars firing at back-projections of marauding Indians. There were also moments of light relief as, for example, when a bullet was fired into a water-keg to provide a stream of water for a man lying wounded underneath – but at least DeMille insisted on a factual conclusion with Hickok being shot in the back and dying. Paramount followed this slice of comic-strip history with Frank Lloyd's static *Wells Fargo* (1937), starring Joel McCrea, and James Hogan's livelier *The Texans* (1938), with Randolph Scott, Joan Bennett and Walter Brennan.

Surprisingly, although three-strip Technicolor was being used by Paramount and other studios on outdoor subjects it was not used in Westerns until *Jesse James* (1939), although a number of Warners' outdoor films – *God's Country and the Woman* (1936), *Gold is Where You Find it* and *Heart of the North* (both 1938) – were almost Westerns. Then two films, Fox's *Jesse James* and Paramount's DeMille extravaganza *Union Pacific* (1939) triggered a great Western boom; the trade paper *Variety* noted the trend early in 1939.

'Out of Hollywood from now until the end of the present production year in midsummer, will flow the rootin', tootin', shootin'est, bowie-knife wielding bunch of ride 'em cowboy, major budget Westerns the picture business has witnessed in a decade. Some $15,000,000 worth of shooting, scalping, train and stagecoach robbing, hyped with

gentle love, mad brawls for the protection of honour and "curse you, Jack Dalton" villains has been budgeted.'

Variety's explanation for the revival of the genre was the cyclical nature of the business and the copy-cat techniques of the studios; all of them were making Westerns for fear of being left out of a forthcoming box-office bonanza. But other factors may have come into play. *Variety*'s report of a 'surge of Americanism' in film subject-matter was only to be expected as the European situation worsened. Key foreign markets were threatened or already lost, and films with strong domestic appeal made sense at the box-office.

Furthermore, cinema attendance figures in the United States had become static despite the rise in population and the studios were consequently making changes in film content in the hope of building new audiences.

One picture has come to stand out from all the rest in the bumper crop of 1939: *Stagecoach*. It was John Ford's first Western since *Three Bad Men* (1926) but was not an outstanding success commercially. *Variety* announced:

'*Stagecoach* at the box-office has not sustained the enthusiastic reviews it received from the press. Lack of strong names in the cast and a trite title are the reasons given for the *Stagecoach* fade.'

But the praise heaped on the film and the evident skill of Ford's direction did have a strong influence on other film-makers: it made the Western a respectable subject for quality films. If the year had not been dominated by *Gone With the Wind*, the film would have won more Oscars than the two it did.

In a dramatic sense *Stagecoach* was not essentially a Western – its carefully assorted band of passengers could have been assembled in any setting and exposed to an equivalent danger to show their reaction under stress. And almost all the scenes involving the leading players were filmed in the studio. But besides John Ford's inimitable use of Monument Valley and his striking chase sequence across salt flats, there was his masterful treatment

Top: Randolph Scott, Kay Francis, Brian Donlevy and Andy Devine were among the familiar names in popular Westerns; here they were teamed in a version of the Daltons legend. Above: the singing cowboy Gene Autry made his feature-film debut in the Western with songs, Tumbling Tumbleweeds

Gun Fights!
Thundering herds!
Prairies ablaze!
Romance!

SAMUEL
GOLDWYN
presents

GARY COOPER

THE WESTERNER

directed by
WILLIAM
WYLER

with WALTER BRENNAN · DANA ANDREWS

Top: on location with The Texans. *The large circular disc is designed to reflect sunlight on the couple in the buckboard – Joan Bennett and Robert Cummings. Top right: Ronald Reagan and Errol Flynn prepare to shoot it out in* Santa Fe Trail. *Above: Wyler's prestige Western based on the life of Judge Roy Bean. Below: Tyrone Power in* Jesse James

of the traditional gunfight on main street. Moreover the dynamic performance of John Wayne, in such moments as the halting of the runaway stage or when he dives to the ground to fire on his opponents in the climactic shoot-out, assured the actor of the front-rank stardom that had eluded him since *The Big Trail*.

Both *Jesse James* and *Dodge City* (1939) eclipsed *Stagecoach* in box-office terms; they had top stars and were in Technicolor. *The Oklahoma Kid* (1939) was another success. James Cagney wore a ten-gallon hat and brought his city-slicker mannerisms to the role of the Robin Hood of Oklahoma, and Humphrey Bogart, dressed in black from tip to toe, played the dastardly villain, but the movie was tongue-in-cheek and deserved its success. *Jesse James* was a romanticized depiction of the celebrated outlaw's life with sympathetic portrayals from both Tyrone Power as Jesse and Henry Fonda as his brother Frank; the two of them take up robbery only after the railroad's representative (played by Brian Donlevy) has burnt down the family farm and killed their mother. Jesse's actual death (he was shot in the back) was retained but the newspaper editor, acting as chorus or commentator, gave the film an upbeat ending eulogizing Jesse:

'We ain't ashamed of him – I don't think even America is ashamed of Jesse James. Maybe it was because he was bold and lawless like all of us like to be sometimes, maybe it's because we understand a little that he wasn't altogether to blame for what his times made him . . .'

The cue had been given for the Old West's other badmen to be covered in Hollywood whitewash. MGM remade *Billy the Kid* (1941) with Robert Taylor; Gene Tierney appeared as the notorious *Belle Starr* (1941) and Universal told of *When the Daltons Rode* (1940).

In contrast *Dodge City* was merely an actionful Western with Errol Flynn dispensing the heroics to a zestful score by Max Steiner. Michael Curtiz's direction displayed its usual panache but the script by Robert Buckner was rather weak. The same combination of star, composer and director were brought in to liven up two more Buckner screenplays: *Virginia City* and *Santa Fe Trail* (both 1940).

DeMille's *Union Pacific* was the epic story of the construction of the first transcontinental railway. No expense was spared to give the film an authentic look: the top track-laying crew of the actual Union Pacific company was recruited to perform in front of the cameras, and there was a spectacular Indian attack on a moving train, staged by Arthur Rosson. The main plot featured Joel McCrea as the overseer fighting saboteurs (led by Brian Donlevy, the period's most hard-working screen villain) while avenging the death of a friend at the same time. The narrative was stronger than that of *The Plainsman* and DeMille gained some inspiration from John Ford's *The Iron Horse* (1924) which had the same historical background.

Even Republic, the leading source of B Westerns, with its singing cowboys Gene Autry and Roy Rogers, decided the time was right to move up-market. Borrowing a star, Richard Dix, a director, George Nichols Jr, and a supporting actress, Joan Fontaine, they made *Man of Conquest* (1939), the story of the pioneer Sam Houston, that culminated in a rousing reconstruction of the battle of San Jacinto. So contagious was the fever for big Westerns that even the 'quality film' specialist Sam Goldwyn succumbed and hired William Wyler to make *The Westerner* (1940), Goldwyn's second (and last) horse opera. The film was a cleverly written account of the relationship between an honest cowpoke (played by Gary Cooper) and the wily Judge Roy Bean (Walter Brennan in an Oscar-winning portrayal).

At the turn of the decade the Western was in such strong shape that it even encouraged the satirical treatment of George Marshall's *Destry Rides Again* (1939), a light-hearted re-working of a Max Brand story that had been filmed straight in 1927 as Tom Mix's first sound film. James Stewart played the apparently naive and helpless Destry who helps clean up a town while Marlene Dietrich was the saloon singer who fell for his good looks and innocent charm.

The astonishing recovery of the genre put it back on its feet for good, but the excitement and vitality of the Westerns of the 1939–41 period was only short-lived.
ALLEN EYLES

How John Ford's West was Won

The heroes of John Ford's films are the frontiersmen, pioneers and peacemakers who dedicated themselves to the founding of the homes and communities that make up America. Ford's vision is a folk vision: a celebration of the ideals that sent wagon trains of settlers westwards in search of freedom and opportunity, but couched in the homeliest of terms – where a dance or a gathering round a graveside speaks volumes more than the dramatic battles and gunfights that were also waged in the winning of the West

Above: Stagecoach, *in which John Ford (inset) first made use of the spectacular mesas of Monument Valley, Utah. The film itself was a landmark in the career of one of the most respected directors in world cinema. Ford (1895–1973) directed his first feature,* Tornado, *in 1917. Born Sean Aloysius O'Feeney, thirteenth child of Irish immigrant parents, in Maine, he had come to Hollywood after failing to get into naval college. He worked his way up as prop man, stunt man and actor*

By the end of the Thirties John Ford already had a hundred films to his name. Whereas a lesser director would have probably burned himself out, the best years for Ford were still ahead. His 'golden age' spanned nearly three decades. It began in 1939 with two films, *Stagecoach* and *Young Mr Lincoln*, and encompassed along the way such milestones as *She Wore a Yellow Ribbon* (1949), *Wagonmaster* (1950) and *The Searchers* (1956). These films are packed with unforgettable sequences and images: the young Lincoln (Henry Fonda) climbing a hill in a storm; Nathan Brittles (John Wayne), the old cavalry captain in *She*

Wore a Yellow Ribbon, riding out of the fort for a final mission and furtively shielding his face from the sun, or Brittles going to his wife's grave in the evening to 'talk' to her. There is the moment when the showgirl Denver (Joanne Dru) flashes a mysterious look at the wagon-train leader Travis (Ben Johnson) in *Wagonmaster*; or when Ethan (Wayne) lifts up and cradles the niece (Natalie Wood) he has sought to kill in *The Searchers*, understanding in those few instants the uselessness of his hatred; or Frank Skeffington (Spencer Tracy) returning home alone after failing to be re-elected as the mayor in *The Last Hurrah* (1958). These

sublime moments in Ford's films reveal more than a thousand critical post-mortems that his art is above all meditative – one might even say symphonic.

The contemplative nature in Ford has rarely been understood. In France, for example, his Westerns have been promoted with pompous phrases like 'heroic charge', 'hellish pursuit' and 'fantastic journey' which suggest that the films somehow belong to the epic genre. Nothing is further from the essence of these fundamentally peaceful works of art. And although Voltaire's assertion that 'Epic authors had to choose a hero whose name alone

Above: Judge Billy Priest (Will Rogers) and other veterans of the Civil War evoke nostalgia for the Confederate States in Judge Priest *(1934). Ford remade the film as* The Sun Shines Bright *in 1953*

would impress itself on the reader' can be applied to certain Ford films like *Young Mr Lincoln* (a splendid evocation of the youth of the American president), it is certainly not applicable to most of his work, including the Westerns. In *My Darling Clementine* (1946), that legendary hero Wyatt Earp (Henry Fonda) is reduced to everyday dimensions; he has no exalted status.

A man's gotta do . . .

It is interesting to compare the socially minded motivation of the typical Ford hero with the personal motivation of the classic Western hero. The classic Western is chiefly built around a ruggedly individualistic vision of the world: Allan Dwan's *Silver Lode* (1954), with John Payne as a man trying to clear his name, and King Vidor's *Man Without a Star* (1955), with Kirk Douglas as a drifter motivated by revenge, are perhaps the most extreme examples of this. Strong feelings, often of physical or psychological violence, predominate; there is hatred, vengeance, rebellion and conquest. A cowboy is usually out to avenge his brother, his friend or his own honour; an outlaw tries to escape from his past; a gunfighter follows his will to kill; a man needs to prove he is not a coward or has to overcome the devil within himself. In short, the genre draws its dramatic force from a few powerful ideas: a confrontation, an opposition, a tearing away. From the films of Raoul Walsh to those of Delmer Daves, Western heroes pitch themselves into a battle by their own free choice. And it is a battle that will allow them to accomplish their purpose – but from which, if they survive, they will emerge permanently scarred. Even if there are no horseback chases or bloody shoot-outs, the dramaturgy of the classic Western is precisely structured and depends on a number of climactic moments.

With Ford, however, the essential motivation is looser, more attenuated, and rarely drawn around an individual emotion or a negative, destructive driving force like vengeance. What predominates at the heart of his Westerns are journeys and wanderings: the slow odyssey of a wagon train, the patrolling of a group of cavalrymen, the crossing of a desert by a stagecoach, or by a group of bandits on the run. Ultimately his films are all odysseys of groups – the stage passengers in *Stagecoach* (1939), farmers and their families escaping from the Oklahoma Dust Bowl in *The Grapes of Wrath* (1940), cavalrymen out on missions in *Fort Apache* (1948), *She Wore a Yellow Ribbon, Rio Grande* (1950) and *The Horse Soldiers* (1959), the Mormon settlers in *Wagonmaster*, Ethan and Martin Pawley (Jeffrey Hunter) searching for Debbie in *The Searchers*. Each group consists of several people who either belong to the same walk of life, or are brought together and bound by the same collective purpose. Ford is only interested in personal

problems in so far as they overlap those of society at large; whereas in Howard Hawks' Westerns, for example, adventure remains the right of the individual and only concerns society by chance or accident. In Hawks' *Rio Bravo* (1959) the sheriff (John Wayne) refuses the help offered to him; Ford's Wyatt Earp, however, accepts it immediately. It is a fundamental difference: the first sheriff seeks to fulfil himself through his duty, the second thinks primarily about helping those around him.

. . . what a man's gotta do

At the same time Ford frequently shows us the dissensions and disagreements that divide communities, and his heroes act only in relation to the environment they live in. It is that environment that provides their task – a duty to fulfil for the good of the community; any personal vendettas are usually subjugated to the communal cause. The notion of having a task or a mission takes precedence over all personal considerations. This is especially true of *Rio Grande* in which Captain Kirby Yorke (John Wayne) puts his duty as a soldier before his marriage and family; and in *The Sun Shines Bright* (1953), in which an old Southern judge (Charles Winninger) risks his reputation in

Most of Ford's films are about men working for a common cause and sharing the hardships incurred. Above: John Qualen, Ward Bond, Jack Pennick, John Wayne and Thomas Mitchell toil on the sea in The Long Voyage Home. *Below: Welsh miners enduring a pit disaster in* How Green Was My Valley, *with Walter Pidgeon and Oscar-winner Donald Crisp*

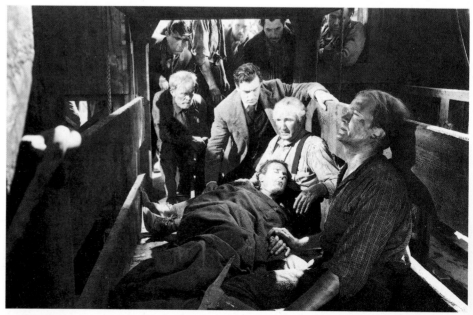

evokes it briefly and objectively, without any indulgence or lyricism; the swift shoot-out at the OK Corral in *My Darling Clementine* and the killing off of the outlaws who threaten the settlers in *Wagonmaster* are good examples.

Even the adventures themselves are non-violent in the way they progress; they are unfolded for us in a rhythm that is at once casual yet majestic. In telling a story Ford takes his time and works like a painter, rather than a strategist or a theoretician.

The true Ford hero has no need to use violence to prove himself. He simply does it, carried along by the collective ideal that leaves no space in his mind for doubt. Perhaps Ford's real heroes are the communities themselves: the unknown soldiers bringing peace to the West; the pioneers who are crossing the country to build new states; the inhabitants of

The story of Ford's films is a great saga of agrarian life: claiming or reclaiming, cultivating and enlarging territorial possessions.

Accordingly Ford's heroes take their character from the peasant, whatever their social origins. Heroes may be Irish peasants, farmers, Welsh miners, soldiers, whatever. In Ford's eyes the soldiers who run a territory in *She Wore a Yellow Ribbon* are involved in the same struggle as the Joad family in *The Grapes of Wrath*. And although the different communities in Ford's films are closed communities governed by their own rules, they are similar in that they share not only the struggles of life but its simple pleasures, too, like a dance, as in *Fort Apache* and *My Darling Clementine*.

The notion of possession accounts for Ford's passion for ceremonies. Celebrations, drunken festivities, dances, even funerals are the tan-

order to rescue a black boy from being lynched. In *My Darling Clementine* Wyatt Earp's vengeance on the Clantons for the killing of his brother is given much less importance than the dance in front of the church and the Shakespearian monologues of the travelling showman (Alan Mowbray). Earp is a supremely calm figure, not someone driven by a nameless hatred (as is the case of the Western heroes in the films of Anthony Mann).

Indeed, violence linked to the notion of a personal quest hardly exists at all in Ford's films. Killings, even woundings, are rare. Not a single Indian is seen to be killed or wounded in *She Wore a Yellow Ribbon*. In *Two Rode Together* (1961), Sheriff McCabe (James Stewart) fires only two revolver shots – the only gunshots in the film. Ford could never conceive a scene like the one in Anthony Mann's *The Man From Laramie* (1955) where Stewart's hand is maimed. Violence is never a goal in Ford's films or a means of self-fulfilment, but a duty or a last resort. When violence is inescapable, Ford

Above: in My Darling Clementine *Henry Fonda portrayed Wyatt Earp as a balanced, pensive peace-loving man. Right: a custodian of the West retires – John Wayne as Captain Brittles in* She Wore a Yellow Ribbon *with Harry Carey Jr, Joanne Dru and Victor McLaglen. Below: Travis (Ben Johnson) and Denver (Joanne Dru) in* Wagonmaster

a township whose chief aim is to establish a society of law and order – all those people who, whether consciously or not, have helped to build the United States and whose names and faces have been forgotten. And so it is their work that the films celebrate. This work may not be exalting; it is often thankless, seldom on a big scale, but it is stamped with a day-to-day heroism.

The homing instinct

Most of Ford's pictures are based on and perpetuate a theme that seems to haunt his last Western, *Cheyenne Autumn* (1964) – his elegy on the dispossessed Indians who seek to reclaim their ancestral lands – and that is the need not simply to build or see something through to its conclusion, but to arrive at the possession of a piece of land, a home or hearth, or perhaps simply a rocking-chair, which is exactly what is sought by Mose (Hank Worden) in *The Searchers*. There is also a need to fight against enemies and the elements to keep possessions in order to understand their complete value.

gible proof of the need to affirm publicly the ownership of a place, especially since it could be taken away at any time – as Lars Jorgensen (John Qualen) remarks in *The Searchers*.

The same motivation underlies Ford's fondness for landscapes that are immutable, notably the desert and rocky outcrops of Monument Valley, his favourite location. It is almost as if the film-maker shares with his characters the desire to possess these vast terrains in order to gain a profound appreciation of stability.

Even that antithesis of the Ford hero, Ethan Edwards in *The Searchers*, who can find no place for himself in stable society, is concerned with its continuation. In this fragmented, poignant film – the only one of Ford's based on a notion of individualism – Ethan sets himself against the ordered life and is seemingly involved in a desperate struggle to remain a loner, a rebel. After a hopeless search for his niece that lasts ten years, Ethan finally understands the uselessness of his revolt. He cannot bring himself to kill the girl when he finds her, tainted though she may be by living with an

Indian 'buck' and therefore a threat to white society. Because he is so concerned to preserve the wholeness of the homestead, he does not realize that the people who made it what it was, and thus its very nature, have changed. There is no place for him and after returning Debbie to the community he disappears, leaving the new generation represented by Martin Pawley to take over.

Exiles and nomads

Ethan is just one of scores of exiles that struggle to preserve society in Ford's films. Others include Irish and European immigrants who dream of gaining some sort of new birthright in America. In *The Man Who Shot Liberty Valance* (1962), restaurant-owner Peter Ericson (John Qualen) actually leaps for joy on hearing the news that he has earned his American citizenship. Ford's universe is also peopled by rootless characters who wander aimlessly – like the sailors in *The Long Voyage Home* (1940). Among these exiles there is even a tribe of Indians: the Comanches of *The Searchers* are Indians who have no territory;

they are constantly on the move. There is also the immigrant prizefighter (John Wayne) returning to his home town after killing a man in the ring in *The Quiet Man* (1952), and families put on the road by the effects of the Dust Bowl to look for new work in *The Grapes of Wrath*.

Other characters are exiled in different ways: the crazed white children and women in *The Searchers* who are refused recognition by their kinsfolk as they have been defiled by Indians. There are also the soldiers for whom the bugle song of retreat in *She Wore a Yellow Ribbon* and *The Wings of Eagles* (1957), or disgrace in *Fort Apache*, sounds a little like exile.

In Ford's films it is not only characters that may be uprooted but entire nations and historical periods. The director has often returned to moments when a social class, or indeed a whole race – in *Cheyenne Autumn* the whole Indian community is oppressed and exiled – is on the brink of extinction. Cheyenne autumn, Welsh twilight – these are both situations from which men and women are forced away to find new means of survival. In *How Green Was My Valley* (1941), industrial strife disrupts the working community and the idyllic family life of the Morgans in the Welsh village where they live at the turn of the century. The youngest son, Huw (Roddy McDowall), whose childhood provides the basis of the story, must finally follow his brothers and move on to pastures new.

Ford portrays people trying to remain faithful to themselves, and to their way of thinking, even when threatened by great historical upheavals. In this respect he may be a spiritual relative of the great Soviet director Donskoi,

Above left: an inaptly titled Belgian poster for The Searchers; *the film is less concerned with Debbie and her 'imprisonment' by Indians than with Ethan, who is a 'prisoner' of his obsession with finding her. Right: the killing of Liberty (Lee Marvin) – but not by Stoddard (James Stewart) – in* The Man Who Shot Liberty Valance. *Below: John Wayne and William Holden in* The Horse Soldiers, *one of Ford's poetic tributes to the US Cavalry*

Filmography

As Jack Ford: **1914** Lucille Love – the Girl of Mystery (serial) (prop man; possible credits for act; stunts; ass. dir); Lucile/Lucille, the Waitress (series of four films: She Wins a Prize and Has Her Troubles; Exaggeration Gets Her Into All Kinds of Trouble; She Gets Mixed Up in a Regular 'Kid Kalamity'; Her Near Proposal) (credited as dir. in some sources); The Mysterious Rose (act. only). **'15** The Birth of a Nation (act. only); Three Bad Men and a Girl (act. only); The Hidden City (act. only); The Doorway of Destruction (act; +ass. dir); The Broken Coin (serial) (act; +ass. dir). **'16** The Lumber Yard Gang (act. only); Peg o' the Ring (serial) (act. only); Chicken-Hearted Jim (act. only); The Bandit's Wager (act. only). **'17** The Purple Mask (serial) (ass. dir); The Tornado (+act; +sc); The Trail of Hate (dir. copyrighted to Ford, no screen credit; +act; +sc); The Scrapper (+act; +sc); The Soul Herder (reissued as short 1922); Cheyenne's Pal; Straight Shooting (reissued as short Straight Shootin', 1925); The Secret Man; A Marked Man; Bucking Broadway. **'18** The Phantom Riders; Wild Women; Thieves' Gold; The Scarlet Drop (GB: Hillbilly); Delirium (co-dir); Hellbent (+co-sc); A Woman's Fool; Three Mounted Men. **'19** Roped; A Fight for Love; The Fighting Brothers; Bare Fists; By Indian Post; The Rustlers; Gun Law; The Gun Pusher (reissued as short 1924); Riders of Vengeance; The Last Outlaw; The Outcasts of Poker Flats; The Ace of the Saddle; The Rider of the Law; A Gun Fightin' Gentleman; untitled one-reel promotion film for personal appearance tour by actor Harry Carey. **'20** Marked Men; The Prince of Avenue 'A'; The Girl in No. 29; Hitchin'

Above: Indian women robbed of their homes in Cheyenne Autumn, *based on the real tragedy of the Cheyenne. It was Ford's last Western and the last of nine films he shot wholly or partially in Monument Valley*

whose films were usually set in a period of social change or revolution. Generally the protagonists do adapt and overcome the crises they face in Ford's films, but they are often required to make costly sacrifices. In *The Man Who Shot Liberty Valance*, Tom Doniphon (John Wayne) kills the outlaw Liberty (Lee Marvin) but makes it seem as though Ransom Stoddard (James Stewart) has done so. For this noble act Doniphon sacrifices the personal glory of the deed and the girl he loves to Stoddard, lives a lonely life and dies alone.

Ford's desire to celebrate collective effort in his later films was tainted with the cynicism of advancing years, and there are hints of bitterness. Between the winning simplicity of *Drums Along the Mohawk* (1939) – Ford's tribute to the spirit of pioneer America on the eve of the Revolutionary War – and *She Wore a Yellow Ribbon*, there is a great difference in outlook. In the latter Nathan Brittles reconsiders his existence as a cavalry officer and begins to question it, and also doubts the validity of his current mission to subdue the Indians even though he continues to pursue it.

Monuments to America

Ford's heroes age with his work. The last shot of *The Man Who Shot Liberty Valance* is of the elderly Ransom Stoddard crying: doubt and uncertainty are bound up with sadness. Perhaps by the early Sixties, the time of *Liberty Valance*, *Cheyenne Autumn* and *Donovan's Reef* (1963) – a kind of melancholic, sometimes comic, reflection on the past, set in the mythical paradise of a Pacific island – Ford had become aware of his own uprootedness and of his own peculiar state of being an exile within American cinema. Perhaps he also realized that the nature of his work would ultimately remain as unchangeable as his own Monument Valley, but that everything around him was crumbling and disappearing. But when he ceased making pictures John Ford left behind him several of his own enduring monuments to the building of a country: a few massive rocks left in the middle of a vast desert.

BERTRAND TAVERNIER

Posts; Just Pals. '21 The Big Punch (+co-sc); The Freeze Out; The Wallop; Desperate Trails; Action; Sure Fire; Jackie. '22 Little Miss Smiles; Nero (uncredited add. dir); Silver Wings (prologue dir. only); The Village Blacksmith; The Face on the Barroom Floor (GB: The Love Image). '23 Three Jumps Ahead (+sc). *As John Ford:* '23 Cameo Kirby; North of Hudson Bay; Hoodman Blind. '24 The Iron Horse; Hearts of Oak. '25 The Fighting Heart (GB: Once to Every Man); Kentucky Pride; Lightnin'; Thank You. '26 The Shamrock Handicap; Three Bad Men (+sc); The Blue Eagle; What Price Glory (uncredited add. dir). '27 Upstream (GB: Footlight Glamour); Mother Machree (+sound version 1928). '28 Four Sons; Hangman's House; Napoleon's Barber; Riley the Cop. '29 Strong Boy; The Black Watch (GB: King of the Khyber Rifles) (silent scenes only); Salute; Men Without Women. '30 Born Reckless (silent scenes only); Up the River (silent scenes only; +uncredited sc). '31 Seas Beneath (silent scenes only); The Brat; Arrowsmith. '32 Air Mail; Flesh. '33 Pilgrimage; Doctor Bull. '34 The Lost Patrol; The World Moves On; Judge Priest. '35 The Whole Town's Talking (GB: Passport to Fame); The Informer; Steamboat Round the Bend. '36 The Prisoner of Shark Island; The Last Outlaw; Mary of Scotland; The Plough and the Stars. '37 Wee Willie Winkie; The Hurricane. '38 The Adventures of Marco Polo (uncredited add. dir); Four Men and a Prayer; Submarine Patrol. '39 Stagecoach (+prod); Young Mr Lincoln; Drums Along the Mohawk. '40 The Grapes of Wrath; The Long Voyage Home. '41 Tobacco Road; How Green Was My Valley. '42 Sex Hygiene (Army training short); The Battle of Midway (doc)

(+co-photo); Torpedo Squadron (private Army film not publicly shown); How to Operate Behind Enemy Lines (Office of Strategic Services training film for restricted showing). '43 December 7th (co-dir) (feature version for Navy; short for public); We Sail at Midnight (doc) (USA-GB: Ford possibly sup. dir. of American version). '45 They Were Expendable (+prod). '46 My Darling Clementine. '47 The Fugitive (+co-prod). '48 Fort Apache (+co-prod); Three Godfathers (+co-prod). '49 Mighty Joe Young (co-prod. only); She Wore a Yellow Ribbon (+co-prod). '50 When Willie Comes Marching Home; Wagonmaster (+co-prod); Rio Grande (+co-prod). '51 The Bullfighter and the Lady (uncredited ed. only); This Is Korea (doc) (+prod). '52 The Quiet Man (+co-prod); What Price Glory? '53 The Sun Shines Bright (+co-prod); Mogambo; Hondo (uncredited 2nd unit co-dir. only). '55 The Long Gray Line; The Red, White and Blue Line (short with footage from The Long Gray Line); Mister Roberts (some scenes only). '56 The Searchers. '57 The Wings of Eagles; The Rising of the Moon (Eire); The Growler Story (short). '58 Gideon's Day (GB) (USA: Gideon of Scotland Yard); The Last Hurrah (+prod). '59 Korea (doc) (+co-prod); The Horse Soldiers. '60 Sergeant Rutledge. '61 Two Rode Together; The Man Who Shot Liberty Valance; How the West Was Won (ep. only). '63 Donovan's Reef (+prod); The Directors (short) (appearance as himself only). '64 Cheyenne Autumn. '65 Young Cassidy (some scenes only); Seven Women. '70 Chesty: a Tribute to a Legend (doc) (+interviewer) (shorter version reissued 1976). '71 Vietnam! Vietnam! (doc) (exec. prod. only).

Directed by John Ford, 1939
Prod co: Walter Wanger Productions/United Artists. **exec prod:** Walter Wanger. **prod:** John Ford. **sc:** Dudley Nichols, from the story *Stage to Lordsburg* by Ernest Haycox. **photo:** Bert Glennon. **sp eff:** Ray Binger. **ed sup:** Otho Lovering. **sup:** Dorothy Spencer, Walter Reynolds. **art dir:** Alexander Toluboff, Wiard Ihnen. **cost:** Walter Plunkett. **mus:** Richard Hageman, W. Franke Harling, John Leipold, Leo Shuken, Louis Gruenberg, adapted from 17 American folk tunes of the 1880s. **mus arr:** Boris Morros. **2nd unit dir/stunts:** Yakima Canutt. **ass dir:** Wingate Smith. **r/t:** 97 minutes.
Cast: John Wayne (*The Ringo Kid*), Claire Trevor (*Dallas*), John Carradine (*Hatfield*), Thomas Mitchell (*Dr Josiah Boone*), Andy Devine (*Buck*), Donald Meek (*Samuel Peacock*), Louise Platt (*Lucy Mallory*), Tim Holt (*Lieutenant Blanchard*), George Bancroft (*Sheriff Curly Wilcox*), Berton Churchill (*Henry Gatewood*), Tom Tyler (*Hank Plummer*), Chris Pin Martin (*Chris*), Elvira Rios (*Yakima, his wife*), Francis Ford (*Billy Pickett*), Marga Daighton (*Mrs Pickett*), Kent Odell (*Billy Pickett Jr*), Yakima Canutt (*Chief Big Tree*), Harry Tenbrook (*telegraph operator*), Jack Pennick (*Jerry, barman*), Paul McVey (*express agent*), Cornelius Keefe (*Captain Whitney*), Florence Lake (*Mrs Nancy Whitney*), Louis Mason (*sheriff*), Brenda Fowler (*Mrs Gatewood*), Walter McGrail (*Captain Sickel*), Joseph Rickson (*Luke Plummer*), Vester Pegg (*Ike Plummer*), William Hoffer (*sergeant*), Bryant Washburn (*Captain Simmons*), Nora Cecil (*Dr Boone's housekeeper*), Helen Gibson, Dorothy Annleby (*dancing girls*), Buddy Roosevelt, Bill Cody (*ranchers*), Chief White Horse (*Indian chief*), Duke Lee (*Sheriff of Lordsburg*), Mary Kathleen Walker (*Lucy's baby*).

NINE ODDLY ASSORTED STRANGERS start out by stagecoach for Lordsburg, New Mexico. Each has his own personal reasons for wanting to get there. Then strange things begin to happen. The telegraph is mysteriously cut . . . the way station burned to the ground. Danger grows steadily more menacing . . . UNTIL . . . As conventions break down, the lives of the travelers are tangled together . . . you live with them this strange adventure . . . tense, full of action . . . deeply moving . . .

A WALTER WANGER Production • Directed by JOHN FORD

Stagecoach has often been credited with reviving the Western in Hollywood in the Forties. Rather, though, it coincided with a whole Western boom, appearing in the same year – 1939 – as *Dodge City*, *The Oklahoma Kid*, *Union Pacific* and *Jesse James*. Even so, when Ford tried to set up the film – his first Western since *Three Bad Men* (1926) – he found the genre was badly out of fashion.

He had bought Ernest Haycox's story, which he found in *Cosmopo-*

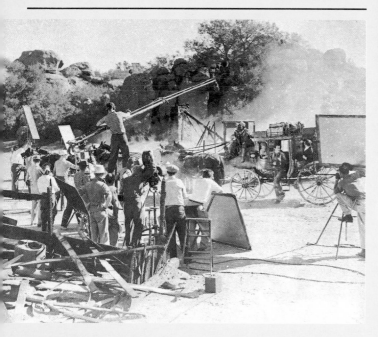

Above: John Ford – standing to the right of the boom-mike operator – filming Stagecoach

Apaches have broken out of the reservation and the telegraph wires have been cut. Nevertheless a varied group of passengers boards the stagecoach from Tonto to Lordsburg: Mrs Mallory, a pregnant wife going to join her husband, a cavalry lieutenant; Hatfield, a shady gentleman-gambler; Dallas, a prostitute run out of town by the 'decent' citizens; the bibulous and disreputable Doc Boone, who takes a keen interest in the samples carried by a timid whisky-drummer called Peacock. At the edge of the town they are joined by Gatewood, the pompous local banker. Riding alongside Buck the driver is Curly, a sheriff in pursuit of the Ringo Kid who has broken jail where he has been serving a sentence for a framed murder charge. Just outside town, Ringo himself joins the party (1). The stagecoach heads into Indian country, stopping shortly afterwards at the first staging post (2–3).

Initially, the group is strictly divided between the respectable and the disreputable, but the hazards of the journey temporarily blur the social barriers. Dallas and Doc Boone take charge of the sudden *accouchement* of Mrs Mallory (4). The Ringo Kid falls in love with Dallas, who is touched by his gallantry to her. The whole party is finally united by the Indian attack (5). The cavalry charges to the rescue (6), but not before Hatfield has been killed.

Arriving at Lordsburg, they go their different ways. The Ringo Kid avenges himself on Luke Plummer, the man who had framed him, and is reunited with Dallas. Curly, instead of arresting the Kid, connives with Doc Boone to speed the couple over the border. 'At least they're spared the blessings of civilization,' reflects the philosophic Doc.

1

RANGE MEN.....

CLAIRE TREVOR · JOHN WAYNE
· MITCHELL·Louise PLATT·George BANCROFT·Donald MEEK·Berton CHURCHILL·Tim HOL

litan magazine, for $2500. 'It wasn't too well developed,' he recalled, 'but the characters were good.' Producers he approached complained that people no longer went to see Westerns: 'Sure it's a Western, I said, but there are great characters

in it. What's the difference whether it's played in the West or wherever?' He took it to RKO where even the powerful Joseph P. Kennedy could not persuade his producers to adopt the project. Walter Wanger, however, who owed a film to United Artists, was finally convinced. Wanger wanted to use Gary Cooper and Marlene Dietrich for the main roles but Ford insisted that it must be cast cheaply, so he hired John Wayne – whose career had so far failed to take off, and who was making five-day Westerns – and Claire Trevor, 'a helluva actress'. Ford surrounded them with fine character players: Thomas Mitchell and Berton Churchill, both stage-trained actors; Donald Meek, George Bancroft, Andy Devine and the cadaverous John Carradine. For every one of them, the role in *Stagecoach* was to prove the most memorable of his career.

Ford himself later drew attention to the faint resemblance of the story to Maupassant's *Boule de Suif*. The critic Welford Beaton was on a better tack, however, when he described the film as '*Grand Hotel* on wheels'. The essence of the story is the interaction of a little group of characters under the stress of a perilous journey.

The structure of the film is very formal. It divides neatly into eight carefully balanced episodes, of which the central and longest is the 24-minute sequence at the Apache Wells staging post with the birth of Mrs Mallory's baby, and the climax is the six and a half minutes of the Indian attack. The expository opening scene, set in Tonto, lasts 12 minutes, during which time every character is carefully and comprehensively introduced.

The characters are also exactly balanced; in one group are the respectable' people – Hatfield, Gatewood (actually an embezzler) and Mrs Mallory; in the other, the 'disreputables' – the Ringo Kid, Doc Boone and Dallas. Buck and Curly, outside the coach, stand aside, a sort of chorus upon the moral debate waged within the coach. The mild little whisky-drummer, too, has a detached function. It is he who states the simple moral of the film: 'Let us have a little Christian charity, one to another.'

The picture was made for $222,000 – $8000 under the assigned budget. The scenes in Monument Valley were completed in four days; the rest was shot on the Goldwyn lot. The Monument Valley days included the extraordinary stunt material staged by Yakima Canutt. Canutt related that after he had performed his most hair-raising feat – jumping onto the stagecoach's lead horse and then, in response to Ringo's rifle shots, falling first to the shafts and then to the ground, allowing six horses and the stage to drive over his prone body – he ran to Ford to ask if the cameras had caught it. 'Even if they didn't,' said Ford, 'I'll not shoot that again.'

At that time there were no specifically equipped camera cars, and ordinary automobiles were used for the amazing scenes where the cameras follow the chase at full speed. The cameramen found to their surprise that in keeping up

with the horses they were driving at 40–42 miles per hour.

'I shot it pretty much as it is written,' said Ford, though Dudley Nichols was on the set throughout the film to write – or more likely to cut – dialogue as required. What is striking is the economy of the script. A broken half-line or two will often brilliantly illuminate a character or a situation. At the end, when the characters are returning to their own worlds, Mrs Mallory makes a hopeless attempt to prolong the brief contact with Dallas. 'If there is ever anything …' she begins awkwardly; 'I know,' says Dallas, understanding, but decisively acknowledging the unbridgeable gulf between them in the hypocritical, rigid society of their times.

Stagecoach stands alone for the epic quality both of its panoramas of the West and its human emotions. At the same time it permanently formed Western style. Ford was the first to make use of the spectacular topography of Monument Valley, and was to return to it many times again himself. The final shoot-out, which he had already used in silent films, and was to use again in *My Darling Clementine* (1946), has, since *Stagecoach*, become a cliché.

'It went back to what Wyatt Earp had told me. Wyatt was a friend of mine – in fact I still have his rifle in the corner of my bedroom.'

Ford has always stayed this close to his own West.

DAVID ROBINSON

3

6

5

The Codes of the West

The Western is perhaps the USA's greatest contribution to cinema. It has adapted with ease to changes in taste and fashion and continues to provide audiences with thrilling entertainment.

Popular cinema's foremost aim is to entertain its audience. Although a film may contain several different pleasurable elements – songs, witty dialogue, spectacular action, romantic love scenes – its main entertainment value lies in its telling a 'good story'. Often this story follows a common three-part structure: at the beginning the audience is presented with a clear image of stability; this is threatened and disrupted by various forces; by the end, a new order is established. This pattern of events involves, grips and, in its generally happy resolution, releases the audience, allowing it to go home contented. It is largely the presence of this pleasure-producing sequence which encourages the cinemagoer to tolerate a range of statements about the law, justice, the community, history and sexuality that may be contained in the film. This does not, of course, rule out the possibility that such statements have a deep ideological effect.

The different methods of working through the three main elements of a story are what determine the various genres of popular cinema – comedies, gangster films, horror films, melodramas, and of course Westerns.

The publicity attendant on the showing of a film (for example, reviews, posters and TV programmes about the cinema) helps to prepare the audience in advance; if that film has been billed and written about as a Western, viewers know more or less what to expect before they arrive at the cinema. The star system reinforces this effect; certain names are strongly linked with certain genres. Thus John Wayne and Randolph Scott (virtually throughout their careers), James Stewart and Charles Bronson (at important points in theirs) were closely associated with the Western.

As soon as the audience takes its seat it has specific expectations which begin to be satisfied even before the narrative sequence has been developed. Thus the most characteristic opening (or ending) of a Western is of a rider coming out of (or disappearing into) a pan-

Top: Charles Bronson, as the half-breed hero of Chato's Land, *adopts the customary pose of the noble savage. Centre: in Gene Autry's films it was easy to tell 'goodies' from 'baddies'. Left: the outlaws find an unusual reception has been prepared for them as they ride into town in* High Plains Drifter

Left: a successful train robbery from Union Pacific. Above left: a gunfighter (Henry Fonda), hired to 'clean up' the town, shoots it out with a couple of cowboys in Warlock. Above: when a well-known 'bad guy' like Lee Marvin (right) sits down to a game of poker, it is not long before more than just money is at stake in Duel at Silver Creek (1952)

oramic landscape. The movement of the rider will invariably be accompanied by a type of music which is different from that which would normally open a gangster movie, a thriller, an epic or a musical. It is a kind of music audiences will immediately comprehend as signifying a Western. The incidental music throughout the film may function as a series of signals easily understood by those members of the audience familiar with other Westerns – for example, the kind of throbbing musical phrase which proclaims that Indians are at hand.

In the early days of the Western the rider's clothes would have conveyed a clear message: good men wore white hats, bad men black. This is less likely nowadays, but as recent a Western as *Once Upon a Time in the West* (1968) endorsed this code by dressing the main villain entirely in black, though it subverted another – that of casting – by having him played by Henry Fonda, the upstanding Western hero *par excellence* of such films as *My Darling Clementine* (1946) and *The Ox-Bow Incident* (1943).

Although the narratives of all Westerns follow the dominant pattern of order, instability and restoration, they do so in a limited and specific number of ways. In a significant group of Westerns, which includes *High Noon* (1952), *Warlock* (1959), *Lawman* (1971) and *High Plains Drifter* (1973), the existing order of a town is disturbed by the intrusion of an outside force, such as a gunfighter. Order is restored only by his death or departure; occasionally, as in *The Fastest Gun Alive* (1956) by him becoming a peaceful member of the community. Another group of Westerns including *Winchester '73* (1950), *Rancho Notor-*

ious (1952), *Last Train From Gun Hill* (1959) and *Chato's Land* (1972), are 'pursuit Westerns', with the central pursuing figures very often motivated by revenge for the killing of their kin. Then there are the Westerns concerned with the opening up of the West such as *The Covered Wagon* (1923), *The Iron Horse* (1924), *Union Pacific* (1939), and *Western Union* (1941). Another key narrative motif has been the journey where a motley group of characters travel together, as in *Stagecoach* (1939), *The Law and Jake Wade* (1958) and *Ride the High Country* (1962); the drama emerges from the internal tensions of the group and the threats to its safety from without.

Clearly these and other key motifs are quite often interwoven. *Shane* (1953), for example, combines the intrusive gunslinger with another common motif – ruthless cattlemen versus peace-loving farmers.

Within the different types of plot provided by the Western it is possible to identify key narrative set pieces (often points of intense action) common to several of them. These include, for example: the gunfighter's arrival in town and the townsfolk's wary response to him in the saloon; the passing on of gun lore from one generation to another; bank and train robberies; a lynch mob storming the town jail. But perhaps the plot device which has most fired audiences' imaginations is the 'face-off', the climactic gunfight out of which new stability is created. In the Western, as in every other genre, there is a constant tension between repetition and innovation, between immediately identifiable iconography and situations and new variations. Together with the 'order/disruption/new order' narrative form, this tension is the main source of

pleasure for the audience. One of the ways the history of the Western could be written is around the different treatments of the 'face-off': in *Stagecoach* it happens largely off screen; in *Winchester '73* it happens in rocky terrain which causes bullets to ricochet wildly; in *Lawman* the normal ethical code of the Western hero is abandoned and the 'hero' indiscriminately kills unarmed, wounded and fleeing men. Such differing treatments offer clues to the social mood and attitudes (for example, with regard to screen violence) that prevailed when these films were made.

Conventionally the Western is set in the period between the end of the American Civil War in 1865, and the closing of the frontier in the late 1880s, although certain films made in the Sixties such as *Ride the High Country* and *Lonely Are the Brave* (1962) were set in later periods and explored the clash between the old and the modern. This would seem to raise the possibility of looking to the Western as a source of knowledge about American history of this period. However to do so would be simplistic and misleading at any other level than the provision of basic fact – for example, that Wyatt Earp was Marshal of Tombstone and that a gunfight did actually occur at the OK Corral. Like every other popular form, Westerns make statements primarily about contemporary ideological problems; they offer statements about the past *for* the present. Just as the Western rarely upsets the viewer's narrative expectations, so it rarely subverts the audience's subjective attitude to what it considers 'right' and 'proper', even if these attitudes may be at variance with the realities of life in the USA. For example, it would be difficult to find a Western that resolved its plot-line in favour of the cattleman and at the expense of the homesteader. This is because the most venerated figure in American films, popular literature and political rhetoric is the individual yeoman farmer ploughing his own land. In reality, of course, large corporate interests have significantly more influence on the machinery of government than small farmers. The ideology of agrarian populism is present in other genres – for example a social comedy like *Mr Deeds Goes to Town* (1936) or a literary adaptation like *The Grapes of Wrath*

(1940), and a melodrama like *All That Heaven Allows* (1955); but by the nature of the thematic terrain traversed by the Western, this ideology is absolutely central – and achieves a religious, almost mystical status in films such as *Wagonmaster* (1950) and *The Westerner* (1940). There is a powerful scene in *The Covered Wagon* in which the wagon train splits, the more sympathetic characters going north to farm land in Oregon, the less sympathetic going south to mine for gold in California. Like many other Westerns *The Covered Wagon* then had to wrestle with two contradictory sets of ideas, each having great force in American culture. Although homesteading confers nobility, it does not confer wealth. Gold mining confers wealth but not nobility. *The Covered Wagon* cleverly negotiates this contradiction by having its hero strike gold in California and then settle down on a homestead in Oregon, thus reconciling the dominant ideologies of the audience: that of closeness to the land and

Top: the American ideal of the poor but proud settler was celebrated in The Covered Wagon. *Centre left: temperatures reach boiling point within the travelling group of* Ride the High Country. *Above: his parents butchered and his home set ablaze by an outlaw gang, Steve McQueen in* Nevada Smith *(1966) vows vengeance. Left: a cattle-drive from* Red River

material success. This same contradiction is negotiated week after week in the TV series *Dallas*. Bobbie, the sympathetic member of the Ewing family is often associated with cattle and ranching, while the unsympathetic one, J. R., is almost exclusively linked with oil and big business. In the absence of homesteading, cattle ranching can assume transcendental significance, underlining the important point that the various narrative motifs of the Western (or any other genre) have no *absolute* meaning, but only acquire meanings by being arranged to conflict with each other within the plot structure of particular films.

The Western, one of the first of the popular film genres to emerge, has entertained audiences for over seventy years. As well as endorsing very traditional American ideologies (such as agrarian populism), it has been pressed into service as a form of allegory when direct statements about certain sensitive political issues were impossible. Thus *High Noon* has been seen as a comment on the social effects of McCarthyism, and *Soldier Blue* (1970) as a parable of the Vietnam War. The Western's future is assured.　　　COLIN McARTHUR

From Peasant to President

The Career of Henry Fonda

John Ford used Henry Fonda to embody the American spirit of liberty – as the pioneer farmer in Drums Along the Mohawk *(above left) with Claudette Colbert, and as the future President in* Young Mr Lincoln *(above)*

Lean, tough and likeable, with a steady lulling drawl, Henry Jaynes Fonda has gracefully aged from portrayals of doomed youths on the wrong side of the tracks and Western heroes to convincing studies of politicians, generals and presidents. He has reached these heights and held his position by avoiding the adulation and studio-processing that nurtured stars like Robert Taylor, Tyrone Power and Alan Ladd, who were then discarded when their box-office draw was fading. 'Hank' Fonda's career continues to grow in stature and to diversify at a staggering pace.

He was born on May 16, 1905, in Grand Island, Nebraska, where his father owned a printing company. Fonda pursued an early ambition to be a writer, majoring in journalism at the University of Minnesota, but he dropped out after two years as he was having to work to pay his tuition fees and could not find enough energies for his studies. Mrs Marlon Brando Sr introduced him to the Omaha Community Theatre where he spent three years, totally stage-struck and often unpaid, before entering vaudeville and appearing in a series of sketches, which he had written himself, with an old Abraham Lincoln impersonator, George Billinger.

Moving on again he joined the University Players, a New England stock company whose members included Joshua Logan, James Stewart and Margaret Sullavan (who became Fonda's first wife). At this stage of his acting career he was equally interested in scenic design but, landing the lead part in the play *The Farmer Takes a Wife* in 1934, his future was decided. Brooks Atkinson, theatre critic of the *New York Times*, realized exactly in which qualities the actor's strengths resided: 'Henry Fonda . . . gives a manly, modest performance of captivating simplicity.' Recalling that shuffling, clean-cut, all-American boy whose naive idealism was matched by his resolute strength of character, Fonda has commented:

'This shy self-conscious boy was not at all self-conscious on the stage. I was behind a mask fashioned by a playwright, and I could do anything because it wasn't me on that stage.

The audiences weren't looking at me. They were looking at whoever my character was.'

He has always prided himself on this anonymity, part of his intuitive instinct for drawing out a character:

'Usually, I don't have a method . . . I either like a part in a script, or I don't, and if I like it, I'll probably do it. I think the writer has done the homework that's necessary to get the specifics of a character, and he's put it there.'

Fonda entered into a contract with Walter Wanger that stipulated he make two films a year, but which allowed him to continue acting on the stage. He was only third choice for the film version of *The Farmer Takes a Wife* (1935), but neither Gary Cooper nor Joel McCrea was available. Fonda has never forgotten the director Victor Fleming's advice on the

different techniques involved in projecting oneself as a film actor as opposed to acting on the stage. Insistent on getting the right parts, he has often had to be talked into a role – he only appeared in Fritz Lang's *The Return of Frank James* (1940) after taking the advice of his friend, director Henry Hathaway.

During the Thirties Fonda made a mixed bag of action and romantic films, society comedies and socially committed stories such as *You Only Live Once* (1937); although the latter was a success, he loathed working with Lang, its director, whom he described as 'a master puppeteer'. But he came into his own with three films for Ford – 'Ford's communication was to chew you out to stop you from acting' – namely *Young Mr Lincoln*, *Drums Along the Mohawk* (both 1939) and *The Grapes of Wrath* (1940). They were all made at 20th Century-Fox, as was Henry King's *Jesse James* (1939), in which he perceptively accepted the second lead to Tyrone Power as he realized that it was the meatier characterization.

At the time, Fonda achieved greater acclaim

Above left: Fonda's first film role was that of an Erie Canal farmer of the 1800s in The Farmer Takes a Wife *with Janet Gaynor. Above: in Vincent McEveety's moody Western* Firecreek *(1968), he played a wandering badman gunning for the town sheriff (played by Fonda's old friend James Stewart)*

for his portrayal of Lincoln than for his Tom Joad in *The Grapes of Wrath*, though his wily studio boss, Darryl F. Zanuck, had used the role of Joad as the bait to lure Fonda into a long-term contract. With the single exception of *The Ox-Bow Incident* (1943), Fonda loathes all the films he made at the studio in this period and was much happier on loan, making *The Lady Eve* (1941) for Paramount and *The Male Animal* (1942) for Warners. Zanuck then delayed Fonda's entry into active naval duty so he could make *The Immortal Sergeant* (1943).

Finally freed by the studio, Fonda served with distinction in the Central Pacific, winning a Bronze Star and a Presidential Citation, and attained the rank of Lieutenant (Senior Grade). After the war he returned to Fox and Ford, scoring a great critical success as a gentle, thoughtful Wyatt Earp in *My Darling Clementine* (1946). But he had an increasing yen to go back to the stage and, after appearing as the disciplinarian cavalry Lieutenant-Colonel Owen Thursday in *Fort Apache* (1948), left the screen until 1955, apart from a guest appearance and some narrations for documentaries

Filmography

1935 The Farmer Takes a Wife; 'Way Down East; I Dream Too Much. **'36** The Trail of the Lonesome Pine; The Moon's Our Home; Spendthrift. **'37** Wings of the Morning (GB); You Only Live Once; Slim; That Certain Woman. **'38** I Met My Love Again; Jezebel; Blockade; Spawn of the North; The Mad Miss Manton. **'39** Jesse James; Let Us Live; The Story of Alexander Graham Bell (GB: The Modern Miracle); Young Mr Lincoln; Drums Along the Mohawk. **'40** The Grapes of Wrath; Lillian Russell; The Return of Frank James; Chad Hanna. **'41** The Lady Eve; Wild Geese Calling; You Belong to Me (GB: Good Morning, Doctor). **'42** The Male Animal; Rings on Her Fingers; The Magnificent Dope; Tales of Manhattan; The Big Street; The Battle of Midway (doc) (narr. only); It's Everybody's War (doc) (narr. only). **'43** The Immortal Sergeant; The Ox-Bow Incident (GB: Strange Incident). **'46** My Darling Clementine. **'47** The Long Night; The Fugitive; Daisy Kenyon. **'48** A Miracle Can Happen/On Our Merry Way; Fort Apache. **'49** Jigsaw (guest). **'50** Grant Wood (short) (narr. only); Home of the Homeless (short) (narr. only). **'51** The Growing Years (short) (narr. only); Benjy (doc) (narr. only); Pictora, Adventure in Art (short series incorporating Grant Wood, 1950) (narr. only). **'52** The Impressionable Years (short) (narr only). **'55** Mister Roberts. **'56** War and Peace. **'57** The Wrong Man; Twelve Angry Men; The Tin Star. **'58** Stage Struck; Reach for Tomorrow (short) (narr. only). **'59** Warlock; The Man Who Understood Women. **'62** Advise and Consent; The Longest Day; How the West Was Won. **'63** Spencer's Mountain; Rangers of Yellowstone (short) (narr. only). **'64** The Best Man; Fail Safe; Sex and the Single Girl. **'65** The Rounders; In Harm's Way; La Guerra Segreta (IT-FR-GER) (USA: The Dirty Game). **'66** A Big Hand for the Little Lady (GB: Big Deal at Dodge City). **'67** Welcome to Hard Times (GB: Killer on a Horse). **'68** Firecreek; The Golden Flame (short) (narr. only); All About People (short) (narr. only); Yours, Mine and Ours; Madigan; Born to Buck (narr. only); The Boston Strangler; C'era una Volta il West (USA/GB: Once Upon a Time in the West). **'69** An Impression of John Steinbeck – Writer (short) (narr. only). **'70** Too Late the Hero; The Cheyenne Social Club; There Was a Crooked Man. **'71** Sometimes a Great Notion (GB: Never Give an Inch). **'73** Le Serpent (FR) (USA retitling for TV: The Serpent/Night Flight From Moscow); Il Mio Nome e Nessuno 11 (IT-FR-GER) (USA/GB: My Name Is Nobody); Film Making Techniques (short) (interviewee only); Ash Wednesday. **'74** Mussolini: Ultimo Atto (IT) (USA: The Last Four Days/The Last Days of Mussolini); Valley Forge (short) (narr. only). **'76** Midway (GB: Battle of Midway). **'77** Tentacoli (IT-USA) (USA: Tentacles); Rollercoaster; The World of Andrew Wyeth (short) (guest); Alcohol Abuse: The Early Warning Signs (short) (narr. only). **'78** Big Yellow Schooner to Byzantium (short) (narr. only); The Swarm; Fedora (GER); Home to Stay (CAN); Elegant John and His Ladies/Last of the Cowboys (reissued as The Great Smokey Roadblock). **'79** Wanda Nevada; Meteor; City of Fear.

'I haven't seen over half my films, but in the ones that I have seen, even those that were received well critically, and those that have won awards, I wish I had had the chance to rehearse more. It is the building of the part that matters; you don't know what you could have done had you done it 18 more times, or 1800 more times.'

Fonda certainly had the chance to perfect *Mister Roberts*, with three years on Broadway and on tour in this famous comedy of life on a battleship during World War II. He then starred in two other Broadway hits, *Point of No Return* in 1951, and *The Caine Mutiny Court Martial* in 1955. There was an outcry when Warners offered Brando the Mister Roberts' role in the 1955 film version, and Ford, who was assigned to direct, insisted on Fonda for the part. Sadly, they fell out over interpretation with Fonda complaining about the injection of what he considered too much low comic relief,

and reputedly blows were struck. Ford, in any case, was ill and had to be replaced.

Although he has never sought publicity, Henry Fonda has never been far away from the public eye – with a string of failed marriages and his stormy relations with his gifted children, Peter and Jane. Off screen, Fonda can be a moody and often angry man, but he kept his cool remarkably when one tactless wife of a producer asked him: 'What was it like to be married to all those women and two of them committed suicide?' He answered softly:

'Well, I loved them all – in a way I still do. I could not have saved one of them and they could not save me. Everyone has to save himself.'

He reached another peak in his career with *Twelve Angry Men* (1957), in which he plays a juror with a dissenting voice of reason who persuades the other jurors to waive a verdict of guilty on a defendant in a murder trial. Fonda

set up his own company to make the film:
'The one chance I had in the cinema was with Sidney Lumet, making *Twelve Angry Men* . . . we got the artists together, most of them theatre actors, and we rehearsed for two weeks like a play . . . the actors had the benefit, and the thrill, of building their parts from the beginning to the end like a graph.'

Henry Fonda is a committed actor. When the strains of a sustained programme of film-making, Broadway, stage touring and a one-man television show proved physically over-taxing, he entered hospital to have a heart pacemaker inserted, and was back on stage within the week. As to the future, he simply intends to carry on as before:

'I'm not sure I have any goals as an actor, other than to be good and real. All any actor can do with the part is to be as good as he can, try to think it out as much as he can, suggest as much as he can.'
KINGSLEY CANHAM

Above: Fonda and Jackie Cooper in the 1940 sequel to Jesse James. Above right: as the malicious killer taken unawares by Charles Bronson in Once Upon a Time in the West *(1968). Below right: with William Powell and Jack Lemmon in* Mister Roberts. *Below left: as 'Juror No. 8' in* Twelve Angry Men

1

Directed by John Ford 1940

Prod co: 20th Century-Fox. **prod:** Darryl F. Zanuck. **assoc prod/sc:** Nunnally Johnson, from the novel by John Steinbeck. **photo:** Gregg Toland. **ed:** Robert Simpson. **art dir:** Richard Day, Mark Lee Kirk, Thomas Little. **mus:** Alfred Newman. **sd:** George Leverett, Roger Heman. **sd eff ed:** Robert Parrish. **ass dir:** Edward O'Fearna. **r/t:** 129 minutes. New York premiere, 24 January 1940.

Cast: Henry Fonda (*Tom Joad*), Jane Darwell (*Ma Joad*), John Carradine (*Casy*), Charley Grapewin (*Grampa Joad*), Dorris Bowdon (*Rosaharn*), Russell Simpson (*Pa Joad*), O.Z. Whitehead (*Al*), John Qualen (*Muley*), Eddie Quillan (*Connie*), Zeffie Tilbury (*Grandma Joad*), Frank Sully (*Noah*), Frank Darlen (*Uncle John*), Darryl Hickman (*Winfield*), Shirley Mills (*Ruth Joad*), Grant Mitchell (*guardian*), Ward Bond (*policeman*), Frank Faylen (*Tim*), Joe Sawyer (*accountant*), Harry Tyler (*Bert*), Charles B. Middleton (*conductor*), John Arledge (*Davis*), Hollis Jewell (*Muley's son*), Paul Guilfoyle (*Floyd*), Charles D. Brown (*Wilkie*), Roger Imhof (*Thomas*), William Pawley (*Bill*), Arthur Aylesworth (*Father*), Charles Tannen (*Joe*), Selmar Jackson (*inspector*), Eddy Waller (*proprietor*), David Hughes (*Frank*), Cliff Clark (*townsman*), Adrian Morris (*agent*), Robert Homans (*Spencer*), Irving Bacon (*conductor*), Kitty McHugh (*Mae*).

The social indignation of John Steinbeck's novel *The Grapes of Wrath* was certainly the finest statement of faith in the common man published in the Thirties. Darryl F. Zanuck's decision to film the book indicated his business acumen and his ability to assess public taste. His courage, vision and careful choice of talents ensured that Steinbeck's work was brought to the screen virtually intact.

Nunnally Johnson's script (doctored by Zanuck) developed the central incidents of the book into a continuous pattern of action and narrative. Though it failed to chart fully the economic, political and social background, the script gained in power and simplicity what it lost in perspective. Johnson retained many lines of dialogue from the novel, but did not hesitate to switch them between characters when it suited the dramatic purposes of the film; he avoided too many long monologues and invested the dialogue with the ring of the people's voice. The script was contractually bound to retain the theme of the book, and Steinbeck passed the script on August 8, 1939. Contrary to popular belief, Henry Fonda was not announced as the star until some time later.

Gregg Toland shot the bulk of the film using only natural light; his unhesitating use of darkness (at a time when most Hollywood films were brightly lit) enhances the picture's emotional power far more than Alfred Newman's unremarkable musical score. Toland's use of long shots punctuates the gruelling journey, both separating its incidents and linking them. His camera plays a more dynamic role in dramatic scenes.

Under John Ford's economical direction the film maintains its impetus until the end; and his knack of placing just the right face in the smallest role dignifies the supporting parts.

Fonda gives a fine, unsentimental performance as Tom Joad, often concealing his emotions beneath a mask of apologetic gruffness. After the death of Casy (John Carradine) – who embodies the religious and political issues of the film – Tom inherits the former preacher's sense of mission; he renounces his personal identity to gain the larger one of 'leader of the people'. In contrast, the casting of Jane Darwell as his indomitable mother was a mistake. Though she won an Oscar for Best Supporting Actress, her plump niceness is plainly at odds with the lean, stringy, rawhide woman of the

4

novel. Ma Joad would have been superbly characterized by Beulah Bondi, who was the original choice for the part.

As the child of Irish parents, Ford was particularly attracted to the project since its story bore a resemblance to a similar situation that arose during the Irish famines of the 1840s; however, his vision became one of American pioneers opening up the West in search of a Garden of Eden. Yet his film breaks new ground by representing in human terms some of the grim costs and results of this pioneering drive. It touches on a few of the effects of land speculation and agricultural mechanization, dramatizing the plight of these victims of American history, and it achieves a more poignant impact than contemporary films like *Our Daily Bread* (1934), *The Trail of the Lonesome Pine* (1936) and *Of Human Hearts* (1938).

Documentaries, such as *The Plow That Broke the Plains* (1936) and *The River* (1938), and books, like *An American Exodus* and *Let Us Now Praise Famous Men*, had highlighted the image of the gaunt,

hungry 'tractored-out' farmer, no longer menaced by Indians in his struggle to survive, but by the pitiless spectre of starvation. This was caused by wholesale evictions from farms by landowners who wished to employ new agricultural machinery. It cannot be said that *The Grapes of Wrath* fully faces up to this serious social issue; for example, the film eliminates the novel's description of the still-birth of Rosaharn's baby, which in context becomes a shocking indictment of society. In addition, the film's depiction of Tom Joad's conversion to the cause of working people is tainted with sentimentality.

At the film's premiere, the first three rows were reserved for officers and directors of the Chase National Bank and their wives. Ironically this was one of the institutions which controlled the western land companies that 'tractored' the Joads, and thousands like them, off their farms. The Bank was about to make further profits from this dramatization of their ex-tenants' plight, since they were also the bankers for the film's production company.   KINGSLEY CANHAM

Returning from a four-year prison sentence for killing a man, Tom Joad finds his Kansas home deserted. His family have been evicted by the land company who wish to farm the dying soil more economically using new agricultural machinery. Tom locates his family at the home of a relative.

They set out for California in a rickety old truck (1), but the 'promised land' soon dashes their hopes (2).

Lured to a miserable township by promises of work as fruit-pickers, they are hounded and exploited by unscrupulous farmers and labour agents and

persecuted by townsfolk and corrupt state police (3). The family's moral strength is tested by death and separation (4). Casy, an unfrocked preacher, attempts to organize a strike for better conditions (5) and is murdered by strike-breakers. Tom revenges his death, but becomes a fugitive from justice, finding only temporary refuge at a government transit camp that is humanely run (6). He tells Ma Joad of his decision to carry on Casy's mission – to fight for the common rights of the working man (7). He leaves his mother determined to hold the remainder of the family together.

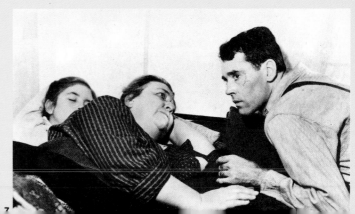

Key films of 1939

Drums Along the Mohawk. USA. **prod co:** 20th Century-Fox. **prod:** Raymond Griffith. **dir:** John Ford. **sc:** Lamarr Trotti, Sonya Levien, William Faulkner, from the novel by Walter D. Edmonds. **photo:** Bert Glennon, Ray Rennahan. **ed:** Robert Simpson. **art dir:** Richard Day, Mark-Lee Kirk. **with:** Claudette Colbert, Henry Fonda, Edna May Oliver, Eddie Collins, John Carradine, Doris Bowdon.

Ford's first colour film, and his only one to deal with the War of American Independence, shows the struggle of colonists against the Indians. It is also his most positive and unambiguous portrait of the growth of a small American community.

Gone With the Wind; directed by Victor Fleming – see special feature in Chapter 18.

Jamaica Inn. Britain. **prod co:** Mayflower. **prod:** Erich Pommer, Charles Laughton. **dir:** Alfred Hitchcock. **sc:** Sidney Gilliat, Joan Harrison, from the novel by Daphne du Maurier. **add dial:** J.B. Priestley. **adap:** Alma Reville. **photo:** Harry Stradling, Bernard Knowles. **ed:** Robert Hamer. **sp eff:** Harry Watt. **art dir:** Thomas N. Morahan. **mus:** Eric Fenby. **mus dir:** Frederic Lewis. **with:** Charles Laughton, Horace Hodges, Hay Petrie, Frederick Piper, Leslie Banks, Maureen O'Hara, Emlyn Williams, Robert Newton, Mervyn Johns.
An unusually elaborate film for Hitchcock and, together with Waltzes From Vienna and Under Capricorn, one of his few period pieces. Laughton's portrayal of the evil Cornish squire Pergallan dominates the film but the sets and decor are also remarkable achievements.

Le Jour se Lève. (Daybreak). France. **prod co:** Productions Sigma. **prod:** Paul Medeux. **dir:** Marcel Carné. **sc:** Jacques Viot, Jacques Prévert. **photo:** Curt Courant, Philippe Agostini, André Bac. **ed:** René le Hénaff. **art dir:** Alexandre Trauner. **mus:** Maurice Jaubert. **with:** Jean Gabin, Jules Berry, Arletty, Jacqueline Laurent, Mady Berry, Bernard Blier.
Containing one of Gabin's most characteristic performances (as a doomed gangster waiting for the end) Le Jour se Lève is also the key film in the Carné–Prévert canon of romantic pessimism. Indeed on the outbreak of war the French authorities banned the film as demoralizing. It was remade as The Long Night in 1947 with Henry Fonda.

Juarez. USA. **prod co:** Warner Bros. **prod:** Hal B. Wallis. **assoc prod:** Henry Blake. **dir:** William Dieterle. **sc:** John Huston, Wolfgang Reinhardt, Aeneas Mackenzie, Abem Finkel, from the play *Juarez and Maximilian* by Franz Werfel and the novel *The Phantom Crown* by Bertita Harding. **photo:** Tony Gaudio. **ed:** Anton Grot, Leo Kuter. **mus:** Erich Wolfgang Korngold. **mus dir:** Leo F. Forbstein. **dial dir:** Irving Rapper. **with:** Paul Muni, Bette Davis, Brian Aherne, Claude Rains, John Garfield, Donald Crisp, Gale Sondergaard.
The most lavish of Warners' biopics, this film dealt with the struggles of the Emperor Maximilian and the Mexican revolutionary leader Juarez against each other and their common foes, the European colonialists. Through this analogy the film pointed up some contemporary parallels like the growth of dictatorships in Europe.

Midnight. USA. **prod co:** Paramount. **prod:** Arthur Hornblow Jr. **dir:** Mitchell Leisen. **sc:** Charles Brackett, Billy Wilder, from the story by Edwin Justus Mayer, Franz Schulz. **photo:** Charles Lang. **ed:** Doane Harrison. **art dir:** Hans Dreier, Robert Usher. **mus:** Frederick Hollander. **with:** Claudette Colbert, Don Ameche, Francis Lederer, John Barrymore, Mary Astor, Elaine Barrie, Hedda Hopper.
A fine screwball comedy in which Colbert plays a hard-boiled dame living on her wits in Paris and Mary Astor plays her scheming rival. The script is one of Wilder and Brackett's most cynical and the superb design testifies to Leisen's early training as an art director.

Mr Smith Goes to Washington. USA. **prod co:** Columbia. **prod/dir:** Frank Capra. **sc:** Sidney Buchman, from the story 'The Gentleman from Montana' by Lewis R. Foster. **photo:** Joseph Walker. **ed:** Gene Havlick, Al Clark. **art dir:** Lionel Banks. **mus:** Dmitri Tiomkin. **mus dir:** Morris W. Stoloff. **2nd unit dir:** Charles Vidor. **with:** James Stewart, Jean Arthur, Claude Rains, Edward Arnold, Guy Kibbee, Thomas Mitchell, Eugene Pallette, Beulah Bondi, H.B. Warner, Harry Carey.
The story of the backwoods political innocent who is elected senator and clashes with the corrupt machinery of government in Washington. This riotous comedy provides Capra with a vehicle for his populist sentiments and his support of the 'ordinary' man against the 'system'.

Ninotchka. USA. **prod co:** MGM. **prod/dir:** Ernst Lubitsch. **sc:** Charles Brackett, Billy Wilder, Walter Reisch, from a story by Melchior Lengyel. **photo:** William Daniels. **art dir:** Cedric Gibbons, Randall Duell. **costumes:** Adrian. **mus:** Werner R. Heymann. **ed:** Gene Ruggiero. **with:** Greta Garbo, Melvyn Douglas, Ina Clair, Sig Ruman, Felix Bressart, Alexander Granach, Bela Lugosi, Gregory Gaye, Rolfe Sedan, Edwin Maxwell, Richard Carle.
Billed as the film in which 'Garbo laughs', Ninotchka is also an excellent example of the 'Lubitsch touch'. The plot revolves around a young Soviet woman on the loose in Paris and provides ample opportunities for razor-sharp satire and wit.

Northwest Passage. USA. **prod co:** MGM. **prod:** Hunt Stromberg. **dir:** King Vidor. **sc:** Laurence Stallings, Talbot Jennings, from a novel by Kenneth Roberts. **photo:** Sidney Wagner, William V. Skall. **ed:** Conrad A. Nervig.

art dir: Cedric Gibbons, Malcolm Brown. **mus:** Herbert Stothart. **sd:** Douglas Shearer. **with:** Spencer Tracy, Robert Young, Walter Brennan, Ruth Hussey, Nat Pendleton, Louis Hector.
Vidor's 'pre-Western' about early American struggles against French and Indian forces around the St Laurence Basin has been variously interpreted as a hymn to colonization and as a vigorous adventure story testifying to Vidor's fascination with American history.

Only Angels Have Wings. USA. **prod co:** Columbia. **prod/dir:** Howard Hawks. **sc:** Jules Furthman, from a story by Howard Hawks. **photo:** Joseph Walker, Elmer Dyer. **ed:** Viola Lawrence. **art dir:** Lionel Banks. **mus:** Dmitri Tiomkin. **with:** Cary Grant, Jean Arthur, Thomas Mitchell, Richard Barthelmess, Rita Hayworth, Sig Ruman, Noah Berry Jr.
A small, tightly-knit, predominantly male group runs a hazardous airmail service in South America – a typical Hawksian situation in which the director's economic style eloquently understates the dramatic situations and the deeply emotional bonds between the characters.

La Règle du Jeu; directed by Jean Renoir – see special feature in Chapter 16.

The Roaring Twenties. USA. **prod co:** Warner Bros. **prod:** Mark Hellinger. **dir:** Raoul Walsh. **sc:** Jerry Wald, Richard Macaulay, Robert Rossen, from a story by Mark Hellinger. **photo:** Ernie Haller. **ed:** Jack Killifer. **art dir:** Max Parker. **mus dir:** Leo F. Forbstein. **with:** James Cagney, Priscilla Lane, Humphrey Bogart, Gladys George, Jeffrey Lynn, Frank McHugh.
An account of the varying fortunes of two World War I veterans faced with unemployment and the lure of money in the bootlegging business. The film's recognition of the social ills produced by the war and the Depression is a product of the New Deal philosophy.

Stagecoach; directed by John Ford – see special feature in this chapter.

The Stars Look Down. Britain. **prod co:** Grafton Films. **prod:** Isadore Goldsmith, Fred Zelnik. **dir:** Carol Reed. **sc:** J.B. Williams, from the novel by A.J. Cronin. **photo:** Mutz Greenbaum, Henry Harris. **ed:** Reginald Beck. **art dir:** James Carter. **sd:** Norman Davis. **with:** Michael Redgrave, Margaret Lockwood, Emlyn Williams, Nancy Price, Edward Rigby, Desmond Tester, Cecil Parker, Allan Jeayes, Linda Travers, Milton Rosmer, George Carney, Ivor Barnard, Olga Lindo, David Markham.
Heralded on its release as a landmark of working-class drama, this film portrayed the struggles of miners in North-East England and featured one man's attempts to become a Member of Parliament in spite of his background.

The Vyborg Side. USSR. **prod co:** Lenfilm. **dir/sc:** Leonid Trauberg, Grigori Kozintsev. **photo:** Andrei Moskvin, G. Filatov. **art dir:** V. Vlasov. **mus:** Dmitri Shostakovich. **with:** Boris Chirkov, Valentina Kibardina, Natalia Uzhki, Mikhail Zharov, Maxim Strauch, Mikhail Gelovani, Yuri Tolubeyev.
The last film in the Gorky trilogy, it deals chiefly with the Bolsheviks' attempts to retain their hold on government after the capture of the Winter Palace. Both Lenin and Stalin are clearly established as heroic figures who are given equivalent responsibility for the Revolution.

The Wizard of Oz. USA. **prod co:** MGM. **prod:** Mervyn LeRoy. **dir:** Victor Fleming. **sc:** Noel Langley, Florence Ryerson, Edgar Allan Woolf, from the book by Frank L. Baum. **photo:** Harold Rosson. **ed:** Blanche Sewell. **art dir:** Cedric Gibbons. **mus:** Harold Arlen. **lyr:** E.Y. Harburg. **mus dir:** Herbert Stothart. **dance dir:** Bobby Connolly. **with:** Judy Garland, Frank Morgan, Ray Bolger, Bert Lahr, Jack Haley, Billie Burke, Charles Grapewin.

The most expensive production of MGM's first fifteen years, originally intended for Shirley Temple but fortunately given to Judy Garland who became a star as a direct result of her performance as Dorothy. One of the most enduring, colourful and delightful of all fantasy films.

Wuthering Heights. USA. **prod co:** Goldwyn-UA. **prod:** Samuel Goldwyn. **dir:** William Wyler. **sc:** Ben Hecht, Charles MacArthur, from the novel by Emily Brontë. **photo:** Gregg Toland. **ed:** Daniel Mandell. **mus dir:** Alfred Newman. **art dir:** James Basevi. **sd:** Paul Neal. **with:** Laurence Olivier, Merle Oberon, David Niven, Flora Robson. Donald Crisp, Geraldine Fitzgerald, Leo J. Carroll.
This full-blooded adaptation of Brontë's classic tale of romantic love set on the Yorkshire Moors is the film that perhaps most accurately sums up the prestige-seeking style of Goldwyn productions.

Young Mr Lincoln. USA. **prod co:** Cosmopolitan/20th Century-Fox. **prod:** Kenneth MacGowan. **dir:** John Ford. **sc:** Lamarr Trotti. **photo:** Bert Glennon. **ed:** Walter Thompson. **art dir:** Richard Day, Mark-Lee Kirk. **with:** Henry Fonda, Alice Brady, Marjorie Weaver, Ward Bond, Donald Meek, Spencer Charters, Arleen Whelan, Eddie Collins, Pauline Moore, Richard Cromwell, Doris Bowdon, Eddie Quilan.
From a contemporary perspective the film's subject was the creation of the Lincoln myth as a corner-stone of American history. The film has also been read (in a crucial analysis by the French journal Cahiers du Cinéma) *as an investigation of the whole myth-making process, in which cinema itself plays such a key role.*

Zangiku Monogatari (*The Story of the Last Chrysanthemums*). Japan. **prod co:** Shochiku. **dir:** Kenji Mizoguchi. **sc:** Yoshikata Yoda, Matsutaro Kawaguchi, from a story by Shofu Muramatsu. **photo:** Shigeto Miki. **mus:** Senji Ito. **with:** Kakuko Mori, Shotaro Hanayagi, Yoko Umemura, Gomjoro Kawarazaki, Tokusaburo Arashi, Kokichi Takata, Ryotaro Kawanami, Nobuko Fushimi.
The first of Mizoguchi's four-film cycle on performing artists and the film by which he freed himself from studio interference, it is a fascinating insight into the tightly enclosed and highly traditional world of the Kabuki theatre.

Chapter 20

Europe at war

When war broke out in 1939 the cinema was mobilized to provide vital footage from the front and morale-boosting propaganda for the home screens

When Archduke Ferdinand was assassinated at Sarajevo in June 1914, precipitating World War I, the movie industry was still in its infancy. Many pioneers were just getting into their stride, exploring the power of the medium and its potential hold over audiences. When Hitler invaded Poland in September 1939, precipitating World War II, a huge, profitable, world-wide industry had long been established with massive resources of equipment, manpower and 'star power'.

European governments had an unparalleled weapon at their command in the film medium. It was vastly popular with the public, it could easily disseminate war information, instruction and, if necessary, lies, through documentaries, newsreels or (most persuasively of all) in dramatic features. The cinema even served a valuable purpose by providing a few hours of escapist fun before audiences stepped out into their beleaguered, blitzed cities. There was no better way of keeping a controlling hand on national morale.

In a way the industry had long been preparing for war, though the bosses – their eyes glued to production schedules and box-office receipts – might not have realized it. Ever since Hitler took control in 1933, studios throughout Europe and America had absorbed directors, producers, cameramen, writers, composers, actors and actresses, all escaping from the threat of persecution under Nazi Germany's anti-Semitic laws.

Hitler himself had partly designed the 1934 Nuremberg rally as a cinema spectacle (duly filmed as *Triumph of the Will*). In place of Hollywood's all-talking, all-singing, all-dancing musicals, here was the Nazi equivalent – all-shouting, all-stomping, all-saluting. For Hitler knew that potent images and the emotional fury of his speeches had far more power to persuade than any rational argument.

The world watched Hitler's activities with unease and incomprehension. He had risen to power by marshalling nationalistic feelings of discontent with the 1918 defeat and the harsh terms of the Versailles treaty. He had rearmed the country and proclaimed the notion of *lebensraum* – the right of the German nation to have enough living space. And by the end of the Thirties Hitler was taking his first steps in this search for extra accommodation by

attacks, annexations and alliances.

Austria was invaded in March 1938. Sudetenland (on Czechoslovakia's borders) in October. Further east, Hitler formed an opportunistic non-aggression pact with Stalin. In the West, Britain's Prime Minister, Neville Chamberlain, naively joined the French in a policy of appeasement and met the Führer at Berchtesgaden and Munich in September 1938. On his return he waved at the newsreel cameramen a bit of paper which promised 'peace in our time'. Unfortunately it guaranteed nothing of the kind. Czechoslovakia fell to Hitler in March; with the invasion of Poland one year later, Britain and France entered the battle and the world war was on.

Britain's television service, only three years old and serving a tiny minority, was promptly shut down. Film-studio space was requisitioned for storing ammunition, greatcoats and all the paraphernalia of war. But the industry continued. Indeed, the experience of working with limited resources under pressure concentrated the minds of many film-makers. And the involvement of the entire country in the war effort – all classes, both sexes – made many old cinema genres and attitudes inadequate. No longer could studios rely upon laboured farces or thrillers featuring stereotypes of the elegant rich or the rude poor.

The transformation, however, did not occur overnight. Alexander Korda's *The Lion Has Wings* (dir. Michael Powell, Brian Desmond Hurst, Adrian Brunel), a hopeful salute to the fighting power of the RAF, was rushed into release in the autumn of 1939. The film was a mixture of newsreel footage, and mocked-up battles but was over-burdened by a quaintly genteel, fictional sub-plot.

Yet slowly the industry buckled to. The Ministry

Top: Douglass Montgomery (left) as an American fighter-pilot teams up with RAF aces David Tomlinson (centre) and Trevor Howard (right) in Anthony Asquith's Battle of Britain film The Way to the Stars. *Above: in Cavalcanti's* Went the Day Well? *a sleepy English village is invaded and occupied by Germans disguised as Royal Engineers, but eventually the British Army and the Home Guard come to the rescue. Left: the San Demetrio was a merchant ship carrying a precious cargo of oil from the USA to besieged Britain. Crippled by enemy fire, the ship limped home to port, a testament to the quiet heroism of the times*

A Great Adventure Story of the sea
SAN DEMETRIO
london
SOS
PRODUCED BY MICHAEL BALCON
Directed by CHARLES FREND Written by ROBERT HAMER & CHARLES FREND
WALTER FITZGERALD · MERVYN JOHNS · RALPH MICHAEL
ROBERT BEATTY · GORDON JACKSON · FREDERICK PIPER

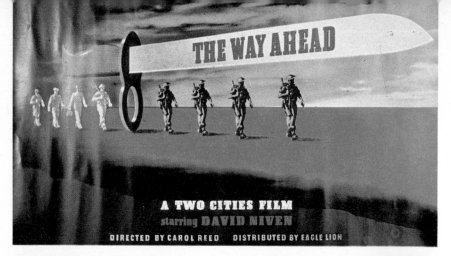

THE WAY AHEAD

A TWO CITIES FILM
starring DAVID NIVEN

DIRECTED BY CAROL REED   DISTRIBUTED BY EAGLE LION

Top: David Niven had trained at Sandhurst in the Thirties and saw active service during the war before returning to films. This one, scripted by Eric Ambler and Peter Ustinov, was a great success and was used at Sandhurst as a training film. Above: The Bells Go Down featured the work of the Auxiliary Fire Service during London's Blitz. Below: The Gentle Sex (1943), showing women's role in the war, was directed by Leslie Howard

together to produce *The True Glory* (1945), a film charting Europe's liberation.

But the greatest changes in British cinema occurred in feature films. Previously the feature industry had been inhibited by American competition, and the presence of so many foreign moguls and visiting directors hardly promoted indigenous product. But with the war, the visitors returned home and rising talent, previously confined to scriptwriting or editing, eagerly moved into the director's chair – David Lean, Charles Frend, Frank Launder, Sidney Gilliat were among them.

All at once there were dramatic subjects to make feature films about: life at RAF and army bases in *The Way Ahead* (1944) and *The Way to the Stars* (1945); war service on the high seas in *In Which We Serve* (1942) and *San Demetrio, London* (1943); and in the munitions factories – *Millions Like Us* (1943). Here was an area where the Americans could not compete. The tone of the films – humorous, quietly heroic – was also unique.

British films found an audience and a popularity they had never enjoyed before. As the war went on escapist entertainment increased in volume and popularity. Traditional tosh was given a topical inflection in *Dangerous Moonlight* (1941), where a Polish concert pianist joined the RAF and played Richard Addinsell's popular 'Warsaw' Concerto.

As the bombs fell on her cities, Britain's cinemas kept open a vital channel of information about the war

Gainsborough studios produced period melodramas like *The Man in Grey* (1943), with ladies and gentlemen behaving amorally, dressed in wigs, masks and riding boots. On a far higher artistic level were the films of Michael Powell and his Hungarian collaborator Emeric Pressburger, who viewed the war through a complex maze of satire and fantasy in bold creations like *The Life and Death of Colonel Blimp* (1943), a film that was loathed by Churchill for its caricature of the army's upper crust. The same team also produced *A Canterbury Tale* (1944). And no world war, however devastating, could halt Gabriel Pascal's determination to film Shaw's *Caesar and Cleopatra* (1945), which began shooting at Denham six days after D-Day, despite the threat of flying bombs and the difficulties of securing nubile young ladies and white peacocks to flit by in the backgrounds.

While British cinema stumbled uncertainly into war production, Germany began with its propaganda machine in top working condition. Ever since Hitler secured control in 1933, his propaganda minister Josef Goebbels had organized the industry to fit Nazi requirements. Jews were banned immediately; a film censor office was established in 1934; film criticism (and all arts criticism) was abolished in 1936, thereafter newspapers could print only facts, not opinions. The independent studios, including the mighty Ufa, were absorbed by the government during 1937. By 1939 many of Germany's best film talents had emigrated; those that remained were regarded as part of the country's fighting forces.

Goebbels sensed how powerful a weapon film could be, but he had known for a long time that audiences resented hard-core propaganda in fictional, dramatic formats. Instead propaganda was channelled into newsreels, compiled or doctored from material shot at the fighting fronts and decked out with animated maps full of pulsating arrows that indicated German advances.

of Information, after many changes of personnel and unfortunate gestures like the slogan '*Your* Courage, *Your* Cheerfulness, *Your* Resolution, will Bring *Us* Victory' (hardly the best way to bind a nation together), established a solid system of film distribution, sending out to cinemas short films on war topics every week. In addition, travelling projectionists showed films in those parts of the country where there were no proper cinemas.

Style and subject in these shorts varied tremendously. Most artistically polished were the poetic essays of Humphrey Jennings, who found in the war an ideal way of expressing his strong feelings for Britain's cultural heritage. Richard Massingham found a similar niche providing crisp, comic illustrations of wartime regulations, such as bathing in only five inches of water.

At the other end of the scale there were filmed lectures given by Ministry men seated behind desks and blinking nervously. These films were so embarrassing that cinema managers occasionally showed them with the curtains tactfully drawn. But it is clear that some of this huge output had considerable effect – particularly abroad, where America was uninvolved in the fighting until Japan attacked Pearl Harbor in December 1941.

Jennings' *London Can Take It* (devised for showing in Allied countries in 1940) filled out its Blitz images with a commentary by the American journalist Quentin Reynolds, full of praise for London's 'unconquerable spirit and courage'. Later, there was much direct film cooperation between the Allies, as each arm of the services prepared photographed accounts of their operations. In the war's last stages Carol Reed and the American Garson Kanin came

The newsreels were eventually lengthened to as much as forty minutes, and there are reports that cinema doors were carefully secured so that there was no possibility of escape. Special productions were concocted to lower the morale of countries about to be occupied: *Feuertaufe* (1940, Baptism of Fire), a film that glorified the Luftwaffe's conquest of Poland, was shown at the German Embassy in Oslo four days before the invasion of Norway in April 1940. The most notorious production of all, however was *Der Ewige Jude* (1940, The Eternal Jew), an illustrated lecture by Dr Fritz Hippler designed to fan the flames of anti-Semitism to inferno proportions.

Once the newsreels were over, audiences could settle down to suffer bombastic, shoddy epics glorifying various sections of the armed forces, or Veit Harlan's viciously anti-Semitic *Jud Süss* (1940, Jew Süss) – a key exhibit in the post-war trials. Other films aimed at influencing the all-important German youth included *Kadetten* (1941, Cadets) which told the story of young Prussians fighting in 1760 during the Seven Years' War. History, in fact, proved a boon for German film-makers who wanted to please their Nazi overlords without being rabidly propagandistic. German history was, after all, well-stocked with belligerently nationalistic heroes. Films about Frederick the Great of Prussia had long formed a separate genre and the actor Otto Gebühr did little else but play him.

Colonial activities in Africa proved a fruitful source of anti-British propaganda. *Ohm Krüger* (1941, Uncle Kruger), though one of the more impressive productions, offered a wickedly coarse caricature of Queen Victoria and blithely credited the British with inventing concentration camps.

Other films slanted the same way included *Titanic* (1943), where the ship hit the iceberg as a result of the sins of Jewish–English plutocracy, and two films by Goebbels' brother-in-law Max Kimmich, portraying British brutalities in Ireland: *Der Fuchs von Glenarvon* (1940, The Fox of Glenarvon) and *Mein Leben für Irland* (1941, My Life for Ireland).

Many other films were simply escapist entertainment with the odd twinge of propaganda. Goebbels spent much money developing Agfacolor so that German audiences would not lose out on colour films while the rest of the world was enjoying the early Technicolor movies.

In celebration of Ufa's twenty-fifth anniversary, Goebbels planned the highly elaborate fantasy film *Munchhausen* (1943) and studied Disney's feature cartoons and Korda's *The Thief of Bagdad* (1940), and almost produced something comparable. But his monumental undertaking was *Kolberg*, begun in 1943 and completed towards the end of 1944. Geared to the declining course of the war, the film shrewdly portrayed the citizens of Kolberg, besieged during the Napoleonic wars and heroically holding out against amazing odds. By the time the film was ready for release in early 1945, it had no value as propaganda for Germany was close to defeat.

Italy, Germany's ally in Europe, went about its film-making as it went about its fighting, with little of the manic fervour displayed by Goebbels. Most of the country's fascist tub-thumping had been performed in the late Thirties, when mammoth spectacles like *Scipione l'Africano* (1937) were mounted to reflect Italy's new image as an imperial, conquering power. Mussolini had ensured that the film industry was well equipped for the task. The vast Cinecittà film studios were built outside Rome and a film school (Centro Sperimentale di Cinematografia) was established. Mussolini's own son Vittorio pursued an active interest in the medium, securing his name on film credits and on the mast-head of a cinema magazine.

Many directors in the war avoided overt propaganda by retreating to unassuming romantic comedies and tales of provincial life. Some talents did manage to cut through the dross. Alessandro Blasetti's *Quattro Passi fra le Nuvole* (1942, Four Steps in the Clouds) focused sharply on the torments of daily life and had a script co-written by Cesare Zavattini, who was later associated with the director Vittorio De Sica and the neo-realist movement. In the same year, Visconti's *Ossessione* (1942, Obsession), a story of adultery and murder, exploded onto the screen with a kind of brute force unseen before in the Italian cinema.

Equally distinctive, though now largely forgotten, were the films of Francesco De Robertis. He was head of the Naval Ministry's film department and made features imbued with the spirit, and often the footage, of documentary, with non-professional players and location shooting.

La Nave Bianca (1941, The White Ship), for instance, began as a straight documentary about the brave work of a hospital ship. When the authorities wanted to boost the Italian entries at the 1941 Venice Film Festival, De Robertis obligingly built in a love story. Despite such compromises, his films had great impact, and his assistant, Roberto Rossellini (nominally the director of *La Nave Bianca*), followed this style in his own wartime films, *Un Pilota Ritorna* (1942, A Pilot Returns) and *L'Uomo della Croce* (1943, The Man of the Cross).

Looking back on the wartime period from the safe distance of 1960, De Sica observed that 'the war was a decisive experience for all of us. Each of us felt the wild urge to sweep away all the worn-out plots of the Italian cinema and to set up our cameras in the midst of real life.' With the studios under allied bombardment, there was also little alternative.

When Italy surrendered to the Allies and declared war on Germany, it only produced more turmoil, with facilities, equipment and talent scattered throughout the country. De Robertis went north, obstinately loyal to Mussolini who was now installed as puppet-head of the short-lived Salò

Top and above: two examples of the virulent anti-Semitic propaganda shown on German screens during the war: Veit Harlan's Jew Süss *was adapted from a novel while* Der Ewige Jude *purported to be a documentary. Left: the disastrous sinking of the Titanic was blamed on the Jews and the English. During the filming, the director Herbert Selpin complained about the interference of several Nazi naval advisers. He was arrested and later found murdered in his prison cell. Below: Ginette Leclerc in Clouzot's* Le Corbeau *made by the German-backed Continental studio in Paris*

Republic. Rossellini went south and helped establish the cinema branch of the Committee of National Liberation.

A few weeks before the Allies entered Rome in June 1944, his film *Roma, Città Aperta* (1945, *Rome, Open City*) went into production. It was a harsh, moving tale of a Resistance leader's betrayal. But the Italian cinema had already encountered its own kind of liberation.

The Soviet Union's path through the war was just as checkered as Italy's. After several years of mounting tension on its western borders with the dismembered parts of the old Austro–Hungarian Empire, Stalin concluded the non-aggression pact with Hitler in 1939. Feature films described the occupation of Poland, the invasion of Finland; items with anti-German leanings such as *Professor Mamlock* and *Alexander Nevsky* (both 1938) swiftly returned to the vaults. But they soon emerged after June 22, 1941, when Germany's shock invasion brought the pact to an end. Film studios were now uprooted from Moscow to safer surroundings. Various Soviet policies were modified and the customary anti-religious bias was abandoned. Suddenly the much-despised Tsarist generals received homage from the cinema for their part in the Napoleonic wars and other conflicts. There were also new forms of presenting films in the Soviet Union during the war. From August 1941 so-called 'Fighting Film Albums' appeared in cinemas every month; these were a mixture of short films that included miniature dramas, satiric japes and war-effort propaganda. Cameramen at the front maintained a constant stream of filmed dispatches which were edited into powerful documentaries. Alexander Dovzhenko supervised and wrote a moving

From 1940 French cinema was made to toe the Nazi line. When Hitler laid siege to Russia, the cinema became a weapon of resistance

commentary for *The Fight for Our Soviet Ukraine* (1943) that reflected his feelings for his homeland.

Soviet features tended to follow the usual propaganda pattern, spotlighting German atrocities or the heroic activities of the partisans. But as in other countries pure entertainment was never neglected, indeed its quantity increased as the war continued. One of the most popular films of 1944 was a musical entitled *At 6 pm After the War.*

The celebrated Soviet director Sergei Eisenstein spent most of the war engaged on *Ivan the Terrible* in Mosfilm's wartime headquarters at Alma-Ata in Kazakstan. By the end of December 1944, the first part of the projected trilogy was ready for release. The film was a ferocious and monumental excursion into Russia's medieval past, with Tsar Ivan bludgeoning his way from childhood to coronation. As a cinematic history lesson, the film was complex and unsettling for audiences.

For those countries occupied by the Germans – France, Denmark, the Low Countries, Norway – there were obviously fewer opportunities to fly their own flag. German films swamped the cinemas; German film censors controlled production. But the censor's limited powers of perception sometimes allowed carefully disguised anti-Nazi sentiments to slip by. When the Danish censor sat through *Kornet Er i Fare* (1944, The Grain Is in Danger) he obviously regarded it as just a boring short about the *sitophilus granariae*, an insect gnawing its way through a whole harvest of wheat. Audiences of a different persuasion realized the insect was also the Nazi

Top: Feuertaufe *celebrated the role of the German air force in the conquest of Poland, offering heroic images of the 'master race' on the attack. Above:* Ohm Krüger *dealt a blow at the British, charging them with great brutality in the course of their imperialist adventures in Africa. Right:* Les Visiteurs du Soir *proved that the French cinema was able to continue its great tradition despite the restrictions imposed upon it by the German army of Occupation*

pest, gnawing its way through Europe.

France was under Nazi occupation from June 1940, though the official French government still existed at Vichy in an uneasy collaboration with the Germans. The main film studios in Paris were taken over by the German company Continental. A few films like *Les Inconnus Dans la Maison* (1942, *Strangers in the House*) betrayed German sympathies, but there was never any concerted effort to promote Nazi propaganda in the course of the film. Continental's output was noted instead for its imitation of Hollywood genre movies, since American films had been banned in France after 1942.

Many of the best French directors were then abroad – Renoir, Clair, Duvivier; those who remained took the obvious way out of their difficult situation by largely avoiding subjects with a topical edge. Simenon's crime stories, boulevard theatre comedies, Maupassant and Balzac all received uncontroversial adaptations. The bulk of film propaganda, in fact, originated from the Vichy government, whose need to foster some spirit of national pride generated a tepid trickle of features in praise of domestic life, hard work and *la patrie*.

Nevertheless, French cinema still managed to develop a special identity and a fighting spirit. New

directors as varied as Robert Bresson, Jacques Becker and Henri-Georges Clouzot embarked on their careers. Some strove to deal with France's problems allegorically: one of the period's most popular films was Jean Delannoy's *Pontcarral, Colonel d'Empire* (1942, Pontcarral, Colonel of the Empire), with its historical colonel fighting the enemy from his barricaded house at the time of the First Empire.

Equally pertinent was Clouzot's *Le Corbeau* (1943, *The Raven*), a thriller about poison-pen letters, produced by Continental. The movie was so bleak and negative in atmosphere that the director and the writer were accused of serving enemy propaganda through their analysis of a town (and, therefore, country) shaken by guilt and suspicion.

Les Visiteurs du Soir (1942, *The Devil's Own Envoy*) took the viewer back to the Middle Ages for a magical story of love conquering the wiles of the Devil, but there was no overt ideological thrust behind Marcel Carné's direction.

Other film-makers and writers (Jean Cocteau included) also luxuriated in fantasy and visual extravagance, though none could match the power and scope of Carné's *Les Enfants du Paradis* (*Children of Paradise*), a period panorama of Paris life begun during the Occupation in 1942 and released in 1945. In its length (three hours) and its lavishness, this film might almost be a symbol of the French film industry's determination not to be cowed by the war but to come up fighting. Most film industries did, all over Europe.   GEOFF BROWN

Them and Us

The propaganda films of Britain and Germany had the same objectives – to denigrate the enemy and inspire the nation to greater efforts. But, in key with the national characteristics of the two sides, their films differed widely both in style and content

At the outbreak of World War II, all cinemas in Britain were closed. However, their value to the maintenance of morale was soon appreciated and they were reopened after about ten days to become one of the principal sources of recreation for the nation at war. Feature films were seen not just as providing escapist entertainment but also instruction and information. Lord MacMillan, the first wartime Minister of Information, issued a memorandum in 1940 suggesting as themes for propagandist feature films: what Britain is fighting for; how Britain is fighting; and the need for sacrifice if the war is to be won. The British cinema responded to these suggestions and in so doing achieved perhaps its finest hour.

A gentleman's game

The earliest British war film *The Lion Has Wings*, rapidly put together by the producer Alexander Korda and on view by November 1939, was a curious amalgam: part illustrated lecture (the German takeover of Europe and the nature of Nazi ideology); part dramatized documentary (the reconstruction of an RAF raid on the Kiel Canal); and part invocation of Britain's heroic past (Queen Elizabeth I's speech to the troops before the Armada). It did not work as a film – indeed pirated copies were shown in Berlin and provoked great mirth – but it did embody many of the themes which

were to be reworked by later and better films. It also established from the British point of view the images of the two sides in the conflict by intercutting scenes of the good-natured, hard-working, decent, democratic British with the regimented, fanatical, jackbooted Nazis marching in faceless formation. Equally to the point was the contrast in leadership the film demonstrated by cutting from the ranting, demonic figure of Hitler addressing a mass rally to the gentle and modest George VI singing 'Underneath the Spreading Chestnut Tree' at a Boy Scout jamboree.

The film looked both to the past and to the future. To the future in the documentary-style representation of wartime operations, and to the past in the staged sequences of a 'typical British couple' (Ralph Richardson and Merle Oberon) responding to the war – scenes which evoked the rigidly stratified class system enshrined in British films of the Thirties. Initially the cinema continued to reflect this tradition, remaining resolutely middle class in tone and values. In films like Carol Reed's *Night Train to Munich* (1940), the war was treated as a gentlemanly jape in which an upper-class hero (here Rex Harrison) runs rings round the humourless, ranting, dunder-headed Hun. The epitome of the romanticized, class-bound and hopelessly out-of-touch war film was Ealing's *Ships With Wings* (dir. Sergei Nolbandov, 1941)

Top left: Michael Redgrave in Way to the Stars *personified the courage and good humour of the British war hero. Above: unswerving loyalty and obedience were lauded in Nazi propaganda like D III 88*

an absurd yarn in which a disgraced Fleet Air Arm officer (John Clements) redeems his honour by undertaking a suicide mission to destroy a dam on an enemy-held island. It received such a hostile press that Michael Balcon, the head of Ealing studios, resolved henceforth to produce essentially realistic stories of Britain at war. He turned, therefore, to the only group in Britain familiar with the evocation of real-life – the documentarists. This group of talented film-makers, nurtured by John Grierson in the Thirties, was committed to the concept of realism in setting, mood, and content and to the dramatization of the everyday experience of ordinary people. Several members, notably Harry Watt and Alberto Cavalcanti, went to work for Ealing studios, and the documentary influence permeated feature-film production.

The image of a nation divided by class barriers was replaced by the concept of 'The People's War', the idea of ordinary people pulling together to defeat a common foe. Ealing's war films exemplified this new image: *The Foreman Went to France* (dir. Charles

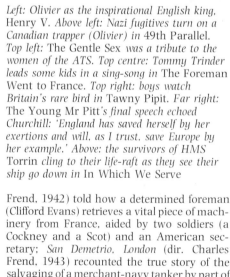

Left: Olivier as the inspirational English king, Henry V. Above left: Nazi fugitives turn on a Canadian trapper (Olivier) in 49th Parallel. *Top left:* The Gentle Sex *was a tribute to the women of the ATS. Top centre: Tommy Trinder leads some kids in a sing-song in* The Foreman Went to France. *Top right: boys watch Britain's rare bird in* Tawny Pipit. *Far right:* The Young Mr Pitt's *final speech echoed Churchill: 'England has saved herself by her exertions and will, as I trust, save Europe by her example.' Above: the survivors of HMS* Torrin *cling to their life-raft as they see their ship go down in* In Which We Serve

Frend, 1942) told how a determined foreman (Clifford Evans) retrieves a vital piece of machinery from France, aided by two soldiers (a Cockney and a Scot) and an American secretary; *San Demetrio, London* (dir. Charles Frend, 1943) recounted the true story of the salvaging of a merchant-navy tanker by part of its crew, a cross-section of various types of men. A similar cross-section made up an army patrol pinned down in a desert oasis in *Nine Men* (dir. Harry Watt, 1943); *The Bells Go Down* (dir. Basil Dearden, 1943) dramatized the work of the Auxiliary Fire Service in London, stressing the comradeship and dedication of the team. Significantly, none of these films had an officer hero. Indeed the personality and attitudes of the old-style officer and gentleman were comprehensively demolished in Michael Powell and Emeric Pressburger's *The Life and Death of Colonel Blimp* (1943). The title figure (played by Roger Livesey), an officer, gentleman and sportsman of the old Imperial school who would rather lose the war than resort to using the methods of the Germans, is shown as a touching but wholly anachronistic figure.

The people's war

Comradeship and cooperation, dedication to duty and self-sacrifice, a self-deprecating good humour and unselfconscious modesty characterized the films of the fighting services. The war produced a masterpiece for each service. For the navy, there was *In Which We Serve* (1942), written, produced, co-directed (with David Lean) and scored by Noel Coward, who also played the lead role. It was based on the true story of HMS *Kelly*, which had been commanded by Coward's friend Lord Louis Mountbatten and had been sunk off Crete. The film focuses on three characters: the captain, a petty officer and an ordinary seaman. Their differences of status, background and situation are submerged by their common loyalty to their ship. The army film – Carol Reed's *The Way Ahead* (1944), scripted by Peter Ustinov

and Eric Ambler – was a semi-documentary account of how a group of conscripts from all walks of life are brought together and welded into a disciplined fighting army unit. And Anthony Asquith's *The Way to the Stars* (1945), scripted by Terence Rattigan, recalled life on a single RAF station between 1940 and 1944 with its joys and losses, its tragedies and its camaraderie. The film also took in the arrival and integration of the Americans into the war in Europe.

The contribution of women to the war effort was vital, and the cinema paid tribute to them, reflecting the dramatic change in their social roles and expectations. Leslie Howard's *The Gentle Sex* (1943) was a female version of *The Way Ahead*, a realistic account of the training of a group of women from all classes and backgrounds in the Auxiliary Territorial Service (ATS). Frank Launder and Sidney Gilliat's moving and memorable *Millions Like Us* (1943) dramatized the experiences of a group of girls drafted to work in an aircraft factory.

These were films with sympathetic and realistic characters and situations to which ordinary people could relate. Much less convincing (though equally well-intentioned) were the films produced as tributes to the oppressed peoples of Europe. The plots were interchangeable – highly romanticized stories of gallant resistance fighters suffering under the yoke of Nazi oppression but doing their bit to speed the day of victory. Realism was not furthered by the casting of such resolutely British types as Tom Walls or Finlay Currie as

partisan leaders. Each country got its tribute – Belgium (*Uncensored*, dir. Anthony Asquith, 1942), Norway (*The Day Will Dawn*, dir. Harold French, 1942), Yugoslavia (*Undercover*, dir. Sergei Nolbandov, 1943), Poland (*Dangerous Moonlight*, dir. Brian Desmond Hurst, 1941), Holland (*The Silver Fleet*, dir. Vernon Sewell, Gordon Wellesley, 1943), France (*Tomorrow We Live*, dir. George King, 1942) and Denmark (*Escape to Danger*, dir. Lance Comfort, Mutz Greenbaum, 1943).

In retrospect, the most redundant propaganda features were those warning against the danger from fifth columnists – simply because there were no fifth columnists in Britain. But warnings against complacency were never wasted and the cycle produced at least two memorable films. Thorold Dickinson's *The Next of Kin* (1942) was a chilling illustration of the slogan 'Careless Talk Costs Lives', demonstrating the way in which a chain of fifth columnists and Nazi spies assemble the information enabling them to destroy a British landing on the French coast. Churchill banned the film on the grounds that it would create alarm and despondency, but a military tribunal reversed this decision. The film was widely shown, and Field-Marshal Alexander told the director: 'This film was worth a division of troops to the British Army.' Alberto Cavalcanti's *Went the Day Well?* (1942) was an equally compelling account of a group of Nazi paratroopers infiltrating and taking over an English village until defeated by the villagers.

This sceptr'd isle

Unlike the Germans, the British did not turn very often to history to point up parallels with the present – possibly because of the unpopularity of historical films with working-class audiences in the Thirties. There were a few notable exceptions. Alexander Korda produced in Hollywood *That Hamilton Woman!* (1941) with Laurence Olivier as Nelson denouncing dictatorship and appeasement with equal vigour and urging the prosecution of the war against Napoleon. In Britain, Thorold Dickinson directed *The Prime Minister* (1941), which had its propaganda value in its account of how Disraeli, Britain's Jewish Prime Minister, outwitted Germany's Chancellor Bismarck. There were definite contemporary parallels in Carol Reed's *The Young Mr Pitt* (1942), which had justly been called 'the finest historical moving picture ever to be staged in this country'. Robert Donat unforgettably played Pitt, who burned himself out leading Britain in her struggle against Napoleon. Laurence Olivier's *Henry V* (1944), dedicated to the commandos, used Shakespeare's heroic poetry as a clarion call to the nation.

Films about *why* Britain was fighting were rarer than films about *how* she was fighting, perhaps because of the difficulty of rendering ideological and philosophical concepts as acceptable entertainment. Perhaps the best programmatic account was provided by Michael Powell's *49th Parallel* (1941). Financed by the Ministry of Information and filmed partly in Canada with an all-star cast, it told the gripping story of the stranded crew-members of a Nazi submarine travelling across Canada towards neutral USA and encountering *en route* various representatives of democracy. An uncommitted French-Canadian trapper (Laurence Olivier) turns against them when they maltreat the 'racially inferior' Eskimos.

A democratic Christian community of Hutterite exiles demonstrate the workability of a system of equality and cooperation. A donnish aesthete (Leslie Howard) beats one of the Germans to a pulp when they burn his books and pictures. Finally a Canadian soldier (Raymond Massey) takes on and defeats the commander of the fugitives (Eric Portman).

Michael Powell (with Emeric Pressburger) also directed *A Canterbury Tale* (1944), a complex, absorbing fable which mystified contemporary critics. It evoked the England of Chaucer and Shakespeare, the Kent countryside, half-timbered cottages and quiet churchyards. The spirit of this England was embodied by Thomas Culpeper (Eric Portman), gentleman farmer and amateur historian, who seeks to communicate its values to a group of latter-day Canterbury pilgrims, all unseeing and unfeeling products of a modern, materialist world. It represented a sense of the living past, the beauty of the English countryside and the enduring relationship of man and the soil.

Less mystical, but no less engaging, was Bernard Miles' *Tawny Pipit* (1944), in which a hierarchical rural society, led by the squire and the vicar, bands together to preserve the nesting place of the rare British bird, the tawny pippit. 'Love of nature and animals is part and parcel of the British way of life,' declares the squire. The defence of the pipits is equated with the defence of freedom against the Germans; the villagers successfully fight off the organized power of the military, the bureaucratic machine and the criminal fraternity to ensure the survival of the pipit.

Anthony Asquith's *The Demi-Paradise* (1943) artfully demonstrated how the preconceived notions about Britain held by an earnest Russian engineer (Laurence Olivier) are dispelled by his actual encounters with the British in peace and war. The film evokes the living power of tradition and indicates what several other films divined as the British secret weapon – their sense of humour. 'If you can laugh, you can be tolerant and freedom-loving,' says the engineer.

The England that these films summoned up was essentially a mythic one – pre-industrial, timeless and hierarchical. It was the dream of a different sort of England that was to lead to the Labour victory of 1945, the logical culmination of those other films which had stressed the lowering of class barriers, the solidarity of ordinary people and the ideals of freedom and justice for the oppressed.

The cinema of hate

German propaganda features identified two sets of enemies – the enemy within (the Jews) and the enemy without (the British). It was not until the outbreak of war that the German film industry produced specifically anti-Semitic and anti-English tracts. But three major anti-Semitic films came out in 1940 and there can be little doubt that they represented the government's cinematic effort to prepare the German public for the full-scale extermination of the Jews, the logical culmination of the race policies of the Third Reich.

The first of these films, *Die Rothschilds*, directed by Erick Waschneck, is a rather dull account of how the Jewish banking family acquired wealth and power in Regency England. It can hardly have done much to stir up German wrath since the victims of the Jews in this case were the British, something

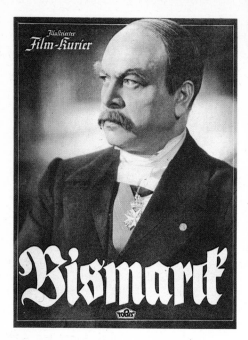

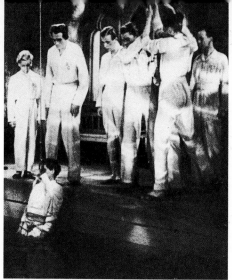

Above: Paul Hartmann as Bismarck *– authoritarian architect of a unified Germany. Centre top: Irish patriots in* Mein Leben für Irland. *Centre right: Emil Jannings as* Ohm Krüger *with a grotesque caricature of Queen Victoria. Right:* Jud Süss *is condemned to death by the citizens of Württemberg. Opposite page: dying for the Fatherland was extolled in both* Kadetten *and* Kampfgeschwader Lützow, *the programme of which saluted its dead pilot hero thus: 'But his ghost lives on in hundreds, in thousands. And his sacrifice will never be forgotten'*

which must have seemed akin to poetic justice. Veit Harlan's *Jud Süss* (Jew Süss) was much more dangerous, brilliantly orchestrating all the themes and archetypes of Nazi propaganda to stimulate the hatred of the audience. The central figure, Süss (Ferdinand Marian), personified the Jewish threat in all its aspects – economic, political and sexual. He acquired considerable wealth, used it to gain control of eighteenth-century Württemberg, brought in the Jews (depicted as scheming, dirty and repulsive) and raped a virtuous German girl. Eventually the honest citizens of Württemberg rose up and destroyed him.

But for sheer, concentrated nastiness, this film was exceeded by the 45-minute documentary *Der Ewige Jude* (The Eternal Jew) compiled by Dr Fritz Hippler. This was a systematic denunciation of every aspect of Jewry. Their appearance was shown to be always scruffy and ugly. They were accused of being responsible for all the ills which had befallen Germany since the end of World War I. They were held to be the source of all degenerate art (Expressionism, Surrealism, Cubism and jazz). Their religious practices were denounced as barbaric. The film ended with Hitler's Race Laws being flashed on the screen. There were no full-length anti-Semitic films after this, but the Jews became standard 'baddies' in conventional films.

Second only to the Jews in Nazi demonology were the British, and indeed Goebbels went so far as to describe them as 'the Jews among the Aryans'. The most memorable of the Nazi anti-British films is without question *Ohm Krüger* (1941, Uncle Kruger), directed by Hans Stein-

hoff. It was a supremely clever and utterly cynical reading of the Boer War, whose importance, so the contemporary film programme assured the audience, lay in the fact that 'for the first time the entire world of culture realized that England is the brutal enemy of order and civilization'. Modelled on Eisenstein's *Battleship Potemkin* (1925), a film Goebbels much admired, *Ohm Krüger* starred Emil Jannings as the Boer President, an all-wise and all-knowing führer-figure, leading the peace-loving Boer farmers in a just war against the military might of a greedy and cruel British Empire. The film is an object lesson in the use of archetypes and presents an unforgettable rogues' gallery of famous British figures. Cecil Rhodes is an oily schemer, his face often seen half in shadow, his voice soft, his eyes gleaming with cunning. Joseph Chamberlain is an aloof, expressionless, impeccably attired scoundrel, a monstrous caricature of British sang-froid. The Prince of Wales is an elderly lecher, ogling dancing girls while his mother lies dying. Kitchener is a beetle-browed sadist ordering total war. Churchill is a bloated despot, running a concentration camp and starving and maltreating the inmates. Queen Victoria is a whisky-sodden old wreck. English missionaries incite the natives to rise against the Boers, handing out Bibles with one hand and rifles with the other.

Much as one may admire the techniques of propaganda, one cannot but be appalled by the sheer cynicism of the exercise. The Nazis were denouncing the British for inventing concentration camps and total war at a time when they themselves were making full use of both.

Similarly, they produced two films, both directed by M. W. Kimmich, *Der Fuchs von Glenarvon* (1940, The Fox of Glenarvon) and *Mein Leben für Irland* (1941, My Life for Ireland) dealing with the oppression of the gallant, freedom-loving Irish by the tyrannical Imperialist British. The films are almost interchangeable with those made by the British depicting the struggles of the gallant, freedom-loving Poles/French/Yugoslavs against the tyrannical Imperialist Germans.

Clever attempts to rewrite the history books occurred in three other anti-British films. *Aufruhr in Damaskus* (Uproar in Damascus, dir. Gustav Ucicky, 1939), showed Lawrence of Arabia stirring up the natives of Syria against the Germans during World War I. *Das Herz der Königin* (The Heart of the Queen, dir. Carl Froelich, 1940), a film strongly reminiscent of *Mary of Scotland* (1936) – made by another anglophobe, John Ford – was a drama about the conflict between the pure, noble and romantic Mary Queen of Scots and the vicious, scheming and vindictive Elizabeth I of England. *Titanic* (dir. Herbert Selpin, Werner Klingler, 1943), a splendid re-creation of the *Titanic* disaster, featured the unsuccessful efforts of the ship's first officer – a German – to prevent the catastrophe in the face of the machinations of corrupt British capitalist aristocrats.

Führers from the past
The German cinema was also concerned to promote those qualities in the people which would sustain the war effort. Above all it promoted the idea of total obedience to an all-wise, all-powerful, all-knowing leader, and for

this purpose leading figures from Germany's history were mobilized as führer prototypes. They were invariably shown as lonely, dedicated warriors, battling for the glory, unity and future greatness of Germany. *Der Grosse König* (The Great King, dir. Veit Harlan, 1942) featured Frederick the Great (Otto Gebühr) and laid great stress on his refusal to make peace with his enemies until total victory had been achieved. Bismarck, Germany's Iron Chancellor, featured in two films directed by Wolfgang Liebeneiner, *Bismarck* (1940) and *Die Entlassung* (1942, The Dismissal) which showed him building up the army, abolishing democratic assemblies, imposing press censorship, outwitting the effeminate and cunning French and Austrians, surviving an assassination attempt by an English Jew and unifying Germany. In the end, he is dismissed by the youthful Kaiser Wilhelm II, but the moral of the film is clear – his unfinished work will be completed by Hitler.

It was not just political leaders but cultural heroes from Germany's past who were utilized to preach the message: poets (*Friedrich Schiller*, dir. Herbert Maisch, 1940), architects (*Andreas Schluter*, dir. Herbert Maisch, 1942), scientists (*Robert Koch, der Bekämpfer des Todes*, dir. Hans Steinhoff, 1939, and *Paracelsus*, dir. G. W. Pabst, 1943), inventors (*Diesel*, dir. Gerhard Lamprecht, 1942), composers (*Friedemann Bach*, dir. Traugott Müller, 1941). All celebrate the struggles and achievements of solitary German geniuses, striving for perfection, refusing to compromise, and sacrificing personal happiness to attain their ultimate goals.

The German people were encouraged to dis-play at all times the qualities of discipline, obedience, comradeship and self-sacrifice. These qualities permeate such films as Herbert Maisch's *D III 88* (1939) and its sequel, Hans Bertram's *Kampfgeschwader Lützow* (1941, Battle-squadron Lützow) which deal with the exploits of the Luftwaffe in peace and war and tell virtually the same story. The comradeship of two pilots is temporarily sundered by their love for the same girl, but they are reunited in time for one of them to die gloriously in the service of the Fatherland. Their commandant tells them in *D III 88*:

'Only through frictionless cooperation and unconditional obedience can our armed forces become an instrument on which our Leader can rely totally in an emergency.'

The same message was specifically directed towards German youth in *Kadetten* (1941, Cadets), a Karl Ritter film set in 1760. It tells of the heroism of a group of boy soldiers during a sneak Russian attack on Berlin while Frederick the Great is away fighting the Austrians.

Dying for the Fatherland

The themes and archetypes of wartime propaganda came together finally in the last cinematic gasp of the Third Reich, Veit Harlan's *Kolberg* (1944). The film was designed to prepare the entire population to fight to the last man, woman and child. It was based on the heroic defence of Kolberg by its citizens against the armies of Napoleon in 1807. The führer-figure is Joachim Nettelbeck, the Mayor of Kolberg (Heinrich George) who makes endless speeches declaring: 'We'd rather be buried under the rubble than capitulate.' Under his leadership, the people pull together to achieve victory, undertaking any sacrifice, including the flooding of part of their town and a comprehensive 'scorched earth' policy to deny the enemy supplies. By the time the film was available for release in January 1945, almost all the cinemas in Germany were closed. Virtually the only people who saw the film were the garrison of La Rochelle, then completely surrounded by the Allies. A print of the film was dropped by parachute to encourage them in their resistance; they surrendered.

With a few notable exceptions, German wartime propaganda features are heavy-handed and stodgy. This is particularly true of the biographical films, staged in a leaden monumental style and replete with lengthy, wearisome Nazi rants, delivered by most of the actors as if they were on the verge of apoplexy. Significantly, the two greatest film-makers for the Nazi party of pre-war years, Leni Riefenstahl and Luis Trenker, were virtually inactive during the war. Comparing British and German propaganda features it is clear that they shared the ideas of an appeal to the heroic past and the need for comradeship, self-sacrifice and dedication to duty in the present. Where they differed was in their central ideas, with the Germans promoting the concept of total obedience to the Leader and the British promoting the concept of a common effort towards mutually agreed ends – but always with the maintenance of a degree of healthy individualism and of a sense of humour and proportion. In the last resort, that conflict of ideologies was what the war was all about.

JEFFREY RICHARDS

Here's the PICTURE from which the SONG SENSATION was taken!

Walt DISNEY'S
DONALD DUCK
in A Nightmare in Nutziland

Der
Fuehrer's
Face

IN MULTIPLANE TECHNICOLOR

From To-morrow—
SIMULTANEOUSLY AT
FOUR BIG
WEST-END CINEMAS!

Greatest Single Reel entertainment novelty since "THE 3 LITTLE PIGS"
Biggest Song Hit since "WHO'S AFRAID OF THE BIG BAD WOLF"

© Walt Disney Productions

The real Adolf was no laughing matter, but nobody in Britain or America was going to admit it – least of all the movie-makers, who generally portrayed him as a figure of fun

Ven der Fuehrer says,
'Ve iss der Master Race',
Ve Heil! (Razz) Heil! (Razz)
Right in der Fuehrer's Face!

In this chorus from the top pop song of 1942, the bracketed instruction 'Razz' indicates, of course, that fruity salute known colloquially as 'the Great British Raspberry' or in America as 'the Bronx Cheer'.

The 'raspberry' had been specifically outlawed by the Hays Code ever since Charles Laughton blew the biggest ever in *If I Had a Million* (1932), but the Hollywood censors could hardly exercise their veto when the latest offender was that family entertainer supreme, Walt Disney. The song, played as a title tune to a Donald Duck cartoon, *Der Fuehrer's Face* (1942), razzed its rowdy way to an Academy Award for composer Oliver Wallace, and won international acclaim for a hitherto obscure comedy band called Spike Jones and His City Slickers. Their million-seller disc also gave them the unique opportunity to star in a second film entitled *Der Fuehrer's Face*,

though this was released as a 'Soundie' for a visual juke-box circuit, rather than to the cinemas.

The excuse to blow raspberries in public was both irresistible and good propaganda, but Donald Duck's 'nightmare in Nutziland' (as Disney publicized the cartoon) was not the first time films had poked a little fun at the Führer and his face. The first cinematic crack at Adolf Hitler, Dictator of Germany, was made by Will Hay as early as 1934, in *Radio Parade of 1935*, a burlesque on broadcasting. Hay played the role of William Garland, fictitious autocratic director-general of the National Broadcasting Group (NBG for short). The character, founded on the BBC's own John Reith, was stern, humourless, and given in quiet moments to admiring his own reflection as he combs down a forelock and holds the comb under his nose. This double gag gave Britain her first film laugh at a face that was already too familiar to be funny in itself, and also made a pointed dig at the 'dictatorship' of Reith's BBC. Hay was to repeat the 'moustache-comb' gag eight years later in *The Goose Steps Out* (1942). This time, with the war on, the laugh was much bigger.

The first actual appearance of Adolf Hitler as a character in a film came as an anachronistic gag in, of all things, the British film adaptation of *The Mikado* (1939). As the Japanese ruler sang of 'making the punishment fit the crime', the film's director, Victor Schertzinger, cut to a close-up in colour of the Führer's face. The actor who, in this brief flash, first portrayed Hitler on the screen was uncredited on the cast list, but whoever he was he had started something big. Soon there was a glut of imitation Hitlers, among them music-hall comedian Albert Burdon, who donned the toothbrush-moustache and Nazi uniform in *Jailbirds* (1939). But it was another anonymous actor who, as Hitler, supported Lord Haw-Haw (played by Geoffrey Sumner and based on the real-life traitorous broadcaster) in 'Nasty Newsreel', a burlesque epilogue to several editions of the Pathé Gazette newsreel from December 1939. And yet another unnamed actor appeared as Adolf in the dream-sequence centre-piece of George Formby's *Let George Do It* (1940), a comedy involving spies and submarines. Billy Russell, a comedian from the variety stage, took on the role in *For Freedom* (1940), Maurice Elvey's epic reconstruction of the rescue of British prisoners from the *Altmark* by the British battleships *Exeter* and *Ajax*, and the subsequent sinking of the *Graf Spee*. This was a curiosity considering Russell's music-hall billing as the man who appeared 'On Behalf of the Working Classes'. But it is possible

Above left: Donald Duck strikes a blow for anti-Nazi sentiment. Right: in The Goose Steps Out *Hay is a schoolmaster-double of a German spy who goes to Germany to steal plans for a secret weapon. While there he teaches his class of German spies to give Hitler the V sign – 'a mark of respect'*

that it was Russell who had portrayed all the 'British Hitlers' right back to *The Mikado*, and he certainly played him again . . . and again . . . and again . . . and all in the same film, *Gasbags* (1940), an outrageous comedy starring the Crazy Gang, which blew the six comedians to Germany on a barrage balloon and incarcerated them in a concentration camp. Here they were baffled by a veritable battalion of Hitler's doubles under training (all Billy Russell) and in due course one of the Gang, Teddy Knox, also became a double for the Führer. All ended crazily when the Gang came home via Hitler's secret weapon – a burrowing submarine!

American imitation Hitlers began with Charlie Chaplin. In *The Great Dictator* (1940), Charlie played a Jewish barber who was the double of Adenoid Hynkel, Dictator of Tomania. This was the first film to introduce caricatures of other Nazi leaders – Goebbels

EALING STUDIOS present
WILL HAY
in
The Goose Steps Out

POKES FUN
AT THE HUN!

produced by
MICHAEL BALCON

directed by
BASIL DEARDEN & WILL HAY

Above: Teddy Knox as Hitler and other members of the Crazy Gang in Gasbags. *Above right: Tom Dugan takes the role in* To Be or Not to Be *with Jack Benny and Carole Lombard. Right: Bobby Watson in* The Devil With Hitler. *Below: Chaplin's Adenoid Hynkel*

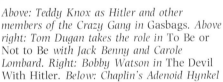

was lampooned as Garbitsch (Henry Daniell), and Göring as Marshal Herring (Billy Gilbert) – while Mussolini was portrayed as Benzino Napaloni of Bacteria (Jack Oakie). Columbia's comedy team, the Three Stooges (Moe Howard, 'Curly' Howard, Larry Fine) starred in a similar burlesque: *You Nazty Spy* (1940) set the slapstick experts in the State of Moronica with Moe as the Dictator and fat 'Curly' as his Göring. Despite lacking Chaplin's satirical intent, the short was such a success that writers Clyde Bruckman and Felix Adler concocted a sequel, *I'll Never Heil Again* (1941). The Three Stooges also repeated their Nazi characterizations in *Higher Than a Kite* (1943).

The first serious portrayal of Hitler in a Hollywood movie occurred briefly and at long range in Fritz Lang's *Manhunt* (1941), adapted from Geoffrey Household's best-selling novel, *Rogue Male*. Walter Pidgeon played a big-game hunter who stalks his prey to the balcony of Hitler's private retreat at Berchtesgaden, only to be nabbed by the Gestapo in the shape of George Sanders.

'What is Adolf Hitler doing in the streets of Warsaw?' was the question posed by the commentator at the beginning of *To Be or Not to Be* (1942). But the seriousness of the early scenes soon gave way to comedy as Adolf was revealed as an actor (Tom Dugan) promoting a play. This rare black comedy, directed by Ernst Lubitsch, produced (somewhat surprisingly) by Alexander Korda and starring Jack Benny and Carole Lombard, disturbed many at the time of its release by seeming to make light of the Polish tragedy. Critical reassessment has

established it as one of the funniest films of World War II. Tom Dugan had a further shot at playing Hitler in Paramount's all-star musical, *Star Spangled Rhythm* (1943). With Paul Porcasi as Mussolini and Richard Loo as Emperor Hirohito, Dugan joined in for a chorus of 'A Sweater, a Sarong, and a Peek-a-Boo' sung by Paulette Goddard, Dorothy Lamour and Veronica Lake.

In *The Devil With Hitler* (1942), a Hal Roach 'Comedy Streamliner' just 43 minutes long, Alan Mowbray appeared as the Devil himself, only outdone in evil by the antics of Adolf Hitler, played by Bobby Watson. Satan pops up in Berlin where, posing as Hitler's valet (Mowbray usually played British butlers), he tries to get his rival to perform one good deed. After

391

THE STRANGE DEATH OF ADOLF HITLER

BEHIND FLAMING HEADLINES LIES THE ENTHRALLING STORY OF A WOMAN'S PLOT TO ASSASSINATE THE WORLD'S GREATEST CRIMINAL!

with
LUDWIG DONATH · GALE SONDERGAARD · GEORGE DOLENZ
FRITZ KORTNER · LUDWIG STOSSEL · WILLIAM TRENK

Screen Play by FRITZ KORTNER
Original Story by FRITZ KORTNER and JOE MAY
Directed by JAMES HOGAN
Associate Producer BEN PIVAR

RELEASED JAN. 10, 1944
A UNIVERSAL PICTURE

some fast-paced slapstick involving the Führer, Mussolini (Joe Devlin), and a Japanese emissary named Suki-Yaki (George E. Stone), the Devil gives up and descends to Hell, only to find Hitler is now in charge of the nether regions. Watson, a middle-aged vaudevillian and a dead ringer for Hitler, rapidly became Hollywood's answer to Britain's Billy Russell. He was rushed into a sequel, *That Nazty Nuisance* (not released until 1943), directed by Glenn Tryon, with Devlin as Mussolini again and Johnny Arthur replacing Stone as Suki-Yaki. In this burlesque, Hitler and company – this time there were also caricatures of Göring (Rex Evans), Goebbels (Charley Rogers) and Himmler (Wedgewood Nowell) – met their match on a tropical island.

Hitler – Dead or Alive (1942), directed by Nick Grinde, was based on the million-dollar reward actually offered by American businessmen for the capture of Hitler, again played by Bobby Watson who was allowed to give a richer performance than his earlier burlesques. Perhaps this hitherto unsuspected power helped Watson win the role of the Führer (instead of original choice Edward G. Robinson) in Paramount's major 'dramatized documentary', *The Hitler Gang* (1944). Rarely revived, this film is a triumph of careful research and reconstruction blended with powerful propaganda. With the end of World War II, Bobby (now Robert) Watson found himself virtually unemployed and unemployable, but after a few small character roles he returned to the screen once more in the part he had made his

Left: The Hitler Gang *starred Martin Kosleck as Goebbels, Victor Varconi as Hess, Bobby Watson as Hitler, Alexander Pope as Göring, and Luis Van Rooten as Himmler. Above:* The Strange Death of Adolf Hitler *featured Ludwig Donath as the Führer. Right: Danny Kaye doing his Hitler in* On the Double. *Below right: Alec Guinness as a doomed Führer in* Hitler: the Last Ten Days

own, playing Adolf Hitler in *The Story of Mankind* (1957).

The last wartime appearance of Hitler in a Hollywood film was in *The Strange Death of Adolf Hitler* (1943), which had Viennese actor Franz Huber (Ludwig Donath, who had already impersonated Hitler's voice in *The Moon Is Down*, made the same year) arrested for ridiculing the Führer, and forcibly operated on to become Hitler's double. His wife (Gale Sondergaard), believing him dead, takes her revenge by shooting Hitler but, of course, kills her husband instead. Conviction was given to this Universal B picture by the authors: ex-Ufa actor Fritz Kortner and ex-Ufa director Joe May were both refugees from the real Hitler.

The first two post-war Hollywood portrayals of Hitler occurred in 1951 with the same actor starring in both films. Luther Adler played Führer to James Mason's Field-Marshal Rommel in *The Desert Fox*, directed by Henry Hathaway, and followed it within a month with the same role in Frank Tuttle's *The Magic Face*. Both films were based on best-selling books, by Brigadier Desmond Morris and William L. Shirer respectively. Shirer's less convincing story concerned an actor, Janus the Great, who murders Hitler, takes his place, loses the war for Germany and finally dies in the rubble of his Chancellery. Intriguingly, both authors played themselves in the films.

The first post-war British film to feature the Führer was *The Two-Headed Spy* (1958). In this believe-it-or-not biography, Kenneth Griffith, an actor hitherto known for his comedy cameos, was Hitler, and Jack Hawkins played General Schottland, a British agent planted in the German army since World War I. Two portrayals of Hitler that appeared in the early Sixties were complete contrasts. Richard Basehart took the role in *Hitler* (1962), virtually a remake of *The Hitler Gang* but with the accent

on sexual perversion. Perversity had been the key note of *On the Double* (1961), with Danny Kaye playing not only Hitler but PFC Ernie Williams, General Sir Lawrence Mackenzie-Smith, a Luftwaffe pilot, a German matron, and Marlene Dietrich as well!

Hitler impressions have continued to alternate between the historic and the comic. Guy Hamilton's spectacular *Battle of Britain* (1969) featured Rolf Stiefel as a serious Führer and Laurence Olivier as Air Chief Marshal Sir Hugh Dowding, while Sidney Miller's Adolf was played strictly for laughs in Jerry Lewis' *Ja Ja Mein General! But Which Way to the Front?* (1970). Alec Guinness made a studied and sombre Hitler in the dramatized documentary, *Hitler: the Last Ten Days* (1973), but it was all out for fun again when Peter Sellers impersonated Hitler in the Boulting Brothers' sex comedy, *Soft Beds, Hard Battles* (1973). Sellers finished one up on Danny Kaye by playing six other characters. And thus the Führer's face became just one in the repertoires of two leading screen comedians.   DENIS GIFFORD

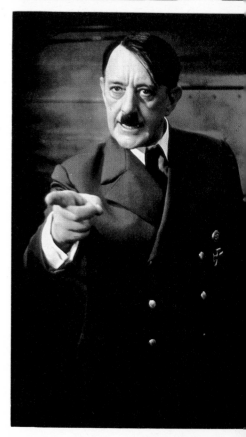

Business as usual

The French film industry survives under the Nazi Occupation, maintains production and scores some of its greatest triumphs

Above left: characters in fancy dress bring a surreal atmosphere to the contemporary setting of Grémillon's Lumière d'Eté. *Above: Gance's costume romance provided safe escapism for the people of Occupied France*

On June 22, 1940, Marshal Pétain, the French Chief of State, signed an armistice with Germany. Under its terms Paris became part of an occupied zone, and was to remain so for just over four years. In June 1944 the Allies landed on the French coast; by August Paris was liberated.

However deep a resentment and humiliation the French people may have felt at their subjugation to Nazism, the French cinema flourished as never before. Something above three hundred and fifty features were made in these fifty months of occupation, including such landmarks of French film as *Le Corbeau* (1943, *The Raven*) and *Les Anges du Péché* (1943, *Angels of Sin*).

Yet there is remarkably little record of overt and willing collaboration by French film-makers with the Nazi Party and its ideologies. Indeed, a number of those artists who remained active – among them the directors Jacques Becker, Jean Grémillon, Jean Painlevé and the actor Pierre Blanchar – were responsible for the formation of the clandestine 'Committee of Liberation of the French Cinema'.

This is not to say that Goebbels did not exert comprehensive control over the French film industry. For years before the war, German films had been successfully infiltrating the French market. With the Occupation – and to an extent through the expropriation of Jewish interests – the Germans acquired complete

economic control of about a third of the industry: production, press, distribution and theatres. French film was subjected to a dual censorship by the German Propaganda Ministry, and by the German-backed Vichy government whose powers in this respect nominally covered only the so-called 'free' zone of France.

Two factors contributed to the freedom allowed to French film-makers. One was the failure of German-made pictures to attract the French public. At the start of the Occupation there was a determined effort to put German films onto French screens, but audiences tacitly boycotted them. As a result, receipts for French films rose considerably, thereby enhancing the financial prosperity of the home industry. Moreover, the Germans looked to French production to replace the films they were no longer buying from Hollywood, and so left film-makers a free hand in the field of what were regarded as purely entertainment pictures.

The only direct injection of German money into French production was through the German-owned Continental company which produced thirty of the more expensive pictures of the period. Continental concentrated particularly on 'American-style' subjects, such as Henri Decoin's light comedy *Premier Rendez-vous* (1941, First Meeting) and detective thrillers. Henri-Georges Clouzot, who had made a number of German versions of French films in Berlin in the early Thirties, scripted two of the

most important of these thrillers: Georges Lacombe's *Le Dernier des Six* (1941, Last of the Six) and Decoin's *Les Inconnus Dans la Maison* (1942, *Strangers in the House*), adapted from a pre-war Georges Simenon novel but turned into an attack on non-Aryans, useful as propaganda for the Vichy government.

Clouzot went on to make his debut as a director with a thriller, *L'Assassin Habite au 21* (1942, The Killer Lives at No. 21), which remains one of his best works. His next film, *Le Corbeau* (1943), based on a real-life story concerning the circulation of poison-pen letters in a French village, became the centre of a bitter controversy when the Nazis used it as anti-French propaganda in Occupied Europe.

Jacques Becker, who also began his career during the Occupation, was a pupil of Jean Renoir and worked in a realist style which combined elements from French pre-war cinema and from the American detective genre. His first film was *Le Dernier Atout* (1942, The Trump Card), a brilliant and commercially successful detective thriller. With *Goupi Mains Rouges* (1943, *It Happened at the Inn*), Becker went beyond his detective-story plot to create a rich portrayal of French rural life. *Falbalas*

393

(1945, *Paris Frills*), completed around the time of the Liberation, was the first of the Parisian subjects on which his later fame was to rest. Set in a top fashion house, the film is a wonderfully detailed description of the French bourgeoisie under the Occupation.

A much-neglected French director, Jean Grémillon, made two of the few strictly realist works of the period. *Lumière d'Eté* (1943, Summer Light) contrasted the life of construction workers on a dam with the decadence of their employers (evidently intended to symbolize the way of life under the Vichy administration). *Le Ciel Est à Vous* (1944, The Sky is Yours), based on the real-life story of two ordinary Frenchmen who achieved a world flying record, was seen by audiences as a symbol of French aspirations towards resistance and liberation.

Other directors were able to follow their individual paths without much hindrance from the Nazis. Sacha Guitry, who was to be arrested and charged as a collaborator in 1944, celebrated his own acting talent in romantic vehicles he directed like *Le Destin Fabuleux de Desiree Clary* (1942), *Donne-moi Tes Yeux* (1943, Give Me Your Eyes) and *La Malibran* (1944). The prolific Abel Gance dedicated *La Vénus Aveugle* (1941, Blind Venus) to Marshal Pétain, and followed it with another work of characteristic romanticism, *Le Capitaine Fracasse* (1942). André Cayatte made as his first film an adaptation from Balzac, *La Fausse*

Maîtresse (1942, False Mistress), and followed up with films of Zola's *Au Bonheur des Dames* (1943) and Maupassant's *Pierre et Jean* (1944).

Robert Bresson commenced a career of unparalleled, uncompromising creative independence with *Les Anges du Péché* (1943), giving cinema audiences their first encounter with his metaphysical and spiritual concerns and his severe, demanding style. It was followed by a no less austere modernization of Diderot's *Les Dames du Bois de Boulogne* (1945), scripted by Jean Cocteau and released on the day after the Liberation of Paris.

The most characteristic films from the Oc-

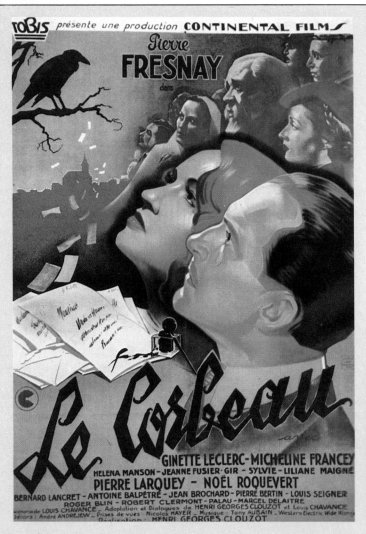

Occupational hazards

André Halimi, whose film *Chantons Sous l'Occupation* (1976) is a highly controversial survey of the French entertainment industry during the Occupation years, offers some reflections on the problems of making films under the Nazi yoke

cupation period, however, are a handful of glittering flights into fantastic worlds or romantic periods – areas where neither Goebbels' nor Vichy's film censors could follow. The veteran Marcel L'Herbier made *La Nuit Fantastique* (1942, *Fantastic Night*), Jean Delannoy followed *Pontcarral, Colonel d'Empire* (1942, *Pontcarral, Colonel of the Empire*) – a historical drama that had clear contemporary references – with *L'Eternel Retour* (1943, *Love Eternal*), a modern version of the legend of Tristan and Iseult. Both the latter and *Le Baron Fantôme* (1943, *The Phantom Baron*), a charming trifle directed by Serge de Poligny, were scripted by Cocteau. Claude Autant-Lara concentrated upon the decorative past in *Lettres d'Amour* (1942, *Love Letters*), *Le Mariage de Chiffon* and *Douce* (both 1943).

Two films above all stand as monuments of the French cinema under Nazi Occupation. Marcel Carné moved into a new phase of his career with *Les Visiteurs du Soir* (1942, *The Devil's Own Envoy*). Visually superb, this evocation of a medieval world, in which the Devil visits a castle at night but is unable to conquer true love, seemed to audiences a symbol of Hitler's final inability to crush the nation's spirit. *Les Enfants du Paradis* (1945, *Children of Paradise*) remains Carné's masterpiece and the most memorable work of the time. This fable of Love and Death, Good and Evil, is set in the Paris of the 1840s. The film's pictorial splendour and the complexity of its intertwining of life and theatre, has lost none of its attraction.
DAVID ROBINSON

Far left: Maria Casarès as a jilted mistress in Les Dames du Bois de Boulogne. *Left: disciples of the devil in* Les Visiteurs du Soir. *Below:* Douce *starred Odette Joyeux as an ingénue. Right: in* Les Inconnus Dans la Maison Raimu *was cast as a barrister*

The cinema of the Occupation had certain characteristics. First, although it was subject to German censorship and, sometimes, German finance, it was dedicated to neither the glory of Nazism nor to the collaborationist policy of Marshal Pétain. It was not free in the full extent, but at least it was free to entertain. This was something in a period when the least show of resistance was ruthlessly suppressed.

On the other hand, Jews – whose influence as producers, scenarists or directors had been considerable – were all blacklisted or denied the right to exercise their profession. The critic Lucien Rebatet, in a text entitled *The Tribes of Cinema and Theatre*, included in a collected work *Jews in France*, declared:

'French films in their entirety, from production to laboratory work and down to the management of the smallest cinema, must inexorably and definitively be closed to all Jews irrespective of class and origin.'

Despite these odious, immoral laws restricting the creative opportunities of artists, a few Jewish writers managed to work under pseudonyms, though with constant anxiety and danger (and frequent changes of address).

Censorship operated at two levels: the Vichy-inspired Board of Control, consisting of representatives of the Ministries of the Family and the Interior, favoured films extolling open-air life, the family, sports and the like; the German censors naturally banned any projects of even the least controversial nature.

Two films were, however, to cause con-

troversy that would haunt their makers in the years after the war. Henri-Georges Clouzot's *Le Corbeau* (1943) dealt with police informers and poison-pen letters in a French village during the Occupation. The publicity slogan for the film was 'Is the law strong enough to punish the writers of poison-pen letters?' The Germans gleefully used the film as anti-French propaganda at home and in other European countries. In France the advertising campaign was modified, as it was clearly in the Gestapo's interest to maintain an atmosphere of paranoia and mutual denunciation among the population. After the Liberation the military censorship body banned *Le Corbeau*, and both Clouzot and his writer Louis Chavance found themselves unable to work in the industry until 1947. Jean Delannoy's *L'Eternel Retour* (1943) – always considered, on account of its script, a Cocteau film – meanwhile aroused deep hostility in post-war Britain. The problem was that the English critics appeared to be unaware that the Tristan and Iseult story, on which the film was based, is an old Breton legend set down by the troubadours Béroul and Thomas: for them Tristan – particularly as played by Aryan-blond Jean Marais – could only evoke the Germanic, nationalist Richard Wagner (whose opera had celebrated the legend). The *Daily Express* branded *L'Eternel Retour* a Nazi film. Its critic wrote:

'There is a mouldy Gothic air, a death-cult mysticism about it. The hero is as blond and vacant as any one of a thousand SS paratroop prisoners I saw in Normandy two years ago. There is nothing French here, but much that is ridiculous and distasteful.'

The *Daily Mail* also spoke of the film's 'heavily Germanic spirit', while the *Daily Telegraph* commented:

'It is a pity M. Cocteau and his associates should have smeared it with marks of German ideology as blatant as so many swastikas.'

Was one obliged to work with the Germans? 'Not at all,' replied Jean Delannoy recently. 'I tried by every possible means to get out of it and avoided problems from the start.'

Michel Duran, another scenarist who worked during the Occupation admitted that he wrote for Continental, but added:

'I worked there by chance since it wasn't to make propaganda films. My job was to write dialogue, and I continued to do so.'

Asked why those who worked for Continental were condemned after the Liberation, he replied:

'There was the usual settling of accounts. Some who had not been able to work for it were probably jealous of us. We never made propaganda films at Continental.'

It was, then, a problem of conscience. There were several degrees of collaboration. Some actively collaborated with the Germans. Others, without actually collaborating in their scripts or films, were willing to accept the finance of German companies like Continental. Others abstained and preferred to remain silent. Some who did not make films, or had problems in making them, took advantage of the situation to denounce Freemasons, Jews, Communists and Gaullists, hoping to step into their shoes.

Most artists worked away as if the Germans had never existed, accomplishing such masterpieces as *L'Assassin Habite au 21* (1942) and *Les Enfants du Paradis* (1945). The masterpieces will remain, long after the settling of accounts and the Frenchmen who were corrupted by the Nazis have been forgotten by history.
ANDRE HALIMI

Far left: in Le Corbeau, *Pierre Fresnay played a doctor victimized by a malicious letter-writer. Left:* L'Eternel Retour, *accused of being pro-Nazi owing to the Aryan look of stars Madeleine Sologne and Jean Marais*

UN FILM DE
MARCEL CARNÉ

1re ÉPOQUE
LE BOULEVARD
DU CRIME

ARLETTY . JEAN-LOUIS BARRAULT . PIERRE BRASSEUR . PIERRE RENOIR

LES ENFANTS DU PARADIS

IMAGES DE ROGER HUBERT
DIRECTEUR DE PRODUCTION FRED ORAIN
avec LOUIS SALOU MARCEL HERRAND *et* MARIA CASARÈS
SCENARIO ET DIALOGUES DE
JACQUES PRÉVERT

Directed by Marcel Carné, 1945

Prod co: Pathé-Cinéma. **prod:** Fred Orain. **prod man:** Raymond Borderie. **sc:** Jacques Prévert. **photo:** Roger Hubert. **ed:** Henri Rust. **art dir:** Léon Barsacq, R. Gabutti, Alexandre Trauner. **mus:** Joseph Kosma, Maurice Thiriet, G. Mouqué. **cost:** Mayo. **r/t:** 195 minutes. Paris premiere, 9 March 1945. Released in the USA as *Children of Paradise*.
Cast: Arletty (*Garance*), Jean-Louis Barrault (*Baptiste Debureau*), Pierre Brasseur (*Frédéric Lemaître*), Maria Casarès (*Nathalie*), Marcel Herrand (*Lacenaire*), Louis Salou (*Count Edouard de Montray*), Pierre Renoir (*Jéricho*), Paul Frankeur (*inspector*), Jane Marken (*Mme Hermine*), Fabien Loris (*Avril*), Etienne Decroux (*Anselme Debureau*), Marcel Pêrès (*director of the Funambules*), Gaston Modot (*File de Soie, the blind man*), Pierre Palau (*manager of the Funambules*), Jacques Castelot (*Georges*), Robert Dhéry (*Celestin*), Rognoni (*director of the Grand Theatre*), Florencie (*gendarme*), Guy Favières (*cashier*), Albert Remy (*Scarpia Borigni*), Auguste Bovério (*first author*), Paul Demange (*second author*), Jean Diener (*third author*), Habib Benglia (*boy from Turkish baths*).

Marcel Carné once said that *Les Enfants du Paradis* (*Children of Paradise*) was a tribute to the theatre, and indeed the film is an evocation of the stage in the days when it still belonged to the people and before it became the haunt of the fashionable upper classes. 'Paradis', in fact, is what in English we should call 'the gods' – the heights sacred to the public sitting in the gallery. And 'the children' are both the actors – beloved (or not) by that audience watching from those heavenly heights – and the audience themselves. The close relationship between public and performer has gone now. It lingered with the music-hall, but the music-hall itself has dwindled and vanished. Perhaps the remembrance of it has helped to give Carné's piece its enormous success.

The idea for the film, it seems, belonged to the actor Jean-Louis Barrault. The second year of the Occupation saw Marcel Carné and his screenwriter, the poet Jacques Prévert, ready to begin making a new film. Working together they had enjoyed great prestige both before the war and during it; but now one of their projects had run into difficulties and they needed a fresh subject. Barrault, whom they encountered in a café in Nice, suggested a film about Baptiste Debureau, the Funambules and the Boulevard du Crime. Debureau had been the most celebrated of French mimes; the Funambules, in the Boulevard du Temple, was the theatre where he performed; the Boulevard du Temple was sometimes called the Boulevard du Crime because it was notorious for murders. Violence, the romance of the popular theatre, and a famous historical figure – everybody agreed that the possibilities were seductive, and work began on the script which, though fictional, was to be based on real-life characters – not only Debureau, but also the stage actor Frédéric Lemaître and the dandy and notorious criminal Lacenaire.

It was a work of happy cooperation. Carné and Prévert, of course, were the chief creators; the designer Alexandre Trauner assisted, as did Joseph Kosma the composer; while the actors, Barrault (Debureau), Pierre Brasseur (Lemaître) and Marcel Herrand (Lacenaire) joined in to discuss their roles. After six months preparation, Carné began shooting.

An authentic setting had to be provided to establish the relation-

1

2

ship between the two actors and their public and to revive the mood and the popular feeling of mid-nineteenth-century Paris. This posed formidable problems; because of the war, materials were scarce – indeed, everything was scarce. Yet somehow a section of the Boulevard du Temple, theatre-fronts and all, was reconstructed – stretching for a quarter of a mile. Carné employed 25,000 extras to act as the carnival crowd, with its entertainers, jugglers, tight-rope walkers and weight-lifters, and the yelling audience of the Funambules theatre.

Les Enfants du Paradis took three years to complete, and at the time was probably the most expensive film ever to be made in France. Certainly it was the grandest of Carné's films; he was never to make another as masterly. It was not a work noted for discovering new talents. Most of the players – Pierre Brasseur, Pierre Renoir, the lovely Arletty – were already established. Barrault, although he made occasional and powerful appearances on the screen, was essentially a stage actor. Only Maria Casarès went on to greater fame, playing the role of Death in Jean Cocteau's *Orphée* (1950).

The film itself, however, was a lasting triumph. For the French, just emerging from years of Occupation, the romantic brilliance of *Les Enfants du Paradis* was a testimony to survival and a reassertion of French elegance and artistry. As Carné said, it was a tribute to the theatre – a French theatre with French performers. It may also be said to have been a declaration of the resilience of France herself.
DILYS POWELL

The story of Garance, a beautiful, independent girl, and the four men who love her unfolds against a background of the popular theatre and the underworld of Paris in the 1840s (1). The girl is saved from arrest for theft by Baptiste, a mime artist, who explains in gestures that she is not guilty; the thief was her criminal companion Lacenaire. Baptiste finds her work in the theatre (2) and shelters her, but out of delicacy refrains from taking advantage of her willingness to love. She becomes the mistress of his friend, the would-be actor Frédéric; later, to save herself from a police charge (3), she accepts the protection of the Count, a rich aristocrat (4), and leaves Paris.

When she returns, Frédéric and Baptiste, now married to Nathalie, a girl from the theatre (5), are both famous. Five years have passed, but Garance and Baptiste are still in love. They are reunited (6) but betrayed by Lacenaire, who in his vicious fashion also loves Garance. He is insulted by the Count (7) and murders him (8). Nathalie discovers the lovers and her pitiful pleas drive Garance to disappear, leaving Baptiste vainly pursuing her through the crowded boulevard.

3

4

5

6

7

8

Alf Sjöberg

Sweden's Hidden Master

Alf Sjöberg's background was the theatre. He studied with Greta Garbo at the Royal School of Dramatic Art in Stockholm and produced plays before turning to the cinema. His films are an uneasy alliance between the fastidious stylization of the theatre and the realism demanded by the cinema, so that, although captivating, they are often disturbingly contradictory. His work provides the link between the Swedish classics of Victor Sjöstrom and those of Ingmar Bergman

Sjöberg's first film, the silent *Den Starkaste* (1929, *The Strongest*), is a tale of seal hunters in the Greenland Sea and their seasonal return to their tranquil farmlands. The film combines documentary footage of Arctic landscapes and whaling expeditions with a humorous treatment of a story of disputed love, trials of strength and avenged honour. Its style foreshadows his later work in the way he builds atmosphere and background with bits of behaviour and decor, and in his taste for combining visual imagery with underlying dramatic movement. Moments of stillness are alternately and expertly contrasted with bursts of movement as quiet conversations give way to swift action.

Excluded for a decade from Swedish cinema because of his unconventional talent, Sjöberg made his second film, *Med Livet soms Insats* (1939, They Staked Their Lives), on the eve of World War II. It has a pacifist theme of individuals caught against their wishes in a net of power and intrigue. The action takes place 'somewhere in Europe' – a deliberately ambiguous location – where democrats fight against a repressive government. He introduces several stylistic features which characterize his work in the next decade – patterned light effects, parodies of thriller clichés and attempts to retain the lucidity of film language developed in the last years of silent cinema.

His style finds its first articulate structure in *Hem från Babylon* (1941). Home From Babylon). Set in three related locations, the narrative is intentionally ironic. A lover returns from war-ravaged 'somewhere in Asia' to the idyllic and remote Swedish countryside where his fiancée is about to leave for the bright lights of Paris. The film closes with pastoral Swedish imagery – a token of the country's neutrality which is both a blessing and a curse.

Himlaspelet (1942, *Road to Heaven*) won several critics to Sjöberg's work. It is an uneasy alliance between a reconstruction of peasant paintings and a modern morality play by the Swedish dramatist Rune Lindström. It freely juggles biblical references which reinforce a bleak Calvinist ethic and make it clear that Sjöberg's God has a tyrannical authority. The shifting narrative framework is interesting – a young and naive peasant (played by Lindström himself) was engaged to a girl who had been falsely condemned and burned as a witch after plague swept their village. Inspired by the murals in a local church, he strides off 'on the road to heaven' to seek justice, during which journey he re-enacts man's progress through temptation to salvation. Finally, as he thanks God for accepting his soul, the camera glides over the paintings on the wall of his new-found home and discovers that they tell the story of the film. This essay in traditionalism, a perfect self-enclosed piece of work, is however less stimulating than many of his earlier films

although it breaks new ground.

Hets (1944, *Frenzy*), starring Mai Zetterling, won international acclaim. It was the film on which Bergman had his first screen credits as both scriptwriter and assistant director, and the resultant unresolved tension between Sjöberg's and Bergman's outlook is a fruitful one. The film is about the tyranny of school life. A teenage rebel harshly criticizes his parents, offends his teachers and makes love to a prostitute in order to pursue his integrity and his right to be unhappy. Caligula, the Latin teacher, is for Bergman a demon figure of evil incarnate, whereas Sjöberg has him read the Swedish Nazi newspaper from behind steel-

Filmography
1928 Adalens Poesi (actor only). **'29** Den Starkaste (GB: The Strongest) (co-dir). **'39** Med Livet soms Insats (+ co-sc); Den Blomstertid (+ sc). **'41** Hem från Babylon (+co-sc). **'42** Himlaspelet (GB: Road to Heaven) (+ co-sc). **'44** Kungajakt (sc. only); Hets (GB: Frenzy; USA: Torment). **'45** Resan Bort (+ sc). **'46** Iris och Löjnantshjärta (GB: Iris) (+ sc). **'49** Bara en Mor (GB: Only a Mother) (+co-sc). **'51** Fröken Julie (GB: Miss Julie) (+co-sc). **'53** Barabbas (+co-sc). **'54** Karin Mänsdotter (+sc). **'55** Vildfäglar (GB: Wild Birds) (+ co-sc). **'56** Sista Paret Ut (GB: Last Pair Out). **'60** Domaren (GB: The Judge) (+co-sc). **'64** On (GB: The Island) (+ co-sc). **'69** Fadern (GB: The Father).

immed spectacles. To Bergman he is a meta-physical villain whereas Sjöberg frames him under a portrait of Karl XII to suggest that here is an authoritarian streak in this sadist. The intricate low-key lighting, the suffocating composition and the disquieting overtones epitomize the Expressionist tradition that aunts the film.

Resan Bort (1945, *Journey Out*), a parody of ife in a small coastal town and the most intri-ate of Sjöberg's essays in 'critical realism', vas largely unacceptable to Swedish critics. Its wo loosely related themes comment on each other. On the one hand Mr and Mrs Bovary, a provincial couple, are visited by a small-time rook (the husband's school friend) who wants o rob the bank where Mr Bovary works – and ncidentally seduces Bovary's wife. At the ame time a young working girl is helping her Norwegian refugee lover to reach England and oin the RAF. Reality, illusion and delusion vork against each other, building a distorted eflection of the characters, criticizing them nd the kind of fiction of which their 'real' life is composed.

Iris och Löjtnantshjärta (1946, *Iris*) is unique n Sjöberg's work for its lightness of touch, its motional delicacy and pungency. It depicts he remnants of an 'important' family as they it through sumptious meals while the fabric of heir society is destroyed by post-war dis-llusionment. The romance between the youn-er son and a servant (Iris) brings their nachronistic mode of life into focus. Although he evil family literally steps on stage from

behind stuffy portraits, and a sexually frust-rated Caligula-like figure prowls around Iris, the film is more romantic than Expressionist. The aristocratic officer and the confident serv-ant girl, despite being stereotypes of male and female social roles, are sensually observed – as when Iris dances in her lover's loose-fitting pyjamas in a room drenched by early-morning sunlight.

After a three-year pause, Sjöberg made *Bara en Mor* (1949, *Only a Mother*) from a novel by Ivar Lo-Johansson. It tells the story of a poor peasant woman who is a victim of her poverty in both social and economic terms. She is an incarnation of the idealized feminine values that in Sjöberg's work unite the life-giving Mary of Christian lore with the militant mother of socialist imagery.

In *Fröken Julie* (1951, *Miss Julie*), his best-known film, he remains faithful to the assump-tions of Strindberg's play while breaking up the text. He uses flashbacks and travelling shots that link characters, movements and looks from the past, present and future without shattering the compact present tense of the action. With methods learnt from the stage he grafts voices or atmospheric sounds from the past onto the present, thus reinforcing the social determinism of the play. Once again the film centres on the sterility of a wealthy family whose traditions crush all challengers. After a pagan outburst on Midsummer's night, Miss Julie and the servant boy, Jean, renounce their love and conform to their fates as he answers the servants' bell and she cuts her throat – a

Below: two scenes from Barabbas *– Sjöberg's religious allegory – in which Ulf Palme takes the title role. Bottom left: a shadow of menace hangs over Mai Zetterling in* Hets *– the film which launched her English-speaking career. Bottom right: Sjöberg's theatrical stylization is epitomized by this scene from* Fröken Julie *– his story of forbidden love*

symbol of her uselessness in contemporary Swedish society.

Fröken Julie's success encouraged the pro-duction company, Sandrews, to embark on an expensive prestige venture – *Barabbas* (1953) – a literary adaptation of the novel of a recent Nobel Prize winner, Pär Lagerkvist. Set free in the place of Jesus, Barabbas witnesses the crucifixion without grasping its evangelical message, and his 'borrowed time' in this world leads him through prisons and catacombs to a cross of his own, whilst running away from the revelation that he has been granted. The film is staggeringly elaborate in allegorical terms, and a complex play between shades of dark-ness and blinding light, but it is also shallowly theatrical in its struggle for significance.

Karin Mänsdotter (1954) is Sjöberg's most original film. But at the time the segmented structure baffled its meagre Swedish audiences and irritated the reviewers. In the first section the child-bride of Erik XIV is presented as the fairy-tale princess of popular Swedish imagery whose progress from rags to riches is enacted in front of painted backdrops. Watery colours suddenly give way to stark black and white as she realizes that, once in the palace, she is supposed to go to bed with Prince Charming. The second part stages, in blunt theatrical strokes, the conflict between the social unrest of the period and the dreamy Hamlet-like monarch caught in a web of shadows and intrigue. The final section is an episodic illust-ration of notes supposedly jotted down on the margins of calendars and Bibles, in the palaces and prisons where Erik and Karin lived in exile. The energy of the previous segment gives way to an elegaic mood that heightens the inherent contradictions. Karin, though in reality de-based, is morally enobled and becomes, in the eyes of her jailers, the queen of her unrealized childish dreams. *Karin Mänsdotter* is a unique film and one of the great unknown works in film history.

Sjöberg then made only five films in the next twenty-five years. They may be seen as tentat-ive gestures towards recapturing the tone of his best-known works in the changed climate of contemporary reality. They are often over-wrought but are compelling even when they are at odds with the taste of their times. Despite his attempts to introduce action and positive change, Sjöberg's characters always seem doomed and bewildered as they react as though obeying some unseen instruction. Any one of them might have spoken the young Count's line in *On* (1964, *The Island*). 'Man is only a chess figure in a game through which he never clearly sees.'

EDGARDO COZARINSKY

Key films of 1940

The Bank Dick. USA. **prod co:** Universal. **dir:** Edward Cline. **sc:** Mahatma Kane Jeeves (W.C. Fields). **photo:** Milton Krasner. **ed:** Arthur Hilton. **art dir:** Jack Otterson. **mus dir:** Charles Previn. **with:** W.C. Fields, Cora Witherspoon, Una Merkel, Evelyn del Rio, Franklin Pangborn, Jessie Ralph.
Arguably Fields' best comedy vehicle: passing a bank, he inadvertently prevents a hold-up and is offered the job of bank detective. Eventually the gags take over the story and Fields reverts to his familiar persona of the idle layabout.

Christmas in July. USA. **prod co:** Paramount. **prod:** Paul Jones. **dir/sc:** Preston Sturges. **photo:** Victor Milner. **ed:** Ellsworth Hoagland. **art dir:** Hans Dreier, Earl Hedrick. **mus:** Sigmund Krumgold. **with:** Dick Powell, Ellen Drew, Raymond Walburn, Alexander Carr, William Demarest, Ernest Truex, Franklin Pangborn.
A thin idea – about a clerk who wins a great sum of money – is turned into a classic Forties comedy by clever characterization and ingenious, rapid-fire direction.

Citizen Kane; directed by Orson Welles – see special feature in Chapter 24.

Dr Ehrlich's Magic Bullet. USA. **prod co:** Warner Bros. **prod:** Hal B. Wallis. **dir:** William Dieterle. **sc:** John Huston, Norman Burnside, Heinz Herald. **photo:** James Wong Howe. **ed:** Warren Low. **art dir:** Carl Jules Weyl. **mus:** Max Steiner. **with:** Edward G. Robinson, Ruth Gordon, Albert Basserman, Otto Kruger, Donald Crisp, Maria Ouspenskaya, Sig Ruman.

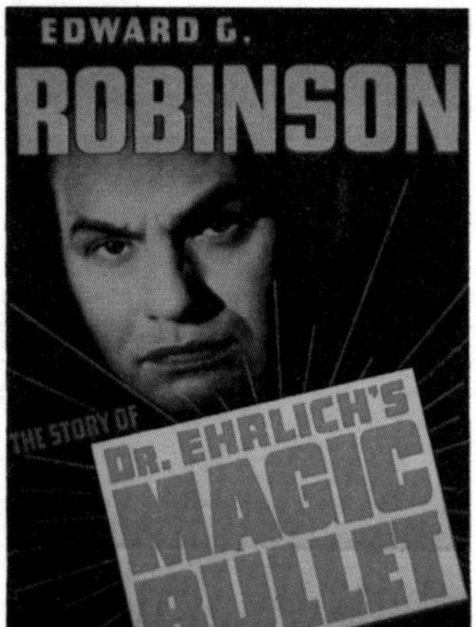

Among the last of the Warners cycle of prestigious screen biographies was this unusual tribute to the man who discovered a cure for syphilis, Dr Paul Ehrlich. Robinson was effectively cast in the comforting role of the dedicated scientist.

Fantasia. USA. **prod co:** Walt Disney. **prod:** Walt Disney. **dir:** Joe Grant, Dick Huemer. **ed:** Stephen Ceillag. **mus dir:** Edward H. Plumb, Leopold Stokowski and The Philadelphia Orchestra. **narr:** Deems Taylor. **mus:** The Nutcracker Suite (Tchaikovsky), Toccatta and Fugue in D Minor (Bach), The Sorcerer's Apprentice (Dukas), The Rite of Spring (Stravinsky), Symphony No. 6 (Beethoven), Dance of the Hours (Ponchielli), Night on a Bare Mountain (Mussorgsky), Ave Maria (Schubert).
Disney's Silly Symphonies had experimented with music and graphics for over a decade when the studio finally produced this feature film. Usually thought of as a partial success only, it is nonetheless remarkable for Stokowski's collaboration in the interpretation of the classics and for its colour and stereo sound.

Foreign Correspondent. USA. **prod co:** United Artists. **prod:** Walter Wanger. **dir:** Alfred Hitchcock. **sc:** Charles Bennett, Joan Harrison. **photo:** Rudolph Maté. **ed:** Otto Lovering, Dorothy Spencer. **art dir:** William Cameron Menzies, Alexander Golitzen. **mus:** Alfred Newman. **with:** Joel McCrea, Laraine Day, Herbert Marshall, George Sanders, Albert Basserman, Robert Benchley, Jane Novak, Edmund Gwenn.
A gripping spy thriller in the best Hitchcock tradition, this film also represented the director's strongest statement about the war. It was as important for the story, with Nazis as stock villains, as for its attempt to encourage America to enter the war.

The Grapes of Wrath; directed by John Ford – see special feature in Chapter 19.

The Great Dictator. USA. **prod co:** Charles Chaplin Corporation. **prod/dir/sc/mus:** Charles Chaplin. **photo:** Rollie H. Totheroh, Karl Struss. **ed:** Willard Nico. **art dir:** J. Russell Spencer. **mus dir:** Meredith Wilson. **sd:** Percy Townsend, Glenn Rominger **with:** Charles Chaplin, Paulette Goddard, Jack Oakie, Henry Daniell, Billy Gilbert, Reginald Gardner, Chester Conklin.
Chaplin, in the dual role of Adenoid Hynkel and the lowly barber from the ghetto, made his political position clearer than any other director in Hollywood at the time. Unfortunately the mixture of pathos and slapstick came in for criticism, but there was no mistaking the brilliance of his Hitler caricature.

The Great McGinty. USA. **prod co:** Paramount. **prod:** Paul Jones. **dir/sc:** Preston Sturges. **photo:** William Mellor. **ed:** Hugh Bennett. **art dir:** Hans Dreier, Earl Hedrick. **mus:** Frederick Hollander. **with:** Brian Donlevy, Muriel Angelus, Akim Tamiroff, Allyn Joslyn, William Demarest, Louis Jean Heydt, Harry Rosethal, Arthur Hoyt.
Preston Sturges' first shot at directing from his own screenplay was a sharp-edged satire on the American political machine. McGinty is elected governor through the all-too-familiar means of corruption, but his career ends abruptly when he succumbs to a moment's honesty. With deliciously fitting irony, he tells his tale to a man whose single moment of dishonesty has branded him an embezzler.

His Girl Friday. USA. **prod co:** Columbia. **prod/dir:** Howard Hawks. **sc:** Charles Lederer, from the play *The Front Page* by Ben Hecht and Charles MacArthur. **photo:** Joseph Walker. **ed:** Gene Havlick. **mus dir:** Morris W. Stoloff. **with:** Cary Grant, Rosalind Russell, Ralph Bellamy, Gene Lockhart, Porter Hall, John Qualen.
One of the most justly celebrated remakes in Hollywood history, Hawks' version of the black comedy about reporters covering a hanging recast the lead reporter Hildy Johnson as a woman and added the element of sex-war to an already bristling script.

Manpower. USA. **prod co:** Warner Bros. **prod:** Hal. B. Wallis, Mark Hellinger. **dir:** Raoul Walsh. **sc:** Richard Macaulay, Jerry Wald. **photo:** Ernest Haller. **sp eff:** Byron Haskin. **ed:** Ralph Dawson. **art dir:** Max Parker. **mus:** Adolph Deutsch. **with:** Edward G. Robinson, George Raft, Marlene Dietrich, Alan Hale, Eve Arden, Frank McHugh, Ward Bond, Barton MacLane, Walter Catlett, Joyce Compton
A drama set among the all-male group of power workers who compete for the love of a nightclub singer. The film's unusual degree of violence was neatly undercut by laconic humour and likeable performances.

The Philadelphia Story. USA. **prod co:** MGM. **prod:** Joseph L. Mankiewicz. **dir:** George Cukor. **sc:** Donald Ogden Stewart, from the play by Philip Barry. **photo:** Joseph Ruttenberg. **ed:** Frank Sullivan. **art dir:** Cedric Gibbons, Wade C. Rubottom. **mus:** Franz Waxman **sd:** Douglas Shearer. **with:** Katharine Hepburn, Cary Grant, James Stewart, Ruth Hussey, John Howard, Roland Young, John Halliday, Virginia Weidler, Mary Nash, Henry Daniell.
A wealthy, domineering divorcee, on the eve of her second marriage, becomes romantically involved with two men – a laconic gossip columnist and her mocking first husband. The film, adapted from a Broadway hit, was a success from the moment of casting and Cukor's direction elicits three strikingly different performances from his stars: Hepburn, Grant and Stewart.

The Power and the Land. USA. **prod co:** US Film Service for the Department of Agriculture. **dir:** Joris Ivens. **sc:** Edwin Locke, Joris Ivens. **photo:** Floyd Crosby, Arthur Ornitz. **ed:** Helen van Dongen. **mus:** Stephen Vincent Benet. **comm:** William P. Adams.
A documentary commissioned to demonstrate the extension of the American electricity network to rural Oklahoma. The tone is strident and hortatory and, for Ivens, surprisingly distant from the human subjects (the dust-bowl farmers), but the film admirably demonstrates the power of his imagery.

Rebecca. USA. **prod co:** Selznick International. **prod:** David O. Selznick. **dir:** Alfred Hitchcock. **sc:** Robert E. Sherwood, Joan Harrison, from the novel by Daphne du Marier. **photo** (Technicolor)**:** George Barnes. **ed:** Hal C. Kern. **art dir:** Lyle Wheeler. **mus:** Franz Waxman. **with:** Laurence Olivier, Joan Fontaine, George Sanders, Judith Anderson, Nigel Bruce, C. Aubrey Smith.
Hitchcock described this, his first Hollywood film, as 'completely British', and indeed the story – a wealthy man remarries and takes his new wife to his country home where suspicious circumstances surround the death of his first wife – is as Gothic as the brooding Cornish settings. The film marked Hitchcock's transition in genre from the thriller to the psychological mystery story.

Remorques. France. **prod co:** SEDIF. **dir:** Jean Grémillon. **sc:** Jacques Prévert, André Cayatte, Charles Spaak, from a novel by Roger Vercel. **photo:** Armand Thirard. **ed:** Louisette Hautecoeur. **art dir:** Alexandre Trauner. **mus:** Roland Manuel. **with:** Jean Gabin, Madeleine Renaud, Michèle Morgan, Fernand Ledoux, Charles Blavette, Jean Marchat.
The poignant story of a sailor who falls for a woman whom he rescues from the sea is powerfully counterpointed by a lyrical and atmospheric evocation of the Brittany coast. The elements and the sea are the major protagonists in the drama.

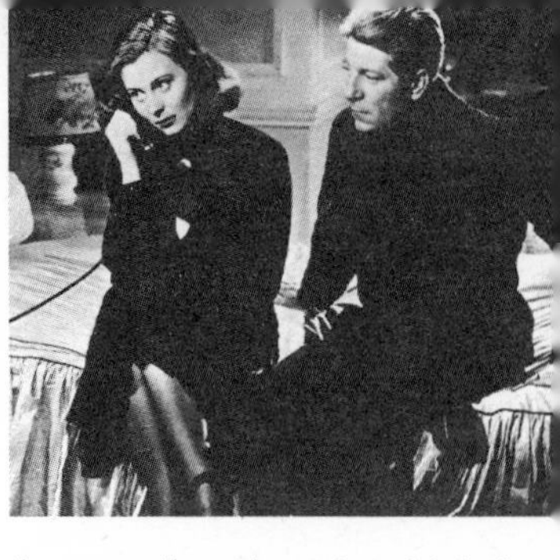

The Return of Frank James. USA. **prod co:** 20th Century-Fox. **prod:** Kenneth MacGowan. **dir:** Fritz Lang. **sc:** Sam Hellman. **photo:** (Technicolor)**:** George Barnes, William V. Skall. **ed:** Walter Thompson. **art dir:** Richard Day, Wiard B. Ihnen. **mus:** David Buttolph. **with:** Henry Fonda, Gene Tierney, Jackie Cooper, Henry Hull, John Carradine, Donald Meek.
Lang's first Western, in soft and luminous colour, is a fascinating analysis of the mythology of the West. The transformation of the legendary outlaw into a hero is reinforced by the persona and performance of Henry Fonda.

The Sea Hawk. USA. **prod co:** Warner Bros. **prod:** Hal B. Wallis, Henry Blanke. **dir:** Michael Curtiz. **sc:** Howard Koch, Seton I. Miller. **photo:** Sol Polito. **ed:** George Amy. **art dir:** Anton Grot. **sp eff:** Byron Haskin, H. F. Koenekamp. **mus:** Erich Wolfgang Korngold. **with:** Errol Flynn, Claude Rains, Brenda Marshall, Flora Robson, Donald Crisp, Alan Hale.
Errol Flynn, as a sea captain with no time for diplomacy, sabotages a Spanish invasion attempt at Good Queen Bess' behest in this Curtiz swashbuckler. The film contains clear analogies with the situation in wartime England.

The Thief of Bagdad. Britain. **prod co:** London Films. **prod:** Alexander Korda. **assoc prod:** Zoltan Korda, William Cameron Menzies. **dir:** Ludwig Berger, Michael Powell, Tim Whelan. **sc:** Lajos Biro, Miles Malleson. **photo** (Technicolor)**:** Georges Pèrinal, Osmond Borrodaile. **sp photo eff:** Lawrence Butler. **ed:** Charles Crichton, William Hornbeck. **art dir:** Vincent Korda, William Cameron Menzies. **mus:** Miklos Rosza. **mus dir:** Muir Matheson. **with:** Conrad Veidt, Sabu, June Duprez, Rex Ingram, Miles Malleson, John Justin, Morton Selton.
This version of the fairy-tale about a quest for a magic chest was even more lavish than Douglas Fairbanks Sr's 1924 spectacular. Begun at Korda's Denham studios, the film was completed in Hollywood owing to the outbreak of war, but the outstanding special-effects work was a triumph of British studio expertise.

Volpone. France. **prod co:** Films Ile de France. **prod:** A. Hertz. **dir:** Maurice Tourneur. **sc:** Jules Romains, from the play by Ben Jonson. **photo:** Armand Thirard. **ed:** Marcel Cohen. **art dir:** André Barsacq, Jean Perrier, Jacques Gut. **mus:** Marcel Delannoy. **with:** Harry Baur, Louis Jouvet, Charles Dullin, Fernand Ledoux, Jacqueline Delubac.
Tourneur had achieved fame as one of the great Hollywood directors in the silent era, but he had been working in his native France since the mid-Twenties. This adaptation of a Jacobean classic comedy was notable for uniting the talents of France's greatest stage actors Louis Jouvet and Charles Dullin.

Chapter 21

Hollywood goes to war

The war had been a tricky subject for American films, but after Pearl Harbor Hollywood opened up with all guns blazing

To understand the way in which America rather tentatively entered World War II it is necessary to appreciate the horrifying spectacle of twelve million men unemployed in the bitter winter of 1932–33 and ten million as late as 1938. The shock to the American psyche was profound and would have long-term effects.

It was Herbert Hoover's contention that the Depression had originated in Europe and that the contagion had somehow been transported to America, possibly in the manner of Dracula coming ashore in Bremen. Since everybody was also aware that most of the European countries had defaulted on their war loans, the isolationist mood of the USA in general and Congress in particular remained essentially unbroken throughout the decade.

The isolationist senator Gerald P. Nye chaired the Congressional Committee which concluded that arms manufacturers, in an unholy alliance with the international bankers and businessmen, had been responsible for the entry of the United States into World War I. Consequently in August 1935 Congress passed the Pittman Neutrality Resolution prohibiting the export of munitions and the shipment of arms on American vessels to foreign belligerents.

America was hardly alone in its introspection. The assembled powers of the world were equally unwilling to act after Italy had invaded Abyssinia in 1935, when Hitler re-occupied the Rhineland in 1936, or when Italy and Germany both sent troops to fight with Franco in the Spanish Civil War.

After the Japanese invaded North China in 1937, Roosevelt made a notorious speech in Chicago in which he called for a 'quarantine' of those nations who were the aggressors (or, in other words, an international embargo against Japan, Italy and Germany) lest the 'disease' of war infect the Western Hemisphere. The allegory instantly outraged a vast spectrum of opinion, both official and unofficial, and thereafter the President kept his anti-fascist feelings to himself. Hollywood, which invariably luxuriated in the warmth of the majority opinion, looked on approvingly as all the political pressures were exerted on the side of caution.

When war eventually broke out in Europe, Roosevelt began 27 months of what he later termed 'walking on eggs'. Congress was immediately called into special session to push through a clause that permitted foreign powers to buy arms from the United States, provided the munitions were paid for in cash and transported on non-American vessels. This was designed to help Great Britain who, unfortunately, had neither the money nor the ships to conform to such requirements.

This was a difficult period for Hollywood. The studio heads read Dr Gallup's poll, which announced that although 84 per cent of all Americans wanted an Allied victory, 96 per cent of them felt that their country should stay out of the conflict. The contradiction almost paralysed the film industry.

In the summer of 1939 all the studios postponed their spy, refugee or anti-Nazi stories. Warner Brothers shelved *Boycott* and *Underground Road* (eventually released in 1941 as *Underground*); Fox held up production on *I Married a Nazi* and Walter Wanger dithered over his dramatization of Vincent Sheean's *Personal History*, which finally saw the light of day as *Foreign Correspondent* (1940). It was felt that a sudden declaration of war or conclusion of peace would ruin the market value of the stories. The events of early September gave the green light to production although there remained the nagging fear, intensified in the wake of the Phoney War in the West, that peace would break out and cause the pictures to be shelved yet again.

Warner Brothers, who had made the one explicitly anti-Nazi film of the pre-war period (1939, *Confessions of a Nazi Spy*), were unofficially told by the government not to make any more such pictures. In April 1940 the news filtered back to Hollywood that several Polish exhibitors who had shown *Confessions of a Nazi Spy* had been hanged in the foyers of their own cinemas.

Warners were thus happy to mute their anti-Nazism by making such films as *The Sea Hawk* (1940) in which Errol Flynn as a swashbuckling privateer rouses a somnolent England to inflict a crushing defeat on the Spanish Armada – a simple parallel with the Luftwaffe and the Battle of Britain.

When the Phoney War of 1939 gave way to the blitzkrieg of 1940, the struggle in America between the isolationists and the supporters of intervention increased in bitterness. Charles Lindbergh, the aviator hero of the Twenties, called passionately for

Left: support for Britain and her allies was evident in Hollywood before the USA joined the war. As well as this airborne adventure, 1941 also saw the release of A Yank in Libya, a film with an equally contrived plot that had an American as hero of a British campaign. Above: cover from The Saturday Evening Post *depicting the role of Hollywood in the war effort; films were shipped to all the fighting fronts and screened in improvised 'cinemas'. Below: British troops were also sustained on a diet of Hollywood cinema. Here ATC cadets attend a show of* I Wanted Wings, *an action movie about young flyers proving themselves in training*

total isolation and warned that American intervention would be a disaster in view of the invincibility of the German armed forces and the inevitability of German domination of Europe.

When President Roosevelt summarily dismissed his opinions, Lindbergh angrily resigned his Commission as a colonel in the Air Corps. Roosevelt ignored the petulant retaliation. In Charlotte, North Carolina, the residents of Lindbergh Drive renamed their street Avon Terrace.

Hitler's victories in the West were undoubtedly bad for Hollywood. In the Low Countries alone 1400 cinemas were immediately closed, representing a loss of $2.5 million in annual revenue to the American film companies. That, added to the losses previously sustained in parts of Scandinavia, Poland, Italy, Spain and the Balkans, meant that they had lost over a quarter of their annual revenue. By the end of 1940, the whole of Continental Europe was closed to US film imports apart from Sweden, Switzerland and Portugal.

Hollywood directly reflected the troubled anxieties of these confusing days. Chaplin's *The Great Dictator* (1940), though ostensibly a satire on Hitler, worked best when it was at its furthest remove from the political parallel and the film's mawkish descent into moral sentimentality in the closing sequence sat unhappily on the preceding farce.

MGM's *Escape* and *The Mortal Storm* (both 1940) doffed their caps in the direction of the horrors of Nazi Germany but they testified to Louis B. Mayer's insistence on avoiding overt condemnation of fascism for fear of political and economic reprisals.

Roosevelt's desperate anxiety to help Britain as she suffered the Blitz and the U-boat war in the Atlantic was tempered by the knowledge that he had decided in 1940 to run for President for an unprecedented third term of office. Only when he had defeated the Republican candidate, Wendell Willkie, could he afford to make sweeping demands of 'Lend-Lease', the Act of Congress which permitted complete and open aid to Britain, short of actual military involvement.

Roosevelt's increasing involvement in the war aided those Hollywood films which touched on the conflict, although most of them treated the issues lightly: there was the Bob Hope comedy *Caught in the Draft*, Abbot and Costello in *Buck Privates* and Tyrone Power and Betty Grable in *A Yank in the RAF* (all 1941). The more serious movies – Robert Taylor in *Flight Command* (1940), Errol Flynn in *Dive Bomber* (1941) and Ray Milland and William Holden in *I Wanted Wings* (1941) – were still far stronger on traditional Hollywood melodrama than ideological content.

It was, therefore, highly encouraging that the coveted place of 1941's top money-making picture was taken by the reflective Howard Hawks film *Sergeant York* (1941), which portrayed a World War I hero (an Oscar-winning performance by Gary Cooper) who overcame his pacifism when he realized that killing for one's country could be also construed as doing God's work. York's rapid elevation to the status of war hero seems to bear divine endorsement, and his decision to fight becomes, by implication, America's decision too.

The easiest way Hollywood could treat the war without offending the isolationists was to make films about Britain for whom sympathy was high in 1941. *That Hamilton Woman!* with Vivien Leigh and Laurence Olivier, was an instant success despite the limited budget on which Alexander Korda made it. The historical parallel of Britain triumphing over the threatened invasion of a foreign tyrant was particularly attractive to Winston Churchill, who took time off from conducting the war to cable Korda with 'helpful' suggestions.

Top right: Gary Cooper played Sergeant York, *the pacifist hick who takes up arms for his country in World War I. The film was a powerfully persuasive argument for American intervention in World War II. Right: it was hardly possible to forget Pearl Harbor, especially as Republic's first contribution to the war effort was released only two months after the event. Below: the film trade papers promoted new alliances (Britain, USA and USSR) through the old alliance between the film distributor and the exhibitors. Bottom: Bob Hope and Dave Willock in* Let's Face It. *Bob ended up a hero and so won a medal*

Despite the marked pro-Allied sentiments in the country at large, Congress still contained a small but significant group of die-hard isolationists. Hollywood was given conclusive evidence of this in October 1941, when Senators Nye and Clark introduced the Senate Resolution 152 which proposed the formation of a committee to investigate:

'. . . any propaganda disseminated by motion pictures . . . to influence public sentiment in the direction of participation by the United States in the . . . European war.'

Of the movies that had caused so much heart-searching in Hollywood during the previous two years, 17 were resurrected and paraded before a collection of unsympathetic politicians. Warner Brothers were condemned for making *Confessions of a Nazi Spy*, *Underground*, *Dive Bomber* and *Sergeant York*. MGM was accused of impure thoughts during the making of *Escape* and *The Mortal Storm* and Fox was keel-hauled for producing *I Married a Nazi* (eventually released as *The Man I Married* in 1941).

Hollywood resigned itself to facing the inevitable rebuke. Ironically it was saved by intervention of the Japanese air squadrons which, in the early morning of December 7, 1941, sank or badly damaged eight battleships and three light cruisers and killed 2400 Americans on the drowsy naval base at Pearl Harbor.

The Pearl Harbor disaster instantly resolved all doubts regarding America's entry into World War II. Hollywood 'enlisted' in a burst of patriotic enthusiasm and economic shrewdness. Paramount changed the title of their picture *Midnight Angel* to *Pacific Blackout* (1942) but it failed to rescue the truly awful nature of the film. David Selznick copyrighted the title *V for Victory* but never got round to using it and in March 1942 Republic Pictures emptied cinemas all over the country with a quickie entitled *Remember Pearl Harbor.*

More significant were the wartime regulations which the government imposed on Hollywood. In December 1941, only two days after Pearl Harbor, army officials moved into all the studios and commandeered the firearms used in any production which were then turned over to civil defence units. All studios were ordered onto a daylight shift of 8 am to 5 pm so that employees could get home before the blackout began and, as a result, night filming was temporarily halted. Most of these instinctive measures were only imposed in the early days of the war when it was still feared that the Japanese were preparing to invade along the vast, undefended coastline of California, but the moves were, at the same time, symptomatic of the government's new involvement in the affairs of the US film industry.

As early as May 1942, the trade paper *Variety* divulged that top-level discussions had resulted in a decision not to portray Hitler and Hirohito as personal symbols of German and Japanese evil. The American public was to be taught that the German and Japanese people were equally to blame for tolerating and cooperating with such leaders.

It was the US government that outlined for Hollywood the six basic patterns for pictures related to the war. The first was the issues of the war itself, into which category fell such diverse movies as *This Above All* (1942) and *Watch on the Rhine* (1943). The second was the nature of the enemy, as exemplified

Once America had entered the war, the Hollywood studios hurled everything into the fight – even star comics and crooners

---

in *Hitler's Children* (1943) and *This Land Is Mine* (1943). Third came the notion of 'United Nations and its Peoples' by which was meant everything from *Mrs Miniver* to *Mission to Moscow* (both 1942) and *Dragon Seed* (1944).

The fourth category focused on the pressing need for increased industrial production, and here the portrayals featured ordinary people engaged in factory work in films like *Wings for the Eagle* (1942) and *Swing Shift Maisie* (1943).

The last two categories were self-explanatory morale-boosting films about the home front and movies dealing with the fighting forces, a genre in which Hollywood had a long and successful record. Even films which were simply composed of military heroics invariably made obeisance to at least one of the categories mentioned.

No genre was excluded from the fight against fascism. The musical made a forceful entry with *Yankee Doodle Dandy* (1942), starring James Cagney as George M. Cohan, the author of the song 'Over There', the one universally acknowledged hit of World War I. Paramount's contribution included *Star Spangled Rhythm* (1943), which served as a passable excuse for a series of flag-waving and eyebrow-raising numbers. More bizarre than most war musicals was *When Johnny Comes Marching Home* (1943), which starred a heroic marine (played by the irrepressible Allan Jones from *A Night at the Opera*), the teenage wonder Gloria Jean and Phil Spitalny's all-girl orchestra.

Basil Rathbone returned to the attack as Sherlock Holmes, chasing Nazi villains in contemporary London (where the head of the Nazi spy ring was, inevitably, Moriarty). Nazis also showed up in Maria Montez's temple (in *White Savage*, 1943) and even attacked a coonskin-clad Errol Flynn in the wilds of Canada in *Northern Pursuit* (1943). They also managed an appearance in the 1943 version of *The Desert Song*, where they signally failed to achieve either victory or a decent song.

The progress of the war itself seemed to follow the traditional narrative line laid down by Hollywood. America's initial experience was a series of desperate defeats. By New Year's Day 1942, the Japanese had made successful landings on Guam, Hong Kong, Borneo, Wake Island and the Philippines. General MacArthur was forced to retreat to the fatal Bataan peninsula from which he was removed while his troops died bravely and helplessly. The names of Bataan and Corregidor became synonymous with death and despair. On May 6, 1942, to prevent even more pointless slaughter, General Wainwright was compelled to surrender the rock with its 11,000 American defenders. It was the biggest capitulation in American history and its effect on the population was profound.

The American film industry had, therefore, to address itself to the unaccustomed atmosphere of military disaster. In an attempt to finish *Wake Island* (1942) on a rousing note, Paramount took the costly step of halting production just before shooting was due to take place on the closing sequences. In this way they hoped that the real military events would permit them a happy ending. They didn't. MGM's *Bataan* (1943) closes with the massacre of the American patrol whose fortunes we have been following, although the end caption points out that from such sacrifices sprang the victory of the Battle of Midway.

Victories in North Africa and Italy in 1943 were followed the next year by the successful invasion of France and, as military events foreshadowed ultimate victory, Hollywood's major problem became how to avoid making war movies which would be immediately outdated if the Germans surrendered before the editing was completed.

In the event it did not really matter. 1946 proved to be the most successful year in the history of the film industry. If the war had driven people into the cinemas to escape, peace sent them there to celebrate. All the major studios did their bit for the war effort, supplying propaganda and escapism in generous helpings. Spectacular profits were their reward. These were indeed the golden years of Hollywood. It was a time, so it was said, when even good pictures made money.   COLIN SHINDLER

Above: the theme and closing hymn of Mrs Miniver *was 'There'll always be an England', but there was no mistaking MGM's all-purpose 'English' mansion as Walter Pidgeon and Greer Garson's home. Below: the last defender in* Bataan. *Bottom: James Cagney helps the RAF in* Captains of the Clouds (1942)

On the Battlefront

Hollywood's finest war films celebrated the courage, loyalty and good humour of the ordinary fighting man, forced to pay the ultimate price of freedom

When the Japanese attack on Pearl Harbor, on December 7, 1941, finally brought the walls of American isolationism tumbling down, Hollywood mobilized for war virtually without breaking step. Encouraged and endorsed by Roosevelt's government, it proceeded to glorify the waging of war in the same way that it had happily exalted the busting of crime syndicates or celebrated the winning of the West. Hollywood's total response to the US government's exhortations and practical cooperation was spectacular: out of approximately 1700 features produced between 1942 and 1945 over 500 were war films of one kind or another.

The qualitative result, however, was somewhat less satisfying. The avowed aims of the American war film were to satisfy the public demand for information about the war, to explain its purposes and why sacrifice was sometimes necessary, and to raise home-front morale by showing, in a positive light, the husbands and sons of America in action. The problem of achieving these aims was that, in contrast to Britain and the rest of Europe, the USA was far removed from the actual theatres of conflict. This fact, combined with the official

guidelines as to what could be shown on the screen, ensured that what the public mostly got were films which (as Leif Furhammar and Folke Isaksson wrote in *Politics and Film*):

'. . . sprang less from reality than from currently popular preconceptions which, in turn, they served to reinforce. War was an exciting adventure; politics a superior form of romance; morality a matter of morale. In this treatment, death was painless, decorative and even, ultimately, a blessing.'

As the war progressed, however, the glamour and escapism began to be replaced by greater honesty and realism. Of all the types of war films that were made, perhaps those which best reflected this progression were the ones which attempted to convey the ordeal of combat, the grim necessity of fighting a 'just' war, the banality of death as well as heroism in

Above: Bataan's study of sacrificial heroism helped Americans come to terms with initial defeat in the Philippines. Right: Cary Grant captains the crew of the submarine that sails into the jaws of death in Destination Tokyo. Below: a band of heroes from all walks of life sheltered together in Guadalcanal Diary

battle, and the one authentic legacy of the soldier – comradeship-in-arms.

The first significant attempt to treat these themes was John Farrow's *Wake Island* (1942), a stirring, semi-fictional account of a doomed, two-week defensive action in the Pacific by a handful of marines in the days immediately following Pearl Harbor.

Although one critic justifiably called *Wake Island* 'a failure in realism', pointing to its over-the-top heroics and sentimentality (represented most jarringly by the presence of a dog-mascot and its litter of puppies), it nevertheless laid the ground rules for all the subsequent successful combat pictures: the immediacy of its true-life theme and the greater confidence in its subject-matter engendered by the USA now having its own exclusive theatre of war; the fact that (because of a War Production Board ban on expensive studio sets) it was made on location and in cooperation with the US Marine Corps; and its concentration on the fighting man, which, though stressing individual characteristics, at the same time implied a oneness against the enemy and a coming-together of the many ethnic strains of American society in a common struggle.

Similar to *Wake Island* in both atmosphere and technique was Lewis Seiler's *Guadalcanal*

Diary (1943), which came close to enacting the spirit of one of the Pacific's bloodiest campaigns and the USA's first major victory. The cross-section of American social types acting in harness without losing their individuality included, this time, a saintly, courageous chaplain (played by Preston Foster).

An interesting sidelight on this and similar films about the Pacific was the image of the Japanese soldier as well-dressed, well-equipped, strong and formidably efficient, whereas later accounts (as in James Jones' *The Thin Red Line*) tell us that they were ragged, half-starved and under-resourced, but totally dedicated.

Another popular film area of operations for American film-makers was the Philippines. Among the most acclaimed films concerned with this theatre of the war was Tay Garnett's

Bataan (1943), an emotive rendering of a supposedly true account of how 13 men fought a desperate, sacrificial rearguard action to aid the withdrawal of General MacArthur's forces.

The Pacific war film also took to the air, most effectively perhaps in Howard Hawks' $3 million epic *Air Force* (1943), the story of a Boeing-17 Flying Fortress and its crew battling their way across the Pacific from Pearl Harbor to an Australian beach, culled by writer Dudley Nichols from factual records made available by General H.H. Arnold of the US Army Air Force. General Arnold's instruction was to tell 'how the Japs laced hell out of us at first; then tell how we fought back. Tell the whole story with its bitterness and sadness and heroism.' Hawks responded with a characteristic paeon to virility and professionalism, and with a heavy concentration on triumphant action set pieces culminating in a re-creation of the Coral Sea naval battle against the Japanese fleet.

Hollywood took particular inspiration from the Doolittle raid, the first bombing attack on Japan which occurred 131 days after Pearl Harbor. Delmer Daves opened the proceedings with his feature debut *Destination Tokyo* (1943), a stirring account of the submarine *Copperfin*'s daring mission to penetrate Tokyo Bay to help set up the raid. The picture was convincing enough to be used later as a navy instructional film. Lewis Milestone followed up with *The Purple Heart* (1944), an indictment of Japanese atrocities against American airmen who had fallen into their hands. But most notable of all the Doolittle films was Mervyn LeRoy's *Thirty Seconds Over Tokyo* (1944), supervised by the leader of the raid himself, Major Ted Lawson, and chronicling all the events from preparation and attack to the final escape of the crew aided by Chinese patriots.

A recurrent problem for American war films was their impact on the British public, who periodically complained of both their quantity and their content. The film most attacked on these grounds was Raoul Walsh's *Objective, Burma!* (1945), the film in which, as several reviewers later described it, Errol Flynn cap-

tured Burma single-handed. Apart from one or two passing references, the film managed to omit any mention of Allied involvement in the Burma campaign, least of all the British 14th Army, made the Burmese jungle look like a national park, and so offended the British public and military personnel alike that Warner Brothers were forced to remove it from English screens. In retrospect, Warners' principal crime seems to have been one of gross mistiming: it was simply the wrong moment to present such a film to a Britain exhausted by six years of all-too-realistic warfare.

More significantly, America's three war masterpieces of 1945 received hardly any attention at all in the UK. These were the heady days of victory and the British had had enough of war particularly in films which took such a grim, melancholy view of the fighting man. John Ford's first war feature, *They Were Expendable* (1945), dealt with the agonized exploits of Commander John D. Bulkeley's (Brickley in the film) small squadron of PT boats in the Philippine withdrawal, coupled with implied criticism of the pre-war military leadership. Despite an apathetic reaction on both sides of the Atlantic, it has survived as a compellingly unglamorous statement of what the British film director Lindsay Anderson has described as 'the time-honoured conceptions of duty, courage and comradeship in arms', and it is now acknowledged as one of the great achievements of American wartime cinema.

Perhaps the two finest depictions of the American infantryman were *The Story of GI Joe* and *A Walk in the Sun* (both 1945). *The Story of GI Joe* (dir. William Wellman) was universally praised but little seen. A hymn of praise to the American soldiers who battled their way from

North Africa to Rome, via Sicily, Southern Italy and Cassino, the film was based on the writings of war correspondent Ernie Pyle (Burgess Meredith) who was later killed at Iwo Jima. There were no mock heroics, only the hunger, misery, fear, boredom and weariness of the foot-soldiers amidst a confusing nightmare of military manoeuvres. The film also dared to show the bodies of dead infantrymen in a low-key finale which was at odds with the euphoria of the time and would account for the wariness with which it was received.

For *A Walk in the Sun* (dir. Lewis Milestone) scriptwriter Robert Rossen took the screenplay almost verbatim from Harry Brown's original novel and conveyed fully the book's verbal cadences and almost folkloric style. The film portrays the confused progress of a single platoon during one morning between landing at Salerno and taking an objective six miles away. This was the ultimate refinement of the group motif, achieved by acute observation of individual characteristics and states of mind, from the frenetic collapse of a shell-shocked sergeant (Herbert Rudley) to the habit of another soldier (John Ireland) of composing letters home in his head as an ironic commentary on the action. In keeping with the predominant vein of Hollywood's final, masterly chronicles of the war period, the film was, as noted by the critic Penelope Houston, 'concerned with the immediate realities of a situation rather than its deeper implications.' The film appeared to accept the fact of war rather than rebel against it.

Thus the American combat film attained maturity and excellence at the very moment that the genre had suddenly become unfashionable, and the masterpieces of the war remained unsung until a later time of rediscovery and reappraisal. CLYDE JEAVONS

Top: American airmen get help from British soldiers in Air Force. *Above right: the restrained performances of John Wayne and Robert Montgomery (centre) helped to make* They Were Expendable *one of Hollywood's finest war films. Right: George Tyne and Richard Conte in* A Walk in the Sun

Howard Hawks rediscovered

Hawks was a much-neglected director until the French critics of the Fifties saluted his personal style of film-making and established him as one of Hollywood's great individual talents

Howard Hawks has created some of the most memorable moments in the history of the American cinema. The problem, however, is how do these moments hang together? Is there a shaping intelligence behind them, or are they merely the accidental benefits of Hollywood movie-making? Until recently the consensus of opinion favoured the latter view. Richard Griffith's remark in 1948, in *The Film Till Now*, that Hawks is 'a very good all-rounder', is representative of the attention paid to Hawks before the French film journal *Cahiers du Cinéma* championed him as *the* American *auteur*. And even after the first rumblings of the *politique des auteurs* (the theory of authorship, by which the creative and artistic credit for a film is attributed to its director) in the mid-

Above: Hawks, seated by the cameraman, directs Gary Cooper in Sergeant York *(1941), and (left) discusses the script of* Gentlemen Prefer Blondes *(1953) with Marilyn Monroe. He was born in Goshen, Indiana, in 1896, and after graduating in engineering from Cornell University in 1917 served in the Army Air Corps during World War I. He then worked as an aircraft builder and pilot and as a racing driver before entering movies in 1922. Although Hawks continued to write, direct and produce films until 1970, flying and driving remained his great passion – revealed in such pictures as* The Air Circus *(1928),* The Crowd Roars *(1931) and* Red Line 7000 *(1965). He died in 1977 – partly from blood poisoning contracted from injuries sustained motorcycling when he was 78 years old*

Fifties, in 1959 *Sight and Sound*, the leading organ of British film culture, had no qualms about not reviewing *Rio Bravo*, a film now acknowledged as one of the great Westerns.

Prior to the *auteur* theory, the mark of a film artist in the American cinema could be found in his choice of subject-matter, in his obvious artistic aspirations, or in his personal visual style. Clearly, by these criteria, Hawks was an unambitious director. In 53 years as a film-maker he was responsible for no major cinematic innovations and was happy to produce pictures that in their sober adherence to the conventions of Hollywood movie-making lack the personal touch of a Hitchcock or the artistry of a Chaplin. Certainly Hawks was a prolific genre director: *Scarface* (1931) is a gangster film; *Gentlemen Prefer Blondes* (1953), a musical; *Land of the Pharoahs* (1955), a biblical epic; *The Dawn Patrol* (1930) and *Air Force* (1943) are war films; *To Have and Have Not* (1944) and *The Big Sleep* (1946), thrillers; *Red River* (1948) and *Rio Bravo* (1959), Westerns; *Bringing Up Baby* (1938) and *Monkey Business* (1952), comedies; and *Only Angels Have Wings* (1939) and *Hatari!* (1962) are just two of his many adventure films.

The breadth of Hawks' films and their consistent commitment to action rather than reflection blinded early critics to the clear pattern of repetition and variation that binds the films together. It was precisely the attempt to trace such a pattern in such a diversity of films directed (and, in most cases, produced) by one man that led 'auteurist' critics to propose Hawks' work as the test case of their theories,

and revealed that behind the mask of Hollywood there lurked artists.

Turning from the ostensible subject-matter of Hawks' films then, it is possible to discern a clear pattern of themes running through them: the group, male friendships, the nature of professionalism, the threats women pose men. Recurring motifs include the passing and lighting of cigarettes for friends, communal sing-songs, and bizarre sexual role-reversals.

Accordingly, rather than relating *Only Angels Have Wings* to the spate of aviator movies that appeared in the Thirties, *To Have and Have Not* to Curtiz's *Casablanca* (1942), and *Rio Bravo* to the development of the Western, it is more useful to relate these Hawks films to each other, or even, as Robin Wood has suggested in his book *Howard Hawks*, to regard them as a loose trilogy in which notions of heroism and self-respect are interrogated.

Band of angels

Only Angels Have Wings is concerned with the problems of a group of mail plane flyers. From the start the group is hermetically sealed off from the outside world by storms, giant condors, mountains and highly dangerous landing-strips – and the action takes place almost entirely in the saloon-cum-office run by Dutchie (Sig Ruman). Here the group is self-sufficient with its members demanding and acknowledging support for each other's actions, as instanced in the talking down of pilots in bad weather, and details like Kid (Thomas Mitchell) passing Geoff (Cary Grant) a cigarette even before Geoff searches for one. Geoff is the leader of the group, who flies when the weather is too bad to send up his comrades.

Into the group comes Bonnie (Jean Arthur), down on her luck but asking for help from no-one. When one of the flyers, Joe (Noah Beery Jr), attempts a landing in bad weather – against Geoff's advice – to keep a dinner date with her, he crashes and is killed. His feelings for a woman have affected his judgment, caused him to behave irresponsibly and let his

Above right: Sergeant York, based on the diary of a pacifist who eventually joined the army and became America's greatest hero of World War I. Released shortly before America joined World War II, it made a powerful call to arms. Below and below right: Hawks' films are full of sing-songs – as in Only Angels Have Wings with Jean Arthur and Cary Grant – and the lighting of cigarettes – as in To Have and Have Not with Humphrey Bogart and Lauren Bacall – and similar gestures of friendship

comrades down by breaching the professional code that binds the flyers together and makes it possible to keep the mail-run going in the face of overwhelming odds. 'Who's Joe?' says Geoff when Bonnie berates him for his callousness in eating the steak that had been prepared for the man who has just died, and goes on to sum Joe up with the words, 'He just wasn't good enough'. The sequence finally ends, however, with the celebratory (and defiant) singing by Geoff and Bonnie of 'The Peanut Vendor', a communal act which has the double function of initiating her into the group as a professional in her own right (she is a singer) and confirming her acceptance of the rules of the game of Hawks' group of flyers.

As the story develops, and Bonnie's love for Geoff deepens, it becomes evident that although suspicious of emotional entanglements – he has been fooled once before – he is, in fact, 'in love' with Kid, his assistant, as his breakdown after Kid's death testifies. At this point the interlocking web of relationships becomes even more complex. Kid's death is, on the one hand, self-inflicted: his eyesight is failing and he flies against Geoff's instructions; but as a grounded flyer he has only a living death to look forward to. At the same time his death is caused by his taking on an important job meant for a flyer whose abilities he distrusts. The flyer, Bat McPherson (Richard Barthelmess), once baled out of a plane leaving a friend of Kid's to die, and has since determined to win back his self-respect by taking on the most hazardous flights possible. This wash of conflicting emotions and loyalties that Hawks

sees as life is only held in check by the sense of what Robin Wood calls 'the constant shadow of death', which in turn demands responsible behaviour and self-respect if the group, or the individual, is to survive.

Loners together

The pattern of relationships in *To Have and Have Not* is similar – but with significant differences. In *Only Angels Have Wings* the group comprises a leader, his friend, the failed professional who is seeking redemption, and an intruder; in *To Have and Have Not* there is the loner Harry Morgan (Humphrey Bogart), Eddie (Walter Brennan) – 'who used to be good' – as a drunken version of Kid, and Slim (Lauren Bacall) as a far more assertive and aggressive Bonnie figure. The equivalent of the McPherson character is Paul de Bursac (Walter Molnar), a man who needs physical assistance from Morgan rather than moral support. And in contrast to Geoff in *Only Angels Have Wings*, who is desperately trying to secure a mail-run contract for Dutchie, Morgan in *To Have and Have Not* is working only for himself. Despite the existence of a group, the characters in *To Have and Have Not* are much more independent and self-motivated than in the earlier film.

Although the bar run by Crickett (Hoagy Carmichael) in *To Have and Have Not* has a communal function in a similar fashion to Dutchie's, the dramatic thrust of the film is provided by the Morgan–Slim relationship. Bogart and Bacall fell in love while making *To Have and Have Not* and their scenes reflect it –

Cary Grant (above), and Elsa Martinelli in Hatari! *(below), learn what it is like to be hunted. Cowpunchers Noah Beery Jr, Walter Brennan and Montgomery Clift enjoy a game of cards in* Red River

especially the one where Slim instructs Morgan to whistle when he wants her ('You just put your lips together and blow') and then excites to the sound of his whistle of surprise. They give the movie a depth of emotion that is missing from the bite-on-the-bullet stoicism of *Only Angels Have Wings.*

In *Rio Bravo* Hawks heightened emotions by having a hero who is completely sexually embarrassed. Previously Hawks had restricted the sexual humiliation theme to the string of crazy comedies he made alongside his adventure films. *Rio Bravo*, though, is a bringing together of comedy and adventure in Hawks' work, a summation of two traditions his films had established.

In his adventure films, the hero is master of all he surveys; in the comedies he is the victim, both of society and of women – who only have marginal roles in the adventure films. The adventure films occupy a world, far from society's grasp, of hunters, fishermen, aviators and so on, who lead their lives struggling against natural hazards; survival depends on every member of the group being 'good enough', and they celebrate that survival through the ritual of sing-songs. Their reaction to death is to pass over the event as quickly as possible. 'We brought nothing into

the world and it's certain we'll take nothing out,' recites Tom Dunson (John Wayne) dryly over a grave in *Red River*. The emotional, romantic reactions of the characters in the adventure films are similarly muted; the women go through elaborate rituals of courtship (usually confiding their love not to the loved one but to his friend) in the course of which they prove themselves as tough as men.

The heroes of the adventure films are emotionally repressed and a current of homosexuality runs beneath the male friendships – in *A Girl in Every Port* (1928) which Hawks himself has described as 'a love story between two men', and erupting closest to the surface in *The Big Sky* (1952).

In the comedies the hero is perpetually humiliated, as often as not by a domineering woman. This humiliation takes two forms: in the regression to childhood – in *Monkey Business* where Barnaby (Cary Grant) and Edwina Fulton (Ginger Rogers) take a rejuvenating drug that turns them – emotionally – back into children, and in the reversal of normal sexual roles, the extreme case being *I Was a Male War Bride* (1949) in which Grant is, for most of the picture, dressed as a woman.

Hunt the man down

In the classic Hawks comedy, *Bringing Up Baby*, the woman is the hunter. Susan (Katharine Hepburn) sees David Huxley (Cary Grant), falls in love with him, pursues him and against all odds – he is engaged to be married – catches him. *Bringing Up Baby* draws a parallel with Hawks' adventure films, extended by the big-game-hunting metaphor that runs through it: Baby (Susan's pet leopard) and a wild leopard are both let loose and hunted during the course of the film. The timid David is constantly humiliated by Susan; at one point he has to dress in a monstrously feminine negligée in order to escape – and is then confronted by a decidedly masculine aunt. But forced to keep company with Susan, he is liberated from the stultifying world of zoological research. Fittingly, the film ends with Susan climbing up the huge scaffolding surrounding the dinosaur skeleton he is completing (in another comic inversion of the big-game-hunting adventure film David 'hunts' dead animals) and bringing down the whole edifice crashing to the floor – and with it David's past dull life.

Rio Bravo, which on the surface is a Western adventure film, has been described by Hawks himself as a comedy, but it is by no means a high farce in the *Bringing Up Baby* tradition. Nevertheless, it is inflected at every stage by the tone of the comedies. For example, there is a strong element of parody, most explicit in Feathers' (Angie Dickinson) sophisticated education of Chance (John Wayne) through a process of sexual humiliation and taunting: thus the scene when she sees a pair of scarlet bloomers being held against him and declaims, 'Those things have great possibilities Sheriff, but not on you'.

Chance meeting

Though the characters of *Rio Bravo* can be traced back to the seminal roles of *Only Angels Have Wings* – Chance to Geoff, Stumpy (Walter Brennan) to Kid, Dude (Dean Martin) to Mc-Pherson and Feathers to Bonnie – the group is no longer a natural formation. It gathers around Chance but for reasons of loyalty rather than professionalism, and at one point, in the communal sing-song that takes place, Chance is even excluded, becoming merely an observer. More significantly, the fear of old age and failing powers, introduced with Kid in *Only Angels Have Wings*, is placed much closer to the centre of *Rio Bravo* in the form of Stumpy, Chance's anarchic, nagging deputy sheriff who performs the tasks of a wife, cleaning and feeding the inhabitants of the jail as they wait for attack from outside. Colorado (Rick Nelson), the young gunman, introduces a theme of youth-versus-age that dominates later Hawks films, notably *El Dorado* (1967) and *Rio Lobo* (1970), which with *Rio Bravo* make up another loose trilogy.

In *Rio Bravo* the squabbling group eventually grows into a kind of 'family' in which the stoical rules of conduct common to previous Hawksian groups are replaced by something closer to family ties. The final shoot-out – photographed like a firework display – becomes a celebration of new-found unity.

In *El Dorado* Hawks goes further, emphasizing the superiority of filial and family loyalties to any professional ethic. But if in *Rio Bravo* Chance is 'not good enough' to overcome his enemies on his own, in *El Dorado* Cole Thornton (Wayne again) isn't 'good enough' even with help. He only kills the professional gunman who opposes him (and who had ironically

acknowledged him with the courtesy that one professional pays another) by trickery. Thornton is even denied the moral authority that Chance possesses in *Rio Bravo*. When he brings the dead body of their son to the MacDonalds – the boy committed suicide when he failed to kill Thornton – there is no shot of Thornton speaking. We simply hear him accepting responsibility for the boy's death. Returning home, he is ambushed and wounded by Maudie (Charlene Holt), the dead boy's sister; her bullet represents the pangs of conscience Thornton has already given voice to, and the paralysis it causes him is an indication of his age. In contrast to Maudie and Mississippi (James Caan) who both exact personal revenge on their enemies, Thornton and the drunken sheriff, J.P. Harrah (Robert Mitchum), have their roots in Kid in *Only Angels Have Wings*. Logically, like Kid, they should have 'grounded' themselves; instead they wearily and farcically – as in the intensely physical (and comic) curing of Harrah's drunkenness with a stomach-turning antidote, compared with the spiritual curing of Dude's in *Rio Bravo* – wend their way through the action.

In *Rio Lobo*, the age of the Wayne character, Colonel McNally, is once again central to the film, though not in the exploitative fashion of

John Wayne leads his men into action in Rio Lobo *(above) and* El Dorado *(below)*

Henry Hathaway's *True Grit* (1969). Hawks gives his 'baby whale' (the fat, aged army officer played by Wayne) the dignity of a revenge quest, as McNally finally capitulates to filial feelings for the son he never had. But Hawks also undercuts this dignity with broad farce in the activities of the group, a group held together purely by the desire for several private revenges and divided equally carefully into young and old characters. The final break from the world of *Only Angels Have Wings*, however, is signalled by the surprisingly elegant, occasionally almost abstract, photography.

Hawks' world is a limited one, lacking, say, the richness and complexity of John Ford's. But his straightforward stories about the stresses and joys of men and women working together in groups, about the nature of friendship, love and professionalism, are stamped with the consistency and highly individual authorship of a great film artist. Howard Hawks has created a body of work that in its laconic optimism is as majestic as the towering mountains Geoff Carter and his foolhardy band of pilots must fly over in the deliciously titled *Only Angels Have Wings*.   PHIL HARDY

only, uncredited). '38 Bringing Up Baby (+ prod); Test Pilot (add. sc. only, uncredited). '39 Gunga Din (add. sc. only, uncredited); Only Angels Have Wings (+ prod); Gone With the Wind (add. sc. only, uncredited). '40 His Girl Friday (+ prod). '41 Sergeant York; Ball of Fire. '43 The Outlaw (some scenes only, uncredited); Air Force (+ co-prod); Corvette K-225 (add. sc. uncredited; + prod; + sup). '44 To Have and Have Not (+ prod). '46 The Big Sleep (+ prod). '48 Red River (+ prod); A Song Is Born (USA retitling for TV: That's Life). '49 I Was a Male War Bride (GB: You Can't Sleep Here). '51 The Thing (co-sc; + sup; + cast dir) (GB: The Thing From Another World). '52 The Big Sky (+ prod); O. Henry's Full House *ep* The Ransom of the Red Chief (GB: Full House); Monkey Business. '53 Gentlemen Prefer Blondes. '55 Land of the Pharoahs (+ prod). '59 Rio Bravo (+ prod). '62 Hatari! (+ prod). '64 Man's Favorite Sport (+ prod). '65 Red Line 7000 (+ co-sc; + prod). '67 El Dorado (+ prod). '70 Rio Lobo (+ prod).

Ingrid Bergman
As time goes by

Discovered in Sweden in the early Thirties, Ingrid Bergman rose to the rank of international star in the Forties, proving herself a brilliant partner to Bogart, Cooper, Grant and Tracy. For many years the seductions of stardom left her unmoved and she never allowed herself to become stereotyped. Today, some fifty years on, and after a series of uneven films, she still commands respect and admiration throughout the industry

Far left: portrait of Bergman in 1942. Above left: her performance in Pä Solsidan *attracted the interest of the American press. Above: star of Selznick's* Intermezzo, *a virtual copy of the original Swedish film. Below: although Bergman's Broadway portrayal of Joan was a triumph, her screen role in* Joan of Arc *was not well received*

Filmography
1935 Munkbrogreven; Bränningar (USA: The Surf); Swedenhielms; Valborgsmässoafton. **'36** Pä Solsidan; Intermezzo. **'38** Dollar; Die 4 Gesellen (GER); En Kvinne Ansikte. **'39** En Enda Natt; Intermezzo: a Love Story (USA) (GB: Escape to Happiness). **'40** Juniatten. *All remaining films USA unless specified:* **'41** Adam Had Four Sons; Rage in Heaven; Dr Jekyll and Mr Hyde. **'42** Casablanca. **'43** Swedes in America (short) (GB: Ingrid Bergman Answers); For Whom the Bell Tolls; Saratoga Trunk. **'44** Gaslight (GB: The Murder in Thornton Square). **'45** The Bells of St Mary's; Spellbound. **'46** Notorious; The American Greed (short) (GB: American Brotherhood Week). **'48** Arch of Triumph; Joan of Arc. **'49** Under Capricorn (GB). **'50** Stromboli, Terra di Dio (IT) (USA: God's Land). **'51** Europa '51 (IT) (USA: The Greatest Love). **'53** Siamo Donne *ep* Il Pollo (IT) (USA: Five Women/of Life and Love *ep* Ingrid Bergman; GB: We Women/We, the Women). **'54** Viaggio in Italia (IT-FR) (USA: Strangers; GB: The Lonely Woman/Journey to Italy); Giovanna d'Arco al Rogo (IT-FR); Angst (GER-FR) (GB: Fear). **'56** Elena et les Hommes (FR-IT) (USA: Paris Does Strange Things; GB: The Night Does Strange Things); Anastasia (GB). **'58** Indiscreet (GB); The Inn of the Sixth Happiness (GB). **'59** The Camp (narr. only) (short). **'61** Goodbye Again (USA-FR). **'64** Der Besuch (GER-FR-IT) (USA: The Visit); The Yellow Rolls-Royce (GB); Stimulantia *ep* Smycket (SW). **'69** Cactus Flower. **'70** A Walk in the Spring Rain; Henri Langlois/Langlois (guest) (doc) (FR). **'73** From the Mixed-Up Files of Mrs Basil E. Frankweiler (GB: The Hideaways). **'74** Murder on the Orient Express (GB). **'76** A Matter of Time (USA-IT). **'78** Herbstsonate (GER) (USA: Autumn Sonata).

Born in Stockholm, Sweden, on August 29, 1915, Ingrid Bergman was brought up by her elderly uncle after the death of her parents, and at 17 joined Stockholm's Royal School of Dramatic Art where she was soon being chosen for the major roles. In 1933, she signed a contract with the Svenskfilmindustri and made her first screen appearance in *Munkbrogreven* (1935, The Count of the Monk's Bridge). By her fifth film, *Pä Solsidan* (1936, On the Sunny Side), she had become a star in Sweden. On this and several other occasions she worked under the direction of Gustaf Molander, who managed to bring out the full range of her talents.

Then, in 1939, David O. Selznick, to whom her growing reputation had been pointed out, brought her to Hollywood and cast her in the remake of *Intermezzo: a Love Story*, (she had already starred in the Swedish version) alongside Leslie Howard. Selznick, a great discoverer and modeller of actresses, was aware of the problems inherent in trying to 'sell' foreign stars to the American public, and astutely decided to place his bets on a fresh, natural and healthy image, relying on, in *Intermezzo*, the sort of story that he knew the public would accept. The gamble paid off and Bergman became an instant success in Hollywood.

However, after only a couple more roles as a pure and loyal woman, Bergman rebelled. Conscious of her potential, she refused to be typecast and fought for the part of Ivy, the barmaid of easy virtue, in Victor Fleming's *Dr Jekyll and Mr Hyde* (1941).

This complete role-change, however, served

only to 'enrich' her screen image. Many of the subsequent Bergman heroines were two-faced and their moral irresolution made them fascinating to watch. This was true of *Saratoga Trunk* (1943), in which she played an illegitimate Creole adventuress in engaging manner, *Notorious* (1946), in which she was a lady of loose morals but admirable intentions, and *Under Capricorn* (1949), in which, while eloping, she murdered her brother who was following her. These films represent the 'black' aspect of her Hollywood character. The heroines are thrown into a booby-trapped, nightmarish world and their physical or mental degradation is all the more suggestive and convincing because the appearance of the actress seems to contradict it.

On the other hand *For Whom the Bell Tolls* (1943), *Spellbound, The Bells of St Mary's* (both 1945) and *Joan of Arc* (1948) – all roles in which she was taking a stand – summarize the positive aspect of the Bergman character. They highlight her idealism, her sincerity and altruism, all of which Selznick had been sensitive to. And yet the ambiguous Bergman characters are preferable to her rather 'toneless' and angelic presentations. In *Casablanca* (1942), the pull of two men, Rick Blaine (Humphrey Bogart) and Victor Laszlo (Paul Henreid), unearths a shaky division of loyalties – on the one hand there is her husband and on the other her commitment to the past.

In spite of the diversity of the studios she worked for and the types of characters she played, Bergman's American career retained a certain unity through the influence of the ever-present Selznick, whose contradictory tastes enabled him to create icy neurotics, fading madonnas and nymphomaniacs. After the break with Selznick in 1946 something was definitely lost from Bergman's style, and nothing new appeared to take its place.

The man who had finally persuaded her to make the break from Selznick was Peter Lindstrom, a Swedish dentist to whom Bergman had been married since the beginning of her career. His intelligent advice in Sweden became sadly misguided in Hollywood. *Arch of Triumph* (1948) sustained considerable losses. In the same year, Bergman saw Roberto Rossellini's *Roma, Città Aperta* (*Rome, Open City*) and, greatly impressed, wrote to him

offering her services.

Curiously, films of the Rossellini period in the Fifties, in spite of some complex narratives, were not so much a denial of the 'Bergman myth' of virginal purity than a change in its essential qualities. *Stromboli* (1950, *God's Land*), was slightly exceptional in that it still partly stemmed from Rossellini's earlier neo-realistic style. Bergman played an unhappy wife escaping from the island of the title. However, all her later films in Italy formed a link with her earlier American films. The temptations of sainthood in *Europa '51* (1951, *The Greatest Love*) are reminiscent of the religious inspiration of *The Bells of St Mary's* and *Joan of Arc*; and the marital hell in *Stromboli* harks back to the tormented wife in *Gaslight* (1944, *The Murder in Thornton Square*) – the film for which she won her first Academy Award, playing a woman blindly in love with a contemptible adventurer. But the more naturalistic approach of Rossellini was not compatible with either actress or theme. In 1950 Bergman finally divorced Lindstrom and married Rossellini, thereby legalizing a relationship that had caused a public outcry against her 'scandalous' behaviour and seriously damaged her career prospects in Hollywood. But when the strain of a series of unsuccessful films proved too much and Bergman decided to return to the stage for a while, Rossellini went to make a film in India and returned with the wife of an Indian director. In 1957, with another divorce, the 'Rossellini period' was over.

20th Century-Fox had offered her the chance of an international comeback with *Anastasia* in 1956, a story about the escape of the Tsar's daughter in 1918. It was a tremendous success, winning Bergman her second Academy Award. There followed a series of roles devised to regain her internationally popular image. In *Anastasia, Indiscreet* (1958, again teamed with Cary Grant) and *Inn of the Sixth Happiness* (1958, as a missionary in China), Bergman achieved respectability. Several later films, of which *A Walk in the Spring Rain* (1970) – an intimate composition in half tones, about the affair of a married and middle-aged woman – was no exception, were not suitable material and did not allow her to attain her true potential, but in 1974 she won another Academy Award, this for Best Supporting Actress, in *Murder on the Orient Express* in which she played a timid and devout missionary.

In 1978, Bergman was cast in *Autumn Sonata* as the self-obsessed mother who is totally involved in her career– the first role worthy of her since the end of the Selznick period. She bravely exposed herself to Ingmar

Above left: Bergman and Bogart, the ill-fated lovers in Casablanca. *Above: in* The Yellow Rolls-Royce, *with Omar Sharif and Joyce Grenfell, Bergman, as a widow crossing war-torn Yugoslavia, outshone in an improbable plot. Below: a lady with a guilty secret in* Murder on the Orient Express

Bergman's scrutinizing eye and achieved, with his complicity, a character of great depth and nuance; this was probably one of the most complete, moving and intelligent creations of the actress' career.

Throughout her years in the cinema, she has maintained regular contact with the stage, playing in about ten plays between 1940 and 1967, including *Joan of Lorraine* (1946), for which she was awarded the Tony Award, *Tea and Sympathy* (1956), *Hedda Gabler* (1962), and *A Month in the Country* (1965), directed by Sir Michael Redgrave at the Yvonne Arnaud theatre in Guildford. In 1958 she married a theatrical impresario, Lars Schmidt.

Ingrid Bergman's career spans a remarkable number of years; they divide into four distinct periods – Sweden, Hollywood, Rossellini and the International period. She survived the disappearance of the Hollywood studios and the Rossellini experience. She also emerged well from several miscasts, thanks to her adaptability and to a thorough discipline that even her least interesting roles exhibit. She remains a combination of femininity, distance, honour and vulnerability, that still seduces us.

OLIVIER EYQUEM

Hollywood's friends and foes

With America facing wars in Europe and the Pacific, the movie capital set about promoting the idea that the Japanese were sadists, the Germans were fools, the British lived in a land of hope and glory, and that the Russians were nearly as brave as the Americans themselves

The first Hollywood feature film to proclaim the evil of Hitler's Germany was Anatole Litvak's *Confessions of a Nazi Spy* (1939). Although the film had prompted a predictably hostile response in German official circles, it had aroused only disfavour or, at most, luke-warm public reaction in the USA.

In the awkward two years which followed the outbreak of war in Europe those movies that did portray Germany or Italy tended to do so from a respectful distance. Mervyn LeRoy's *Escape* (1940), though set largely inside a concentration camp (designed by Cedric Gibbons), even managed to avoid the mention of the words 'German' or 'Nazi'. Fritz Lang's *Manhunt* (1941), which opens with a British hunter (Walter Pidgeon) seeing if it is possible to assassinate Hitler, rapidly retreats into the story of a chase. Increasing Japanese militarism, meanwhile, made even less of an impression on Hollywood than it did on the American government before the events of December 7, 1941.

Above: The Purple Heart, *a piece of inspired guesswork about the fate that befell brave American pilots captured by the Japanese.*
Right: The White Cliffs of Dover, *regarded by* Newsweek *as 'Anglophile . . . with knobs on'.*
Far right: Casablanca, *a wartime fairy-tale*

From Hollywood's point of view the disaster at Pearl Harbor was mitigated by the fact that the studios now had a clear political line to follow. They sprang into action with such topical 'turkeys' as *Remember Pearl Harbor, Little Tokyo, USA* and *Secret Agent of Japan* (all 1942). By the end of 1942 *Across the Pacific* and *Wake Island* had indicated that the quality of films made about the Japanese was likely to improve during the course of the war – though not necessarily the view taken in them of the enemy's essentially evil and duplicitous nature. It was an attitude that reinforced the public's hostility towards Americans of Japanese extraction living in the United States;

they found that their insurance policies were arbitrarily cancelled, their cheques bounced, the milkman refused to deliver and shopkeepers declined to serve them.

In 1943 20th Century-Fox made *The Purple Heart*, best of the anti-Japanese pictures. Written and produced by Darryl F. Zanuck and directed by Lewis Milestone, it was intended to strengthen public hatred of the Japanese at a time when it appeared as if the war in Europe were stealing all the headlines. The film was not finally released until 1944 when the War Department was prepared to concede officially that the Japanese had indeed been torturing American POWs. Zanuck would have been

ganda nor as comedy. In the Thirties McCarey had graduated from directing Laurel and Hardy two-reelers to improvising with considerable success around the sophisticated talents of Cary Grant and Irene Dunne in *The Awful Truth* (1937). The issues of World War II proved beyond McCarey's grasp, however, and his depiction of a concentration camp in which Grant and Ginger Rogers are wrongly held made no attempt to arouse in his audience any sense of the despair and degradation that permeated such places. It was simply a setting for a case of sub-comic mistaken identity.

As the war continued, the portrait of the Nazi enemy progressed via the Nazi beast to the compliment of the 'good' German, the 'real' inhabitant of the land of Bach and Beethoven. Perhaps supreme among Nazi beasts of the cultured variety was Conrad Veidt who starred in *Escape* (1940), Jules Dassin's *Nazi Agent* (1942), and played the much loved Major Strasser in Curtiz's *Casablanca* (1942). Erich von Stroheim, who was the grudgingly admired Rommel in Billy Wilder's *Five Graves to Cairo* (1943), went on to depict another 'good', but flawed, German in Milestone's *The North Star* (1943). Also in 1943, in an adaptation of John Steinbeck's novel *The Moon Is Down*, directed by Irving Pichel, Cedric Hardwicke plays a German officer who has the hostages in a Norwegian village shot, but only with terrible feelings of guilt. The government, which kept a watchful eye on Hollywood's treatment of the war, nodded approvingly both at straightforward portraits of Nazi beastliness and at more reflective examinations of the issues of the war. *Hitler's Children* (1942), a hugely successful low-budget production directed by Edward Dmytryk, was superficially just another ramble over the territory of Nazi methods of enslavement, using the device of an attractive American girl (Bonita Granville) who was, unfortunately for her, born in Germany and is therefore subject to German authority. The masterstroke was the advertising still which showed Miss Granville in a state

Above left: Russian peasants surrounded in The North Star *which starred Erich von Stroheim (left). who had been playing cruel German soldiers since World War I, as a Nazi officer complete with scar. Bottom: Skippy Homeier as an orphaned Hitler Youth adopted by an American family in* Tomorrow the World

quite prepared to wait until the end of the war to release his picture – so strongly did he feel about it.

The Purple Heart originated – as did MGM's *Thirty Seconds Over Tokyo* (1944) – in the sensational raid in April 1942 made by a group of B-25 bombers which took off from an aircraft carrier in the Pacific and attacked Tokyo. The damage this caused was slight but the boost to American morale was considerable. Though based on no hard factual evidence (none of course existed), the film supposes that the American flyers shot down in the raid were tried, tortured – with due emphasis on sadistic humiliation – and executed.

In a sense, the Nazis, perhaps because they were European and therefore better 'known', fared somewhat better in Hollywood as the war progressed. But their movie image did not get off to an auspicious start. Early in 1942 two comedies appeared suggesting that the Nazis were fools to be outwitted by simple tricks. Ernst Lubitsch's *To Be or Not To Be* is admittedly a very funny film, starring Jack Benny and Carole Lombard as Joseph and Maria Tura – a husband-and-wife acting team in Poland who are able to use their stage techniques to triumph over the Gestapo. Sig Ruman, the Teutonic stooge from the Marx Brothers films, plays the redoubtable Concentration-Camp Erhardt ('I do the concentrating, they do the camping'). Benny in disguise asks his opinion of Tura as an actor. 'Ah yes,' recalls Ruman, 'I saw him once before the war. Believe me, what he did to Shakespeare we are now doing to Poland.'

Perhaps not surprisingly, *To Be or Not To Be* was released to a barrage of hostile notices which declared the film to be in the grossest of bad taste. One critic went so far as to call Lubitsch's comedy 'propaganda for Goebbels'.

No such charge was levelled against Leo McCarey's *Once Upon a Honeymoon* (1942), but it was successful neither as anti-Nazi propa-

of undress being publicly flogged by the Nazis for her refusal to submit to their licentious suggestions.

The Broadway stage was perhaps a more fitting arena for a debate on the differences between democracy and fascism. Lillian Hellman's play *Watch on the Rhine* did not translate particularly well to film when it was made by Herman Shumlin in 1943; and James Gow's *Tomorrow the World* (1944), though less stage-bound in its direction (by Leslie Fenton), appealed principally through its story of the havoc created in an American household when a 12-year-old Nazi boy is brought to live there. Ironically, the dawning maturity of film audiences and their receptivity to 'ideas' persuaded Steinbeck and Hitchcock to devise *Lifeboat* (1944), in which the survivors of a torpedoed ship are cast adrift in an open boat. The film outraged critics, who saw in Walter Slezak's portrait of the sole Nazi member of the boat a more eloquent advocate of his political system than the inept quarrelsome products of democracy – his fellow passengers – were of theirs. While the best of the films dealing with the enemy came towards the end of the war, Hollywood's tribute to America's allies diminished in power as the war continued. The pro-British sentiment which had been built up in so many films of the early Forties – *The Sea Hawk* (1940), *That Hamilton Woman!* (1941) and so on – reached an all-time peak in 1942 when MGM made *Mrs Miniver*. William Wyler's universally popular, finely wrought film has undeservedly fallen into critical disrepute because of its lack of 'realism' (though this doesn't seem like much of a charge when one starts to examine *Casablanca* for *its* realism). Mrs Miniver (Greer Garson) captures a German pilot, hiding his gun behind the Welsh dresser, while Mr Miniver (Walter Pidgeon) is off rescuing British troops from the beach at Dunkirk. The village's last moments before global warfare breaks out are spent at the local flower-show where the British aristocracy in the person of Dame May Whitty is revealed as a crab apple with a core of solid gold.

Mrs Miniver opened at the Radio City Music Hall in New York on June 4, 1942. Within ten weeks it had attracted a million and a half spectators. In all it grossed $6 million in North America alone and swept the board at the Academy Awards where it took four of the top five Oscars. On an even higher level President

Roosevelt told Wyler that *Mrs Miniver* had appreciably lessened the political problems of increasing aid to Britain; and Frank Knox, Secretary of the US Navy, thought that the film was as valuable in terms of morale as a flotilla of battleships.

So pleased were MGM with their triumph that the studio ordered the same writing-production team to repeat the success. In 1944 they came up with *The White Cliffs of Dover* with Irene Dunne replacing Greer Garson as MGM's compulsory matronly heart-throb and Clarence Brown directing. Unfortunately, though equally laudable in aim and professional in execution, the film was only a pale shadow of the great *Mrs Miniver*.

Throughout the war the British remained the American film industry's favourite ally. RKO provided free facilities for the making of *Forever and a Day* (1943), basically the story of a house to which every Hollywood-based British actor donated his or her services; the proceeds went to the British Red Cross. Margaret O'Brien's glutinously compelling performance in Woody Van Dyke's *Journey for Margaret* (1942) successfully pleaded for the adoption by American households of endangered British children. There followed an instant demand for little English girls – six years old and preferably with blonde hair. It must have come as a shock to Americans when they were confronted with the offspring of Cleckheaton and Wapping.

Anatole Litvak's *This Above All* (1942), an adaptation of Eric Knight's bitter novel about an aggressive British soldier who deserts because he feels the war is being waged to preserve the stagnant and repressive British class system, is in some ways the most interest-

Above left: undaunted – an English family at war in Mrs Miniver, *starring Greer Garson, Teresa Wright, Walter Pidgeon and Richard Ney. Left: Cary Grant and Ginger Rogers in* Once Upon a Honeymoon. *Below: US envoy's daughter (Eleanor Parker) impressed by Russian ski-troops in* Mission to Moscow

Americans: Robert Taylor, as an orchestral conductor on tour of the Soviet Union in 1941, marvels at the collective wheat farm which reminds him of the Mid-Western wheat farm on which he was raised. Susan Peters plays the beautiful concert pianist with whom he falls in love – to the accompaniment of endless thunderous variations on Tchaikovsky's B Flat Piano Concerto. At some point the Germans invade the Soviet Union and unsportingly interrupt a blossoming relationship – but fortunately love conquers all, including the German Panzer divisions.

On a more serious level was Samuel Goldwyn's *The North Star* (1943), written by Lillian Hellman and originally to have been directed by William Wyler on location in Russia. Litvinov (Soviet ambassador to the USA) pointed out, when asked for permission,

Left: Ruth Warrick and Kent Smith in the Union Jack-waving Forever and a Day. *Below: Norwegian villagers prepare to face a Nazi firing squad in* The Moon Is Down. *Bottom: Robert Young and Laraine Day with William Severn and Margaret O'Brien as the British war orphans in* Journey for Margaret

ing of all the pro-British films to come out of Hollywood during the war years. Darryl F. Zanuck cast Tyrone Power as the dour Yorkshire anti-hero and, predictably, dictated that there should be a happy ending in which the soldier's patriotism is revived by his girl.

In the long run, Hollywood's films showing solidarity with the brave Russian people were to have the most dramatic impact on the American film industry. The most famous of them was *Mission to Moscow* (1943), adapted from the memoirs of Joseph E. Davies, the former American ambassador to the USSR. According to Jack Warner, the film was made by Warner Brothers on the direct order of President Roosevelt, an allegation which proved useless when Warner was under attack by the House Un-American Activities Committee in 1947.

The essence of *Mission to Moscow* is the conviction that Russians are just like Americans with fur hats, and that the ideological divisions between the two nations are more apparent than real. The film was brilliantly directed by Michael Curtiz, skilfully blending newsreel with dramatic reconstruction, but it is riddled with such political bias as to make *Triumph of the Will* look like an objective documentary. Trotsky, Nazi Germany and Japan are all conveniently linked to outbreaks of sabotage in the USSR and the Stalin purges of 1937 and 1938 are thereby justified on the grounds of national security. Even the Non-Aggression Pact with Germany is easily explained as a reaction to misguided British and French appeasement of Hitler at Munich which had left the USSR defenceless on her eastern border.

On its release, in 1943, *Mission to Moscow* aroused instant controversy, attracting violent criticism from the Right (particularly from the Hearst press) and Left (especially those who took exception to the film's pro-Stalinist attitudes). It was therefore not surprising to find that MGM's contribution to this new genre *Song of Russia* (dir. Gregory Ratoff, 1943), concentrated on Russian music and a love story. It was another film which emphasized the essential similarities of Russians and

that there was enough shooting already going on in the Soviet Union in 1943, and with Wyler's departure for the armed forces Lewis Milestone took over the direction. Despite Lillian Hellman's best intentions, *The North Star* still suffers from the idea perpetuated in all Hollywood films about the Soviet Union that the country is a slightly abnormal version of America. The villagers in *The North Star* look and sound like characters in *Oklahoma!* and the cavalier treatment of political ideology means that the Nazi invasion of June 1941 is made to seem like a cattle raid by organized rustlers.

Both *The North Star* and *Song of Russia* were cited in 1947 as evidence of Communists at work in Hollywood. Sam Goldwyn and Louis B. Mayer, like Jack Warner, maintained that such pictures were only part of the war effort and that although they were self-evidently pro-Soviet in attitude the films were simply expedient propaganda exercises.

Hollywood has usually managed to bend with the political wind. Its portraits of America's allies and enemies during World War II remain as clear evidence of contemporary official policy and wider public attitudes.

COLIN SHINDLER

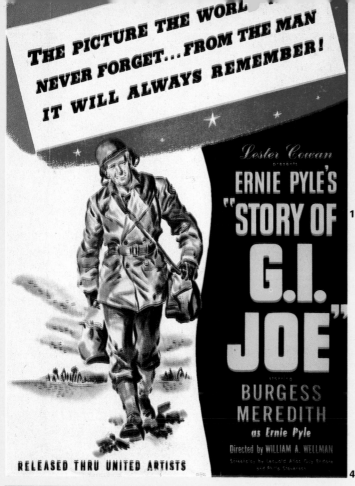

Directed by William Wellman, 1945

Prod co: Lester Cowan Productions/United Artists. **prod:** Lester Cowan. **assoc prod:** David Hall. **sc:** Leopold Atlas, Guy Endore, Philip Stevenson, from the book by Ernie Pyle. **photo:** Russell Metty. **ed:** Otho Lovering, Albrecht Joseph. **art dir:** James Sullivan, Edward G. Boyle. **mus:** Ann Ronell, Louis Applebaum. **mus dir:** Louis Forbes. **sd:** Frank McWhorter. **ass dir:** Robert Aldrich. **r/t:** 109 minutes. Re-released as *War Correspondent*.

Cast: Burgess Meredith (*Ernie Pyle*), Robert Mitchum (*Lt Walker*), Freddie Steele (*Sgt Warnicki*), Wally Cassell (*Pte Dondaro*), Jimmy Lloyd (*Pte Spencer*), Jack Reilly (*Pte Murphy*), Bill Murphy (*Pte Mew*), Tito Renaldo (*Lopez*), William Self ('*Gawky' Henderson*), Yolanda Lacca (*Amelia*), Dorothy Coonan (*Red*), 'and as themselves, combat veterans of the campaigns in Africa, Sicily and Italy'.

'Many things in the film move me to tears – and in none of them do I feel that I have been deceived, or cynically seduced or manipulated, as one usually has to feel about movies.'

So wrote James Agee in a rapturous review of *The Story of GI Joe* on its original release in 1945. And Sam Fuller, himself no mean chronicler of the brutalities of war in *Fixed Bayonets*, *The Steel Helmet* (both 1951) and *Merrill's Marauders* (1962), has commented that:

'Except for Wellman's *GI Joe*, with its feeling of death and mass murder, all war films are kind of adolescent, completely insincere.'

Today's viewers may feel a little less enthusiastic than Agee and Fuller. Vietnam brought into the open one of the rarely acknowledged facts about war: that not all officers are resourceful leaders, and that their tired and frightened men may be as likely to shoot them as to obey them. But *The Story of GI Joe*, devoting itself to the propo-sition that Captain Walker is one of the good officers, careful and caring about the lives of his men, proceeds to demonstrate it with such quiet conviction that one feels a genuine sense of loss at his death. The closing sequence then shows Private Dondaro – last seen resentfully digging latrines as punishment for neglect of duty – weeping as he holds his dead captain's hand. Here, at least, we are being 'seduced or manipulated', not cynically but sentimentally.

In fairness to Agee, it must be remembered that in 1945, in the context of Hollywood's insistence on flag-waving and rampant heroism in all war movies, *The Story of GI Joe* came as a breath of honest, clean air with its infantryman's angle on war as a meaningless vista of mud, muddle and fatigue ending very probably in a wooden cross. And in fairness to the film itself, it should be added that the final sequence is its only serious lapse. Elsewhere, what Fuller de-scribes as its feeling of death and mass murder comes over with an astonishing power, more effective than all the anti-war sentiments of *All Quiet on the Western Front* (1930) because the terrible carnage of war is implied, never stated.

The film's masterstroke is its use of the war correspondent Ernie Pyle as an intermediary between us and the action: his commentary supplies the emotional significance that the scenes themselves are not required to carry. Much of the film is therefore shot in documentary style, not imitating newsreel images so much as *interpreting* them while this documentary approach is barely marred by the character sketches and personal conflicts used by most war movies to ensure audience involvement.

In the film's exemplary opening sequence, for instance, we sense not so much fear as a terrible vulnerability as the men are told that they are going into the line and almost lose their talisman, a little dog. That night, vague characterizations – with nostalgia evoked by music from a radio ('This is Berlin bringing you the music of Artie Shaw') – begin to emerge with Dondaro expounding on his favourite topic of women, Murphy grieving that he is too tall to become a pilot, and so on. But by the time battle comes, after weary days of endless marching through rain and grey dawns, anonymity has taken over again; and as the shells scream, Pyle's voice speaks for all of them:

'This was their baptism of fire; it was chaos . . . each boy facing the worst moment of his life, alone.'

Thereafter, as one battle gives way to the next, the audience is chiefly aware that some faces have disappeared to be replaced by others, that familiar faces have suddenly become older and warier, that all are blanketed by an overwhelming fatigue and despair.

But Ernie Pyle is himself a participant in this drama as he wanders around with his typewriter, his next dispatch always in mind. Harassed by tiredness and the apprehension of death as he watches these men, he grows to love them and faces the almost impossible task of making sense of what is happening to them in the stories he writes for their families at home.

This explains the abrupt shift in manner with the bravura sequence in the Italian town; it begins with the snipers being cleared from the church (the last one, shot by Walker as Warnicki kneels to pray, clutches a bell-rope to toll an ironic knell as he falls), then continues with Warnicki finding a gramophone, Dondaro finding a complaisant Italian girl, and Murphy's wedding.

These scenes function as the random personal impressions out of which Pyle builds a meaningful basis for his tale of the terror of war. We hear the beginning of one of his dispatches after Murphy's death: 'He was just a plain Hoosier boy [a native of Indiana]; you couldn't imagine him ever killing anybody . . .' Sentimental, yes; but *The Story of GI Joe* cancels out all mawkishness by showing exactly why Pyle felt as he did about the GI who 'lives so miserably, dies so miserably'.

TOM MILNE

```
ERNIE PYLE

SOMEWHERE IN ITALY (BY WIRELESS)


I HAD LONG AGO COME TO THINK OF PRIVATE

"WINGLESS" MURPHY AS AN OLD, OLD FRIEND.

HE WAS JUST A PLAIN HOOSIER BOY.

YOU COULDN'T IMAGINE HIM EVER KILLING
```

6

8

War correspondent Ernie Pyle watches as Lt Walker, leading a company of untried GIs into action, allows them to take along a pet dog (1). After sharing their miseries and their baptism of fire, while recording it all in his dispatches (2), Pyle begins to look upon the boys as his special family. He is later parted from them but, after the North African and Sicilian campaigns, they are reunited in Italy.

Entering an enemy-held Italian town, Walker (now a captain) and Sgt Warnicki (3) clear German snipers from the bell-tower of a ruined church. Warnicki, whose wife has sent him a record of his child's voice, finds a gramophone in a shattered house (4) but it has no needle. In the bombed church, Pyle gives away the bride when Murphy and an army nurse are married by the chaplain.

Finding their way blocked by a hilltop monastery held by the Germans, the frustrated GIs dig in. Murphy is killed and Pyle's moving story about him (5) wins him the Pulitzer Prize. At Christmas, Pyle insists his 'family' get turkey and whisky (6).

Warnicki at last gets to hear his son's voice but succumbs to battle fatigue and has to be put under restraint (7). Walker leads the rest of the company in a desparate assault on the monastery. As the exhausted survivors sit on the road they have cleared to Rome (8), mules bring the dead down from the hilltop. Walker is among them (9).

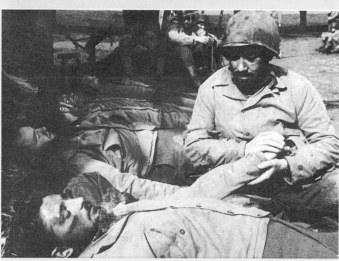

9

Keeping Up Morale

Hollywood's instinctive reaction to the outbreak of World War II was to ignore it in the same way as it had previously glossed over other important social and political developments. However it was quick to capitalize on the impetus war gave to technology, which resulted in improvements in film-stock processing, sound recording, and lighting in colour films. The public was hungry for entertainment and the studios swung into action with renewed vigour. Each one had a different approach: MGM, for example, concentrated on family pictures and musicals; Warner Brothers preferred fast-paced war films and melodramas; 20th Century-Fox made bold, brassy colour films. By mid-1941 box-office receipts showed a noticeable increase.

But pressure from Roosevelt's government and from within the film industry itself, gradually induced Hollywood to play a more and more active role in building and maintaining morale at home and abroad. Certain stars joined the armed forces amid fanfares of publicity that encouraged the general public to follow suit. James Stewart signed up for active service in the navy when he discovered that his boss, Louis B. Mayer, head of MGM, was trying to protect his studio's 'assets' by keeping him out of the draft. The film director Woody Van Dyke, who had received a commission in the Marine Reserves in 1934, was asked to make his outfit – the 22nd Battalion Marine Corps – operational in 1940. With many Hollywood workers in its ranks, the Battalion went abroad, where Woody earned the nickname of 'Steam Engine in Breeches' for his dynamism. However he was eventually forced to resign his commission because of heart trouble (from which he later died).

Many big names took part in the Stars Over America shows, which were put on extensively at hospitals and army camps in the USA and overseas. The stars also became involved in nation-wide tours to promote the buying of War Bonds. Bette Davis, for instance, recalls one tour in Missouri and Oklahoma during which a portrait of her in *Jezebel* (1938) fetched

Above left: the million-dollar legs of Betty Grable, the forces' favourite pin-up, in their finest hour. Below left: Lt Gable of the USAAF. Below: James Stewart takes the oath of allegiance with other draftees

Hollywood movies and Hollywood stars lifted the hearts of Americans at home and in the front line, temporarily allowing them to forget the horrors of war

guest appearances by everyone from Harpo Marx to Gracie Fields.

After the USA entered the war in 1941, Hollywood's biggest successes were the patriotic, all-star extravaganzas – *Star Spangled Rhythm*, *This Is the Army* (both 1943) and *Follow the Boys* (1944). These films offered loose apologies for plots (often on the lines of boy tries to date girl) with music, and were showcases for a studio's roster of talent. Undoubtedly the finest of these musical, flag-waving celebrations was *Yankee Doodle Dandy* (1942), a glowing tribute to the patriotic song-writer George M. Cohan (played by James Cagney) and the American way of life.

Victory for all the family

Undue sentimentality marred the majority of the earliest attempts at 'serious' portrayals of the home front. A comedy like *The More the Merrier* (1943) came much closer to the truth with its depiction of the accommodation shortage which forces a working girl (Jean Arthur) to share a small apartment with two bachelors (Cary Grant and Charles Coburn). However, the following year saw the appearance of two of the most superior, polished and effective morale-boosting dramas to emerge from the American cinema during World War II – *Since You Went Away*, and *Meet Me in St Louis* (both 1944). The script of *Since You Went Away* was rewritten, updated and expanded by David O. Selznick to provide a sweeping portrait of America at war, played with genuine, tender conviction by a large cast. The film kept the more unpleasant details of war to a minimum, effectively focusing characterization and narrative on the 'unconquerable fortress of 1943 – the American family'.

Minnelli's *Meet Me in St Louis* was a classic showcase for all the virtues of a closely knit family. It was a superbly constructed musical, with fine songs and a fabulous street set that enhanced the nostalgic re-creations of a

Far left: Cagney leads a patriotic chorus in Yankee Doodle Dandy. *Top: the stars' morale-boosting work was celebrated in* Hollywood Canteen. *Left: Sgt Carl Bell, the millionth serviceman to enter the Canteen, is congratulated by (from left) Lana Turner, Deanna Durbin and Marlene Dietrich. Below: Bing Crosby in* Star Spangled Rhythm, *a musical showcase for Paramount's stars*

$250,000 worth of bonds and her autobiography $50,000. Although she raised $2 million in two days, she remained aware of the ambiguous nature of her achievement, commenting later that 'It seemed outrageous... that motion picture stars had to seduce people into buying bonds to help their country'.

Carole Lombard became Hollywood's first 'victim' of the war when the plane she was in crashed while returning from a bond-selling tour in Indiana. Shortly afterwards, amid a blaze of publicity, her husband Clark Gable joined the US Army Air Force. His fans followed him everywhere – even to the extent of keeping pace with him on the other side of the compound fence when he was on guard duty. The army was forced to announce:

'Lieutenant Gable will appreciate it if the public will not interfere in his training. He wishes to be treated like every other member of the public.'

The effect that Gable's decision to join up had on building American morale may be measured by a story – widely believed – that alleged that Göring had offered the equivalent of $5000, plus promotion and leave, to the flyer who managed to shoot him down.

In 1942, following the success of the New York Stage Canteen, the Hollywood Canteen

was set up in Los Angeles. It was founded by Bette Davis and John Garfield who raised the initial capital from the sale of $25 tickets for a premiere and a party. The building was equipped and decorated by volunteers from all the guilds and unions in Hollywood, and the Canteen opened with the public paying $100 apiece to sit and watch the first troops crossing the threshold. Like its East Coast counterpart, the aim of the Canteen was to give GIs on leave some fun and relaxation. They could eat from a menu devised by the famous chef Milani and cooked by Marlene Dietrich, be entertained by Bing Crosby, and be asked to dance by Rita Hayworth – all for free. By the end of the war the Hollywood Canteen had entertained an estimated three million servicemen. The studios made sure that an even wider audience had a share of the fun (though *not* for free) by producing two films, *Stage Door Canteen* (1943), from United Artists, and *Hollywood Canteen* (1944), from Warners; the movies contained

bygone era lovingly given new life by the colour camera. The performances of Judy Garland and Margaret O'Brien injected a feeling of warmth, happiness and optimism.

At home and overseas, movies formed a staple part of the troops' ration of entertainment. Statistics in 1943 show that 630,000 men in the armed services were seeing Hollywood films each night. Some of these – including *Saratoga Trunk* (1943), and *The Two Mrs Carrolls* (1945) – were viewed by them quite a few years before their commercial release. The soldiers also provided a captive audience for instructional short films like John Ford's *Sex Hygiene* (1942), a graphically documented treatise on VD.

Perhaps fortunately, the men in the front line did not have to depend solely on the silver screen for distraction; they could still hope for the personal appearance of one of their favourite stars. After Pearl Harbor, Al Jolson immediately campaigned to be allowed to go abroad and entertain the troops, saying, 'My name's Jolson and I sing. Let me sing to the boys. I'll pay my own fare'. When the United States Entertainment Organization was formed, Jolson was one of the first to be sent overseas. He tells the story of how, on his first appearance, it had been rumoured that Lana

Above: Marlene Dietrich said, 'The war gave me the opportunity of kissing more soldiers than any other woman in the world'. Below: Al Jolson sings his heart out for the troops. Bottom: Vernon Cansino (far left) shows army buddies a photo of his sister – Rita Hayworth

Turner was to appear. The disappointment that greeted Jolson – who had not sung before a live audience for many years – when he stepped out onto the stage was immense. But he won them over, crying, 'Hallo boys – I'm Al Jolson. You'll see my name in the history books'. He sang all the old favourites – 'Dixie', 'Buddy, Can You Spare a Dime?', 'Give My Regards to Broadway' – but unless pressed by his listeners, he would not sing 'Sonny Boy' as he found that it tended to reduce audiences to tears. As was the case with all the stars who ventured abroad, stories circulated about his courage. One famous one tells of how, when sheltering during an air raid, he joked about not being scared. He was only there, he said, because 'I'd look awfully silly singing "Mammy" with just one arm'.

The voices of Hope and 'Uncle Sam'

Bob Hope and Bing Crosby (who was known as 'Uncle Sam Without Whiskers') were two tireless entertainers despite frequent narrow escapes in the air and on the ground. Not content with singing to the assembled troops, Crosby would travel round the front finding more boys to shake hands with.

Hope broadcast from a military base each week. His main problem was that as each show was received by the Allied forces everywhere, he continually had to rewrite his gags. One of his most famous openings was:

'Hallo everybody. Thank you very much. Thank you for the applause and please point your guns in the other direction.'

In the excitement of the concert, the soldiers had forgotten to disarm.

In addition to the French *Légion d'Honneur*, Marlene Dietrich received the Medal of Freedom – the highest American civilian decoration – for her efforts to 'bring pleasure and cheer to more than 500,000 American soldiers'. Her shows often began with a comedian coming on stage and announcing that Miss Dietrich would be unable to appear as she had gone to dinner with an American colonel. As a cry of disappointment went up from the audience, a voice would call out from the back of the auditorium, 'No, I'm here'. A moment later the slim, immaculate figure of Dietrich would run down the centre aisle. The highlight of her act was when she played the saw with a violin bow. She always wore khaki, and refused to pose for 'leg' pictures while 'in uniform'. She lived as the soldiers did, washing her face in snow and eating out of mess tins. Although working exclusively for the Allied cause, Dietrich was popular with soldiers on both sides during the war, so the Office of Political Warfare asked her to record her hit songs in German – but rewritten with a propaganda twist. She considered this her greatest contribution to the war effort.

A personal appearance by a celebrity was a rare release from the bitter routine of war; for the rest of the time GIs had to make do with pin-ups of their favourites. The two most popular darlings of the forces were Betty Grable and Rita Hayworth. It was considered the ultimate compliment to a star when a photograph of Hayworth in a black lace and white satin negligée was pasted on the side of the first nuclear bomb, tested on the Bikini Atoll in 1946 – a gruesome tribute perhaps, but a symbol of Hollywood's invaluable contribution to American morale during the war.

KINGSLEY CANHAM, SALLY HIBBIN

Chapter 22

Documents of war

During the war the people back home craved information, and film was a fast, effective means of reporting the war's progress. For some documentary film-makers, it was their finest hour

From the outset of World War II, Britain, Germany, the USA, the USSR and Japan all mobilized their cameras as well as their guns in the battle to win people's minds and to stimulate morale, recalling, perhaps, Stalin's words that 'the cinema is the greatest means of mass propaganda'. As authentic records of the war, many of the official films and newsreels thus produced have still to be properly analysed. They were often composed of reconstructed material – model and studio work was mixed in with actuality footage which was itself subject to rigorous censorship – and they continue to pose problems for film historians whose task is to sort out the mock from the genuine.

Indeed one has to delve deep into the archives to find the 'real' war – unadulterated shots of sailors relaxing after D-Day, bomb-disposal experiments in London's Richmond Park, a day's activities on a British bomber-squadron airfield, and so on – usually recorded by amateur cameramen with no propaganda axe to grind.

Of course it was rarely the prime intention of the official war documentary or newsreel to present a genuine, straightforward account of combat or home-front conditions. Many of them did offer a stark portrayal of war, but in retrospect they are chiefly of interest and importance as exercises in propaganda and as reflections of national attitudes at a time of intensive crisis and global turmoil. Their purpose was not simply to record the war (which in part they did) but to 'interpret' it to the soldier and civilian on whose behalf it was being fought. It is no accident that Frank Capra's propaganda masterpiece of the war was called *Why We Fight* and not 'How We Fight'.

In Britain the war documentary has come to be recognized as a high point in the country's cinema, a happy marriage of official need and artistic film-making which created a national cinematic identity and indigenous style. It was, in essence, the maturing of the Grierson-inspired documentary movement of the Thirties. The style appeared to thrive on austerity as well as the brilliance of its exponents, and its exposition of the war was a beguiling blend of facts and lyricism, news and motivation.

The film-makers also quickly recognized how the war had unified the British in an unusual way, lowering class barriers, providing a common cause, and engendering in the people a modest self-respect and determination to safeguard the white cliffs of democracy. Confronted with arrogant German notions of 'superiority', the British took a collective pride in being 'ordinary', and the films of the period cleverly conveyed the phenomenon of an entire populace mentally rolling up its sleeves to get down to the serious business of survival. They were also gritty, realistic, wryly humorous, informative, emotionally restrained, largely free from expressions of overt nationalism, and even relatively tolerant towards the enemy, who nevertheless had to be taught a lesson.

As the war began, the government and armed-services film units were linked together and, along

with the best of the independent documentary companies, were placed under the control of the Ministry of Information. Numerous instructional films were turned out, ranging from the practical (how to cope with food, health, weapons, machinery) to the political (war information, ridicule of the enemy, moral preparedness, and so forth). The Ministry of Information increased access to their films by showing them in the towns and villages of Britain (often where no cinemas existed), and even projecting them in factories, where shift-work prevented people from seeing films at normal times.

At first there was a lack of co-ordination among the documentary film-makers working under the aegis of the Ministry of Information. In the first year of the war the only projects of note were those completed on the independent initiative of the talented members of the GPO Film Unit. These included *The First Days* (1939), a mood piece depicting London's reaction to the declaration of war, made by Humphrey Jennings, Harry Watt, Pat Jackson and Alberto Cavalcanti. Watt followed this with a GPO film officially commissioned by the Ministry of Information, *Squadron 992* (1939), a simple, strikingly photographed study of an RAF barrage-balloon unit in training and protecting the Forth Bridge.

In 1940, the situation improved with the creation of the Crown Film Unit (absorbing the GPO Film Unit) which, together with many other sponsored units, such as those of the oil company Shell and Paul Rotha's independent team, settled down to a planned policy by which they would pump out propaganda in films ranging from two-minute flashes to feature-length documentaries. It is an interesting sidelight to note how many of the film-makers involved in this corporate, Establishment effort had been known in the Thirties for their radical political views.

Above: Coastal Command *was made by J. B. Holmes for the Crown Film Unit and set to music by Vaughan Williams. It showed how the RAF and the Royal Navy protected British merchant-ship convoys as they continued their hazardous work. Below: the image of a nation going about its daily business amid the bombing of the Blitz was emphasized in* London Can Take It, *a film that saw the emergence of a major new director – Humphrey Jennings*

Above: The Silent Village, *a portrait of a Welsh mining community, was made as a tribute to the people of the Czech mining town of Lidice who had been massacred by the Nazis in retaliation for the assassination of the SS General Heydrich. Top left:* Desert Victory, *directed by Roy Boulting, focused on the British advances through Egypt and Libya. Top centre:* Tunisian Victory *was an Anglo-American account of the latter stages of the North African campaign. It was co-directed by Roy Boulting and Frank Capra and the commentary was shared between Bernard Miles and Burgess Meredith. Top right:* The True Glory *was a resumé of the war in Europe from the D-Day invasion to the final victory. This epic documentary was given a human perspective by focusing on individual soldiers*

The poet and genius of the British documentary movement was Humphrey Jennings whose films, with their warmth and spontaneity of feeling, evoked more than any others the atmosphere of Britain and the mood of its people in wartime. He achieved this by eschewing the more pragmatic approach of his colleagues and recalling instead the sights and sounds of Britain and its people, their culture and their traditions.

Jennings made his mark as assistant director on *London Can Take It* (dir. Harry Watt, 1940), which told the story of the first big bombing raid on London at the beginning of the Blitz. Its chief purpose was to dramatize to those abroad – particularly Americans – how their own democracy might likewise be threatened. Jennings followed this in 1941 with a trilogy of impressionistic film poems, portraying Britain at war – *Heart of Britain, Words for Battle* (both 1941) and *Listen to Britain* (1942). His acknowledged masterpiece, however, was *Fires Were Started* (1943), a memorial to the firemen of London which captured all the tragedy and heroism of civilians at war.

Jennings developed a more symbolic, semi-fictional technique in his next two films, *The Silent Village* (1943) and *The True Story of Lilli Marlene* (1944), with less appealing results. He then reverted to his more characteristic style with *80 Days* (1944), an account of the V-1 flying-bomb attacks on England, and *A Diary for Timothy* (1945), a picture of Britain in the last months of the war that reflected on an uncertain future. Jennings' final commentary on the war, *A Defeated People* (1945), was a characteristically sympathetic study of the German experience after the armistice.

Jennings' contribution to war documentaries may have been unique but many other documentaries of the period were notable for their style. Some films contained a pleasing leavening of satire, as in *Lambeth Walk* (1941) in which shots of Germans goose-stepping were cut in time with the famous popular song. Cavalcanti made a memorable caricature of Mussolini in *Yellow Caesar* (1940), and Len Lye's *When the Pie Was Opened* (1941) was an imaginative, lively presentation of a wartime recipe for vegetable pie. Paul Rotha's *World of Plenty* (1943) was a potent piece of film journalism which surveyed the global food problem in a style similar to the *March of Time* newsreels. Finally Anthony Asquith's *Welcome to Britain* (1943), a shrewd guide to the British for the benefit of

US servicemen, used traditional, self-deprecating British humour.

Among the best and most popular British documentaries of the war were those depicting actual operations and combat. Early examples were Harry Watt's *Target for Tonight* (1941), a reconstructed account of a routine bombing raid, and Pat Jackson's colour film *Western Approaches* (1944), a tribute to Britain's merchant seamen. Both films portrayed men facing extreme danger with calm and courage. At the same time the Services Film Units contributed a morale-boosting series of 'Victory' films: *Desert Victory, Tunisian Victory* (both 1943) and *Burma Victory* (1945); British director Roy Boulting worked on all three films.

The culmination of the combat documentaries was *The True Glory* (1945), an ambitious, Anglo-American collaboration, directed by Carol Reed and Garson Kanin. The film celebrated the part played by the ordinary fighting men of all the Allied Nations in the final defeat of the Germans on the Western Front. It provided a fitting climax to what might most aptly be described as Britain's finest hour of film-making.

'Documentary is at once a critique of propaganda and a practice of it' wrote Grierson, summarizing the wartime role of his former colleagues

In Germany as early as 1933 the Nazi regime had exercised strict bureaucratic control over the ideological content of every film made there. Goebbels had been shrewd enough to realize that the way to keep the cinemas well attended was to lay emphasis on escapism, but he ensured that all cinema programmes were supplemented with a regular quota of propaganda newsreels and shorts. The latter were mostly simple, direct presentations of a limited number of approved themes: anti-Semitism, Aryan superiority, war heroism, Germany's glorious past, loyalty to the Fatherland and worship of the Führer.

With the outbreak of war this efficient propaganda machine simply continued its now familiar function, although naturally the emphasis was shifted to the conflict itself, highlighting the sweep of German victories in Europe.

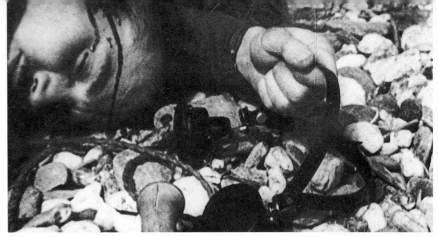

Numerous short record films described aspects of the war effort, such as the work of the Nazi Army Hospital Service or the activities of U-boats. A regular newsreel, *Die Deutsche Wochenschau* (The German Weekly Review) was produced and continued up to the end of the war. In 1940, the first German victories were celebrated in heady dynamic documentaries like H. Bertram's *Feuertaufe* (1940, Baptism of Fire) and Fritz Hippler's *Feldzug in Polen* (1940, Campaign in Poland) and *Sieg im Westen* (1941, Victory in the West). But what the public was permitted to see and what was actually filmed often differed markedly.

In addition to straight documentary there was also pseudo-documentary: Fritz Hippler's *Der Ewige Jude* (1940, The Eternal Jew) was an insidiously skilful film on 'the problems of world Jewry' that aimed to expose the alleged decadence of the Jewish people and, through explicit climactic scenes in a kosher abbatoir, their inherent barbarity. One later commentator called it 'probably the most evil film ever made'.

In the USSR, where the Revolution of 1917 had inspired the cinema's most successful coupling of artistic achievement and overtly propagandist intentions, there was rather little experience of documentary film-making to draw upon when the country finally engaged in war with Germany.

Undeterred, however, Soviet film-makers responded eagerly to the exhortations of the All-Union Cinema Committee 'to help in the moral, political and military defeat of Fascism'. Throughout the war, the Russians produced some remarkable documentaries and newsreels depicting their country's resolute defence and the defeat of their enemy.

Once at war, they shot numerous propaganda films. Outstanding talents such as Alexander Dovzhenko, Leonid Varlamov, Roman Karmen and Yuli Raizman contributed films to an ambitious cycle of documentaries. Dovzhenko made *Defeat of the Germans Near Moscow* (1942) and *Victory in the Ukraine* (1945) and his wife Solntseva made *Battle for Our Soviet Ukraine* (1943) with Dovzhenko supervising and briefing the front-line cameramen.

Karmen directed *Leningrad Fights* (1942); and other notable compilations included *Liberated France* (1945) by Yutkevich, *Defeat of Japan* (1945) by Zarkhi and Heifitz, and Varlamov's *Stalingrad* (1943). Varlamov had also supervised *A Day of War* (1942), perhaps the most elaborate of these documentaries, which was compiled from the contri-

butions of over a hundred cameramen who sent film back from the entire Soviet front.

Undoubtedly the most elating film of all was Yuli Raizman's *Berlin* (1945), photographed by Karmen and 40 other cameramen and showing the final triumphant capture of the *Reichstag* after bitter street-fighting. These films were all spectacular exercises in patriotism and Soviet audiences saw none of the retreat, disaster and death which the combat cameramen frequently recorded.

The USA also lacked a strong tradition of documentary film-making when it entered the war. As in the Soviet Union, established feature-film directors were called upon to step in and make propaganda films. For the US War Department the peculiar problem was to explain or 'sell' the war to a public that had little idea why it was becoming embroiled in something happening 6000 miles away.

At the same time there was a call for war-related films which, as one critic has put it, 'were an honest expression of national resolve and a clear indication of realities, unadorned with Hollywood hoop-la'. The US War Department not only harnessed the talents and experience of the entire American film industry, it also prepared itself to spend $50 million to ensure it got what it wanted. In the fighting areas, massive amounts of combat footage were shot and used for military study as well as being edited into newsreels for cinema consumption.

The most persuasive and influential of the US War Department's indoctrination films was Major Frank Capra's *Why We Fight* series (1942–45). It

Top: Jennings' 80 Days dealt with the German V-1 flying-bomb attacks on Southern England. The American broadcaster Ed Murrow narrated, but the most telling moments on the soundtrack were the ominous silences just before the 'doodlebugs' hit their targets. Above: Jewish profiles offered as 'documentary' evidence in support of Nazi theories on race in Der Ewige Jude. Below: the German weekly wartime newsreel

Nr. 49

Die neuesten Frontberichte unserer Propaganda-Kompanien

Die deutsche WOCHENSCHAU

1. Der Duce besichtigt die Rüstungswerke

2. Graf Ciano auf dem Berg

3. General ... Berlin

4. Brennstoffnachschub für unsere Luftwaffe

was originally intended solely for military purposes but was eventually shown in cinemas throughout the USA and abroad. The aims of Capra's seven films were to counterpoint the lessons of politics and war by focusing on the key events of the conflict.

The result was an expertly sustained series of documentaries which transcended their original purposes and proved highly influential, both in terms of promoting a public 'understanding' of the war, and in terms of documentary techniques in general, whether wartime or peacetime.

The extent to which Hollywood responded to the US government's exhortations to contribute to the war effort can be gauged by the activities of one studio in particular, Walt Disney. By 1943, Disney had virtually abandoned straight entertainment films in favour of war-oriented product, turning out military and home-front propaganda films on an unprecedented scale. Disney's work at this time culminated in the extraordinary *Victory Through Air Power* (1943), a controversial hard-sell polemic for winning the war in the air.

The most enduring war documents of the period were those that stemmed from major Hollywood film-makers who were called up for the specific purpose of recording the conflict. Chief among these were John Ford, William Wyler and John Huston. Shooting often in colour, and with results which were frequently at odds with the wishes of the authorities, these directors contributed a small but remarkable group of documentaries impregnated with their creators' personal attitudes and artistic styles. John Ford led the way with *The Battle of Midway* (1942) and *December 7th* (1943). Wyler joined a USAF bombing raid over Germany to make *The Memphis Belle* (1944) and Huston set aesthetic and moral standards in his wartime film-work which have never been equalled.

As in the USA, documentary film-making was a seriously under-developed area in the Japanese cinema at the outbreak of World War II. Like the Americans, they called on their feature-film directors to service propaganda requirements. Japan's output of militaristic films was prodigious in the years immediately preceding the global conflict, but these were dramatic presentations rather than straight documentaries. Themes were heroic, and the films made strong appeals to the concept of duty, laying little stress on the issues at stake and never questioning the rectitude of Japan's position. These films did, however, avoid the super-heroism of their German counterparts, preferring to depict 'ordinary' fighting men and not shirking from the

Above: The Siege of Leningrad *was a feature-length documentary showing how the city's four million inhabitants built defences in the streets and maintained a precarious food-supply line across the frozen Lake Ladoga. Below:* Stalingrad *depicted the other great siege in the history of the Eastern Front. Supervised by the director Varlamov, the film was released less than six weeks after the German capitulation. Bottom: the Soviet army of liberation in Raizman's* Berlin

unpleasant realities of death and distress.

Japanese war films had their own distinctive style: much use of tracking shots, highly mobile camerawork, striking compositions and grainy images that added a touch of realism to battle scenes. The enemy was usually unseen and Japanese fighting units often appeared to be operating in a vacuum. There were few shots of close combat and much use of long-distance, panoramic camerawork that gave an impression of victorious advances. In contrast to American techniques, Japanese war films tended to depersonalize the war to a point which deeply impressed Frank Capra who commented, 'We can't beat this kind of thing'.

Strongly representative of these characteristics were the films of Tomotaka Tasaka, notably his fictional and somewhat ambiguous accounts of the Sino-Japanese war, *Gonin No Sekkohei* (1939, *Five Scouts*) and *Tsuchi to Heitai* (1939, *Earth and Soldiers*). Later on in the war Tasaka reverted to a more conventional format with *Navy* (1943), a depiction of military training in a camp setting. Yoshimura's *Nishizumi Senshachoden* (1940, *The Story of Tank Commander Nishizumi*) was a rare personal study of a fighting man. The film was not aggressively militaristic and was remarkable for the stark, documentary style of its war scenes and the humanistic attitude towards enemy civilians.

Cameramen did not flinch from recording the Nazi atrocities in Russia – the footage made strong propaganda for the besieged people

From 1940 onwards, the Japanese government enforced a stricter code of film-making to take account of war preparation and to encourage the 'national Japanese philosophy . . . and the spirit of complete sacrifice for the nation'. The rest of Japan's cinematographic war was dominated by nationalistic battle movies of which the leading exponents were Yutaka Abe and Kajiro Yamamoto.

Documentaries were a lesser feature of Japan's wartime film-making. The Japanese film expert John Gillett recently made a major rediscovery at the Toho studios when Fumio Kamei's *Fighting Soldiers* (1940) was unearthed. This hour-long documentary shot in China recorded conventional manoeuvre scenes but also contained moments of implicit sympathy for the Chinese peasants and refugees. Gillett has compared the film to John Huston's wartime short *San Pietro* (1944) and indeed the Imperial Japanese authorities found the film far too humanistic in its attitude to the enemy. It was banned and all copies were supposed to have been destroyed, but one print fortunately survived.

Impressive for more conventional reasons was Yamamoto's *The War at Sea From Hawaii to Malaya* (1942), half drama, half documentary, which extolled 'the navy spirit as culminated at Pearl Harbor' and was judged top Japanese film of its year. This film mixed actuality and reconstruction to great effect – the attack on Pearl Harbor being put together entirely with model work – and evidently convinced some US military advisers in Japan that it was genuine footage of the raid.

Film production units of all kinds – feature, newsreel and documentary – were mobilized to serve each nation's war effort. The results add up to a unique, unprecedently thorough record of the world's largest battle-at-arms. But this mass of reportage is also a significant compendium of differing national attitudes caught in a period of turmoil and conflict.   CLYDE JEAVONS

Pulling Together

Plunged into war in 1939, the British people expended blood, toil, tears and sweat in defending their nation and defeating Germany – and the documentary film-makers were on hand to record how they did it

It is tempting to see the British documentary film-makers on the eve of World War II as a tight little group of pioneers, a family almost, working together on common principles under the stern, paternal guidance of John Grierson, and believing in cinema not as entertainment or distraction, but as the 'creative interpretation of actuality'. Grierson himself had written in 1937:

'It is worth recalling that the British documentary group began not so much in affection for film *per se* as in affection for national education.'

In other words, Grierson was suggesting that the group was not inspired by fiction and the romance of the movies, but by the romance of social advance, community and the technological society.

The truth is different. By the time war broke out, Grierson had left for Canada where he conceived, founded and guided a whole new national cinema through his invention of the Canadian National Film Board. The GPO Film Unit, base of the British documentary movement, was by then being run by Alberto Cavalcanti, much less of an ideologue, much more of an artist than Grierson. Among the talented young men working for him was the turbulent, rough-edged Harry Watt, a Scotsman, who had already distinguished himself with the classic *Night Mail* (1936), on which he collaborated with Basil Wright, and *North Sea* (1938), a vivid and exciting picture of Aberdeen fishermen battling against a storm. He didn't have much time for Grierson or his theories; his instinct was for drama. Humphrey Jennings and Pat Jackson were his young colleagues, chafing for chances.

Britain was at war, but little happened. A Ministry of Information (MOI) was formed, but it clearly had no idea how to use Cavalcanti's film-makers. In fact the first wartime 'documentary' came from the feature industry – a propaganda piece called *The Lion Has Wings* (1939), flung together by Alexander Korda in a rush of patriotism. It offered a prestigious cluster of stars and some appalling dialogue (Merle Oberon to Ralph Richardson: 'We must keep our land darling – we must keep our freedom. We must fight for the things we believe in – Truth and Beauty . . . and Kindness'). Grierson, perhaps feeling guilty from afar, spoke respectfully of *The Lion Has Wings*: 'This work of film documentation was Britain actually at war, zooming and roaring above the clouds.' But the intemperate Harry Watt more accurately called it 'a ghastly, bloody film'.

A phoney war of their own

'Nothing happened for six weeks,' Watt told Elizabeth Sussex (author of *The Rise and Fall of British Documentary*). 'We sat on our backsides looking out of the window, watching the tarts in Savile Row . . . Then Cavalcanti took it upon himself to send us out . . .'

They went out and shot a 'record of events' called *The First Days* (1939), a kind of cinematic scrapbook of London at the beginning of the war. All the film-makers at the GPO shot material, and although there is no real shape to the film, there is charm and wit and feeling in the picture they built up of evacuees and young recruits; Londoners in their braces filling sandbags; a little group on a suburban street gathered round a car radio to hear

Above: Fires Were Started, *a dramatic reconstruction of London firemen in action. Below: young evacuees with gas-masks, but few other belongings, leave London in* The First Days. *Bottom:* Squadron 992 *showed a barrage-balloon unit in training*

Above and below right: London Can Take It *took the form of a news bulletin that showed the capital stoically facing up to the Blitz. Above right: the intrepid British airman, 'played' by a real member of Bomber Command in* Target for Tonight, *which dramatized a raid on Germany. The aircraft interiors were shot through holes cut in the fuselage of a wrecked Wellington brought to Denham studios*

Chamberlain announce the outbreak of war. *The First Days* captured – in the plain, ordinary faces confronting catastrophe – the poetry and pathos that Jennings in particular was to make memorable in later work.

The fight begins

The same humane, characteristically English accent distinguishes further early war documentaries: *Squadron 992* (1939), *Dover Frontline* and *Christmas Under Fire* (both 1940). The Blitz came, and the whole team collaborated on another picture under Watt's directorial supervision: *London Can Take It* (1940). This moving account of a night of raids, from sunset to sunrise, with its theme of endurance and resilience and an effective commentary narrated by the American journalist Quentin Reynolds, proved extremely successful in exciting sympathy and support in the USA. Here again there is a sharpness and sensitivity of observation, as well as a humour and understatement (much more powerful than rhetoric) which often take the picture far beyond mere record into poetry.

The Crown Film Unit, as the former GPO Film Unit had been renamed in August 1940, was soon going out beyond the Home Front, to bring people at home the feel of the war on the battlefronts. *Men of the Lightship* (1940), *Merchant Seamen* (1941), *Coastal Command* (1942) – the titles tell the stories. Particularly rousing was Harry Watt's *Target for Tonight* (1941). 'We were getting very tired of the "taking it" angle,' Watt has recalled, and he and his colleagues decided to make a film about the war that Bomber Command was carrying into the heart of Germany. Simple, unpretentious and dramatic, this tells the story of a typical night raid – from the photo-reconnaissance that provides the planners with the necessary information, to the return of 'F for Freddie', limping home injured to land in heavy fog.

Watt did not use actors. The preface to *Target for Tonight* announces: 'Each part is played by the actual man or woman who does the job'. But sets were constructed: the pilots' changing-room was 'in a little subsidiary studio in Elstree', and the huge Bomber Command control was designed by Edward Carrick and built at Denham. A model was used to show the bombs landing on railway stock-yards and real British soldiers stood in as German anti-aircraft gunners. Dialogue was written, and generally played with great naturalness and modesty by the airmen. The result was a film which caught most powerfully the courage and undemonstrative resolution of the RAF. Making his report at the end, pipe in mouth, the pilot apologizes with the lightest of ironies, 'I'm afraid I didn't see very much. I was rather busy at the time'. There is nothing affected about his understatement: it has the dignity of truth, and it still has the power to move.

ALL THE PLAYERS IN THIS PICTURE ARE OFFICERS AND MEN OF THE MERCHANT NAVY. THE NARRATOR IS A MEMBER OF ONE OF THE SHIP'S CREW.

MERCHANT SEAMEN

Directed by **J. B. HOLMES**
Photography by **H. E. FOWLE**
Technical work by **EDWARD CARRICK**
TRADE SHOW
G.F.D. PRIVATE THEATRE
MAY 27 at 11 a.m., 1.15 & 3 p.m.
Released June 30

GENERAL FILM DISTRIBUTORS LTD.

Target for Tonight, dramatically constructed, shows how far Crown – and particularly Harry Watt – had diverged from Griersonian principle. Pat Jackson showed a similar inclination towards the fictional with *Western Approaches*, made in 1944. This was the ambitious story of an Atlantic convoy, and a boatload of survivors from a torpedoed merchantman. Perhaps it was too ambitious, for the result somehow lacks the simple conviction of Watt's picture. All the characters are played by real seamen, but the story, involving staged scenes on a U-boat, a melodramatic climax and a last-minute rescue, smacks too strongly of artifice. And Jack Cardiff's accomplished colour photography lacks the simple black-and-white authenticity of *Target for Tonight*. Perhaps here documentary was edging too close to the theatrical.

The third of those young men who sat watching the tarts in Savile Row in September 1939 had little in common with the fictional bent of Watt and Jackson. Humphrey Jennings had an approach that was entirely his own, and one which he developed through a series of wartime films until he had become by far the most individual, imaginative and powerful of Britain's documentary directors. *Heart of Britain* (1941) was the first of these, a somewhat tentative portrait-in-miniature of the North of England at war, lyrical in feeling, personal in style. The same could be said of his next film, *Words for Battle* (1941), in which he used a collection of literary texts complemented by images of great beauty and originality to celebrate national pride. *Listen to Britain* (1942) developed the style with sounds and images alone, and is wonderfully evocative in

its impression of a Britain at war. This, perhaps Jennings' most completely successful work, got him into trouble with his colleagues, suspicious of the 'arty' and the 'intellectual'. Reviewing it in the *Spectator*, Edgar Anstey described *Listen to Britain* as 'the rarest piece of fiddling since the days of Nero', and added, 'It will be a disaster if this film is sent overseas.' Jennings' *Fires Were Started* (1943) was more safely recognizable in genre (though no less original) – a masterly tribute to London's fire service, strongly affectionate, intensely poetic, the 'public film' at its most creative. This superb sequence of documentaries closes with *A Diary for Timothy* (1945), a tender, closely-wrought, impressionist chronicle of the last year of the war.

Humphrey Jennings made more films before his tragic death in 1950 at the age of 43, but none of them really achieved the intensity of his wartime work. His colleagues were perhaps right to suspect him of aestheticism; he was certainly an intellectual. But in his war films he at least proved himself an artist, with a power of communication that has survived undiminished and which has won a place for him in the history of the British cinema.

Filming for victory

Of course, to pick out a few titles like this is to give a misleading impression of the documentary movement's contribution to Britain's wartime effort. For instance, the torrent of films produced by Basil Wright (who unfortunately spent the war years producing instead of directing) and Edgar Anstey at Film Centre, which Grierson himself had set up when he left the GPO in 1937, had great practical value and were certainly closer to Grierson's ideas. They made instructional films for Civil Defence, for the fire service, for agriculture, for the Ministry of Labour. Other units produced films for the forces, for the hospital services, for the government. The MOI distributed a new five-minute subject free to the cinemas every week, which meant that documentaries were now reaching audiences of over twenty million people. So a vast new public was introduced and accustomed to the

Above left: John Holmes' box-office success Merchant Seamen *followed the fortunes of a crew whose ship is torpedoed. Below: RAF staff in* Words for Battle *and (left) a member of the Observer Corps in* Heart of Britain *watch the war in the air. Jennings backed these films with rousing music and poetry, evoking Britain's pride in its heritage*

THE MUSIC OF A PEOPLE AT WAR

LISTEN TO BRITAIN

A Ministry of
Made by the
Directed by
and Stewa
Produced by

Trade S

CAMBRIDGE
Thursday, FEB. 12

Above: scenes from Jennings' Fires Were Started, *which covers a night in the life of a National Fire Service unit during the Blitz. Jennings gave an affectionate portrayal of each fire-fighter in the company and, as in his previous film* Listen to Britain *(above right), revealed the team spirit and fortitude of the British people facing up to danger during World War II*

idea of a cinema of fact rather than fantasy.

Another highly successful genre was the compilation film, made up from footage shot on the battlefronts. One of the first of these, *Wavell's 30,000* (1942), showed the British advance into Libya. Cavalcanti, who had since moved to Ealing to produce features, supervised a satirical demolition of Mussolini's regime in *Yellow Caesar* (1940). And the victorious campaigns from Africa to the Far East to the Second Front were celebrated in a series of fine compilations: *Desert Victory*, *Tunisian Victory* (both 1943), *Burma Victory* and *The True Glory* (both 1945). Photographed with skill and daring and edited with outstanding craftsmanship, these films from the Service Film Units showed the emergence of classic documentary techniques spreading beyond Crown to inspire a whole new generation of film-makers.

Compilation provided a basis for the work of another highly individual film-maker. Paul Rotha, one of the most talented mavericks of the British documentary movement, was an early member of the Grierson group, but his style and viewpoint were always firmly his own. Rotha set up his own unit in 1941 with the resolution not to compete with Crown on battlefield subjects but to 'make film about what was happening in Britain under the influence of a world war'. This resulted in a flow of films about public health, schools, day nurseries, education. Then came further and greater inspiration. With the writer Eric

Knight, Rotha conceived the idea of a film about the problems of world food – a brave attempt to initiate debate and spread knowledge on a subject which was going to be a matter of life and death to millions in the post-war world. It was partly the nature of the subject and partly the need for economy in time and money that dictated the style of *World of Plenty* (1943). A hard-hitting script, uncompromising in its argument as well as in its statistics, was the blueprint for a powerfully effective montage of library material. It included a persuasive commentary, spoken by actors, as well as interviews with such distinguished authorities as Sir John Boyd-Orr, the nutritionist. If Rotha's plea for a world food plan, based on the right of men to eat, failed to achieve its object, the fault was certainly not in *World of Plenty*. Documentary could lead, enlighten and inspire. It could not work miracles.

What did it all mean? It was Rotha – often prickly, always outspoken – who said of the documentary movement generally: 'I don't think the films themselves are the least bit important. What is important is the sort of spirit which lay behind them.' Perhaps this reflects the anti-art impatience which, since Grierson, seemed so often and so unnecessarily to reflect documentary thinking. Rotha's view certainly plays down the documentary movement's major achievements. It is not true that all the films made in the Thirties and Forties survive today on their own terms –

perhaps only *Song of Ceylon* (1934), *Night Mail*, *London Can Take It*, possibly *Target for Tonight*, Jennings' films from *Words for Battle* to *A Diary for Timothy*, probably a handful more – but this was work that fulfilled an honourable function in its day, and that still illuminates the moment of history that produced it.

The documentary influence

Just how influential these films were on the 'other' British cinema is another question. During the war there were certainly instances where feature directors profited from the experience and the understanding of the documentarists. Rotha claims that *Night Shift* (1942), made by his unit about women working in a Welsh factory, inspired Frank Launder and Sidney Gilliat's *Millions Like Us* (1943); Carol Reed's *The Way Ahead* (1944) was developed out of an army training film called *The New Lot* (1942); and Basil Wright has recalled how Noel Coward studied wartime documentaries when he was scripting *In Which We Serve* (1942). Films like *San Demetrio, London* (1943), too, and Asquith's *We Dive at Dawn* (1943), were certainly affected by the documentary tradition.

But it was not a lasting influence. Documentary directors like Watt, Jackson and Jack Lee, who went across to features, hardly managed to make much of a dent in established tradition; and Paul Rotha had a hard time as an independent producer of his own features. Jennings never made a fiction film, and on the evidence of dramatized documentaries like *The Silent Village* (1943) and *The Cumberland Story* (1947), would not have been very successful if he had.

Cavalcanti claimed that 'perhaps the most important result of the documentary movement' was the imposition of workers as 'dignified human beings' on a British cinema in which the working classes had traditionally been considered as fit for nothing more than comic relief. But it is interesting to find exactly the same charge being levelled, ten years after the end of the war, by members of the Free Cinema documentary group.

The wartime documentary movement performed a worthy service and made some fine films, but it did not change things. Nor did the movement go forward into peacetime with much vitality. Perhaps one of the reasons was that, having spent the Thirties as anti-establishment dissidents, the survivors found that the war had turned them into propagandists for tradition. They were certainly no longer in any sense radical. Perhaps, too, the scorn for 'intellect' and 'art', which had once signified a healthy impatience with pretension, had become too much of an excuse for complacency. When Churchill's Conservative government ungratefully and unimaginatively disbanded the Crown Film Unit in January 1952, no-one really seemed to care. The chapter had already ended.

LINDSAY ANDERSON

Below: as the war draws to its close a mother holds in her arms Britain's hopes for the future in A Diary for Timothy. *Bottom: three scenes from Rotha's* World of Plenty, *a study of world food problems that combined library material with new interviews, and also with what Rotha himself has described as 'black market' footage from secret sources*

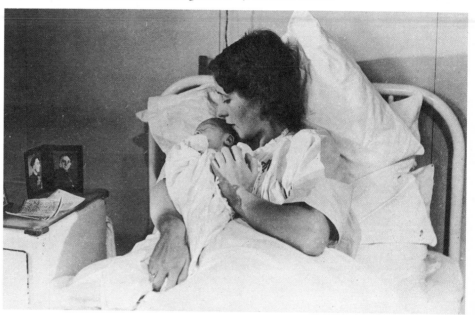

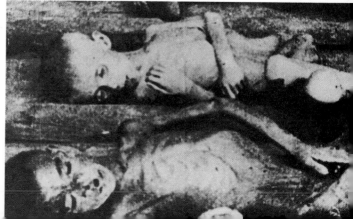

The Battle of Midway

John Ford's famous documentary was edited by Robert Parrish, who describes here how he and Ford (above centre) put the film together

Personnel from the US Navy, Marine Corps, Army and Air Force await an attack by the Japanese Imperial Fleet on Midway Island, a coral atoll in the Pacific 1300 miles north-west of Honolulu. Shots of the men preparing for action – a navy patrol plane landing in the water, the Marine Colour Guard marching (1) – are interspersed with the birds of the island. Guards gaze out at the sunset on the eve of the battle (2).

The next morning – June 4, 1942 – an enemy fleet is sighted and a council of war is held. At home, mothers sit anxiously but calmly (3) as their sons get ready to do their duty. The Japanese attack begins and the battle rages for two days (4–6); it switches from the air to the sea as the Americans launch a counter-offensive and ends with the Japanese fleet in retreat.

The American planes return to their carriers and the pilots, tired and relieved, climb out from their cockpits, 'home from the day's work' (7). Wounded survivors are brought back after days without food or water. The heroic dead are buried (8). The film ends with the official report of the Japanese losses.

Lt-Commander John Ford brought back eight cans of 16mm colour film from the Battle of Midway to my cutting room in the OSS (Office of Strategic Services) headquarters in Washington. 'Do you think we can make a twenty-minute record of the attack on Midway from that?' he asked me. I said, 'Do you want a factual film for the record, or do you want a propaganda film?'

'It's for the mothers of America,' he said. 'Do you think we can make a movie that the mothers of America will be interested in?'

I told him I thought we could make a very moving twenty-minute film that would interest not only the mothers of America, but also the fathers. He said the fathers already knew about the war because a lot of them were fighting it. He wanted the mothers to see how brave their sons were. 'Take the film to Hollywood,' he said. 'Don't report to anyone.' I was wearing dungarees,

United States Navy Documentary.
Directed by Lt-Commander John Ford, USNR, 1942
Prod co: US Navy/20th Century-Fox (Motion Picture Industry War Activities Committee). **photo:** John Ford. **add photo:** Jack McKenzie, Sp 2c, USNR. **ed:** Robert Parrish, Sp 2c, USNR. **mus:** Alfred Newman. **narr sc:** John Ford, Dudley Nichols, James Kevin McGuinness. **narr:** Donald Crisp, Henry Fonda, Jane Darwell, Irving Pichel. **r/t:** 17 mins.

3

1

2

so I replied, 'OK. I'll get changed and leave as soon as my orders are ready.'

'Never mind the orders,' he said, 'and don't bother to change. Just get on a plane and take the film to your mother's house in Hollywood and hide there until you hear from me. I don't want anyone from the Navy Department to know about this.' I reminded him that they would find out eventually and he said, 'It will be too late then. We'll already have our picture made. Besides, I'll tell them that it's not my fault if an enlisted man steals eight cans of top-secret film and runs home to his mother.'

My mother was delighted to see me. 'Where is your luggage and why are you travelling in dungarees?' she said. I told her I was on a secret mission and had been assigned to work with the OSS. She said, 'What's the SOS, some kind of dungaree outfit?' I was in the OSS for four years and she always called it the SOS.

Two days later Dudley Nichols phoned and said Ford would arrive that night to run the film with him. When Ford arrived, I asked him about my orders. He said I would get my orders in due course and that the only important thing was to get on with the work. Nichols, Ford and I ran the film and discussed ideas for the continuity and narration. Nichols went away to write and Ford said to me, 'Lock yourself in your cutting room and get to work. I'll have a sleeping bag and some sandwiches sent in to you. If anyone from naval intelligence comes around and asks what you're working on, tell 'em it's none of their goddam business.'

He asked another writer, James K. McGuinness, to add some ideas and then got Donald Crisp, Jane Darwell, Henry Fonda and Irving Pichel to record the narration for the film.

'Al Newman will write some music for you,' he said to me. 'Use about half of whatever he gives you, but be sure to include ''Red River Valley'', and ''My Country 'tis of Thee'', as well as ''Anchors Aweigh'', ''The Air Force Song'', and ''The Marine Hymn''. Get it all together and bring it to me in Washington.'

I said, 'What about my orders? If I get picked up with no orders, they'll toss me in some crummy navy brig in Chavez Ravine and the mothers of America will be disappointed, especially mine.'

'The Shore Patrol doesn't cover cutting rooms,' he answered. 'You'll get your orders when you need them. In the meantime, don't let anyone see any of the film, especially anyone from the Navy Department.'

He went to Washington that night. Three weeks later, I put the negative under the bed at my mother's house and followed Ford with the first complete print of The Battle of Midway. Ford took the film to the White House and ran it for President and Mrs Roosevelt, Harry Hopkins, Admiral Leahy, Stephen Early and certain members of the Joint Chiefs-of-Staff. When the lights came up, the President turned to Admiral Leahy and said, 'I want every mother in America to see this picture.'

My mother took the negative from under her bed and delivered it to the Technicolor lab, where a record 500 prints were made and rushed to cinemas across the country. I attended the opening at the Radio City Music Hall where there were a number of sobbing women in the audience – and most of them looked like mothers. I don't know how many mothers saw The Battle of Midway, but I know one who didn't. Two years later, when I next saw my mother, she said, 'Whatever happened to that dungaree movie you were making for the SOS?'

ROBERT PARRISH

Condensed material produced with permission of the Bodley Head from Growing Up in Hollywood by Robert Parrish.

4

Documentary Footage
Its uses and abuses

The immense amount of film shot during the war has been utilized in many ways – for propaganda, for dramatic sequences and for documentation. This article explores the ways that footage of the war has been used to mislead as well as to inform

World War II was unique in history – not only for the murderousness with which it was fought, but also for the thoroughness with which it was recorded on film. When the war ended, all the material shot, whether edited or in the form of rushes, became part of the historical record of the conflict. Though archives did their best to catalogue and identify the material entrusted to them, they were starved of funds and staff. Even today only about half the filmed record of the war has been positively identified. As with any other such records it was at the mercy of those who used it and, even in peacetime, not all film-makers are particularly fastidious.

Many scrupulous records do exist. The Wehrmacht (the German military command) painstakingly recorded its advance into Russia and shot similar footage of the campaigns in Poland, the Low Countries and France. The British recorded the Eighth Army from Normandy to the Danish border. The US Marine Corps filmed all of its amphibious operations and it recorded the invasions of Iwo Jima and Okinawa in colour. The US air force not only filmed its own operations, but recorded the advance of the American armies into southern Germany and Czechoslovakia – also in colour. There is colour film of the liberation of Prague, the link-up between the Russians and the Americans at Torgau, and of the surrender of an entire SS division to the American Sixth Army. There is also colour film of what the Americans found when they liberated the concentration camp at Buchenwald. There is even British film of bread-baking and a German film of igloo-making.

Despite the amount of resources deployed and the 500 million feet of film shot, there are unexpected gaps in the record. There is virtually no film of the British fleet in the first six months of the war. The Admiralty did not have its own film units and yet would not allow civilians to film its activities, so there is little film of the departure of the British Expeditionary Force to France or of its evacuation from Dunkirk – only a few hundred feet shot by civilian newsreel cameramen exists. The vessel carrying most of the film of D-Day back to England for processing was sunk, and there is hardly any film of the Japanese attack on Pearl Harbor from either the American or the Japanese side.

Nor is there much film of black American troops or of American service women (black or white). Their contributions to the war may not have been highly regarded. There is little Soviet film of the battle of Stalingrad – and what exists should be treated with suspicion since the army commander, General Chuikov, never allowed cameramen into the sector where the heavy fighting was. There is virtually no filmed record of the extermination of Europe's Jews and gypsies – the Nazis saw no purpose in recording that – and the victims had no opportunity to show what was happening to them. The few records which do exist are either the work of amateurs – grisly home movies dating from before the systematic ex-

Above left: picking up the pieces after a bomb attack – from British documentary footage.
Below left: the Soviets re-invaded Berlin, street by street, in order to film it. Below: courage in the face of adversity – the Soviet image in films – from the Story of Stalingrad

termination began – or show conditions in transit or concentration camps, not the actual extermination camps, crematoria or gas chambers.

During the war itself the footage obtained was used in many different ways. Feature film-makers, newsreel outfits, armed forces, scientific research establishments, industries, organized pressure groups and public and private organizations of all kinds made films about the war to serve their own purposes. Not surprisingly, different groups used the footage in different ways.

The coverage of the war by various bodies on the Soviet/German battle lines is an interesting example. In Nazi Germany several powerful institutions recorded their own version of what went on. For the newsreel cameramen who were ultimately responsible to Goebbels' Propaganda Ministry, the invasion of the Soviet Union in the summer of 1941 was a classic blitzkrieg: Panzers and motorized infantry and Stuka aircraft cut through Soviet defences and raced towards Moscow. The SS slightly modified their film version of events. Wherever the fighting was toughest or the advance was swiftest, there could be found Waffen SS tanks and armoured personnel carriers. But the Wehrmacht knew better. The German army was not highly motorized. While its handful of Panzers did race ahead, the great mass of the German army fought as it had a generation before. Its units were shipped by troop train to points hundreds of miles from the front. From there they marched on foot and their supplies were brought up in horse-drawn wagons. The Wehrmacht left the job of impressing civilians to the newsreels. It was more interested in learning from its mistakes. How did equipment stand up to the heat and dust of a Russian summer? How exhausted were the troops after a week's forced march? Why could Russian ponies and iron-wheeled carts keep going in terrain that brought German draught-horses and rubber-tyred wagons to a standstill? So the Wehrmacht cameramen diligently recorded exhausted troops, broken-down machines and all the other consequences of inadequate equipment and incompetent planning; meanwhile audiences back home

Above: a British Spitfire chasing a German Heinkel in the Battle of Britain. *The Heinkels were borrowed from the Spanish air force and fitted with Rolls-Royce aero engines for the film. Below: a post-war shot of Auschwitz from* The World at War

marvelled at the speed and smoothness of the triumphal advance.

On the other side of the battle line much the same thing happened. Soviet combat cameramen recorded retreat, panic flight and disaster, while newsreel audiences behind the lines saw nothing but resolute defence, calm assurance and single-minded patriotism.

Authorities in each of the combatant countries also had the difficult task of controlling what sort of non-fictional material was shown to the ordinary cinema-going public. Every country had a centrally controlled censorship mechanism, whose interventions ranged from vague exhortations to explicit instructions. German newsreels, for instance, were never allowed to dwell on the effects of the Allied bombing offensive on German cities; to do so would be to call attention to the inadequacy of German aerial defences. But British newsreels took urban destruction as an important theme in 1940 and 1941 (carefully following government guidelines, that any pan shots of bombed-out streets should begin and end on buildings which were intact) to show that the British could take it. The Italians, who never claimed to have impregnable air defences, showed their cities in flames to rouse popular feeling against the cultural barbarism of their enemies.

The job of publicly exhibited newsreels and documentaries, though the methods varied in each country, was to support the war effort and to sustain the morale of the millions of civilians who went to the cinema each week. All other considerations were secondary. Thus, though there might be disagreement about what would best sustain morale at any given time, no-one in authority ever doubted that a film which did not do that should not be made, and if it somehow were made, it should certainly not be exhibited. This led to awesome discrepancies between the war as fought and

the war as portrayed. Harry Watt's *Target for Tonight* (1941), which used Royal Air Force air crew and ground personnel, was produced at a time when RAF night bombers were known to be unable to drop more than ten per cent of their bomb loads within an eight-mile radius of their aiming points. Yet it showed a single aircraft destroying an entire oil refinery and marshalling yards with a single stick of bombs. *Desert Victory* (1943) was made to celebrate the second battle of El Alamein which was rightly expected to be the last great land battle to be fought in the West without the assistance of the American troops. Some of it was filmed in Egypt; much of it was filmed on the back-lot at Pinewood studios. Some night shots recorded the tracer-bullet arcs of the Eighth Army in Egypt, but lighted matches thrown a few feet away from the camera looked equally impressive.

One of the most elaborate scenes from *Stalingrad* (1943), shows the link-up of the two Soviet armies who cut off the German troops besieging the city. The scene shows long lines of infantry running towards each other across snow-covered fields, embracing and cheering as they meet. But in reality the first units to link up with each other were motorized and they met in fog.

Why We Fight (1942–45) was a series of hour-long films directed by Frank Capra, to be shown to all American conscripts during their basic training. By explaining the nature of the societies of both America's adversaries and allies, it was intended to commit those young Americans who saw it to the war they were waging and the role that they were playing in it. The War Department, which sponsored it, was so pleased with the series that it was cleared for theatrical release. However, it was unwilling to allow Capra to describe in any detail the role of the Communist Party in twentieth-century China and, in order to preserve balance, decided that the activities of Chiang Kai-Shek should not be given undue emphasis either. With the most important single issue in Chinese politics simply left out of the *Battle of China* (1944), the film was crippled. Even the government came to realize this, and so withdrew it.

We do not know what effect any of these films had. Most studies of audience behaviour were conceptually unsophisticated or frankly anecdotal. What evidence there is does not support the idea that audiences were mindlessly passive or capable of easy manipulation by skilled or unscrupulous film-makers. American GIs in basic training appreciated film shows of all sorts – with the lights out they could catch up on their sleep. When German audiences left their cinemas they couldn't help noticing that their cities had been reduced to rubble. British audiences appreciated that it was difficult for RAF cameramen to film the destruction of German marshalling yards from the ground so they cheerfully accepted the destruction of a model. As always, audiences used films – they saw what they wanted to see and heard what they wanted to hear; if that coincided with what the film-makers wanted, everyone was content. It was certainly not a time for fastidious film-making.

So for thirty years Germans in tanks have continued to slice through Russia like a hot knife through butter and the Soviet Army has surrounded them with its infantry at Stalingrad under clear skies. In the BBC's *The Commanders* (1972) London was bombed with American transport aircraft and British troops were evacuated from Dunkirk with an aircraft carrier. More recently, in *The Secret War* (1977) Luftwaffe pilots blitzing Coventry in 1940 saw

beneath them fires started by the RAF when they bombed Germany in 1945. Independent television companies have been equally imprecise. In Granada Television's *Cities at War* (1968), a scene of a worker in a Leningrad factory was step printed (i.e. every third frame was printed twice) to make him appear to have slowed his pace in the bitter cold of the siege. In Thames Television's *The Hunting of Force Z* (1977) the HMS *Repulse* and the HMS *Prince of Wales*, which are sent to the bottom of the sea by the Japanese air force, were models that were first sunk in a 1942 Japanese drama-documentary.

Films made directly for the cinema have also cut corners. Alain Resnais in *Nuit et Brouillard* (1955, *Night and Fog*) showed the horrors of Auschwitz with film taken in Holland before Auschwitz was built. In *Swastika* (1973) experts claimed to have been able to lip read what was said in Eva Braun's silent home movies and provided speeches even for guests whose backs were turned to the camera. In reality, guests facing the camera had a habit of talking more about the afternoon's entertainment than exterminating European Jewry.

It's not hard to see why such things are done. Except when making films for knowledgeable, critical specialists, most film-makers – including documentary film-makers – have never been much interested in authenticity for its own sake. They have been more concerned

with what they see as inner truths than in surface appearances. Their arguments are both practical and aesthetic. Practically, there are very few shots of advancing tanks that have been taken from the point of view of the enemy, or top shots of troops crawling on their bellies under fire, or close-ups of high-explosive shells on impact, or of the first wave of an amphibious force seen from the standpoint of the beach defenders. If such scenes are to be shown at all they must necessarily be staged. The aesthetic argument is related to this: if the point of a scene is to show cold, wet, miserable troops, it doesn't really matter whether they are filmed on manoeuvres or in combat as long as their cold and misery is genuine. What counts is the emotion, not how it is induced.

This is why documentary film-makers have always been prepared to use reconstructions, training films and even excerpts from feature films to flesh out what they see as the bare bones of their visual material. John Huston, for example, cut re-shot material into *San Pietro* (1944), Frank Capra shot Nazi classroom scenes in the United States and the Soviets re-fought parts of the battle for Stalingrad after the Germans surrendered, and reconquered Berlin four years after the end of the war.

Yet documentary film-makers have always been uneasy about such practices. Documentaries, after all, make claims to tell the truth and their credibility suffers if the material they incorporate is shown to be other than what it purports to be. That is why so many go to great lengths to conceal the origins of their material – even to the point of degrading picture quality to give the impression that scenes were shot under hazardous circumstances many years beforehand.

The production team responsible for *The World at War* made for Thames Television between 1971 and 1974 did not accept that documentary accounts of World War II need necessarily rely on unauthentic material or on material used unauthentically to make the film effective. The executive producer was Jeremy Isaacs, I was the associate producer and we thought it was possible to be faithful to actuality film as shot and yet make films which

Above left: in Patton *large numbers of Patton tanks converge – but they were, in fact, built long after the war had ended. Below left: the bombing of Pearl Harbor was restaged for* Tora! Tora! Tora! *Below: an American plane attacks a Japanese aircraft carrier in* Midway *– a reconstructed sequence from the film*

Above: four scenes from the original D-Day footage used in Overlord. *The makers went to great pains to use shots of the best technical quality without presenting them in contextually implausible ways*

were more than chronicles. We saw no reason why the impact of the series would be diminished if it faithfully acknowledged and critically evaluated the material from which it was made. But such positive identification of material was expensive, difficult and time consuming: it meant being systematically sceptical towards all previous use of material, and being particularly vigilant where compilation films were concerned. (Those who believe that 'if you've seen one Stuka you've seen them all' had a habit of sending the same one into action against Warsaw, Rotterdam, Biggin Hill and Stalingrad.) Though *The World at War* was a critical and popular success and earned more money for Thames than any other project it has undertaken, the challenge of its production methods does not appear to have been taken up by others dealing with World War II.

Feature film-makers have never been worried in the same way about distinctions between authentic and unauthentic material and its use. Being concerned with dramatic impact, they have had no hesitation about blurring distinctions to suit their needs. Budgetary considerations are often paramount: assembling a naval armada to invade the European continent strained the combined industrial resources of the United States and Britain, so not surprisingly producers have tended to use actual footage of the D-Day landings rather than try to re-create the whole

show. There is the question of danger as well: front-line filming is among the most hazardous possible. An explosive charge planted underground and detonated has different characteristics from one which results from the impact of a high explosive shell. The pilots of ground-support aircraft pressing home an attack will fly differently from stunt pilots doing their best *not* to kill the camera crew. No wonder *Midway* (1976) used material shot by John Ford and his crew when they were in the line of real fire in 1942.

Another use of actuality material is to propel a narrative forward or to establish locations. *La Traversée de Paris* (1956, *A Pig Across Paris*) made no attempt to suggest that it had been filmed under German Occupation: it simply used the well-known films of the German victory parade down the Champs Elysées as its title sequence to establish economically where and when the story was going to take place.

All these practices have their dangers: actuality material that is striking enough to use in the first place may end up stealing the show from the fictional material in which it is embedded. Who could take even a Francis Ford Coppola D-Day seriously once they'd seen what the real armada looked like? Could anyone feel that the studio Third Reich which collapsed around Alec Guiness' head told them more about the fall of Berlin than Soviet actuality film which punctuated his impersonation of the Führer in *Hitler: the Last Ten Days* (1973)? And could anyone looking at the brief snatches of film of Japanese aircraft taking off from their carriers to bomb Pearl Harbor – the only such film which exists – be impatient to return to the travelling matte

world of *Tora! Tora! Tora!* (1970)?

Some makers of feature films have taken that lesson to heart. There is no actual footage in *Patton* (1970) – the fictional presentation of America's most-photographed tank general. Audiences won't be tempted to wonder how he managed to win his victories with tanks which were built long after his death.

Actuality film is inconspicuous in many other war spectaculars because genuine footage could hardly be intercut with scenes in these films. For *The Battle of the River Plate* (1956), the American navy lent Michael Powell a cruiser but wouldn't let him sink it or, for that matter, replace the Stars and Stripes with a German naval battle flag. *The Battle of Britain* (1969) equipped its Heinkels and Messerschmitts with the same aero engines as the Royal Air Force had. (The Germans still lost!) The cameramen who filmed the liberation of Paris in 1944 were tactless enough to neglect their fellows who subsequently became ministers in de Gaulles' Fifth Republic, so their material was not really welcome in *Paris Brûlet-il* (1969, *Is Paris Burning?*).

Can fiction and actuality film ever be successfully integrated? Admirers of *Overlord* (1975) think it is a model of how such a thing might be done, but if it showed a way, no-one has yet followed it. Certainly the enterprise is fraught with difficulties and there is no point even attempting it until film-makers stop thinking of archives as visual breakers' yards from which to get the odd shot of a Stuka or an invasion, and begin to think of the filmed record of World War II as something to respect. If past experience is any guide, that time might be some way off.   JERRY KUEHL

Britain's Secret Weapon

The British sense of humour was perhaps more central to the war effort than the Spitfire or the Bren gun. Film-makers certainly found that a liberal dose of laughs was often the best way to get over vital information to the public

Britain's sense of humour was jocularly called its secret weapon in Leslie Howard's feature film *Pimpernel Smith* (1941), though the Nazi general, played by Francis L. Sullivan, did not think much of it: after wading through Lewis Carroll, Edward Lear and *Punch* magazine he concluded with Teutonic solemnity that the weapon was useless. The British film industry plainly thought otherwise, and exploited it

constantly. Established comics like Will Hay and George Formby appeared in features fighting fifth columnists and other enemies with slapstick and buffoonery. But the most revealing use of the British sense of humour occurred in the short propaganda films produced for the Ministry of Information. These were shown at all public cinemas; they came on after the first of the two features, in between

the newsreel and the trailer for whatever was coming next week.

The government had a mountain of information to get across to the public in an effort to keep the Home Front secure: newspapers, posters and leaflets, as well as films, exhorted people to keep lips buttoned about troop and munition movements ('Careless talk costs lives'); to save any metal scrap for salvage; to turn cast-off clothes into new creations ('Make do and mend'); to turn the flowerbeds over to vegetables ('Dig for victory'); to eat plenty of potatoes, plenty of National Wheatmeal Loaf and plenty of carrots.

It was hard work persuading the public that

Above: Halas and Batchelor's Dustbin Parade *illustrated the importance of conserving household rubbish for the war effort. Left:* Pimpernel Smith *(Leslie Howard, third from left) baffles the Nazis with his sense of humour and helps refugees escape their clutches. Below: Richard Massingham's foot ruler from* The Five-Inch Bather

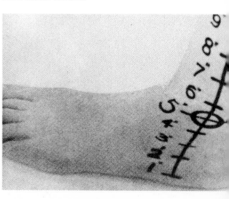

Above: a home-grown turnip does a little dance in Filling the Gap. *Right and bottom right: Sydney Howard before and after the bomb drops in* Mr Proudfoot Shows a Light, *which showed the perils of not observing blackout regulations, thereby providing an easy target for German night bombers. Bottom: Will Hay calmly fills a bucket with water in order to deal with an incendiary bomb in* Go to Blazes! – *another 'how not to do it' film*

these measures were important. The cartoonist Fougasse, who designed many of the period's most memorable posters, made a succinct analysis of the obstacles to be overcome in his book *A School of Purposes*, published in 1946. There was:

'. . . a general aversion to reading any notice of any sort; secondly, a general disinclination to believe that any notice, even if it was read, can possibly be addressed to oneself; thirdly, a general unwillingness . . . to remember the message long enough to do anything about it.'

But here was where Britain's secret weapon came in: if the same message was presented simply, and in a humorous, original way, it was far more likely to be remembered.

Film-maker Richard Massingham certainly realized this. One of the British cinema's true oddballs, he gave up a career in medicine to make sponsored shorts, often appearing in them himself – a bulky, friendly figure with a face forever plunged in lugubrious gloom or beaming with childlike joy. Cinema audiences took to him at once – he was no starchy government official sitting at a desk giving dull instructions, but a comic, human character in comic, human situations. When the Ministry of Fuel, Light and Power wanted to persuade

people to bathe in no more than five inches of water, Massingham appeared in a bath-tub, singing 'What Shall We Do With the Drunken Sailor?', with the five, vital inches marked off on his foot (*The Five-Inch Bather*, 1942). He even capitalized on the public's inbuilt resistance to obeying instructions. In his series of films on the dangers of spreading germs (*Coughs and Sneezes*, 1945, was the first), he looked at a handkerchief as though it was an object from Mars, spreading diseases by vaguely using it to polish a table and pick fruit.

He also showed a nimble wit when working solely as a director. World War II has no more ingenious propaganda film than *In Which We Live* (1943). Not to be confused with Noel

Coward's *In Which We Serve* (1942), which was the story of a destroyer and its crew, this is the story of a suit of clothes narrated on the soundtrack by the suit itself. Its history unfolds in a series of vignettes, from purchase off the peg through various stains and tribulations to its death and rebirth as short trousers for the children. 'To sleep, perchance to dream . . .', the suit quietly quotes as the housewife's scissors do their work. Massingham continued to flourish after the war, when the Labour government's complicated legislation and the continuance of rationing made film propaganda still necessary.

Comic personalities from feature films were not neglected in these propaganda shorts. Will Hay explained how to put out an incendiary bomb by demonstrating how *not* to do it in *Go to Blazes!* (1942); Arthur Askey promoted the correct use of the handkerchief in *The Nose Has It* (1942); Sydney Howard bumblingly ignored blackout regulations in *Mr Proudfoot Shows a Light* (1941). Another tiny film offered audiences the chance of *Eating Out With Tommy* (1941), which showed Tommy Trinder eating at one of the new chain of British restaurants set up all over the country to provide solid, cheap food. 'They never let bygones be rissoles!' he said.

Experimental film-maker Len Lye used a more sophisticated brand of humour to advertise the delectability of vegetable pies: *When the Pie Was Opened* (1941) flavoured its cooking

recipe with a soundtrack that included snatches of Louis Armstrong's music, train noises and the sound of wood being sawn (synchronized with a knife cutting through the pie crust). The techniques of animation were under-used during the period, although the team of John Halas and Joy Batchelor, subsequently famous for their feature *Animal Farm* (1954), established themselves with a film about the need for home-grown foods, *Filling the Gap* (1942) and one about salvage, *Dustbin Parade* (1943). They also supplied Middle East troops with animated explanations of the dangers of food poisoning and VD. The war proved that Britain's secret weapon could be aimed at any target.   GEOFF BROWN

When the US government called on the directors of Hollywood to make propagandist documentaries to further the war effort, the results were not always quite what it had bargained for

Unlike Britain, the USA had little or no tradition of documentary film-making when it was plunged into world war in 1941. With the exception of Louis de Rochemont and his relatively conservative *March of Time* newsreels, documentarists – such as Pare Lorentz, Joris Ivens and Robert Flaherty – were widely regarded as dangerous radicals. A typical establishment view was that of the director Frank Capra who described them as 'longhaired kooks'.

The events of Pearl Harbor did little to remove this prejudice, with the result that the US government, shocked by the potency of German film propaganda, turned not to the established exponents of documentary but to Hollywood to fulfil its war propaganda needs. Thus major Hollywood directors, such as Capra, John Ford, John Huston and William Wyler, were called up for military service whence they were to lead the cinema into battle with cameras instead of guns.

For this reason the films these directors created, instead of acquiring a collective style comparable with that of the British Crown Film Unit, were usually highly individualistic, frequently contentious, and judged, as often as not, by the same standards applied to commercial feature films. At their best, however, they were brilliantly and heroically photographed and stand as vivid records of war.

A handful of documentaries attempting to portray the grim realities of the war in Europe had been produced during the USA's ambivalent isolationist period, but it was not until after it entered the war that the flow of authentically American war documentaries began in earnest. The first – that is, the first intended for release to the general public – was John Ford's *The Battle of Midway* (1942). It set a style for front-line film-making, and

provoked debate, in contrast to Ford's only previous propagandist effort, an army training film called *Sex Hygiene* (1942).

With some alacrity Ford had joined the navy as a lieutenant-commander in charge of the Field Photographic Branch of the Office of Strategic Services, into which he recruited Hollywood colleagues like Robert Parrish, Gregg Toland and Robert Montgomery. For *The Battle of Midway* – an account of the first significantly successful American action in the Pacific – Ford headed the photographic unit himself, getting so close to the battle that the camera recorded the jolts of bombing and he sustained wounds which later led to a partial loss of eyesight. The film won an Academy Award as the best short documentary of 1942. It was an entirely personal blend of stark reality and Fordian myth-making; an exercise in patriotic fervour and a deeply felt

essay on 'war, and peace and all-of-us', appealing to the heart rather than the mind. Its main enduring strength was its concentration on individuals, the brave boys who fought and died to defend small-town America.

Ford's second documentary of the war the only other one of note he was able to complete during his wartime career – was *December 7th* (1943). This account of Pearl Harbor had been commissioned at the highest levels of government and planned as a feature-length morale-booster. Ford, however, took the opportunity to attack America's lack of preparedness in the Pacific (in a tone which presaged his later angry war feature, *They Were Expendable*, 1945), concentrating on supposedly subversive activities by Japanese elements in Hawaii while the US navy slept. Most of it was

Above: a pall of smoke hangs over Pearl Harbor, devastated without warning by Japanese planes – a reminder of why the USA was at war from December 7th. *Below: a small Italian boy stands amid the rubble of his 'liberated' village,* San Pietro

I SWEAR REVENGE UPON THE ENEMY...

photographed and directed by cameraman Gregg Toland, whom Ford had sent with a crew to the island. Ford later put together a provocative 85-minute version composed largely of mocked-up battle scenes (the only actuality footage available to him showed the aftermath of the attack) and dramatized critical comment. This proved unacceptable to the authorities and what finally appeared in the cinemas was a 20-minute 'incentive' version which, ironically, earned Ford his second wartime Oscar.

In direct contrast to Ford, Frank Capra was in perfect accord with the military and the government. Thanks in large part to his reputation as a popular and sympathetic observer of the American national character, Capra had been given the rank of major and, somewhat to his bewilderment, put in charge of the US War Department's film programme. His response was the acclaimed and highly influential *Why We Fight* series, seven innovative documentaries produced between 1942 and 1945.

They focused on the key events in the development of the conflict. The first, *Prelude to War* (1942), recorded the rise of fascism in Italy, Germany and Japan before Pearl Harbor and the basic reasons for America's entry into the war; the second, *The Nazis Strike* (1943), traced German aggression up to the fall of Poland; *Divide and Conquer* (1943) described the conquest of Denmark, Norway, the Low Countries and France; *The Battle of Britain* (1943) showed the British resistance to German bombing; *The Battle of Russia* (1943) detailed the bitter struggle on the Eastern front culminating in the German defeat at Stalingrad; *The Battle of China* (1944) reviewed Japanese aggression in China; and *War Comes*

Above: four eloquent scenes from the Why We Fight *series. Children learn how to handle a field gun* (Prelude to War, *top left*); Luftwaffe *bombers head for Britain's cities* (The Battle of Britain, *top right*); *a church is laid waste* (The Nazis Strike, *above left*); *a Russian patriot vows to avenge the invasion of his homeland by the forces of fascism* (The Battle of Russia, *above right*)

to America (1945) examined American values and showed how they were threatened by the forces of facism.

Employing an unprecedented and increasingly complex montage of words, music, diagrams and film from a wide variety of sources, including enemy footage and feature films, Capra achieved an expertly sustained and persuasive propaganda package which succeeded (in the words of the film historian Leslie Halliwell) in 'turning unpleasant facts into breathtaking entertainment'. Having set new standards in the use of film for propaganda purposes, Capra left army service in 1945 smothered in military honours and having achieved the rank of lieutenant-colonel.

One of Capra's inspirations in the making of the *Why We Fight* series had been to use the Walt Disney studio for the animation of maps. This was, in fact, a comparatively minor chore for Disney, whose studio had, by 1943, become almost exclusively concerned with the production of films under government contract. This was significant for Disney in more ways than one, for not only did it mark an unprecedented degree of involvement by an entertainment studio in the government's propaganda programme, but it also provided an opportunity for considerable experimentation in animation

styles and techniques and, as the war continued, rescued Disney from serious financial and labour problems.

Disney's war output ranged from training films to public information shorts and 'Good Neighbour' exercises like *The Three Caballeros* (1945). Minnie Mouse exhorted the American housewife to save kitchen fat in *Out of the Frying Pan Into the Firing Line* (1942). Donald Duck satirized Hitler in the Oscar-winning *Der Fuehrer's Face* (1942) and explained how to fill in tax forms in *Spirit of '43* (1943); the studio even designed military insignia and a Mickey Mouse gas-mask. The most remarkable of Disney's wartime films, however, was the deadly serious *Victory Through Air Power*, a feature-length cartoon, completed in 1943, which strongly promoted the then unfashionable opinion of a Russian immigrant, Major Alexander de Seversky, that air domination was the only way to win the war. Often fanciful and simplistic (it envisaged the war carrying on until at least 1948, and bombers being developed as invulnerable super-weapons), it was received with decidedly mixed feelings (evaluations ranged from 'Disney's greatest film' to 'the wickedest film in the world'). Nevertheless the film made a considerable impact in high places, exciting both Roosevelt and Churchill. It was one of the most extraordinary pieces of work to emerge from the stable which had sired *Snow White and the Seven Dwarfs* (1937) and *Bambi* (1942).

More conventional, but no less powerful, material emerged from those directors involved with the fighting at the front line as the tide of war turned in 1944. Such films were frequently concerned not only with victory itself but also with the price of victory. A

Above: a gunner of The Memphis Belle. *Right: Disney's depiction of the first forms of aerial combat from* Victory Through Air Power. *Bottom: a 'heroic' verse commentary was added to* The True Glory *when the film went on show with* Henry V *(1944)*

  WALT DISNEY presents **VICTORY THROUGH AIR POWER** in TECHNICOLOR U

notable example was *The Battle for the Marianas* (1944), a lucid, harrowing account of a phase of the American counter-attack in the South-Western Pacific which, the film takes pains to point out, cost the lives of 4470 US Marines and countless Japanese.

A favourite method of presenting the conflict was also to follow the fortunes of a single fighting unit. William Wyler used this technique to eloquent effect in *The Memphis Belle* (1944), a first-hand account of a B-17 Flying Fortress and its crew in bombing raids over Germany, with Wyler and cameraman William Clothier themselves shooting the aerial combat scenes on an actual mission over Wilhelmshaven. Even more spectacular was *The Fighting Lady* (1944), the story (narrated by Robert Taylor) of an aircraft carrier and its 3000-man crew in Pacific waters, photographed by Edward J. Steichen and memorable for its use of cameras synchronized to dive-bombers' guns, which recorded, among other things, the massacre of an alleged 360 Japanese aircraft in a single day.

Perhaps the most honest, telling and poignant of the documentaries which depicted the American fighting man were those from the camera of John Huston, who began his war career with *Report From the Aleutians* (1943), a low-key study of ordinary soldiers on a remote and unsung posting in the North Pacific known as the 'Bridge of Asia', and followed with his reportage masterpiece, *San Pietro* (1945). Huston's singular attitudes to the war invited controversy and censure. *San Pietro*, an on-the-spot account of the 143rd Infantry Regiment's tortuous and costly attempts to take a German-held village in the Liri valley in Italy, contrasted military objectives with the price paid in human courage and death. 'These lives', said Huston himself on the soundtrack, 'were valuable. Valuable to their loved ones, to their country and to the men themselves.' Death, moreover, was plainly seen, most movingly in scenes showing bodies wrapped in sacks, and the result was that the War Department condemned the film as pacifistic and demoralizing and cut Huston's 50-minute version down to 30 minutes – although in so doing they failed to suppress

It's your story of your victory told by your guys!

VICTORY THE PICTURE YOU HELPED TO MAKE... Now on the screen in all its thrilling glory!

Gen. **Dwight D. Eisenhower's** **THE TRUE GLORY**

Exploit it to the skies – with the help of the War Department and the OWI!

Capt. GARSON KANIN · CAROL REED
Distributed by COLUMBIA PICTURES

fully the film's sorrow at the waste of war.

Huston's third and last contemporary statement about the war, *Let There Be Light* (1946), was received even more harshly. Asked to make a film about the treatment of soldiers suffering from war-induced neuroses, to reassure potential employers that these men were not permanently insane, Huston replied with an intensely human document which again implicitly condemned the war and its terrible effects on the mind and the spirit. This time the film was banned outright, and has not been exhibited until recently.

As if to unite at last the disparate paths taken by the British and American war documentaries, the British Ministry of Information and the US Office of War Information combined forces in 1945 to produce the final blockbuster account of the Allied victory in Europe, *The True Glory*. Directed by Carol Reed and Garson Kanin, the film was photographed in action by 700 cameramen (of whom 32 were killed, 16 reported missing and 101 wounded) who shot an alleged 6.5 million feet of film. It was a tribute to the soldiers of all the Allied nations who took part in the final rescue of democracy, cleverly emphasizing the comments of the troops themselves and only marred by snatches of an inappropriate blank-verse commentary.

The True Glory was universally praised and admired, particularly for its notions of international alliance and comradeship in the cause of freedom, but it was largely untypical of the war documentaries of the USA, where, perhaps more than in any other country, film had (in the words of the film historian Lewis Jacobs) 'served as a potent instrument of national policy'. In 1945, at the conclusion of European hostilities, Hollywood assumed its obligations to the government to be at an end, abruptly ceased its interesting flirtation with documentary and returned to its own battle-front – the box-office.   CLYDE JEAVONS

Chapter 23
Realism, Italian-style

After the false rhetoric of the Fascist regime had been exposed, Italian film-makers went in search of the truth and found it in everyday life

When the great Italian director Roberto Rossellini was asked to define neo-realism, he said:

'For me it is above all a moral position from which to look at the world. It then became an aesthetic position, but at the beginning it was moral.'

w To understand both the moral and aesthetic position which informed neo-realism, as well as the forces which helped destroy it, it is necessary to begin with the economic, political, and social context in which it was born.

There were, of course, harbingers of a 'new realism' before Rossellini's *Roma, Città Aperta*

(1945, *Rome, Open City*). But when that film burst upon the international cinema scene in the immediate post-war years, neo-realism proper can be said to have begun. *Rome, Open City* was a direct product of the 'War of Liberation' taking place in Italy in 1945.

During 1943 and 1944, Italy had been torn apart. Mussolini's government had fallen, the new Badoglio government had surrendered to the invading Allied armies in the South while the Germans had occupied the North; anti-fascist Italians of every political and religious persuasion had been involved in the fighting to liberate their country and had been united by the struggle against fascism.

To film-makers and all other artists of the period it was clear that if the lies and empty rhetoric of the Mussolini government had brought Italy to agony, then a confrontation with reality, an encounter with 'truth' would save Italy. In terms of the cinema this meant the rejection of what had gone before, for although there were few blatant propaganda films made under the Fascist regime, the films that were produced in Italy during the war years had

little to do with Italian reality.

Some long-term benefits emerged from the Fascist government's control of the film industry. The huge studio complex of Cinecittà had been built and the Italian film school, Centro Sperimentale di Cinematografia, had already trained many important Italian film-makers. Not every film made under the Fascist regime was poor but none of them came close to touching the social reality of Italy; for the most part, they were slick, glossy, vacuous melodramas made entirely in the studios and featuring upper-middle-class characters. Collectively they were known as 'white telephone' films, a nickname that has come to typify film production in Italy under the Fascists.

Inspired by the 'War of Liberation', film-makers rejected the old cinema and its conventions. Their belief in showing 'things as they are' was placed in the service of the construction of a new Italy. In this way the moral and aesthetic principles of neo-realism were united. The manner and style of the new cinema was to be as much a statement as its subject-matter.

The theory of neo-realism was formulated in part from basic assumptions about the nature of cinema and its function in society, and in part from the early films of the movement. Theory and practice rarely coincided in one film and many were only superficially neo-realist films. Some astute Italian critics decried the use of neo-realist mannerisms to disguise purely commercial ventures (usually exploitative sexual melodramas) and the forcing of material which cried out for a different treatment into a neo-realist style.

Cesare Zavattini, the writer of Vittorio De Sica's major films, and a director himself in the Fifties, formulated the theory of neo-realism: cinema's task was no longer simply to 'entertain' in the usual sense of the word, but to confront audiences with

Above: Massimo Girotti in Visconti's Ossessione. *A stranger in a remote rural district, he finds casual work with a couple who run a roadhouse, seduces the wife and plots with her to murder the husband. Left: the hurried burial of a partisan in Rossellini's six-part film* Paisà, *about the resistance and liberation of Italy in 1944–45. Below: production shot from De Sica's* The Children Are Watching Us *(1943), not strictly a neo-realist film but one that anticipates the style, notably through its use of exterior shots and urban settings*

found in newspapers. Zavattini cited the example of a woman buying a pair of shoes to show how simple such narratives could be and how social problems – poverty, unemployment, poor housing – could be illustrated within a fiction film.

Although most of the problems presented in neo-realist films were susceptible to political solution, the neo-realists never presented a clear political programme. Their party affiliations were, after all, quite diverse: a number of writers and directors were Marxists but just as many were Christian Democrats, or held various other political ideas.

The theorists, especially Zavattini, insisted that there was a natural affinity between the cinema and 'reality', despite the fact that a camera will record whatever is in front of the lens and that the processed film will then (depending upon the skill of the film-maker) convince a spectator of the 'reality' of what he is seeing. But it was never quite so simple and Zavattini frequently made it clear that, for him, the entire question remained ambiguous, that cinematic 'realism' was merely a convention, and that the neo-realist method was only one possible approach to cinema.

Above: a starkly realistic scene from La Terra Trema, *filmed several years before the term 'kitchen sink' was used to describe realist drama. The actors were non-professionals and the details of life in the Sicilian fishing community were totally authentic. Right: father and son (Lamberto Maggiorani and Enzo Staiola) walk the rain-soaked streets in* Bicycle Thieves. *Below right:* Sperduti nel Buio (Lost in Darkness), *a melodrama filmed in the slums of Naples, provides evidence of a realist style in Italian cinema as early as 1914. With its scrupulous attention to detail, its cracked walls and worn steps and its use of natural light, this film influenced several generations of Italian film-makers*

Inevitably audiences become accustomed to cinematic conventions, even those as initially 'shocking' as open-air shooting on real streets with non-professional actors. In *Rome, Open City* real locations were used for almost the entire film but no-one has complained (and very few people even knew) that the priest's room, the Gestapo headquarters and one apartment were constructed entirely in a studio and therefore broke the rules of authenticity. Similarly the theoretical principle that roles be played by 'real people' – which was partly an over-reaction to the artificiality of movie stars – became a convention in itself.

In De Sica's *Umberto D* (1951), the non-actor playing the role of the unemployed government official was in real life an elderly professor. He was highly praised for the 'reality' of his performance, but it was a performance; the professor had nothing in common with the character except age.

The only neo-realist film which followed the theory by having the entire cast made up of non-professionals was Visconti's *La Terra Trema* (1948,

Pure neo-realism lasted only for a few short years, although the style was soon absorbed into Italian popular cinema

The Earth Trembles). In that film, however Visconti rehearsed his village fishermen over and over again until they delivered the performances he wanted. They were effective, not so much because they were fishermen, but rather because they had been formed into good actors.

For some critics and film-makers, 'reality' meant 'social reality' and in particular the representation of the the conditions of the poor and unemployed. Later, when directors like Rossellini and Visconti moved away from the working classes, they were denounced as 'betrayers of neo-realism', as if the middle classes were not a part of 'social reality'.

Social criticism was hardly lacking in neo-realist films, but it was rarely their major thrust. In De Sica's *Ladri di Biciclette* (1948, *Bicycle Thieves*) the camera pans along rows of pawned sheets while the protagonist attempts to pawn those belonging to his wife. Throughout the film we are made aware of the thousands of people like him, all seeking work. Yet the problem of unemployment is never analysed. Instead the story takes a dramatic turn as the protagonist steals a bicycle and is thus criminalized

their own reality, to analyse that reality, and to unite audiences through a shared confrontation with reality. The most disheartening thing for the neo-realist film-makers must have been that this basic goal was not achieved, simply because Italian audiences remained indifferent or hostile to the films, preferring instead pure escapism. They had no desire to confront on the screen the depressing reality of their everyday lives.

If cinema was to present things 'as they are', it meant that fiction, particularly that derived from novels and plays, would have to be replaced by looser, rather 'open ended' narratives, based on real experience familiar to the film-makers or, perhaps,

by his poverty. He is subsequently humiliated and finally 'redeemed'. At the end of the film we are moved by the man's plight, but we are no closer to an understanding of his social reality.

Visconti's *La Terra Trema* comes closest to being the perfect neo-realist film: it achieves a clear understanding of how the fishermen are exploited and of how this 'social reality' works to oppress people generally. Ironically, while the theory of neo-realism was fulfilled by *La Terra Trema*, Visconti violated one of Zavattini's fundamental tenets by basing the film on a novel, *I Malavoglia*, by the nineteenth-century writer Giovanni Verga, who is often mentioned by critics and film historians as one of the possible sources of Italian neo-realism.

Most of the arguments and polemics surrounding neo-realism had already been rehearsed in the nineteenth century. At that time the literary movements of the *verismo* novelists concerned themselves primarily with the lower classes and their problems. One of the stated goals of the verist writers was the social education of their readers. Such work, however, rarely reached the class which might have drawn benefit from it.

Most verist novelists, like the neo-realist directors, sought to increase their popularity by recounting routine shop-girl fantasies, cloaked in the mantle of realism. But a small core of film-makers remained faithful to the principles of neo-realism; among them were Giuseppe De Santis, who made *Caccia Tragica* (1947, *Tragic Pursuit*), a tale of robbery at a collective farm and *Roma Ore Undici* (1952, *Rome, Eleven O'Clock*), a memorable film of a real-life incident in which a staircase collapsed under the weight of two hundred girls who had all applied for the same job.

In tracing the origins of Italian neo-realism, 'realist' film styles can be detected in the early Italian cinema: even the historical spectaculars which gave Italian cinema its international reputation contain a vividly realistic streak.

The American cinema may also be evidenced as an antecedent of Italian neo-realism: it is clear, for example, that everyone working in Italian cinema of the Forties was familiar with such 'realist' classics as Vidor's *The Crowd* (1928) and Stroheim's

Greed (1929). Also influential was the so-called 'poetic realism' of Jean Renoir and his fellow film-makers in France during the Thirties. Visconti's own training as an assistant on *Toni* (1934) and his close study of Renoir's films is echoed in films like *Ossessione* (1942, Obsession) and *La Terra Trema*.

The 'War of Liberation' may have temporarily united Italians of diverse political beliefs and provided an inspiration for the neo-realists but the honeymoon was short-lived. After the liberation, anti-communist propaganda took root in Italy.

Although the social criticism of neo-realist cinema was essentially mild and non-Marxist, the films did illuminate problems in Italy that remained unsolved. In the immediate post-war climate, 'anti-fascist' had come to mean much the same thing as 'communist' and the government did not take too kindly to the image of the country that the neo-realist film-makers were projecting. For its part, the Church claimed that such films were unsympathetic to the clergy and even blasphemous.

Some neo-realist films had great success at the box-office, but for the most part they depended on foreign receipts to cover the costs of even the small budgets involved. The huge popularity of American films all but destroyed whatever financial basis the domestic market had for Italian films, neo-realist or otherwise. Gradually the producers, too, became hostile to the neo-realist style.

When the government appointed Giulio Andreotti as the head of Direzione Generale dello Spectacolo (an agency for overseeing the performing arts), he was given wide-ranging powers over the cinema. Andreotti controlled bank loans: he restricted them to 'suitable' films and vetoed loans on films which were 'infected with the spirit of neo-realism'. His powers went even further: Andreotti could, and often did, ban public screenings of films that he decided were 'not in the best interests of Italy'. Even more harmful were the bans on the exportation of films that maligned Italy. And it was these moves as much as anything else that brought about the demise of the neo-realist movement.

The immediate inheritance of the neo-realist movement was to be evidenced in the Fifties, the decade that also saw the break up of the original core of directors – Rossellini, Visconti, De Sica and the young Antonioni. As their careers diverged and the political realities of Italy in the Fifties went through several changes, the Italian cinema gradually shed its mantle of neo-realism.

DAVID OVERBEY

Top: in Riso Amaro (Bitter Rice) *Silvana Mangano and Vittorio Gassman try to steal the rice crop from a small valley in the North of Italy. The film portrayed the painful labour of rice-growing with a documentary zeal, but its success at the box-office, both at home and abroad, was probably due to its erotic content (below left). Above:* Stromboli, *made in 1949, is a transitional film that bears the vestiges of the documentary style so beloved of the neo-realists, but also indicates the shift in Italian cinema towards the use of international stars in sensational dramas set against a background of rural poverty*

VITTORIO GASSMANN
DORIS DOWLING
SILVANA MANGANO
RAF VALLONE
Regia di
GIUSEPPE DE SANTIS

un film LUX

LUX FILM

riso amaro

The films of

Roberto Rossellini

Rossellini is commonly known as the 'father' of the neo-realist movement. Yet this convenient critical label does not do full justice to a director who, in the face of widespread criticism, continually sought to redefine the relationship between the film-maker and his audience and to create a new, vital role for cinema in society

Rossellini made his first full-length feature films during the period that the Fascist regime held sway in Italy. For this reason, many of the director's later admirers were uncomfortable when he talked blithely and frankly of his work on *La Nave Bianca* (1941, The White Ship), *Un Pilota Ritorna* (1942, A Pilot Returns) and *L'Uomo della Croce* (1943, The Man of the Cross). Indeed, *La Nave Bianca* was produced under the supervision of the dedicated Fascist Francesco De Robertis at the Naval Ministry.

These films have been described as 'fascist propaganda', mostly, of course, by people who have never seen them. However, in Rossellini's defence it must be remembered that anyone working in the cinema at that time was forced to operate under tight restrictions. Obviously no anti-fascist films were made; on the other hand, few overtly propagandist features were made either (the radio was far more extensively used for such purposes). Few film-makers indulged in the kind of fascist rhetoric to be found in Alessandro Blasetti's *Vecchia Guardia* (1934, *The Old Guard*) or Mario Camerini's *Il Grande Appello* (1936, The Great Roll-Call).

La Nave Bianca is half documentary and half

fiction. A romance between a sailor and a schoolteacher-turned-nurse links the film's two sections. The first shows the sailor's ship leaving port (with a few shots indicating the power of the Italian navy), sailing into battle and being severely damaged. The second section deals with the rescue of the wounded – including the sailor – and their fine treatment on a hospital ship, where the sailor is reunited with his beloved. The film's ideological fault is not that it is openly fascist in outlook but that it achieves its aim of promoting the illusion that all is well in Italy in 1941.

Any attempt by a film-maker to present life as it was lived was bound to be frustrated

during the Fascist period, as most of the future neo-realists soon found. However, their very frustration with this state of affairs made them reject fascism on moral and aesthetic grounds; thus the neo-realist movement partly owes its origins to the disenchantment of certain film makers with the restrictions placed on artistic freedom in Fascist Italy.

Above left: Rossellini in 1949, when rumours of his romance with Ingrid Bergman were rife. Above: an American GI meets a Naples urchin in Paisà. *Below: a village under fire in* L'Uomo della Croce, *one of Rossellini's films made during the Fascist regime*

By 1942 De Robertis and Rossellini had quarrelled – first over Rossellini's refusal to work from a detailed scenario, and then over politics. Two years later, Rossellini was in Rome, the representative of the Christian Democrats in the film branch of the Committee of National Liberation. It was then that neo-realism was born with *Roma, Città Aperta* (1945, *Rome, Open City*). Rossellini is often said to be the father of neo-realism which, considering the influence *Rome, Open City* and his next film, *Paisà* (1946, *Paisan*), had on film-makers in Italy and all over the world, is not surprising. However, it must be remembered that neo-realism had a number of antecedents, sprang from a number of sources, and that the same influences working on Rossellini were also felt by other film-makers, some of whom were already aiming at similar goals. Rossellini himself was unhappy with the title; it resulted in his work being attacked as it moved away from dealing exclusively with the Italian experience of World War II:

'It was the war itself which motivated me; war and resistance are collective actions by definition. If from the collective I then passed to an examination of personality, as in the case of the child in *Germania, Anno Zero* (1947, *Germany, Year Zero*) and the refugee of *Stromboli* (1950, *God's Land*) that was part of my natural evolution as a director.'

That 'evolution' was often branded 'involution' and 'betrayal of neo-realism' by a good many critics at the time.

Rossellini's personal life undoubtedly had a strong impact on the subsequent development of his work. One of the reasons he made *L'Amore* (1948, *Love*) was his long-standing relationship with the actress Anna Magnani:

'The phenomenon to be examined was Anna Magnani. Only the novel, poetry and the

cinema permit us to rummage through a personality to discover reactions and motives for actions.'

In the second part of the film, *Il Miracolo*, (*The Miracle*), Magnani plays a simple peasant woman who is made pregnant by a vagabond she believes to be St Joseph. It caused a scandal everywhere. Rossellini's wish to return to a 'more optimistic subject' led to *Francesco, Giullare di Dio* (1950, *Flowers of St Francis*), a film about St Francis in the form of a fable. Instead of winning back support from those who had attacked him as a blasphemer after *Il Miracolo*, the new film merely antagonized those who had liked the previous one.

Ingrid Bergman had seen *Rome, Open City* and *Paisà* in the winter of 1947–48. She wrote to Rossellini expressing a strong desire to appear in one of his films. A few months later they met to discuss the making of *Stromboli*.

Bergman was disenchanted with her marriage and career at the time and a love affair rapidly developed between her and her idol which shocked her American fans – accustomed to Bergman's 'spiritual' image – and provided good copy for gossip columnists for some time. Following the birth of a son, Bergman's husband, Dr Lindstrom, divorced her and she and Rossellini were married. The partnership led to six of his finest films, particularly *Stromboli* and *Viaggio in Italia* (1954, *Journey to Italy*). *Stromboli* has Bergman cast as a Lithuanian refugee who marries a peasant to escape from an internment camp after the end of World War II. When he takes her to his island home, she finds herself even more imprisoned. Seeking to escape, she climbs over the island's semi-active volcano, Stromboli. Exhausted and in despair she sinks to the ground and cries out to God. In *Journey to Italy*, she and George Sanders play an English couple whose marriage is gradually breaking down. They travel to Italy in order to sell a house bequeathed to them in a will. Gradually they fall under the influence of the unfamiliar Italian environment, and are ultimately reconciled during a religious parade in a small village. Both films were unsuccessful at the box-office, and have led to a great many misunderstandings about the nature of Rossellini's religious beliefs. He has pointed out that the refugee's crying out to God at the end of *Stromboli* is merely an instinctive act that anyone at the end of his strength might commit, and that the couple's reconciliation at the end of *Journey to Italy* is at best only temporary; any religious significance the scene may possess is probably ironic.

Although Rossellini's films found fewer and fewer paying customers and were often dismissed by the majority of critics who bothered to review them (with the French being a happy exception), his influence on other film-makers continued to be felt. *Journey to Italy* encouraged Michelangelo Antonioni to make *L'Avventura* (1960, *The Adventure*); certainly both François Truffaut and Jean-Luc Godard have admitted their debt to Rossellini during this period. Rossellini was simply a decade ahead of his time, and audiences were just not

Above: St Francis and his brother friars in Flowers of St Francis, *which explored the idea of saintliness through a naturalistic evocation of history. Right: Ingrid Bergman as Karin, the oppressed wife of a Sicilian fisherman in* Stromboli

ready to accept or understand what he was attempting to do.

For a very short period Rossellini attempted to work within the commercial cinema, making *Il Generale Della Rovere* (1959, General Della Rovere), a heavily scripted, sentimental, pseudo-realist film, and *Vanina Vanini* (1961, *The Betrayer*), based on stories by Stendhal. While the first did very well with audiences and critics, the second was a failure. Rossellini himself was happy with neither, and decided to give up the cinema and work in the popular medium of television, making historical and scientific meditations – which he described as 'studies of ideas as they burst upon history'. *L'Età del Ferro* (1964, The Age of Iron) was followed by *La Prise de Pouvoir par Louis XIV* (1966, *The Rise of Louis XIV*), which had a surprising international success in cinemas. The series continued with *Atti Degli Apostoli* (1969, Acts of the Apostles), *Socrate* (1970, Socrates), *Il Messia* (1975, The Messiah), and was to include a film on Karl Marx.

Just before his death in 1977 at the age of 71, Rossellini was looking forward to the publication in France of his book on education and society, *Un Esprit Libre ne Doit Rien Apprendre en Esclave*. In many ways that title – which in English means 'A free spirit will learn nothing from slavery' – sums up his life and career. When asked at Cannes what he thought his role and function was in world cinema, he replied with a laugh: 'As I see it my role is to be a constant pain in the ass to everyone.' And so he was – if all pejorative connotations may be removed from the phrase. He never let anyone alone; he pushed, questioned, probed, and analysed constantly. To be in his company – or viewing one of his films – invariably forced one to re-examine and reconsider everything, from the role of a director in the cinema, to current definitions of 'reality' and 'truth'.

He was constantly curious, and serious, about everything. When he began thinking about a new film – particularly in the latter part of his career when he dealt primarily with historical figures and their ideas – he would read all he could find on the subject. He would also stop people in the street and ask them detailed questions about their jobs, their ideas, and their lives. He loved to provoke others by making deliberately outrageous comments –

Above: two scenes from Rossellini's rarely-seen documentary India, *which concentrates on the relationship of Man and Nature – a theme that the director explored throughout his work. Right: Jean-Marie Patte as the all-powerful king in the TV film* The Rise of Louis XIV, *which combined opulence with a high degree of realism*

his eyes twinkling with playfulness – to stir up reaction and debate.

All the praise heaped upon him by critics immediately after his death would, without doubt, have amused him highly. He was, after all, hardly used to universal praise when he was alive. From the beginnings of his career to the time of his last feature film, *Il Messia*, he was criticized by practically everyone for practically every reason. The Left attacked his early films, calling them apologies for fascism; it also complained about *Anno Uno* (1974, *Italy, Year One*), an analysis of Italy after World War II based upon the remarkable career and personality of the politician Alcide de Gasperi, leader of the Christian Democrat Party. After he had made *Stromboli*, the Right claimed he was:

'. . . the head of a gang directed by the Kremlin and Mao Tse-tung which has the sole goal of destroying the brains of American filmgoers.'

His personal morality and religious views also came under fire: he had 'insulted all Italian women' and made a 'blasphemous' film with *Il Miracolo*, the second part of *L'Amore*; at the same time he was described as a 'spokesman for the Church and a slave of the clerics' when he made *Flowers of St Francis* and *Journey to Italy*. Save for a small handful of works, the general public tended to ignore Rossellini's films. As he saw his function as film-maker as partly that of a teacher who wanted people to use their brains and their eyes in new ways, he felt the lack of a popular audience keenly, though he was never surprised by it. He commented:

'As I see it, the only chance is to make films intended for a much smaller audience, to reduce costs as much as possible, and to think carefully how best to launch a film made outside the usual formula. There is always a small public who will come to see films which say something new.'

Rossellini saw film as an instrument for examining moral values in order to arrive at a definition of 'the truth'. Over the years, he came to believe that 'the truth' could only be found by allowing audiences the widest possible freedom to experience a film. From the first he distrusted traditional narrative forms, believing them to be too manipulative of emotions and ideas and falsifications of the 'cinematic reality' he aimed for. Over the years he reduced narrative to a bare minimum, presenting instead a carefully selected series of fragments which illustrated 'the movement of ideas in history'. Yet when examining a concept he never insisted on a single point of view. His idea in making *Il Messia*, for example, was to examine Christ's 'revolutionary idea that the Law was made for Man, rather than Man for the Law'. Yet by allowing his camera to roam – often with apparent aimlessness – over his reconstruction of a 'past reality' he allows the audience freedom to choose some 'stray detail' which might then set off a chain of new ideas or interpretations. Thus, in addition to

his examination of how power functions in *The Rise of Louis XIV*, a viewer could also become aware of a 'stray detail' such as the distance between kitchen and dining-hall at the Palace of Versailles, which meant that Louis probably never had a hot meal.

Although in his later years Rossellini claimed to feel little personal contact with his earlier work, he continued to maintain that there were 'constant elements' running through his films and that 'in *La Nave Bianca* I had the same moral position as in *Rome, Open City*'. He himself pointed to 'the documentary attitude of observation and analysis', to a 'perpetual return to fantasy', and to an 'effective spirituality' (as opposed to specific religious faith) as themes which recur throughout his work.

Rossellini mistrusted the use of 'the beautiful shot' for its own sake. He observed:

'A film must be well-directed; that is the least one can expect from a film-maker, but a single

Filmography

1936 Fantasia Sotto-Marina (short). '37 Prelude à l'Après-midi d'un Faune (short). '38 Daphne (short); Luciano Serra, Pilota (co-sc; 2nd unit dir. only). '39 Il Tacchino Prepotente (short). '40 La Vispa Teresa (short). '41 Il Ruscello di Ripasottile (short); La Nave Bianca (co-dir; +co-sc). '42 Un Pilota Ritorna (+co-sc). '43 L'Invasore (sup; +co-sc. only); L'Uomo della Croce (+co-sc). '45 Roma, Città Aperta (+co-sc) (USA: Rome, Open City: GB: Open City). '46 Paisà (+prod; +co-sc) (USA/GB: Paisan). '47 Germania, Anno Zero (+co-sc) (IT-GER) (USA/GB: Germany, Year Zero). '48 L'Amore: episode one/Una Voce Umana, episode two/Il Miracolo (GB: The Miracle) (+co-sc); La Macchina Ammazzacattivi (+prod) (USA/GB: The Machine That Kills Bad People). '50 Francesco Giullare di Dio (+co-sc) (USA/GB: Flowers of St Francis); Stromboli/ (Stromboli,Terra di Dio) (+co-prod; +co-sc) (USA: God's Land). '51 Europa '51 (+co-sc) (USA: The Greatest Love). '52 I Sette Peccati Capitali ep L'Invidia (+co-sc) (IT-FR) (USA/GB: The Seven Deadly Sins ep Envy); Medico Condotto (sup; +co-sc. only); Dov'è la Libertà? (+co-sc) (USA/GB: Where Is Liberty?). '53 Siamo Donne ep Il Pollo (+co-sc) (USA: Five Women/Of Life and Love ep Ingrid Bergman; GB: We Women/We, the Women). '54 Amori di Mezzo Secolo ep Napoli '43; Viaggio in Italia (+co-sc) (IT-FR) (USA: Strangers; GB: The Lonely Woman/Journey to Italy; Giovanna d'Arco al Rogo (+sc) (FR-IT) (USA/GB: Joan of Arc at the Stake); Angst (GER-IT) (GB: Fear). '55 Orient-Express (sup. only) (FR-IT-GER). '59 India (+sc); Il Generale Della Rovere (+co-adapt) (IT-FR). '60 Era Notte a Roma (+co-sc) (IT-FR) (USA/GB: It Was Night in Rome). '61 Viva l'Italia (+co-sc) (IT-FR); Vanina Vanini (+co-sc) (IT-FR) (USA/GB: The Betrayer). '62 Benito Mussolini (prod; + uncredited sup. only); Anima Nera (+co-sc). '63 Les Carabiniers (co-sc. only) (FR-IT) (USA/GB: The Soldiers); RoGoPaG/Laviamoci il Cervello ep Illibatezza (+sc) (IT-FR). All subsequent films were initially made for Italian TV unless specified. '64 L'Età del Ferro (sup; +comm. sc only). '66 La Prise de Pouvoir par Louis XIV (FR) (USA/GB: The Rise of Louis XIV). '67 Sicilia: Idea di un'Isola (short). '69 Atti degli Apostoli (+co-sc). '70 La Lotta dell'Uomo per le Sua Sopravivenza (sc; +ed; +comm. only); Socrate (+co-sc) (film) (IT-FR-SP) (USA/GB: Socrates). '72 Blaise Pascal (+co-sc); Agostino di Ippona (+co-sc). '73 L'Età di Cosimo; Cartesius (+co-sc). '74 Anno Uno (+co-sc) (GB: Italy, Year One). '75 Il Messia (+co-sc) (IT-FR). '76 Concerto per Michelangelo (short). '77 Beaubourg, Centre d'Art et de Culture Georges Pompidou (short).

Above: the Apostles' first supper after the death of Jesus from Atti degli Apostoli, *which chronicles the disciples' struggles to preach Christianity. Right: Christ crucified –* Il Messia

shot need not be beautiful.' He felt instead that the most important aspect of technique – which can't be learned' – was 'rhythm': 'You feel when the point is made, how long to maintain a sequence, or you don't'.

He also mistrusted scenarios that were complete down to the last detail, saying that 'they are only useful to reassure producers'. He preferred to depend upon the 'inspiration of the moment, of the place, of the actors.'

He was the fount from which all important Italian cinema has sprung since the war, and a major force in international film-making. He had his failures – films which did not work on any level – however, as a lasting creative influence on the art of our time, he was a major figure of this century.   DAVID OVERBEY

LONDON FILM PRODUCTIONS LTD. PRESENT

The International Prize-winning Drama

OPEN CITY

(A)

ANNA MAGNANI
ALDO FABRIZI

DIRECTED BY
ROBERTO ROSSELINI

WITH ENGLISH SUB-TITLES

1

Left: Open City *was an early British title for* Rome, Open City

Directed by Roberto Rossellini, 1945
Prod co: Excelsa Film. **sc:** Roberto Rossellini, Federico Fellini, Sergio Amidei, from a story by Sergio Amidei, Alberto Consiglio. **photo:** Ubaldo Arata. **ed:** Eraldo Da Roma. **art dir:** R. Megna. **mus:** Renzo Rossellini. **sd:** R. Del Monte. **r/t:** 100 minutes. Released in the USA as *Rome, Open City*.
Cast: Anna Magnani (*Pina*), Aldo Fabrizi (*Don Pietro Pellegrini*), Marcello Pagliero (*Manfredi*), Maria Michi (*Marina*), Harry Feist (*Major Bergmann*), Francesco Grandjacquet (*Francesco*), Giovanna Gallotti (*Ingrid*), Vito Annichiarico (*Marcello*), Carla Revere (*Lauretta*), Nando Bruno (*Agostino)*, Carlo Sindici (*police superintendent*), Joop van Hulzen (*Hartmann*), Akos Tolnay (*Austrian deserter*), Eduardo Passerelli (*policeman*), Amalia Pelegrini (*landlady*).

Rossellini's *Roma, Città Aperta* (*Rome, Open City*) was the first significant film in the neo-realist style. Thus, aside from its own many qualities, it is one of the most important films in the history of the cinema in terms of its wide influence on other film-makers.

In 1944, a wealthy Roman lady commissioned Rossellini to make a brief documentary about a priest who had been killed by the Germans. She then suggested a second short on the Resistance activities of Roman children. The director decided to combine both themes into a single, feature-length fiction film based on the real events and the experiences that the Romans lived through between 1943 and 1944; the action of the film, however, was to be confined to a three-day period. Rossellini and the writer Alberto Consiglio (who had collaborated with him on *L'Uomo della Croce*, 1943, The Man of the Cross) wrote the first draft of the script; this was then substantially added to by the writer Sergio Amidei, with further additions by the then cartoonist (and future director) Federico Fellini.

Money was a constant problem as Rossellini's sponsors ran out of funds. He managed to raise small amounts which enabled him to continue shooting for a time, but eventually he was reduced to selling his furniture and his clothes. Film stock was very hard to come by – even when he had money to pay for it – so Rossellini was forced to use pieces

4

of 35mm newsreel stock of varying lengths and quality. Due to a lack of equipment, and for economic reasons, the film was shot mute with the actors dubbing their dialogue later. Most of the footage remained undeveloped until shooting was completed because Rossellini could not afford laboratory costs. Nonetheless, such technical limitations worked to the final advantage of the film. *Rome, Open City* has the 'real' appearance of a newsreel, which led to the oft-repeated tale (unfounded in fact) that the film was shot with concealed cameras before the Germans had left Rome.

Except for three small studio reconstructions, the entire picture was filmed where the events on

6

7

2

3

5

In Rome, the Fascist regime of Mussolini has fallen; the Allied armies have invaded Italy but have not yet reached the capital; meanwhile, the Resistance is more active than ever.

A communist Resistance leader, Manfredi, escapes a police raid and takes refuge with fellow-communist Francesco, a printer. The following morning Francesco is due to marry the widow Pina who is already pregnant with his child. Pina's sister, Lauretta, works as a part-time prostitute at a music-hall with Marina, Manfredi's former mistress (1).

Don Pietro, a local priest (2), is against the communists but nevertheless acts as a messenger for the Resistance and is respected by everyone – including the one-legged Romolo and his gang of boy saboteurs.

Manfredi escapes another German raid, but Francesco is arrested. Pina protests (3,4) and is shot (5). Later, Francesco escapes and hides with Manfredi in Marina's apartment. The lovers quarrel, and in anger, and to obtain drugs, Marina betrays Manfredi to her friend Ingrid (6), an agent of Bergmann, head of the Gestapo (7). Manfredi is arrested when visiting Don Pietro and both are taken to headquarters. Manfredi is tortured to death (8) in front of the priest who is then shot.

While Marina and Lauretta are lost in drugs and prostitution, Francesco, and Romolo and his gang (9) continue the fight.

which it was based took place; the city thus played a major part in the action. While the cast was a mixture of experienced actors (such as Anna Magnani and Aldo Fabrizi) and non-professionals, there is a raw, natural quality to the performances which belies acting. This is aided by the equally 'raw' images produced by the cinematographer Ubaldo Arata, who worked with available lighting. The fragmented construction of the narrative, with many scenes seemingly unfinished, nourishes an excitement that might well have been dissipated by a more polished script.

Rome, Open City is a direct portrait of the time in which it was made; life as it was then lived is reflected on the screen with great

authenticity. As important as the historical moment in the film are the characters, who seem to have lives that extend beyond the brief periods that the film captures. It is this quality above all which continues to give the film its power to move modern audiences.

According to Rossellini, when the film was eventually completed, everyone he showed it to hated it. 'For want of anything better' the Italians entered it at the Cannes Film Festival, where the director claims it was ignored by everyone. However, it was bought for international distribution 'for a crust of bread', and opened in Paris to rave reviews and booming business. This success was soon surpassed in the USA. 'I suddenly went from

artistic cretin to international genius in a matter of weeks,' Rossellini commented wryly some years later. The film then did well in Italy on the basis of its foreign reputation, but the pattern had been set, both for neo-realism and Rossellini. With each new film he would be denounced as a 'cretin' in his own country; neo-realist films would remain most popular outside Italy, finding special favour in France and Britain.

The elements that made *Rome, Open City* into a bombshell which blasted apart the cinematic conventions of 1945 were those that were to make up the theory, and often the practice, of the many neo-realist films that followed it.

DAVID OVERBEY

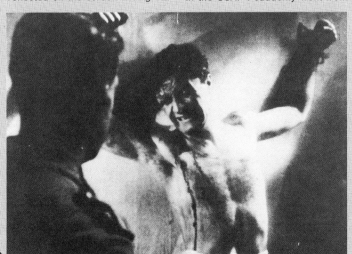

8

9

MAGNANI!

'I put the name in caps with an exclamation mark because that is how she "comes on" . . . In a crowded room she can sit perfectly motionless and silent, and still you feel the atmospheric tension of her presence, its quiver and hum in the air like a live wire exposed, and a mood of Anna's is like the presence of royalty.'

Tennessee Williams

Left: Anna Magnani – the flamboyant actress who became the screen's epitome of Italian motherhood – loud-mouthed, brash and gesticulating but also sexy, earthy and loving. Above: a different image for Magnani – as a music-hall artist in Teresa Venerdi. *Above right: she is typecast as the hard, vulgar and overbearing mother who tries to push her daughter into the movies in* Bellissima

Anna Magnani was not so much an actress as a phenomenon of the type that only the film medium could produce. She must rank among those 'big names' in the history of cinema, alongside Garbo and Keaton who, in spite of professional acting backgrounds, would probably have never become famous if they hadn't turned to the screen. Magnani had studied at the Eleonora Duse drama school but her reputation in Italy seemed destined to be restricted to the music-hall and even to the kind of music-hall which triumphed on the Italian stage during the Twenties. She might well have remained there if it hadn't been for a cinema genuis – himself, at the time, little more than a competent professional – who was inspired enough to give her a dramatic role in the fictionalized documentary that he was making. It was a story of a priest who, in the Rome of 1944 which was occupied by the German army as it retreated northwards after the Allied invasion of Sicily, died a martyr in the name of the anti-fascist Resistance. The film was *Roma, Città Aperta* (1945, *Rome, Open City*) and the director was Roberto Rossellini.

In legend, Magnani has become as Roman as the she-wolf on the Capitoline Hill or the Colosseum itself, despite the fact that her biographers are not quite sure whether she was born in Rome in 1908 or in Alexandria in 1903. She was always indignant when it was suggested that she was not really a 'Roman of Rome'. Yet there was some mystery surround-

ing her birth. Her father, or at least her mother's husband, was certainly Egyptian. Her mother was from Rimini which was also Fellini's birthplace. But whether Magnani was born in Rome or Alexandria does not really matter. Either of the two backgrounds, each of which are the homes of two great Mediterranean historical cultures, gives her credentials for a romantic entry into the world.

In the cinema, Magnani's adventures began in a typical melodrama of the period – *La Cieca di Sorrento* (1934, *The Blind Woman of Sorrento*). She was offered her second film role two years later by Goffredo Alessandrini who was later to become her husband. The film was *Cavalleria* (1936, Cavalry) and after it was made he told her that she wasn't 'a cinema type'. Discouraged by her husband's judgment she returned to the stage, mainly to music-hall, and, apart from a few breadwinning screen appearances, did not get a good break for some time. In 1941, Vittorio De Sica, a matinée-idol-turned-director, used her to play a music-hall artist in *Teresa Venerdi (Doctor, Beware)* – one of his first essays into 'serious' directorial activity. She was noticed by a Milanese playboy intellectual who was also about to break into film-making – Luchino Visconti. He wanted to turn a sordid American novel about adultery and murder in a roadside café, called *The Postman Always Rings Twice*, into a stark naturalistic Italian tragedy – *Ossessione* (1942, Obsession). Visconti had the intuition to recognize

Magnani's potential as a believable heroine suited to the emerging neo-realist style of cinema and wanted to use her as the star. But her own private life intervened – she was pregnant by Massimo Serrato, the most handsome young Italian actor of the day – and the role was played instead by Clara Calamai.

Even if Magnani was not the star of the film, which ranks as an early milestone of the neo-realist school, she became the epitome of Italian motherhood in Rossellini's *Rome, Open City*: the film that was to show the world what was happening in the Italy which had heroically stood up to the humiliation of Mussolini's imperialistic regime and the neo-barbarian influences of Hitler's Nazi hordes. The scene in which Magnani runs screaming through the streets of Rome as the Nazis carry her partisan husband away in a truck, before she is shot down by a German gunman, remains not only the most vivid image of the neo-realist cinema but also a document, the record of an epoch. Magnani's later performance in Visconti's *Bellissima* (1951) confirms her stature as a

Filmography
1934 La Cieca di Sorrento (GB: The Blind Woman of Sorrento); Tempo Massimo. **'36** Cavalleria; Trenta Secondi d'Amore. **'38** La Principessa Tarakanova. **'40** Una Lampada alla Finestra. **'41** La Fugitava; Teresa Venerdi (USA: Doctor, Beware). **'42** Finalmente Soli; La Fortuna Viene dal Cielo. **'43** L'Avventura di Annabella; Campo dei Fiori (USA: The Peddlar and the Lady); L'Ultima Carrozzella. **'44** La Vita È Bella; Il Fiore Sotto Gli Occhi; Quarletto Pazzo. **'45** Roma, Città Aperta (USA: Rome, Open City); Abbasso la Miseria! **'46** Il Bandito (USA: The Bandit); Un Uomo Ritorna; Davanti a Lui Tremvata Tutta Roma (USA: Before Him All Rome Trembled). **'47** Abbasso la Ricchezza (USA: Peddlin' in Society; GB: Down With Riches); L'Onorevole Angelina (USA: Angelina) (+ co-sc). **'48** L'Amore: episode one/Una Voce Umana, episode two/Il Miracolo

lifelike heroine who steps outside a film's images in a way that no heroine could step out of the pages of a book. The Italian novelist Corrado Alvaro wrote of this performance as Maddalena Cecconi, the Roman mother, who wanted her little girl to be chosen as 'the most beautiful Roman child':

The protagonist passes from domestic tenderness to the delicate subterfuge of a merely hinted-at sentimental idyll, from rage and desperation to a comic gesture, offering us once again a down-to-earth and deeply human portrait of an Italian woman who is certainly more pagan than Christian, who is noisy, prepossessing and extrovert.'

Magnani's magnificent capacity for understatement, so rare in Italian acting, contrasted with her extrovert portrait in this performance. On the stage in Zeffirelli's production of Verga's *La Lupa* (1964–65), she almost succeeded in maintaining the balance between flamboyancy and realism but she was afraid to accept roles like Cleopatra and Mother Courage. Tennessee Williams wrote *The Rose Tattoo* (1955) for her and it won her an Oscar, even though she had not been at all at ease with either living or working in Hollywood. She would not do *Orpheus Descending*, which was also written for her, on Broadway but she did appear in the film of it – *The Fugitive Kind* (1960) – directed by Sidney Lumet and co-starring Marlon Brando, whom she called a 'sadistic egocentric'. Hollywood offered her many more roles but she refused most of them.

She made two other American films – Cukor's *Wild Is the Wind* (1957) and *The Secret of Santa Vittoria* (1969), playing opposite Anthony Quinn in both – but neither was successful.

She will be remembered for her Italian films that followed *Rome, Open City* – Zampa's *L'Onorevole Angelina* (1947, *Angelina*) and *L'Amore* (1948, *Love*) the two-part film which Rossellini dedicated to her art. She enacts the society woman's 40-minute monologue from Cocteau's *La Voix Humaine* (The Human Voice) and the realistic parable *Il Miracolo* (*The Miracle*) which bore the distinctive mark of the Fellini script. The other films she made, even when they bore the names of great directors, were Magnani shows, for instance Renoir's *Le Carrosse d'Or* (1952, *The Golden Coach*) or Pasolini's *Mamma Roma* (1962). On the night she died in September 1973, an Italian television network had by coincidence programmed one of the films she made for TV – *Correva, l'Anno di Grazia 1870* (1971, In the Year of Our Lord 1870) – a somewhat pedestrian film directed by Alfredo Ciannetti, which was brightened by the presence of

Above: in The Fugitive Kind *Magnani plays a free-living exhibitionist virago who gets herself involved with a Mississippi drifter – Marlon Brando. Below: a typical caricature of a shrewish Italian wife in her last American film,* The Secret of Santa Vittoria. *The film, about a village which hides its enormous stores of wine from the occupying Germans, contains elements of grim brutality and hilarious comedy*

Magnani's 'pagan' woman. Her real swan-song took her back to the streets of Rome in the brief scene at the end of *Fellini's Roma* (1972) when the phoney television crew catch up with her at the door of the Roman palazzo where she lived most of her life. Like the other personalities who were being interviewed on what they thought about Rome, she had her answer ready. She closed the door of Palazzo Alteri in Fellini's face, affectionately rude and to the point. Once again she had epitomized the relationship between real-life and the cinema; a fitting finale to the actress who showed that the neo-realist cinema needed realistic heroines.

JOHN FRANCIS LANE

(GB: The Miracle); Lo Sconosciuto di San Marino; Molti Sogni per la Strade (GB: Woman Trouble); Assunta Spina (USA: Scarred). '49 Vulcano. '51 Bellissima. '52 Camicie Rosse (USA: Anita Garibaldi; GB: Red Shirts); Le Carrosse d'Or/La Carrozza d'Oro (USA: The Golden Coach) (IT-FR). '53 Siamo Donne (USA: Five Women/Of Life and Love; GB: We Women/We, the Women). '55 Carrosello di Varientà!; The Rose Tattoo (USA). '56 Suor Letizia (USA: The Awakening; GB: The Last Temptation). '57 Wild Is the Wind (USA). '59 Nella Città l'Inferno (USA: . . . and the Wild Women; GB: Caged) (FR-IT). '60 The Fugitive Kind (USA); Risate di Gioia. (GB: The Passionate Thief). '62 Mamma Roma. '63 Le Magot de Josefa (FR-IT). '66 Made in Italy (IT-FR). '69 The Secret of Santa Vittoria (USA). '71 Correva, l'Anno di Grazia 1870. '72 Fellini's Roma (IT-FR).

Luchino Visconti: opening shots

A grim, compelling study of adultery and murder; a portrait of a man struggling to keep his integrity in the face of hardship and exploitation – these are the subjects with which Visconti began his career as a director

Luchino Visconti – or to give him his full title, Conte Luchino Visconti di Modrone – came from one of the most illustrious families of the Milanese aristocracy. Though he professed himself to be a dedicated Marxist, this was hardly borne out by his elegant lifestyle; he dwelt in a superb Roman *palazzo* decorated with priceless tapestries where white-gloved Sicilian servants waited at table.

In his early years he gave no sign of developing into one of the cinema's boldest and most fastidious talents. His first passion was for breeding and training race-horses.

The famous couturière Madame 'Coco' Chanel, who had been travelling back with Visconti from a race-meeting in England, had the idea of introducing him to the film director Jean Renoir. The outcome of this meeting was that Visconti became one of Renoir's assistants (the others were Jacques Becker and Cartier Bresson) on *Une Partie de Campagne* (1936, A Day in the Country) and *Lés Bas-Fonds* (1937, The Lower Depths). Subsequently when Renoir, disgusted by the French reception of his masterpiece *La Règle du Jeu* (1939, The Rules of the Game), left his native country vowing to work elsewhere, Visconti co-scripted with him the ill-fated *La Tosca* (1940), on which Renoir worked for only a few days before being replaced by Carl Koch.

Visconti's first film, *Ossessione* (1942, Obsession) was a deliberate gesture of defiance against authority. Under Mussolini's totali-

tarian regime, it had been decreed that neither crime nor immorality was to be depicted on the screen so as to propagate the impression that the government had successfully eradicated these social evils. *Ossessione* was a sombre story of lust, infidelity and murder, loosely based on James M. Cain's novel *The Postman Always Rings Twice*. In the flat, bleak landscapes of the Ferrarese region of northern Italy, where the film was shot, and in the searingly accurate observation of the main characters' sordid motives and behaviour, lie the true seeds of the movement that was later to become known as neo-realism.

The tale of a casual labourer, who becomes infatuated by a woman and allows himself to become her accomplice in the murder of her middle-aged husband, pulsates with a dark sensuality rarely equalled on the screen. The depiction of the husband as an affable, trusting creature lends an added poignancy and harshness to the woman's ruthless pursuit of her own gratification. Clara Calamai plays the role of the woman to perfection; the final shots of her, dead and dangling in her lover's arms like a rag-doll, are unforgettable.

After *Ossessione* Visconti devoted himself to the theatre, and it was not until 1948 that he returned to the cinema to make an even more uncompromising work, *La Terra Trema* (1948, The Earth Trembles).

The new project was conceived along grandiose lines. *La Terra Trema* was to be the first part of a trilogy. This saga of life in a small Sicilian fishing-village was to be followed by another dealing with people in the city, with a third about workers in the fields. The general theme was the plight of humble people at the mercy both of their environment and those intent on exploiting them.

La Terra Trema was filmed entirely in the coastal village of Aci Trezza and enacted by the local inhabitants. The leading character, 'Ntoni, a young fisherman, is sick of being

Left: Visconti was 36 when he made his first feature Ossessione. *Below, far left: the lovers, Giovanna and Gino. Below: having murdered Giovanna's husband, the couple seek to escape the police, but their car goes out of control and Giovanna is killed*

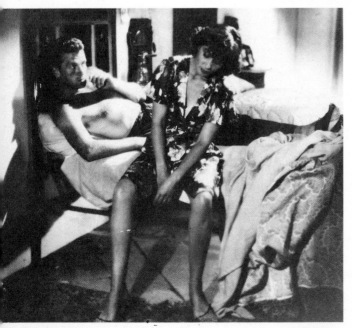

box-office and the rest of the trilogy was consequently abandoned. But one might say that Visconti was still pursuing his original conception years later with *Rocco e i Suoi Fratelli* (1960, *Rocco and His Brothers*), a tale of Sicilians fighting to survive in Milan.

Visconti was, in all respects, a law unto himself. He was frank and open about his homosexuality at a time when it was far from socially acceptable to be so. When he attended a film premiere in Rome with his entourage, one had the distinct impression that royalty had consented to grace the occasion. And at the Venice Festival, when everyone else would be staying across the water on the Lido where the event took place, Visconti preferred to remain at a patrician distance, installed in the exclusive Bauer-Grünwald hotel. News of the Festival's progress would be conveyed to him by messengers speeding across the lagoon. His sardonic wit was feared. He was also a fervent patriot. He deplored what he viewed as the Italian tendency to take their vast cultural heritage for granted and to allow their magnificent architectural achievements to fall into disrepair. 'The Italians don't deserve Italy,' he once remarked. His exhaustive quest for visual perfection often went to exaggerated lengths. When shooting *Il Gattopardo* (1963, *The Leopard*), he demanded a series of retakes under the boiling Sicilian sun because a horse, on the edge of the frame, persistently swished its tail, which, in the opinion of the Master, marred the composition of the shot.

Visconti knew how to bide his time and most of the projects he held dear he eventually managed to realize. The great exception, about which he had dreamt for years and frequently seemed close to setting up, was Marcel Proust's *A la Recherche du Temps Perdu*. That elegant work and this meticulous director were surely meant for each other.   DEREK PROUSE

Visconti's work following La Terra Trema *will be dealt with in detail in a later chapter*

sometimes seems to detract from the force of the social protest. In his determination to show the proximity of the fisher-folk to their environment, no stone, as it were, remains unturned. Pebbles, rippling water and facial expressions are long and lovingly dwelt on to the point of over-indulgence, with the result that the film's rhythm becomes decidedly slow. But there are many sequences which achieve greatness, such as the scene in which black-cowled women, perched on the rocks like gaunt birds, await the men's return from the rough sea. Then, again, there is 'Ntoni's race through the rain in search of refuge in the little house he is about to lose.

Although the film received a prize at the Venice Film Festival for its masterly stylistic qualities, *La Terra Trema* was a failure at the

exploited by the wholesale fish-dealers and decides to strike out on his own. He plans to salt his own fish, employ his own men and make his own arrangements for the disposal of his produce. But one stormy night his boat is wrecked and he is deprived of his livelihood. He tries desperately to find work but the wholesale dealers boycott him to punish him for his rebellion. When he is unable to meet his mortgage dues, the bank evicts him and his family from their house. One sister becomes a prostitute and the other, out of pride and humiliation, refuses an offer of marriage. Finally, 'Ntoni manages to get work as a fisherman for one of the wholesalers but remains a stubborn outsider.

The film is superbly shot by the brilliant cameraman G.R. Aldo, but Visconti's obsession with the creation of a formal pictorial style

These scenes from La Terra Trema *show the film's protagonist 'Ntoni with his son (above); 'Ntoni refitting his boat for a fishing expedition (top); and the women of the village anxiously awaiting the return of their menfolk from the sea (right)*

1

2

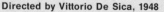

3

4

Directed by Vittorio De Sica, 1948
Prod co: Produzione De Sica (PDS). **prod:** Vittorio De Sica. **prod man:**
Umberto Scarpelli. **sc:** De Sica, Oreste Bianco, Suso Cecchi d'Amico,
Adolfo Franci, Gherardo Gherardi, Gerardo Guerrieri, adapted by
Cesare Zavattini from the novel by Luigi Bartolini. **photo:** Carlo
Montuori. **ass photo:** Mario Montuori. **ed:** Eraldo da Roma. **art dir:**
Antonino Traverso. **mus:** Alessandro Cicognini. **mus dir:** Willy Ferrero.
ass dir: Gerardo Guerrieri. **r/t:** 90 minutes. Italian title: *Ladri di
Biciclette*. Released in USA as *Bicycle Thief*, in GB as *Bicycle Thieves*.
Cast: Lamberto Maggiorani (*Antonio Ricci*), Enzo Staiola (*Bruno Ricci*),
Lianella Carell (*Maria Ricci*), Vittorio Antonucci (*the thief*), Elena Altieri,
Gino Saltamerenda, Giulio Chiari, Michele Sakara, Carlo Jachino,
Nando Bruno, Fausto Guerzoni, Umberto Spadaro, Massimo Randisi.

7

With *Bicycle Thieves*, Vittorio De Sica came very close to perfecting the kind of realist film to which he hoped to dedicate himself as a director. His previous film, *Sciuscià* (1946, *Shoeshine*) had shown him freeing himself from the theatrical influences that had shaped his earlier work, and had also established the importance of the contribution that writer Cesare Zavattini could make to his films. It was Zavattini who adapted *Bicycle Thieves* from the novel by Luigi Bartolini. 'I had liked Bartolini's book,' said Zavattini in 1980. 'I thought it would make the basis for a good film. I think it was an inspired film idea, even if it was completely different from the book which was based on the author's own experience. Later, when the film came out, Bartolini made a bit of a fuss, prompted by someone in the bourgeois press who hated the film. But Bartolini was quite aware of what we were going to do to his story when we paid him for the title.'

De Sica had to go the rounds of the producers trying to raise money to make *Bicycle Thieves*. He acted out all the parts for them to try and catch their interest, but no-one would back his picture. He went to France, where *Shoeshine* had been very successful, but the French producers said they'd be delighted to buy the film – after they had seen it. In London De Sica met the director-producer Gabriel Pascal who kept him locked up in his country home for a weekend to prevent him from going to Korda with the film, but then Pascal only offered £5000. In the end De Sica found three Italian businessmen who were prepared to finance him.

In order to capture the kind of 'reality' that he and Zavattini felt was essential to the telling of the story, De Sica insisted on using only non-professional actors. He had even turned down a generous offer from David O. Selznick who was prepared to finance the film if Cary Grant played the central role of the bill-sticker.

To find the right non-professional for the main part, however, was not easy. In the end De Sica used a workman, Lamberto Maggiorani, who had brought his child to be auditioned for the part of the bill-sticker's ten-year-old son.

If in *Shoeshine* De Sica could still lapse into sentimentality, particularly in the ending, in *Bicycle Thieves* he showed restraint and a firm grip of film narrative. The subject-matter is grim and De Sica lets the bare facts dictate the style of the film. He avoids sentimentality even in the fade-out with the father and son – reunited after the humiliating scene in front of the stadium – walking off into the distance with a Chaplinesque resignation to life's pitfalls.

The Rome of *Bicycle Thieves* is not that of Mussolini's heroics, or of the German Occupation, or of Hollywood's many 'Roman Holidays' to come. Though the workman's bike is stolen in a street in the centre of the city, only a stone's throw from the Spanish Steps, the Rome that De Sica shows is that of the embankments by the sluggish and muddy Tiber, the flea markets in the rain, the ugly suburban houses. It is a harsh setting and a sad story but De Sica enlivens it often with characteristic touches of humorous observation – the scene, for example, in the restaurant when Bruno tries to manage a knife and fork and is looked down on by the well-behaved middle-class boy; the caricatures of the fortune-teller and her clients, the charity helpers in the church, and the rowdy women protecting the thief in the brothel. Despite the intensity of Zavattini's political commitment and his own social conscience, De Sica was still able to make a film that, although a powerful cry of despair, never lapses into a shout of propaganda. It was clearly the work of an artist who had mastered a medium that for so long had only given him the chance to show his professional competence. He has commented:

'What is so important about a bike in the Rome of 1948 where so many bikes are stolen every day? Yet for a worker who loses his means of support a stolen bike is a very tragic circumstance. Why should we, film-makers, go in search of extraordinary adventures when we are confronted in our daily lives with facts that cause genuine anguish? Our literature has already explored this modern dimension that puts an emphasis on the smallest details of everyday life which are often dismissed as commonplace. The cinema has at its disposal the film camera which is the best medium for capturing this world. That's what I think this much-debated question of the new realism is all about.'

JOHN FRANCIS LANE

Antonio Ricci is an unemployed workman in his thirties, married with two children. He is offered a job as a bill-sticker on condition that he has his own bicycle. Ricci does have a bike but it is in a pawn shop. He has to pawn the family bed linen to get it out (1).

He goes to work the next day, but while he is sticking up a poster of Rita Hayworth (2) his bike is stolen (3). Many bikes are stolen every day in Rome and the police suggest he looks for the thief himself. Ricci, accompanied by his ten-year-old son Bruno, first searches the flea markets (4) where stolen bikes and parts are on sale. They see the thief talking to an old man whom they follow into an almshouse (5), but he slips away from them. Ricci takes Bruno to eat in a smart restaurant in order to forget their problems for a while (6).

When Ricci sees the thief again he follows him into a brothel (7), but the young man denies the charge. In the street the crowd turns on Ricci and the thief has an epileptic fit. Nobody can prove anything. In despair, Ricci and Bruno sit outside the football stadium and listen to the crowd roaring inside. Ricci sends Bruno away and on an impulse steals an unguarded bike (8). He is caught immediately but the owner doesn't bring charges. Bruno has watched his father's humiliation. They walk away – at first separated, but then together as Bruno offers his hand in comfort and solidarity (9).

5

6

8

9

Vittorio De Sica

seeker of truth

Children grubbing for a living on the rain-swept streets of Rome and Naples, a bicycle thief having a fit outside a whorehouse, an old man looking for his dog among the abbatoirs – this was the 'real' Italy depicted by De Sica in his early films. One of the qualities he brought to them was a sparse but undeniable charm – which later shed its grim and gritty flavour in the glossy pictures he made with Sophia Loren

Vittorio De Sica (1902–74) was born in Sora, in the Ciociaria region half-way between Rome and Naples – the setting for his later success *La Ciociara* (1961, *Two Women*). But he was really a Neapolitan: both his father, a poor clerk called Umberto (like the old man in his 1951 film, *Umberto D*), and his mother Teresa came from Naples. De Sica began his career as an actor in films when he was persuaded to play the young Clemenceau in *L'Affaire Clemenceau* (1918, The Clemenceau Affair) which starred the great Italian film actress Francesca Bertini, and he made his stage debut (as a waiter) in 1923 with the theatre company of Tatiana Pavlova. He went on to score great successes in musicals and sophisticated comedy, and, indeed, it was as a debonair comedian that he became a star – in Mario Camerini's *Gli Uomini, Che Mascalzoni* (1932, *What Rascals Men Are!*). Between 1931 and 1940 De Sica acted in 23 films.

De Sica's debut as a director came with *Rose Scarlatte* (1940, Red Roses). He said that he began making his own films as the result of wounded pride:

'I had played in Gallone's film of *Manon Lescaut* (1940) but the critics did not like me. This hurt because I knew they were right. I had felt my own mistakes and had pointed them out to Gallone but he wouldn't listen. That's

why I felt I wanted to take responsibility for my own performance and directed myself.'

After several potboilers, De Sica made *I Bambini ci Guardano* (1943, *The Children Are Watching Us*), collaborating for the first time with writer Cesare Zavattini, thereby forming a partnership that was central to what became known as the Italian 'neo-realist' cinema – a cinema committed to the realistic treatment of the problems of urban life in impoverished, post-war Italy. Their next two films, *Sciuscià* (1946, *Shoeshine*), the story of two shoeshine boys, and *Ladri di Biciclette* (1948, *Bicycle Thieves*), about an Italian workman's search for the stolen bicycle that keeps him in a bill-sticking job, are shot in drab street-locations and concerned with the difficulties faced by the poor in simply earning enough money to survive, and despite the callous indifference of society.

'It isn't as if one day Visconti and Rossellini and the rest of us were sitting at a cafe and suddenly Zavattini came along and said "Let's create neo-realism",' De Sica has said. 'But when a producer offered me the idea of *Shoeshine*, though I didn't like the way he had conceived it, I saw its possibilities and asked Zavattini to help me get it into shape.'

In spite of the prizes and international acclaim which greeted *Shoeshine* and *Bicycle*

Above left: De Sica directs Umberto D. *Above: in* Shoeshine *the young delinquents Pasquale (Franco Interlenghi) and Giuseppe (Rinaldo Smordoni) take a brief respite from the troubles of the world before they are faced with betrayal and death. Interlenghi later turned professional and starred in Fellini's* I Vitelloni *(1953)*

Thieves, neither film opened the way for De Sica to continue making the kind of films that he and Zavattini were dreaming about. De Sica had to work for several years acting in a mixed bag of films in order to raise the money to make *Miracolo a Milano* (1951, *Miracle in Milan*). Though not all the Italian critics liked or understood the film, it was a success with the public. It also provoked a political reaction and there were vicious attacks on De Sica and Zavattini in the 'Cold War' climate of Italian politics. Even so, they managed to make *Umberto D* (1951), which was produced by Angelo Rizzoli.

Rizzoli backed *Umberto D* in the hope that De Sica would direct *Il Piccolo Mondo di Don Camillo* (1952) for him. Although De Sica – much tempted by the large sum of money Rizzoli offered him – did not accept the chore, he was, in subsequent years, to accept many compromises with producers, usually dragging Zavattini along with him. The pair had

become bitter about the way top-level Italian political figures had poured scorn on their work, among them future Prime Minister Giulio Andreotti, who had accused De Sica of washing Italy's dirty linen in public with *Umberto D*. The film was not included in the Italian Film Week in London in 1954 to which De Sica had been invited as the actor playing opposite Gina Lollobrigida in Luigi Comencini's *Pane, Amore e Fantasia* (*Bread, Love and Dreams*), a film that travestied the whole neo-realist idea. But a private showing of *Umberto D* for English critics resulted in rave reviews and De Sica's film eclipsed all the others that had been officially put on show by the Italians.

Although Zavattini says today that his relationship with De Sica first became strained during the making of *Un Mondo Nuovo* (1966, *A Young World*), there had been several rifts before. These were often due to compromises into which De Sica was driven by producers such as David O. Selznick on *Stazione Termini*

(1953, *Indiscretion of an American Wife*), or Dino De Laurentiis on *Il Giudizio Universale* (1962, *The Last Judgement*), or Carlo Ponti on the pictures made with Sophia Loren. There was even a rather startling collaboration between De Sica and Zavattini on *I Sequestrati di Altona* (1962, *The Condemned of Altona*), an adaptation of Jean-Paul Sartre's play, with actors like Fredric March and Maximilian Schell seeming somehow uncomfortable in De Sica's hands despite Zavattini's valiant attempt to be faithful to Sartre.

The last neo-realist film from the De Sica–Zavattini stable was really *Il Tetto* (1956, *The Roof*). At the time De Sica said:

'*The Roof* is a love story rich in poetry. What ever people say, neo-realism is poetry, the poetry of real life. For that reason neo-realism is not dead and will never die.'

De Sica was right. Neo-realism did not die. But it was neither he nor Zavattini who were to keep it alive – either as a political manifesto or as poetry. The directors who inherited these

two aspects of neo-realism were Francesco Rosi and Ermanno Olmi who, at the end of the Seventies, were still making films about the poetry – and the politics – of real life. Yet some of De Sica's successes in subsequent years had professional dignity even if they took him and Zavattini further and further away from neo-realism. Films like *Two Women* (1961), for which Sophia Loren won an Oscar, and jovial comedies like *L'Oro di Napoli* (1954, *Gold of Naples*) and *Matrimonio all'Italiana* (1964, *Marriage Italian Style*) projected the Loren image of earthy dynamism throughout the world, doing discredit to neither actress nor director.

Below: in Miracle in Milan *a boy able to work miracles turns a field to ice with hilarious results. Bottom:* Montgomery Clift in Indiscretion of an American Wife. *Bottom left: the old man (Carlo Battisti) and his only friend in* Umberto D. *Below left: father and son search for the stolen bike in the streets of Rome in* Bicycle Thieves

Above: the love affair in A Place for Lovers. with Marcello Mastroianni and Faye Dunaway. is threatened by the girl's illness. Left: Loren as a prostitute in Marriage Italian Style. Below left: a scene from Lo Chiamaremo Andrea. Below right: Giovanna (Sophia Loren) searches a Russian military cemetery for her husband's grave in Sunflower

Top, from left to right: lovers Christien Delaroche and Nino Castelnuovo in Un Mondo Nuovo; Shirley MacLaine as the wife out to get her own back on her husband in the Amateur Night episode of De Sica's only American film, Woman Times Seven; gold smuggler Peter Sellers posing as a film director in Caccia alla Volpe, which was scripted by Neil Simon

Cesare Zavattini

Later on, though, De Sica seemed unable to avoid more glossy and sophisticated images of Loren, as in the unfortunate Russian-Italian co-production *I Girasoli* (1970, *Sunflower*) and *Il Viaggio* (1974, *The Journey*). And *Woman Times Seven* (1967), starring Shirley MacLaine, was a disaster – the only one of his films that De Sica ever actually admitted was bad. There was one final triumph: *Il Giardino dei Finzi-Contini* (1970, *The Garden of the Finzi-Continis*), an adaptation of Bassani's novel about Jews in Ferrara under Fascism and a film of great visual beauty and human depth. But it is for his neo-realist films that De Sica will be remembered.   JOHN FRANCIS LANE

Filmography (films as director)
1940 Rose Scarlatte (co-dir; +act); Maddelena Zero in Condetta (+dial; +act). **'41** Teresa Venerdi (+co-sc) (USA/GB: Doctor, Beware). **'42** Un Garabaldino al Convento (+co-sc; +act). **'43** I Bambini ci Guardano (+co-sc) (USA/GB: The Children Are Watching Us). **'44** La Porta del Cielo (+co-sc) (USA/GB: Shoeshine). **'48** Ladri di Biciclette (+co-sc) (USA/GB: Bicycle Thieves). **'51** Miracolo a Milano (+co-sc; +co-prod) (USA/GB: Miracle in Milan); Ambiento e Personaggi (short) (+co-sc; +act) (never shown); Umberto D (+co-sc; +co-prod). **'53** Stazione Termini (+co-prod) (IT-USA) (USA: Indiscretion of an American Wife; GB: Indiscretion). **'54** L'Oro di Napoli (+co-sc; +act in *ep* Il Giocatori) (USA/GB: Gold of Naples). **'56** Il Tetto (USA/GB: The Roof). **'61** La Ciociara (+co-sc) (IT-FR) (USA/GB: Two Women). **'62** Il Giudizio Universale (+act) (IT-FR) (USA/GB: The Last Judgement); Boccaccio '70 *ep* La Riffa; I Sequestrati di Altona (IT-FR) (USA/GB: The Condemned of Altona). **'63** Il Boom. **'64** Ieri, Oggi, Domani (IT-FR) (USA/GB: Yesterday, Today and Tomorrow); Matrimonio all'Italiana (IT-FR) (USA/GB: Marriage Italian Style). **'66** Un Mondo Nuovo (IT-FR) (USA/GB: A Young World); Caccia alla Volpe (+guest appearance) (USA/GB: After the Fox). **'67** Le Streghe *ep* Una Sera Come le Altre (IT-FR) (USA: The Witches *ep* A Night Like Any Other); Woman Times Seven (FR-USA). **'68** Amanti (+co-sc) (IT-FR) (USA/GB: A Place for Lovers). **'70** I Girasoli (IT-USSR) (USA/GB: Sunflower); Il Giardino dei Finzi-Contini (USA/GB: The Garden of the Finzi-Contini). **'71** Le Coppie *ep* Il Leone. **'72** Lo Chiamaremo Andrea. **'73** Una Breva Vacanza (IT-SP) (USA: The Holiday; GB: Brief Vacation). **'74** Il Viaggio (USA/GB: The Journey).
De Sica also acted in 153 films from 1918–74.

Novelist, scriptwriter and diarist Cesare Zavattini (b.1902) is regarded as one of the fathers of the neo-realist cinema for his decisive role as scriptwriter on Vittoria De Sica's early films *The Children Are Watching Us* (1943) and *Shoeshine* (1946). Their partnership bore its greatest fruits in the great trilogy *Bicycle Thieves* (1948), *Miracle in Milan* and *Umberto D* (both 1951), and it was in these films that Zavattini's declaration that 'the artist's starting point must not be art but life itself' found its most poetic expression. Zavattini recalls how they first came to work together:

I first met De Sica when he was acting in *Darò un Milione (I'll Give a Million)* in 1935. The director was Mario Camerini whom I had tried to convince to cast Buster Keaton for the role that was to be played by Luigi Almirante. I hadn't seen De Sica on the stage but knew of his fame as an actor in comedy. We had only a polite professional relationship on that occasion and did not discuss ideas. I don't think he had more than a superficial influence on that film; for him it was a professional engagement.

We didn't have any further contact until 1939 when a theatre critic, Adolfo Franci, brought him to my home. I didn't mix in theatrical circles but Franci (rightly as it turned out) thought that De Sica and I could work together. De Sica bought a story of mine but it was never filmed. Our partnership began, so to speak, when he was making *Teresa Venerdi (Doctor, Beware)* in 1941. The film was written by Aldo De Benedetti, an excellent dramatist but not very practical when it came to films. De Sica called me and asked me to help. I think I did help him to get the story out of its theatrical atmosphere.

De Sica was afraid of being unfaithful to his theatre friends, but when he came to make *The Children Are Watching Us* in 1943 he broke from the stage. *The Children Are Watching Us* – the title was my idea by the way – was our first real collaboration. It was based on a novel, *Pricò*, by C.G. Viola – another of De Sica's theatrical friends. I worked almost 'underground' with Vittorio (his friends were jealous of me, a young

man who had come from the Milan publishing world and claimed to have ideas how films should be made!) and never went on the set. Indeed, in years to come when my position as scriptwriter was much more official, I still rarely came near the set.

After the preliminary script discussion and revisions, Vittorio and I would always talk on the phone every night; that kind of collaboration began during the making of *The Children Are Watching Us* and continued to the end. De Sica didn't need any advice in choosing his cast or on shooting the film. Sometimes, later, I would visit him when he was editing. With *Bicycle Thieves* and *Shoeshine* I did in fact follow the cutting quite closely since the unpredictable conditions under which those films were shot meant that much of the dialogue had to be written over the movieola before the post-synchronization began.

The idea of *Shoeshine* was not mine. It came from the producer Paolo William Tamburella, an Italian-American. I was working with other directors at the time. Vittorio had started preparing the film without me, but again he felt uneasy with his theatrical writers. I was able to dedicate two entire days to this script, which was inspired by the stories of two boys whom everyone had seen in the Via Veneto area in those years. One was called Scimmietta ('little monkey') and he slept in an elevator at night and shined shoes on the sidewalks during the day.

After *Bicycle Thieves* De Sica and I made *Miracle in Milan* and *Umberto D* together; Vittorio used to say that these two films were, respectively, his homage to me (*Miracle* was based on a novel of mine, *Toto il Buone*, which I was very attached to), and mine to him (*Umberto* was the name of Vittorio's father whom he loved dearly – he had wanted so much to make a film about being old). More than that, however, I see the two films as a continuation of what we had started with *Bicycle Thieves*: the completion of a trilogy about different aspects of Italian reality – men in society (*Bicycle Thieves*), the escape from the harshness of life (*Miracle*) and old age (*Umberto D*).
                                        CESARE ZAVATTINI
From an interview with John Francis Lane, March 1980

Key films of 1941

Ball of Fire. USA. **prod co:** Samuel Goldwyn Productions. **prod:** Samuel Goldwyn. **dir:** Howard Hawks. **sc:** Charles Brackett, Billy Wilder. **photo:** Gregg Toland. **ed:** Daniel Mandell. **art dir:** Perry Ferguson. **mus:** Alfred Newman. **with:** Gary Cooper, Barbara Stanwyck, Oscar Homolka, Henry Travers, S.Z. Sakall, Tully Marshall.

Brackett and Wilder's spoofed version of Snow White and the Seven Dwarfs has seven professors sheltering Barbara Stanwyck – a striptease artist on the run. She shatters their tranquility and Cooper is forced down from his ivory tower to win her.

La Corona di Ferro. Italy. **prod co:** ENIC-Lux. **prod:** Leo Menardi. **dir:** Alessandro Blasetti. **sc:** Alessandro Blasetti, Corrado Pavolini, Guglielmo Zorzi, Giuseppe Zucca, Renato Castellani, from a story by Renato Castellani, Alessandro Blasetti. **photo:** Vaclav Vich, Mario Craveri. **ed:** Mario Serandrei. **art dir:** Virgilio Marchi. **mus:** Alessandro Cicognini. **with:** Elisa Cegani, Luisa Ferida, Gino Cervi, Massimo Girotti, Osvaldo Valenti, Paolo Stoppa, Primo Carnera.
A baroque fantasy about the struggle for a stolen crown imbued with supernatural properties. This exuberant film stood out against the anodyne comedies with which Italian cinema was then over-run.

Dumbo. USA. **prod co:** Walt Disney. **prod:** Walt Disney. **sup dir:** Ben Sharpsteen. **sc:** Aurelius Battaglia, Dick Huemer, Joe Rinaldi, Bill Peet, Webb Smith, George Stallings. **seq dir:** Samuel Armstrong, Norman Ferguson, Wilfred Jackson, Jack Kinney. **art dir:** Donald DaGradi, Dick Kelsey, A. Kendell O'Connor, Herbert Ryman, John Hubley, Ernie Nordli, Charles Payzant, Terrell Stapp, Al Zinnen, Claude Coats, Ray Lockrem, Joe Stahley, Al Dempster, Gerald Nevius, John Hench. **anim dir:** Arthur Babbitt, John Lounsberry, Wolfgang Reitherman, Ward Kimball, Fred Moore, Vladimir Tytla. **char des:** James Bodrero, John P. Miller, Elmer Plummer, John Walbridge, Joe Grant, Maurice Noble, Martin Provenson. **mus/songs:** Ned Washington, Frank Churchill, Oliver Wallace.
The story of the baby elephant who learns to fly with his oversize ears; it is one of Disney's liveliest and most inventive medium-length cartoons. Filmed in Technicolor, it includes the delightful and famous sequences of pink elephants dancing and crows singing raucously.

49th Parallel. Britain. **prod co:** Ortus Films/Ministry of Information. **prod/dir:** Michael Powell. **sc:** Emeric Pressburger. **photo:** Frederick Young. **ed:** David Lean. **art dir:** David Rawnsley. **mus:** Ralph Vaughan Williams. **mus dir:** Muir Mathieson. **with:** Richard George, Eric Portman, Raymond Lovell, Niall MacGinnis, Peter Moore, John Chandos, Basil Appleby, Laurence Olivier, Finlay Currie, Anton Walbrook, Glynis Johns, Leslie Howard, Raymond Massey.
An unusual wartime film in which Powell avoids the customary flag-waving. The survivors of a sunken U-boat trail across Canada and the characters that they meet stimulate a debate between fascism and democracy that remains stubbornly ambiguous and unresolved.

Genroku Chusingura Part I (The Loyal 47 of the Genroku Era). Japan. **prod:** Shintaro Shirai, **dir:** Kenji Mizoguchi. **sc:** Yoshikata Yoda, Kenichiro Hara, Seika Mayama, from a story by Seika Mayama. **photo:** Kohei Sugiyama. **art dir:** Hiroshi Mizutani. **mus:** Shiro Fukai. **with:** Yoshisaburo Arashi, Manpo Mimasu, Ganyemon Nakamura, Seizaburo Kawazu, Hiroshi Sawamura.
The most famous version of the often-filmed legend of the 47 Ronin samurai who committed hara-kiri after finally avenging their late master's honour. In this major Japanese wartime production, (Part II was made in 1942) Mizoguchi avoids the usual tribute to the wartime bushido code and makes a highly personal, sober elegy and tribute to the spirit of the dead.

How Green Was My Valley. USA. **prod co:** 20th Century-Fox. **prod:** Darryl F. Zanuck. **dir:** John Ford. **sc:** Phillip Dunne, from the novel by Richard Llewellyn. **photo:** Arthur Miller. **ed:** James B. Clark. **art dir:** Richard Day, Nathan Juran. **mus:** Alfred Newman. **narr:** Rhys Williams. **with:** Walter Pidgeon, Maureen O'Hara, Donald Crisp, Anna Lee, Roddy McDowall, John Loder, Barry Fitzgerald.
The film is based on a prestigious novel about a Welsh mining village which is facing the prospect of industrialization and unionization. As the tensions between the individual and the community interests mount, Ford's ambivalent attitude towards social progress is revealed.

The Lady Eve; directed by Preston Sturges – see special feature in Chapter 35.

The Little Foxes. USA. **pro co:** RKO-Samuel Goldwyn Productions. **prod:** Samuel Goldwyn, **dir:** William Wyler. **sc:** Lillian Hellman, from her own play. **photo:** Gregg Toland. **art dir:** Stephen Gooson. **ed:** Daniell Mandell. **mus:** Meredith Wilson. **with:** Bette Davis, Herbert Marshall, Teresa Wright, Richard Carlson, Patricia Collinge.
The story traces the wranglings of a rich and powerful Southern family. Its claustrophobic atmosphere of evil owes much to Toland's camera expertise and to Bette Davis' powerful portrayal of an emotional woman.

The Maltese Falcon; directed by John Huston – see special feature in Chapter 29.

Never Give a Sucker an Even Break. (What a Man). USA. **prod co:** Universal. **dir:** Edward Cline. **sc:** John T. Neville, Prescott Chaplin, from a story by Otis Criblecoblis (W.C. Fields). **photo:** Charles Van Enger, Jerome Ash. **ed:** Arthur Hilton. **art dir:** Jack Otterson, Richard H. Riedel. **mus:** Frank Skinner. **mus dir:** Charles Previn. **sd:** Bernard B. Brown. **with:** W.C. Fields, Gloria Jean, Billie Lenhart, Margaret Dumont, Kenneth Brown, Anne Nagel, Franklin Pangborn.
This film is pure anarchy as the tipsily self-propelled Fields is provocatively cast against a cloying child actress. A wifully perverse series of encounters and fantasy episodes ends up with a madcap car chase.

One of Our Aircraft Is Missing. Britain. **prod co:** British National. **prod/sc:** Michael Powell, Emeric Pressburger. **dir:** Michael Powell. **photo:** Roland Neame. **art dir:** David Rawnsley. **ed:** David Lean. **with:** Godfrey Tearle, Eric Portman, Hugh Williams, Bernard Miles, Hugh Burden, Emrys Jones, Pamela Brown, Joyce Redman, Googie Withers, Robert Helpman, Peter Ustinov.
The crew of a crashed British bomber are sheltered by the Dutch Resistance, providing an opportunity for a series of representations of 'everyday fascism'. It is a beautiful and marginally shocking, but effective, propaganda film which was dedicated to the people of Holland who had suffered at the hands of the Nazis.

The Palm Beach Story. USA. **prod co:** Paramount. **prod:** Paul Jones. **dir/sc:** Preston Sturges. **photo:** Victor Milner. **ed:** Stuart Gilmore. **art dir:** Hans Dreier, Ernst Fegte. **mus:** Victor Young. **with:** Claudette Colbert, Joel McCrea, Mary Astor, Rudy Vallee, Sig Arno, Robert Warwick, Torben Meyer, Jimmy Conlin, William Demarest.

The wife of an impoverished engineer leaves him to look for excitement and the 'high-life', which she finds with a gullible millionaire and her zany sister. The husband turns up, and the sister takes a fancy to him – but so does his wife. A sophisticated screwball comedy with a whirl of romantic complications.

Sergeant York. USA. **prod co:** Warner Bros. **prod:** Jesse L. Lasky, Hal B. Wallis. **dir:** Howard Hawks. **sc:** Abem Finkel, Harry Chandler, Howard Koch, John Huston. **photo:** Sol Polito. **ed:** William Holmes. **art dir:** John Hughes. **mus:** Max Steiner. **with:** Gary Cooper, Walter Brennan, Joan Leslie, George Tobias, Stanley Ridges.
Gary Cooper plays the agonized Christian pacifist, Alvin York, whose turkey-shoot marksmanship carries him to unwanted heroism in the trenches of World War I. A portentous film for Hawks but one which struck a timely chord with the American public and earned Cooper an Oscar.

The Shanghai Gesture. USA. **prod co:** Arnold Pressburger Productions. **prod:** Arnold Pressburger. **assoc prod:** Albert de Courville. **dir:** Josef von Sternberg. **sc:** Josef von Sternberg, Geza Herczeg, Karl Vollmoeller, Jules Furthman, from the play by John Colton. **photo:** Paul Ivano. **ed:** Sam Winston. **art dir:** Boris Leven. **mus:** Richard Hageman. **with:** Gene Tierney, Walter Huston, Victor Mature, Ona Munson, Phyllis Brooks, Albert Basserman.
A melodrama of a casino proprietress taunting her ex-husband about his daughter's degradation. The circular plot matches the circular decor of the casino as Sternberg once again explores the elusive nature of the feminine mystique.

Sullivan's Travels. USA. **prod co:** Paramount. **prod:** Paul Jones. **dir/sc:** Preston Sturges. **photo:** John Seitz. **ed:** Stuart Gilmore. **mus:** Leo Shuken. **with:** Joel McCrea, Veronica Lake, Robert Warwick, William Demarest, Franklin Pangborn, Porter Hall.
A film director says farewell to Hollywood and escapist entertainment and takes to the road as a hobo to research his projected 'realist' masterpiece. But, chastened, he discovers the point where life and the movies diverge. This barbed satire on Hollywood's apparent vogue for 'social concern' fluctuates wildly between sophisticated comedy and tragedy.

Suspicion. USA. **prod co:** RKO. **prod/dir:** Alfred Hitchcock. **sc:** Samson Raphaelson, Joan Harrison, Alma Reville, from the novel Before The Fact by Francis Iles. **photo:** Harry Stradling. **ed:** William Hamilton. **art dir:** Van Nest Polglase. **mus:** Franz Waxman. **with:** Cary Grant, Joan Fontaine, Nigel Bruce, Sir Cedric Hardwicke, Dame May Whitty, Isabel Jeans.
Hitchcock called it 'the second English picture I made in Hollywood' and the film was his first failure with the American public. But its portrayal of a woman convinced that her husband wants to murder her can now be seen as a chronicle of a death wish bred of sexual frustration.

Swamp Water. (The Man Who Came Back). USA. **prod co:** 20th Century-Fox. **prod:** Irving Pichel. **dir:** Jean Renoir. **sc:** Dudley Nichols, from the novel by Vereen Bell. **photo:** Peverell Marley. **ed:** Walter Thompson. **mus:** David Buttolph. **with:** Walter Brennan, Walter Huston, Anne Baxter, Dana Andrews, Mary Howard, John Carradine.
A fugitive hiding in the swamps troubles the peaceful lives of the local townspeople. It was Renoir's first American film and marked the beginning of a transformation of his style in which his lyricism was gradually replaced by self-effacement and austerity.

A Woman's Face. USA. **prod co:** MGM. **prod:** Victor Saville. **dir:** George Cukor. **sc:** Donald Ogden Stewart, Elliot Paul, from the play Il Etait Une Fois by Francis de Croisset. **photo:** Robert Planck. **ed:** Frank Sullivan. **art dir:** Cedric Gibbons. **mus:** Bronislau Kaper. **with:** Joan Crawford, Melvyn Douglas, Conrad Veidt, Osa Massen, Reginald Owen, Albert Basserman.
This story, set in Sweden, of a nursemaid scarred in childhood and determined to avenge herself on the world, is marked by a Crawford performance of sombre intensity. For Cukor, the film is unusually bleak and dark and has the quality of an evil, Scandinavian fairy-tale.

Chapter 24
Tools of the trade

The refinement of film stock, the introduction of tape recording and the invention of new highly mobile cameras in the Forties revolutionized film-making

Scientific research and technical development are, as in any industry, essential features of the film business. The innovations of the late Thirties and the Forties – faster film, magnetic tape recording and reflex cameras – gave cameramen greater freedom and enabled them to achieve visual effects that had far-reaching implications for cinema.

Every picture, every frame, still told a story, but those film-makers who had mastered the innovations realized the opportunities for establishing and developing narrative and character through new effects of lighting and subtleties of composition.

One film that displays such mastery of technical innovations is *Citizen Kane*. Other films exploited the new tools of the trade, especially the sophisticated cameras, by returning to real-life locations and shooting in the streets. Either way, the 'look' of Hollywood cinema was changing once again.

The invention of reflex cameras was a major technical advance; later in the Forties, smaller, more mobile cameras like the German Arriflex brought a new flexibility to camerawork

For many years motion-picture cameras like the Mitchell NC (and the BNC model) allowed the cameraman to focus his subject by means of a 'rackover' system: the body of the camera (containing the film magazine, camera drive and motor) could be shifted sideways at the touch of a lever. This action brought into position (behind the lens) an optical viewfinder which gave the cameraman an uninterrupted view of his subject while taking the shot.

In the design of motion picture cameras one priority has always been that the cameraman should be able to have a continuous view of what he is shooting, through the taking lens during filming. This facility for 'reflex viewing' (focusing and viewing as one operation at one and the same time) was built into movie cameras in the late Thirties.

In 1937 the Vinten camera incorporated a revolutionary viewfinding system: a rotating mirror was placed in front of the film at an angle of 45°. The mirror acted as a shutter to keep out the light while the film was advanced between exposures, but at the same time the mirror reflected the image onto a piece of ground glass in the viewfinder, thus enabling the cameraman to check his focus constantly.

In 1938 Arnold and Richter, camera makers in Munich, Germany, developed the Arriflex camera whose great advantage was that it was light enough to be hand-held. It also incorporated a shutter reflex viewfinder mechanism based on the principle of the rotating mirror as pioneered by Vinten. Arriflex reflex cameras were used extensively by German newsreel cameramen during

World War II and became highly prized trophies when captured by Allied war correspondents. The basic pre-war Arriflex design has continued in production with remarkably few modifications for over forty years.

The Cameflex (as distinct from the American Cameraflex) was produced by the French Eclair company. It comprised many innovations in motion-picture camera design. The film was moved in the camera by a ratchet mechanism that gave much steadier pictures but was rather noisy to operate and did not permit the film to be run in reverse. Mounted on the front of the camera was a lens turret with three lenses attached to it; a lens of the appropriate focal length could be selected by simply turning the turret. The Cameflex also featured an eyepiece which could be rotated to any angle (so that the cameraman could view his picture even if the circumstances of shooting obliged him to work in awkward positions). Loading the camera was made easier by the invention of a 'clip on' magazine which could be attached and removed even when the camera was running. Like the Arriflex, this camera was light and portable, though Cameflex instruments were designed to be operated from the shoulder rather than held in the hand.   DAVID SAMUELSON

Tape recording as we know it today developed from a sound-recording system perfected in Germany during World War II. The German Magnetofon company developed a plastic tape coated with magnetic materials that would act as a medium for recording sounds. The implications for motion pictures were twofold: tape provided a new recording medium and a new form of soundtrack on the

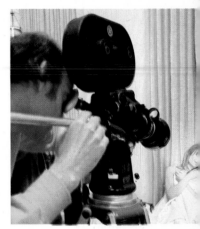

Top: the Arriflex camera, first introduced in 1938 and scarcely modified in over forty years' use. Centre: the Vinten camera. Above: the Cameflex, with its lens turret. Left: the Mitchell NC

film itself. The advantages of using tape were immediately apparent.

Magnetic sound gradually replaced the old optical system for all studio and location film-making because of its facility for instant playback, erasure of errors and re-use. No longer did a sound engineer spend a sleepless night wondering whether an expensive actor or an even more expensive orchestra had had a day's labour ruined by a technical slip in the recording. The results of their work were there on tape, to be checked and, if necessary, corrected on the spot. Magnetic tape was in experimental use in Hollywood from 1947 onwards and by the Fifties all studios were using it for their sound recording.

Magnetic recording brought greater flexibility to sound shooting and saved recordists many a sleepless night wondering about the quality of the sound

However, the adoption by the film trade of magnetic soundtracks was beset with problems. At a time when audiences were declining, cinemas were unwilling to lay out the cost of re-equipping their projectors for magnetic 'stripe' soundtracks, even though these were proved to be of higher fidelity than optical soundtracks.

When the CinemaScope revolution occurred in the early Fifties, 'directional' sound (that is, sound that came from, or moved to, a specific point on the screen) was best achieved by the use of magnetic soundtracks. The biblical epic *The Robe*, for example, was released in CinemaScope in 1953 carrying four magnetic soundtracks. The effect was moderately impressive but the cost of re-equipping 35mm projectors to reproduce magnetic soundtracks was exorbitant. The four-track, magnetic stereophonic film with its costly alteration to the projection mechanism and its hazardous maintenance, soon fell into disuse.

In the studios, however, magnetic recording was making great advances. PVC plastic was developed to make the tape more robust. The great sound trucks with their massive batteries and generators became obsolete as the highly portable tape recorders gained in usage. By the end of the Forties, optical sound was no longer used for recording during filming but released prints were of course supplied to the exhibitors with optical soundtracks just as they had always been.

Optical sound had scored at least one major success in the Forties. Disney's breathtaking *Fantasia* (1940) was released in stereophonic sound: it had three principal optical soundtracks. A fourth track carried a pattern of electronic cues and was used for control of volume levels. The sound engineers on *Fantasia* were working on the idea of making the sound come from different parts of the screen.

In 1951, the Festival of Britain's Telekinema (later to become the National Film Theatre) gave a demonstration of stereoscopic films coupled with an attempt at stereophonic cinema sound. The experiment was not wholly successful, but it provided sufficient interest to catch the attention of many cinemagoers and proved that people were beginning to care about the quality of sound that they were hearing in cinemas.   KEN CAMERON

When panchromatic film stock was introduced to motion pictures in the mid-Twenties, it marked a significant improvement in black-and-white movies: it was sensitive to all the colours of the spectrum and thus gave more faithful reproduction. In 1939, vastly improved panchromatic negative films came on the market and opened up great possibilities for the creative motion-picture cameramen of the Forties.

The new panchromatic films were more sensitive to light – in technical terms they were 'faster' and permitted photography under poor lighting conditions. They were also less 'grainy' than previous films which meant that the images looked sharper. As more and more 'exterior' scenes were being photographed indoors, using back projection and studio live action, the finer-grain, faster films greatly enhanced the quality of the images. Moreover, fast films allowed cameramen to 'stop down' their lenses, thereby increasing 'depth of field' (the distance both in front of and behind the point being focused within which other objects will remain in acceptably sharp focus).

Faster films operated under lower lighting levels. The benefits of this were several-fold: smaller, more compact lamps could be used, giving the cinematographer better control over lighting; a 50-percent saving was achieved in power consumption; and fewer lamps meant less heat on the set with a consequent improvement in working conditions.

The use of colour for motion pictures advanced at a tremendous rate during the Forties. At the start of the decade, three-colour photography was dominated by Technicolor (the system used by most of the major studios), although in the field of two-colour photography many companies (Cinemacolor, Cinecolor, Magnacolor, Trucolor) were very active. The quality of two-colour processes did not match that of the Technicolor process but they were often used for B pictures and were felt acceptable for certain subjects, especially Westerns.

In 1945 the patents of the German Agfacolor system were circulated abroad and the process was imitated by several film manufacturers. Among these derivative systems was Ansco Color, a multi-layered film with three emulsions (each with differ-

Left and centre: sound recording in the Forties, showing the most portable tape recorders of the day. Above: a reel of nitrate film in an advanced state of chemical decomposition

ent sensitivities to colour), was introduced. Instead of the colour being produced from three strips of film (as in Technicolor), this process was based on one strip which was coated with three layers of emulsion, one on top of the other. It meant that standard cameras could now be used for full-colour photography. Normal processing and printing equipment was also usable, with a minimum of modification.

Black-and-white films may have been superior in quality to colour movies of the time but the increased sophistication of film stock meant that cameramen had to be more precise in judging the correct exposure. The development of exposure meters was, therefore, of major importance. The photo-electric exposure meter, for instance, was used to establish 'key' lighting (the main lighting on the set) and to maintain consistent light levels; with the commercial availability of these precision instruments, films attained a uniform standard in the printing, despite the widely varying types of lighting under which they may have been shot. Also available were new lenses coated with an anti-reflective substance that cut down light loss and thus provided further lighting controls.

The usable life of a film print was greatly extended by the introduction of a new lacquer that helped prevent abrasions and could be removed and replaced with a new coating whenever necessary.

Since the beginning of cinema, film stocks had been nitrate-based. Such film was highly inflammable and was notorious for causing fires in laboratories and projection booths. Early in the Forties, however, a gradual change to 'safety' acetate films was under way in Germany and France. Other countries followed, and in 1943 refinements were made in the chemical base of the 'safety' film.

With this increased safety came drawbacks. Acetate films were subject to a greater degree of shrinkage which caused problems in printing and projection; they also had less resistance to tearing than the old nitrate films and frequently broke during handling.

By the end of the decade, however, research into safety films resulted in the introduction of 'triacetate' films with physical properties similar to those of nitrate films. A side benefit of this development was the reduction in fire-insurance costs, but what mattered was that film had become safer to work with.   DENNIS KIMBLEY

Below: Orson Welles directing Citizen Kane – *in this scene Susan Alexander makes her operatic debut. Bottom: low-key lighting and deep-focus photography in* Citizen Kane

Citizen Kane was, in many ways, the showcase of the new movie technology. And the Forties vogue for location shooting was no less important for film style

Orson Welles' original contract with RKO gave him unlimited power over any film that he directed, with the sole proviso that the studio had the right to reject any presentation of a completed script. Such unprecedented freedom accorded to a not entirely humble newcomer to Hollywood was one of the causes of the hostility directed at Welles even before he began shooting Citizen Kane.

Welles had proposed two scripts to RKO which they had rejected. The first was based on Joseph Conrad's *Heart of Darkness*, but its projected costs and the enormous technical problems it posed led RKO to turn it down. The second proposal, *Smiler With a Knife*, from a novel by Nicholas Blake, hit problems over the lack of a suitable leading lady. Herman J. Mankiewicz then suggested to Welles the subject which was to become Citizen Kane.

Welles asked Mankiewicz to develop a treatment and a script, but the controversy is still raging as to who exactly wrote what. Nonetheless, the shared screen credit (and Oscar) seems to be just; Mankiewicz wrote the actual script but enough of Welles' ideas were incorporated during production for him to deserve at least a co-author credit.

Citizen Kane has long been hailed as original and innovative, chiefly for its synthesis of cinematic and narrative elements which had not co-existed before. Its influences, however, are worth noting too. Fritz Lang once called the film 'a scrapbook of expressionist devices' and though the judgment may be unfair, it is quite clear what Lang meant.

Welles had spent a long time studying the films of Lang, as well as those of John Ford, Frank Capra and others. There are elements of all those directors' styles in Citizen Kane, but the most obvious influence is the German-style lighting and the kind of camera placement to be found in Lang's films.

Gregg Toland and Russell Metty brought to the film their experience with lighting, deep-focus photography, coated lenses and the newly developed fast film stock. They devised techniques of building sets to allow for the low camera angles and the special lighting that Welles wanted.

Welles had made himself a master of sound during his work in radio, and, in many ways, the use of sound in Citizen Kane is the most innovative aspect of the film. The dialogue is made to overlap and thus provide continuity, and Welles creates irony out of the conjunction of sound and image. A major part of the film's success comes from the score by Bernard Herrmann who worked on the music reel by reel as the film was being edited.

The filming began before the script was actually approved by the studio. Welles was supposedly shooting 'tests' but he managed to film half a dozen sequences that found their way into the final film. These included: part of the picnic sequence, the scene in the projection room and the 'March of Time' newsreel (which was composed of old footage and newly shot material that had been specially 'aged' in the laboratories).

Even when shooting started officially on June 30, 1940, the plot of the film was meant to be a secret. It soon became an open secret, however, and the fact that it was based on the life of the newspaper magnate William Randolph Hearst excited much controversy. Ironically the relationship of Hearst to the film often gets in the way of considering the film in a fresh perspective. At the time, critics who would tear an ordinary Hollywood biopic to shreds for its departure from fact were outraged by Citizen Kane's similarities to Hearst's life.

Although Hearst himself had read the script in 1940, he later became incensed over the film's alleged blackening of his name. What made matters worse was that his gossip columnist, Louella Parsons, had become hysterically obsessed by the film. At first Hearst forbade any other mention of Citizen Kane, or, for that matter, any other RKO films in his newspapers, although he proceeded to attack it just before it was due to open. In addition he threatened Hollywood in general, saying that he would expose immorality in the film industry and play up any scandals that were found there.

MGM's Louis B. Mayer tried to buy the original negative for $842,000 in order to destroy it. But Henry Luce, Hearst's newspaper competitor, was equally interested in buying it so that he could release it. RKO's production executive George J. Schaefer denied that Citizen Kane was about Hearst, and Welles mischievously added that they were nonetheless planning such a film.

The film was completed towards the end of 1940 and was scheduled to open in February 1941 but

Since the cinema was invented, the majority of films were made on studio sets or on locations conveniently close to the studios which 'doubled' for places where the action was supposed to be taking place.

There was, after all, nothing which could not be duplicated, more or less realistically, with sets. Moreover, studio shooting provided complete control over every technical aspect of filming. There were always those directors who insisted that one paid heavily for that control with a loss of realistic atmosphere but, with few exceptions, they were overruled by imagined 'technical limitations' and the cost of going on location.

Whatever film-makers and audiences understood by realism – a concept that consistently defies definition – there appeared to be a direct relationship between the artificiality of sets, the lack of 'real-life' subjects and the treatment of those subjects in the majority of Hollywood films.

Veteran directors returning from their experiences in World War II with an altered perception of 'reality' were joined in Hollywood by younger directors who wanted to treat American society and its problems in a realistic fashion. Concurrently, Italian neo-realism burst upon the international film scene, with its mixture of actual locations, realistic acting and its treatment of post-war life. After *Rome, Open City* (1945) some film-makers found it impossible to return to their sets and the subjects which those sets represented. On the economic level of American film-making, the neo-realist style also made its mark: it was suddenly possible to produce good and profitable films without big stars and huge budgets, and film-makers could save money by shooting carefully on real streets in real cities.

Louis de Rochemont, throughout the Thirties the producer of the *March of Time* newsreels, clearly anticipated the new American movement towards realism with his production of *The House on 92nd Street* (dir. Henry Hathaway, 1945). This semi-documentary spy film was shot all in New York with plenty of real-life locations. Two years later he produced *Boomerang* (dir. Elia Kazan, 1947) a thriller about incompetence in municipal government. Kazan maintained much the same approach in his *Panic in the Streets* (1950), about the public health service, which was shot on the docks of New Orleans. Kazan's major contribution to the post-war realist movement was his mixture of professional and non-professional actors and to his use of young actors from the New York stage trained in the 'realist' school of acting.

Jules Dassin's treatment of a formula prison-escape story in *Brute Force* (1947) was tough and realistic and made the film seem more hard-hitting than it was in retrospect. His subsequent thriller *The Naked City* (1948) was one of the most influential crime films of the decade: the New York settings and the grimy, unromantic aspects of normal police procedure overshadowed the murder plot, and the atmosphere created by shooting in the streets and unglamorous offices and apartments paradoxically brought a freshness to the genre.

For a time, realistic shooting and settings encouraged a more-or-less realistic treatment of social problems: *Crossfire* (1947) and *Home of the Brave* (1949) dealt with racial discrimination; the problems of soldiers readjusting to civilian life were focused in *The Men* (1950); corruption in the boxing-ring was the subject of *Body and Soul* (1947) and in the political arena in *All the King's Men* (1949). Other genres, notably Westerns, benefitted from the realist trend: films like The *Gunfighter* (1950) favoured increased location shooting and a greater degree of psychological realism.

DAVID OVERBEY

was postponed when the RKO board over-ruled Schaefer's decision to release it.

In March, Welles called a press conference to point out that his contract gave him the right to demand that the film be released within a certain period of time, otherwise, he said, he might sue the studio. In spite of Louella Parsons' demands that the governor of New York ban the film, it did open in New York City on May 1, 1941, at the Palace cinema.

The myth that *Citizen Kane* was savaged by the critics and flopped disastrously is simply not true. The film attracted highly enthusiastic reviews and did enough business in major cities to break even. Since its first release *Citizen Kane* has, of course, proved quite profitable and is still widely shown today. It won several Oscar nominations and the Best Screenplay Award for 1941, although the film, like its maker, remained unpopular in Hollywood.

Film scholars and critics insist that *Citizen Kane* had a tremendous effect on everyone who saw it – audiences and film-makers – but exactly why it is a masterpiece is hard to define. Certainly the radically different use of narrative techniques, the deep-focus photography, the overlapping sound and the complex cutting contribute to the film's uniqueness.

Top: filming The Naked City *on the real locations where the story was supposed to have happened was a breakthrough in Hollywood style. Above:* The House on 92nd Street *also used genuine locations, but the story was routine spy fiction. Right: the poster for Jules Dassin's* The Naked City *proclaims that the movie was 'actually filmed on the sidewalks of New York'. Ironically, the cameraman was William Daniels who had been responsible for some of the most stylized photography of Garbo earlier in his career at MGM*

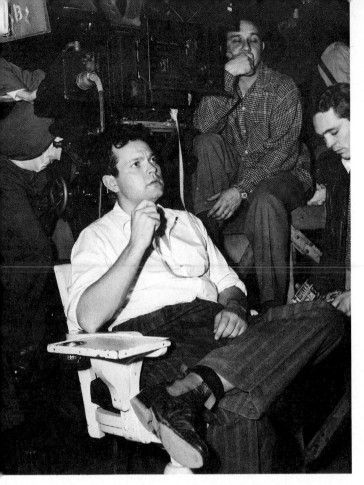

The Immortal Story of Orson Welles

'There but for the grace of God, goes God.' This famous quip by the writer Herman Mankiewicz sums up the mixture of awe and resentment that greeted the arrival in Hollywood of Orson Welles, for whom the word 'genius' seemed to have been newly minted

Orson Welles came to Hollywood having soared to prominence as a producer of stage and radio. Given *carte blanche* by George J. Schaefer, president of RKO studios, Welles was determined to create something highly personal for his film debut. He had considered and reluctantly discarded an adaptation of Joseph Conrad's *Heart of Darkness* and been forced to abandon a project based on Nicholas Blake's *The Smiler With a Knife*, owing to the aversion of Carole Lombard and Rosalind Russell – the film's potential stars – to working with an untried director.

Undeterred, Welles decided that he would play the lead in an original story, *Citizen Kane* (1940), concocted by Herman Mankiewicz and himself. Despite the risks involved, Schaefer stood by Welles and turned over the resources of his studio to him. But prior to release, the film ran into unexpected problems. Louella O. Parsons, head of the movie department of Hearst's newspaper empire, had been one of the first to view the film and had complained to Hearst that *Citizen Kane*'s story was nothing but an unflattering version of Hearst's liaison with his mistress, Marion Davies. The Hearst newspapers refused to run advertisements for

---

'The cinema has no boundaries. It's a ribbon of dream'

---

the film. As a result, *Citizen Kane* did not have a nationwide release and some cinemas even cancelled their bookings. In spite of a number of intelligent and enthusiastic reviews, it was not the runaway box-office hit the studios had hoped for.

RKO was concerned, therefore, about Welles' second venture, *The Magnificent Amber-sons* (1942), a film version of Booth Tarkington's novel, which was already in production. Welles did not act in *The Magnificent Ambersons*, preferring to concentrate his talents on directing the picture. He was thoroughly conversant with his material; in 1939 he had played the part of the unsympathetic young hero, George Amberson Minafer, on the radio. He cast Tim Holt in this role for the film and devoted all his energies to re-creating a nostalgic picture of American life in the nineteenth century.

To those few who were lucky enough to see the sneak preview of the completed film at the United Artists Theatre in Pasadena, *The Magnificent Ambersons* was a stunning, never-to-be-forgotten event, in every way as important cinematically as *Citizen Kane*. However, the film was sent back to the editing room as the studio felt further cutting was necessary.

Welles was meanwhile staggering production on two films, *Journey Into Fear* (1942) – a version of the Eric Ambler novel, which Welles was directing with Norman Foster and also acting in – and a semi-documentary about South America made with the cooperation of the US government, *It's All True*.

The worst thing that could have happened to Welles' career in Hollywood then hit with the suddenness of a Californian earthquake: Schaefer, Welles' sponsor, was replaced as head of production at RKO by Charles J. Koerner, a man who knew how to distribute and exhibit movies, had great taste, but no patience with failure at the box-office. Welles, busy shooting in South America, was summarily fired, and all the film he had shot for *It's All True* was deposited in the RKO vaults where it remained until June 1978 when a portion of it was shown for the first time.

On July 1, 1942, *The Magnificent Ambersons*,

a third of its original length edited out – and with it much of its bitter-sweet drama – opened in Los Angeles as part of a double bill with a 'programmer' called *Mexican Spitfire Sees a Ghost* (1942). The Hollywood career of Orson Welles seemed to have ground to a halt; he was regarded as an expensive eccentric.

When *Journey Into Fear* was released it had been even more mangled by RKO's editors than *The Magnificent Ambersons*. Wisely, Welles left Hollywood. His name had been linked with the beautiful Dolores Del Rio, but when she saw what remained of her work in *Journey Into Fear*, she threw up her hands in

Above: Welles plans a scene for The Lady From Shanghai. *Below: an atmosphere of unease is superbly evoked by this angled shot from* The Magnificent Ambersons

Above: Rita Hayworth, then Welles' wife, played the beautiful, bewitching murderess in The Lady From Shanghai. *Below: the killing of King Duncan in* Macbeth, *the first of Welles' Shakespearean adaptations*

despair and returned to her native Mexico.

When Welles returned to Hollywood, he did so solely as an actor. He was cast in *Jane Eyre* (1943) as the moody Mr Rochester, who conceals his insane wife in the attic of his house. The production had been set up by David O. Selznick and then sold with two other potential Selznick productions (*Claudia*, 1943, and *Keys to the Kingdom*, 1944) to 20th Century-Fox because Selznick desperately needed ready money. Selznick had set up Robert Stevenson as director of *Jane Eyre*, and he had supervised the script prepared by Aldous Huxley and the production designs of William Pereira. From the beginning, *Jane Eyre* was to star Joan Fontaine; the role of Rochester had been styled for an older actor, such as Ronald Colman. Colman, however, was ill, and another candidate, Laurence Olivier, was in war service for his own country. Welles was an unexpected choice for the part, but was approved by all concerned. His Rochester was young and handsome, and he played the character with great theatrical bombast. Colman and Olivier might have chosen to act the part with more subtlety, but Welles invested it with a romantic fury, more closely

akin to another Brontë hero – Heathcliff in *Wuthering Heights*.

Jane Eyre was well received, and Welles had no difficulty getting other acting roles. He was believable in a mysterious soap-opera romance, *Tomorrow Is Forever*, playing opposite Claudette Colbert, and he was even allowed to direct *The Stranger* (both 1946), in which he played the lead – a Nazi war criminal attempting to conceal his murky past. He, however, has never thought much of that picture.

In 1947 he directed his wife Rita Hayworth (they had married in 1943) in *The Lady From Shanghai*, an exotic melodrama – now regarded as a classic – that at the time attracted a small coterie of admirers. They chose to disregard Louella Parsons when she named Welles 'awesome Orson, the self-styled genius' and informed fans that he was not only 'washed up' in Hollywood, but was finished as Rita's husband. She was right in her latter accusation, for Hayworth and Welles soon divorced, Miss Hayworth declaring: 'I can't take his genius any more.'

'A film is never really good unless the camera is an eye in the head of a poet'

Welles may have been surprised to find that Hollywood – at least his own peers – was sympathetic to his previous misfortunes as a director. His first two films had many admirers. Vera Hruba Ralston, wife of the head of Republic studios, Herbert Yates, is rumoured to have persuaded her husband to put both Welles and John Ford on the Republic lists to give the studio some real class. Yates let Welles direct a production of Shakespeare's *Macbeth* (1948), which he made in just 23 days and on a remarkably low budget. It is an uneven but extremely effective picture, and one of the best presentations of the play on film.

Macbeth was Welles' last film directed within the old Hollywood studio system. His subsequent career was erratic but often brilliant – a fitting reflection of this flamboyant figure's idiosyncratic genius.   DeWITT BODEEN

Filmography
1940 Swiss Family Robinson (narr. only); Citizen Kane (+co-sc; +act). '**42** The Magnificent Ambersons (+sc); Journey Into Fear (actor; +uncredited dir). '**43** Jane Eyre (actor only). '**44** Follow the Boys (actor only). '**46** Tomorrow Is Forever (actor only); The Stranger (+act; +uncredited co-sc). '**46** Duel in the Sun (narr. only). '**47** The Lady From Shanghai (+act; +sc). '**48** Macbeth (+act; +sc; +co-cost). '**49** Prince of Foxes (actor only); The Third Man (actor only); Black Magic (actor only). '**50** The Black Rose (actor only); La Miracle de St Anne (short) (FR); La Disordre (narr. only) (FR). '**52** Othello (+act; +sc); Return to Glennascaul (actor only) (short); Trent's Last Case (actor only). '**54** Si Versailles M'Etait Conté (actor only) (FR) (USA/GB: Versailles); L'Uomo, la Bestia e la Virtù (actor only) (IT); Trouble in the Glen (actor only) (GB); Mr Arkadin/Confidential Report (+act; +sc; +cost). '**55** Three Cases of Murder *ep* Lord Mountdrago (actor only) (GB); Napoléon (actor only) (FR); Out of Darkness (narr. only) (doc). '**56** Moby Dick (actor only). '**57** Man in the Shadow (actor only) (GB: Pay the Devil). '**58** The Long Hot Summer (actor only); Touch of Evil (+act; +sc); The Vikings (narr. only); South Seas Adventure (narr. only) (doc); Come to the Fair (narr. only)

(doc); The Roots of Heaven (actor only). '**59** Les Seigneurs de la Forêt (co-narr. only) (BEL) (USA/GB: Lords of the Forest); Compulsion (actor only); Ferry to Hong Kong (actor only) (GB). '**60** David e Golia (actor only) (IT) (USA/GB: David and Goliath); Crack in the Mirror (actor only); Austerlitz (actor only) (FR-IT-YUG) (USA/GB: The Battle of Austerlitz). '**61** I Tartari (actor only) (IT) (USA/GB: The Tartars); King of Kings (narr. only). '**62** Lafayette (actor only) (FR-IT); Le Procès (+act; +sc) (FR-IT-GER) (USA/GB: The Trial). '**63** River of the Ocean (narr. only) (doc) (GER); The VIP's (actor only) (GB) (USA: International Hotel); RoGoPaG (actor only) (IT-FR). '**64** The Finest Hour (narr. only) (GB). '**65** La Fabuleuse Aventure de Marco Polo (FR-IT-EG-YUG-AFG) (USA/GB: The Fabulous Adventures of Marco Polo/The Magnificent Marco Polo) (USA retitling for TV: Marco the Magnificent). '**66** Chimes at Midnight/Falstaff (+act; +sc; +cost) (SP-SWIT); Paris, Brûle-t-il? (actor only) (FR) (USA/GB: Is Paris Burning?); A Man for All Seasons (actor only) (GB). '**67** Casino Royale (actor only) (GB); Sailor From Gibraltar (actor only) (GB); I'll Never Forget What's-'is-Name (actor only) (GB) (USA retitling for TV: The Takers). '**68** Histoire Immortelle (+act) (FR)

(USA/GB: Immortal Story); Oedipus the King (actor only) (GB); House of Cards (actor only). '**69** L'Etoile du Sud (actor only) (FR-GB) (USA/GB: Southern Star); Tepepa (actor only) (IT-SP); Barbed Water (narr. only) (doc) (GB); Una su Tredici (actor only) (IT-FR) (USA/GB: 12+1). '**70** The Kremlin Letter (actor only); Start the Revolution Without Me (narr. only) (USA-CZ); Catch-22 (actor only); Waterloo (actor only) (IT-USSR); A Horse Called Njinsky (narr. only) (doc) (GB). '**71** Sentinels of Silence (narr. only) (short) (English version of Mexican short Sentinelas del Silencio); Directed by John Ford (narr. only) (doc); A Safe Place (actor only); La Decade Prodigieuse (actor only) (FR) (USA/GB: Ten Days' Wonder). '**72** Treasure Island (+act; +co-sc) (GB-GER-FR-SP); Malpertuis (actor only) (BEL-FR-GER). '**73** Get to Know Your Rabbit (actor only) (USA); Vérités et Mensonges/F for Fake/Question Mark/Nothing but the Truth) (+act; +sc) (FR-IRAN-GER); '**75** And Then There Were None/Ten Little Indians/Ten Little Niggers/Death in Persepolis (GER-FR-SP-IT). '**76** Voyage the Damned (actor only) (GB); The Late Great Planet Earth (narr; +act. only). '**78** Filming 'Othello' (+narr). '**79** The Muppet Movie (actor only) (GB).

Apart from isolated peaks of achievement, Welles' later career has failed to fulfil its early promise. He remains a charismatic figure who seems to invite audiences to reflect on what might have been had the right opportunities come his way

After *Macbeth* he began to film *Othello*. The work was to become the kind of odyssey which was henceforth to characterize Welles' life. The filming dragged on from 1949 to 1952, moving from location to location across Morocco and Italy. When money ran out, work would stop – to recommence when funds came in and the cast could be reassembled.

If the difficulties of production again show in the uncertainty of the overall conception, at least here Welles could call on more talented associates than he had been able to for *Macbeth*; his old friend and early mentor from his youthful days as an actor in Dublin, Micheál MacLiammóir, creates a wonderful, feline Iago whose malice, the film infers, is the product of sexual impotence.

Welles now seemed doomed to endless wandering, leaving in his wake a host of uncompleted or abortive projects. In 1955 he began to film *Don Quixote* in Mexico and Paris, with himself as the Don and Akim Tamiroff, one of Welles' favourite actors, as Sancho Panza, but the film was never completed. Other projects talked of along the way include the biblical stories of Noah, Abraham and Salome; two more Shakespeare subjects, *King Lear* and *Julius Caesar* (eventually produced in 1953 by an old Mercury Theatre collaborator, John Houseman, with Joseph Mankiewicz as director); *Pickwick Papers* and (ironically) *The Odyssey*; *Catch-22*, which was eventually made by Mike Nichols in 1970, with Welles himself playing General Dreedle.

Even in the days of his childhood encounters with Shakespeare, Welles showed a special affection for larger-than-life characters. *Mr Arkadin* (1954) is a monster on the lines of *Citizen Kane*, a man of great wealth and power, who, unlike Kane, hires his own investigator to reconstruct the history of his mysterious career. This is, it is revealed, a test to establish if Arkadin's ultimate secret, the past guilt he

Left: Welles as General Dreedle on the set of Catch-22. *Below: to avenge the murder of his wife, detective Quinlan (Welles) prepares to 'execute' Grandi (Akim Tamiroff) in* Touch of Evil. *He plans to throw blame for the deed on Susan (Janet Leigh), wife of Quinlan's enemy – a Mexican police chief*

Although he was to return to Hollywood once more to make *Touch of Evil* (1958), Welles' *Macbeth* (1948) may be taken to mark his final divorce, as director, from the film capital. This was the first of his series of screen encounters with Shakespeare. To admit that it is also the least satisfactory of them is not to deny that it is, at the same time, one of the most imaginative of the cinema's adaptations of the playwright, comparing with Kurosawa's *Kumonso-Jo* (1957, *Throne of Blood*) and towering, in its imaginative force, over Polanski's later version made in 1971. But the restrictions of time and money show, and the performances are uneven. Welles' collaborators seemed to find it hard to follow his imaginative flights.

This is hardly surprising: Welles has spent sixty years of his life brooding on the mastery and mysteries of Shakespeare, and reshaping them to find new interpretations. It is said that his bed-time stories at the age of two were Charles Lamb's *Tales From Shakespeare*. At three he rejected these in favour of the original texts. By seven he knew *King Lear* by heart, and by ten he had learnt all the great tragic roles.

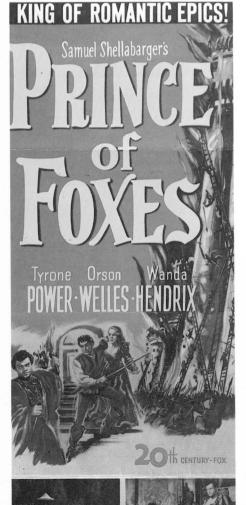

Above: Falstaff cuddles Doll Tearsheet – Welles and Jeanne Moreau in Chimes at Midnight. *Below and below right: costume melodramas like* Prince of Foxes *and* The Tartars *allowed Welles to revel in villainous roles, which he invested with sinister power*

KING OF ROMANTIC EPICS!

Samuel Shellabarger's

PRINCE of FOXES

Tyrone Orson Wanda
POWER · WELLES · HENDRIX

20th CENTURY-FOX

with MARINA BERTI · EVERETT SLOANE · KATINA PAXINOU · FELIX AYLMER

Directed by HENRY KING Produced by SOL C. SIEGEL

most wants to conceal, is safe from detection. When it proves not to be, Arkadin realizes that the man must be silenced for good.

For many of Welles' admirers *Touch of Evil* (his last attempt to come to terms with the Hollywood studio system) is his masterpiece. Welles plays Hank Quinlan, a fat, decaying, crack cop, whose sense of deistic superiority leads him to frame people whom his 'infallible' instinct tells him are guilty. Welles sets the action in a border town of nightmare seediness, whose other inhabitants include Marlene Dietrich as a languidly philosophical madame, apparently a one-time flame of Quinlan's, and Akim Tamiroff as the patriarch of a bizarre gang of hoodlums.

For years *Touch of Evil* was regarded as yet another example of Hollywood's legendary humiliation of creative genius: Universal studios' editors were alleged to have butchered Welles' original version. More recently, however, this has been reconstituted, and it is arguable that the Universal conception was actually an improvement; by leaving out some too-literal explanatory scenes, the cuts enhanced the sense of mystery and metaphysic

which is the film's great attraction.

Le Procès (1962, *The Trial*), a Franco-Italian-German co-production, was shot in Paris and Zagreb. Much admired on its first appearance, it now seems one of Welles' least successful works. His own evident philosophical distance from Kafka results not so much in invigorating

---

'Every time I bring out a new movie, nobody bothers to review it . . . They don't review my work, they review me'

---

tensions as in excessive debate: for an Orson Welles picture it is, unusually, often tediously talkative. Visually the film is remarkable. Much of it was shot in the abandoned buildings of the Gare d'Orsay in Paris; the old railway station, often bathed in swirling mists, provides some stunning images.

Thanks to Spanish and Swiss finance, Welles was next able to return to Shakespeare with a film that may well remain, alongside

Citizen Kane, his monument – *Chimes at Midnight* (1966). In a textual adaptation so brilliant that even the most demanding Shakespearean cannot fault it on grounds of scholarship, Welles assembled scenes from *Richard II*, *Henry IV Part I* and *II*, *Henry V* and *The Merry Wives of Windsor*, along with a commentary taken from the *Chronicles* of the Elizabethan historian Holinshed, to create a wholly new work which might be alternatively titled 'The Tragedy of Sir John Falstaff'. Without any violence to Shakespeare's own, essentially comic, vision of Falstaff, Welles extracts a character that is heroic in his humour, generosity and goodness, flawed perhaps, but finally tragic in his incomprehension of the ingratitude of the great and powerful.

Over the years Welles acted indefatigably – often appearing in two or three films per year. Some of his roles – in *Jane Eyre* (1943), *The Third Man* (1949), *Compulsion* (1959) and *Catch-22*, for example – are memorable; all are enjoyable; none is without a conscientious intelligence. Often, however, Welles' willingness to accept parts in the most inconsiderable material – from TV commercials to *Casino Royale* (1967) – looks positively cynical. His majestic, unflawed performance as Falstaff, however, demonstrated that, to whatever extent he might have prostituted his talent to the service of much lesser creators, he had kept intact and pure his gifts as an interpreter.

Histoire Immortelle (1968, *Immortal Story*), adapted from a tale by Isak Dineson (the pseudonym of Karen Blixen), provided him with another of the monsters he loves: a man like Kane and Arkadin, rich and powerful in the worldly sense but troubled by a secret sense of incompleteness. This old man, Mr Clay, is the embodiment of the traditional sailors' legend of the rich man of Macao who invites a young mariner to sleep with his beautiful wife (played by Jeanne Moreau), and fulfil the marital function of which he is himself incapable. Brief, classical and near-perfect, this film is, to date, Welles' last completed formal story film.

His wanderings continued. He acted in Bondarchuk's *Waterloo* (1970) and Chabrol's *La Decade Prodigieuse* (1971, *Ten Days' Wonder*). His rich, inimitable voice and superb diction were constantly in demand for film com-

mentaries; and it was thus that he came to work with François Reichenbach. Out of their collaboration came the delicious, enigmatic *Vérités et Mensonges* (1973, *F for Fake*). Welles was fascinated by some 16mm footage Reichenbach had shot for a TV series on fakers, with the celebrated art forger Elmyr de Hory and Clifford Irving, who, subsequent to the original Reichenbach film, had become famous as the faker of Howard Hughes' 'autobiography'. To these, Welles added his own fakes (in which he included his role in the radio production of *War of the Worlds* which, over thirty years earlier, had fooled thousands of Americans into thinking that the USA was under attack by Martians). Welles orchestrates this material so as to entice the spectator into a fascinating labyrinth.

Old now but still exuding boyish mischief, Welles relishes his film persona of magician and charlatan, amiably deceiving his willing audience with wonderful sleight of hand. Yet his place in movie history is nearer, in reality, to one of his tragic characterizations. Potentially one of the most gifted figures of world cinema, his output in forty years has been

Above, far left: Welles abridged Shakespeare's tragic study of sexual jealousy for his version of Othello. *Here, he attends to the poisonous counsel of Iago (Micheál MacLiammóir). Above left: F for Fake – Welles' most recent film as director. Above and below: Welles as a TV reporter in Huston's* The Roots of Heaven, *and as the isolated Cardinal Wolsey, swept aside by the caprices of Henry VIII, in Zinnemann's* A Man for All Seasons

miserably small, a constant story of frustrated or abortive projects. This may be detected in the tale he told himself in *Filming 'Othello'* (1978) – his contribution to which undoubtedly went further than mere commentary and interview. In recent years the list of incomplete projects has grown. Between 1967 and 1979 he was at work filming *The Deep* off the Dalmatian coast. Since 1970 he has been at work on *The Other Side of the Wind*; but nothing of that film, either, has ever been seen publicly. 'I do not work enough', he confessed to an interviewer in 1965, in a moment of unusual self-revelation, 'I am frustrated. Do you understand?'
DAVID ROBINSON

Directed by Orson Welles, 1940
Prod co: Mercury Productions/RKO. **exec prod:** George J. Schaefer. **prod:** Orson Welles. **sc:** Herman J. Mankiewicz, Orson Welles. **photo:** Gregg Toland. **sp eff:** Vernon L. Walker. **ed:** Robert Wise, Mark Robson. **art dir:** Van Nest Polglase, Darrell Silvera, Hilyard Brown. **cost:** Edward Stevenson. **mus:** Bernard Herrmann. **sd:** Bailey Fesler, James G. Stewart. **ass dir:** Richard Wilson. **r/t:** 119 minutes. New York premiere, 1 May 1941.
Cast: Orson Welles (*Charles Foster Kane*), Joseph Cotten (*Jedediah Leland*), Dorothy Comingore (*Susan Alexander*), Everett Sloane (*Mr Bernstein*), Ray Collins (*James W. Gettys*), George Coulouris (*Walter Parks Thatcher*), Agnes Moorehead (*Kane's mother*), Paul Stewart (*Raymond*), Ruth Warrick (*Emily Norton*), Erskine Sandford (*Herbert Carter*), William Alland (*Thompson; newsreel reader*), Fortunio Bonanova (*Matisti*), Gus Schilling (*head waiter*), Philip Van Zandt (*Mr Rawlston*), Georgia Backus (*Miss Anderson*), Harry Shannon (*Kane's father*), Sonny Bupp (*Kane III*), Buddy Swan (*Kane age 8*), Richard Barr (*Hillman*), Joan Blair (*Georgia*), Al Eben (*Mike*), Charles Bennett (*entertainer*), Milt Kibbee (*reporter*), Tom Curran (*Teddy Roosevelt*), Irving Mitchell (*Dr Corey*), Edith Evanson (*nurse*), Arthur Kay (*conductor*), Tudor Williams (*chorus master*), Herbert Corthell (*city editor*), Benny Rubin (*Smather*), Edmund Cobb (*reporter*), Frances Neal (*Ethel*), Robert Dudley (*photographer*), Ellen Lowe (*Miss Townsend*), Gino Corrado (*Gino the waiter*), Alan Ladd, Louise Currie, Eddie Coke, Walter Sande, Arthur O'Connell (*reporters*).

Charles Foster Kane utters his final word, 'Rosebud', and dies on his massive, crumbling estate, Xanadu (1).

Newsreel journalists prepare a film showing Kane's rise and fall, but it lacks an angle. A reporter is sent to find out who Rosebud may be. He interviews Susan Alexander (2) (Kane's second wife), Bernstein (3) and Jed Leland (two old employees) and Kane's butler, Raymond. Through them the jigsaw of Kane's life is pieced together.

Five-year-old Kane has inherited an immense fortune; at his mother's wish he is placed under the guardianship of banker Walter Thatcher (4) and is taken away from his Colorado home.

Thirty years later Kane buys up the New York *Inquirer* and begins his career as a scandal-sheet publisher (5). He marries Emily Norton (6) but later meets Susan Alexander (7) and establishes a love-nest with her. His attempt to run for governor (8) is shattered along with his marriage when political enemy Jim Gettys (9) exposes the affair.

Kane marries Susan and launches her on a disastrous career as an opera singer. But her failure and the set-backs he suffers during the Depression force him to retreat to his castle, Xanadu (10).

Susan, bored by the isolation of Xanadu and by Kane's autocratic behaviour, eventually leaves him. Kane dies and his chattels are disposed of, among them a childhood sled bearing the painted-on name of Rosebud (11).

1

2

3

7

8

9

Up to the Forties, orthodox Hollywood camera style consisted of diffused lighting and soft focus, even for such brutally realistic films as *I Am a Fugitive From a Chain Gang* (1932). Photographed in this way a typical sequence might consist of a long or medium establishing shot with cuts to close-up shots to show detail. Orson Welles' *Citizen Kane* (1940), however, signalled the beginning of a new period in American cinema. Composition in depth, obtained by increased depth-of-field photography, meant that images on several planes could all be held in sharp focus. The dramatic effects of a scene were created by images within the composition itself rather than by editing; and because both foreground and background remained in focus, the spectator could see everything there was to see in a single shot.

Depth of field in *Citizen Kane* results from a number of factors including the use of faster film and wide-angle lenses. These lenses possess certain inherent optical properties which can dramatically affect the appearance of a composition. As well as keeping foreground and background in focus, they create the illusion of perspective by exaggerating the relative scale of objects on different planes – objects closer to the camera appear much larger than those further away.

The relationship between visual style and narrative content seems almost inseparable in the film. The character of Kane is revealed not so much by what he says and does as by how he is made to appear in the context of his surroundings.

Early in the film there is a scene where Walter Thatcher has come to Colorado to take the young Kane away with him. In one of the shots (picture 4) Mrs Kane sits reading the terms of her son's inheritance in the foreground and at the right of the frame. Thatcher is seated slightly behind and to the right of her, and Kane's father stands at the left of the frame in the middle distance. By their position and size the three figures appear to be visually and dramatically at the centre of the scene. Initially their relative sizes on the screen seem to indicate their relative narrative importance: Mrs Kane, the mother who is trying to do the best for her son, is the dominant personality; Thatcher is the interloper; and the elder Kane, ineffectively voicing his opposition, is a figure of weakness. After looking through the foreground diagonally to the middle distance, attention centres on a window at the very back of the room. Through it can barely be identified the figure of a young boy who is all but obliterated by falling snow.

The boy may at first appear to be the least important figure in the composition, but the opposite is true. Much greater dramatic coherence is given to the scene when it is scanned in reverse order, from background to foreground. The smallest figure becomes the focal point of the narrative – it is Kane's future his parents and Thatcher are discussing, *his* life that, from that point onwards, will be irrevocably changed.

Time and again in the film secondary figures are positioned to act as a frame within the film frame in order to concentrate the spectator's attention on Kane in the distance. But a point occurs during the political rally sequence where, although a similar framing technique is used, the dramatic effect is suddenly reversed. Kane is giving the supreme performance of his career: his magnificent rhetoric about protecting working men, slum children and ordinary citizens alike captivates the audience. The scene ends, however, with a shot (picture 9) that dispels this effect and signals the beginning of the end for Kane. Political boss Jim Gettys is seen standing high up in a balcony, his figure filling the right side of the frame. To the left and far below, Kane is finishing his speech to wild applause. But the exaggerated perspective and the disproportionate size of Gettys foreshadows the despairing events about to befall Kane.

Up to this point in the film Kane is depicted as being in control of space on the screen. The spectator's attention, manipulated by the expressive dynamics of the composition and lighting, is unerringly drawn to him. But from the time he loses the election to the end of the film, his presence is made to seem increasingly insignificant in relation to his surroundings. This is most noticeable in the concluding scenes of Kane and Susan's self-imposed exile in Xanadu where Kane appears dwarfed by the volume of the rooms and the sheer depth of the huge, gaping fireplace. Space in the cavernous mausoleum of Xanadu now controls Kane and isolates him in a void of darkness.

ARNOLD DESSER

5

6

10

11

Here's looking at you
The work of the Hollywood cameramen

From our present perspective, informed as it is by the concept of a director's cinema, it is sometimes hard to imagine a time when the director concerned himself with the actors and it was the cameraman who put his signature on the finished film. In the early days of the silent cinema, however, the art of the film was founded in this close relationship between the man who directed the actors and the man whose job it was to make them look beautiful.

By the Twenties, the art of the cameraman had been emphatically established. Pioneer cinematographers like Billy Bitzer and Victor Fleming had begun their careers in the movie business; others, like Arthur Edeson and James Wong Howe, had come to films from portrait photography. Now that film-making had become a highly specialized craft and, in some cases, an art form, the man behind the camera was at the very least a highly prized technician and occasionally something approaching a magician.

Cameramen had to do their own special effects and optical work. They also needed a keen sense of design and sometimes had to invent the new technology of movie-making as they went along, modifying and adapting their equipment to cope with the ambitious demands of the directors.

A good cameraman always needed a good

handsome, tragic or heroic. From this background emerged the first generation of great motion-picture cameramen.

Above: some of Arthur Edeson's finest cinematography was seen in Casablanca *and other films for Warners during the Forties. Left: in* The Cameraman *(1928) Buster Keaton parodied the craft of cinematography, but as a director he favoured camera movement*

director, but he also benefitted from the skills of a good designer. Cecil B. DeMille's *The Cheat* (1915), designed by Wilfred Buckland, is an early example of such collaboration. The film contains a scene where two actors are framed against what appears to be a wall in the background; the scene is dark and the actors are illuminated by one patch of light that is criss-crossed with prison-type bars. The whole effect is achieved with light and shadow and is extremely atmospheric.

In the Twenties, cameramen began using panchromatic stock which gave an excellent visual texture. The fact that film was made on a nitrate base also gave it a special luminous quality that was particularly noticeable in the black tones. Later acetate-based films never looked as rich in their blacks as did nitrate. Handling celluloid was a dangerous job for which there was no training. Most cinematographers simply coped with the hazards and taught themselves their trade.

As the variety of films in the silent era expanded – Westerns, comedies, romances, spectaculars – cameramen learned to change their style to suit the story they were making. Lighting for a domestic drama, for example, would be 'flatter' (more two-dimensional) than that designed for a lustrous, historical pageant.

This mobility between the various genres is a crucial factor in the history of cinematography. At first sight it may seem strange that the cameraman Lee Garmes, for example, could switch from Rex Ingram's exotic *The Garden of Allah* (1927) to William A. Seiter's 'realist' drama *Waterfront* (1928) and to the Eddie Cantor musical *Whoopee!* (1930), but Hollywood was an industry that made a wide range of products, and cameramen, like anyone else, were hired to make the best use of their skills on whatever film they were assigned by the studio.

If adaptability was essential to the role of the cameramen, it was also vital that he remain susceptible to new ideas. Cinematography developed so rapidly between the years 1915 and 1930 that virtually everything known about the art today was discovered in that period.

Given the flexibility of cameramen, it seems surprising that mobility of the camera was one of the last developments to be made. In the majority of silent films, motion-picture photography was just that. People and things moved in front of the camera, and highly elaborate effects were created in the camera, but the instrument itself moved comparatively little.

There were exceptions, of course, notably in the films of Buster Keaton. He conceived his comedy around a succession of dynamic, highly mobile gags: the railway engine in *The General* (1926) and the studio-built waterfall in *Our Hospitality* (1923) are fine examples of the way Keaton uses camera movement, especially tracking shots, as an integral part of the comic narrative.

The other great actor-director of the period, Erich von Stroheim, preferred static camerawork, though he displayed a great sensitivity to light and shade. Ben Reynolds was one of Stroheim's cameramen on *Blind Husbands* (1918), *Foolish Wives* (1922), *Greed* (1923) and *The Wedding March* (1928), and achieved some remarkable contrasts of opulence and poverty through his knowledge of how various surfaces reflected and absorbed light. Stroheim's sets were so elaborate that he insisted his audience be allowed the time (in the shot) to

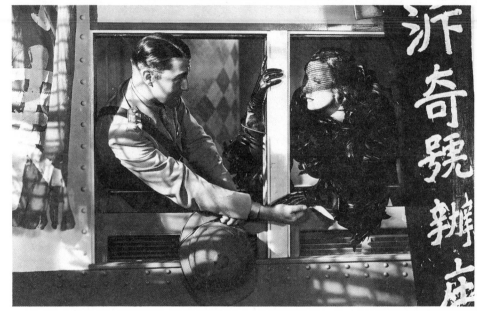

feast their eyes on the decor and to absorb all the movement going on within the frame.

The real 'liberation' of the camera took place in the late Twenties and was especially remarked upon in the work of the German director F.W. Murnau. In this respect both *Der Letzte Mann* (1924, *The Last Laugh*), made in Germany, and *Sunrise* (1927), Murnau's first American film, are key examples of how, towards the end of the silent period, directors were making the camera work to move the film's story along.

The achievement is not solely attributable to Murnau. In France, for example, Marcel L'Herbier's *L'Argent* (1928, *Money*) contains several elaborate tracking sequences and some sequences of expertly shot, hand-held camerawork; and in Japan, Kinugasa's 'experimental' films *Kurutta Ippeiji* (1926, *A Page of Madness*) and *Jujiro* (1928, *Crossroads*) reveal a sophisticated awareness of camera mobility.

Ironically, the newly acquired freedom of movement in camerawork was unexpectedly interrupted, in Hollywood at least, by the arrival of talkies and the need for cameras to be sound-proofed within bulky, almost unmovable booths. It was a retrogressive, though mercifully brief, stage in the history of cinematography.

By 1930, however, the booths were banished; cameras (like the new Mitchell) were blimped and once again free to move. For the next decade the art of the cameraman was largely a refinement and sophistication of the expertise already acquired. The musicals had their heyday and, as dance-directors like Busby Berkeley designed ever more elaborate numbers, cameramen like George Folsey and Joseph Ruttenberg learned to devise new kinds of shots and angles. The movie camera had never been so mobile. At the major studios the roster of top cameramen remained as it had been in the days before the talkies. Lee Garmes and Victor Milner were at Paramount, William Daniels at MGM. The 'vocabulary' of the movie cameraman was more or less unaltered: crisp, clear shots were used for action scenes, flattering soft-focus for close-ups, and so on.

Perhaps the finest example of this continuity of style is evidenced in the series of 19 Greta Garbo films photographed by William Daniels. Daniels himself told Charles Higham (in *Hollywood Cameramen*):

'Even my lighting for Garbo varied from picture to picture. There wasn't one Garbo face in the sense that there was a Dietrich face.'

But a close comparison of the seduction scene in *The Mysterious Lady* (1928) and the bedroom scene in *Queen Christina* (1933) reveals a consistent lighting style: a fondness

for simulating firelight and candlelight, a tendency to throw shadow onto the star's eyes to increase her aura of mystery.

Lee Garmes' photography of Marlene Dietrich in the films they made with Josef von Sternberg testifies to a similar working relationship, though in *Morocco* (1930), *Dishonoured* (1931) and *Shanghai Express* (1932), the style of Sternberg's direction is more self-conscious than that of Clarence Brown in the Garbo films, and the famous 'slatted' light effects of these exotic-looking films may be more properly attributed to Sternberg than to Lee Garmes.

Nevertheless Garmes was one of the most painterly of all Hollywood cameramen. A great admirer of Rembrandt, he claimed to have borrowed the painter's technique of 'north light' – whereby the main source of light on the set always comes from the north. Garmes clearly shares with Rembrandt a predilection for low-key lighting and in a film from later in his career, *Caught* (dir. Max Ophuls, 1948), he achieves some remarkably suspenseful effects. In one scene Barbara Bel Geddes meets her lover in an old boathouse. The only illumination comes from her flashlight and, as the scene develops into a quarrel, the shadows become genuinely menacing.

The partnership on this film of the versatile Garmes and the virtuoso Ophuls was one of the happy accidents of the Hollywood system. In the Thirties, Garmes had tried his hand at directing in partnership with the screenwriters Ben Hecht and Charles MacArthur, but in the

Top left: John Gilbert and Greta Garbo in Flesh and the Devil *(1927) photographed in luminous black and white by William Daniels, who created similar effects for the same duo in* Queen Christina *(top). Above: Clive Brook and Marlene Dietrich in* Shanghai Express, *shot under Lee Garmes' exotic lighting*

post-war period he returned behind the camera to work with Hitchcock, Ophuls, Wyler and Ray, among many other directors.

Whereas the Thirties and early Forties saw William Daniels' career reflect, and in some measure determine, the MGM house style, his post-war work with Jules Dassin could not have been more different. *Brute Force* (1947) and *The Naked City* (1948) were starkly realistic pictures for Hollywood, and though Daniels would later be reunited with two of his favourite directors, Clarence Brown and George Cukor, he responded with expertise and enthusiasm to the idea of shooting in the streets, over-exposing the new extra-fast film to adjust the contrast between daylight exteriors and (deliberately) drab interiors.

The Forties was the decade of the *film noir* whose principal visual characteristic was, as the name implies, a predominance of dark settings sparingly illuminated by 'low-key' lighting. The 'key' light is the primary light on a set (all other lamps in use are collectively termed 'fill' lighting). To position the key light as near to the floor of the set as possible was to create an effect of long, tall shadows, obscure shapes and dark enigmatic faces. The atmos-

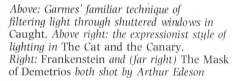

Above: Garmes' familiar technique of filtering light through shuttered windows in Caught. *Above right: the expressionist style of lighting in* The Cat and the Canary.
Right: Frankenstein *and (far right)* The Mask of Demetrios *both shot by Arthur Edeson*

phere evoked in this way was unique but the techniques had been around Hollywood ever since cameramen like Karl Struss, Eugen Schüfftan, Karl Freund and Franz Planer had introduced elements of the German Expressionist style into their work.

One of the earliest beneficiaries of this shadowy, often sinister, use of black and white had been Universal, whose cycle of horror films in the Thirties was clearly influenced by the German horror movies of a decade or so earlier. On the staff of Universal at that time was the cinematographer Arthur Edeson, who had begun his film career with Douglas Fairbanks Sr and had pioneered the use of filming on location with the unwieldy new sound cameras.

By the time Edeson had completed his first (war) film at Universal (*All Quiet on the Western Front*, 1930), the studio's style in horror films was a tamer version of the fiercely expressionistic films like Paul Leni's *The Cat and the Canary* (1927). Edeson photographed *Frankenstein* (1931), *The Old Dark House* (1932) and *The Invisible Man* (1933) and confirmed his reputation as one of the finest black-and-white cameramen of his generation.

When the vogue for low-key lighting resurfaced in the Forties, Edeson assimilated it to the prevalent house style at Warners, where he worked from 1936 to 1947. His camerawork on *The Maltese Falcon* (1941), *Casablanca* (1942) and *The Mask of Demetrios* (1944) bears evidence of the *noir* influence, but is at the same time a glossy refinement of the distinctive Warners visual style pioneered by Tony Gaudio and Sol Polito in gangster films and melodramas throughout the Thirties.

Another survivor from the earliest days, and a man of arguably greater talent than Edeson, was John F. Seitz. During the Twenties, Seitz was one of the highest-paid cameramen in Hollywood. An expert in the use of intense, low-key lighting, Seitz found his perfect professional match in the director Rex Ingram. The partnership yielded three extraordinary films, each of them displaying an unprecedented visual flair and sophistication: *The Four Horsemen of the Apocalypse* (1921), *Scaramouche* (1923) and *Mare Nostrum* (1926).

In the Forties, Seitz found himself working

with Preston Sturges at Paramount. He photographed *Sullivan's Travels* (1941), *The Miracle of Morgan's Creek* (1943) and *Hail the Conquering Hero* (1944), but, though these comedies were minor masterpieces in the genre, they did not make exceptional demands on Seitz's unique talent for 'painting with light' (to borrow cinematographer John Alton's phrase).

Working with Billy Wilder, however, Seitz formed a relationship that was as fruitful, in its own way, as the one with Ingram in the Twenties. Their first film together was *Five Graves to Cairo* (1943) which genuinely looks as if it had been lit in a silent-film style. The whole screen is suffused with patterns of light, filtered through shutters into darkish interiors. For *Double Indemnity* (1944), Wilder's only *film noir* proper, Seitz was a logical and happy choice. The scene where Fred MacMurray calls at Barbara Stanwyck's house to discuss the insurance on her husband is a fine example of the almost tangible atmosphere Seitz's delicate lighting could create.

There followed *The Lost Weekend* (1945) and *Sunset Boulevard* (1950), in which Seitz was faced with the challenge of suggesting 'private worlds' for Ray Milland's desperate alcoholic and Gloria Swanson's faded movie star. He succeeded admirably but, looking back on his career, Seitz averred that *Five Graves to Cairo* was his favourite piece of work.

The advent of three-strip Technicolor in the mid-to-late Thirties was of major importance in the history of cinematography, but colour

itself was no novelty and many cameramen had previous experience of working in the medium. On the whole, Hollywood was slow to switch to colour and it was not until the late Forties that a distinctive mastery of the new colour technology could be detected in the work of the cinematographers. There were, of course, those who had gained early experience: Ray Rennahan, for example, was the Technicolor company's full-time cameraman. He filmed the first feature in Technicolor, *Becky Sharp* (1935), and was adviser on *Gone With the Wind* (1939).

James Wong Howe shot his first Technicolor sequence in an otherwise black-and-white musical, *Hollywood Party* (1934) and in 1938 photographed his first Technicolor feature, *The Adventures of Tom Sawyer*, for David Selznick. Howe's career behind the camera had begun in 1921 and during the silent era he worked with a couple of cameramen-turned-directors – Victor Fleming and Bert Glennon. His credits in the Thirties include films with Howard Hawks, W.S. Van Dyke and John Cromwell, but it is the photography in his Forties work that is most memorable.

Howe shot some of the classics of the *film noir*: Lang's *Hangmen Also Die!* (1943), *Pursued* (dir. Raoul Walsh, 1947) and *He Ran All the Way* (dir. John Berry, 1951). *Pursued* is a dark and sombre Western that depends on effective visual devices to express childhood traumas, whereas *He Ran All the Way* is set in the rainswept streets of New York under the pitiless light of streetlamps. Both films demonstrate Howe's versatility in black and white, but the latter film also reveals his ingenuity: for, in the course of a scene in an indoor swimming pool, Howe (standing up to his waist in water) utilized the daylight reflected from the water's surface to add a strange texture to the actors' faces. He considered this among his finest work, but he was no less inventive when shooting *Body and Soul* (dir. Robert Rossen, 1947). While a team of extra cameramen shot footage of the climactic boxing match from a distance, Howe took advantage of his height (he was a little over five foot) to duck and weave in and out of the fight, even using the old silent cameramen's trick of being pushed around on roller skates to get his close-ups.

By the end of the Forties, colour was becom-

Above: shooting The Miracle of Morgan's Creek *with Eddie Bracken and Betty Hutton; second from left is the cameraman John Seitz, at far right of film crew is the director Preston Sturges. Above right: Seitz's distinctive silent-cinema lighting for Ramon Novarro in* Scaramouche. *Right: essentially the same lighting style in* Five Graves to Cairo

ing firmly established in Hollywood. 20th Century-Fox were leaders in the field but all the major studios displayed confidence in colour. Henry King's musical *Margie* (1946), photographed by Charles Clarke, is an outstanding example and one that lacks the garishness occasionally found in other Fox musicals of the Forties. The finest cameraman on the Fox lot at the time was undoubtedly Leon Shamroy whose skills are nowhere better exemplified than in *Wilson* (1944), Henry King's biopic about the US President who fought to establish the League of Nations.

Shamroy worked closely with Technicolor's Ray Rennahan on films like *Down Argentine Way* (1940) and *That Night in Rio* (1941) and this collaboration gave him the grounding that was to make him the premier Technicolor cameraman of the Fifties: *The Snows of Kilimanjaro* (1952), *The Robe* (1953), *South Pacific* (1958) and *Porgy and Bess* (1959).

Black-and-white cinematography did not go out of fashion overnight. At some studios in the Forties 'quality' meant black-and-white pictures. It is significant, for example, that the major Goldwyn productions of the decade (*Little Foxes*, *The Westerner* and *The Best Years of Our Lives*) were all black-and-white produc-

tions and that the falling-off of the Goldwyn style appears to coincide with the growth of colour features. For black-and-white cinematography, Goldwyn's top cameraman Gregg Toland was much in demand and has become one of the art's most famous practitioners.

Toland had begun as an assistant to Arthur Edeson in the Twenties, but it was with *Dead End* (1937) and *Wuthering Heights* (1939) that he made his reputation and did much to contribute to the elegant house style of Goldwyn films.

The critical acclaim showered on *Citizen Kane* (1940) has tended to exaggerate Toland's status as a cinematographer. He did not, of course, invent deep-focus photography, which had existed from the beginnings of cinema, but he did perfect a system of adding drilled metal stops ('Waterhouse stops') to the lens in order to alter depth of focus while the camera was on the move. Toland is also to be credited with being one of the first cameramen to use the new fast film stocks introduced in the Forties and his work on *Citizen Kane* is nothing if not innovative. Camera style rarely calls attention to itself and, as a result, Toland's work tends to appear more self-conscious than that of his fellow cinematographers. In *The Grapes of Wrath* (1940), for example, the viewer is made conscious of the way the light falls across Henry Fonda's face, making a composition. *Wuthering Heights* also suffers from direction and camerawork that is inclined to strike poses rather than move the story along.

RKO was the other bastion of black and white in the Forties. The indelible image of the studio was *film noir* thrillers and the horror films produced by Val Lewton. This consistency of style is, as always, the result of several contributory factors, but since so much depends on the distinctive, chiaroscuro lighting, the work of Nicholas Musaraca on such films as *Cat People* (1942), *The Seventh Victim* (1943), *The Spiral Staircase* (1945), *The Locket* (1946), and *Out of the Past* (1947) must be ranked alongside his more frequently praised contemporaries. The Forties was, after all, the last great period of black-and-white motion pictures. They just will not make them like that again.   MARTYN AUTY

With acknowledgments to John Gillett for his assistance

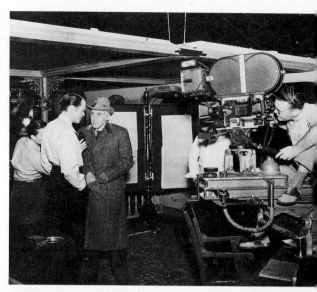

Top: James Wong Howe supervising an outdoor shot on Hombre (1967) starring Paul Newman. Top right: Gregg Toland lines up a shot on Citizen Kane beneath the extra-low ceilings that deliberately forced the camera into the corners of the set. Right: Leon Shamroy's delicate lighting on Wilson. Below: The Spiral Staircase shot by Nicholas Musuraca

Oscars for the British

In Britain in the Forties, cameramen had emerged as major creative artists in their own right. Freddie Francis, a leading cameraman in post-war Britain and director of several notable horror movies, recalls what distinguished the roles of British cameramen from their opposite numbers in Hollywood

I have been a cameraman and director all my life, but when I began in the business in 1939, the cinematographer worked for the studio first and the director second. This meant that cameramen could be taken off one production and put on another, just like that – they were interchangeable. But things did change because the studio system, such as it was, was never as rigid as that in Hollywood. And for this reason British cameramen tended to free themselves from the system sooner than their American counterparts.

When Jack Cardiff won an Oscar for his photography on *Black Narcissus* (dir. Michael Powell, Emeric Pressburger, 1947), it gave everybody hope that you didn't have to be American to win awards and those of us who were cameramen in Britain were becoming a force to be reckoned with.

Later on Robert Krasker won an Oscar for *The Third Man* (1949). He had done his training under Korda at London Films where he was camera operator on *Rembrandt*, *Things to Come* (both 1936), *The Four Feathers* (1939) and *The Thief of Bagdad* (1940). He was already pretty familiar, then, with the Technicolor process and made a fine job of *Henry V* (1945). On *The Third Man* Krasker took everything off level and made the film exciting for its use of odd angles. He was greatly encouraged by the director Carol Reed, in much the same way as David Lean encouraged Freddie Young. It all comes down to a director having confidence in his cameraman and then giving him the freedom to create.

On the whole the vogue for low-key lighting in Hollywood did not influence British cameramen too much, though *Brighton Rock* (1947), photographed by Harry Waxman, did favour lots of shadows and contrasting black and white. What seemed to have more influence in Britain was the continental style of Georges Périnal, who was brought over by Korda to shoot *The Private Life of Henry VIII* (1933) and stayed for the rest of the decade. Everyone loved Périnal's style and it contributed enormously to the lavish look of Korda's productions. After all, a cameraman's job is to give the director the best canvas on which to paint his picture.

From an interview with THE MOVIE. *February 1980*

John Garfield

Reading about the life and work of John Garfield can be a depressing experience. He died young in tragic circumstances and his reputation seems to have hardened into a set of tired clichés: East Side kid makes good; the first angry young man; the original rebel without a cause; the forerunner of Brando and Dean . . . and so on. There is now a heavy layer of glib journalistic varnish over his whole career and it has become difficult to believe in a real man

that the young love to hear but seldom dare to act on. Above all he was attractive – passionate, intense, sullen, even insolent, his vitality and his sexual drive almost burst out of the screen. *This* is what he had in common with the young Brando, with Dean, with Valentino in his day and with the Finney of *Saturday Night and Sunday Morning* (1960).

His success as Micky inevitably led to similar roles – a boxer on the run in *They Made Me a Criminal* (1939), an ex-reform-school boy in *Dust Be My Destiny* (1939) and a broke and impractical inventor in *Saturday's Children* (1940). But he also played a variety of other parts from the war-blinded veteran of *Destination Tokyo* (1943) to Lana Turner's murderous lover in *The Postman Always Rings Twice* (1946). He formed his own production company for a brief period during which time he starred in *Body and Soul* (1947) as a boxer corrupted by success.

But the rebel label stuck, and his unhappy experiences with the House Un-American Activities Committee, which arose mainly from his habit of supporting liberal causes (while not actually accused of anything, he was blacklisted as an unfriendly witness), sealed the stereotype. Unable to obtain work in Hollywood he returned to the theatre and ironically achieved his ambition to play the lead in *Golden Boy* only a few weeks before his death of a heart attack at the age of 39.

Garfield was a serious, hard-working actor who might well have matured into a character player in the Tracy class. He deserves to be remembered as a talented and engaging man, not merely as a symbol of adolescent rebellion.

BRENDA DAVIES

As so often happens the publicity and press stories about Garfield had a basis in fact. He was born Jules Garfinkel (Julie to his friends) on New York's Lower East Side in 1913. His parents were Jewish immigrants from Russia and his mother died when he was seven. He came close to becoming a juvenile delinquent before being influenced by a brilliant teacher who was able to channel his excess energy into acting. As a youth he bummed across the States with a friend, taking whatever job came up and learning the realities of working life.

He then returned to New York and joined the Group Theatre in 1934. He was featured in many of their productions, but when they produced Odet's *Golden Boy* in 1937 Garfield, who had originally been offered the lead, was relegated to a supporting role. This disappointment led to his signing a seven-year contract with Warner Brothers who had been making him offers for some time. He insisted, however, that he should be allowed to make a return to the theatre every year.

At 24, therefore, he was on his way to Hollywood, a successful young actor in line for featured roles with a big company, his theatrical career safeguarded by contract. Within a year he was a star, thanks to Warners who cast him as the rebellious young musician Micky Borden in *Four Daughters* (1938).

This was where the Garfield legend began –

John Garfield – the loser – in We Were Strangers *(top),* They Made Me a Criminal *(above) and* He Ran All the Way *(right)*

the interweaving of fact and fiction that led, in the end, to such a confusion between the actor and his roles that his name now stands for an attitude rather than a man. Garfield himself had little reason to be bitter or rebellious. He had had a tough childhood, he had seen the poverty and distress of the Depression years and his association with the Group Theatre indicated his left-wing sympathies. But he had been very lucky, was happily married and enjoyed his work. It was Micky Borden who was bitter and twisted. Micky was a cynical no-hoper who believed that the world was against him and who proudly wore an outsize chip on his shoulder. His eruption into the sweetly antiseptic world of *Four Daughters* was nicely calculated but far from new. He was the 'Heathcliff figure' that recurs regularly in romantic fiction and his appeal to young girls, both in the film and the audience, had little to do with his views or his talent but everything to do with sex. Micky was the personification of a teenage (at the time the word would have been 'bobbysoxer') dream. Scruffy and unshaven, a cigarette drooping from his lip, he sat at the piano despising everyone and articulating all the anti-authority arguments

Filmography

1933 Footlight Parade (extra). **'38** Four Daughters. **'39** Blackwell's Island; They Made Me a Criminal; Juarez; Daughters Courageous; Dust Be My Destiny; Four Wives. **'40** Castle on the Hudson (GB: Years Without Days); Saturday's Children; Flowing Gold; East of the River. **'41** The Sea Wolf; Out of the Fog; Dangerously They Live. **'42** Tortilla Flat. **'43** Air Force; Thank Your Lucky Stars; The Fallen Sparrow; Destination Tokyo. **'44** Between Two Worlds; Hollywood Canteen. **'45** Pride of the Marines (GB: Forever in Love). **'46** The Postman Always Rings Twice; Nobody Lives Forever; Humoresque. **'47** Body and Soul; Daisy Kenyon (guest); Gentleman's Agreement. **'49** Force of Evil; Jigsaw (USA retitling for TV: Gun Moll); We Were Strangers. **'50** Under My Skin; The Breaking Point. **'51** He Ran All the Way.

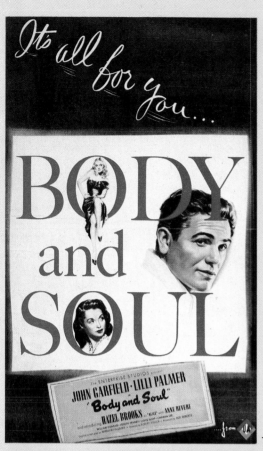

It's all for you...

BODY and SOUL

The ENTERPRISE STUDIOS present
JOHN GARFIELD · LILLI PALMER
'Body and Soul'
HAZEL BROOKS as 'ALICE' with **ANNE REVERE**
and introducing
WILLIAM CONRAD · JOSEPH PEVNEY · LLOYD GOFF · CANADA LEE
Original screen play by ABRAHAM POLONSKY · Directed by ROBERT ROSSEN · Produced by BOB ROBERTS
...from UA

Charley Davis, middleweight champion of the world, has agreed to 'throw' his last fight for cash. On the eve of the fight he visits his mother's house where his estranged girlfriend Peg lives. He takes her in his arms but his mother tells him to leave (1).

Charley recalls the past when, as an ambitious Jewish boy from New York's Lower East Side, he graduated from the amateur boxing ranks with the encouragement of his manager Quinn and his pal Shorty (2). These were the days when he had Peg's love (3) – before he signed on with the crooked promoter Roberts (4), before success and money went to his head. Later Shorty had told him that the fight which made him champion had been fixed, and warned him to break from Roberts. Rescued by Charley from a beating by one of Roberts' men, Shorty was knocked down and killed by a taxi shortly after.

Back in the present, Charley goes into the ring intending to lose the fight. But he recovers his integrity in the final round, knocks his opponent out (5), loses his money but wins back Peg and his self-respect.

Below left: James Wong Howe gets a close action shot of the fight

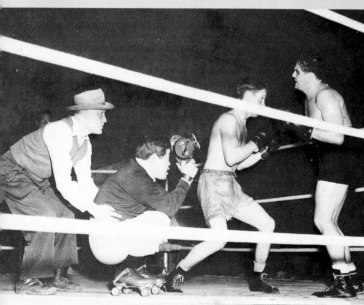

Directed by Robert Rossen, 1947
Prod co: Enterprise Studio. **prod:** Bob Roberts. **sc:** Abraham Polonsky. **photo:** James Wong Howe. **ed:** Robert Parrish. **art dir:** Nathan Juran, Edward J. Boyle. **mus:** Hugo Friedhofer. **mus dir:** Rudolph Polk. **mus cond:** Emil Newman. **song:** 'Body and Soul', by Johnny Green, Edward Heyman, Robert Sour, Frank Eyton. **montages:** Gunther V. Fritsch. **ed adviser:** Francis Lyon. **ass dir:** Robert Aldrich. **r/t:** 106 minutes.
Cast: John Garfield (*Charley Davis*), Lilli Palmer (*Peg Born*), Hazel Brooks (*Alice*), Anne Revere (*Anna Davis*), William Conrad (*Quinn*), Joseph Pevney (*Shorty Polaski*), Canada Lee (*Ben Chaplin*), Lloyd Goff (*Roberts*), Art Smith (*David Davis*), James Burke (*Arnold*), Virginia Gregg (*Irma*), Peter Virgo (*Drummer*), Joe Devlin (*Prince*), Shimin Ruskin (*grocer*), Tim Ryan (*Shelton*), Mary Currier (*Miss Tedder*), Milton Kibbee (*Dan*), Artie Dorrell (*Jack Marlowe*), Cy Ring (*Victor*), Glen Lee (*Marino*), John Indrisano (*referee*), Dan Tobey (*fight announcer*).

Body and Soul would have been just like any other boxing picture but for the inspiration of cameraman James Wong Howe. Robert Parrish, who won an Oscar for editing the film, reveals how it managed to pack a bigger punch than any of its predecessors

Body and Soul was originally titled *Tiger, Tiger, Burning Bright* and based on the life story of Barney Ross, three-time welter-weight boxing champion of the world, war hero and model for American youth. When Ross confessed to addiction to heroin, which he was first given as a pain-killer during World War II, the executives at the brand-new Enterprise Studio decided to cancel the picture. Robert Rossen, who had been assigned to direct, threatened to sue unless production went ahead as scheduled. So the title was changed and announcements were made saying that the picture had nothing to do with Barney Ross.

Production started three weeks later and went smoothly until a week before the end. On the Sunday afternoon before the last week of shooting, Rossen, James Wong Howe (the cameraman), and I (the editor) ran the cut material. When we finished, Rossen said:

'I'm worried about the end of the picture. Polonsky (the screenwriter) wants Garfield [John Garfield was in the star part as boxer Charley Davis] to win the big fight and tell the gangsters to go to hell. I'm not so sure he's right. I have an idea that maybe the picture should end with Garfield losing the fight and being shot by the gangsters as he leaves the stadium.'

'Why don't you shoot it both ways?' asked Jimmy Howe.

'I hardly have time to shoot *one* ending,' said Rossen. 'I have to shoot the final fight next week and I haven't made up my mind how I'm going to end the picture. It's an expensive set with lots of extras. I don't know how I'm going to get enough coverage within the schedule, even if I don't shoot my new ending.'

Jimmy and I sat silent for a few moments, then Jimmy said, 'I may have an idea for you.' Rossen looked at him hopefully. 'Don't tease me,' he said. Jimmy got up and started to walk around the projection room. Finally he spoke: 'The war produced a lot of good cameramen, but none of them can get in the union unless his father is a cameraman.'

'What does that have to do with the end of our picture?' Rossen said hoarsely.

Jimmy went on as if Rossen hadn't spoken. 'I'd like to pick four good ex-combat cameramen from the war and get them waivers from the union to work on this one job. I'm sure I can do it. We'll give each of these guys an Eyemo hand-held camera and 1000 feet of negative each morning. We'll tell 'em that they can shoot anything they want as long as they don't turn in any unexposed negative. We'll have 4000 feet of surprises to choose from each day. Most of it will probably be unusable, but the law of averages will give us some shots that we could never get shooting in the normal way.' He paused while Rossen eyed him suspiciously.

'Go on,' said Rossen.

'Parrish and I will run everything each evening and put the good footage aside. Then, when we're all finished shooting in the stadium, we'll run everything with you and Abe and make an ending to the picture from it. I'm sure the combat guys I pick will give us some unique material, and when cut with what you and I shoot, we'll have a hell of an ending.' He looked at Rossen with his expressionless eyes, 'It'll work Bob, you just make any ending you want in the cutting room instead of on the set.'

Rossen grumbled, 'And what will you and I be doing while these four combat cameramen are running around shooting stuff that's mostly unusable?'

'We'll be shooting close-ups of Garfield and the other principals. I'll put on a pair of roller skates and let the grip pull me around so that our stuff will have the same quality as the combat footage. If a few shots are out of focus, so much the better. We'll have a real fight on the screen for the first time.'

Rossen finally agreed and it worked just the way Jimmy predicted. I got 12,000 feet from the combat cameramen and 5000 from Jimmy Howe and Rossen. We cut the 17,000 down to 600 and Rossen shot two endings. When it came time to decide which one to use, Polonsky and Rossen had their private fight and Rossen lost. The movie that almost wasn't made ended the way Polonsky had originally written it and the fledgling Enterprise Studio wound up with their first successful film.

ROBERT PARRISH

Condensed material produced with permission of The Bodley Head from Growing Up in Hollywood *by Robert Parrish*

3

5

Final page from camera script of *Body and Soul*: REVISED 1/13/47

Scene no.   *Page no.*
                                                                      121

294   CLOSE SHOT – CHARLEY IN RING
        his face dazed, sweaty, bloody.

295   FULL SHOT – RING
        as the pandemonium moves from the crowd into the ring, the disappointed gamblers, the squad of cops surrounding the winner.

296   CLOSE SHOT – RINGSIDE
        As Charley comes through the ropes and down and is congratulated by the joyous Arnold.

297   AISLE PANNING SHOT
        Peg fights her way through the crowd.

298   CORRIDOR AND RAMP IN ARENA
        As policemen form a line to keep the excited crowd from pouring through the corridor, which leads to the dressing rooms, Charley and his entourage come through the police line and down the steps into the corridor. As Peg reaches him, locks arms with him, Roberts is waiting. As Charley comes by, Roberts turns to him. In the b.g. we see Quinn and Alice looking over the line of police. The spectators yell to Charley as they pass.

ROBERTS
(ironically)
Congratulations, Champ!

Still at the height of his emotion, Charley wheels, looks furiously at Roberts, and takes a swing at him. Roberts catches Charley's gloved hand and pulls him in close.

299   TIGHT TWO SHOT – ROBERTS, CHARLEY
        To the bystanders an ordinary conversation.

ROBERTS
What makes you think you can get away with this?

CHARLEY
(smiling)
Whatta you going to do, kill me?
Everybody dies.

He and Peg break away from Roberts through the reporters and into the depth of the corridor.

FADE OUT:

THE END

Key films of 1942

L'Assassin Habite au 21 (*The Killer Lives at No. 21*). France. **prod co:** Continental Films. **prod:** J.A. Liote. **dir:** Henri-Georges Clouzot. **sc:** Stanislas-André Steeman, Henri-Georges Clouzot, from a story by Stanislas-André Steeman. **photo:** Armand Thirard. **art dir:** André Andrejew. **mus:** Maurice Yvain. **with:** Pierre Fresnay, Suzy Delair, Jean Tissier, Pierre Larquey, Noël Roquevert, René Génin.
Clouzot's first feature as a director and one of this three adaptations from the novels of S-A. Steeman. Fresnay is the detective assigned to reveal the true identity of the self-advertised murderer 'M. Durand' from amongst the lodgers of a Parisian boarding house – only to find himself faced with three guilty men.

The Battle of Midway; directed by John Ford – see special feature in Chapter 22.

Casablanca. USA. **prod co:** Warner Bros. **prod:** Hal Wallis. **dir:** Michael Curtiz. **sc:** J.J. Epstein, P. G. Epstein, Howard Koch, from a play by Murray Burnett, Joan Alison. **photo:** Arthur Edeson. **ed:** Owen Marks. **mus:** Max Steiner. **song:** Herman Hopfeld. **mus dir:** Leo F. Forbstein. **with:** Humphrey Bogart, Ingrid Bergman, Claude Rains, Peter Lorre, Sydney Greenstreet, Paul Henreid, Conrad Veidt.
'You must remember this . . .' Sam plays it again as (war)time goes by in Rick's American Café. Bogie and Bergman replay their doomed romance to its tearful airport finale. This classic combination of intrigue, excitement, suspense and humour won three Academy Awards.

The Cat People; directed by Jacques Tourner – see special feature in Chapter 36.

The Foreman Went to France. Britain. **prod co:** Ealing Studios. **prod:** Michael Balcon. **dir:** Charles Frend. **sc:** Angus McPhail, John Dighton, Leslie Arliss. **photo:** Wilkie Cooper. **ed:** Robert Hamer. **art dir:** Tom Morahan. **mus:** William Walton. **mus dir:** Ernest Irving. **with:** Tommy Trinder, Constance Cummings, Clifford Evans, Robert Morley, Gordon Jackson, Ernest Milton.
A Welsh foreman's secret mission provides the basis for one of Britain's more populist wartime films. Charles Frend used his talents as a director of action films to bring to life this realistic drama behind enemy lines.

Der Grosse König (*The Great King*). Germany. **prod co:** Tobis. **dir/sc:** Veit Harlan. **photo:** Bruno Mondi. **ed:** Franz von Puttkammer. **art dir:** Erich Zander, Karl Machus. **mus:** Hans-Otto Borgmann. **sd:** Hans Rutten. **with:** Otto Gebühr, Kristina Söderbaum, Paul Wegener, Gustav Fröhlich, Hans Nielson, Claus Clausen.
This was the last of several Third Reich films that celebrated Frederick the Great's life and military campaigns, and was a clear allegory of Hitler's leadership. Goebbels said of it 'the film works extremely well as political education. We need this today. We live in a time which could do with more of Frederick's spirit'.

Hellzapoppin; directed by H.C. Potter – see special feature in Chapter 35.

Himlaspelet (*The Road to Heaven*). Sweden. **prod co:** Wivefilm. **prod:** Per Önner. **dir:** Alf Sjöberg. **sc:** Alf Sjöberg, Rune Lindström, from a story by Rune Lindström. **photo:** Gösta Roosling. **ed:** Oscar Rosander. **art dir:** Arne Åkermark. **mus:** Lillebror Söderlundh. **with:** Rune Lindström, Eivor Landström, Anders Hendrikson, Holger Löwenadler, Gudrun Bost.
Sjöberg's classic medieval tale follows author-actor Lindström's quest for heaven by way of a part-realistic, part-symbolic pilgrimage through faith, corruption and repentance. A highly stylized film whose core of religious mythology pre-figures the work of Ingmar Bergman.

In Which We Serve. Britain. **prod co:** Two Cities Films. **prod:** Noel Coward. **assoc prod:** Anthony Havelock-Allan. **dir:** Noel Coward, David Lean. **sc/mus:** Noel Coward. **photo:** Ronald Neame. **ed:** Thelma Myers. **art dir:** David Rawnsley. **sd:** C.C. Stevens. **with:** Noel Coward, John Mills, Bernard Miles, Celia Johnson, Joyce Carey, Kay Walsh, Michael Wilding.
The lives of the crew of a sunken destroyer in the Mediterranean are reconstructed through flashbacks to show how all men may contribute to the war. It was very much a product of the 'Dunkirk spirit' and has been described by the critic Raymond Durgnat as an 'archetypal essay in the stiff upper lip, bravely bleak for its times'.

The Magnificent Ambersons. USA. **prod co:** Mercury/RKO. **prod dir:** Orson Welles. **sc:** Orson Welles, from the novel by Booth Tarkington. **photo:** Stanley Cortez. **ed:** Robert Wise. **art dir:** Mark-Lee Kirk. **mus:** Bernard Herrmann. **with:** Joseph Cotten, Dolores Costello, Anne Baxter, Tim Holt, Agnes Moorehead, Ray Collins.

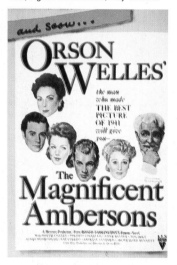

Welles' ambitious fresco of family conflict portrays an American dynasty in decline. Despite its savage cutting by RKO and considerable reworking by Robert Wise – without Welles' permission – it was a critical success.

The Major and the Minor. USA. **prod co:** Paramount. **prod:** Arthur Hornblow Jr. **dir:** Billy Wilder. **sc:** Billy Wilder, Charles Brackett, from the play *Connie Goes Home* by Edward Childs Carpenter. **photo:** Leo Tover. **ed:** Doane Harrison. **art dir:** Hans Dreier, Roland Anderson. **mus:** Robert Emmett Dolan. **with:** Ginger Rogers, Ray Milland, Rita Johnson, Robert Benchley, Diana Lynn, Edward Fielding.
A dazzling comedy of disguise in which a romance flowers between Milland, as a short-sighted army major, and Rogers, who hilariously
sustains an impersonation of a 12-year-old child. The film bears Wilder's first credit as a director in Hollywood.

Mrs Miniver. USA. **prod co:** MGM. **prod:** Sidney Franklin. **dir:** William Wyler. **sc:** Arthur Wimperis, George Froeschel, James Hilton, Claudine West. **photo:** Joseph Ruttenberg. **ed:** Harold F. Kress. **art dir:** Cedric Gibbons. **mus:** Herbert Stothart. **with:** Greer Garson, Walter Pidgeon, Teresa Wright, Richard Ney, Dame May Whitty, Henry Travers, Reginald Owen, Henry Wilcoxon, Rhys Williams.
A Hollywood portrait of how a British middle-class family copes with the trials and tribulations of war. Wyler's view of war-struck Britain is a peculiar never-never land of village fêtes and bombed churches, but the film aroused a good deal of support in America for the British war effort.

Ossessione. Italy. **prod co:** ICI. **prod:** Camillo Pagani. **dir:** Luchino Visconti. **sc:** Luchino Visconti, Mario Alicata, Giuseppe De Santis, Gianni Puccini, from the novel *The Postman Always Rings Twice* by James M. Cain. **photo:** Aldo Tonti, Domenico Scala. **ed:** Mario Serandrei. **art dir:** Gino Franzi. **mus:** Giuseppe Rosati. **with:** Clara Calamai, Massimo Girotti, Juan de Landa, Dhia Cristiani, Elio Marcuzzo, Vittorio Duse.
This film of love and murder has been acclaimed as the harbinger of the neo-realist style in its use of locations, its emphasis on grittiness in players and sets and its portrayal of greed and malice as underlying human motives. The image of Italian life it presented did not meet with the Fascist Party's approval and the film was banned until after the war. In 1946 the source novel was filmed in Hollywood with Lana Turner and John Garfield.

They Died With Their Boots On. USA. **prod co:** Warner Bros-First National. **prod:** Hal B. Wallis. **dir:** Raoul Walsh. **sc:** Wally Kline, Aeneas MacKenzie. **photo:** Bert Glennon. **ed:** William Holmes. **art dir:** John Hughes. **mus:** Max Steiner. **with:** Errol Flynn, Olivia de Havilland, Arthur Kennedy, Charles Grapewin, Gene Lockhart.

A glorious example of the 'print-the-legend' biopic, this romanticized account of the life and death of George Armstrong Custer uses many cavalry-movie clichés and creates even more. The result is a palatable and durable myth of the West.

This Gun for Hire. USA. **prod co:** Paramount. **prod:** Richard M. Blumenthal. **dir:** Frank Tuttle. **sc:** Albert Maltz, W.R. Burnett, from a story by Graham Greene. **photo:** John Seitz. **ed:** Archie Marshek. **art dir:** Hans Dreier. **mus:** David Buttolph. **with:** Veronica Lake, Robert Preston, Laird Cregar, Alan Ladd.
Harsh lighting contrasts, laconic dialogue and Ladd's edgy performance as the double-crossed hired gun make this a masterly film noir. With Lake's slinky support, he exposes an un-American conspiracy.

To Be or Not To Be. USA. **prod co:** Romaine Film Productions/United Artists. **prod/dir:** Ernst Lubitsch. **sc:** Edwin Justus Mayer, from a story by Ernst Lubitsch, Melchior Lengyel. **photo:** Rudolph Maté. **ed:** Dorothy Spencer. **art dir:** Vincent Korda. **mus:** Miklós Rózsa. **mus dir:** Werner Heyman. **with:** Carole Lombard, Jack Benny, Robert Stack, Felix Bressart, Lionel Atwill, Sig Ruman, Tom Dugan.
A Shakespearian troupe turn their questionable talents to the impersonation of German officers in order to help the Polish Resistance. The film was pilloried on its initial release for 'bad taste', despite its treatment of fascism through farce.

Les Visiteurs du Soir (*The Devil's Own Enemy*). France. **prod:** André Paulvé. **dir:** Marcel Carné. **sc:** Jacques Prévert, Pierre Laroche. **photo:** Roger Hubert. **ed:** Henri Rust. **art dir:** Georges Wakhévitch, Alexandre Trauner. **mus:** Maurice Thiriet, Joseph Kosma. **with:** Arletty, Jules Berry, Marie Déa, Fernand Ledoux, Alain Cuny.

Carné switched abruptly from pre-war, downbeat poetic realism to escapist poetic fantasy with this celebrated medieval romance, in which one of two emissarian sent back to earth by the Devil to disrupt a courtly wedding falls in love with the bride-to-be.

Went the Day Well? Britain. **prod co:** Ealing. **prod:** Michael Balcon. **dir:** Alberto Cavalcanti. **sc:** John Dighton, Diana Morgan, Angus MacPhaill, from a story by Graham Greene. **photo:** Wilkie Cooper. **ed:** Sidney Cole. **art dir:** Tom Morahan. **mus:** William Walton. **with:** Leslie Banks, Basil Sydney, Frank Lawton, Elizabeth Allan.
Cavalcanti diagnoses the potentially corrupting effect of war on the British psyche in this, for its time, uncommonly ambiguous film. It focuses on the cold-blooded revenge wreaked by mild-mannered villagers on the disguised German paratroopers who have occupied their homes.

The Young Mr Pitt. Britain. **prod co:** 20th Century Productions. **prod:** Edward Black. **dir:** Carol Reed. **sc:** Sidney Gilliat, Frank Launder. **photo:** Frederick Young. **ed:** R.E. Dearing. **art dir:** Vetchinsky. **mus dir:** Louis Levy. **with:** Robert Donat, Robert Morley, Phyllis Calvert, John Mills, Raymond Lovell, Max Adrian.
Writers Launder and Gilliat struggled vainly to humanize this portrayal of Pitt and his patriotic rallying call to counter the Napoleonic threat. The film is a deliberate inspirational parallel to the wartime situation and British history is rewritten accordingly.

Chapter 25
Trouble in Hollywood

When the war was over the movies enjoyed a boom, but a new battle was about to be waged – this time for the political soul of Hollywood

There never was a year like 1946 for Hollywood. Servicemen waiting for demobilization were trapped in camps across America, eager for films to pass the time. When they finally got home, they were courting and going out to the movies. American cinemas sold more than 4000 million tickets – producing a box-office take of nearly $1700 million. The latter figure was not matched again until 1974, when cinemas sold only a quarter of the number of tickets. After the wonderful year of 1946, only inflation made Hollywood's take look good.

In the four years following the end of the war, however, Hollywood went from boom to nervous disarray, its structure radically altered by law, its morale shattered by paranoia, its audience thinned away. Those captive servicemen went home, married, built a suburban lifestyle away from the downtown cinemas. They wanted entertainment in the home and, when they could get it, they wanted television.

Lifestyles which had been denied by the Depression and the war were now embraced with wild relief. The women who had worked in the munitions factories went home, settled down, had babies and stopped going out to the distant, inconvenient movies.

Between 1946 and 1948, even before television was nationwide, movie admissions dropped by 16.9 per cent. In the inner councils of the industry, moguls and bankers alike saw estimates that the fall-off would exceed 25 per cent. They did not publish the figures, but they took action. In 1946, MGM had already decreed a slimming of its product. It was to be a little less long, a little less lavish. Anticipating keener competition for dwindling audiences, 20th Century-Fox concentrated its resources on fewer but bigger inducements to draw audiences back to the cinemas. Columbia and Universal, on the other hand, tried to make their product more glamorous. Everyone felt cold competition coming.

Fewer admissions were bad enough. Worse, for the majors, was the continuing interest of the US Department of Justice in the financing of Hollywood and in particular the cosy cartel operated by the big studios.

From the early Thirties, the Department of Justice had been trying to break the stranglehold of the majors over independent cinemas. Its aim was to force the film production and distribution companies to sell off their highly lucrative cinema divisions. Since most of the majors made almost all their money in film exhibition, rather than in distribution or production, Hollywood resisted as long as it could.

Cases were brought before the courts in 1938 and 1940 but the war delayed their impact. In 1946, the Department of Justice began to strip away the major privileges (and major profits) of the big-league motion-picture companies. The change was even more radical than most observers admit. Along with new tax laws (the biggest external influence on movies), the anti-trust decisions of the late

Forties changed the basis and nature of movie financing, and so of movie-making.

By 1946 the pattern of the business was changing: the small-town cinema owner was no longer confronted with a salesman who would make him take everything a studio might produce, on pain of getting nothing at all. He did not have to accept prices before seeing movies and he could bid competitively. It would be naive to suggest that this made for open competition in the movie business, but it did mean movies were not automatically guaranteed success. They had to convince cinema owners first.

Independent producers now had a better chance of selling their movies. The new tax laws made it wise for stars and star directors to form themselves into independent corporations. Frank Capra, making movies for Liberty Films, paid only corporation tax on earnings (at 60 per cent) instead of personal income tax (at the post-war rate of 90 per cent). If each movie project were a corporation in its own right, sold, when completed, to a distributor for a profit, then the profit would attract only 25 per cent capital-gains tax. The majors had to compete for these independent productions and for stars who also wanted their independence.

The majors were made to sell their cinema chains by a series of legal settlements reached between 1949 and 1959. These sales took away the largest element in profit and cash-flow from the studios. Banks were short of lending money in the immediate post-war period and were thus inclined to examine individual movie projects as well as corporate credits. In this way the idea of the 'bankable' star emerged. The strict hierarchy of first-run and second-run cinemas was shaken and this too altered the financial base of movie-making.

World War II had effectively closed most of

Above: at least the second musical remake of a mistaken-identity tale; this version was designed as a vehicle for the Brazilian star Carmen Miranda in the hope of capturing new audiences in Latin America. Below left: a contemporary advertisement (painted by John Falter) for bottled beers, showing the prominence of television in the 'average' American home at the beginning of the Fifties

Above: violence erupts during a strike by workers at the Warner Brothers studio in 1946. A similar strike at RKO (right) in the same year proved that, while the major studios were enjoying their most profitable year ever, discontent was widespread, particularly among the craft unions. Below: Adolphe Menjou, who, in 1947, warned the House Un-American Activities Committee of 'communist acting' that made propaganda 'by a look, by an inflection, by a change in the voice'. Below right: Walt Disney, who told the Committee that communists were even 'drawing' propaganda in cartoon studios

America's traditional markets for film, except Britain. Attempts were made to open up larger business in South America, notably with Carmen Miranda in musicals like *Down Argentine Way* (1940), *That Night in Rio* (1941) and *Weekend in Havana* (1944). Such moves did not, however, compensate for the loss of European markets. One of the problems with South America was the difficulty of shipping films there during wartime.

MGM had calculated rightly that the domestic US market was at saturation point in 1946. Abroad, American movies never had such a success as they did in the late Forties. But this did not bring money back to the studios.

When, in 1946, the world opened up again, only the USA had generous supplies of film stock – the raw materials with which to carry on the trade of film-making and win new markets. Alongside the 20 films made in the Soviet Union in 1948 and the mere 54 that Italy completed at the height of the neo-realist movement, Hollywood's total of 432 was staggering. Furthermore, the American film industry had a backlog of movies from the war years still unreleased in many foreign territories. Even though the US Department of Commerce announced 'only the movies which put America's best foot forward will be sent abroad', the stage was set for American domination of the world film trade.

There was a catch in this apparently open-ended market. American films covered the screens of Europe but the revenue was going back across the Atlantic and European exhibitors enjoyed none of the profits of their cinema boom. In 1946, the French authorities conceded that three-quarters of

the nation's screen time should be filled by Hollywood product, but in 1948 they insisted that only $3.6 million out of an annual $14 million take could be sent back to the USA. For their part, the British allowed $17 million to leave the country each year but $40 million remained blocked by foreign-exchange regulations. Hollywood needed the cash but could not touch it. In time these blocked funds would form the basis of 'runaway' productions – American movies made outside America. Until this money could be made into new movies, Hollywood had a wild but profitless success on its hands.

Back in California the system was breaking up: PRC, a minor major, collapsed and United Artists tore itself apart – Pickford and Chaplin bad-mouthing each other across the nation, threatening to sell their shares and suing their absentee partner David O. Selznick. When a masterpiece of a film like *Red River* (1948) went $12 million over budget, United Artists could not support it. The production passed to an independent company. Such visible troubles did not help confidence. As a result of their experiences after 1948, at least half a dozen banks left the movie industry alone.

Labour trouble was the next problem to hit Hollywood. Post-war prices demanded new wage scales. Clean-ups in the craft unions in the early Forties had made the usual studio policy of buying off the union leaders impracticable. Those leaders were fierce and liberal, yet at the same time they included men like Ronald Reagan.

All this change and trouble and decline made for bad nerves, especially where Wall Street bankers or government support were involved. It was this nervousness that produced the sordid business of blacklists and blackmail. The political paranoia in Hollywood in the late Forties was fed by the uncertainties that abounded in the industry.

Hollywood had been blooded politically in the Thirties, with the vicious resistance to the author and screenwriter Upton Sinclair who ran for Governor of California. Prominent figures within the industry had taken part in a campaign of blatantly reactionary propaganda. Its political mood was always conciliatory to those in power, eager to avoid trouble, dissension or scandal. The flimsy wartime alliance between the USA and the USSR was terminated with the end of the war. The Left was characterized as both enemy abroad and

enemy within. It was not surprising that when the House Un-American Activities Committee, bearing the banner of the right wing, came out to investigate, Hollywood caved in. HUAC, as it was generally known, calculated quite shrewdly that Hollywood names would make headlines, and resistance would be soft. They were right.

Early investigations in 1940 had been 'promising'. In 1947, HUAC opened its attack and from the start they had help from the studios. Jack L. Warner, eager to explain away a handful of pro-Soviet movies made during the war years, warned that communist writers were 'poking fun at our political system' and picking on rich men. Adolphe Menjou alerted the Committee to 'communist acting', which made propaganda, he said, 'by a look, by an inflection, by a change in the voice'. Walt Disney told how he had been pressured by communists (in the unlikely guise of the League of Women Voters) to accept communists. His evidence, however, was such manifest and hurtful nonsense that it had to be retracted by cable.

The Committee looked and sounded absurd. The Mississippi congressman John Rankin, a man whose vocabulary depended on the words 'kike' and 'nigra', delightedly discovered that the protesting liberals had something to hide. 'One of the names is June Havoc', he reported. 'We have found that her real name is June Hovick. Another is Danny Kaye, and we found that his real name is David Daniel Kamirsky.'

The Committee was an arm of Congress. As such it was able to compel cooperation. It began to ask for names: 'I could answer that,' the screenwriter Ring Lardner Jr said, 'but I would hate myself in the morning.' Ten people refused to cooperate, and were cited for contempt of Congress. These ten witnesses, who had refused the Committee's questions, were suddenly suspended without pay; actually firing them could have led to lawsuits.

Hollywood's top moguls promised to employ no subversives; they asked for the support of the law, 'since the absence of a national policy, established by Congress with respect to the employment of communists in private industry, makes our task difficult'. The declaration also said: 'There is the danger of hurting innocent people. There is the risk of creating an atmosphere of fear.' Hurt and fear followed. The ban on ten men became a general blacklist, informally applied and therefore beyond challenge. To escape the list, a suspect had to name his 'undesirable' contacts before some self-appointed rightist like the projectionist Roy Brewer, head of the craft union IATSE. The unions joined the moguls and, as the Korean war escalated, polarizing the issue of communism, their all-industry council denounced those who refused to tell all (or invent all) for the House Committee.

Paranoia entered Hollywood's soul. It made necessary a sort of public jingoism which embarrassed almost everyone; the quietest people were suspect. It crept into movie texts, often appearing in the guise of science fiction. It curtailed the string of social melodramas which had followed the war. John Wayne hit the screen as a heroic investigator for the Committee in *Big Jim McLain* (1952). The appalling *I Was a Communist for the FBI* (1951) inflated the Cold War rhetoric and spawned radio and television versions like *I Led Three Lives*. The studios' decision to surrender to HUAC in 1947 allowed the Committee to stamp on liberals throughout the entertainment business, but once sacrifices had been made the publicity-hungry politicians clamoured for fresh victims and the more famous the name, the better. Far from escaping, Hollywood was actually setting itself up,as a prime target for the witch hunts of the late Forties. By the time

Senator McCarthy arrived on the national scene in 1951, Hollywood was 'clean' politically.

If there was subversion in Hollywood in the post-war years, it was either implicit in the pessimism of the *film noir* or explicit as in the social-problem movies that dealt with racialism and allied subjects.

Edward Dmytryk's *Crossfire* (1947), for example, originally intended as an examination on homosexuality, changed its focus to anti-Semitism. The subject of Mark Robson's *Home of the Brave* (1949) was changed from hatred of the Jews to hatred of blacks. In more sentimental form, oppression of Jews surfaced in Kazan's *Gentleman's Agreement* (1947), which was mostly concerned to show that Jews are exactly like everybody else. Race also formed the dramatic problem in Kazan's *Pinky* (1949), a tale of a black girl trying to pass for white.

The idea that it might be hard to adjust to peace, a thought utterly taboo in wartime, came to the surface in *The Best Years of Our Lives* (1946). Political corruption, once completely forbidden by the Production Code, was allowed to be shown in Rossen's *All the King's Men* (1949) and also formed the subject of Kazan's *Boomerang* (1946).

Essentially, this revival of interest in social conscience had minimal political content. It was an extension of the black mood of crime melodramas and was perhaps equally romantic in nature. These films reflected a pervasive pessimism rather than activism; they spoke of subjects rather than analysed them. The Production Code would not be softened until the Fifties: in the American remake of *Le Jour se Lève* entitled *The Long Night* (1947), the criminal is obliged to surrender himself rather than commit suicide as he does in the original.

Certain subjects had, however, been opened by the war. Psychosis, induced by the strain of war, became a respectable subject because it had a visible cause. Social strain in the wake of the war was also discussed in films. This apparent liberalization was a fine illusion; it assimilated some of the uncertainties produced by the war but was swiftly reversed by the black-and-white moral certainties of the Cold War.

At the end of the decade television continued to pose a threat to Hollywood but its mass availability was delayed by various factors including the Korean War. Hollywood went about its regular work and more movies were made in 1950 than in 1946, despite the slump in attendances and the box-office gross. It was not TV that broke the movies in the Fifties and the Sixties; it was the post-war years, when Middle America established its suburban lifestyle and stopped going to the movies.

MICHAEL PYE

After the war, the American Congress began to investigate the 'communist bias' of the film industry. Films that had once been patriotic were labelled potentially subversive. Everyone who showed the slightest left-wing views became a suspected Communist sympathizer. The witch hunt was on!

In 1947, Congressional politics invaded Hollywood. The House Un-American Activities Committee (HUAC) subpoenaed 19 'unfriendly' witnesses – writers, directors, producers and actors. From then on, the film industry was to operate in an atmosphere of a very real fear of outside control, an atmosphere that stultified creative independence and from which Hollywood never fully recovered.

Politicians wanted headlines, and votes. No congressional investigation ever achieved the sensationalized worldwide coverage in the media that became possible with an attack on the glamorous world of the stars. HUAC had been formed in 1937 and was officially re-established in 1945. It exploited public ignorance and hysteria about a 'communist-inspired conspiracy'. Officially, its members had the power only to suggest alterations to any law. In fact, they had the power to destroy

people's lives, using innuendo, hearsay and malice, under the aegis of a right-wing press.

Public interest in 'the communist threat' had subsided during World War II, but the beginnings of the Cold War made possible new opportunities to highlight and justify the hearings of HUAC. Two of the most active members, John Rankin, who was blatantly anti-Semitic, and the chairman, J. Parnell Thomas, who was rabidly anti-New Deal, had long memories. They recalled the 'intellectuals' of the Thirties: the writers, teachers and lawyers who had been attracted to leftist activity.

As many of these writers and lawyers were now working in the film industry, Hollywood was an obvious target. The hearings opened privately in the spring of 1947 with the appearance of helpful witnesses, like Ginger Rogers' mother, Lela, who revealed her daughter's stubborn refusal to speak the line 'Share and share alike – that's democracy', in *Tender Comrade* (1943). More influential friendly witnesses included Jack L. Warner, Louis B. Mayer, Walt Disney, Gary Cooper, Robert Montgomery, Ronald Reagan, George Murphy, Robert Taylor and the self-appointed Hollywood expert on communism, Adolphe Menjou. After six months of psychological pressure within the industry, the public hearings were held in October. They lasted only two weeks, with testimonies from 23 friendly witnesses, and ended after 10 of the 19 unfriendly witnesses had been called before the Committee. The Hollywood Ten were John Howard Lawson, Dalton Trumbo, Lester Cole, Alvah Bessie, Albert Maltz, Ring Lardner Jr, Samuel Ornitz, Herbert J. Biberman, Edward Dmytryk and Adrian Scott.

The Ten

Writers were predominant among them. At that time, Lawson and Trumbo were the most prominent figures. Lawson had edited a paper in Rome for many years, and had also held the post of publicity director for the European division of the American Red Cross, before achieving success as a Broadway playwright. After a spell as a contract writer at MGM, he freelanced for Wanger, Goldwyn and 20th Century-Fox, working on anti-fascist and/or anti-Nazi films like *Blockade* (1938), *Sahara* (1943) and *Counter-Attack* (1945), as well as melodramas such as *Smash-Up* (1947). He was a founder member of the Screen Writers' Guild.

Trumbo was a former reporter and editor, who graduated from cheapies like *Road Gang* (1936) to become the highest-paid scriptwriter in Hollywood by the mid-Forties: *Tender Com-*

Above left: on the picket line in support of the Hollywood Ten – the scriptwriters and directors who were indicted for contempt of Congress – from the film Hollywood on Trial *(1976), which used footage that was shot during the course of the hearings. Left: the Ten and their lawyers arrive at the district court in Washington. Front row, left to right: Herbert J. Biberman, attorney Martin Popper, attorney Robert W. Kenny, Albert Maltz and Lester Cole. Middle row: Dalton Trumbo, John Howard Lawson, Alvah Bessie and Samuel Ornitz. Back row: Ring Lardner Jr, Edward Dmytryk and Adrian Scott*

was formed to organize the film industry's protest against the trial's infringements of the rights and freedoms of the American constitution. The chairman, John Huston, William Wyler and Philip Dunne organized a planeload of stars, including Humphrey Bogart, Lauren Bacall, Danny Kaye, Gene Kelly, and Jane Wyatt, to go to Washington and see that their people had a fair hearing. They arrived in a blaze of publicity and it was partly because of the row they caused that the hearings came to an abrupt, though temporary, halt.

The hearings

This was only the beginning. The hearing opened with Paul McNutt, special counsel for the 19, daring HUAC to list those films made in the past eight years with supposed communist propaganda content, and threatening to exhibit all those pictures immediately. Another defence lawyer directly attacked HUAC:

'The purpose of the inquiry is to build hysteria to the point of putting the power to employ or fire in the motion picture industry into the hands of this Committee, thus making the very art of producing pictures subject to political censorship.'

Led by John Howard Lawson, the Ten persistently refused to answer the question 'Are you, or have you ever been, a Communist?' and were cited for contempt of Congress. Rather than refuse to testify on the grounds that they might incriminate themselves (according to the Fifth Ammendment), they regarded the Committee itself as unconstitutional.

The Committee for the First Amendment now felt obliged to issue statements dissociating themselves from Lawson and the Ten's belligerent stance. Lawson stated in court that it was America that was on trial, not the Ten. Abraham Polonsky described in 1970 how the Committee was:

'. . . ripped asunder when the thing exploded

Dagger. Samuel Ornitz was the least known of the Ten, with *Three Faces West* (1940) as his only major credit.

There were also two directors and one producer. Herbert Biberman came to Hollywood from the New York theatre. He was a founder member of the Hollywood Anti-Nazi League, and of the Academy of Motion Pictures Arts and Sciences. He directed and/or scripted minor action films – *One Way Ticket* (1935), *The Master Race, Action in Arabia* (both 1944). Dmytryk joined Paramount in 1923, while still at school, spending the Thirties as an editor until he started directing B films in 1939, but he was well established at RKO by the mid-Forties, having worked on *Murder, My Sweet* (1944), *Back to Bataan, Cornered* (both 1945), *Crossfire* (1947). Adrian Scott also had stage experience before starting as a scriptwriter in 1940, and settling at RKO as a producer where he made *Murder, My Sweet, Cornered* and *Crossfire* all with Dmytryk.

The Committee for the First Amendment

Right: Gary Cooper giving evidence about communism – 'From what I hear, I don't like it because it isn't on the level'. Far right: Robert Montgomery testifying – 'I gave up my job to fight a totalitarianism called fascism. I am ready to do it again to fight the totalitarianism called communism'

rade, *A Guy Named Joe* (both 1943) and *Thirty Seconds Over Tokyo* (1944) were among his best-known credits.

Lester Cole was a freelancer who is probably best remembered for *Objective, Burma!* (1945). Bessie, who scripted *Northern Pursuit* (1943) and worked with Cole on *Objective, Burma!* and Maltz, who scripted *This Gun for Hire* (1942) and *Cloak and Dagger* (1946), were successful contract writers.

Ring Lardner Jr had been a reporter and publicity writer for David O. Selznick before achieving recognition as a scriptwriter. Among the films he worked on were *Woman of the Year* (1942), *The Cross of Lorraine* (1943), *Tomorrow the World* (1944) and *Cloak and*

in Washington. General Beadle Smith was sent to Hollywood and he met the important Hollywood owners. A policy was laid down to call these actors and directors off – the important ones. Pressure was put on them through their agents and the whole thing melted in about two weeks. I finally went to a meeting and Humphrey Bogart turned around and looked up a half empty room; the first meetings were held at George Chasen's, and you couldn't get in – it was like an opening night at the opera – everybody wanted to be in on this. Anyway, Humphrey Bogart looked round this room and said: "You don't think I'm going to stand up there all by myself and take a beating – I'm getting out too," and he walked out of the room. Then Huston said: "Well, it's hopeless, fellows," and left for Europe. The final meeting was held, and the only people present were Willie Wyler, the permanent secretary, myself and one other. Wyler said: "Well, I think we can use our time better than this." And it was true.'

There was no help for the victims to be had from the industry as a whole. On November 24, 1947, the Association of Motion Picture Producers met at the Waldorf-Astoria Hotel in

New York to discuss their attitude to the Ten and formulate their policy for the future. The Association declared that, since the Ten had 'impaired their usefulness to the industry', they would not be employed again until they had purged themselves of the contempt and sworn under oath that they were not Communists.

The pledge

They pledged that the industry would 'Not knowingly employ a Communist or a member of any party or group which advocates the overthrow of the Government of the United States by force, or by any illegal or unconstitutional method'. This was the beginning of the blacklist that was to grow longer and longer as the hearings continued well into the Fifties.

There were exceptions to the capitulation of the moguls. In his book, *The Hollywood Tycoons*, Norman Zierold tells how Sam Goldwyn, who loathed Russia and communism:

'watched the proceedings... with increased dismay because he felt this was not the American way of doing things; no Congressional committee should be the arbiter of a man's right to work. He felt that producers like Mayer, who were loudest in their outcries

were themselves responsible if the charges were true. After all, they had made the pictures, approving each step of production. Goldwyn felt the entire industry was being hurt by the charges. He heard the Committee was planning to call his close friend Robert Sherwood in order to examine certain suspect scenes in *The Best Years of Our Lives* (1946).'

Goldwyn then sent a telegram explaining his views to J. Parnell Thomas and stating that he wished to appear before the Committee to elaborate his views personally. He threatened to make his views public if he did not get a reply from Thomas. Goldwyn's stand has been credited as a factor in Thomas dropping his investigation.

The result

Legal proceedings dragged on for more than two and a half years before any of the Ten actually served time in prison. John Berry produced and directed a short film in 1950 in their defence, entitled *The Hollywood Ten*. But, during this period, there was constant pressure from groups such as the Motion Picture Alliance for the Preservation of American Ideals to reopen the hearings, and 'clean up' Hollywood.

HUAC capitalized on the fact that, during the Thirties and Forties, there had been some card-carrying members of the Communist Party in Hollywood (including several of the Ten), and that a number of household names had contributed to liberal causes and funds, some of which had proved to be Communist 'front' organizations. These names formed the basis of the lengthening blacklist.

The Alger Hiss trial, American involvement in the Korean War, but above all, the rise to prominence of Senator Joseph McCarthy, who repeatedly threatened to name names of Communists serving in the State Department, produced a hysterical right-wing paranoia that built up in the public mind the supposed influence of these 'Reds under the beds' out of all proportion. Trash sheets like *Red Channels* began publishing the names. The people con-

cerned were put on the spot by their employers, and the HUAC hearings reopened in 1951 to examine those on the blacklist.

Box-office receipts had been declining since 1947 and were further affected by the advent of television, and expensive studio gimmicks like 3-D were failing to stem the tide, so the moguls put tremendous pressure on their employees to 'confess' or else face being blacklisted. For example, Abraham Polonsky was fired after several weeks of editorials in Hollywood papers, following his being called to stand before HUAC.

The 'grey' list was also set up by the American Legion, listing names of suspected Communists or sympathizers. Every artist was by now afraid of being on somebody's 'list'. If you didn't get a job for some time, fear ate into the soul. As Polonsky commented: 'You never doubt your talent, you doubt your ability to get jobs for some strange reason.' Workers in Hollywood always faced the risk of being named by cooperative witnesses, for those on the list could 'buy' themselves off it. The 'cleaning' process required them not only to admit their own guilt, but to list publicly all their friends and colleagues who had ever shown the slightest left-wing sympathy. Clearance letters then had to be begged from the American Legion and other patriotic groups, and the price often included producing anti-communist articles. (One was John Garfield's 'I Was a Sucker for a Left Hook', written shortly before his death, with his career already totally ruined). Only then was employment once more assured.

An estimated 320 people suffered directly as a result of this cleansing process. A few brave individuals like Trumbo, Polonsky and Howard Da Silva refused to compromise or cooperate, but one of the Ten, Dmytryk, even went as far as naming John Berry, who had

Left: Cole and Bessie, who wrote the patriotic Objective, Burma! were charged with un-American activities. Below: the miners' strike from the independent film Salt of the Earth

**Tell them that old Indian fighter got his.
Tell them I'll kill if I have to.
Tell them they'll never take me alive.**

Tell them Willie Boy is here

UNIVERSAL PRESENTS **Robert Redford · Katharine Ross
Robert Blake · Susan Clark**

"Tell Them Willie Boy Is Here"

Co-starring Barry Sullivan Screenplay by ABRAHAM POLONSKY · Directed by ABRAHAM POLONSKY · A JENNINGS LANG PRESENTATION · A PHILIP A WAXMAN PRODUCTION TECHNICOLOR® PANAVISION®

instead of the $75,000 he had earned a decade earlier, Trumbo never made less than $18,000 in any of his own depression years.'

However, Corliss admitted that the cost was more then financial:

'It would be pleasant to think that Trumbo and his blacklisted brethren wrote, under psuedonyms, the finest Fifties films. But with the exception of Michael Wilson – who had scripted *A Place in the Sun* (1950) and *Five Fingers* (1952), before being blacklisted, and *Salt of the Earth* (1954); *Friendly Persuasion* (1956): *The Bridge on the River Kwai* (1957) and *Lawrence of Arabia* (1962) afterwards – their output was prolific but hardly profound. The political and administrative pressures that obsessed most leftist writers in the Forties became murderously oppressive in the Fifties, and most of the blacklisted screenwriters' work came through subterranean channels, and went into substandard productions.'

The comeback

In the Sixties, some of The Ten had their own names back on the screen. Trumbo was the first to come out of the wilderness in 1960 when Otto Preminger gave him screen credit for *Exodus*. Herbert J. Biberman had directed the independent film, *Salt of the Earth*, but did not re-emerge until *Slaves* (1969), Lardner had to wait until 1965 for his official screen credit on *The Cincinnati Kid*, and then went on to script *M*A*S*H* (1970). Lawson had retreated to Moscow.

J. Parnell Thomas himself ended up joining one of the Ten who was still in prison, serving a sentence for fraud. Yet HUAC continued its investigations until it was formally wound up in 1966. But its ghost has never been finally laid to rest. During the Nixon administration Jane Fonda, Gregory Peck and other Hollywood celebrities found themselves named 'enemies' of the President. The year 1947 was a black one in the history of the industry. It established a precedent for effective outside control over movie content and personnel.

KINGSLEY CANHAM

Above: Abraham Polonsky did not return to film direction until 1969 when he made Tell Them Willie Boy Is Here. *Left: Zero Mostel, who was himself blacklisted, plays a writer unable to get work in Hollywood in* The Front *(1976).
Below: Lardner's first screen credit after the trial was for* The Cincinnati Kid

problems. Or he or she could use a pseudonym. Dalton Trumbo wrote *The Brave One* (1956) under the pseudonym Robert Rich, and even received an Oscar for it.

The film critic Richard Corliss admired Trumbo's 'winning combination of businessman and craftsman' which kept his career alive in the blacklisted Fifties:

'The ruin that other writers took as malefic destiny, Trumbo took as a challenge. Writing as quickly as ever, but for $3000 per script

made the film *The Hollywood Ten* in his defence! Elia Kazan, Sterling Hayden, Robert Rossen (another of the original 19) and others paraded through the witness box, and employment ended for Larry Parks, Zero Mostel, Gale Sondergaard, Marsha Hunt, Jeff Corey and many others. Actors and actresses remained out of work. Writers and directors like Berry, Joseph Losey and Carl Foreman, who had been named but refused to testify, left for Europe.

But for those writers who stayed in America, like Trumbo and Polonsky, business carried on. As Trumbo commented in *The Nation* in 1957: 'The studios, while operating a blacklist, were in the market purchasing plays and other material without crediting the authors.' Producers and directors still went to the writers they knew were competent. A writer could use the name of a friend, which often created

1

Directed by Billy Wilder, 1945

Prod co: Paramount. **prod:** Charles Brackett. **sc:** Billy Wilder, Charles Brackett, from the novel by Charles Jackson. **photo:** John F. Seitz. **sp eff:** Gordon Jennings, Farciot Edouart. **ed:** Doane Harrison. **art dir:** Hans Dreier, Earl Hedrick, Bertram Granger. **mus:** Miklós Rózsa. **mus dir:** Victor Young. **sd:** Stanley Cooley. **ass dir:** C.C. Coleman. **medical adv:** Dr George N. Thompson. **r/t:** 99 minutes.

Cast: Ray Milland (*Don Birnam*), Jane Wyman (*Helen St James*), Howard da Silva (*Nat*), Philip Terry (*Wick Birnam*), Doris Dowling (*Gloria*), Frank Faylen (*Bim*), Mary Young (*Mrs Deveridge*), Lillian Fontaine (*Mrs St James*), Anita Bolster (*Mrs Foley*), Lewis L. Russell (*Charles*), Helen Dickson (*Mrs Frink*), David Clyde (*Dave*), Eddie Laughton (*Mr Brophy*).

Don Birman, an aspiring novelist, but an alcoholic, avoids a weekend with his brother Wick by getting drunk. Wick and Helen, Don's devoted girlfriend, have found his booze (1) and had his credit withdrawn at his haunts. But Don pilfers money left for his cleaning lady and goes to Nat's bar (2) where he reminisces about the past three years. He decides to turn his experiences into a novel called *The Bottle*, but after a false start he goes to a nightclub where he is caught stealing a woman's purse (3). Desperate for money, he tries to pawn his typewriter, but finds all the shops closed (4). He loses the typewriter and blacks out, waking to find himself in an alcoholic ward (5). During the night he escapes and steals a bottle from a liquor store, returning home to experience horrific hallucinations (6). The next morning he pawns Helen's expensive coat to get a gun to kill himself. Helen arrives and tries to talk him out of it, and when Nat suddenly returns the lost typewriter Don resolves to write the novel at last, dropping his cigarette into his whisky.

Until *The Lost Weekend* alcoholics in the movies were just plain drunks. Tottering downstairs bottle in hand, slurring their words, belching at inopportune moments, lying in the gutter singing Irish ballads – they could always be guaranteed to provide a laugh. Billy Wilder's film, if not the first on the subject, was the one that changed Hollywood's and moviegoers' conceptions of alcoholism. The hero of *The Lost Weekend* falls downstairs and lands in 'Hangover Plaza', as the drying-out ward of New York's

Bellevue Hospital is called, a nightmare world run by sadistic male nurses and peopled with pathetic social outcasts, screaming and convulsing as the DTs take hold.

After reading Charles Jackson's best-selling novel, while on the train from New York to Los Angeles, Wilder cabled ahead to his screenwriting partner Charles Brackett to open negotiations for the film rights. *The Lost Weekend* was not a project that Paramount found very attractive, and had not Brackett and Wilder already achieved a certain power and prestige, the film might never have been made. The studio's production executives vigorously opposed the project until

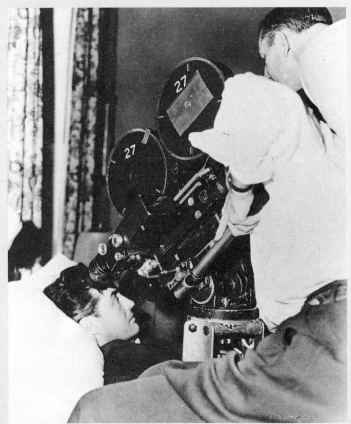

Left: cameraman John Seitz lines up a close-up shot during the filming of The Lost Weekend

2

3

4

5

6

Paramount's New York-based president, Barney Balaban, intervened and gave Brackett and Wilder the go-ahead.

One crucial alteration to Jackson's original was made: in the novel the hero's drinking stems from his failure to come to terms with his homosexuality; in the film, Don Birnam, played by Ray Milland, is a novelist and his drinking is a symptom of his artistic inadequacy. One of Wilder's biographers, Maurice Zolotow, has suggested that Birnam was based on Raymond Chandler, with whom Wilder worked on *Double Indemnity* (1944), but Hollywood clearly offered innumerable examples of failed writers who sought solace and escape through drink. By making their hero a writer, Brackett and Wilder could obviously lend authenticity to their characterization, but this led to a conflict of interest in the film between the analysis of a character close to the writers' hearts and the denouncing of a sickness in more detached terms. It is the failed writer who interests Brackett and Wilder, not the alcoholic, and the ending reveals this imbalance all too clearly. Birnam is saved from suicide by the miraculous return of his typewriter, which he had thought lost. This makes for a weak ending since his

inability to write does not simply begin and end with the material means to do so.

If the genre forced Wilder into structural sleights-of-hand like this, the visual impact of the film is impressive enough, reflecting both Wilder's European origins and stylistic movements then popular in Hollywood. The decision to strive for total realism produced some fine location footage: Ray Milland's famous walk down Third Avenue in search of a pawnshop was shot in a single day with concealed cameras; 'Hangover Plaza' really was at Bellevue Hospital (the staff of which, outraged by the way Wilder portrayed them, refused permits for a subsequent production); P.J. Clarke's bar on East 55th Street became Birnam's watering place, though it had to be re-created in Hollywood halfway through shooting as New York's December snowfall ruined the illusion of a sweltering summer. The gritty realism, which tips over into Expressionist nightmare for the delirium tremens sequence when Birnam has his vision of a mouse being eaten by a bat, is entirely consistent with the tormented world of *film noir*, where the architecture of the city and chiaroscuro lighting envelop the characters and create a fatalistic and claustrophobic mood. *The Lost*

Weekend was not all gloom though; Wilder's mordant sense of humour is present in a number of sequences, notably in the flashback to the opera when the drinking song in *La Traviata* becomes too much for Birnam to take, or the irony of Yom Kippur closing the pawnshops.

The Lost Weekend was previewed in Santa Barbara, California, and the result was disastrous. In place of Miklós Rózsa's dramatic score the studio had, in its haste, dubbed on inappropriate library music and, as soon as the audience saw Birnam's whisky bottle hanging hidden below his window, accompanied by the flip music, the cinema rocked with laughter. Wilder was away on military ser-

vice, but Brackett and Rózsa persuaded the front office not to shelve the picture. With Rózsa's score added to the print the second preview was a massive success. On March 7, 1946, *The Lost Weekend* collected four Academy Awards – three going to Brackett and Wilder for Best Picture, Best Director and Best Screenplay, and the fourth to Milland for Best Actor.

The Lost Weekend provided what Hollywood has always loved, a big commercial hit made out of a social message (the 1975 film *One Flew Over the Cuckoo's Nest* is the modern equivalent), demonstrating that the studios have a social conscience as well as a commercial instinct.

ADRIAN TURNER

Ray Milland
Star for all seasons

For a star so well-known and so perennial, Ray Milland has had an oddly undistinguished succession of films to contend with in his long career. The man himself – the personality – is so memorable, so clearly an important part of Hollywood during the Forties, that it comes as something of a surprise to discover how unmemorable most of his films were. He is a classic case of the star being greater than the sum of his parts

Ray Milland's career turned on one of those mid-stream changes of direction that is an indication of the Hollywood passion for drama in life as well as on the screen. So many Oscars have been won, so many careers transformed, by virtue of some feat which, coolly considered, was merely average; it was not so much that it was well done as remarkable that it was done at all. And Milland's Oscar for *The Lost Weekend* (1945) must certainly come in that category. Up to 1945 he had nearly always been associated with light comedy and romantic drama. Then he was suddenly called upon to pull out all the stops in Billy Wilder's very outspoken story of a crisis in the life of a confirmed alcoholic.

The film was a creditable attempt to handle what was, by the Hollywood standards of the time, a distasteful and uncommercial subject. But distasteful and uncommercial subjects are usually, when it comes to the point, very commercial indeed, and daringly offbeat casting – like Ray Milland playing a drunk – usually pays for itself in terms of advance audience interest. In the event, Milland gave a solid, slightly monotonous reading of the part, determinedly serious and putting any hint of comedy far behind him. Many another actor could have done it better, but the element of surprise would have been missing – and it was surprise more than anything that brought Milland his Oscar and the New York Critics' Award.

In most respects *The Lost Weekend* proved to be the high point of a career that started very quietly. Born Reginald Truscott-Jones in Neath, Glamorgan, in 1905, Milland seems to have had no particular acting ambitions; but in 1929, when he was a handsome young guardsman and man-about-town, he happened to visit his friend, film actress Estelle Brody, while she was making *The Plaything*, and was offered a small part. This led to other small parts, a couple of stage appearances, and some slightly larger roles in early British sound films, including the first version of *The Informer* (1929), with Lya de Putti and Lars Hanson, and the male lead in *The Lady From the Sea* (1929). Fortified by this, he was put under contract to MGM and set off for Hollywood, where he was given minor roles in several films – most notably *Payment Deferred* (1932).

His contract was not renewed and he returned to Britain. But in 1934 he was back in Hollywood, this time joining Paramount, which was to remain his home studio for nearly twenty years. Paramount – true to their practice with long-term contractees – built Milland up slowly, giving him second leads in mainstream films like *We're Not Dressing* (1934), making him the romantic interest in comedies like George Burns and Gracie Allen's *Many Happy Returns* (1934), and occasionally throwing him top billing in a B picture. By 1936 he was playing leads in relatively big pictures like *The Jungle Princess*, discovering Dorothy Lamour and her sarong out in the Tropics, and *Bulldog Drummond Escapes* (1937), where he was, naturally, Bulldog Drummond. He became a star with Mitchell Leisen's crazy comedy *Easy Living* (1937), in which he finally managed to win the heroine (Jean Arthur), and had a couple of return matches with Lamour – *Her Jungle Love* and *Tropic Holiday* (both 1938) – as well as a part as one of the heroic brothers in *Beau Geste* (1939).

His new status was confirmed when Paramount sent him back to England in 1939 to be the star of their film of Terence Rattigan's

comedy *French Without Tears*, for which Milland received the best notices of his career up to that time. Back in Hollywood he was constantly on call as an all-purpose smoothie – among his films were *Irene* (1940), in which he stood by as Anna Neagle burst into colour to sing 'Alice Blue Gown', and Leisen's *Arise My Love* (1940), in which he and Claudette Colbert coped, rather ambiguously, with the Spanish Civil War. He was even to have an underwater battle with a giant squid in DeMille's blockbuster *Reap the Wild Wind* (1942). More significant, however, was his appearance in Billy Wilder's first solo outing as a director, a comedy called *The Major and the Minor* (1942), co-starring Ginger Rogers; his happy experience working with Wilder on this film led the director to cast him in *The Lost Weekend*. But before that, Milland starred in *The Uninvited* (1944), an excellent, but unacclaimed, ghost story, and in *Ministry of Fear* (1944), Fritz Lang's effective adaptation of Graham Greene's novel. He was also re-teamed with Ginger Rogers in *Lady in the Dark* (1944), a lavish but not very successful version of the stage musical.

After *The Lost Weekend* he was taken more seriously, at least in principle. The trouble was that in practice the films he was given had little quality, and he was seldom again to find himself working with a director of Wilder's calibre. Leisen's *Golden Earrings* (1947), with Marlene Dietrich as an anti-fascist gypsy fortune-teller, was foolish but fun, and *The Big Clock* (1948), if primarily an opportunity for Charles Laughton to overact, was still very good of its kind with Milland as a reporter trying to solve a murder. But *A Life of Her Own* (1950), with Lana Turner, was one of George Cukor's least successful films, and *Something to Live For* (1952), with Milland and Joan Fontaine both playing alcoholics, foundered under George Stevens' direction.

Finally separated from Paramount in 1953, Milland found more interesting roles in more interesting films. He was a retired tennis champion who plots the murder of his wife (Grace Kelly) in Hitchcock's *Dial M for Murder* (1954), and the architect Stanford White, victim of a crime of passion in *The Girl in the Red Velvet Swing* (1955), a somewhat laundered version of the celebrated murder case. And he was able to fulfil a long-standing ambition to direct when he made some intriguing low-budget pictures, usually starring himself, such as the Western *A Man Alone* (1955), and the science-fiction story *Panic in Year Zero* (1962). More stage work, a television series and a definitive transition to character roles as the

Filmography

1929 The Flying Scotsman (GB); The Lady From the Sea (GB); The Plaything (GB); The Informer (+sharp-shooting stunts). **'30** Way for a Sailor (uncredited); Passion Flower (uncredited). **'31** The Bachelor Father; Just a Gigolo (GB: The Dancing Partner); Bought; Blonde Crazy (GB: Larceny Lane); Ambassador Bill; untitled advertising short (GB). **'32** The Man Who Played God (GB: The Silent Voice); Polly of the Circus; Payment Deferred; Once in a Lifetime (uncredited). **'33** Orders Is Orders (GB); This Is the Life (GB). **'34** Bolero; We're Not Dressing; Many Happy Returns; Charlie Chan in London; Menace; One Hour Late. **'35** The Gilded Lily; Four Hours to Kill; The Glass Key; Alias Mary Dow. **'36** Next Time We Love (GB: Next Time We Live); The Return of Sophie Lang; The Big Broadcast of 1937; The Jungle Princess. **'37** Three Smart Girls; Wings Over Honolulu; Easy Living; Ebb Tide; Bulldog Drummond Escapes; Wise Girl. **'38** Her Jungle Love; Tropic Holiday; Men With Wings; Say It in French. **'39** Hotel Imperial; Beau Geste; Everything Happens at Night; French Without Tears (GB). **'40** Irene; The Doctor Takes a Wife; Untamed; Arise My Love. **'41** I Wanted Wings; Skylark. **'42** The Lady Has Plans; Reap the Wild Wind; Are Husbands Necessary?; The Major and the Minor. **'43** Star Spangled Rhythm (guest); The Crystal Ball; Forever and a Day. **'44** The Uninvited; Lady in the Dark; Till We Meet Again; Ministry of Fear. **'45** The Lost Weekend; Kitty. **'46** The Well-Groomed Bride; California. **'47** The Imperfect Lady (GB: Mrs Loring's Secret); The Trouble With Women; Golden Earrings; Variety Girl (guest). **'48** The Big Clock; So Evil, My Love (GB); Miss Tatlock's Millions (guest); Sealed Verdict. **'49** Alias Nick Beal (GB: The Contact Man); It Happens Every Spring. **'50** A Woman of Distinction; A Life of Her Own; Copper Canyon (+sharp-shooting stunts). **'51** Night Into Morning; Circle of Danger (GB); Rhubarb; Close to My Heart. **'52** Bugles in the Afternoon; Something to Live For; The Thief; Jamaica Run. **'53** Let's Do It Again. **'54** Dial M for Murder. **'55** The Girl in the Red Velvet Swing; A Man Alone (+dir). **'56** Lisbon (+dir; +prod). **'57** Three Brave Men; The River's Edge. **'58** The Safecracker (+dir) (GB); High Flight (GB). **'62** The Premature Burial; Panic in Year Zero (+dir). **'63** The Man With the X-Ray Eyes. **'65** The Confession (reissued as Quick, Let's Get Married/Seven Different Ways). **'68** Hostile Witness (+dir) (GB). **'70** Company of Killers (shot as TV film but shown in cinemas); Love Story. **'72** The Big Game (SA); Embassy (GB); Frogs; The Thing With Two Heads. **'73** The House in Nightmare Park (GB); Terror in the Wax Museum. **'74** Gold (GB). **'75** Escape to Witch Mountain. **'76** The Swiss Conspiracy (GER-USA) (GER: Per Saldo Morte); Aces High (GB-FR); The Last Tycoon. **'77** The Uncanny (GB-CAN); Slavers (GER) (German and English-language versions). **'78** Battlestar Galactica; Oliver's Story. **'79** Game for Vultures (GB). **'80** Survival Run.

father in *Love Story* (1970), marked by a ritual discarding of his toupée (though it was back on in the 1972 film, *Frogs*), have followed and have kept Milland a busy actor.

He seems, throughout his long career, to have taken himself and his world with an admirable lack of seriousness, well mirrored in his autobiography *Wide-Eyed in Babylon*. No doubt that attitude has allowed him to stay near the top for so long, and to leave such a pleasant mark on our memory.

JOHN RUSSELL TAYLOR

Above, far left: Beau Geste starred Milland, Robert Preston and Gary Cooper as three brothers who join the Foreign Legion and leave behind the girl they all love (Susan Hayward). Left: in Hotel Imperial Milland is a Hungarian soldier involved in romance and intrigue. Below left: with Gail Russell and Ruth Hussey in The Uninvited, a haunted-house story set in Cornwall. Below: helping Oliver (Ryan O'Neal) face up to tragedy in Love Story. Right: directing Frankie Avalon in the after-the-holocaust yarn Panic in Year Zero. Above right: as Sire Uri in the outer-space adventure-movie Battlestar Galactica

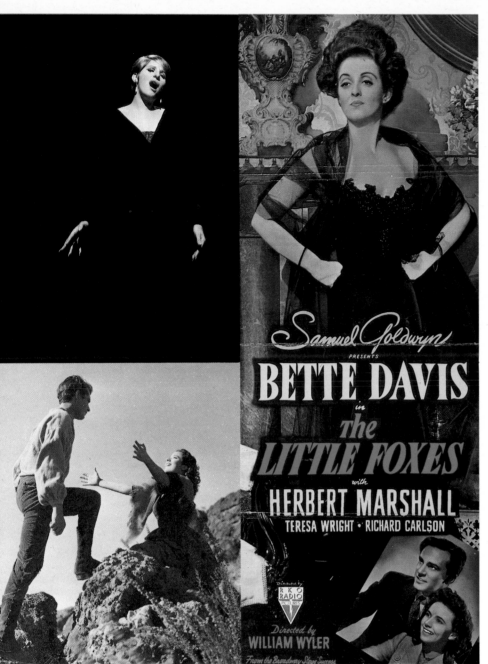

Samuel Goldwyn
PRESENTS
BETTE DAVIS
in
The LITTLE FOXES
with
HERBERT MARSHALL
TERESA WRIGHT · RICHARD CARLSON

RKO RADIO PICTURES

Directed by
WILLIAM WYLER

From the Broadway Stage Success

markably eclectic in his choice of subject. There appears to be no consistent philosophy of life running through his films. Often he seems to have been attracted to a theme simply because it represented a technical or personal challenge: as he had never made an epic, he might as well make *Ben Hur* (1959); since he had never made a musical, he would try his hand at *Funny Girl* (1968); because Hollywood traditionally shied away from presenting racial themes, he would tackle them in *The Liberation of L. B. Jones* (1970).

Wyler's most evident line of consistency as a director is in the development of a style based on sustained shots and great depth of field, so that something going on in the far background is just as clear as something in foreground close-up. This technique begins with *These Three* in 1936, and continues until *The Best Years of Our Lives* in 1946. Yet this style cannot be solely attributed to Wyler. *These Three*, after all, was the start of Wyler's collaboration with the cinematographer Gregg Toland and the producer Sam Goldwyn for whom most of his finest films were made during the next ten years – *Dodsworth* (1936), *Dead End* (1937), *Wuthering Heights*, *The Little Foxes*, *The Best Years of Our Lives*. (*The Best Years of Our Lives*, coincidentally, was the last time Wyler worked with either.)

At first sight it appears as if Wyler has been given credit for a collective enterprise (although certainly he did not claim it). Yet all the elements in Wyler's films hold together in a way which seems to argue that he was, at the very least, their overall guiding force. Toland may have been interested in experimenting with deep focus, but this was precisely what made him especially useful to Wyler, because shooting in that way was perfect for Wyler's treatment of actors; it accorded with his desire to produce sustained performances from them, rather than shooting in short takes which,

Left: Wyler is renowned for films that brought added prestige to the wide range of talents that appeared in them, including Bette Davis in The Little Foxes, *Barbra Streisand in* Funny Girl *(top far left) and Laurence Olivier and Merle Oberon in* Wuthering Heights *(far left).*
Below: Wyler became Davis' favourite director; here the pair confer during the making of The Little Foxes

The winning ways of William Wyler

William Wyler is renowned as the actor's director *par excellence* and as the supreme Hollywood craftsman, turning well-written scripts into award-winning movies with the aid of first-rate casts and technicians

There is no doubt that Wyler has done extremely well by his actors, and that they have done extremely well by him. The long succession of acting Oscars won in his films include two for Bette Davis and Walter Brennan, and one each for Olivia de Havilland, Audrey

Hepburn, Fredric March, Barbra Streisand, Charlton Heston and Greer Garson. Many actors have testified how Wyler tortured their performances out of them; although he could not or would not explain to them exactly what he wanted, somehow, mysteriously and bit by bit, it all came right. Both Laurence Olivier and Bette Davies began by detesting him and ended by adoring him. Rightly so, for they have seldom shown to better advantage on screen than in *Wuthering Heights* (1939) and *The Little Foxes* (1941) respectively.

It is undeniable that Wyler has been re-

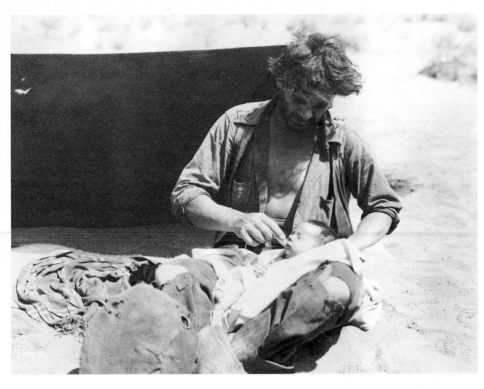

Hopkins and Walter Huston, but comes through, in *These Three*, in the playing of Merle Oberon (a beauty, to be sure, but seldom much of an actress outside Wyler's films); then in *Dodsworth* Ruth Chatterton, a has-been making a comeback in an unromantic, middle-aged role as Fran Dodsworth, gives one of the great performances of the American cinema.

In the next few films with Toland, Wyler continued to explore the various expressive possibilities of his style (or their joint style): in *Dead End* it took on the harsh look of grimy urban realism; in *Wuthering Heights*, romantic chiaroscuro; in *The Little Foxes*, a stifling, turn-of-the-century intricacy. The two films he

Left: a tough cowboy (Charles Bickford) plays nursemaid in Hell's Heroes. *Below: Merle Oberon and Miriam Hopkins as the maligned schoolteachers of* These Three. *Bottom: Audrey Hepburn and Gregory Peck in* Roman Holiday. *Bottom left: Leslie Crosbie (Bette Davis) shoots her lover in* The Letter

through careful editing, could later be fused into a performance.

Although the earlier part of his career remains obscure – and therefore largely ignored by film historians – Wyler was, in fact, functioning as a director in Hollywood from 1926. He was born in Alsace in 1902, and educated in Lausanne and Paris (where he seemed destined to become a professional musician). He then abruptly left for the USA, following a chance encounter with Carl Laemmle, head of Universal studios. His first films were two-reel Westerns, of which, he alleges, he made nearly fifty in two years. His first film to attract attention did not come until 1929 when he made *Hell's Heroes*, a shamelessly sentimental drama about three hard-

ened cowboys who find and save a baby in the desert; it impressed critics because of its (for the time) imaginative use of sound. But *These Three* and *Dodsworth* showed him at last really coming into his own.

Both had substantial subjects: *These Three* was based on Lillian Hellman's play (*The Children's Hour*) of a lesbian relationship in a girl's school; *Dodsworth* was adapted from Sinclair Lewis' novel about an American couple whose view of life is changed by a trip to Europe. Both are treated with an ease and fluidity which frees them from the curse of being stagey or bookish. Moreover, with these two films Wyler asserted his special ability in handling actors. This is not so much in evidence with reliable performers like Miriam

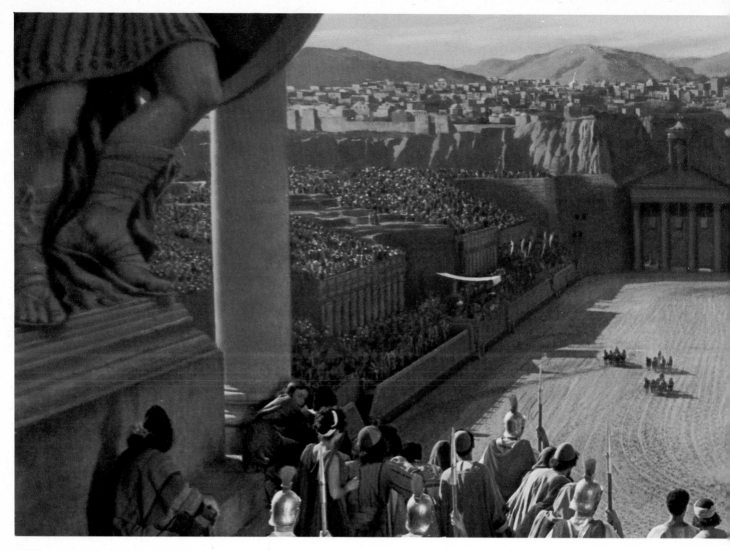

Above: the magnificent arena for the spectacular and fiercely realistic chariot race in Ben Hur, *which won 11 Oscars, including one for Wyler. Below: Terence Stamp as the psychopath who adds the beautiful Samantha Eggar to his collection of butterflies in* The Collector *(1965), which was based on John Fowles' novel*

made outside this collaboration, both Bette Davis vehicles for Warners, were less interesting, visually and otherwise: *Jezebel* (1938) allowed Davis to play a bitchy Southern belle; *The Letter* (1940) incited her to chew the scenery in Somerset Maugham's old shocker of adultery and murder set in Malaya. All the

same, the performances still stand up: even by this stage in her career, Bette Davis could be execrably mannered, but Wyler knew how to keep her in reasonable check.

During World War II, Wyler first found himself making a somewhat fulsome and starry-eyed tribute to beleaguered Britain; his *Mrs Miniver* (1942) was a glossy picture which has dated badly. He was then drafted into the US Army Air Force to make training and propaganda films. One of these, *The Memphis Belle* (1944), was generally regarded as one of the most satisfactory American official films to have come out of the war. And there is no doubt at all that Wyler's first film on his return to civilian life, *The Best Years of Our Lives*, was the finest about the home front and the veteran returning from the battlefront. Finely structured despite being on a large scale (the film ran for 160 minutes), its screenplay, by Robert E. Sherwood, miraculously avoids being sentimental, glib or patronizing. Wyler managed a large cast with consummate ease, and the film represents in many respects the height of his achievement. It was loved by audiences in America and abroad, who felt that it spoke simply and unaffectedly of their problems and emotions.

Although thereafter he operated without the support of Goldwyn (who subsequently produced few films of distinction) and of Toland (who died in 1948, at the age of 44), Wyler's career showed few signs of decline. *The Heiress* (1949) put back into the simplified

stage version of Henry James' *Washington Square* some of the original Jamesian complexity, although a superb performance by Ralph Richardson as the tyrannical father was not matched by the total miscasting of Montgomery Clift as the fortune-hunting suitor. *Carrie* (1952), an intensely depressing film, contained another of Laurence Olivier's fine screen performances, and captured with astonishing accuracy the essence of Theodore Dreiser's realist novel, *Sister Carrie*. There was also much to be said for the romantic charms of *Roman Holiday* (1953), which introduced Audrey Hepburn to the American public, the knowing rusticities of *Friendly Persuasion* (1956), and the wide open spaces of *The Big Country* (1958). His second, franker version of *The Children's Hour* (1961) was a decided improvement on the first, and *Funny Girl*, on which he was assisted by Herbert Ross as dance director, was the best musical of the Sixties as well as an ideal showcase for its star, Barbra Streisand.

With Wyler it has always been necessary to listen to the songs and not be too concerned with the singer. Perhaps his films *are* impersonal, but in a Hollywood where the directors are increasingly eager to be superstars in their own right, a little impersonality becomes in itself the mark of a strong and individual personality. If, in the final analysis, Wyler is not accounted a great director, there is no question but that he has made a fair handful of great films. JOHN RUSSELL TAYLOR

Below: the grisly closing sequence of The Liberation of L. B. Jones, *in which a black undertaker becomes the brutalized victim of Southern racism as personified by a vicious, bigoted white cop*

Filmography
1923 The Hunchback of Notre Dame (ass. dir. only). **'25** Crook Buster; Ben Hur (prod. ass. only). **'26** The Gunless Badman; Ridin' for Love; The Fire Barrier; Don't Shoot; The Horse Trader; Lazy Lightning; Stolen Ranch; Martin of the Mounted; The Two Fister. **'27** Kelcy Gets His Man; Blazing Days; Tenderfoot Courage; The Silent Partner; Hard Fists; Galloping Justice; The Haunted Homestead; Shooting Straight/Straight Shootin'/Range Riders; The Lone Star; The Ore Raiders; The Home Trail; Gun Justice; The Phantom Outlaw; The Square Shooter; The Border Cavalier; Daze of the West; Desert Dust; Thunder Riders. **'28** Anybody Here Seen Kelly? (GB: Has Anybody Here Seen Kelly?); The Shakedown. **'29** Love Trap; Hell's Heroes. **'30** The Storm. **'32** A House Divided; Tom Brown of Culver. **'33** Her First Mate; Counsellor at Law. **'34** Glamour. **'35** The Good Fairy; The Gay Deception. **'36** These Three; Dodsworth; Come and Get It! (reissued as: Roaring Timber) (co-dir. only). **'37** Dead End. **'38** Jezebel. **'39** Wuthering Heights. **'40** The Westerner; The Letter. **'41** The Little Foxes. **'42** Mrs Miniver (+prod). **'44** The Memphis Belle (+prod; +sc; +co-photo) (short); The Fighting Lady. **'46** The Best Years of Our Lives. **'47** Thunderbolt (co-dir. only). **'49** The Heiress (+prod). **'51** Detective Story (+prod). **'52** Carrie (+prod). **'53** Roman Holiday (+prod). **'55** The Desperate · Hours (+prod). **'56** Friendly Persuasion (+prod). **'58** The Big Country (+co-prod). **'59** Ben Hur. **'61** The Children's Hour (+prod) (GB: The Loudest Whisper). **'65** The Collector (USA-GB). **'66** How to Steal a Million. **'68** Funny Girl. **'70** The Liberation of L. B. Jones.

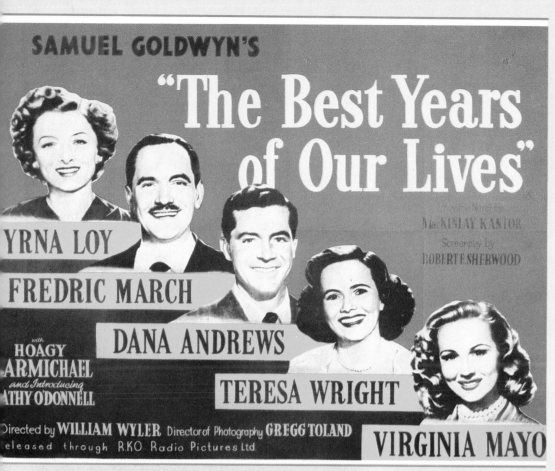

SAMUEL GOLDWYN'S

"The Best Years of Our Lives"

From the Novel by
MacKINLAY KANTOR

Screenplay by
ROBERT E. SHERWOOD

YRNA LOY

FREDRIC MARCH

with
HOAGY
ARMICHAEL
and Introducing
ATHY O'DONNELL

DANA ANDREWS

TERESA WRIGHT

VIRGINIA MAYO

Directed by WILLIAM WYLER Director of Photography GREGG TOLAND

eleased through R.K.O. Radio Pictures Ltd.

Homer, Fred and Al first meet on the plane taking them home to Boone City (1). They are all unsure of how their recent war experiences have changed them and Homer, who lost his arms in a torpedo blaze, worries about the inevitable pity his disability will arouse in Wilma, his fiancée. After predictably awkward reunions, the three men and Al's family gather that night to reminisce in the bar owned by Butch, Homer's uncle (2).

Al starts to drink heavily when he returns to his former job as a banker (3), while Fred and Marie soon recognize their mutual incompatability (4). Fred is forced to go back to his humiliating pre-war job in a department store (5). By now he has fallen in love with Peggy, Al's daughter, who is moved by his current plight and his recurrent nightmares of being shot down (6).

Millie, who is also finding it hard to adjust to peacetime with Al, is upset that her daughter is attempting to break up Fred's failing marriage. Homer, meanwhile, is doubting the wisdom of marrying Wilma (7), but she manages to convince him of her complete understanding. At their wedding, Fred, who has left his wife and is now working in a junk yard, meets Peggy again as Al and Millie look on, powerless to intervene.

1

2

5

6

The last months of World War II found Hollywood in a difficult position. The end of the war was obviously near – but how near? Any 'peacetime' film put into production might have to sit on the shelf for months before VJ day arrived. The single exception was the subject of the rehabilitation of the fighting man, since this was a predictable problem that would affect Americans from every walk of life.

Sam Goldwyn had read an article in *Time* which foresaw huge difficulties for returning soldiers. Sensing that the subject-matter could be translated into feature-film material, he commissioned the writer MacKinlay Kantor to supply a 50-page treatment to serve as the basis for a future screenplay on the subject. With the war over, President Truman, to the great delight of Goldwyn's publicity department, set about demobilizing as quickly as he could. By May 1946, over seven million men had been demobbed.

Kantor, having spent the $12,500 Goldwyn had originally paid him, reappeared some three months later with a 268-page novel entitled *Glory for Me*, written in free verse. Goldwyn, once the total horror of the situation had dawned on him, threw a terrible rage which culminated in Kantor's getting another $7500 to write a screenplay from his novel. When this, too, proved to be a disaster, Goldwyn handed the project over to his most trusted lieutenants – the director William Wyler and the writer Robert E. Sherwood.

Both men accepted the responsibility somewhat nervously. Sherwood had spent much of the war writing speeches for Roosevelt, and Wyler had been making documentaries in the combat zone, in the course of which he had gone deaf in one ear. At the same time as they were losing touch with commercial film-making, a new generation had taken their places in Hollywood – a town with a notoriously short memory.

Fortunately, Goldwyn's trust was not misplaced and *The Best Years of Our Lives* was an instant hit both critically and commercially, brushing aside the challenge of Frank Capra's *It's a Wonderful Life* (1946) to make virtually a clean sweep of the year's Oscars. Certain left-wing groups (particularly in the newly-published journal *Hollywood Quarterly*) dug into *Glory for Me* to prove that *The Best Years of Our Lives* was a fraud because Sherwood had softened the almost unrelieved misery Kantor had inflicted on his characters. However, the film's durable reputation has effectively answered most of the criticism.

Much of the credit is due to the actors, all of whom gave inspired performances. Fredric March was never better than as Al, the army sergeant who cannot face life at home or at his old job in the bank

without frequent recourse to alcohol. At a pompous formal dinner given by the bank in his honour, Al makes a drunken speech full of mixed metaphors while Myrna Loy (in her first middle-aged role) ticks off on the tablecloth the number of drinks he has consumed.

Unlike March and Loy, Dana Andrews was a Goldwyn contract star whose previous career had given no hint of the success he was to achieve in this film as Fred Derry, the dashing young air force major. Fred simply wants 'a decent job and a little house for my wife' but returns, like so many others, to find only menial work available and to discover that his wife had fallen in love with the glamorous pilot and not the unglamorous civilian.

The remaining member of the returning trio is a sailor, Homer, who has lost both his arms below the elbow. This fate had indeed befallen Harold Russell (though in different circumstances from those

described in the film). Wyler had first seen Russell in a training film designed to rehabilitate such men. On the most propagandist level, Russell's role in *The Best Years of Our Lives* once again merely shows the practical achievements still possible for men so handicapped, but Sherwood and Wyler are not afraid to explore the emotional difficulties which inevitably occur. Thus, in context, Homer's decision to marry Wilma, after considerable doubt on his part, perhaps becomes the film's most positive statement.

Despite the criticism levelled at the film for its false optimism (Fred finds a job and faces life with Peggy, Homer marries and Al and Millie seem to have conquered most of their readjustment difficulties), *The Best Years of Our Lives* succeeds because its treatment of a particular social problem is accomplished with the wit and sensitivity of truly great artists.

COLIN SHINDLER

Directed by William Wyler, 1946
Prod: Samuel Goldwyn. **sc:** Robert E. Sherwood, adapted from the verse novel *Glory for Me* by MacKinlay Kantor. **photo:** Gregg Toland. **ed:** Daniel Mandell. **art dir:** Perry Ferguson, George Jenkins, Julia Heron. **cost:** Sharaff. **mus:** Hugo Friedhofer. **mus dir:** Emil Newman. **sd:** Richard DeWeese. **r/t:** 182 minutes.
Cast: Myrna Loy (*Milly Stephenson*), Fredric March (*Al Stephenson*), Dana Andrews (*Fred Derry*), Teresa Wright (*Peggy Stephenson*), Virginia Mayo (*Marie Derry*), Cathy O'Donnell (*Wilma Cameron*), Hoagy Carmichael (*Butch Engle*), Harold Russell (*Homer Parrish*), Gladys George (*Hortense Derry*), Roman Bohnen (*Pat Derry*), Ray Collins (*Mr Milton*), Minna Gombell (*Mrs Parrish*), Walter Baldwin (*Mr Parrish*), Steve Cochran (*Cliff*), Dorothy Adams (*Mrs Cameron*), Don Beddoe (*Mr Cameron*), Victor Cutler (*Woody*), Marlene Aames (*Luella Parrish*), Charles Halton (*Prew*), Ray Teal (*Mr Mollett*), Howland Chamberlain (*Thorpe*), Dean White (*Novak*), Erskine Sanford (*Bullard*).

Samuel Goldwyn

'I've always been an independent even when I had partners'

Left: Samuel Goldwyn and his wife Frances – 'She's the only real close partner I've ever had'. Below: The Kid From Brooklyn (1946) starred Danny Kaye – one of Goldwyn's many discoveries. Bottom: Roman Scandals was devised for another find – Eddie Cantor

Samuel Goldwyn is remembered both as the producer of some of Hollywood's most distinguished pictures, and as a purveyor of malapropisms and *non sequiturs* known as Goldwynisms – although his family and close associates deny ever hearing him utter one. Goldwyn's eccentric language became almost as well known to the movie-going public as the familiar portly figure of Alfred Hitchcock

Samuel Goldwyn, who, to quote Bob Hope, 'did more for movies than dark balconies' had the standard movie-mogul background. Born in a Jewish ghetto in Warsaw in 1882, he arrived penniless in America at the age of 15. His real name sounded to the immigration officials like Samuel Goldfish and that is what he became.

His English, learnt in his teens, often contained a curious usage of words which, in later life, became highly publicized. He laughed at the sayings that were attributed to him (like 'Gentlemen, include me out' and 'In two words: im . . . possible') because, as he wryly put it, 'Well, I'd be the only one if I didn't'.

After prospering in the glove trade, he persuaded Jesse Lasky (who, at the time, was his brother-in-law) to go into film-making. Goldfish, Lasky and Cecil B. DeMille founded Jesse Lasky Feature Plays. They made *The Squaw Man* (1913) and discovered a new location – Hollywood. Sam sold the Lasky output to exhibitors throughout the world. The company prospered and merged with Adolph Zukor's Famous Players; the new company was later to become Paramount.

Sam clashed with Zukor and sold out. He then formed Goldwyn Pictures Corporation with Broadway's Edgar Selwyn – the company name being formed from *Gold*fish and Sel*wyn* – and, tired of the jokes associated with being a Goldfish, he took the joint name, legally, for his

own. The company lacked major stars and tried to compensate by hiring 'Eminent Authors' like Rex Beach and Mary Roberts Rinehart to write its pictures. The arrangement did not work out because the writers failed to understand the visual primacy of the silent film, but it demonstrated Sam's lifelong policy of hiring the best regardless of cost. New partners were then brought in to provide additional financing, but Sam soon feuded with them and quit the company in 1922. With its lion trade mark and motto '*ars gratia artis*' it went on to become Metro-Goldwyn-Mayer.

In 1923, Goldwyn, realizing that he was not endowed with sufficient patience to tolerate partners and was wealthy enough not to need them, set up in business on his own. He embarked on a series of highly popular romantic films, made a hot box-office combination

---

'Verbal contracts are not worth the paper they are written on'

---

out of Ronald Colman and Vilma Banky and invented a new slogan to celebrate his success: 'Goldwyn pictures griddle the earth!' He was now his own master.

In 1930, he made a lavish, two-colour Technicolor musical, *Whoopee!*, that brought screen stardom to Eddie Cantor, introduced Busby Berkeley to Hollywood, and led to the creation of the Goldwyn Girls. Sam had it in

unfilmable. But he outwitted his critics and remained true to the spirit if not the lesbian detail of the powerful play. Goldwyn was not allowed to retain the original title, but audiences knew full well that *These Three* (1936) was based on *that* play, due to the publicity it had received, and they were eager to see what Goldwyn and director William Wyler had made of it.

'I had a monumental idea this morning, but I don't like it'

Goldwyn's career would have been much less notable without Wyler. Despite the many films they made together, Goldwyn and Wyler were constantly feuding. 'I made them – Willie Wyler only directed them,' Goldwyn would say, while Wyler often refused to direct what he, usually rightly, considered were poor properties, happily going on suspension to back his judgment. Goldwyn could be tight-fisted: he

mind to become the Florenz Ziegfeld of the screen (Ziegfeld helped him make *Whoopee!*) and his productions of the next two decades featured a number of lightweight musical-comedy extravaganzas. He made five more with Cantor, including *The Kid From Spain* (1932) and *Roman Scandals* (1933), and he tried to start a series of annual revues with *The Goldwyn Follies* (1938). Sam rarely employed established stars, preferring to create his own. He signed up the stage actor, Danny Kaye, had his hair dyed blond, and starred him in six pictures from *Up In Arms* (1944) to *Hans Christian Andersen* (1952). Goldwyn's musicals were the profitable backbone of his output, the films most in line with his policy of providing entertainment for all the family.

But Goldwyn also made more serious pictures as part of his annual film schedule. These were almost always based on plays or novels. There was *Street Scene* (1931), a drama of New York tenement life that Elmer Rice adapted from his stage play, and *Arrowsmith* (1931), about the idealism of a doctor; *Dodsworth* (1936) about a middle-aged automobile manufacturer taking stock of himself; and *Dead End*

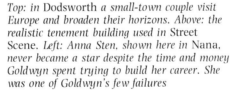

Top: in Dodsworth *a small-town couple visit Europe and broaden their horizons. Above: the realistic tenement building used in* Street Scene. *Left: Anna Sten, shown here in* Nana, *never became a star despite the time and money Goldwyn spent trying to build her career. She was one of Goldwyn's few failures*

(1937), another story of the slums. Such films brought the studio prestige more often than profit and probably reflect the influence of Frances Goldwyn, Sam's wife since 1925, a lady of shrewd and cultivated taste who had early on taken over the reading of books and scripts submitted to her husband.

Sam was never scared to tackle a difficult project. However, with the prohibitions of the Hays Office, he could hardly have remained faithful to Emile Zola's study of vice when he made *Nana* (1934). It was shaped as a vehicle for his new discovery, the Polish actress Anna Sten, whom audiences decisively rejected. He bought Lillian Hellman's play *The Children's Hour*, which was considered by many to be

once recovered two weeks of Wyler's salary when the director quit a picture and jokingly offered him his money back. However, Sam spent whatever it took to make a good picture and Wyler respected him for that. Wyler's greatest triumph was persuading Goldwyn to make *Wuthering Heights* (1939). It took two years to overcome Goldwyn's dislike of a story with an unhappy ending, and even then Goldwyn had the final say: just before the film opened, and without telling Wyler, he sneaked in a final shot of the film's two lovers reunited in the hereafter.

But Goldwyn also respected Wyler and rallied to his defence when Myrna Loy was reluctant to work on *The Best Years of Our Lives* (1946) with a director she had heard was sadistic towards his actors. 'That's not true,' declared Goldwyn 'he's just a very mean fellow.' Despite Hollywood's belief that there would be no interest after the war in a serious film about returning airmen's problems of readjustment to civilian life, Goldwyn staked over $2 million of his own money and was

Above: holding the Oscars for The Best Years of Our Lives are Samuel Goldwyn (Best Film) – he also received the Irving Thalberg Award for services to the industry – Harold Russell (Best Supporting Actor) and William Wyler (Best Direction). Below: Guys and Dolls was one of Goldwyn's last films

amply rewarded when the film was a box-office success and won seven Oscars.

Goldwyn was always concerned with making his films as good as they could possibly be. He stopped production on *Nana* and *The Bishop's Wife* (1947) when he did not like the rushes and started afresh with new directors, regardless of the cost. He also had Wyler re-shoot the last half of *Come and Get It* (1936) as he wasn't entirely satisfied with the material produced by Howard Hawks.

The Goldwyn studios were run in the same way as the majors but on a smaller scale. His various departments were headed by top talent, although, in fact, he and Mrs Goldwyn took charge of the story department to the chagrin of those who tried to run it according to his often contradictory dictates. It is certainly to his credit that he encouraged the brilliant cinematographer Gregg Toland, who later worked on *Citizen Kane* (1940), to experiment; part of *The Wedding Night* (a 1935 Anna Sten picture) was test shot by Toland in 3-D, and the deep-focus images of *The Little Foxes* (1941) and *The Best Years of Our Lives* came about through Goldwyn's interest in advancing technical standards. The great art director Richard Day designed almost all of Goldwyn's pictures from 1930 to 1938 – including *Dead End* with its celebrated set of a New York slum. Goldwyn was initially disappointed: 'This slum cost plenty – it shouldn't look like any ordinary slum' he complained (or so legend has it). He was concerned that audiences should have the best that money could buy. Alfred Newman was another notable figure on the Goldwyn lot, the composer or music director of nearly every Goldwyn film in the Thirties. Goldwyn could even match the major studios in such intricate, expensive areas as special effects – which he proved when he gave art director James Basevi a free hand in creating the climactic sequence of *The Hurricane* (1937).

Even more important was Goldwyn's roster of stars. He had Gary Cooper, David Niven, Joel McCrea, Miriam Hopkins, Merle Oberon, Teresa Wright, Dana Andrews and Virginia Mayo under contract. Because of his limited output, he kept them busy by loaning them to other studios, either pocketing the profit of the transaction himself or acquiring another star in exchange. He got Bette Davis for *The Little Foxes* by providing Warner Brothers with Gary Cooper for *Sergeant York* (1941).

Goldwyn did not handle his own distribution although he was occasionally tempted to do so. In the Thirties he contributed to the success of United Artists as a member-owner, letting that company handle his pictures. In 1941, he went to RKO where his quality films propped up that ailing studio for more than a decade. Even so, Goldwyn kept a close eye on where his pictures were shown and on what terms. He even went to court to wrestle a fair deal from a circuit that was freezing his films out and helped create the climate in which the American government forced the major studios to divest themselves of theatre chains. Goldwyn's scrutiny extended overseas too: *Porgy and Bess* (1959) opened more than two years late in London because Sam decreed that only the Dominion Theatre was suitable and was prepared to wait until he could have it.

Like the major studios, Goldwyn seemed to lose his sureness of touch towards the end of the Forties. Films like *Enchantment* (1948), *Roseanna McCoy*, *My Foolish Heart* (both 1949), *Our Very Own*, *Edge of Doom* (both 1950) and *I Want You* (1951) failed to make a great impression on audiences, which were dwindling anyway. His star power was diminished and his new discoveries, like Farley Granger and Joan Evans, were not becoming major draws. His subjects tended to be too American for worldwide appeal. Even re-shooting key scenes in *Edge of Doom* after its opening failed to turn it into a success.

Goldwyn was 70 when his last Danny Kaye picture, *Hans Christian Andersen*, was released in 1952. He then relinquished all his contract

'Our comedies are not to be laughed at'

artists. There were two more special pictures. The first was *Guys and Dolls* (1955), which linked him for the first time with the company that bore his name – Metro-Goldwyn-Mayer – and which cost him an all-time record sum for the screen rights to the Broadway show. He daringly cast Marlon Brando and Jean Simmons in lead roles, alongside the more conventional casting of Frank Sinatra. It was expensive, but well-received both by critics and audiences.

Finally, Goldwyn made *Porgy and Bess* (1959). The problems were immense: he had to counter black opposition to the project, fearing it would be full of 'Uncle Tomism'; he had to rebuild his huge Catfish Row set after a fire; he changed directors and the film lost millions.

Not quite through with movie-making, Goldwyn made some trips to the Middle East in connection with a film he was contemplating. But he was an old man and a series of strokes confined him to a wheelchair. He died in 1974, aged 91, leaving a fortune estimated at $4 million. Not bad going for a Polish runaway who thrived on independence and often said 'I make my pictures to please myself'.

ALLEN EYLES

Chapter 26
Picking up the pieces

In the aftermath of World War II, film industries in Europe and the Far East were resurrected and played a vital role in building new societies

On September 3, 1943, four years to the day after the outbreak of hostilities between Britain and Germany, Italy unconditionally surrendered to the Allied powers. On May 7, 1945, General Jodl signed the document of Germany's surrender. Alone of the Axis powers, Japan fought on a few weeks more. On August 6, 1945, a United States B-29 bomber dropped an atom bomb on the city of Hiroshima, and less than a month later Japan finally surrendered. The war, in which 15 million military personnel and countless civilians had perished, was over. Out of the wreckage of the old, a new world had to be built, and the men who made the movies were everywhere conscious of their role in this reconstruction.

The Liberation found the French cinema at a complete standstill. German preparations for the Allied advances had paralysed the life of Paris, closing all the city's cinemas and halting film production. Nevertheless, despite chronic shortages of equipment and energy, production did recover and rose in 1946 to 96 films – not far short of pre-war levels – though, in most cases, post-war budgets were smaller.

In the following year, however, an agreement with the Americans to relax pre-war quota controls on the importation of Hollywood films caused French film production to plummet sharply. Imported films, dubbed into French, dominated the market and handicapped home-made product for 12 months until the quota was re-established. The subsequent recovery of the cinema industry was assisted by the introduction of two government measures: the Loi d'Aide à l'Industrie Cinématographique (1949) and the Loi de Développement de l'Industrie Cinématographique in 1953.

If the French cinema's economic situation was shaky, its prestige still rated highly. A series of notable films of the Occupation period, including Marcel Carné's Les Visiteurs du Soir (1942, The Devil's Own Envoy) and Les Enfants du Paradis (1945, Children of Paradise) and Robert Bresson's Les Anges du Péché (1943, Angels of Sin) were all revealed after the Liberation to worldwide acclaim.

Of the pre-war masters, Jacques Feyder was dead and Jean Renoir had stayed in America. Only René Clair resumed work in France and made Le Silence Est d'Or (1947, Man About Town), an attractive and mature reflection on old age. Claude Autant-Lara rose to fame with a series of literary adaptations – the exquisite Le Diable au Corps (1947, Devil in the Flesh), from a novel by Raymond Radiguet, about a youth's first love, and Occupe-toi d'Amélie (1949, Keep an Eye on Amelia) from a play by Feydeau.

Jean Cocteau, whose wartime film L'Eternel Retour (1943, Love Eternal) had been wrongly suspected of purveying 'German mysticism', pursued his own idiosyncratic way with the magical La Belle et la Bête (1946, Beauty and the Beast) and Les Parents Terribles (1948), adapted from his own play.

René Clément's La Bataille du Rail (1945, The Battle of the Railway Workers), one of the first French films released after the war, portrayed

railway workers fighting for the Resistance and suggested, through its spare shooting style, that French films might have developed a neo-realist movement similar to that of Italian cinema in the post-war years. Clément himself followed this film with another war subject in the realist mode, but Les Maudits (1947, The Accursed) did not find favour with audiences and Clément's example was not followed by other film-makers.

French directors seemed, in fact, more inclined to take up where they had left off, resuming the fatalistic style of pre-war films like Quai des Brumes (1938, Quay of Shadows) and Le Jour se Lève (1939, Daybreak). Carné made Les Portes de la Nuit (1946, Gates of the Night), a drama set in the wartime black market. Clément added to the melancholic mood with Au Delà des Grilles (1949, Beyond the Gates), and several other films echoed the 'noir' atmosphere – doomed lovers playing out their lives in gloomy surroundings; these included: Duvivier's Panique (1946, Panic) and Clouzot's Quai des Orfèvres (1947, Jenny Lamour).

Of the French directors who came to the fore in the immediate post-war years, the most notable was Jacques Becker. His first success was a light-hearted, unsentimental film, Antoine et Antoinette (1946), about a lost lottery ticket. This was followed by Rendez-vous de Juillet (1949, Rendezvous in July), in which Becker examined post-war youth through the interwoven stories of several young actresses. Edouard et Caroline (1951) portrayed a Parisian, bourgeois marriage and confirmed Becker's reputation as an expert maker of everyday comedies.

The documentary film-maker Georges Rouquier

Top left: Quai des Orfèvres *(the Paris police HQ), an atmospheric thriller in which a music-hall artist is accused of a crime passionnel, starred Louis Jouvet as a police inspector in one of his most celebrated roles. Top:* Panique *contained an outstanding performance by Michel Simon as an aged eccentric pursued by a suspicious community. Above:* Farrebique, *a highly acclaimed story that traces the fortunes of a rural family through the four seasons of the farming year*

Top: Jean Marais and Josette Day in Cocteau's La Belle et la Bête, *a surrealistic fantasy based on the age-old fairy-tale. Above:* Le Blé en Herbe *(1954, Ripening Seed) dealt with the awkwardness and hesitancy of young love. Top right: the story of the artist Utamaro and his unique art of body-painting is told in Mizoguchi's* Five Women Around Utamaro. *Above right: Denjiro Okochi in Kurosawa's* They Who Tread on the Tiger's Tail. *The title is taken from a proverb: 'From the mouth of a serpent, they had a narrow escape. No less hard way they went, than walking on a tiger's tail'*

made a single feature-length, dramatized documentary, *Farrebique* (1947), about the life of a farming family in the Massif Central. The film owed much to the style of the American documentarist Robert Flaherty, and the same tendency was perceptible in the post-war work of Roger Leenhardt – *Les Dernières Vacances* (1947, Last Holidays) and Louis Daquin, whose outstanding film *Le Point du Jour* (1948, First Light) dealt with the lives of the miners of northern France.

However progressive these films may have been, the popular fare was bourgeois comedy in which stars like Fernandel, Bourvil and Noël-Noël were consistently popular. Alongside such traditional offerings, the debut of Jacques Tati in *Jour de Fête* (1949, Day of the Fair) – combining the influences of Chaplin, neo-realism and French rustic comedy – was a singular and welcome innovation.

The end of the war found Japan, the last Axis enemy, in a desperate situation. Most cinemas were closed, and though the studios had remained theoretically open, the shortage of materials and equipment was acute. The whole country was placed under the regulations of the Supreme Command Allied Forces in the Pacific (SCAP) whose officers drafted and implemented the rules about what films should and should not be made.

Existing films about militarism, feudal loyalty, ritual suicide and the oppression of women were placed on the banned list. As to new projects, uplifting, recommended subjects included the peaceful organization of trade unions, respect for individual rights and the emancipation of women. The latter category provided the pretext for Mizoguchi's *Utamaro O Meguro Gonin No Onna* (1946, Five Women Around Utamaro). Meanwhile

the SCAP authorities industriously burned negatives and prints of some 225 forbidden films, which included works by outstanding directors like Kinoshita, Ichikawa and Kurosawa. Many prominent people in the industry were condemned as war criminals and removed from their posts as a result of SCAP investigations. Industrial troubles and strikes further undermined the structure of the Japanese film industry in the late Forties, most seriously affecting the giant company Toho.

Under the Occupation, subjects and styles of filmmaking changed radically. The period film practically disappeared, though old chivalric stories were often updated as modern gangster films, to which SCAP registered no objections. The much-favoured films about the new, emancipated woman resulted in some major works like Mizoguchi's *Joyu Sumako No Koi* (1947, *The Loves of Actress Sumako*) and Kinugasa's *Joyu* (1947, *The Actress*). Kurosawa's *Tora-no-o* (1945, *They Who Tread on the Tiger's Tail*) had the distinction of being banned both before and after the defeat of Japan. But Japan's recent past was examined in the same director's *Waga Seishun Ni Kuinashi* (1946, *No Regrets for Our Youth*).

Other major directors analysed post-war society, its problems and its victims: Mizoguchi in *Yoru No Onnatachi* (1948, *Women of the Night*) and Ozu in *Kaze No Naka No Mendori* (1948, *A Hen in the Wind*).

The Occupation brought one incidental but novel revolution to the Japanese cinema – the kiss. By the late Forties it had become an essential, sensational ingredient of any film with box-office ambitions. But even despite such dramatic Western innovations, the full revelation and flowering of post-war Japanese cinema was delayed until *Rashomon* (1950) brought Japan to the attention of the moviegoers abroad.

Germany was defeated, destroyed, demoralized and artificially divided into zones under the control of the British, American, French and Soviet conquerors. By the end of the war the number of operative cinemas had dwindled to a fraction. But, as the occupying powers realized, the value of cinema in the rehabilitation of a defeated people, they set about reopening movie houses and promoting production.

In the American zone the entertainment permitted to the Germans was strictly limited to Hollywood escapism. There was little reminder or re-examination of the recent war. Production, too, was closely supervised by the military government, which was rigorous in excluding suspected ex-Nazis.

In 1947 production was licensed at the Geiselgasteig Studios in Munich and at the old Templehof Studios in Berlin. Apart from some footage shot for

Hollywood films like *Berlin Express* and *A Foreign Affair* (both 1948) and a notable success with Robert Stemmle's *Berliner Ballade* (1948, *The Ballad of Berlin*), a satire on post-war Germany, no truly distinguished films emerged from the Berlin studios in this period.

The British Control Commission was more relaxed about the film entertainment permitted the defeated people. Old German films were allowed, if they were thought to be clean of Nazi content. Foreign films, too, were re-introduced after their long wartime absence and were shown in both subtitled and dubbed versions; among them were British war pictures like *The Foreman Went to France* (1942) and *San Demetrio, London* (1943).

A number of German productions dealt frankly with recent history and contemporary problems. Wolfgang Liebeneiner, who had been an active director during the war years, portrayed a young woman's gradual disillusionment with Hitler in *Liebe '47* (1947, *Love '47*): she falls in love with a man suffering from war wounds and her faith in humanity is restored. Rudolph Jugert's *Film Ohne Titel* (1947, *Film Without a Title*) adopted a humorous approach by posing the question of how to make a comedy for German audiences who were suffering the tribulations of the post-war period. On the other hand, Arthur Brauner's *Morituri* (1946, *Those About to Die*) confronted the reality of the death camps.

Although these films used plenty of location footage and adopted a straightforward shooting style, they were never part of the mainstream of neo-realism. One German film, however, can be properly termed neo-realist: Rossellini's *Germania, Anno Zero* (1947, *Germany, Year Zero*), a grim and desolate description of a young boy's degradation in the social conditions of the defeated land.

The Eastern zone, under Soviet control, began with considerable advantages. The newly formed Defa (Deutsches Film Aktiengesellschaft) inherited

German film-makers – whether in the East or the West – seemed more preoccupied with the legacy of the war than with plans for peacetime

the old Ufa organization, the Neubabelsburg and Johannistal Studios and the Agfa laboratories along with the Agfacolor process. Everything received full state backing. In the immediate post-war years some of the best and most progressive German directors were attracted to work for Defa. Wolfgang Staudte's *Die Mörder Sind Unter Uns* (1946, *The Murderers Are Among Us*) examined varying attitudes to former war criminals and was perhaps the best of the group of films set in the ruins of Berlin that earned the generic name *Trümmerfilme* ('rubble films'). Other notable examples were Gerhard Lamprecht's *Irgendwo in Berlin* (1946, *Anywhere in Berlin*), a film about the plight of children in the aftermath of defeat, and Kurt Maetzig's *Ehe im Schatten* (1947, *Marriage in the Shadows*), based on the story of the famous actor Gottschalk who, together with his Jewish wife, committed suicide in Nazi Germany.

Slatan Dudow, who had directed *Kühle Wampe* (1932, *Whither Germany?*), from a Brecht scenario, before fleeing from Nazi Germany, returned to make *Unser Tägliche Brot* (1949, *Our Daily Bread*), a somewhat schematic film about socialist reconstruction. Dudow was later to direct a striking feature, *Stärker als die Nacht* (1954, *Stronger Than Night*) about Nazi oppression of communists.

Defa was now headed by the Moscow-trained Sepp Schwab. Bureaucracy took root and the best of

Above: the legacy of the Nazi regime was shown in Stronger Than Night, *a film that revealed how communists were interned in concentration camps. Left: Robert Stemmle's* The Ballad of Berlin *made post-war German society and the occupying forces objects of satire. Gert Frobe played 'Otto Nobody', a 'little man' picking his way through the black marketeers, the rationing and the rubble of Berlin. Below: cold-war politics prompted a succession of anti-American films; the Soviet* Meeting on the Elbe *was typical of such propaganda*

film was suppressed (it finally emerged more than a decade later). The intended third part was finally abandoned. Eisenstein never worked again and died, at the age of 50, in 1948.

The films that did meet with approval were, for the most part, historical fabrications. Highly favoured, of course, were those that deified Stalin, like Mikhail Chiaureli's appalling *The Vow* (1946), *The Fall of Berlin* (1949) and *The Unforgettable Year of 1919* (1951). Other films, like Abraham Room's *Court of Honour* and Mikhail Romm's *The Russian Question* (both 1948), Alexandrov's *Meeting on the Elbe* (1949) and Chiaureli's *Secret Mission* (1950) attacked the American character and US imperialist aims, as well as 'cosmopolitanism' in general.

Under Zhdanov's control Soviet film production dropped gradually until 1952 when only five feature films appeared in the year. The preference was more and more for apparently 'safe' subjects and this explains the seemingly endless output of idealized historical biographies, direct records of stage productions (favoured by Stalin, who liked the theatre but had become increasingly paranoid about appearing in public), children's films and technical novelties like a version of *Robinson Crusoe* (1946) made in 3-D.

The Polish cinema was nationalized in November 1945, with Aleksander Ford, a notable pre-war director, as head of the new organization called Film Polski. The first post-war Polish feature, Leonard Bucskowski's *Forbidden Songs*, did not appear until 1947 but fast became a great hit at the box-office. The film popularized folk ballads that had been banned under the Nazis and is still one of the most successful films ever made in Poland.

Bucskowski followed it with a contemporary story of post-war reconstruction, *Skarb* (1948, *The Treasure*). This film, starring Danuta Szaflarska who had appeared in *Forbidden Songs*, dealt in a gently humorous manner with the acute housing shortage in post-war Poland. Aleksander Ford, himself a Jew, made *Ulica Granicza* (1948, *Border Street*) about the solidarity of Jews and Poles which culminated in the Warsaw ghetto uprising of 1943.

Wanda Jakubowska drew on her own recent memories of Auschwitz for *Ostatni Etap* (1948, *The Last Stage*). This small group of films was a remarkable start of a new-born industry, but in 1949 the Polish Workers Party assumed power and a congress of film-makers at Wisla laid down the new, strict dogmas of socialist realism: interest in imaginative and stylistic devices was condemned along with the portrayal of introspective characters; instead 'the positive hero of the new Poland' was to be made the subject of films that dealt with everyday life in the new socialist state.

Above: Polish Resistance fighters defend their ground in Border Street, *a re-creation of the Warsaw ghetto uprising of 1943. Below: Adám Szirtes in* The Soil Beneath Your Feet, *a man with marital problems. Below right:* Somewhere in Europe, *about a band of homeless Hungarian children who wander from town to town amid the rubble of post-war Hungary*

the directors, who had provided a brief renascence in East Germany, crossed to the West: Arthur Maria Rabenalt, Gerhard Lamprecht, Erich Engel and finally – after completing three more films for Defa – the gifted Staudte. Even after the death of Stalin in 1953, the revival of East German cinema was to be slow and reluctant.

The developments in East Germany, paralleled throughout the whole of socialist Europe, were primarily the result of the strengthening influence of the Soviet Union. In the USSR the ending of the war brought a renewal of the grim repressions that had marked Stalin's domination in the Thirties. A. A. Zhdanov, a prominent member of the Politburo, had become Stalin's mouthpiece and led the campaign to bring art and artists into order, making them serve the precise and immediate needs of the Party. A Resolution of the Central Committee in September 1946 condemned the second part of Leonid Lukov's film *A Great Life* (1946) for its realistic treatment of the people of the Donbas coal basin during the war. What was now officially required was an idealized image of Soviet history.

Other films came under attack: Kosintsev and Trauberg's *Plain People* (1945) was alleged to have dealt too frankly with the war, and V.I. Pudovkin suffered criticism for his historical biography of *Admiral Nakhimov* (1946). Eisenstein, too, was a victim of the prevalent ideology. In the second part of *Ivan the Terrible* (1946) his portrait of the Tsar as an iron ruler surrounded by a secret army was evidently too close to being a likeness of Stalin. The

In Hungary the path of cinema history, from euphoria to reconstruction and from reconstruction to disillusion, was very much the same, if more complex. Production had continued in Budapest during the war, though by 1945 it had fallen to only three films a year. After the war the great film theorist Béla Balász returned from a quarter of a century of exile to teach at the newly founded Academy of Dramatic and Film Art. The classic Soviet films were shown in Hungary for the first time and film-makers also had the chance to see large numbers of Hollywood films. But from 1947 film production permits were granted only to the leading political parties. Two outstanding films resulted from this period: István Szöt's *Enek a Búzam-ezökröl* (1947, *Song of the Cornfields*) and Géza Radványi's *Valahol Európában* (1947, *Somewhere in Europe*). The latter was scripted by Béla Balász and told the story of a group of delinquent war orphans through a touching, idealistic fantasy that owed much to the Soviet film *The Road to Life* (1931).

In March 1948 the Hungarian film industry was

In the post-war period, the film industries of Eastern Europe revived, but the films' subject-matter was often dull and dogmatic

nationalized and the first films produced by the state were auspicious: Frigyes Bán's *Talpalatnyi Föld* (1948, *The Soil Beneath Your Feet*) Imre Jeney's *Egy Asszony Elmdul* (1949, *A Woman Makes a New Start*) and Felix Mariassy's *Szabóné* (1949, *Anna Szabó*) which dealt compassionately with problems of adjustment to the new socialist world.

Soon, however, Hungarian film-makers, too, found their work forced into the schematic moulds of socialist realism. The script, which had to be approved in advance, became paramount. Béla Balász was removed from his post at the Academy. Pudovkin was sent from Moscow as an adviser on film affairs and Hungary moved into the most sterile period of her long film history.

No other Eastern European cinema began the post-war period with greater optimism than that of Czechoslovakia. A well-established film industry had survived the war and was nationalized in August 1945. A body of expert and experienced directors was assembled, among them Otakar Vávra, a specialist in historical and literary subjects. Jiří Weiss returned from London, where he had worked with the Crown Film Unit, and made his first feature film *Uloupená Hranice* (1947, *Stolen Frontier*). The Czech cinema was given a great moral boost when Karel Steklý's *Siréna* (1946, *The Strike*) won the Golden Lion at the first post-war Venice Film Festival.

Similar patterns evolved in the Romanian cinema (nationalized in 1948 but barely past the stage of primitive comedy and socialist morality films) and the Bulgarian film industry, though in 1948 the celebrated Soviet director Sergei Vasiliev was loaned to the Bulgarians to make *Geroite na Shipka*, (*Heroes of the Shipka*) about the liberation of Bulgaria from Turkish rule in the nineteenth century.

In post-war Yugoslavia it had been necessary to create a national cinema from scratch – rather as the state itself had been established. The separate republics that made up Yugoslavia had their own languages and their own cultural character. In the summer of 1945 a state film enterprise was established. Promising young people were sent abroad to film schools and film centres were established in Belgrade and in the major cities of the six republics.

The first productions of this newly-formed in-

dustry were documentaries, but in 1947 a feature film *Slavica* (dir. Vjekoslav Afrić) was released. The film dealt with the partisans' struggles against the Nazis and this theme has remained a dominant preoccupation of Yugoslav cinema. Similar partisan films from the same period included Radoš Novaković's *Decak Mita* (1948, *The Boy Mita*) and Vojislav Nanović's *Besmrtna Mladost* (1948, *Immortal Youth*). Despite the break with the Soviet Union in 1948, Yugoslavia itself evolved a dogma of socialist realism, though here it was defined as 'national' realism. Whatever the name, the image of Eastern European cinema in the late Forties was one conditioned by the political situation – namely the Cold War.   DAVID ROBINSON

Top: a dramatic scene from Stolen Frontier, *a post-war Czech account of the German occupation of the Sudetenland. Above: the wives of striking steel workers in the Czech film* Siréna; *the film was based on a novel by the popular author Marie Majerova. The end of the war saw the start of a feature-film industry in Yugoslavia; the aspirations of the new country were often expressed in films about youth;* The Boy Mita *by Radoš Novaković (below) was typical of this trend*

505

The Third Man

Directed by Carol Reed, 1949
Prod co: (Alexander Korda, David O. Selznick for) London Films. **prod:** Carol Reed. **assoc prod:** Hugh Perceval. **sc:** Graham Greene. **photo:** Robert Krasker. **add photo:** John Wilcox, Stan Pavey. **ed:** Oswald Hafenrichter. **art dir:** Vincent Korda, Joseph Bato, John Hawkesworth. **mus:** Anton Karas. **sd:** John Cox. **ass dir:** Guy Hamilton. **r/t:** 104 mins.
Cast: Joseph Cotten (*Holly Martins*), Orson Welles (*Harry Lime*), Alida Valli (*Anna Schmidt*), Trevor Howard (*Major Calloway*), Paul Hoerbiger (*porter*), Ernst Deutsch (*Baron Kurtz*), Erich Ponto (*Dr Winkel*), Wilfred Hyde White (*Crabbit*), Bernard Lee (*Sergeant Paine*), Siegfried Breuer (*Popescu*), Geoffrey Keen (*British policeman*), Annie Rosar (*porter's wife*), Hedwig Bliebtrau (*Anna's 'Old Woman'*), Harbut Helbek (*Hansl*), Alexis Chesnakov (*Brodsky*), Paul Hardtmuth (*hall porter*).

After they had completed *The Fallen Idol* (1948), director Carol Reed and writer Graham Greene dined with Alexander Korda, who was anxious for them to work on a new film together. Although they agreed on a setting – post-war Vienna – they were stuck for a story until Greene produced an old envelope on which years before he had written a single sentence:

'I had paid my last farewell to Harry a week ago, when his coffin was lowered into the frozen February ground, so it was with incredulity that I saw him pass by, without a sign of recognition, among the host of strangers in the Strand.'

This became the basis of Reed's *The Third Man*, a film that was to take the Grand Prix at the Cannes Film Festival and earn him a third successive British Film Academy Award for Best Picture.

Greene drafted the story as a novel and then, working closely with Reed, turned it into a screenplay. Although it is in many ways a classic Greene tale, with its themes of guilt and disillusionment, corruption and betrayal, Greene himself has been quick to accord to Reed credit for many of the film's memorable qualities. It was Reed who insisted on the bleakly uncompromising ending where Anna, as she leaves Harry's funeral, walks not

Left: Carol Reed directs the chase scene in the sewers

into Holly's arms in the conventional final clinch, but passed him, staring impassively ahead. It was Reed who discovered the zither-player, Anton Karas, whose 'Harry Lime theme' gave the film a special haunting quality. It was Reed who prevailed on a reluctant Orson Welles to play the comparatively small but pivotal part of Harry Lime. Welles became so enthusiastic about the film that he contributed to the script a much-quoted justification of Harry's criminal activities:

'In Italy for thirty years under the Borgias they had warfare, terror, murder, bloodshed. They produced Michelangelo, Leonardo da Vinci and the Renaissance. In Switzerland they had brotherly love, five hundred years of democracy and peace. And what did that produce – the cuckoo clock. So long, Holly.'

It was, of course, also Carol Reed who gave remarkable visual life to Greene's brilliantly wrought script, a perfect marriage of word and image, sound and symbol. Holly's odyssey in search of a truth that is to destroy his oldest friend, the girl they both love and, in a sense, Holly himself, is conducted against the background of post-war Vienna, unforgettably evoked by Robert Krasker's powerful chiaroscuro photography which won him a deserved Oscar. The vast, echoing, empty baroque buildings that serve as military headquarters and decaying lodging houses are a melancholy reminder of the Old Vienna, the city of Strauss waltzes and Hapsburg elegance, plunged, in the aftermath of war, into a nightmare world of political intrigue, racketeering and murder. The shadowed, narrow streets and the jagged bomb-sites are the haunt of black marketeers, vividly portrayed inhabitants of a dislocated society. There is a powerful symbolism, too, in the places where Harry makes his appearances: a giant ferris wheel from which he looks down contemptuously at the scuttling mortals, and the Viennese sewers where, after a breathtaking and sharply edited final chase, he is cornered, rat-like, and dispatched.

The angled shooting, atmospheric locations, and sombre shadow-play eloquently convey the pervading aura of tension, mystery and corruption. It is an aura enhanced rather than dissipated by flashes of black humour, such as the sequence in which Holly, bustled by strangers into a car and believing himself kidnapped, discovers he is being taken to address a cultural gathering, the members of which think he is a famous novelist.

The cast is superlative, with the four stars outstanding: Joseph Cotten as decent, dogged, simple, faithful Holly; Alida Valli as the wonderfully enigmatic Anna; Trevor Howard as the shrewd, determined, quietly spoken military policeman Calloway; and Orson Welles as the fascinating Harry Lime. *The Third Man* was one of the peaks of post-war British filmmaking and remains a flawlessly crafted, timelessly perfect work of art.
JEFFREY RICHARDS

1

2

3

Holly Martins, a writer of hack Westerns, arrives in Vienna to look for his friend Harry Lime, only to be told that Harry has been killed in a street accident. Holly attends the funeral (1) and is questioned by military policeman Major Calloway (2), who tells him that Harry was a racketeer selling penicillin so diluted that it caused the deaths of sick children.

Holly sets out to find the truth and visits Harry's girlfriend, actress Anna Schmidt (3), who suggests that Harry's death may not have been accidental. An elderly porter reports seeing a mysterious third man at the scene of the accident (4); next day the porter is found dead. Holly is chased by two thugs but escapes. Leaving Anna's apartment, he sees Harry in the shadows (5) and realizes he is 'the third man'. Harry's coffin is exhumed and found to contain the body of a police informer.

Harry arranges to meet Holly and offers to buy his silence (6). But when Calloway arrests Anna (7) (who has a forged passport) and plans to deport her behind the Iron Curtain, Holly, who is in love with her, betrays Harry to the police in return for her release. A chase through the sewers underneath the city (8), ends with Holly shooting Harry dead. Anna attends the funeral and then walks away past Holly without speaking to him (9).

4

5

6

7

Ivan the Terrible

Eisenstein's project to make a film about Tsar Ivan IV – *Ivan the Terrible* – was accepted for production at Mosfilm in 1941 but inevitably delayed by the German invasion of the USSR which began in June of that year. When filming finally started in 1943, Moscow was still under attack, so the film was shot at the Alma Ata studios in the heart of Central Asia.

The scenario was conceived in two parts, but in production Eisenstein extended the piece to become a trilogy, a decision which was to cause the authorities to misunderstand the nature of the film and view a part of it with grave disapproval.

Ivan IV was the ruler who in the sixteenth century completed the task (begun by his grandfather Ivan III) of uniting the Russian lands under a single autocrat or Tsar. In the process he overcame rival feudal princes, drove out the Tartars and paved the way for an opening for the province of Rus upon the Baltic Sea – finally achieved 150 years later by Peter the Great.

As with his previous film, *Alexander Nevsky* (1938), Eisenstein certainly intended *Ivan the Terrible* to arouse patriotic pride in Russia's past achievements and heroes as part of the preparation for the coming German onslaught. What especially interested him was the human aspect of this historical recreation; he was fascinated by the personality of a man who combined constructive idealism with growing ruthlessness.

Was Ivan indeed 'Terrible' – a monster? Had he been so the project would have been far less interesting. Undoubtedly the struggle for national identity and royal absolutism led to the committing of vile deeds. But, as Eisenstein reminds us, the century that Ivan lived in was one of widespread bloody and bitter conflict throughout Europe. It is only in recent times that the word 'Terrible' has acquired its evil overtones in English. The Russian word applied to Ivan – *Grozny* – has much more the meaning of 'awe-inspiring'. It was this awe of majesty that Eisenstein sought to create throughout the film.

He adopted many special devices for this purpose. The acting is in an intense, almost ritualistic style, quite unlike the realistic use of natural settings, persons and movements for which he became famous in his early work. To em-

phasize the complex duality of his subject he used two master cameramen, adding to the limpid clarity of Tissé's exteriors the glitter and darkness of Moskvin's interiors, so expressive of intrigue. He used colour in one reel, and in an unusual way, not to imitate nature but to heighten the drama. The composer Prokofiev and he married the rhythms of music and image more closely than ever before. He also used a new method of cutting away towards the end of a character's speech so that his closing lines were superimposed on the image of the listener – thus focusing attention on his reaction and redoubling the impact of the words.

The exact action as filmed can be studied in the script published beforehand. It is set out in a series of magnificent episodes: Ivan's assertion of authority against his regents while yet a boy; his self-coronation as Tsar in the Cathedral of the Assumption at the age of 17; his luxurious wedding, and the quelling, by his personal domination alone, of a panicky crowd; the defeat of Tartar might at the city of Kazan; the treachery of the boyars (nobles) and disloyalty of his friends when he lies ill; the poisoning of his consort by his foes; his withdrawal from Moscow and triumphant return to the city.

Here ends *Part One*. It reached the Soviet screen at the end of 1944, and two years later was awarded the Stalin Prize First Class for cinema for that year.

Part Two of the scenario depicts Ivan's terrible revenge. He draws closer around him his 'iron ring' of guards – the *oprichniki* or 'men apart' – to slaughter his enemies. He frustrates a plot by his kinsfolk to assassinate him in an amazing cathedral scene. Finally, despite corruption and treachery even within the ranks of his own 'Tsar's men',

he eventually leads his troops against the Teutonic castles to reach the Baltic shore.

Inevitably, by dividing the intended second part, and separating off its beginning of claustrophobic horror as *Tale Two: The Boyars' Plot*, with the end, the attainment of the goal of unification, to come in yet a third, Eisenstein obscured, so far as practical viewing was concerned, the balance of the whole.

Tale Two was ready in 1946. In the circumstances it was not altogether surprising that, when the Central Committee of the Soviet Communist Party decided to take several famous directors to task, they sharply criticized this film for untruth. Ivan, they said, had become Hamlet-like, 'a man of no will and little character,' and his guards 'Klu Klux Klan-like degenerates'. It is ironical that *Pravda* published this criticism just as Eisenstein and his friends were celebrating the award for *Part One*. Purely coincidentally, without yet knowing of this, he collapsed with a heart attack while dancing alone at the festivities. He recovered slowly in the VIP's hospital, and it was agreed that when well enough he should work on completing *Ivan the Terrible* as a two-part film using sequences from *Tale Two*, reels already made for 'Three' – four of which are said to have been finished but have disappeared – and shooting final scenes on the Baltic shore. But his convalescence was slow; he wrote and lectured a little, then died from a second attack in 1948 while writing an article on the film's use of colour.

The ban on *Tale Two* was lifted only in 1958, after 12 years' waiting, and immediately had an overwhelming success at the International Fair in Brussels, completing the extraordinary, though unfinished, legacy of this remarkable director.

IVOR MONTAGU

1 The coronation of Ivan, the young Grand Duke of Muscovy, as Tsar of Rus.
2 The royal wedding feast of Ivan and his bride Anastasia.
3 Ivan at the siege of Kazan, at which he defeats the Tartars.
4 Ivan swears vengeance on the coffin of his wife, poisoned by the nobles.
5 Ivan secludes himself in a monastery, but the people of Moscow beg him to return and rule over them.

6 The Tsar's aunt plots to kill Ivan and place her son, Vladimir, on the throne in his stead.
7 At a banquet, Vladimir, fuddled, incautiously reveals his aunt's plot.
8 Apparently in high spirits, Ivan calls for the royal regalia and persuades Vladimir to head the procession to evening prayer clad in the royal robes.
9 The assassin, hired by the aunt to kill Ivan, strikes her own son by mistake.

Directed by Sergei Eisenstein. Part One, 1944; Part Two (Tale Two: The Boyars' Plot), 1946
Prod co: Mosfilm. **sc:** Sergei Eisenstein. **photo:** Andrei Moskvin, Edouard Tissé. **art dir:** Isaak Shpinel. **mus:** Sergei Prokofiev. **lyr:** V. Lugovsky. **ass dir:** B. Sveshnikov, L. Indenblom. Moscow premiere of Part One, 30 December 1944.
Cast: Nikolai Cherkasov (*Ivan*), Ludmila Tselikovskaya (*Anastasia Romanovna, the Tsaritsa*), Mikhail Zharov (*Malyuta Skuratov*), A. Buma (*Alexei Basmanov*), M. Kuznetsov (*Fyodor, Basmanov's son*), Serafina Birman (*Euphrosyne Staritsky, the Tsar's aunt*), Pavel Kadochnikov (*Vladimir Staritsky, her son*), Mikhail Nazvanov (*Prince Andrew Kurbsky*), Andrei Abrikosov (*Boyar Fyodor Kolychev, later Metropolitan Philip*), Alexander Mgebrov (*Pimen, Archbishop of Novgorod*), V.I. Pudovkin (*a beggar fanatic*), A. Balashov (*Peter Volynets*), Pavel Massalsky, (*King Sigismund of Poland*), Eric Pyriev (*Ivan as a boy*).

Double Adaptors

The screenwriters Aurenche and Bost specialized in adapting classic French novels for the screen and were responsible for the predominantly literary nature of post-war French cinema

From the end of World War II to the late Fifties, the cinema in France was characterized by films which were high-quality products of skilful adaptation, rather than works bearing the unmistakable stamp of a particular creator. It is true that this period saw a number of features by veterans who had already established themselves as film artists in the Thirties – Jean Renoir, René Clair (both of whom had worked abroad during the Occupation), Marcel Carné and Jean Cocteau. It is also true that Robert Bresson and Jacques Tati made films that, though few in number, were both highly personal and cinematically original. The centreground of the French cinema was, however, occupied by a succession of features that were the work of an extraordinarily fruitful partnership between the screenwriters Jean Aurenche and Pierre Bost.

Both men began to work in the cinema before World War II. Jean Aurenche (born in 1904) joined an advertising agency in the

Twenties where, with the future playwright Jean Anouilh, he wrote screenplays for publicity films. After co-scripting and co-directing two documentaries in 1933, he started to script features in 1936. Pierre Bost (1901–75) entered the civil service in the Twenties. In his spare time he became a moderately successful novelist and first applied his talents to the cinema in 1939 with a film called *L'Héritier de Mondésir* (The Heir of Mondésir). The two men joined forces in 1943 and, together with the director Claude Autant-Lara, wrote the script of *Douce* (1943), based on a mediocre novel by a minor author, Michel Davet.

Like many films made during the Occupation, *Douce* was set in a historical period that was comfortably distant from France's contemporary situation. Social or political comment was eschewed in favour of psychological interest. The film shows how two fortune-seekers (a middle-aged man and woman) win the hearts of a sheltered girl and her widowed father, a retired army officer. The young girl, Douce, falls in love with one of them and her father with the other, but both are betrayed when it is revealed that the fortune-seeking

Above left: Michèle Morgan and Pierre Blanchar, as the Protestant minister who falls in love with her, in La Symphonie Pastorale. Above: Odette Joyeux and Marguerite Moreno in the bitter romance Douce. Far left: an original poster for La Symphonie Pastorale. Left and below: poster and shot from Occupe-toi d'Amélie, an entertaining period farce

Above: in Le Diable au Corps, Gérard Philipe and Micheline Presle are lovers who scandalize French society during World War I. Top: Georges Poujouly and Brigitte Fossey playing their 'forbidden games' in Clément's Jeux Interdits. Top right: travellers sit down to eat at an inn whose owner is a murderer in L'Auberge Rouge

newcomers are themselves lovers. What gives this elegant, apparently conventional film an extra dimension is the implicit view of a cruel world, where the privileged long for love while the underprivileged envy their material comfort.

This bitter, satirical tone, which was to become a feature of the films created by the close collaboration of these three minds, is not present in Autant-Lara's previous works, even in those where he worked with Aurenche alone.

The chemistry of this working relationship was complex and volatile. Pierre Bost was non-conformist by the very fact of his Protestant background. Jean Aurenche was raised by Jesuits and harboured strongly anti-clerical sentiments; his politics were socialist. For his part, Autant-Lara became notorious for his militant atheism and anarchist sympathies.

Script collaborators seldom own up to enquiries about who actually did what, but it appears that Aurenche tended to concentrate on the main lines of the scenario, while Bost specialized in writing the dialogue. Above all, however, it was a group effort, as Aurenche explained in an interview in the journal Positif:

'I like working in collaboration because I like people. For me, the ideal combination is an adaptor, a dialoguist and a director working in unison. When there are three of you, you have many more ideas.'

Film of the book

Aurenche and Bost virtually cornered the market in adaptions from novels. As their work progressed into the Fifties, a pattern was established that confirmed the literary nature of the mainstream of French cinema. Their second collaboration was based on a much more distinguished piece of fiction than the source of Douce: the book was André Gide's La Symphonie Pastorale (The Pastoral Symphony). The film, directed by Jean Delannoy, enjoyed commercial success when it was released in 1946, although many felt that it did not fully capture the spirit of the original. The novel is written in the form of a diary which reveals the self-deception of a Protestant minister who does not realize that he is falling in love with the blind girl he and his wife have adopted. In the screen version, the pastor is portrayed rather two-dimensionally as a hypocrite and the psychological attention is focused on the girl, admirably played by Michèle Morgan.

After completing their work on La Symphonie Pastorale, Aurenche and Bost again teamed up with Autant-Lara to work on an adaptation of Le Diable au Corps, the penultimate novel by Raymond Radiguet who had died very young in 1923. The story, set in

World War I, is of the doomed love affair between an adolescent and an older woman whose husband is fighting in the trenches. Aurenche and Bost's version shocked many people on account of its close parallels with recent wartime experiences. Nevertheless Le Diable au Corps (1947, Devil in the Flesh) was a commercial and critical success, thanks mainly to the sensitive acting of Gérard Philipe and Micheline Presle in the leading roles. The critic Lo Duca praised the writers:

'The scenario is definitely, even violently cinematographic and this is the finest tribute that can be paid to the work of Aurenche, Bost and Autant-Lara.'

Despite a few dissenting voices, Le Diable au Corps was seen as proof that it was possible to bring a work of literature to the screen without betraying the original text but, at the same time, without sacrificing cinematic values.

Their reputation now firmly established, Aurenche and Bost had no difficulty in finding work, either singly or as a team. With Autant-Lara, they adapted the Feydeau farce Occupe-toi d'Amélie (1949, Keep an Eye on Amelia) and wrote L'Auberge Rouge (1951, The Red Inn) which was, for once, an original screenplay based on an idea by Aurenche. In the film a monk, played by Fernandel, saves a group of bourgeois travellers from a murderous innkeeper and his wife but then unwittingly causes their death. Aurenche's anti-Catholic feeling comes to the fore when the monk, who has heard the killer's confession, is shown to be unable to warn the guests directly of their danger because of his vow of secrecy.

Aurenche and Bost's next assignment was the equally scandalous Jeux Interdits (1952, Forbidden Games). This film was in a quite different register from L'Auberge Rouge and depicted the strange games of two children during World War II, who create a cemetery for animals and insects, stealing crosses from their parents and the church graveyard. The director was René Clément, with whom Aurenche and Bost had already worked on Au Delà des Grilles (1949, Beyond the Gates), a melodrama set in Genoa from a story originally written by Cesare Zavattini and Suso Cecchi d'Amico.

The Aurenche and Bost scenario for Le Blé en Herbe (1954, Ripening Seed) was adapted from a novel by Colette about the relationship between a teenage girl and a boy, the latter being initiated into the mysteries of love by an older woman. The British critic Gavin Lambert commented on their adaptation:

'There is more of the real Colette in some of the scenes in Marc Allégret's Lac aux Dames (for which she wrote the screenplay) than in any film directly derived from her own work. In Le Blé en Herbe, the scriptwriters Aurenche and

Above: Danielle Darrieux, who has lost her lover, in Le Rouge et le Noir. *Right: a family funeral in the Zola-adaptation* Gervaise. *Below: in* La Traversée de Paris *Jean Gabin and Bourvil are black marketeers who carry an illicit pig across Paris*

Bost have been reasonably faithful to the letter but Autant-Lara's handling, alas, betrays the spirit. The film sadly lacks the elliptical grace and sensibility of *Le Diable au Corps*.'

Mature talents and young Turks

Although *Le Blé en Herbe* and other texts which they had adapted did suggest a tendency to treat certain taboo subjects, film criticism was about to take a new turn, and Aurenche and Bost were surprised to find themselves villified as pillars of the cultural establishment. François Truffaut, writing in the journal *Cahiers du Cinéma*, led this critique of dominant French cinema. He refuted the claims that their adaptations of literary works were imaginative but faithful transpositions of the original texts. Truffaut rejected their statements that what they had created were the cinematic equivalents of passages in novels which could not be filmed directly. He went on to suggest that in their various adaptations, numerous scenes from the source works were unjustifiably distorted to convey their own anti-clerical, anti-bourgeois views. Nor might it be allowed that such recurrent features entitled them to be classified as 'auteurs' (according to the theory of film authorship then being defined by *Cahiers du Cinéma*). They hid, he alleged, behind successful works of fiction so as to assure themselves of a public and wrote scripts that were literary or academic, to which the films' directors merely added the images.

This attack astonished Aurenche and Bost,

especially as the latter had received Truffaut in a most friendly fashion, lending him the rejected script of *Le Journal d'un Curé de Campagne* (*Diary of a Country Priest*), which the young critic had proceeded to use as a weapon against both writers. They did not counterattack, but in an interview in 1955 Bost did point out that adaptation was in part adoption and that an adopted child often absorbed the characteristics of its new parents.

In the meantime, Aurenche and Bost had worked with Autant-Lara on a version of Stendhal's *Le Rouge et le Noir* (1954, The Red and the Black). The film was an extremely expensive Franco-Italian co-production, starring Gérard Philipe, which was cut by over an hour for foreign release and was only moderately successful at the box-office. As the critic of *Time* magazine put it, the effect of the film was 'to vulgarize Stendhal's passionate parvenu as a sort of angry young man in grey flannel culottes'.

A much more satisfactory adaptation of one of the 'classic' novels of nineteenth-century literature was their version of Emile Zola's *L'Assomoir*, directed by René Clément and retitled *Gervaise* (1956). As Clément himself made clear, the change of title represented a shift of emphasis: attention was to be focused on the main character rather than on the problem of alcoholism in a working-class family at the end of the last century. It could be argued that this is, in fact, what the novel actually does, despite Zola's theories of pursuing scientific method in literature. Another change from the source novel is the introduction of a strike, but this element is in keeping with the political aspect evident elsewhere in Zola's 'Rougon-Macquart' family saga of which the novel *L'Assomoir* is just a part. If anything is missing from *Gervaise*, it is some form of cinematic equivalent for the poetic

quality created by the novelist's rich imagery.

Aurenche and Bost returned to work with Autant-Lara for their next screenplay, *La Traversée de Paris* (1956), a rather free adaptation of a novella by Marcel Aymé. The film follows the adventures of a petty blackmarketeer, played by Bourvil, and an artist in search of excitement, played by Jean Gabin, as they trek through the night across Paris. The setting is the Occupation, and the two men are carrying a consignment of pork in suitcases. Neither they nor the various people they meet are particularly admirable human beings and, despite the touch of humour and the addition of a happy ending, this film is perhaps the most perfect expression of the misanthropic vein that runs through all the products of Aurenche/Bost/Autant-Lara collaboration.

End of an era

Their next combined effort, *En Cas de Malheur* (1958, In Case of Misfortune), starring Jean Gabin, Edwige Feuillère and ('in a serious role') Brigitte Bardot, was an adaptation of a Georges Simenon novel and, though it was reasonably close to the narrative line of the original text, it failed to capture its stifling atmosphere. Ironically, François Truffaut praised both these films, but by 1958 the cinema according to Aurenche, Bost and Autant-Lara was on the way out. Roger Vadim had pointed the way with his 1956 hymn of praise to Bardot, *Et Dieu Créa la Femme* (*And God Created Woman*), Louis Malle had followed with *L'Ascenseur Pour l'Echafaud* (*Lift to the Scaffold*) and in 1959 the *nouvelle vague* was attracting public attention.

Although the two scriptwriters continued to work, individually or as a team, throughout the Sixties, their names were soon forgotten in a cinema where the director had been raised to the status of a superstar. In 1973, two years before Bost's death, the Aurenche and Bost partnership was brought back into the limelight by Bertrand Tavernier, a representative of the post-*nouvelle vague* generation who asked them to co-script his first feature *L'Horloger de Saint-Paul* (*Watchmaker of Saint-Paul*), adapted from a thriller by Simenon.

The film was extremely successful and the critics paid compliments to the contribution of Aurenche and Bost. Interviewed shortly after the release of *L'Horloger de Saint Paul*, Jean Aurenche took little credit for the film's success and affirmed that in his eyes the true artist in the cinema is the director, the role of the scriptwriter being 'to throw ideas in his direction'. Nevertheless, the 'rediscovery' of Aurenche and Bost does serve as a reminder that, whoever is ultimately the 'auteur', a film is also a work of collaboration.

ALISTAIR WHYTE

Cinema of the Rising Sun

Against all odds, the Japanese film industry made a dynamic recovery in the years after the war. Its commercial progress was matched by the new cultural and artistic trends set by directors like Ozu, Kurosawa and Mizoguchi, who were making bold attempts to reflect contemporary attitudes in their films

The dropping of the atomic bombs on Hiroshima and Nagasaki in August 1945 brought an already weakened Japan to its knees. Within a few days the American occupying forces under the leadership of General MacArthur had accepted Japan's surrender and commenced the process of 'democratizing' what the Allies regarded as an essentially feudal state. This entailed breaking down all the old feudal allegiances in commerce, politics and society in general, and the establishing of equal rights for all. The changes in the structure and operation of industry that were forced on the defeated country affected virtually every aspect of life. The cinema did not escape the upheavals.

Japan had tended to depict its long tradition of a highly structured, feudalistic society very firmly in its films. Prior to the war many films had been made which roused and reinforced the people's loyalty to the Emperor and the ideals of the nation. During the war such movies had become more overtly propagandist, and it was these to which the new American censors turned their attention. Of the 554 films from the war years, 225 were judged to be feudal or anti-democratic and were ordered to be destroyed. The Occupation forces not only censored completed films, but also kept a watchful eye on new scripts. Kon Ichikawa's puppet film *Musume Dojiji* (1946, *Girl at the Dojo Temple*) was burned simply because he had not submitted the script for approval.

At the start of the war all Japanese film companies had been amalgamated, but afterwards they were allowed to start up production as independent studios again. Censorship control was handed to the Civil Information and Education Section (CI & E) of MacArthur's Supreme Command Allied Forces in the Pacific (SCAP) in March 1946. Japanese films were subject to its rulings for the next four years but, freed from this yoke, production exploded in the Fifties and Sixties. Another reason for this boom was the physical rebuilding of the industry, especially the cinemas. In October 1945 there were only 845 cinemas in operation; more than half of the pre-war cinemas had been destroyed in the bombing, although the majority of the studios had miraculously escaped damage. By January of 1946 the number had increased to 1137 cinemas; this rate of building continued so that by 1957 it had reached the astonishing total of 6000.

There were, however, negative and destructive influences at work, including the search by the CI & E for war criminals. The task of naming these was given to the Japanese Motion Picture and Drama Employees Union; but the Americans, failing to realize that this union was largely communist-controlled, thereby unleashed a wave of political revenge rather than justice, and many who were banned from the industry had to fight for twenty years or more for reinstatement.

Meanwhile, the democratization process (which gave workers the initiative to seek greater powers), coupled with a colossal, crippling tax on the box-office returns, caused

Left: poster from Hiroshi Inagaki's Musashi Miyamoto *(1954–55, Samurai), a three-part colour remake of his 1941 version. The earlier film was one of the better-quality Japanese films to survive the post-war censorship purge by the American occupying forces*

513

terrible strife in the studios and strikes resulted. Toho, the company that gained a virtual monopoly after the war, suffered a spectacular 'work-in' in 1948 which was eventually broken by two thousand police supported by a cavalry company, seven armoured cars and three planes from the US Eighth Army. Few films were produced during this period and it was not until 1949 that a balanced pattern emerged with five major companies carving up the market between them; these were Toho, Toei, Shochiku, Daiei and Shin Toho. Toho, for example, became the main distributors for period films. Daiei had previously specialized in military films, so obviously, in the post-war climate, had to seek new material; the choice of films full of sex and violence may not have made them readily exportable, but their product was sufficiently popular at home to allow the company to rebuild its finances. Shochiku survived on domestic comedies, but in the Fifties these lost favour with audiences and the studio suffered a few lean years until it developed its enormously popular *yazuka*, or gangster films. With these new trends, Japanese film production expanded from 67 films in 1946 to the staggering total of 547 in 1960, by which time 18 companies were in business (the five majors plus a series of small independent companies).

After the war, all the precepts by which the Japanese had lived were being questioned, and writers, artists and film-makers had to cope with new ideas imposed by the West. Some indulged in recrimination; some, like Yasujiro Ozu, retreated to the conservatism of what might be called an essentially Japanese view of life; while others, like Akira Kurosawa, sought to find a balance between old and new values. Despite the problems they faced, some of the greatest talents in Japanese – and world – cinema worked throughout this period and prepared the ground for the glories of the Fifties and Sixties.

Whereas before and during the war the predominant mode of thought in Japan was of group identity (nation, family or company), the post-war turmoil generated what was for the Japanese an unfamiliar concept: that each person had to work out his or her own future. Film-makers started to examine the new ideo-

logies, and the radical importance of this can only be fully appreciated in realizing the strength of the traditionalist views of parental power in Japan, of the obedience of children and the veneration of the family as a unit, and especially the great extent to which pre-war cinema had upheld these beliefs.

Ozu acknowledged the fragmentation of the traditional group ethic in *Nagaya Shinsi Roku* (1947, *Record of a Tenement Gentleman*) in which a boy, roaming the streets amongst physical and moral disorder, seeks and finds his father. The failure of the family to provide the virtues of stability are exemplified in the boy's rejection of his father and the foster mother's 'un-Japanese' reaction to the loss of the boy (in setting up a home for war orphans she moves outside the accepted family support structure). Yet at the same time the family group remains the only hope there is for stability and order. *Kaze No Naka No Mendori* (*A Hen in the Wind*), made the following year, is a melodramatic story of a mother, awaiting the return of her husband from the war, who is compelled to become a prostitute to support her sick child. It was not until 1949 with *Banshun* (*Late Spring*) that Ozu returned to the narrative style that he had begun to develop before the war. His best films have little or no story but examine a quality that has been

termed *mono-no-aware* – an acceptance of things as they are. This view of life is not fatalistic but depends rather on a calm belief in a world that changes slowly around one. At the end of *Late Spring*, a daughter has gone to be married and her father is left alone, resigned but content. The quiet, controlled style of this and other Ozu films was to become better known in the West after the success of *Tokyo Monogatari* (1953, *Tokyo Story*).

Daisuke Ito had previously specialized in the period film, but after the war he became one of the first directors to expose the resurgence of the gangster in urban life in his film *Oshó* (1947, *The Chess King*). Tadoshi Imai, who had shown his support for Japanese Imperialism in such films as *Boro No Kesshitai* (1943, *Suicide Troops of the Watch Tower*), turned against the feudal code with *Minshu No Teki* (1946, *An Enemy of the People*), a call for communist-based political action. A more humanistic approach was evident in his later film, *Aoi Sammyaku* (1949, *Blue Mountains*), which examined teenage love and parental authority. The popularity of this particular film may have resided in its attack on the rigid views of the parents – a stance unthinkable before the war – and thereby on the basis of the family. Keisuke Kinoshita's *Yabure-Daiko* (*Broken Drum*), made the same year, showed the

Far left: the filming of Kurosawa's crime story Stray Dog. *Left: a father (Chishu Ryu) prepares to give away his daughter (Setsuko Hara) in Ozu's* Late Spring. *Above: Ito's* The Chess King. *Above right: Imai's* Blue Mountains, *which explored the generation gap in post-war Japan*

futility of a father trying to hold a family together with feudal authority. Kinoshita had attacked traditional family values two years earlier with *Kekkon* (1947, *Marriage*), showing that a girl can make up her own mind to marry the man of her choice.

Part of the search for new ideas – some of which bordered on the anarchic – led to the reconsideration of the woman's place in Japanese society. Directors such as Kenji Mizoguchi had long been concerned with the plight of women, but few had dared to make honest exposés of their subservient position. The new post-war freedom encouraged the fight for women's liberation. Mizoguchi in *Joyu Sumako No Koi* (1947, *The Loves of Actress Sumako*), and Teinosuke Kinugasa, in *Joyu* (1947, *The Actress*) both celebrated the heroic figure of Sumako Matsui, an actress who had earlier struck a major blow for the emancipation of women by playing Ibsen heroines in the newly formed *Shingeki* theatre. This had been the first entry of social drama into a traditional theatre dominated by *onnagatu*, male actors playing female roles.

Already famous before the war for his studies of women in such films as *Naniwa Ereji* (1936. *Naniwa Elegy*). *Gion No Shimai* (1936. *Sisters of the Gion*) and *Zangiku Monogatari* (1939, *The Story of the Last Chrysanthemums*),

Far left: prostitutes in Women of the Night. *Left: a political prisoner in* My Love Has Been Burning. *Both films were typical studies of women by Mizoguchi. Below: Kinoshita's* Broken Drum, *which traced the breakdown of parental authority. Below right: Toshiro Mifune in* Drunken Angel

Mizoguchi had avoided the worst excesses of nationalism during the war by setting his stories back in history and making them intensely personal. During the immediate post-war years he made *Josei No Shori* (1946, *Women's Victory*), a long-promised film about women fighting for and gaining professional posts with the law courts, and *Waga Koi Wa Moeru* (1949, *My Love Has Been Burning*), dealing with the part played by women in active politics. The competence and strength of women is a subject that threads its way through many of Mizoguchi's films, particularly those with a modern setting.

Even his *Utamaro O Meguro Gonin No Onna* (1946, *Five Women Around Utamaro*), the story of a famous artist set in feudal times, deals with the way in which women are exploited, and his most famous film of this period, *Yoru No Onnatachi* (1948, *Women of the Night*), is an unsentimental portrayal of the life of post-war prostitutes – a film largely instrumental in changing the laws governing prostitution.

Kurosawa, after an apprenticeship with Kajiro Yamamoto, directed his first film, *Sugata Sanshiro* (1943, *Sanshiro Sugata – The Judo Story*), during the most nationalistic period. Immediately after the war he made a series of films each of which concentrated on an individual having to work out a course of action for him or herself. There is much of the humanist in Kurosawa, but there is also something essentially feudal. In his early films the *sensei-deshi*, or master-pupil, relationship on which many, but not all, of his later films were to pivot is clearly discernible. Perhaps Kurosawa's greatest gift, supporting his great narrative strength, is his psychological insight into character. It is rare to find clearly defined 'good' or 'bad' people in his films.

Waga Seishun Ni Kuinashi (1946, *No Regrets for Our Youth*) looked back to the political turmoil that had preceded the war and centred on a young woman who, when her illusions of people are shattered and the man she loves dies in prison, chooses to live the life of a peasant

with the man's parents. The villagers turn out to be as harsh and unjust as those people she had known in politics, yet she makes a conscious choice to stay and carry out what she sees as her duty.

The conflict between will and honour or duty, the key to much Japanese literature, is turned by Kurosawa, in his films, into a modern, self-determined driving force. *Yoidore Tenshi* (1948, *Drunken Angel*) tells the story of a gangster (the first starring role for Toshiro Mifune) befriended by an alcoholic doctor who tries to cure him of his tuberculosis; the action centres round a festering pond that symbolizes the rotting heart of the lower depths of society. At the end the gangster is killed and, although little seems to have changed, along the way the story gives several lessons in humanity by showing how, though morally tarnished, people still help each other. *Shizukanaru Ketto* (1949, *The Quiet Duel*) is about a doctor (Mifune) who, during an operation, becomes infected with syphilis from a patient. From this point his own life has to be reassessed as he turns away from the woman he loves and tracks down the infected man. It is a flawed film, however, lacking the psychological strength evident in his next film, *Nora Inu* (1949, *Stray Dog*). This is based on a true story of a detective (Mifune again) whose gun is stolen. With his section chief (Takashi Shimura), he follows a chain of clues deeper and deeper into the criminal underworld. The thief is not seen until the end of the film, yet it is the relationship between the three characters that opens up aspects of human will and perseverance. After a fight in a paddy field the detective eventually captures the thief but, by this time, they are all so covered with mud that 'good' and 'bad' are indistinguishable. This fine film, with its questions about who is really on the side of law and justice, was a precursor to *Rashomon* (1950), the film with which Kurosawa entered a new decade and thrust the Japanese cinema before a worldwide public once more.   RICHARD TUCKER

Germanía, Anno Zero

After the huge success of *Roma, Città Aperta* (1945, *Rome, Open City*) in Paris in 1946, Roberto Rossellini's artistic (and commercial) reputation had risen much higher in France than in his native Italy. The French government gave him permission, and a French production company (Union Générale Cinématographique) gave him the money to visit Berlin to investigate and develop an idea for the third 'panel' of his triptych on World War II. He had already made films about Roman suffering and the Resistance (*Rome, Open City*) and about the movement of the Allied forces up the Italian peninsula (*Paisà*, 1946); he was now interested in finding out what had led the German people ('human beings like the rest') to embrace Nazism, thus sowing the seeds of their own downfall.

Throughout Rossellini's career, his interest in, and analysis of, ostensibly political subjects was focused on psychological, moral and emotional matters which became political only by implication. The director was later fond of describing his films as studies of the 'movement of the soul'. It was logical, therefore, for him to have chosen a child as the protagonist of his meditation on Germany – a figure who is confronted with, and corrupted by, distorted ideas as he moves through a nightmare landscape. When what Rossellini termed the child's still unextinguished 'little flame of morality' leads him to realize that the murder of his father was not the act of heroism he had believed it to be, 'he commits suicide to escape this malaise and contradiction'.

Germania, Anno Zero (Germany, Year Zero) was finally a German-Italian co-production. The film was not well-received, although it had its few supporters and some success outside Italy. Rossellini, whose experience led him to have respect for very few film critics, later pointed out that most journalists had failed to understand what he had made, preferring to write about what they thought about Germany rather than his film. Even late in his career, when he said that he 'felt very little personal contact' with his earlier films, he continued to have an affection for *Germania, Anno Zero*, and reiterated his own earlier judgment that he had made the film as he had wished to and that his analysis of Germany had been 'just, not complete, but just'.

Germania, Anno Zero was the first film to bring neo-realist theory and practice to a non-Italian subject, although there were obvious parallels between the post-war sufferings of Berliners in this film and the Romans of *Rome, Open City*. Despite being made by an Italian director, *Germania, Anno Zero* may be placed within the context of German films made during the late Forties which attempted to come to terms with the German experience of World War II. Within that context, however, the film is something of a maverick, remaining outside the German tradition of filming under the controlled conditions of a studio.

In retrospect, *Germania, Anno Zero* marked an expansion of neo-realism, one which became clearer in Rossellini's *Stromboli* (1950, *God's Land*), *Europa '51* (1951, *The Greatest Love*) and *Viaggio in Italia* (1954, *Journey to Italy*). While physical and social 'reality' remained a constant, as did the original moral vision of neo-realism, the tendency to concentrate on purely factual events gave way to meditations on a higher spiritual reality – the movement of soul.

DAVID OVERBEY

Directed by Roberto Rossellini, 1947
Prod co: Tevere Film/Sadfilm. **prod:** Roberto Rossellini, Alfredo Guarini. **sc:** Roberto Rossellini, Carlo Lizzani, Max Kolpet, from a story by Rossellini. **photo:** Robert Juillard. **ed:** Eraldo Da Roma. **art dir:** Roberto Filippone. **mus:** Renzo Rossellini. **sd:** Curt Dubrowsky. Released in the USA as *Germany, Year Zero*.
Cast: Edmund Meschke (*Edmund Koeler*), Eric Gühne (*Herr Henning, the schoolteacher*), Ernst Pittschau (*Edmund's father*), Ingetraud Hinze (*Eva*), Franz Kruger (*Karl-Heinz*).

In Berlin, just after the German defeat in World War II, desolation is everywhere (1), from the rubble of the city to the general pervasion of corruption and despair. The black market, prostitution, robbery, shortages and a sense of loss of purpose define the environment in which the boy Edmund grows up. His family's small apartment is oppressive: Edmund's bed-ridden father (2) whines and quarrels constantly; his elder brother Karl-Heinz (3), who fought on the Eastern front as a convinced Nazi, has taken refuge in the flat; his sister Eva drinks with Allied soldiers to obtain cigarettes (4), which can be exchanged for food, and is on the brink of prostitution.

Herr Henning, Edmund's former schoolteacher (recently dismissed for his strong Nazi views) is a pederast who controls a small gang of children engaged in selling stolen goods for him. He tells Edmund that 'the weak should die' (5). Unable to bear his father's return from the hospital and the new quarrels it will bring, Edmund kills his father with poisoned tea (6). Reduced to despair by guilt, Edmund wanders the streets (7). When he confesses his murder to Henning, he is slapped and pushed away. Climbing ever higher in a ruined building, he looks down to see his father's body being taken away (8) and his brother and sister departing for the funeral. He leaps to his death (9).

8

2

3

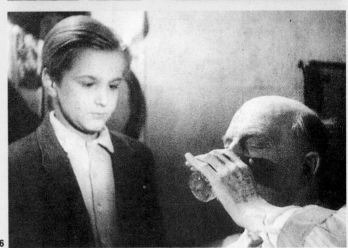

4

5

6

9

1

4

The film critic of the satirical weekly paper *Le Canard Enchaîné* threatened to fight a duel with anyone who professed to prefer *Jour de Fête* (1949, Day of the Fair) to *Les Vacances de Monsieur Hulot* (1953, *Monsieur Hulot's Holiday*). Today many would still cheerfully take up the challenge. *Jour de Fête*, although Jacques Tati's first feature-length film, is also his masterpiece.

Unlike Tati's other films, *Jour de Fête* is not uncomfortably episodic: it preserves the classical unities of place and time. The place is the little town of Sainte-Sévère-sur-Indre, in the Touraine. The time, the most important 24 hours in the year, is the day of the annual fair. The film opens with the arrival of the showmen's wooden horses in their trailer, and closes with their departure. Giving the film even more the feel of a classical bucolic comedy is a chorus: the bent old woman, with her goat, who introduces the principal characters to us and comments upon their actions.

Tati has spoken of his admiration for Jean Renoir's *Une Partie de Campagne* (1949, A Day in the Country), and *Jour de Fête*, although it cannot be considered as homage, reflects some of the sensual quality so characteristic of Renoir. In 1949 it was still unusual to shoot a movie entirely on location, but Tati confidently captures the lush coun-

tryside, the heat of the day, and the heavy grace of the farmers and villagers. The sound was tape-recorded, a technique that was only just in the process of development, but if the dialogue is at times inaudible that is because it would be so from where the action is shot: Tati has succeeded in creating the effect of a modern television street interview.

It is a fortunate accident that the film is in black and white. All Tati's films since *Monsieur Hulot's Holiday* have been in colour, but none has been technically satisfying. *Jour de Fête*, actually shot in the new Thomson-Color, was not successfully processed. Happily, a black-and-white negative was made at the same time, and the film was printed from this.

Tati began as an entertainer in the annual revue staged by the Racing-Club de France – the rugby club for whom he played – and the mime characters that he first developed were sporting ones. Fired with success, he took to the music-hall, becoming an international name. Before long some of his sketches were recorded as short films. In 1936, René Clément directed him in a one-reeler entitled *Soigne ton Gauche* (Guard Your Left). In this film are found some of the essential elements of *Jour de Fête* – the rural naturalness of the location shooting and the first appearance of the village postman.

In 1939, Tati's career was abruptly interrupted. Mobilized into the French army, he took refuge in Sainte-Sévère after the French surrender. Here he first conceived the idea of a film, to be entitled *Mon Village*, or *Fête au Village*.

After the war, Tati slowly made his way in the world of the movies. He was remarkably miscast in *Sylvie et le Fantôme* (1945, Sylvie and the Ghost) – in which he played a tall and surprisingly ungraceful ghost in love with a 'real' girl – and in 1947 had planned a one-reeler with René Clément, entitled *L'Ecole des Facteurs* (School for Postmen). When Clément fell ill Tati took over direction and found his *métier*.

But recognition as a director did not come easily. His one-reeler did not have wide distribution, so Tati decided to remake the story as a feature. The villagers of Sainte-Sévère were enlisted as extras, and shooting was completed in three months. The distributors unanim-

ously turned the film down, and if Tati had not had the idea of staging a preview in the Parisian suburb of Neuilly, and had it not been *un succès fou*, perhaps we would have heard no more of François the postman, or even of Monsieur Hulot.

Not, indeed, that so very much more *was* heard of François. For five or six years *Jour de Fête* enjoyed a growing reputation, enhanced by the popularity of *Monsieur Hulot's Holiday*. Then Tati's finest feature vanished from the screen. Nobody – except Tati – knows the true reason, but in January 1958 Charles de Gaulle became President of France. Tati, tall and lanky, was always uneasily aware of his superficial resemblance to the General, a resemblance heightened by the cap of the village postman. Perhaps, in 1958, it did not seem too tactful to underline this with a comic film?

BRIAN INNES

Directed by Jacques Tati, 1949
Prod co: Cady Films. **prod:** Fred Orain. **sc:** Jacques Tati, Henri Marquet, René Wheeler. **photo:** Jacques Mercanton, Marcel Franchi. **ed:** Marcel Moreau. **art dir:** Rene Moulaert. **mus:** Jean Yatove. **r/t:** 70 minutes. Paris premiere, 11 May 1949.
Cast: Jacques Tati (*François, the postman*), Guy Decomble (*Roger, a showman*), Paul Frankeur (*Marcel, a showman*), Santa Relli (*Roger's wife*), Maine Vallée (*Jeanette, the young girl*), Roger Rafal (*the barber*), Beauvais (*the cafe owner*), Delcassan (*the old lady*), and the inhabitants of Sainte-Sévère-sur-Indre.

2

3

Every year, on July 3 at 9.30 am the fair comes to Sainte-Sévère (1). The carousel is erected and the showmen set up the stalls round the square, watched by the oldest villager and her goat (2). François, the village postman (3), takes time off from his round to supervise the raising of the flagpole (4); then, egged on by his companions, he stays to drink several glasses too many of the local wine. In the cinema tent they are showing a US mail-service documentary: 'Neither snow, nor rain, nor heat, nor gloom of night stays these couriers from the swift completion of their appointed rounds.' François is teased unmercifully about his delivery service, and eventually leaves (5).

Later in the evening he has an unhappy encounter with a fence (6) that will not let him remount

his bicycle, and at last he falls asleep in a railway wagon. At dawn the teasing continues as the showmen encourage François to practise vaulting on and off a bicycle (7). Determined to prove the French postal service as good as the US mails, François sets off on a lightning delivery. Stopping for nothing, he delivers letters on to ends of pitchforks and into harvesting machines, doing his deskwork on a speeding lorry's tail-board. Faster and faster he goes, overtaking some racing cyclists until, in blind frenzy, he rides into the river. Rescued by the old lady with the goat, he takes her advice: there are more urgent matters than the post. Taking off his jacket he joins the harvesters (8).

Every year, on July 4 at 9.30 am, the fair leaves Sainte-Sévère. . .

5

7

6

Key films of 1943

Les Anges du Péché. France. **prod co:** Synops-Roland Tual. **prod:** Roland Tual. **dir:** Robert Bresson. **sc:** Robert Bresson, Father R. P. Bruckenberger, Jean Giraudoux. **photo:** Philippe Agostini. **ed:** Yvonne Martin. **art dir:** René Renoux. **mus:** Jean-Jacques Grunenwald. **with:** Renée Faure, Jany Holt, Sylvie, Mila Parély, Marie-Hélène Dasté.
In his first feature film, Robert Bresson established his unique style of Christian parable. Set in a Dominican convent, the film concentrates on the intense spiritual relationship between a novice nun and a convicted murderess.

I Bambini ci Guardano (*The Children Are Watching Us*). Italy. **prod co:** Scalera. **dir:** Vittorio De Sica. **sc:** Gherardo Gherardi, Cesare Giulio Viola, Adolfo Franci, Cesare Zavattini, Margherita Maglione, Vittorio De Sica, from the novel *Pricò* by Cesare Giulio Viola. **photo:** Giuseppe Caracciolo. **art dir:** Vittorio Valentini. **mus:** Renzo Rossellini. **with:** Emilio Cigoli, Isa Pola, Adriano Rimoldi, Luciane de Ambrosis.
An adulterous triangle is seen through the eyes of a child, the ultimate victim of his parents' quarrels. The film reflects the growing naturalism and social awareness that anticipated the neo-realism of the post-war period.

The Bells Go Down. Britain. **prod co:** Ealing. **prod:** Michael Balcon. **dir:** Basil Dearden. **sc:** Roger MacDougall, Stephen Black. **photo:** Ernest Palmer. **ed:** Sidney Cole. **art dir:** Michael Relph. **mus:** William Walton. **mus dir:** Ernest Irving. **with:** Tommy Trinder, James Mason, Mervyn Johns, Philippa Hiatt, Finlay Currie, Philip Friend.
A comedy drama in which Trinder joins an East End fire-fighting unit as the Blitz rages. Cockney humour is used as an image of native pluck and resilience.

Le Corbeau (*The Raven*). France. **prod co:** L'Atelier Français. **dir:** Henri-Georges Clouzot. **sc:** Louis Chavance, Henri-Georges Clouzot. **photo:** Nicolas Hayer. **art dir:** André Andrejew. **mus:** Tony Aubain. **with:** Pierre Fresnay, Pierre Larquey, Noël Roquevert, Bernard Lancret, Antoine Balpêtre.
Clouzot's dark and bitter mood was already much in evidence in his second film, the story of a small French town which is flooded with poison-pen letters. Its vitriolic portrait of provincial life led to its banning in France after the war and the blacklisting of Clouzot until 1947.

Day of Wrath. Denmark. **prod co:** Palladium Film. **dir:** Carl Theodor Dreyer. **sc:** Carl Theodor Dreyer, Mogens Skot-Hansen, Poul Knudsen, from the play *Anne Pedersdotter* by Hans Wiers-Jenssen. **photo:** Karl Anderssen. **ed:** Edith Schlüssel, Anne-Marie Peterson. **art dir:** Erik Aaes, Lis Fribert. **mus:** Poul Schierbeck. **with:** Lisbeth Movin, Thorkild Roose, Sigrid Neiiendam, Preben Lerdorff Rye.
A young woman in seventeenth-century Denmark is accused of witchcraft when her husband dies. Dreyer evoked in this powerful picture, still as relevant as Orwell's 1984, all the terror of a mind being twisted and brainwashed.

L'Eternel Retour (*Love Eternal*). France. **prod co:** André Paulvé. **prod:** André Paulvé. **dir:** Jean Delannoy. **sc:** Jean Cocteau. **photo:** Roger Hubert. **art dir:** Georges Wakhevitch. **mus:** Georges Auric. **with:** Jean Marais, Madeleine Sologne, Jean Murat, Yvonne de Bray, Junie Astor.

This modern version of the Tristan and Iseult myth, much favoured by the Nazis, caused its makers some embarrassment after the war. Its feeling for magic and fantasy is more typical of Cocteau than Delannoy.

Five Graves to Cairo. USA. **prod co:** Paramount. **prod:** Charles Brackett. **dir:** Billy Wilder. **sc:** Charles Brackett, Billy Wilder, from a play by Lajos Biro. **photo:** John Seitz. **ed:** Doane Harrison. **art dir:** Hans Dreier, Ernst Feyte. **mus:** Miklós Rózsa. **with:** Franchot Tone, Anne Baxter, Akim Tamiroff, Erich von Stroheim, Fortunio Bonanova, Peter van Eyck.
Wilder's spy melodrama, set in the days following the fall of Tobruk, was his highly individualistic contribution to the war effort. Like La Grande Illusion *it is more concerned with questions of national identity than with conventional topics or flag-waving propaganda.*

For Whom the Bell Tolls. USA. **prod co:** Paramount. **prod/dir:** Sam Wood. **sc:** Dudley Nichols, from the novel by Ernest Hemingway. **photo** (Technicolor): Ray Rennahan. **ed:** Sherman Todd. **art dir:** Hans Dreier, Haldane Douglas. **mus:** Victor Young. **with:** Gary Cooper, Ingrid Bergman, Akim Tamiroff, Arturo de Cordova, Joseph Calleia, Katina Paxinou.
The producers secured Franco's approval for their beautifully photographed but otherwise pedestrian adaptation of this Hemingway novel of doomed love in the Spanish Civil War. Sam Wood recalled the problems of the location in the Mexican Sierras: 'We even uprooted wild flowers and greenery to prevent the harsh landscape from becoming "pretty".'

Hangmen Also Die! USA. **prod co:** Arnold Pressburger Productions/ United Artists. **prod:** Arnold Pressburger. **dir:** Fritz Lang. **sc:** Fritz Lang, Bertolt Brecht, John Wexley. **photo:** James Wong Howe. **ed:** Gene Fowler. **art dir:** William Darling. **mus:** Hans Eisler. **with:** Brian Donlevy, Walter Brennan, Anna Lee, Gene Lockhart, Dennis O'Keefe, Alexander Granach.
This account of the assassination of the Nazi Reinhard Heydrich, known as the Hangman of Prague, was one of the rare films on which the celebrated dramatist Bertolt Brecht worked. His influence is evident mainly in the didacticism and directness of the script. The collaboration with Fritz Lang, however, was not very cordial.

Heaven Can Wait. USA. **prod co:** 20th Century-Fox. **prod/dir:** Ernst Lubitsch. **sc:** Samson Raphaelson, from the play *Birthdays* by Laszlo Bus-Fekete. **photo** (Technicolor): Edward Cronjager. **art dir:** James Basevi, Leyland Fuller. **mus:** Alfred Newman. **with:** Gene Tierney, Don Ameche, Charles Coburn, Marjorie Main, Laird Cregar, Spring Byington.
Henry van Cleve, a rich American Casanova, finds himself in Hell and narrates his life story to 'His Excellency'. Lubitsch's first colour film is a typical mixture of romantic passion and sly satire at the expense of the lifestyle of monied America in the late nineteenth century.

I Walked With a Zombie. USA. **prod co:** RKO. **prod:** Val Lewton. **dir:** Jacques Tourneur. **sc:** Curt Siodmak, Ardel Wray, from a story by Inez Wallace. **photo:** J. Roy Hunt. **ed:** Mark Robson. **art dir:** Albert S. D'Agostino, Walter E. Keller. **mus:** Roy Webb. **mus dir:** C. Bakaleinikoff. **with:** James Ellison, Frances Dee, Tom Conway, Edith Barrett, Christine Gordon, James Bell.
A visually seductive and poetic horror film that presents the human unconscious as a supernatural threat. The conflict between reason and the unknown is enacted through the central characters – a Christian nurse and the Voodoo-stricken wife of a Caribbean planter.

The Life and Death of Colonel Blimp. Britain. **prod co:** Independent Producers/The Archers. **prod/dir/sc:** Michael Powell, Emeric Pressburger. **photo** (Technicolor): Georges Périnal. **ed:** John Seabourne. **art dir:** Alfred Junge. **mus:** Allan Grey. **with:** Roger Livesey, Anton Walbrook, Deborah Kerr, Roland Culver, James McKechnie, Albert Lieven.
Powell and Pressburger incurred the wrath of Winston Churchill with this (potentially subversive) epic tapestry on the British military ethos before, between and during two world wars. The film is part analysis and part celebration of the famous cartoon character, and is acutely perceptive of the British way of life.

Lumière d'Eté. France. **prod co:** André Paulvé. **prod:** André Paulvé. **dir:** Jean Grémillon. **sc:** Jacques Prévert, Pierre Laroche. **photo:** Louis Page. **ed:** Louisette Hautecoeur. **art dir:** Max Douy, L. Barsacq. **mus:** Roland-Manuel. **with:** Madeleine Renaud, Pierre Brasseur, Madeleine Robinson, Paul Bernard, Georges Marchal, Aimos.
A bitterly satirical, poetic drama about a sad group of failures who live in a remote Alpine hotel on the edge of an abyss. Made during the Occupation, when Grémillon was a member of the underground Comité de Libération du Cinéma Français, the film is a metaphor for the state of Vichy France.

Millions Like Us. Britain. **prod co:** Gainsborough. **prod:** Edward Black. **dir/sc:** Frank Launder, Sidney Gilliat. **photo:** Jack Cox, Roy Frogwell. **ed:** R. E. Dearing. **art dir:** John Bryan. **mus:** Louis Levy. **with:** Eric Portman, Patricia Roc, Anne Crawford, Gordon Jackson, Basil Radford.
This 'Home Front' film tells of the difficulties of a middle-class girl in adapting to her job in a factory. The film historian Roy Armes described it as 'a key document of the period, posing questions about class and the durability of national unity.'

The Miracle of Morgan's Creek. USA. **prod co:** Paramount. **prod/dir/sc:** Preston Sturges. **photo:** John Seitz. **ed:** Stuart Gilmore. **art dir:** Hans Dreier, Ernst Fegte. **mus:** Leo Shuken, Charles Bradshaw. **with:** Betty Hutton, Eddie Bracken, Diana Lynn, William Demarest, Brian Donlevy, Akim Tamiroff.
A pregnant girl seeks a father for her offspring. The volunteer father gets more than he bargained for when the girl gives birth to sextuplets. It is a biting satire on small-town life from the director whom the critic Andrew Sarris describes as the 'Brueghel of American comedy directors'.

Nine Men. Britain. **prod co:** Ealing. **prod:** Michael Balcon. **assoc prod:** Charles Crichton. **dir:** Harry Watt. **sc:** Harry Watt, from a story by Gerald Kersh. **photo:** Roy Kellino. **ed:** Charles Crichton, Sidney Cole. **art dir:** Duncan Sutherland. **mus:** John Greenwood. **with:** Jack Lambert, Gordon Jackson, Frederick Piper, Grant Sutherland, Bill Blewett, Eric Micklewood.
Watt's tale of a lost army unit fighting across the North African desert was an early example of the 'drama-documentary' approach to film.

The Ox-Bow Incident; directed by William Wellman – see special feature in Chapter 34.

The Seventh Victim. USA. **prod co:** RKO. **prod:** Val Lewton. **dir:** Mark Robson. **sc:** Charles O'Neal, DeWitt Bodeen. **photo:** Nicholas Musuraca. **ed:** John Lockert. **art dir:** Albert S. D'Agostino, Walter E. Keller. **mus:** Roy Webb. **mus dir:** C. Bakaleinikoff. **with:** Kim Hunter, Tom Conway, Jean Brooks, Isabel Jewell, Hugh Beaumont, Erford Gage.
Opening with a quotation from Donne 'I ran to Death and Death meets me as fast, and all my pleasures are like Yesterday', the film develops into a chilling tale of diabolism in Manhattan. The heroine, who has come under the influence of Satanists, commits suicide at the end of the film – a bleak conclusion, probably unique in Hollywood movies of the time.

Shadow of a Doubt. USA. **prod co:** Universal. **prod:** Jack H. Skirball. **dir:** Alfred Hitchcock. **sc:** Thornton Wilder, Alma Reville, Salley Benson, from a story by Gordon McDonnell. **photo:** Joseph Valentine. **ed:** Milton Carruth. **art dir:** John B. Goodman, Robert Boyle, R. A. Gausman, L. R. Robinson. **mus:** Dmitri Tiomkin. **mus dir:** Charles Previn. **with:** Joseph Cotten, Teresa Wright, MacDonald Carey, Patricia Collinge, Henry Travers, Hume Cronyn.
This is one of the few Hitchcock films in which the central character is the villain. Charlie Oakley, on the run for murder, plants himself on his unsuspecting sister's family. The result is a classic film noir set in small-town America.

This Land Is Mine. USA. **prod co:** RKO. **prod:** Jean Renoir, Dudley Nichols. **dir:** Jean Renoir. **sc:** Dudley Nichols. **photo:** Frank Redman. **ed:** Frederic Knudtson. **art dir:** Albert S. D'Agostino, Walter E. Keller. **mus:** Lothar Perl. **mus dir:** C. Bakaleinikoff. **with:** Charles Laughton, Maureen O'Hara, George Sanders, Walter Slezak, Kent Smith, Una O'Connor, Philip Merivale.
Charles Laughton gives a fine performance as the mild schoolteacher who finally asserts his right to freedom in Nazi-occupied France. It is an ambitious attempt by the exiled Renoir to come to terms with the question of neutrality and collaboration among his compatriots.